Privatization, Regulation and Deregulation

The last fifteen years have been unparalleled in the privatization and deregulation of key industries. Professor Michael Beesley has played a unique role in these changes. He conducted the first public inquiry on liberalizing telecommunications and advised government on forthcoming legislation in telecommunications, buses and water, as well as advising the new regulators. Equally important, he has made significant contributions to the basic economic arguments underlying the reforms.

In this second edition of *Privatization, Regulation and Deregulation*, the author has updated and augmented the original material to take account of developments over the last five years. This volume includes ten completely new chapters, replacing papers which have been overtaken by further work or cover the same ground, all with the added advantage of hindsight. With coverage of the critical period from 1981 to the present, the book provides a unique insight into the privatization and regulatory procedure. In addition, the work presents a significant contribution to the basic economic arguments underlying these reforms. As such, it will be an invaluable guide to both students and practitioners involved in privatization and regulation.

Professor M. E. Beesley is a Founding Professor of Economics at the London Business School. He has been Lecturer in Commerce at Birmingham University, then Reader in Economics at the London School of Economics; he became the Department of Transport's Chief Economist for a spell in the 1960s. Now Emeritus, his main teaching interest was in the contribution of economics to developing organizations' strategy. He started the Small Business Unit at the London Business School. At the other end of the scale, he has advised companies on problems of monopoly and restrictive trade practices and on the relationship between nationalized industries and their ministries. His widely known work in transport economics and telecommunications policy has taken him to a wide range of countries. A member of the Monopolies and Mergers Commission since 1988, he was Economic Adviser to the government on water privatization in 1988/9, and from 1989 has been Economic Adviser to OFFER (Office of Electricity Regulation). He was made a CBE in the 1985 Birthday Honours List.

Privatization, Regulation and Deregulation

2nd Edition

M.E. Beesley

Published in association with the Institute of
Economic Affairs

First edition first published
by Routledge in 1992
Reprinted 1993, 1995

Second edition
first published 1997
by Routledge
11 New Fetter Lane, London EC4P 4EE

Simultaneously published in the USA and Canada
by Routledge
29 West 35th Street, New York, NY 10001

© 1997 M.E. Beesley

Typeset in Times by Pure Tech India Ltd, Pondicherry
Printed and bound in Great Britain
by Mackays of Chatham PLC, Chatham Kent

British Library Cataloguing in Publication Data

A catalogue record for this book is available from the British Library

Library of Congress Cataloging in Publication Data

A catalogue record for this book has been requested

ISBN 0–415–16452–4 (hbk)
ISBN 0–415–16453–2 (pbk)

To an inspiring teacher,
Arthur Shenfield

Contents

Figures

Tables

Acknowledgements

In republishing the papers, I acknowledge with gratitude the part played in several of them by my collaborators. Partnerships based on complementary skills are usually enjoyable, as these certainly have been. I well recognize the indispensable contributions they have made. I have particularly appreciated Stephen Littlechild's eye for the questions needing answering and his insistence on unfettered argument; Stephen Glaister's patience with the deficiencies of a mathematical innocent, and his modelling skills; and Bruce Laidlaw's unrivalled grasp of issues concerning telecoms' licensing and how technical developments in telecoms will emerge into commercial prospects. Most of all, however, I have simply enjoyed arguing the toss with them. They have been wise as well as generous in debate. I thank them for encouraging me to republish the essays.

General note

The material in this book appears as it was originally published; references are therefore often contemporaneous.

1 Introduction

M.E. Beesley

FORMATIVE INFLUENCES

The essays in this collection represent ten years' involvement in privatization and regulatory affairs. They appear at a time when, having become London Business School's first emeritus professor, reflections on one's early formative influences are expected. A previous collection of essays – on urban policy – was published in the early 1970s. Those essays reflected my preference for market-oriented solutions to policy issues, but in truth I had little hope of their being influential. At that time no one could have foreseen the political changes which were to promote markets to a central place in economic policies. The changes were particularly welcome to me.

Arguments in favour of free markets were implanted in my undergraduate days at Birmingham from 1942 to 1945, by Arthur Shenfield's unfailingly brilliant defence of the competitive paradigm. He had plenty of opportunity to show its very wide application, as in those wartime years he had perforce to shoulder much of the economics teaching. He, in turn, had been much influenced by Hayek and others at LSE. So we undergraduates were immediately in the thick of the problem of the legitimate scope of the state in economic affairs. And the debate was a serious one: leading up to the 1945 election there really was a choice for or against a massive increase in state control. In that election, I well recall arguing vehemently that what was wrong with the coal industry, for example, was the lack of competition, not too much. Both Tory ideas of centralized control of the pre-war coal cartels and the Labour idea of nationalization were equally wrong. Later, in 1950, I was an unsuccessful Liberal candidate, but gave up active campaigning after that. For me, 1950 was the last occasion on which that party could truly claim to be intellectually descended from Gladstonian liberalism. From my viewpoint, politics had then deteriorated into an unedifying competition to manage a corporate state, leaving free-market ideas to live on in such stalwarts as Ralph Harris and Arthur Seldon of the IEA.

But I also had a highly practical interest in industry. I had originally embarked on a B.Com. degree because of a youthful ambition to succeed in business. Many years before, there had been a small but prosperous family concern which my grandfather had sold. It was clearly a matter of regret to my father that he had not been taken into it, an elder brother having thoroughly disillusioned my grandfather by having a good time in the USA instead of negotiating useful printing rights. To run one's own firm, I thought, was the way to get the profits; to be an executive like my father was insufficient.

As a practical training for business, Birmingham turned out to be something of a disappointment. The Faculty of Commerce had failed to develop along the lines foreseen by the founding spirits, among them Sir William Ashley and Joseph Chamberlain, whose support for Birmingham's aspirations was contingent on creating such a faculty. Before 1914 it had a good claim to be effectively the first UK business school. Between the wars it had become a fairly conventional economic and social sciences school. It still had, however, a commitment to learning about, and observing, industry. Here, P. Sargant Florence, lecturing from what appeared to be a compost heap of notes, provided a sharp contrast to Arthur Shenfield, who prided himself on never bringing as much as a single sheet to class. But Florence convinced me of the need to supplement economic insight with the careful development and interpretation of data. More important, it became clear that immersing oneself in the facts was often a useful method of developing new questions for analysis.

These intellectual influences were to surface in academic work later. Graduating, I duly followed the course I had mapped for myself. Rejecting the offer to stay on for a Ph.D., I and my father found a firm of metal workers located in the old jewellery quarter in Hockley, Birmingham. They did not want the small capital I was able to offer, but the three directors had no children to follow and so wanted an assistant with a view to succession. The firm, Henry Jenkins and Sons Limited, quoted on the Birmingham Stock Exchange, boasted an issued share capital of £16,666.13s.4d. (This odd figure, so tradition had it, was the result of an unwise speculation in stamping medals in the Boer War. In those days, adversity had to be met head on. Henry Jenkins and Sons had been incorporated at £50,000.)

To my dismay, I discovered that business, in 1945/6, was not a chance to deploy economics for strategic reasoning in the interests of the firm. It was, rather, a matter of progress chasing, of attempting to keep output up by whatever means came to hand. It had some instructive lessons in rationing, of which we were both the victims and the perpetrators. But intellectual starvation played a large part in persuading me to return to the university after 15 months to take up the Ph.D. offer.

Nevertheless, the experience left an indelible mark. For one thing, the firm itself had practically every known kind of non-ferrous metal forming and shaping, and had never, it seemed, quite abandoned any process in its long history. For example, we occasionally used an oval turning lathe to form the edges of blanks for silver-plated platters. Curiosity led me one day to scrape its stock. The date 1825 appeared. Thus began a practical scepticism for accounting valuations. I was also given a task deemed appropriate for a fresh graduate, namely job costing and pricing. I would meticulously weigh and measure, time and enquire, producing what were by common consent far more accurate job costs than ever before seen in the firm. On receiving one, the managing director would say 'Very good, Beesley. Now, we don't want that one. Add 100 per cent.' To the next he would say 'This is important, add 25 per cent.' These sessions caused me to reflect deeply on the nature of accuracy in costing: but I soon realized what my essential function was – to save him from making too low a quotation. He obviously had a keen appreciation of what each 'market' would bear.

He also had a favourite maxim: 'There are three good livings in this business, my boy. It's our job to protect them.' Coupling this with latter-day sophistication in pricing theory, one might well describe his policy as a kind of private sector application of Ramsey pricing, where the 'good livings' and plant overheads represented the required gross profit constraint. But because of material shortages, and rationing, this would perhaps be to express the short-run view. Everyone looked forward to the return of pre-war days of opportunity, when, especially on Saturday mornings when cheap return rail fares were to be had from London, people with ideas for new products would canvass the Birmingham 'metal bashers' for production and backing. At all events the experience was enough to make me most sceptical when back at university of the notion, widely held in the late 1940s, and often revived since, that it was not sensible to assume profit maximization as a working hypothesis in analysis. However rough and ready, here was a practical demonstration of preferring more profit to less, with a clear, if intuitive, appreciation of elasticity in demand and avoidable costs.

The jewellery quarter was also a living monument to R.H. Coase's view of the firm. Firms' boundaries were indeed manifestly driven by trading off the advantages of arm's length dealing against the advantages of administrative relations. Not only did the quarter's firms embrace every imaginable constellation of integration, Henry Jenkins and Sons itself had one operation within its walls – metal spinning – in which the head spinner recruited and paid his own labour whilst working with Henry Jenkins's machines and materials, for a negotiated price. Thus was nurtured a scepticism about issues of the 'benefits' of firm scale and, in particular, about the immutability of integration and of labour contracts.

Back at university, I embarked on a Ph.D. suitable for one convinced that what was then principally needed in government-industry relations was an effective anti-trust law and not the other modes of government interventions then beginning to proliferate. I wanted to study cartel (trade association) activity and perhaps work out effective countermeasures. This was hardly in the spirit of the times. I well recall Mrs Joan Robinson earnestly advising me against pursuing the topic, chiefly on the grounds, it appeared, that all that could usefully be said on the topic of collusion had already come to light in the Robinson-Chamberlin debate on imperfect or monopolistic competition. I always had some difficulty in connecting these views with her appearance as one of the first members of the newly formed Monopoly and Restrictive Practices Commission. Indeed the Commission itself seemed to me an aberration for a Labour government, until I later read the parliamentary debate leading up to its formation. From this, it seems likely that establishing the Commission was a reward to the Co-operative allies of Labour, then numerically important, who had suffered considerable disadvantages at the hands of trade associations. Many of these regarded co-operatives as vehicles for undercutting fixed retail prices and many organized refusals to supply them. Collective resale price maintenance duly occupied much of the early years of the Commission.

Despite the heavyweight advice, I persisted for some time with the Ph.D. topic. I had one big stroke of luck. A university friend's father happened to be an enthusiast for 'orderly marketing', involving alliances between manufacturers and distributors. He was the chief executive of a large Birmingham non-ferrous concern. He thought he could correct my misguided references to 'collusion' etc., by showing me what really happened in these associations. So he invited me to read the series of minutes, from their foundations, of about eight manufacturing associations in different products his firm made. I was spellbound. I had heard that Birmingham businessmen were often valued according to their success in organizing associations. Here the skills were revealed. In association A, on Monday, he or his representative (depending on whether 'trouble' was expected or not) might, for example, throw his weight behind arguments to form a 'fighting fund' to discourage newcomers. On Tuesday, in association B, he might be earnestly resisting the idea of agreements on advertising outlays. On Wednesday, he might be resisting the notion that, since association C had been so beneficial to members up to now, it would be useful, henceforth, for members to bring new products to the meeting for approval. On Thursday, in association D, he might be agreeing to develop more information to enforce the association's price agreements.

These histories were illuminating in several ways. One's economic training had stressed the industry as the unit of interest. What I had found ran counter to the idea, then quite prevalent, that there was in a given group of firms forming an association an inevitable progression to complete collusion. Here was a warning that one must consider individual firms' interests and limitations to understand collusive behaviour. More important, it suggested that a more interesting focus for enquiry might be the firm, in its several manifestations, rather than the industry. In each product there was an optimum scope for association activity, depending on its value to the company. Unfortunately, when I showed no sign of embracing the collectivist faith the facility was withdrawn, and with it any hope of getting permission to publish any analysis of the phenomena. However, it did greatly influence my teaching of 'industrial organization' later, in the 1950s. When I occasionally meet students who sat in those classes, if they remember anything of what they were taught, it is always my accounts of how to manage collusion in the Birmingham brass trades!

Not progressing as I had hoped, I left Ph.D. studies for a spell in regional town and country planning with the West Midlands and North Staffordshire Plans. These were the heady days of physical planning, when economists in all seriousness were asked to predict, as in my case, how the future development of the motor car industry would affect town development in the West Midlands and North Staffordshire. I soon discovered that 'planning' did not mean, as I rather thought it would, combining different disciplines to arrive at a larger, more satisfactory, model. At the time, I thought that others' refusal to take on board economists' reasoning was some failure of the intellect. With hindsight, I realized that the function of economists was essentially to provide the men in charge – in that case the eminent architects Sir Patrick Abercrombie and Herbert Jackson – with some reassurance that their vision of interdependent urban and rural physical development would not be undermined by adverse economic change. On a somewhat grander scale, this resembled the function my costings had provided for Henry Jenkins's managing director in his pursuit of good business.

Perhaps the most important by-product of that experience for me was access to the individual data on plants, from the Factory Inspectorate, which I saw could form the basis for a greatly revised Ph.D., and which enabled me to finish it by 1951, the Plans having been completed in 1949. The Ph.D. was on Interlocking Directors. The question was, what influence, if any, would be made to computations of concentration in industries if, instead of taking ownership as the basis for control, one took common boardroom membership? I still think this an interesting notion and I duly found that it did make a lot of difference to computed concentration, depending on the industry and the directness of the interlocking (for instance, what if firm A was interlocked to firm B indirectly through firm C?). I have to admit that much as the measurement of concentration has developed, and despite the fact that questions about its limitations are still standard fodder for examination questions, ownership stubbornly remains the underlying criterion of control in such studies. But more baffling at the time was how to interpret the phenomenon of interlocking directly. By collating board memberships of the companies in what amounted to a census of plants in West Midlands metal industries, I had come up with the result that at least one-third of all activity was interlocked, at least at some remove.

Colleagues at Birmingham were equally baffled, but respectful of what had obviously been a gruelling job. (No computer aids in those days. Collation had to be done laboriously, by clipping cards and using needles to shake out possible interlocks.) My own interpretation was not particularly strong. Clearly it was quite implausible to suggest that this was a web of active control mechanisms. It was far too diverse, and I remembered the behaviour of the large Birmingham brass-founder. I thought that the probable significance was essentially as a risk-reducing device. When substantial investment was mooted by an individual firm, the network was used to signal intentions, mark territories, and learn of possible conflicts. The important learning for me lay in the fact that I found propositions about the theory of the firm in a comparative static framework simply inadequate to grapple with the problem. My interpretation, tentative as it was, meant that I had to consider the origins of change in the conditions facing firms. I also had to understand better the idea of 'power', which I thought best approached in a negative way, as the relative absence of constraints (a 'near' interlock was more influential than a distant, indirect one).

As a result of my Ph.D., I was offered, and accepted, a lectureship in commerce, eventually inheriting, in 1955, Sargant Florence's responsibility for lectures on industry. This was during what its members now think of as the great age of Birmingham's Faculty of Commerce and Social Science. Alan Walters gives its flavour in his essay on 'The life philosophy of eminent economists'. With Terence Gorman, Frank Hahn, Alan Walters himself, and Esra Bennathan it was a powerhouse for economic thought. It also boasted sociologists and social psychologists, especially Chelly Halsey and Josephine Klein, well able to stand up for themselves in debate. We took the Faculty's business traditions seriously. For example, in a cross-disciplinary group, we turned our attention to the mysteries of decision making, by taking it in turns to present papers. Esra Bennathan summed up the proceedings succinctly when he said on one occasion 'at least we have learned that decisions are the by-product of hysteria'. We concluded, wisely, that we should each concentrate on his or her own relative advantage. It was not the first, but also not the last, occasion on which the limitations of interdisciplinary discussion in social science were exposed.

For me, the most difficult question of this period was how to reconcile the obviously powerful competitive paradigm, as presented in an increasingly well-thought-out neo-classical framework, with Schumpeter's persuasive criticisms in *Capital, Socialism and Democracy*. His characterization of capitalism as driven by incentives of creating monopoly, but subject to the perennial gale of competition, rang very true when I first read the book as an undergraduate, and it was probably the beginning of an active curiosity about how to analyse firm behaviour. The subsequent experiences in business, recounted earlier, and a continuing interchange with businessmen did nothing to dim Schumpeter's appeal: on the contrary. Specifically, it offered an explanation for the existence of profits as an outcome of innovation: that is new products, services and production methods. The 'perennial gale' ensures that the profits, to use the neo-classical term, would become a quasi-rent stream, not a permanent rent.

I do not think that anyone has since improved on Schumpeter's account of the source of profits. It certainly seemed to me a great improvement on the utter shiftiness involved in using the idea of 'normal' profits, which rather mysteriously were supposed to keep neo-classical firms' noses to the grindstone. Yet at the same time, like nearly everyone else, I had to accept the logic and the usefulness of the idea of resource allocation for which the idea of the firm in neo-classical economics had been invented. As I shall recount below, I now think I have come to terms with, and find useful, both modes of thought. But it took many more years to do so.

The mark of a 'coming' economist in the 1950s was that he or she would receive an invitation to visit, and usually teach for a year in, a well-known American university department. One by one, my promising Birmingham colleagues duly did so. I got mine, at last, in 1959. Through Gilbert Walker's good offices, I was invited to the Wharton School in Philadelphia, to be an associate professor for a year. It was duly a watershed. More than that, it introduced me to the fully professional business school; and Gilbert asked me while in the United States to make the rounds of other eminent schools, as far west as Chicago, to advise on what Birmingham's developments should be. When I got back, I advised that it was necessary to concentrate on postgraduate education, not undergraduate, and to have a two-year M.B.A or equivalent as the academic backbone, but that it was also necessary to generate a lot of shorter courses (of much less intrinsic academic merit) to make financing the whole operation feasible. This was a formula Birmingham was unable, in the event, to adopt at that time. But it still has validity, I think, for describing much of the essential business of business schools.

Soon after I arrived in Philadelphia a graduate student at Wharton introduced himself to me on campus one day saying, 'I know you – you are a footnote in Florence.' This was Jim Ball, referring to his reading of one of Sargant Florence's books. This started a friendship which was to lead later to Jim's invitation in 1965 to join the nascent London Business School. In doing this, he was careful to predict that London Business School would indeed conform to the basic specification I had outlined in Birmingham, notwithstanding the considerable pressures from the founding fathers of LBS to specialize in post-experience programmes and at most a one-year master's programme.

Critical to career progress as Philadelphia was, I cannot claim that it broadened one's intellectual horizons in the manner of Birmingham in the 1950s. Rather, it introduced the concept, entirely new to me, of student-oriented teaching. Not for Wharton the idea that the lecturer commented critically on the arguments in the latest journals. Not for it the cavalier handing out of reading lists containing all relevant wisdom, or the idea that examinations were tests of the student's absorption of all this. Students expected to be instructed, on specifically assigned readings, class by class. The burden of proof for failure in tests rested, to one's consternation, on oneself. The students actually questioned their grades! And horror of horrors, a campus magazine appeared, giving advice to students on which courses and individual instructors to select, or, more important, which to avoid. The orientation considerably helped my own subsequent adaptation to business school life in London. But the consumer-oriented view it reflected was but one manifestation of that wider phenomenon, a consumer-oriented society.

Looking back, it seems to me that, whatever the formal statistics tell us, a point somewhere towards the end of the 1950s marked the biggest absolute difference between the UK and USA in perceived consumer standards. Rationing was still a recent memory in the UK and, of course, such wonders as self-service supermarkets, drive-in cinemas, and basement bargains in department stores were all most welcome when making do on $6,500 a year for a household of six. But the most striking thing was the basic attitudes; the consumer in the USA really was made to feel the king. Markets certainly worked, as promised by enthusiasts for the American way of life. Everyone, it seemed, started from the assumption that the consumer should be helped. (Even doctors, at this point, still visited one's home in Philadelphia.) My distant admiration of the USA's attitude to micro-economic affairs had been confirmed. Amongst the Democrats we immediately befriended in West Philadelphia, I found myself frequently in a most unaccustomed position of arch-conservative, in the particular American meaning of defending the purity of the 1776 Constitution. They did not realize, I thought, what a marvellous thing this was compared to any other order on the globe; one tinkered with it at one's peril. The years since have done little to diminish this enthusiasm for the USA, not least the fact that my old friends there still refuse to adopt my position. And I have never lost my fascination with, and admiration for, the USA as the world's laboratory for exploring arrangements between governments and economic agents.

While in the USA I was invited to apply for the Rees Jeffrey fellowship in transport economics at LSE, newly established by Gilbert Ponsonby, the university reader there in that topic. This offered the prospect of working full time on transport problems; no teaching was required. Much of my research to that point had been in transport, the result primarily of Gilbert Walker's own interest in that area. I had, for example, helped the Road Research Laboratory with one of the earliest of cost–benefit studies, on the economics of the M1. A collaborator, on occasions, had been Alan Walters, whose seminal work on transport was similarly stimulated by Gilbert Walker. ('Seminal' is a term of hindsight, of course.) What impressed me most at the time was Alan's extraordinary gift for spotting what evidence is relevant to a problem and then applying it. This included a wily device for securing a near 100 per cent response rate to a survey of company users of transport. It was to pick an extremely pretty and intelligent research assistant, whose arrival at a target company's address was timed exactly to follow that morning's post, in such a way that no one could deny having received it, but no one had had time to work out what answering it entailed. An offer to be of assistance proved irresistible. (Alas, such a stratagem would be ruled out nowadays by at least two factors: one cannot be so overtly chauvinistic; and the post cannot be relied upon!)

I was duly asked to take the fellowship up and, forgoing tenure at Birmingham, I accepted the risk of a contract renewable for a maximum of seven years from 1961. This was the opportunity to explore cost–benefit analysis (CBA) more deeply as a means of public decision making, reflected chiefly in the work with Christopher Foster on the Victoria Line. While holding the fellowship, I was able to produce what also later came to be regarded as a pioneering empirical work: namely estimates of the valuation of time spent travelling. Transport economics in general was enjoying a boom, and was rapidly extending its relevance to policy making. For example, the Smeed Committee on Road Pricing, by 1964, had worked out the practical applications of social cost pricing on congested roads. For me, working in both CBA and the pricing work with the Smeed Committee, this was the occasion to develop more clearly the relations between two very different modes of public intervention – that of direct decision making represented by CBA and that of repairing defective markets – as in road pricing. What I then lacked was direct appreciation of the tasks as government itself saw them. This was made good in 1964 by a happy accident – London University's rules for appointing readers.

Gilbert Ponsonby wished to retire, and a successor had to be appointed. The rules called for overkill in the matter of eminent assessors, who had to be present at the interview. One of these happened to be Alex Cairncross, then Government Chief Economic Advisor. As one of only two serious candidates, I got into a vigorous argument with him about road pricing, which had to be truncated by the chairman. I was offered and accepted the readership, but more to the present point, was soon asked by Cairncross to be the Ministry of Transport's Chief Economic Advisor on a part-time basis, a post which I carried on when becoming one of the founding professors of economics in London Business School, in 1965.

The time as the adviser, from 1964 to 1970, was an important first period of instruction about the economist's role in government – chiefly, then, for defining what the relative skills of civil servants and economists are. I found it increasingly implausible for economists to assume the textbook role of the god-in-the-machine, prescribing for best choices among defined options in response to a recognizable, if implicit, welfare function. This last was not a useful way to describe the role of real politicians, who it appeared to me were operating in a far more dynamic and opportunistic political market-place than their party rhetoric allowed. The civil servants, I found, were engaged in a very difficult task of devising policies to meet what were often, contingently at least, quite incompatible requirements. This needed very high intellectual capacity and imagination, which the 'generalist' civil servants with whom we dealt often displayed. Their art lay in inventing new courses of action consistent to a plausible degree with the requirements, the acid test of which was their acceptance in Cabinet. There was more to it than this, of course, and I have often regretted the failure of political scientists to produce a good theory of the Minister, in which private and party ambitions have to be satisfied. But the experience left me with the feeling that in micro-economic affairs at least, economists had only themselves or their profession to blame if they were not listened to attentively.

Economists began to be employed by government on a large scale in the 1960s. This was the high-water mark of belief in technocratic solutions to public problems. That belief then extended to the contribution expected of economists. When Barbara Castle became Minister of Transport in 1965, she made a condition of taking the job that there should be a much enlarged economic input to policy making. Christopher Foster was brought in as Director-General, at the unprecedentedly high level for a departmental economist of deputy-secretary equivalent. I had been brought in a year before on the civil service initiative I have described as an under-secretary equivalent under Tom Fraser, who did not hold Cabinet rank. We found at that time, 1964–5, that if transport policy was being made anywhere, it was not in our department. Morale was low among the administrators; Barbara Castle's clout and combative, open style were highly welcome. I was happy to carry on my half-time assignment with Christopher, and a rapid build-up of economist professionals ensued. I suppose that, collectively, our greatest effort in the period was found in the 1968 Transport Act. This was a tribute to what turned out to be a brief period of apparent technical dominance over political dogma, in its simultaneous enactment of road freight transport deregulation and the nationalization of the largest bus companies to form the National Bus Company. We ardently pushed for more radical economic solutions, perhaps the most prominent of which was road pricing to deal with congestion, already worked out to a highly sophisticated degree, both as to hardware and as a new form of tax, by the Smeed Committee.

At the time, economists looked set fair to begin a great leap forward. But there were several reasons why this was a false dawn for economists' influence in transport policy, as elsewhere in micro-economic policy. The first was the precarious nature of the political marketplace which would allow room for both a market solution and more economic centralization in one Act. It will be recalled that Barbara Castle's down-to-earth view of economic needs did not survive her translation to her next job at the Department of Employment, when 'in place of strife' became the issue. She found that challenging union power head on was quite a different order of difficulty from quietening union misgivings about freight deregulation.

The second reason was that when it came to formulating specific policies at the level at which we were engaged, an economist's underlying political preferences had to surface, and indeed were seen by many as a condition of access to the inner circle of policy making. This gave rise to disagreements about the proper use of analysis. A good example was in the 'use' or 'abuse', depending on one's viewpoint, of CBA for deciding on road invest-ment priorities. CBA as a technique had recently been much improved, for example, by measuring explicitly values of time saved in travelling (as in my work referred to earlier). These values were, however, derived from evidence of choices made by individuals trading off time against cash. Values were thus dependent on, or at least heavily influenced by, incomes. How, if at all, should CBA applications by the department 'correct' for this? Some took the view that corrections to offset income variation should be built in as routine automatically, using road investment to 'correct' for the underlying income distribution. Others adhered to a strict efficiency objective. The several values of time should not be adjusted. Income distribution should be done directly, not through what was regarded as an insidious insertion into administrative processes at the Department of Transport's level.

Looking back now, I would emphasize more the nature of economists' training. I do not think that, by and large, economists over the years since this late 1960s flowering have much increased their essential influence on policy making in transport. Our economic team at the department was by and large quite unskilled at those very things that made the generalist civil servant so useful to Ministers. It was not only that communication skills were lacking (I recall we had to be given a superb example of a 'generalist' – Peter Lazarus – to translate our thoughts into understandable memoranda) but also that too many of us lacked alternative modes of analysis to that imagined by the standard textbooks.[1]

In 1965, I transferred the academic half of my job to London Business School, having been recruited by Jim Ball to join him as one of the two founding professors of economics there. My decision was strongly influ-enced by principles of location, as was fitting for an economist then special-izing in transport. Two postgraduate schools of business studies had simultaneously been set up, in London and Manchester. I had no doubt at all that London would prove to be the superior location for this kind of activity. It was not that Manchester, so far as I know, had any interest in me. It was simply that we were clearly in for a rapid expansion of the business school industry, in which London must have the competitive edge.

By the late 1960s, I was a member simultaneously of two quickly growing organizations – The Directorate of Economics at the Department of Trans-port, and the London Business School. Each side was very tolerant of the difficulties, but I felt increasingly dissatisfied with a life of chasing from one meeting to another with what seemed like ever shorter time to do either justice. Not wishing to become an ever more specialist transport economist, I opted for LBS. Moreover, without much interest in macro-economics, there was little hope I would feel comfortable in the higher reaches of the economic civil service. A departmental economist, however expert in its affairs, was of little use to the Minister if he or she could not give quick and defensible opinions about the implications of the latest disturbance to the UK general economic policy. The more true this would be the higher the

Minister's Cabinet ranking. But the period was an invaluable training in how the higher civil service worked. Above all, for an economist to have influence, his or her advice must, it seemed to me, anticipate policy needs, be produced quickly when needed, and be couched in easily understood terms. In other words, it had to be tradeable in the very hard markets of interdepartmental interchange and negotiation.

These, then, were some of the main early formative influences, which doubtless are reflected in the essays of the 1980s. For me, the 1970s was a period of little direct influence on micro-economic policies. I maintained my interest in competition policy, producing for example a critique of merger policy for the IEA which, in taking the line that it was preferable to attack consequent abuse of a market position rather than judge mergers *ex ante*, had considerable interest for specialists. But market solutions were out of fashion. Civil servants were busy devising 'better' means for the central guidance of economic affairs. In any case, London Business School was a most challenging place to be. Nowhere was this more so in the difficult matter of teaching micro-economics to graduate students of average age 27, with very high IQs, often with little background in economics, and with large amounts of their own (or their spouse's) money at stake for the training. Like any other business, this was a difficult one to learn, and I certainly had not completed my self-instruction when becoming emeritus.

The technique of teaching had to be different, to begin with. I well remember our scepticism in 1966 when the first business policy teacher at the school, Basil Denning, was trying to persuade us to adopt the Harvard case method. We, traditional university teachers, by contrast, were certain that what was required was to be (temporarily at least) the world's greatest expert on a given topic and then be able to deliver a full series of lectures of $1\frac{1}{4}$ hours each. (The time of $1\frac{1}{4}$ hours was adopted in obedience to United States business school schedules. For recruits from university posts, used to the standard 55 minutes, it was a tough extension. It was even tougher for the class.) I, for example, really did know everything worth knowing about anti-trust economics, for a period, and duly held forth for the required time. Of course, in the end, most of us had to recognize that cases and, more widely, interaction with the class were essential, and so we developed or adapted cases which underlined the principles we wished to convey for discussion in class.

But there were more fundamental problems, in my opinion, and these took years to come to terms with. What, I increasingly had to ask myself, is the service we economists should be giving to the students? It was true that the standard neo-classical tests gave a rigorous way of thinking which was clearly of value in itself to masters' students destined for top business jobs. Moreover, American business schools regularly relied on orthodox micro-economics as a staple offering in the M.B.A. Yet it all seemed to turn out as so much formal instruction. Most students did not absorb it into their basic thinking about business situations. The solution was slow to arrive, but it was that micro-economics should be explicitly taught as a foundation course for business policy, the course designed to bring together the students' skills in role playing for business decisions. For that the focus should, I thought, be shifted to profit. Economics should have a great deal to contribute there, yet in standard texts 'profit' got little specific treatment. Typically, it would appear early on under the guise of the maximizing principle. Some interesting material on what it *was* would appear only at about page 500+, often alongside accounts of the Marxian view of capitalism.

So I thought a course should be arranged around profit – in three respects. First, how the opportunity to make it may arise; second, what would be involved in negotiating to realize it; and third, what is involved in defending it. These phases, treated as sequential, would involve different but complementary economic ideas. The analysis would take the firm's viewpoint: in effect the Schumpeterian scenario should be played out – the initial search for profit, the establishing of monopoly, and the defence of the (quasi-)rent against the perennial gale. In the first phase, the broader Austrian view of economic processes would be to the fore, stressing disequilibrium, market signals and the creation of information, alongside wisdom derived from economic history. The second phase would in part be a typically Austrian concern (namely, why have markets not produced this opportunity before?) and partly neo-classical, in that the essential problem is how to assemble the necessary resources without giving away in advance the profit one hopes to realize. Static comparative accounts of the impact of the firm's proposals on relevant markets are certainly useful in this connection. Third, one would enter the 'defence' phase. This is where modern developments of industrial economics in particular come into their own. Some 'game' has to be played against the other competitors. Hence, for example, one needs a flexibly applied account of oligopolistic relations. But the course must not reflect the weight given to these phases in the literature, because, in an important sense, once the problem is to confound competitors, the more interesting early gains from being the sole mover are past. More usefully, competitor analysis should be deployed to restart the Schumpeterian cycle.

All this, in one sense, is just a rearrangement and different emphasis within very familiar themes. Yet its principal requirement is to run with two quite different modes of economic thought: Austrian (including for this purpose Schumpeter) and neo-classical. Most professionals, in my experience, find this a difficult proposition. It is not helped by the typical bias in early training, but neither is it encouraged by the feeling one sometimes receives that Austrian-minded economists are engaged in some form of holy war. At all events, to combine both describes the direction of my own teaching efforts; not surprisingly, students with no previous economic training often found the shifts of viewpoint easier to manage than those with it. One of the perennial difficulties in the course was to find suitable texts. In the end, we tended to solve them by writing notes to precede classes. One of these days, perhaps there will be the time to turn my own efforts into a textbook.

THE CONTEXT OF THE ESSAYS

As I have explained earlier, the onset of practically oriented market policies from 1979 onwards owed nothing to my being in any sense an adviser of politicians. But I have no doubt that my 'sound grasp' (as one side might put it; the other would say 'prejudice in favour') of markets made me one of few relatively old hands who would survive the process of sounding out opinion when someone was needed to take the lead in exploring a difficult issue. Fortunately for me, one such issue was the impending liberalization of the use of British Telecom's network, in 1980. Minds were sufficiently open to make this a public inquiry, which I duly conducted for the then Secretary of State for Industry, Sir Keith Joseph. It was 'fortunate' in two senses. It made me tackle an industry I barely knew beforehand, which turned out to be endlessly productive of new problems. Second, it turned out to need tackling with ideas of business economics well to the fore. Much of the analysis of the report on the inquiry is reproduced in Chapter 14.

It had to be completed in three months, so there was a prospective bonus for those whose opinions were well formed enough to put forward evidence quickly. To my surprise, it turned out that easily the most well-informed evidence came from the Post Office Engineering Union, who were strongly against any freeing of the existing constraints on the leasing of BT's capacity. BT itself seemed less well prepared. It may well have expected the debate to centre on principles of pricing. Uppermost in its mind was the likely disturbance competitors would cause to the existing structure of cross-subsidy inherent in its pricing system. In the event, I took the line that one first had to consider what, if any, entry was likely in response to possible changes in the rules. Entry depended on projected profit and future competitive responses. One could not isolate the point of departure of the inquiry – the terms of resale for BT's capacity – from other matters affecting entry. One then derived one's views on issues such as effects on BT's prices via pressure on BT's profits. Moreover, entry was contingent on competitive rules of conduct, such as discrimination, at that time largely unarticulated for dominant firms in the UK. (The 1980 Competition Act was itself hardly on the statute-book.)

One of my incorrect assumptions in consenting to a three-month inquiry limit was that there would be readily available a worked-out rationale in the Department of Industry for more competition in telecommunications. In fact, I cannot recall receiving more than one and a half pages of such elucidation. This was less surprising when I learned that the manpower in the department devoted to telecommunications' affairs was about four and a half, the half being on the input of an economist. BT itself was still in many ways the official source for conducting government affairs, as it had been when part of the Post Office. So, in effect, my report was the first reasonably long rationale for the government's announced policy of more competition, with the result that I immediately became a recognized, if quite unofficial, champion of competition in telecoms, a role which still characterizes my position, as also shown in Chapters 14 to 16.

In 1981, the report's conclusions were strong stuff, even for the government. They were strongly opposed, of course, by BT itself and the unions. I was taken to task by some fellow academics for not 'solving' the pricing problem, by which they meant in particular applying a model in which the principal arguments would be the significance of scale economies for correct pricing. The extracts below will show why I thought concerns about 'economies of scale' were misplaced. I think I can claim that the report did propose the right agenda for policy making in telecoms and that much of its material is still relevant, particularly on resale. This is partly because I took seriously the technological implications of digitalization for regulation of entry, and partly because no one from a business school could resist emphasizing the problem of how to develop new business in a market with an incumbent having a 100 per cent market share.

As a result of this report, I became an adviser to the department on competitive aspects of telecoms. The privatization of BT, announced in a White Paper in July 1982, altered the competitive outlook considerably, so presenting a new series of problems. Foremost among these was the setting up of new, independent regulatory machinery, which would have a dual problem of management of prices and of emergent competition. These and subsequent developments are reflected in the other essays. But there remains an intriguing unanswered question: what would have happened had policies in favour of entry been rigorously pursued while still retaining BT's public corporation status? Most economic critics of privatization, and they outnumber the approvers, think that promoting product and service competition, where possible, does more for economic efficiency than privatization, the essence of which is exposure to competitive capital markets. This debate, too, is reflected in the essays below. To me, however, it seems probable that such views posit what is so far an empty political box, namely one party in the UK's two-party system which is willing to allow a public monopoly simply to wither away via competition.

Critics of privatization are fond of pointing out the apposition between allowing more competition and getting a good price for the sale of the assets. The government has, in fact, been more eclectic in this matter than most critics allow, as Chapter 3 points out. The simultaneous deregulation of the local bus industry and the privatization of the National Bus Company in 1985 are a counter-example. I have included in the essays my own paper recommending a policy of bus deregulation in late 1982 at Chapter 10, and subsequently became one of the principal advisers to the government in the lead-up to the White Paper of 1984 which announced the new bill. The White Paper incurred the displeasure of most professional transport economists and the subsequent debate is referred to in the 1989 ECMT paper, republished here as Chapter 13. This was one of the episodes which has increasingly indicated to me the need for economists to be prepared to use both Austrian-inspired notions of competition and the indications from neo-classical models. Another relevant experience has been that on the Monopolies and Mergers Commission (MMC), which I joined in 1988. In this, it has often appeared to me that, whereas the questions posed by applying (neo-classical) textbook analyses of competitive processes are extremely useful in establishing possible deviations from the desirable outcomes expected from competition, when it comes to devising remedies, analyses directed to sources of profit and their changes are equally essential.

When water privatization was carried forward in 1988, I was asked to assume the point of view of the regulator, in order that the manner in which his job would be best performed could be reflected in the legislation and the licensing procedures. This called for the production of papers, as required, on pressing issues as they arose. They had to be short, understandable to generalists and, above all, useful in departmental negotiations. One example is Chapter 6 on the required rate of return, which was the focus for discussions with water and other interests in preparation for the flotations. Questions about the required rate of return are common to all privatizations, of course, but water also presented quite a different industrial situation from telecoms and buses. In these industries competition – its prospects and development – was a central issue, calling for particular levels of regulatory response. In water, by contrast, there was the prospect of water authority PLCs with virtually permanent monopoly powers. It seemed to me that a critical need was at once to maximize exposure to the capital market and thus encourage challenge to incumbent managements through takeover and, at the same time, to maximize the regulator's ability to control prices and service quality in the industry through critical comparisons between the regulated companies. This view was expressed in the policy paper which is reproduced at Chapter 5.

It will be seen that the paper argued for a *per se* rule against water mergers and, otherwise, no ban on takeovers. Ministers finally negotiated this to the position taken in the Water Act, namely that there should be automatic reference of water mergers to the MMC, whose judgement was to be taken explicitly in the light of the regulator's need to maintain effective comparisons across the industry. (Subsequent cases before the MMC have already indicated that the policy is working as intended.) As to takeovers, the result of the negotiations was that golden shares in the English water authorities were to be limited to five years, after which there would be no constraint other than the horizontal merger provisions. Welsh water was an exception, with a permanent golden share, an illustration of the fact that privatization is not simply the concern of the main sponsoring department – Scotland and Wales have important independent influences in their own territories.

Over the several utility privatizations of the 1980s, from telecoms to electricity, the UK has devised its own methods of regulation to meet two kinds of regulatory problems. The first is the question of how to avoid the inefficiencies widely held to accompany rate of return regulation and the second is how to accomplish a transition to competition from the initial dominant incumbent position. In the paper reproduced as Chapter 4, Stephen Littlechild and I set the problems in the context of the contrast with United States regulation. We point out the very different implications for the development of regulation for the cases where substantial competition will be possible from those in which one can envisage a more or less permanent exemption from it. We also argue that the task of managing the transition to competition calls for analyses of consequent regulatory action, requiring the applications of both neo-classical and profit-oriented modes of thought. A similar concern for prediction of likely entry underlies the analysis Bruce Laidlaw and I made in an IEA monograph on the then forthcoming duopoly review in telecoms, part of which is reproduced, alongside an update of our arguments, presented in July 1990, in Chapter 16.

Privatization is a learning process for government as well as for analysts. It is salutary to reflect on a great concern which preceded BT's privatization in 1984 about the effect on the gilt markets, and therefore on the government's own cost of borrowing, of such an unprecedented large flotation (I recall opinions to the effect that the gilt market could be 'upset' for as long as 6 months!). All this, I surmise, had its influence on the decision to sell only 51 per cent of the shares and to stagger shareholders' payments. The opinions puzzled believers in a near-perfect capital market at the time, and I do not think that this kind of worry is held to be important now. There has also been learning about the need to avoid a 100 per cent dominance in the opening market structure, such as was followed in British Airports and Gas. Hence the decision with electricity to commence with at least two privatized generators and the recognition that, even with strong geographical monopolies as in water and electricity distribution, it is preferable to have more independent operators than fewer.

The next major area for the application of learning is, predictably, the relation between the utility regulators and the more general pro-competitive institutions and legislation, itself developing. In the important area of influencing the conduct of large firms, the UK has developed a set of institutions, the utility regulators, whose powers to deal with their industries reflected the perceived weakness of the 1980 Competition Act in particular. The Act did not offer a direct connection between possible abuse of a dominant position and protection for potential competitors against it. Hence the inclusion in licences of clauses designed to give such protection, directly enforceable by the regulator concerned. Within the confines of their particular legislation, and the subsequent licensing provisions, they have arguably been an effective and necessary complement to the wider law. But now that the latter is being developed, along with other things, to embrace

EEC modes of dealing with dominant abuse, the question will arise about redividing labour among the institutions. My own position is that 'learning' is indeed the key; it would be wise to let the separate utility regulators run as they are for a period before seeking to modify their remits substantially. In particular, their experience in dealing with issues of price discrimination and anti-competitive incumbent moves should be drawn upon in formulating the more general framework. The UK has never before had the continual experience in dealing with market power in a specific industrial area which the utility regulators represent, but they too are as yet comparative new-comers to the problems.

One way of summarizing the experiences which, as I have described, have helped to shape the chapters of this book is to say that, over the years, I have learned to distinguish more carefully the different analyses useful for tackling applied economic problems, to respect their limitations, but be willing to take new approaches on board. What I hope I have resisted is the temptation to shape the 'problem' to fit the analysis. This, I fear, is endemic in the profession. With the pressures to get publications in good journals, it is understandable that so much of industrial economics, for example, consists of deriving propositions from simple statements about entry conditions, and then experimenting to see how the 'conclusions for policy' might be modified if the assumptions were changed. It is often admirable, rigorous work, well calculated to yield the expected number of 'good' articles for the next promotion review. I have found that to be effective as an adviser on economic problems one has to be prepared to build up a considerable capital in the form of digging in and around the industrial circumstances. One can only hope to surface every now and again to turn these into a publishable article.

The incentives facing professional academic economists do not encourage useful policy-oriented work. When in 1987 I was asked to contribute a piece to celebrate the twentieth anniversary of the *Journal of Transport Economics and Policy*, itself very much a product of the resources newly put into transport research in the 1960s, I asked myself the question whether the needs of policy making were fundamentally at odds with the way in which incentives in the economics profession operate.

Reviewing the subject matter published in the journal over the two decades, I noted that there had been little tendency to match publications with new policy concerns. Still less did they anticipate policy needs with analysis. Academic advancement, above all, involved publishing articles which showed one's competence in teaching economics and, better still, being cited widely in other economics journals. So transport was of less interest in itself than for the bearing it might have on more general, textbook-centred, propositions. An investigation of the contents and cita-tions of the journal's articles confirmed this view. I lamented the relative paucity of articles which probed the business economics of the individual transport modes.

A major problem with the mode of thought engendered by standard texts, and the supporting professional infrastructure of articles which eventually will illumine the texts, is that policy comparisons are often conceived of as measuring deviation from a 'best' state of the world represented, for example, by the outcomes expected of perfect competition. This formulation is interesting and useful for clarity of thought, but it is not the problem that faces the politician/decision maker. The latter's problem is to judge whether, from where we now stand, a particular (admittedly imperfect and necessarily negotiated) proposal will improve welfare. This is essentially a cost–benefit formulation, in which the difficult matters for analysis are likely to be characterization of the starting position, prediction of the 'without change' condition and a clear understanding of how the proposal(s) will actually alter things. Here again, one has to analyse with higher-level matters of resource allocation in mind, including measures of benefits and costs, at the same time as trying to make solid predictions about particular economic actors' behaviour in response to policy change. The more elevated the policy issue, the less specific can the analysis of reaction to change be, but the method remains that of applying cost–benefit principles.

An example of such a high-level issue is the first paper in the series, Chapter 2, on what priorities should guide the government's ordering of privatization. Stephen Littlechild and I wrote this out of a feeling that the then new policy of privatizing large public sector firms should be given overall shape. Its timing just before the 1983 general election was quite fortuitous and it became perhaps the most frequently quoted of all our privatization work. It did not, it must be said, influence the actual sequence of privatizations actually adopted. Three of our favourite candidates – coal, railways and posts – remain in the public sector so far. But work at that level of economic abstraction is often useful for stirring up argument. Its particular appeal lay in the approach of putting all candidates together for analysis, comparing them along dimensions which included market prospects and competitive potential. This approach corresponded well to the way in which different responsible departments might wish to open their case for or against privatization of 'their' industries at a particular time.

The several phases of policy development are indeed represented in the essays which follow. The papers on transport covered the generation of ideas through economic argument, as in Chapters 8 and 9 on the relevant industry economics for decisions about regulation; the paper designed for consumption by policy makers, as in the 1982 paper for the Department of Transport (Chapter 10); and the appraisal of policy, as in the 1989 ECMT paper (Chapter 13). The 1982 paper did not prove to be an input to active policy immediately, but it was revised for consideration when political interest subsequently turned again to deregulating buses. The 1989 paper, in principle at least, should stimulate questions of whether policy needs revision.

Two of the papers, for me, represented more than their intended contributions to economic policy debates, because they marked progress in analytical problems which had been troublesome for a considerable period. They were the 1983 EJ paper with Stephen Glaister and the JTEP paper in May 1986, respectively Chapter 9 and 12.

As one intensely interested in different interpretations of the meaning of 'competition', I was particularly eager to be clearer about the circumstances in which it might be justifiable to intervene in markets which did not display deviations from the classical competitive conditions, that is where market failure in the usual senses did not prevail. A practical case seemed to be London taxis, known to be atomistic and characterized by highly elastic supply, for reasons explained in the earlier JTEP paper, reproduced as Chapter 8. Entry standards raised costs somewhat, but did not constrain supply. Price control, designed to follow changes in an index of costs, did not materially affect underlying supply conditions. Technological development and capital labour ratios were remarkably unchanging over time. Stephen's and my particular interest in the industry had been stimulated in the first place by a consultancy assignment from the Prices and Incomes Board in the late 1970s. We were asked the straightforward question – if the PIB allowed prices to rise in this industry, what would happen to output? Would it rise or fall? We found ourselves unable to give a straight answer at the time, so felt obliged to come back to the problem for our own satisfaction later.

We were led to set up the model described in the paper, which had to deal with the main stumbling block, namely that demand and supply were not independent in this industry. Demand depended both on price and service elements. Profits depended on price received per mile and the probability of being hailed. We of course found that similar kinds of problems had been tackled in other industries, notably in aviation, and we found this helpful. We were then able to answer, in a highly conditional manner, the questions we had failed to answer a few years before, as will be seen. But there were two important by-products. The first was that it became clear that, measured in conventional CBA terms, subsidy could improve welfare in the unconstrained industry. It could add to consumer surplus while leaving profits unchanged, that is at the level measured by the options open to the drivers to earn in their alternative occupations. This was basically because the stock of available but unused cabs necessary to sustain service standards would not increase proportionately as the industry's scale became larger. I had to accept that intervention *could* improve on unaided markets, even in conditions approaching perfect competition.

This was most useful, because it then focused attention on the real issue – in what circumstances *would* a regulator be likely to identify and develop the opportunity to intervene beneficially? In other words, what were the chances of avoiding failure in regulation? At least one necessary condition for this would be generating the appropriate information; and we investigated this very carefully. Our conclusion was that even in the simplest of conditions, a very heavy burden would rest on the regulators. A fair view seemed to be that the chances of beneficial intervention would be low.

This reinforced the point that the legitimate concern of policy makers, bent on improvement, should not be comparison with some ideal solution, but the more relevant cost–benefit-oriented question of what will a proposed change do to the welfare of consumers and production. Also it raised the question, further taken up in the 1989 Beesley–Littlechild paper, Chapter 4, of the conditions under which regulators could be supposed to acquire information at a faster rate than the regulated players in the industry. In other words, a view of the conditions for a regulator's effectiveness began to take shape, a view which continuing experience in regulatory affairs is still helping to form.

The 1986 JTEP paper, Chapter 12, was an outcome of an attempt to enter the air charter market, with a newly formed company called London Express Aviation Ltd. By the time the article was written, I had become the company's chairman, and it was written a few months before we had to admit defeat and withdraw from the market. The essential reason was that the tour operator's innovatory contracts, on which we relied, and as described in the article, did not happen. But the experience, though costly, principally in time absorbed, was well worth while for the new insights it gave me into the problems of raising risk capital, dealing with regulators as a 'customer' intending to enter and dealing with other participants in a high-return (hopefully), high-risk project. It was no less instructive on the purely academic side, in that it caused me to think more carefully about the status of 'sunk', or as I preferred to call them 'committed', costs in entry problems.

Such costs had, by the early 1980s, become the centrepiece of new theorizing about 'contestable markets', part of a much heralded new era of more rigorous analysis of firms' behaviour. I had encountered earlier developments in that theory, concerning non-sustainable natural monopoly as part of the arguments surrounding entry into telecoms, as the extracts from 'Liberalization of the use of British Telecommunications' network', Chapter 14, show. The JTEP article will speak for itself about the usefulness of the concept for industrial economists' usual concerns. My own conclusion from it is that the idea of sunk costs has no content unless the passage of time and some change in the initial conditions are explicitly recognized. This means, of course, that Austrian concerns must enter.

Another, most useful, lesson I drew from the work was the realization that I had never, until that point, seriously asked myself the question: if one is proposing to enter a new venture of any kind, be it with a new organization or not, what capital does one *have* to raise? That is, how much unfettered cash will one need in prospect in order to begin the process of negotiating with other potential suppliers of resources? This is a question which can only arise out of innovation or market disequilibrium. There are many capital suppliers willing to supply part of the capital needed, but nearly all that we encountered wished to hedge to some degree by subordinating our money, taking what we regarded as too high a residual equity interest etc. However, we had one important marker – the Civil Aviation Authority's requirements for available free cash before giving the licence. As explained in the paper, this estimate of 'the hole' – the amount the entrepreneurs would have to be prepared to lose in adverse circumstances – turned out to have a connection with, but was not wholly comprised by, 'sunk costs' as the literature defined them. I think the CAA was simply encapsulating for us the process of rationalizing the required equity – the necessary statement of commitment before we could be taken seriously as a possible service provider.

POSTSCRIPT: FIVE YEARS LATER

In putting together this collection, I have taken the opportunity to replace chapters that have been overtaken by further work, covering the same ground, but with the further advantage of hindsight. This applies to the telecoms sector, in which Chapter 16 supplants three of the older pieces on the development of telecoms regulation.

Since the first edition's publication, my intensive course in real-time regulation has continued, with Offer,[2] MMC[3] and Ofgas.[4] The intensity owes much to the vastly increased volume of criticism of how UK privatized utilities work. One of the largely unanticipated effects of privatization was a revolution in popular access to information about the industries – not merely about what has happened but, perhaps even more important, about what it is thought now should happen, as inherent in an $RPI - X$ price regulation system. It is all a far cry from the days when serious criticism of utilities was based on rather sparse and always out-of-date government publications.

$RPI - X$ as a way of regulation has, so far, survived increasing exposure rather well. Critics almost universally come to the conclusion – 'could do better' – with the critics' emendations – not that it should be abandoned. Meanwhile, 'founding fathers' like me think of the Acts passed at privatization as incomplete or flawed in important respects (the politicians were partially deaf) and the enterprise one in which in any case a determined, long-lasting effort would be necessary to build effective regulation, not least because of the great cultural change implied for the utilities themselves.

Argument at home and calls to explain what is involved in setting up regulatory offices from abroad have helped to focus on the essential requirements. This is reflected in the new chapters included in this edition. Chapter 7 harks back to water privatization in 1998. I have placed it alongside others (Chapters 5 and 6) from that era. I had completely forgotten having written it when Chris Bolt, a colleague in that episode and subsequently chief economic adviser to Ofwat, drew it to my attention when moving to Ofrail in 1995. It turns out to have foreshadowed much of what in practice has been Ofwat's procedures in building the necessary information exchange with the industry. Papers written in the heat of the endeavour are often forgotten, but as will be evident from parts of further papers appearing here, central ideas used in them are remarkably resistant to change.

Chapter 17 considers what have proved to be difficult regulatory bed-fellows: the tasks of regulating via $RPI - X$ in the business hard to challenge via entry, the 'non-contestable pipes and wires businesses'; and the potentially competitive ('contestable') activities, bundled with them on privatization. The regulator, doing his or her best with the tools given by an Act, has first to promote competition – i.e. provide the conditions in which entry can occur – and then, in principle, retreat from the scene to let the more normal laws on competition take over. One implication of this grand design is a clearer focus for the remaining regulatory task – that of regulating the pipes and wires. In telecoms, the facts of development in technology have made this division of labour particularly hard to do, and Chapter 17 gives my views on the central task at about 1993.

The opportunity to lay out what a regulator of a utility should aim for in the case in which there is a prospect of satisfactory isolation of the contestable from the non-contestable activities has come with an assignment in 1996 for the Australian Consumer and Competition Commission (ACCC). The ACCC has the task of overseeing the regulatory principles to be applied by the several state utilities, privatized or government owned, to add to its duties in the field of competition law and administration. Here, I felt there was a particular need to show how the information requirements relevant to both tasks could be formulated for use in a consistent manner, and this occupies much of Chapter 18. I have appended to it answers to questions on the paper which ACCC asked about it.

Back in the UK, the paper on Gas (Chapter 19) was produced at a time when the arguments about British Gas TransCo prices for 1997 to 2002 were joined. TransCo, as a separate arm of British Gas, was essentially the creation of the MMC 1993 investigations into British Gas's monopoly. I was a member of the group which produced the report, which many commentators have regarded as MMC's largest task in its 40-year existence. We advocated (among many other things) the total divestment of British Gas's trading activities from its pipes right down to the domestic burner tips.

This, an innovation in the world gas scene, was of course strongly opposed by British Gas; but we thought it an essential precursor to free competition in gas sales using the pipes. (In practice, in the UK, divestment of privately owned companies in the interests of competition must involve MMC; it cannot be done using the privatization Acts themselves.) The MMC's recommendation was formally turned down by the Secretary of State in 1993; but his alternative involved ring-fencing of TransCo to a standard of physical and accounting separation we had advocated as a preliminary to divestiture. This created the same effect in regulatory terms. Since then, British Gas has announced that it now intends to recognize the change by itself divesting trading activities (with some holdings of gas) from the rest in 1997.

I thought I discerned, in TransCo's response to Ofgas's first consultation document of the Review which started in 1995, an attempt to evade first principles of such a review, and so produced the application of Chapter 18's principles in the Gas context in Chapter 19. As I write, the final Ofgas decision on what has been widely regarded as tough initial proposals is still to be made.

When the utilities were privatized, it was realized that UK's existing competition laws, and in particular the Competition Act 1980 which was meant to discipline large firm power, would be inadequate for the task of dealing with emerging competitive relationships after privatization. The utility regulators were accordingly given powers to act in this area through the respective licence conditions which bear on competitive moves, particularly by the incumbent operators. It is very doubtful, however, whether the full extent of the impending competition problem was realized. Indeed, antitrust law all over the world would find it difficult to cope with a situation in which, typically, an owner of non-contestable pipes or wires was starting competitive life with a 100 per cent initial market share downstream – the customers. This was an incumbent versus entrant problem of unprecedented magnitude. As regulatory power has begun to bite, and the necessary conditions – notably the effective separation of the two types of activities, the non-contestable and potentially contestable – have been better realized, incumbents in particular have made the case that the utility regulators should yield their powers on competitive conduct to the general UK competition law. This raises important questions again about how effective that law is.

Over the years I have kept up an active interest in the development of UK competition law and administration. This is also the field offering greatest challenge to those who regard markets and competition through Austrian as well as neo-classical eyes. Practical regulation, I argue, must involve using Hayekian and Schumpeterian insights. Competition – in particular entry – *is* a necessary means for disclosing new sources of gain to the consumer; but, at the same time, competitors – in particular, entrants – must be able to foresee the creation of profits which will not be eroded so quickly as to foreclose a payout. The key point is the effect of regulatory processes and initiatives on the incentives of incumbents and would-be and actual entrants, respectively, largely motivated by prospective effects on profits. This view is applied in Chapter 21, Abuse of Monopoly Power, which deals with what I think are needed UK competition law reforms; and is evident in the early, sceptical paper on merger control (Chapter 20).

The perception that government regulation is often competition's worst enemy, so evident in the earlier chapters on transport, is taken up in another field – that of concern about concentration in the media – Chapter 22. It also illustrates, in my view, the potential for mischief inherent in established governmental divisions, the prime example in this case being the two bureaucratic worlds inhabited by the biggest UK media operator, BBC, on the one hand and the commercial media on the other.

The final paper (Chapter 23) was intended as a tribute to an old hero, Schumpeter. Even this arch-sceptic of the usefulness of government intervention in markets would, I think, have felt obliged to give advice, if asked the question today, about what government's policy in an area of great public concern should be. I think the effort, and perhaps the gall, needed to apply his actual thoughts on monopoly and competition (not the reified versions of what he is alleged to have thought) might indicate useful lessons for how to conduct regulation in this field. The reader must be the judge.

NOTE

1 As Christopher Foster has reminded me, Peter's function was also to act as a minder for these rather exotic civil servants. After six months' minding, we were judged to be sound enough to be left on our own.
2 The Office of Electricity Regulation: I started as Economic Adviser in 1989.
3 Mergers and Monopolies Commission: I was a member from 1988 to 1994.
4 The Office of Gas Regulator: I have been an Economic Adviser since leaving MMC in 1994.

2 Privatization
Principles, problems and priorities[1]

M.E. Beesley and S.C. Littlechild[2]

What principles should guide a further programme of privatization? What kinds of problems will be encountered, and where should the priorities lie? Economists have not written much on these issues. We hope to provide an explicit structure in which relevant questions can be identified and answered.

'Privatization' is generally used to mean the formation of a Companies Act company and the subsequent sale of at least 50 per cent of the shares to private shareholders. However, the underlying idea is to improve industry performance by increasing the role of market forces. Many other measures can contribute to this, notably freeing of entry to an industry, encouraging competition and permitting joint ventures. Market forces can also be increased by restructuring the nationalized industry, to create several successor companies which may be publicly owned. To secure maximum benefits, a whole set of measures must be designed for each industry, including privatization as a key element.

In this article we seek criteria to decide: (1) whether a particular nationalized industry is a serious candidate for privatization; (2) how the industry should be structured and the regulatory environment designed; and (3) what should be the priorities for privatization among the industries.

CRITERIA FOR PRIVATIZATION

It is helpful to structure the problem as a cost–benefit analysis. In principle, one might examine the effects of each alternative privatization proposal on different interest groups such as existing and potential customers, taxpayers, suppliers of labour and capital, etc. Trade-offs between these interest groups could be established and decisions made accordingly.

We propose to short-circuit this procedure somewhat by specifying a single criterion, namely the present value of aggregate net benefits to UK consumers. This is measured primarily by lower prices of currently available goods and services (offset by any price increases). Effects on the level of output, the quality and variety of goods and services available, and the rate of innovation will also be important. Typically, there will be release of resources, benefiting the consumer in other ways. Changes in the distribution of benefits (e.g. by geographical area) and effects on employees, suppliers, exports and taxpayers must also be considered. None the less, the criterion of aggregate net benefit to consumers seems a simple and appropriate starting point. Unless this promises to be considerable, the political costs of change will scarcely be worth incurring. (Public opinion on privatization is probably changing. Political 'costs' may prove significantly less than they once appeared.)

We do not assume that privatization is desirable in itself. Respectable arguments support such a view – for example, that political freedom depends on private property, or that government intervention should be minimized, because the larger the government sector, the larger the threat to liberty. Here, privatization is strictly an economic instrument. Privatization in certain industries (or parts thereof) could be ruled out as simply not beneficial to consumers.

Our criterion excludes the stock-market value of the successor company or companies. This value could clearly be artificially increased (e.g. by granting a monopoly or announcing lesser restrictions on entry), but this would be counter-productive to consumers. Similarly, the (alleged) poor proceeds of sale, realized or in prospect, should not in themselves deter privatization. The right sale price is simply that which investors are prepared to pay, once conditions and timing of sale have been determined by the criterion of consumer benefit.

Though it should not influence the decision to privatize, the sale value is not unimportant. The proceeds are the price at which the present owners of the company's assets (i.e. the taxpayers) transfer these assets to the future owners (i.e. the shareholders). The method of flotation should aim to minimize oversubscription or undersubscription. There is no merit in making a gift to 'stags' or imposing losses on underwriters. The difficulties of estimating future stock-market prices are great, as witness Amersham, Britoil and Associated British Ports. There is therefore a strong case for supplementing professional advice by the organization of some form of futures market, for example by distributing to customers limited quantities of shares to be traded in advance of the main flotation.

The criterion of benefit to consumers should be used to design the privatization scheme as a whole. Consider some of the things to be decided in order to write prospectuses for floating one or more successor companies:

1 the number of companies, the assets and liabilities of each, and their intended aims and scope of business;
2 the structure of the industry in which the company (or companies) will operate, especially the conditions of new entry;
3 the regulatory environment, including competition policy, efficiency audits, controls (if any) on prices or profits;

4 non-commercial obligations (e.g. with respect to employment, prices or provision of services) and sources of funding for these obligations (e.g. direct subsidies from government or local authorities);
5 the timing of the privatization scheme, including the flotation date and the times at which new competition is allowed and/or regulation instituted;
6 future levels of government shareholding, and ways in which the associated voting power will be used.

Potential investors will translate this package, which is designed to maximize benefits to consumers, into a stock-market price. Successful flotation requires an accurate forecast of this price, and a limited futures market in the shares can help.

BENEFITS AND COSTS

Our criterion involves benefits for two sets of consumers: actual or potential consumers of the industry; and other consumers, who benefit from savings in resources which may accompany privatization. Thus, if lower subsidies are paid, other consumers will benefit via lower taxation. Subsidies represent real resources which could be consumed elsewhere.

Privatization will generate benefits for consumers because privately owned companies have a greater incentive to produce goods and services in the quantity and variety which consumers prefer. Companies which succeed in discovering and meeting consumer needs make profits and grow; the less successful wither and die. The discipline of the capital market accentuates this process: access to additional resources for growth depends on previously demonstrated ability. Selling a nationalized industry substitutes market discipline for public influence. Resources tend to be used as consumers dictate, rather than according to the wishes of government, which must necessarily reflect short-term political pressures and problems of managing the public sector's overall demands for capital.[3]

But gains are not all one way. Privatization is intended to change motivations of management towards profit-making. A privately owned company will have greater incentive to exploit monopoly power commercially. To the extent that this is not limited, consumer benefits from privatization will be less than they might be. Second, a privatized company will be less willing to provide uneconomic services. The resources so released will be used more productively, but particular sets of consumers will lose by the change. This raises the question of how such losses, often thought of as social obligations, should be handled. Third, eliminating inefficient production and restrictive labour practices means the release of resources. This will benefit taxpayers and consumers outside the industry, but some employees and suppliers will suffer. The short-cut criterion does not explicitly recognize these losers. Ways of coping with these three problems are discussed below.

Some have argued that ownership is largely irrelevant. But could the benefits of privatization be obtained without the change in ownership? We have already argued that ownership *does* matter because consumers in general will be better served. Also, for political reasons, privatization may be a necessary accompaniment to competition. The additional liberalization of entry into telecommunications announced in February 1983 would not have been politically feasible if the transfer of British Telecom to private ownership had not by then been in process. Furthermore, competition policy is (or certainly could be) more effective against a private company than against a nationalized industry.

Alternative ways of increasing market pressure are politically limited. The benefits of privatization derive partly from the ability to diversify and redeploy assets, unconstrained by nationalization statutes. These statutes might be relaxed without transferring ownership, but rival firms and tax-payers fearing government-subsidized competition or uncontrolled expansion would undoubtedly oppose this. Again, efficiency might increase if governments refrained from intervening in the industries, but as long as the industries are nationalized, such self-restraint is implausible. The industries might be asked to act commercially, but nationalization itself delays inevitable adjustments to market forces. The substantial reductions in over-manning in British Airways and the nationalized manufacturing industries could surely not have been achieved if the intention to privatize had not already been expressed.

Nationalized industries were deemed appropriate vehicles for a wide variety of social policies. But most consumer's interests were adversely affected, and nationalization often proved inadequate for the social purposes too. It is now necessary to reform the industries while meeting social needs. This is always a politically difficult exercise, and impossible with nationalization. Privatization, properly designed, makes it possible to decouple the two tasks, and to focus social policy more effectively.

COMPETITION

Competition is the most important mechanism for maximizing consumer benefits, and for limiting monopoly power. Its essence is rivalry and free-dom to enter a market. What counts is the existence of competitive threats, from potential as well as existing competitors. The aim is not so-called 'perfect' competition; rather, one looks for some practical means to intro-duce or increase rivalry. The relevant comparison for policy is between the level of competition that could realistically be created, and the present state of the nationalized industry.

Certain features of nationalization need attention whatever the ownership form finally adopted. The artificial restrictions on entry embodied in the statutory monopolies granted to most of the earlier nationalized industries should be removed. Government-controlled resources (e.g. wayleaves and radio spectrum; airspace, routes, and landing rights; harbour facilities; mineral rights on land and sea, etc.) should be made equally available to new entrants, without favouring the incumbent nationalized concerns.

The starting structure for the successor private company or companies is extremely important. In some cases, different parts of the industry could compete if formed into horizontally separate companies. Resources or assets could be transferred to potential entrants. Vertically separating the industry into different companies would also generate rivalry at the inter-face. If, for example, British Telecom's International Division were separated from the Inland Division, each would encourage alternative sources of supply (including self-supply).

Splitting up an organization might involve sacrificing economies of scale or scope. Increased costs of production or transacting may offset the gains from increased competition. This argument is dubious for present national-ized industries, since they have been determined largely by political or administrative, not market, forces. However, in the absence of competition, one cannot know in advance precisely what industry structure will prove most efficient. Therefore, as far as possible, the future growth of the industry should not be fixed by the pattern established at flotation. Com-panies should be allowed to expand or contract, diversify or specialize, as market forces dictate. Where there are very few existing outside compet-itors, or none at all, the starting structure should be designed to create effective competition. When in doubt, smaller rather than larger successor companies should be created, and allowed to merge thereafter, subject to rules of competition policy discussed below.

REGULATION AND COMPETITION POLICY

Even the introduction of such competition as is feasible may still leave the incumbent with significant monopoly power in some industries. How should this be dealt with? Government will no longer have the direct and indirect control associated with nationalization, but alternative means of influencing or regulating conduct are available (besides the promotion of competition).

One favourite idea is to influence the successor company's prices by limiting the profits earned, expressed as a rate of return on capital. The United States has had much experience of this; the result has generally been higher rather than lower prices. Some defects are well known: disincentives to efficiency, a 'cost-plus' mentality and expensive enforcement. Other defects are gradually becoming better understood: the vulnerability to 'capture' of the regulatory commission by the regulated industry, and the associated tendency to limit competition among incumbents and to restrict new entry. In fact, US regulation embodies a philosophy similar to nation-alization, with similar effects. Rate-of-return regulation should not be thought of as a relevant accompaniment to privatization.

There is considerable pressure for efficiency audits or value for money audits, on the grounds that monopoly industries will have inadequate incentive to increase efficiency. Without sanctions for non-compliance, such audits are likely to be ineffective. However, if they are used for setting tariffs and controlling investment plans, the system essentially amounts to rate-of-return regulation, itself defective for the reasons just indicated. Pressure of competition and the firms' own incentive not to waste resources are likely to be more effective inducements to efficiency than the creation of a government nanny.

Another possibility is to limit prices directly by means of explicit tariff restrictions. For example, it is proposed that the price of a bundle of telecommunications services should not increase by more than X percentage points below the retail price index (the RPI $- X$ formula) for a period of 5 years. This could be applied to any set of services, perhaps weighted as in the bills of a representative consumer. The level of X would, in practice, be the outcome of bargaining between BT and the government; an exhaustive costing exercise is not called for.

The purpose of such a constraint is to reassure customers of monopoly services that their situation will not get worse under privatization. It 'holds the fort' until competition arrives, and is inappropriate if competition is not expected to emerge. It is a temporary safeguard, not a permanent method of control. The 'one-off' nature of the restriction is precisely what preserves the firm's incentive to be efficient, because the firm keeps any gains beyond the specified level. Repeated 'cost-plus' audits would destroy this incentive and, moreover, encourage 'nannyish' attitudes towards the industry.

A preferable alternative to detailed regulation of costs, profits or prices is greater reliance on competition policy. Predatory competition should be discouraged, both to curb monopoly power and to allow new ownership structures to emerge after privatization. In the UK at present, potential anti-competitive practices have to be considered in turn by the Office of Fair Trading, the Monopolies and Mergers Commission and the Secretary of State. In the case of hitherto-nationalized industries a stronger and speedier policy is required. The main aim should be to protect existing and potential competitors likely to be at a disadvantage when competing with a dominant incumbent, who in the past has generally had the advantage of statutory protection, and who even now probably has significant legal and other advantages (e.g. rights of way). Certain practices (e.g. price discrimination, refusal to supply, full-line forcing) should be explicitly prohibited if they are used by the dominant incumbent to eliminate or discipline specific competitors. Parties adversely affected should be able to sue in the courts, perhaps for triple damages.

The 1983 Bill privatizing British Telecom exhibits some awareness of the problem. Present monopoly control has been supplemented by an Office of Telecommunications, and BT's licence will require published tariffs and prohibit predatory price discrimination. However, encouraging future entry and reliance on competition policy instead of regulation have yet to be as firmly established as would be desirable.

NON-COMMERCIAL OBLIGATIONS

Nationalized industries provide various services which are uneconomic at present prices and costs. Not all are necessarily uneconomic and some could be made viable by a private company or companies operating with increased efficiency. However, there will also be attempts to raise certain prices and/or reduce certain services. Since a main aim of privatization is to guide resources to the most highly valued uses, the companies should not be prevented from doing so. Nevertheless, it may well be felt socially desirable or politically necessary to ensure that certain prices or services are maintained (e.g. in rural areas).

Procedures for establishing non-commercial obligations need to be clearly specified. Each privatization act should define which services are potentially of social concern. Any company claiming that such a service is uneconomic should be required to provide relevant financial data to support its case, accompanied by a request to withdraw unless a subsidy is provided. A specified public body (e.g. a local authority) will then consider whether the case is plausible, whether another operator is willing to provide the service, and whether a subsidy should be provided.

Where should this subsidy come from? One of the prime aims of nationalization was to facilitate cross-subsidies from more profitable services. However, cross-subsidization largely hides the extent of the subsidy and opens the door to political pressures. Also, it inevitably entails restrictions on competition so as to protect the source of funds: cross-subsidization and unrestricted competition are mutually incompatible. For these reasons, economists have long recommended that explicit public subsidies should be provided in preference to cross-subsidies.

What if the government is unwilling to do this? Explicit subsidies have admittedly not proved politically popular to date. Other possibilities have to be explored. In telecommunications it is currently envisaged that BT will charge an access fee to other networks; this will be used to finance emergency services, call-boxes and certain loss-making services in rural areas. This amounts to a tax on telecom operators to support particular socially sanctioned outputs. So long as the scope of these 'social' services is narrowly defined, stringent tests of loss making are applied, and the access fee is applied to all relevant operators, the tax will remain low and competition should not be seriously damaged. Such compromises may well have to be worked out for many cases of privatization in which protection of particular consumers is deemed important. They will reduce total net benefits to consumers; but political realities have to be faced. Unless safeguards are provided for adversely affected interest groups, privatization itself could well be jeopardized. Once again, the design of the privatization scheme is crucial.

Privatization is often opposed on the grounds that it leads to unemployment. But even state-owned firms cannot in practice finance overmanning over long periods. Large-scale redundancies have already occurred in those which have failed to match international competitors' efficiency. Where the effects of privatization promise to be severe, generous redundancy payments should be made. However, remaining employees' prospects will be brighter in privatized industries, which have a superior ability to adapt, diversify and grow.

PRIORITIES

We have argued that a nationalized industry should be privatized if the net benefits to consumers from doing so are positive. Many industries will meet this criterion, yet it would be impossible to privatize all of them at once, if only because of the constraints imposed by the parliamentary timetable. Which industries should then be given priority? Leaving aside political considerations, our criterion indicates those industries where the consumer benefits of privatization are greatest. How can this be determined?

First, other things being equal, a larger industry offers larger potential scope for savings. That is, if costs and prices can be reduced by an average of x per cent, an industry with a turnover of £2 billion offers twice the potential benefit of an industry with a turnover of £1 billion. Table 2.1 lists the nationalized industries in order of turnover. It shows that the largest three industries (electricity, telecommunications and gas) account for nearly half the total turnover in the nationalized sector. At the other end of the list, there is relatively little to be gained by privatizing the smallest seven industries, whatever percentage gains each one could generate, since together they account for less than 6 per cent of total turnover in the nationalized sector. Of course, other things are *not* equal, and the industries offer significantly different scope for generating benefits, as we show in a moment. None the less, the criterion of size must be constantly borne in mind. For example, to match a 1 per cent saving in capital employment in the electricity industry, it would be necessary to achieve a saving of 2 per cent in telecoms, 5 per cent in coal, 12 per cent in steel or 24 per cent in posts.

Second, industries will offer less scope for savings if they have already been subject to severe remedial action, and more scope if they are as yet relatively untouched. The last column of Table 2.1 shows the percentage changes in manpower over the last two years. By this criterion, the 'manufacturing' nationalized industries (British Steel, BL, Rolls-Royce, British Shipbuilders) plus British Airways and the bus companies probably have relatively small further savings to offer compared to the other industries, particularly since press reports suggest that yet more redundancies are already in train.

Table 2.1 Nationalized industries,* 1981/2

Name	Turnover £m	Capital employed (CCA basis)£m	Workforce 000s	% Change in workforce since 1979/80
Electricity industry[1]	8,057	32,605	147	−8
British Telecom	5,708	16,099	246	+2
British Gas	5,235	10,955	105	0
National Coal Board	4,727	5,891	279	−5
British Steel	3,443	2,502	104	−38
BL	3,072	1,521	83[5]	−31
British Rail	2,899[2]	2,746	227	−7
Post Office[3]	2,636	1,347	183	0
British Airways	2,241	1,338	43[4]	−24
Rolls-Royce	1,493	992	45	−23
British Shipbuilders	1,026	655	67	−18
S Scotland Electricity Board	716	2,817	13	−5
National Bus Company	618	508	53	−16
British Airports Authority	277	852	7	−7
N Scotland Hydro Electric	270	1,981	4	−3
Civil Aviation Authority	206	162	7	−2
Scottish Transport Group	152	157	11	−17
British Waterways Board	16	50	3	−2
Total	42,792	83,178	1,627	

* These are the organizations classed as nationalized industries in the public enterprise division of the Treasury, as reflected in the White Paper *Government Expenditure Plans*, Cmnd 8789, with the addition of BL and Rolls-Royce.

Notes:
1 Including CEGB, Council and Area Boards. Figures for CEGB alone are £6,364m, £23,357m, 55,000, − 11%.
2 Including government contract payments of £810 million.
3 Including Giro and postal orders.
4 Reportedly 37,500 as at March 1983.
5 UK only; overseas approximately 22,000.

Third, benefits to consumers are likely to be greater in so far as competition rather than monopoly is likely to predominate. Competition could come from multiple ownership in the same industry, from abroad, or from rival products. However, in order to ascertain which industries, or parts of industries, are susceptible to competition it is necessary to examine more closely the demand and cost conditions under which the industries are likely to operate.

These ideas may be clarified by conceiving of each nationalized industry as located in a simple 2 × 2 matrix. Demand prospects for typical services and products are classified as 'Good' or 'Bad', depending on long-term trends, and supply prospects are classed as conducive to 'Single' or 'Multiple' (competing) ownership depending on developments in technology. This of course oversimplifies the situation, but the contrasts between the industries are great enough for the divisions to be useful.

Demand prospects

		Good	Bad
Supply prospects	Single	**A** Electricity distribution (Area Boards and Grid) Telecoms (local) Gas distribution Airports	**B** Rail Post (or possibly C?) Waterways
	Multiple	**C** CEGB (excl. Grid) Telecoms (excl. local) Gas production Coal British Airways	**D** Steel BL Rolls-Royce Shipbuilding Buses

Figure 2.1 Classification of nationalized industries post-privatization

Figure 2.1 shows our own conjectures as to the quadrant in which each industry would be located *if appropriately privatized*. These are not necessarily the same quadrants as the one in which the industries would currently be placed. As we shall shortly argue, privatization may well be necessary in order to shift an industry from an 'inferior' quadrant to a 'better' one, that is to one which offers greater benefits to consumers (and, often, to employees also). In some cases, too, it is appropriate to place different parts of an industry into different quadrants (e.g. electricity production and distribution). We now consider each quadrant in turn – for convenience, in the order D, C, A, B.

Quadrant D

Industries in this quadrant need present no problems of monopoly power, since multiple ownership is quite feasible within the UK. Moreover, the manufacturing industries among them – British Steel, BL, British Shipbuilders and Rolls-Royce – are already subject to international competition, which secures prices as low as can be expected, given the current excess capacity on a world scale. Operating efficiency – or lack of it – in the UK industries is a relatively minor factor in determining prices. Labour monopoly power has surely been much reduced. There may be expansion as the depression ends, but there will probably be increasing competition from superior sources abroad, so these industries are always likely to occupy quadrant D. Thus, consumers in these manufacturing industries will gain little *directly* from privatization.

Consumers will, however, gain indirectly from privatization, notably as taxpayers. Private owners will be more willing and able than the government to identify and rectify inefficiencies and to exploit new opportunities. Privatization will reduce the liability to losses and free resources for better use elsewhere. It should not be deferred merely to get the industries 'into the black', by further subsidies, so that a 'respectable' flotation price can be achieved.

Of all the nationalized industries, bus operations are least suited to the scale of operations which nationalization implies. Nevertheless, the prospective gains are greater from encouraging competition than from privatization. An important element of NBC is long-distance traffic. Here deregulation occurred in 1980, leading to increased competition, better service and lower prices. Further gains would follow from removing further obstacles to competition (e.g. by facilitating access to favourable terminal locations). In urban areas, the principal short-distance markets, quite different conditions prevail. The incumbent operators are owned by local authorities, and to a much lesser extent by NBC, and entry is still toughly regulated. Here, there would be a large gain from deregulation, not least in the redistribution of bus resources towards the more favourable routes. Methods of subsidy should also be changed to stimulate competition so as to promote efficiency among all kinds of operators (e.g. by shifting subsidies to users, not paying them to producers).

In sum, privatization of the manufacturing industries in quadrant D will yield positive but small net benefits to consumers, so a high priority is not indicated. In the bus industry, preference should be given to facilitating competition where it is at present restricted.

Quadrant C

Industries in this quadrant are characterized by good long-term demand prospects. They happen to be very large, and (with the exception of British Airways) are relatively untouched as yet, so they presumably offer considerable scope for improvements in efficiency. They need present no significant problems of monopoly power, because multiple ownership is viable. Thus, they are prime candidates for privatization.

Interestingly, however, none of the four industries is organized as if it were in quadrant C at present. The CEGB and British Telecom are each a single organization (though Mercury should begin to offer a challenge to the latter). The NCB is a single organization whose prospects in the absence of privatization are somewhat dim. British Airways is part of a multi-ownership industry, but again its prospects without privatization are unclear. Currently, these industries would probably be put in quadrants A, B and D respectively. Privatizing them involves recognizing that, wholly or partly, they could belong to quadrant C, and that benefits for both consumers and employees can be secured without generating severe problems of monopoly power. However, careful attention needs to be given to their structure after privatization.

In the case of the CEGB, the national grid should remain in public ownership for the present, perhaps as a common carrier. (It might be integrated with the Department of Energy.) The generating stations should be sold to separate buyers, so as to establish competition in production. Firms would be allowed to bid for a group of stations (and coal mines) so as to achieve economies of integration, but sufficient independent entities would be created to make competition workable.

Privatization of the British coal industry would follow a similar pattern. Consumers would benefit directly from the lower prices due to competition, including the removal of restrictions on imports. The prospects for the British coal industry itself would also be greatly improved. There are currently very dramatic differences in costs between different pits. Resources of capital and labour would be reallocated so that the more efficient pits – which would command the highest prices on privatization – would expand. There would also be benefits from a severe reduction in the monopoly power of labour. The relatively low capital–labour ratio (£21,000 capital employed per man in 1981/2) could profitably be increased. Because long-term trends in demand are favourable to coal (particularly when synthetic fuels become viable), and because Britain has many favourably placed locations for coal mining, the industry could once again become an expanding one. Employment could then increase in the British coal industry as a whole. In practice, privatization seems necessary to secure these benefits. Of the pits which are presently extra-marginal, some would become viable as a result of more efficient management. Widespread closure of the least efficient pits would necessitate a generous policy to cope with social adjustment. As noted earlier, a merit of privatization is that it divorces the problem of industrial development from that of discharging society's debts arising from the past.

The 1983 Bill enabling the privatization of British Telecom does not envisage the restructuring of British Telecom. The present analysis would indicate the creation of several successor companies. Local distribution (which we place in quadrant A) presents the chief monopoly problem. The Bill does explicitly recognize the need for developments in competition policy to prevent the exploitation of a dominant position, and the government has concurrently announced limited measures to facilitate competition from new entry, though more could be done. Overall, most of the industry is prospectively in quadrant C.

The British Gas Corporation is already subject to competition in the discovery and extraction of gas. It has hitherto held a favoured position as sole buyer; this has recently been discontinued. Competition and efficiency would be further increased if some of the extremely valuable existing contracts were auctioned to new entrants, if the production side of the Corporation were completely separated from the national grid and local distribution, and if restrictions on gas exports were removed. Whether privatization of gas production would create direct as well as indirect benefits for consumers is not clear.

No special steps are necessary to achieve a competitive market structure for British Airways, though fewer restrictions on routes and allocation of airport landing slots on a more competitive basis would facilitate competition. However, as with the manufacturing industries, it is not clear that the further gains to consumers from privatizing BA would be substantial. Thus, in quadrant C, the prime candidates are the CEGB, British Telecom and the NCB.

Quadrant A

The industries in this quadrant are characterized by good demand prospects but the supply prospects do not favour multiple competing ownership. Local distribution systems for electricity, gas and telephones are characterized by high sunk costs. With the possible exception of telephones, they do not face much immediate technological challenge, and will be sustainable as local monopolies. Consumers are therefore at risk.

Cannot the market process be used even if successor entities are sustainable monopolies? Some have argued for auctioning franchises to private bidders, thereby encouraging competition for the monopoly privileges. Franchising would transfer the value of the inherent monopoly power to the seller – in this case the government. This benefits the taxpayer, but does little to help the consumer. There are practical snags, too, in awarding the franchise to the bidder offering the lowest price to consumers, as witness experience in the United States with franchising cable TV. It is difficult to specify in advance the appropriate pattern and quality of output, and the costs of negotiating and monitoring contracts are substantial. Furthermore, it is difficult to sell a franchise on the premise of sustainable (natural) monopoly alone. Bidders will usually demand statutory monopoly privileges, which will create formal exemption from risks of entry and engender a position from which to exact further concessions from governments. Though the franchising option is not ruled out, it needs far more analytic attention before positive recommendations can be made.

This does not mean that nothing can be done to generate benefits for consumers in these industries. Restrictions on new entry can be removed, so as to pare down the monopoly to a minimum. This has recently been done for gas and electricity, but entry into local telephone networks (e.g. by cable TV companies) is still highly restricted. Dividing utility distribution systems into regionally independent units would create market pressures on supplies of factors of production, not least in providing alternative opportunities for hiring and rewarding management talent, and would facilitate competition on the production side. Between airports, there is some, but not much, scope for direct competition for customers. It would be quite feasible, and beneficial, to organize the more important airports as separate entities.

To summarize, privatizing the industries in quadrant A will pose problems in curbing monopoly power. It would be more fruitful to encourage competition by removing restrictions on entry and restructuring the industries, even if the successor companies remain as nationalized, municipal or other public bodies.

Quadrant B

The industries in this quadrant have declining demand prospects while their supply conditions favour a single organization. Monopoly power may be a problem in some services, but it is generally not severe because the reason for the decline in demand is the emergence of substitutes preferred by consumers. Nationalization was seen as a means of resisting decline: it led to continued injections of new capital and the financing of losses. The aim of privatization would be to facilitate the movement of resources out of these industries and/or use existing resources more fully by developing new products and services. However, social and political problems will accompany the withdrawal of services. Privatization schemes will need to be designed with careful thought to non-commercial obligations.

As far as rail operations are concerned, British Rail would remain in quadrant B after privatization. These operations are not easily divisible below reasonably sized and geographically separate sectors, such as the old regions. No one is likely to want, or to be able, to emulate such successor railway supply companies, so their monopolies will be technically sustainable. However, demand is adverse, and will increasingly be so. This particular combination of circumstances BR shares with British Waterways. But BR is marked off from the other nationalized industries by the exceptionally high alternative use value of its assets. Its territory is immense, and in many parts very valuable indeed. Privatization here would indeed be called an asset stripper's paradise, not just for selling land, but for all the myriad deals which can be constructed, based on locational advantage.

In the case of a declining industry of high alternative use value, asset stripping is very much in the general consumer's interest. However, railways are perhaps the most politically sensitive of all the nationalized industries. Wholesale withdrawal of services would not be politically acceptable. A practical compromise therefore presents itself. Successor companies could be floated which, in return for command over assets, would have to bind themselves to a minimum programme of rail output. This output would be heavily passenger oriented and would, in effect, be financed by profits from other activities. Because of privatization, the required output would be achieved in a much more economical way than at present, thereby freeing up many stations, marshalling yards and miles of track. The alternative use value of these assets is so great that a quite considerable passenger output could be insisted upon. The Serpell report thought it necessary to severely curtail the rail network in order to achieve financial viability. With the present approach, a much higher rail output could be attained. Thus, privatization would open up social solutions not possible under nationalization.

Demand for postal services is probably decreasing, partly because of more direct competition from telecommunications. However, there are attractive market possibilities in new forms of collaboration with new techniques. In fact, though most would now place the Post Office in quadrant D, there are opportunities for its eventual emergence in quadrant C. Mainly because it is so labour intensive – capital employed is the lowest of all the industries in Table 2.1 at £7,600 per man – there is considerable scope for labour substitution and redeployment. The basic distribution network has great potential for development outside traditional Post Office work. A useful form of privatization would be a successor national company, or several regional companies, which essentially would franchise the local operations to individual small groups. One could therefore expect not only an improvement in postal services, but also a willingness to diversify into such services as security and delivery work.

CONCLUSIONS

Privatization is not merely a matter of selling shares in a nationalized industry. The underlying intent is to improve industry performance by increasing the role of market forces. To achieve this, other devices for promoting competition must also be adopted. Each act of privatization must be part of a whole scheme tailored to the particular conditions of each industry.

The following general considerations should guide policy:

1 Privatization schemes should be designed to maximize net consumer benefits, measured primarily by lower prices and improved quality of service, rather than stock-market proceeds. A futures market for shares would facilitate flotation.
2 The promotion of competition – by removing artificial restrictions on entry, making resources equally available to potential entrants, and restructuring the existing industries – is the most effective means of maximizing consumer benefits and curbing monopoly power.
3 Stricter competition policy is preferable to rate-of-return regulation, efficiency audits and related forms of government 'nannying'.
4 Clear ground rules should be laid down concerning the criteria for providing uneconomic services and the sources of finance for these.
5 Compensation should be paid for serious transitional unemployment, though in the longer run employees' prospects will be enhanced by privatization.

6 Priority should be given to privatizing those industries where consumer benefits are likely to be greatest. Potential benefits will depend upon the size of the industry, whether it has already received attention, and whether competition rather than monopoly is likely to ensue.

The scope for privatization is substantially greater than is commonly believed. Consumers would benefit, directly or indirectly, from appropriately designed privatization schemes in industries covering over four-fifths of the presently nationalized sector. In the remaining industries, notably buses, airports and local distribution of electricity, gas and telephones, the main benefits would derive from restructuring into smaller units and facilitating new entry.

The announced intention to privatize British Airways and the manufacturing industries has already helped to increase efficiency, and privatization should not be delayed merely to increase the proceeds from flotation. Nevertheless, these industries are no longer first priorities. Greater benefits to consumers would derive from privatizing the Central Electricity Generating Board (excluding the national grid), British Telecom, the National Coal Board, British Rail and the Post Office. Apart from British Telecom, these industries are seldom thought of as candidates for privatization. However, the bulk of the consumer benefits that can be expected to follow from privatization could be achieved by appropriately designed policies for these five industries alone.

NOTES

1 *Lloyds Bank Review*, July 1983.
2 At the time of writing Michael Beesley is Professor of Economics at the London Graduate School of Business Studies and Stephen Littlechild is Professor of Commerce in the Department of Industrial Economics and Business Studies at the University of Birmingham. This article was written before the 9 June General Election was announced.
3 To support this argument, there is growing empirical evidence, mainly from the USA, that privately owned companies make more efficient use of labour, capital and other resources, and are also more innovative. See, for example, De Alessi (1974, 1980)

BIBLIOGRAPHY

Privatization

Barlow, W. (1981) 'The problems of managing nationalized industries', in *Allies or Adversaries*, London: Royal Institute of Public Administration.
Heald, D. and Steel, D. (1981) 'The privatization of UK public enterprises', *Annals of Public and Co-operative Economy* 52, 351–68.
——(1982) 'Privatizing public enterprise: an analysis of the government's case', *Political Quarterly*, July, 333–49.
Littlechild, S.C. (1978) *The Fallacy of the Mixed Economy*, Hobart Paper 80, Institute of Economic Affairs.

Littlechild, S.C. (1981) 'Ten steps to denationalization', *Journal of Economic Affairs* 2 (1) October.
Pryke, R. (1981) *The Nationalized Industries*, Martin Robertson.
Redwood, J. (1980) *Public Enterprise in Crisis*, Oxford: Blackwell.
—— and Hatch, J. (1982) *Controlling Public Industries*, Oxford: Blackwell.

Evidence on regulation and ownership

Breyer, S. (1982) *Regulation and its Reform*, Cambridge, Mass.: Harvard University Press.
Chandler Jr, A.D. (1980) 'Government versus business: an American phenomenon', in J.T. Dunlop (ed.) *Business and Public Policy*, Boston: Harvard University Press.
De Alessi, L. (1974) 'An economic analysis of government ownership and regulation', *Public Choice* XIX, Fall.
—— (1980) 'The economics of property rights: a review of the evidence', *Research in Law and Economics* 2.
Jarrell, G.A. (1978) 'The demand for state regulation of the electric utility industry', *Journal of Law and Economics*, October.
Stigler, G.J. (1971) 'The theory of economic regulation', *Bell Journal of Economics* 2 (1) Spring, reprinted in G.J. Stigler (1975) *The Citizen and the State*, Chicago: University of Chicago Press.

Nature of competition

Hayek, F.A. (1948) 'The meaning of competition', in F.A. Hayek (ed.) *Individualism and Economic Order*, Chicago: University of Chicago Press.
—— (1978) 'Competition as a discovery procedure', in *New Studies in Philosophy, Ethics and Economics*, London: Routledge Kegan and Paul.

Competition policy

Beesley, M.E. (1973) 'Mergers and economic welfare', in Arthur Selden (ed.) *Mergers, Takeovers and the Structure of Industry*, IEA Readings no. 10, pp. 73–80.

3 Privatization
Reflections on UK experience[1]

M.E. Beesley

INTRODUCTION

Privatization has been a consistent element in the Conservative government's policy since 1979, but it was only with the privatization of British Telecom in 1984 that it assumed the political importance it now has. Up to the election of 1987, over £15 billion had been raised by the Treasury by the sale of publicly owned assets. This transfer of ownership is the essential feature of 'privatization' in the UK, and distinguishes it from other ways of transferring activity to the private sector, such as requiring nationalized industries to put out certain of their operations to private tender.

Privatization was, and is, part of the political ambition to roll back the scope of the state. But what gave the opportunity to broaden political aims was the (at the time) radical proposals to 'sell off' very large nationalized industries normally thought of as belonging naturally to the public sector. Thus the successive privatization of British Telecom (BT), British Gas (BG), British Airports Authority (BAA) and now, as announced in the Conservative June manifesto, Water Authorities and (probably in the 1989/90 session) Electricity. The key political insight was that very large, safe-looking enterprises gave the opportunity to add a significant dimension to the private ownership of shares, so reinforcing the aim of building a 'property-owning democracy'. Millions of people have indeed become shareholders for the first time through the big privatizations; though how many will survive as shareholders is a matter for debate, there is no doubt that an important political constituency has been created.

Moreover, the new shareholders included many workers of the nationalized industries involved, over 90 per cent in British Telecom's case. The existence of these two groups of shareholders has an important economic effect. It greatly reduces the risk that, with a change of government, renationalization would occur on terms unfavourable to shareholders. (As things now stand, after the June election, such a risk appears doubly hedged!)

British Telecom and British Gas alone have accounted for one-half of the realizations on privatization to date, even though only 49 per cent of British

Telecom shares have been sold (so far – the rest may follow in whole or in part later). We might guess that BAA will raise above £1,200 million, and, very speculatively, the Water Authorities and Electricity roughly £7 billion each. The scale of these firms and their assumed degree of monopoly power have generated great interest in how their market conduct can or should be regulated.

Most economists have been critical of what has emerged so far from the privatization programme.[2] I shall explain in this paper why I think much of this criticism has missed important points or has been mistaken. More helpfully, I hope, I shall try to provide a way of analysing the phenomenon, elements of which may well be transferable to non-UK privatization proposals. A further theme will be the conspicuously absent candidates for privatization, prominent among them British Coal, the Post Office and British Rail. Why should they – as apparently they do – present particular difficulties to a radically minded government?

HOW SHOULD ANALYSTS REGARD PRIVATIZATION?

There is an unfortunate tendency among economists to approach the question of privatizing a nationalized industry in terms of a comparison between private sector firms and public organizations *per se*. One sets out generalizations about behaviour in the two types, assumes that the particular cases fit these types and draws conclusions about whether transfer from one to the other is likely to be desirable. This method may be useful in deciding in general whether a policy of privatization ought to be entertained at all, but it is a poor basis for prediction in particular cases. Privatization involves a change from the one condition to the other, requiring careful attention to where one starts, the nationalized industry in question, and to the emerging firm, the privatized entity and, moreover, to what is actually proposed to affect its behaviour. Once the particular shift has been identified, it becomes possible both to make predictions about whether welfare in general will be increased by the change, and to learn from the experience after the event. I shall refer later to an example of the former question, which in effect is a cost–benefit analysis of the proposed change of policy. But I wish in this chapter to concentrate on what we can learn from events so far.

First, in the UK, privatization is observed to involve substantial change in factors affecting managerial and therefore corporate behaviour. It is best to think of the change not in terms of ideal types, but as involving essentially a redrawing of what might be called the 'social contract' between the government and the industry involved. In this change, some terms of the contract are dropped, and others are added. In the UK cases, these greatly affect the scope for managerial action.

Second, because the government has to deal with established (nationalized) firms, there normally has to be a negotiation between the government and top management (conducted through the chairman and responsible Minister) which precedes privatization. In this, the Minister is trying to achieve certain economic aims – lower real prices, better services, etc. – and he or she faces political constraints arising from party ideology, for example private power must be seen to have curbs. The chairman, on the other hand, is engaged in starting a process of shifting an organization steeped in public sector ways into a more flexible, but more uncertain, future. He or she may or may not have been appointed as nationalized industry chairman with a remit to privatize. To review the big UK cases so far: the BT chairman was appointed to head BT as a nationalized industry in 1980 when its secession from the Post Office was in train. BG's and BAA's chairmen were long-serving nationalized industry men. British Airways' chairman, on the other hand, was appointed with a view to privatization.

Whatever their background or their degree of enthusiasm for privatization – and this has varied – the chairmen see their task similarly: to get the terms which will secure a trouble-free financial period while necessary internal change is accomplished. In all these major recent cases this has involved a uniform attitude about the structure of the emerging firm – that this must be kept intact. So far, each chairman has resisted any proposal to break up the industry. The chairmen's major weapon in the negotiation is asymmetry of information – they have complete access to what can be gleaned. The Ministers have formal access to information, but cannot go much beyond what they have conventionally received to discharge their responsibilities for nationalized industries to the House of Commons. Specifically, once the negotiations have started, chairmen are not obliged to speculate for Ministers about outcomes under privatization. The Minister has to have his or her own separate advice on this.

The terms of the new 'social contract' have to be known by the capital markets before flotation. Most of the terms appear in the prospectus, but any ministerial statement after the announcement of a privatization timetable is relevant. Every large privatization case has involved an Act of Parliament to set up the 'contract'. A ministerial statement may bear on any legal question after the Act about the further interpretation of its clauses. In contrast to the normal expectations in nationalized industries, the terms of the 'contract' are expected by both sides to hold for a considerable period ahead. Thus privatization has 'solved' one of the most thorny problems in the history of government – nationalized industry relationships, namely the industries' perennial complaint that objectives are not clear and are subject to unforeseeable ministerial pressures.

But perhaps the most important aspect of the process of privatization is that all the relevant terms of the 'social contract' have to be recognized *simultaneously*. When drawing up the prospectus and related statements, no major factor which might affect valuation can be safely left aside. The markets, in determining the flotation's value, will appraise uncertainties alongside the financial prospects. The consequence is that many aspects of policy which have been neglected or left implicit have to be explained. The requirement for simultaneous treatment means of course that there are many hastily contrived or incomplete answers to questions posed by privatization, leaving unforeseen consequences. A good example is the duopoly policy announced as a prelude to BT's privatization. The role of the second public network (Mercury) had to be announced. So had the decision taken to treat it in principle equally with BT, made with the assurance that the duopoly would last at least five years, that is to 1990, when a change might be possible. The many unforeseen consequences of this on competition between BT and Mercury, and of other potential entrants to the market, are now being played out.

But the point here is that, for better or worse, with privatization all main aspects of the nationalized industries' future have to be given at least attempted answers and, for better or worse, these must be adhered to for a considerable time. This in itself makes a sharp break in the way in which ministerial–nationalized industry relationships have been conducted. In the UK at least – and I suspect it may be very widely true – when Ministers are responsible ultimately for industries, the making of decisions affecting them is essentially sequential. Nationalized industries have to respond to the latest political need, but at the same time are working to be as independent as possible. The last thing each side wants is to be forced to be consistent in every aspect of an industry's actions. Privatization is thus a means – some will say bought too dearly – of breaking free from these constraints, making consistency at least possible in practice.

EXPECTATIONS ABOUT PRIVATIZATION

The most important elements expected in a change to privatization concern (1) a shift into profit-seeking behaviour by the industry's management and (2) changes in the scope to pursue profit, implied both by an escape from political objectives and consequences just noted, and, as indicated earlier, explicit changes in rules about what the industry can do. The implications are far reaching.

Increased profit seeking as an overriding aim will sharply increase the influence of the private market for managerial talent. Those on the old regime with abilities to pursue the new opportunities will gain; others will lose. Recruitment has to be more open. Reward systems will shift towards private industry norms. The stereotyped five-year contract for chairmen and other board members is dropped. There is some evidence of these expectations being fulfilled. In BT's case (the example having the longest track record) management changes at top level have been remarkably speeded up. At the beginning, in 1984, there was also great uncertainty about what management structures would be appropriate, reflected in many changes since. Some notion of the drastic changes in management required can be seen by reference to BT's information about its large customers. When conducting my inquiry of 1980/1,[3] I found that BT could not specify the total business done with any large multi-locational customers; the accounts were monthly, on a cash-in, cash-out basis. A major subsequent task for BT has been to attempt to get informed commercially about its own business.

The large-scale nationalized industries were normally created as supply monopolists. In order to safeguard contiguous private enterprise, restrictions were placed on their ability to enter new areas, so confining them in effect to their original bases. All of the large-scale privatizations have increased the scope for transactions markedly. The formal limitations on integration or disintegration have been largely removed. Privatization shifted the issue of monopolistic behaviour to be dealt with by anti-trust-type rules, on which more comment is made later (see p. 51). Nationalized industries were also of course subject to Treasury financing rules as part of the Public Sector Borrowing Requirement (PSBR) mechanism. Whether a borrower or lender in this system, the change to complete freedom to finance one's own capital requirements represented both major opportunity and a test, in that the capital markets now had to be satisfied.

On the buying side of their operations, a strong, if normally informal, pressure had always been put on nationalized industries to buy from British suppliers, with important results in restricting buying opportunities and relations with the suppliers. The results of this have been extremely uncomfortable, for example for major BT suppliers. But by far the most important, if informal, expected change concerned the position of the labour unions in nationalized industries. All have been opposed to privatization, for economic as well as (in some cases) ideological reasons. The degree to which their bargaining power would be affected depended in each case on the extent to which monopolistic power would be transferred to the privatized firm, but all stood to lose the special position accorded to them in access to Ministers and to direct political pressures via the process of parliamentary accountability.

The objectives of privatization therefore were, and still are, to create circumstances in which management would: (1) exploit all sources of profit including any monopoly right it might inherit or it might be able to create; and as part of this (2) seek to reduce costs both with respect to productive arrangements and by seeking new or neglected ways to improve costs (i.e. to eliminate X inefficiency as understood in the monopoly literature); and (3) similarly, on the demand side, seek out new products, new price/quantity combinations hitherto foreclosed or discouraged by the rules. (That is, to eliminate what I have elsewhere christened Y inefficiency.) Profit seeking is indifferent with respect to monopoly exploitation or eradication of X and Y inefficiencies; if one increases the search for profit, one is expecting each to be pursued, and, indeed, failure by management to pursue any one would be a sign of failure of privatization.

But here, of course, we encounter the trade-offs which have so dominated economic discussions of privatization. In economic welfare terms, privatization involves, so the critics say, an expected loss from (1) extra monopoly exploitation (the Marshallian 'dead losses' to consumers), against gains from (2) and (3), which would be split between producers and consumers (which economists would call 'gains in producer and consumer surplus'). Though all admit it is as yet early to judge, there are considerable fears that (1) is more important than (2) and (3). I find this extremely implausible, for the following reasons.

IS THERE A PRIVATE MONOPOLY POWER PROBLEM?

There are signs that there will be substantial gains from elimination of x and y inefficiencies. There has been a marked speeding up in adoption of available but hitherto neglected technical improvements, related to the removal of capital and constraints on raising capital and purchasing. BT, for example, has chosen to speed up and considerably modify its programme of digitalization of its network, involving among other things substantial change in its previous efforts to pioneer and develop a system which has received virtually no support in export terms. British Gas has recently announced unexpected cuts in gas prices, in which increased efficiency played a significant part. On the cutting of Y inefficiency, BT has been, if anything, too frenetic in its search for new product and services development, while BAA has already begun seriously to address the main misallocation of resources under the old regime, namely that of the competing uses for its extremely valuable land, especially in and around Heathrow and Gatwick. (Land had been occupied by a host of suppliers with little or no regard for their differing ability to pay for advantage of being located on the airport.)

The actual and potential gains have largely yet to develop and may well be difficult to measure, but the main weight of criticism of privatization has been on the side of monopoly exploitation. I would argue that there are several reasons to believe that these fears are exaggerated. First, one cannot have the prospective gains without incurring the risk of losses. Both are tied to the profit motive. Second, the expectation of economists should be influenced by the literature on measuring monopoly gains and losses. This tends to encourage the view that elimination of X inefficiency is more important than Marshallian dead loss. *A fortiori*, the case is stronger if we add, and I believe we should, gains from eliminating Y inefficiency. Third, if one inspects the actual price changes associated with privatization, one has to recognize the possibility that there may, for a considerable time, be a coincidence between raising prices to get more profits and a move towards a 'better' set of prices from the welfare viewpoint. This can occur because most of the industries produce multiple products or services. Under nationalization these were typically priced in ways not reflecting respective marginal costs, and with an arbitrary requirement to create an overall surplus. More logical, profit-based pricing, reflecting costs *and* exploiting the relative demand elasticities, could well have resulted, so far, in a constellation of prices more in line with welfare maxims.

But these are rather esoteric, economists', points. In fact, in every case where there *is* substantial risk of consumer 'exploitation', there are provisions in the respective Acts to deal with it. These are breaking new ground in the UK, and represent one of the most interesting, and significant, developments privatization has stimulated. The means are new forms of price regulation and new bodies both to oversee price control and to enforce licence conditions which bear on the competitive behaviour of the privatized firms. Thus we have for telecoms, Oftel; for gas, Ofgas; for BAA, an expanded CAA, the existing regulatory body; and for the future, Ofwat, to cover the water industry. Other privatizations have not been deemed to require special provisions of this kind. Thus in BA's case competitive pressure in airlines was thought sufficient to ensure the consumer interest. Instead the change for the industry involved is to become subject to the UK's competition laws, to which, as nationalized industries or public corporations, they were not fully – indeed hardly at all – exposed.

Table 3.1 shows how privatization cases, so far, correspond to the distinction between those having special regulatory mechanisms and those which do not. The list includes BAA's anticipated flotation in August 1987. They are ranked by actual or expected size of yields on flotation. The special measures to limit 'exploitation' thus cover more than half of the privatizations by the pound measure. The upcoming water and electricity cases will sharply increase that proportion.

The principles of the price controls adopted differ markedly from most past examples of utility regulation. First, they are targeted to what were thought to be the most vulnerable consumers, for example residential consumers in the case of BT and BG, and to airline passengers (via the charges made to airlines for landing, takeoff and passenger handling). Industrial consumers, it was judged, would be capable of driving their own bargains. In terms of coverage of revenue by the price control measures, the approximate proportions are BT 55 per cent, BG 64 per cent and BAA 37 per cent. The firms are free to charge outside these 'baskets' of services, and, so long as the overall constraint is observed, to vary the prices within a basket. The formula used in each case is $RPI - X$, where RPI indicates the retail price index, expressed as a percentage change over a year, and X a number determined in negotiation with the government. X is 3 for BT, 2 for BG and 1 for BAA. (BG also has a Y, having the effect of exonerating it from the profit risk arising from price fluctuations in the principal raw material, gas supplies, which are outside its control and subject to government taxation policies.) The control disallows rises in the weighted average of the controlled prices or products which exceed RPI minus the negotiated X. (Negotiation of X is one of the principal issues between Ministers and nationalized industry chairmen before flotation.)

Table 3.1 Privatization and special regulatory mechanisms

Privatization cases involving special regulatory provisions	£m	Privatization cases assimilated to existing private sector competition legislation	£m
British Gas	4,145	Trustee Savings Bank	1,498
British Telecom (51% shares)	3,910	Cable and Wireless	1,015
British Airports Authority	1,225	British Airways	900
		British Petroleum (remainder of shares)	819
		Britoil	449
		Brit. Aerospace	393
		Enterprise Oil	380
		Jaguar Cars	297
		Wytch Farm (gas)	215
		Associated Brit. Ports	96
		Inmos	95
		Sealink (Ferries)	66
		Amersham Int.	64
		Int. Aeradio	60
		Ferranti (50% shares)	55
		British Sugar (24% shares)	44
		Int. Computers Ltd	37
		British Rail Hotels (91% shares)	34
		Fairley	22
		Miscellaneous	503
Totals	9,280		7,042

Thus, a second feature of the control is that, unlike most regulated utilities, it is aimed at prices, not at rates of return on capital. The latter form of regulation was rejected at an early stage in the privatization process because it would lead to exploitation of the regulators and therefore consumers, by dextrous use of superior information, and because it would give incentives to management contradictory to the general aims of privatization, among them to increase efficiency. In British Telecom's case, where effective competition was predicted to increase sharply after privatization, the option to abandon the price control mechanism by 1990 (giving it a 5-year run) was retained. A last, essential, feature of price control was its intended stability. Having made the bargain about X in each case, the government undertook not to revise it in material ways before a five-year period had elapsed.

The nature of these price controls has attracted much attention, some of it favourable. The second leg of the monopoly control provisions has passed most critics by. Yet it is in many ways more significant. Formally, the privatized firms are licensed by the relevant Secretary of State to provide their goods or services. The licences contain provisions which essentially and substantially *extend* the ambit of competition law normally faced by large (and other) firms in the private sector. This was largely a practical reaction to the fact that UK competition law is weak in its treatment of single-firm monopoly power. These licence provisions are designed to anticipate possible anti-competitive actions by the newly privatized firms. Among the provisions common to all are those designed to favour transparent accounting procedures, safeguarding against 'undue' discrimination in dealing with customers and suppliers, and review of proposals for merger, to engage in joint ventures, etc. These provisions, like the price controls, are monitored by the respective directors-general of the new offices. They have already been shown to have teeth. Professor Carsberg, the Director-General of Telecommunications in 1985, advised the Secretary of State not to permit proposed joint ventures between BT and IBM, which he thought had anti-competitive implications, particularly with respect to the development of telephony standards. His advice was taken.

The difference in treatment between the newly privatized firms and other large firms in the private sector is that it is *assumed* in the former case that there will be attempts to forestall competition. Measures have been devised, before the event, to try to circumvent this. By contrast, other large firms' conduct can be investigated by the Monopolies and Mergers Commission (MMC) and remedies proposed, but only after triggering a reference to it. As the author of the Telecoms Act once put it to me, in framing the pro-competitive provisions of the licence he imagined that an MMC investigation had been held, finding BT to have been guilty of anti-competitive behaviour against the public interest. He then drafted the appropriate remedies, in advance. In effect, therefore, privatization has introduced a *de facto* extension of UK pro-competitive law, and may well in the future serve as a model for wider reform.[4] Even well-disposed critics have worried that Oftel, Ofgas, etc. will be 'captured' by their large regulated firms. There is a great deal of influence. But to pose the problem as an increase in capture is wrong. All started off with virtually 100 per cent capture. The question is how far have they reduced the level of capture, and (to those who want more competition) what should be done to continue the trend?

THE TRANSFER OF GOVERNMENT RIGHTS

It remains true, however, that the most important aspect of the monopoly problem in privatization is the question of whether or how far, on privatization, government rights and privileges which the nationalized industries have enjoyed are passed on to the privatized firm. By 'rights' and 'privileges' is meant a large number of advantages – such as government-inspired restrictions on land development, negotiating rights with overseas governments and firms, etc. The treatment of these is a leading question in planning for privatization. It is possible to conceive of extinction of the rights along with privatization, so deliberately attempting to reduce the value of the firm, or its assets, to competitive levels. In practice, the bargaining over privatization will normally have to leave the potential for the capital market to perceive some source of monopoly profits. Also politicians perceive a privatization (especially at the start) as a risky exercise. The real question is, how far should one go in handing over or modifying the rights?

Despite the impression often given by those who stress the extent of the monopoly powers handed over on privatization, choices here have varied considerably in the UK. To take the privatizations since 1984, the position, in bald summary, is as follows.

In BT's case the previous exclusive monopoly for all telecommunications has been drastically changed. Post-privatization restrictions on entry are basically confined to the switched-voice market, in which a duopoly is allowed, with Mercury, a subsidiary of Cable and Wireless, as BT's potential competitor. This duopoly policy has been announced to hold until 1990, when it will be reviewed and possibly modified. Thus in other services and products, for example in the provision of value-added services, and in the attachments to services, (the telephone equipment market), substantial competition has emerged. This represents what BT at least thinks of as a revolutionary change.

In the case of British Gas, by contrast, the essential underpinning of market power was not affected by privatization. This consists of the gas distribution grid, the ownership of which conveys cost advantages to the incumbent and, because of this, leeway to price without fear of entry. The former nationalized industry monopoly right *per se* added no value; this was, rather, inherent in the economics of entry. Even if the government were to offer licences to newcomers there would be no takers as long as BG stays within the limit prices, which are considerably above current prices. The former BG monopoly of gas purchases was rescinded in 1981. Since then, it has been in principle possible for large industrial customers to use their own suppliers and to pipe over BG's grid. Until privatization, no instances of contracts of this kind had in fact occurred. The privatization licences held provisions designed to help to encourage these contracts, for example requiring the disclosure of BG's own contract terms and conditions. In effect, therefore, we have in this respect a further *de facto* extension of pro-competitive policy as applied to large private firms.

BAA represents perhaps the clearest case of a wholesale transfer of government right for exploitation by the privatized concern, reinforced by the decision to include all seven BAA airports in one privatized firm. BAA's strong market position arises from locational controls on the entry of rival airports, particularly in the London region. These have effectively excluded competitive entry over the whole period of air travel development, and are maintained intact. Of all the cases of privatization, this is easily the safest bet to generate a secure and growing profit stream.

This does not mean, of course, that there will not be major net economic benefits from privatization. On the contrary, it could persuasively be argued that, on the one hand, passengers are very well protected by the RPI − X formula, backed up by individual airline's pressures on landing fees at Heathrow and, more importantly, by the earning power of activities outside the price control 'basket' of services. On the other hand, the clearest economic losses under nationalization arose from failure to subject the very valuable and expensive land under BAA's control to the price mechanism. This will, predictably, be rectified; BAA will become expert land developers. Indeed, there were clear signs of this development even before the flotation, and in anticipation of it. (BAA has about 7,500 employees; 70,000 people are employed on its land.)

The remaining case of privatization since 1984 has not yet been noticed in this paper because of its comparatively small size. This is the National Bus Company (NBC) which provided (and still does) much of the local bus services outside London and the other main conurbations, together with much of the principal inter-city bus links. In this case, the government took the decision to extinguish government rights at the same time as privatizing. The Transport Act of 1985 abolished quantity control over entry into local bus operations outside London, and withdrew the exemption which the bus industry had hitherto enjoyed from UK competition laws. All observers agree that this is by all odds the most radical privatization package yet from the viewpoint of promoting competition. Protection from entry in local buses had existed for over fifty years, essentially untouched (inter-city bus operations had been deregulated in 1981). The consequence is that the NBC (under a new chairman) is in effect a realization agency. NBC has been broken up into seventy companies for separate disposal, many to management buy-outs. At the time of writing, some thirty companies have been disposed of.

So the track record of the Conservative government in dealing with government rights has varied considerably, and with different effects in each industry. But clearly critics are right in most cases, and to varying degrees, to say that the government missed important chances to create more competitive conditions alongside privatization. Of the recent cases, except NBC, they did not break up nationalized companies for separate flotation, thus directly affecting market structure. In BT's case, it could be argued that, technically, a break-up was impossible because the information on financial prospects could not have been constructed for the flotation of separate companies in a timescale compatible with political needs. In British Gas, the distribution grid was a natural monopoly. Nevertheless, one has to concede that more could have been done. Moreover, more could have been done in BT's case in particular to encourage entry by modifying inherited rights. The main bone of contention, still being argued over, was limitations of the resale of BT's capacity. Provision of switched voice over any lines leased from BT is still prohibited, at least until 1989.

Many regrets have been expressed that an alternative line of development was missed. This was to retain a nationalized industry in public ownership, but to liberalize it by removing controls on entry, thus avoiding the need to concede quasi-rents on change of ownership. My own opinion is that this is an interesting, but empty, theoretical box. In UK conditions (and probably elsewhere), so long as a Minister has responsibility for an industry, he or she will always act to maximize his or her potential influence over it, or, at the very least, to safeguard his or her rights of effective intervention. Privatization implies the political decision to give up the direct responsibility *and* accept drastically diminished direct influence on the industry.

A more interesting line of criticism is that which anticipates that the managers of the nationalized industry, who are assumed to survive the change, so far from being ruthless seekers after profits, including 'exploitation' of consumers, will impute the gains to themselves via increased 'managerial slacks', for example by enjoying the quiet life possible in a protected market situation. The argument goes that, especially because the industries are normally sold intact, and are often very large, there is little for managers to fear from the disciplines of the capital market, specifically takeover threats. But recent events in these markets have greatly diminished the force of this argument. Very large private firms, in an increasingly internationalized capital market, feel themselves increasingly vulnerable to takeover. The newly privatized firms will have to pay equal attention to their share prices, to criticisms of large investors, and to consider their future needs to go to the capital market to raise money.

More important, top managements perceive the change to privatization as itself a liberation, to enter a competitive world. Their mission, as they see it, is to change other managerial attitudes in their firms towards commercialism, the search for profit. When the chairmen welcome the prospect of 'competition', as they frequently do, they are not being hypocritical. In a real sense, they perceive such external threats as a lever for needed internal change. (Not *too* much competition *too* soon, of course!) Here we have a central problem of government policy towards their newly privatized creations. The public interest generally will require more competition, and therefore less weight to incumbents' economic interests. In practice, however, time must be allowed for reform in very large organizations not least because this was the essence of the deals struck with chairmen when embarking on an innovative course. Those of us who are firmly in the pro-competitive camp must hope that, as time passes, it will be deemed increasingly more practicable for the government to increase competitive pressures. Given the underlying ideology prompting the changes, this is a question of not appearing to rewrite the 'social contract' in favour of more competition too soon.

FUTURE PRIVATIZATION? THE MISSING CANDIDATES

It will be useful, in conclusion, briefly to consider conspicuous nationalized industries not so far on the government's agenda for this Parliament, and probably unlikely to be. When Stephen Littlechild and I in 1983 considered which of all the nationalized industry candidates were most worth privatizing, in terms of prospective real benefits to consumers, we picked out BT, Electricity, Water, British Rail and the Post Office, both because of their scale and the improvability of their activities.[5] BT has been privatized and Electricity is on the agenda. The others are not. They are large industries in many countries. What puts them so low on the list in UK practice?

The common factor is that they pose particular degrees of difficulty in mounting a privatization move. British Rail's (BR's) exclusive right to run railways in the UK is worth very little; no one would wish to challenge through entry. The market for non-subsidized rail operations is nowadays small, confined to some inter-city passenger routes and siding-to-siding freight. By contrast, subsidized commuter rail operations are deemed very important, and their demise unthinkable. Privatization without a subsidy implies severe contraction in politically highly sensitive markets. In 1985/6, subsidy accounted for 40 per cent of BR's total revenues. On the other hand, maintaining a permanent subsidy means that there cannot be the required arm's-length dealing with the practices concerned. Ministers must and will interfere. It follows that, if privatization in the fullest sense of transfer of all railway assets to private ownership is to be accomplished, a substitute source of subsidy must be found. An appealing, but radical, solution would be to make full use of the fact that railways in the UK are still large landowners, specifically in London and the major conurbations. Were railways to be privatized as essentially property companies, with full rights to develop, sell or buy property, the prospective proceeds might well suffice to allow an additional constraint to be imposed. This would be an obligation to maintain the socially necessary rail output. Variation in this, year by year, could be argued through a regulatory process. Such a package might well appeal to the capital markets sufficiently to raise acceptable bids for, say, five successor companies.

Coal, with its many production units, lends itself readily to treatment by a realization agency, akin to the NBC procedure. Many sources of bids can be anticipated – from firms seeking backward integration, from management buy-outs, and independent stock-market flotations. Of all nationalized industries, coal has the most diverse production and therefore cost conditions. The worth of successor firms is set by the difference between these costs and the world price for coal deliveries in the UK and export markets.

The drawbacks to coal privatization are political, one inherited from the bitter strike of 1984 and one to do with having unsold coal properties remaining on one's hands after privatization, which would be deemed a political failure. The former factor will fade with time, the latter will continue. The risks can be reduced, as just indicated by implication, by having a variety of treatments for the privatized units. This in itself would pose new demands on information and bargaining ability. With withdrawal of all forms of subsidy, some contraction would be probable, increasing the uncertainty. Charting the future of the labour force would be difficult before the event. For all these reasons, coal presents exceptional political risks, and without, in this case, the political comfort of a substantial increase in shareholder numbers.

The Post Office is in many ways the most intriguing case of all, because of all nationalized industries it most depends for its existence as a large, unified concern on the existence of the government-granted monopoly, which exempts it from competition for letters and packages sent for £1 or less. Bereft of the monopoly right, it could not sustain anything approaching its current scale, profitable as it now is. Yet it would be politically extremely difficult, indeed unthinkable, to privatize and keep the monopoly explicit and intact. On the other hand, the industry pressures to retain the organization as it is on privatization are just as strong, and well entrenched, as in the other cases. A compromise, new to the privatization process, suggests itself – namely to privatize as it is, but to couple the flotation with the stated intention to lower the £1 monopoly limit to zero in stages, say over five years. This would give top management the leverage required to reduce costs towards competitive levels, would be an important derogation from the monopoly, and would, in all probability, be a basis for a flotation to be successful in the capital market.

The reasons why these economically good candidates for privatization are far down the UK list illustrate aptly a main theme of this chapter. Privatization is a negotiated process, in which political requirements and constraints interact with economic ones. If the candidates are eventually to be included, innovation in means and willingness to shoulder rather greater potential political costs are needed. But what has been done so far has itself involved political boldness, and the deals which have been struck are by no means as favourable to the industries' vested interests as often imagined. Fundamentally, if one wishes market pressures to drive a firm, that firm must be open to all available market pressures. This must imply privatization. Transition from nationalized to private status has its costs, and these will normally include some shelter, hopefully temporary, from full competition. The true test of UK privatization is still to come – will competition be progressively encouraged as time progresses? Perhaps the clearest and soonest test will be the treatment of constraints on competition in telecoms, on which the debate is now starting. In two or three years' time, we shall know whether the commitment to freer markets, the political inspiration of much that has happened, wins out.

NOTES

1 Paper for ADEBA Conference, Buenos Aires, August 1987.
2 Much of the tone of this was set by Kay and Thompson's paper on privatization in the *Economic Journal*, March 1986.

3 Beesley, M.E. (1981) *Liberalisation of the use of British Telecommunications Network*, London: HMSO.
4 The privatized firms are still subject to the normal laws governing the reference of a single firm's power to the MMC. So there is, as it were, a fallback position for the regulators.
5 Beesley, Michael and Littlechild, Stephen (1983) *Privatization: Principles, Problems and Priorities*, Lloyds Bank Review, July.

4 The regulation of privatized monopolies in the United Kingdom[1]

M.E. Beesley and S.C. Littlechild[2]

SUMMARY

This article examines the experience in the United Kingdom with the regulation of privatized monopolies. Its conclusions are (1) that there are significant differences between RPI $-$ X (or price-cap) and US rate-of-return regulation, which provides greater scope for bargaining in the former system: (2) that UK regulators have taken seriously their duty to promote competition, but that the existing economic literature is of limited help in this task: (3) that price regulation is likely to be more effective where technology is changing slowly and/or where there are many firms in an industry, whereas the promotion of competition is indicated where technology is changing rapidly; and (4) that the case for RPI $-$ X price-cap, rather than rate-of-return regulation, is strongest in telecommunications, gas supply and electricity supply and least strong in gas and electricity transmission grids.

INTRODUCTION

Since 1979, the Conservative government has transferred over two dozen public enterprises into private ownership. Most of them previously operated in more or less competitive industries, but three of the largest – namely, British Telecom (BT), British Airports Authority (BAA) and British Gas (BG) – had market shares approaching 100 per cent for their core activities. These three companies now operate under licences containing many obligations and constraints. Independent regulatory authorities, each headed by a director-general, monitor and enforce compliance with licence conditions. The impending privatization of the water and electricity industries will follow a similar pattern, although in these two industries there will be a number of successor companies rather than a single major one. Thus, in the UK there is now a set of five major privatized industries which (in the US context) would normally be thought of as regulated utilities.

The statutory duties of the regulators include protecting the interests of producers (licensees), of consumers of various kinds, and of employees and third parties (e.g. environmental concerns). The wording varies but, for present purposes, three main objectives may be identified in the respective privatization Acts: (1) to ensure that all reasonable demands are met, and that licensees are able to finance the provision of these services; (2) to protect the interests of consumers with respect to prices and quality of service; and (3) to enable or promote competition in the industry. Strictly speaking, the duties of the regulator are not a direct obligation to achieve the stated objectives, but rather require the regulator to carry out his or her statutory functions in the manner which he or she believes is best calculated to achieve these objectives.

Economists may find it helpful to analyse privatization as the instrument of change in a cost–benefit appraisal. The privatization Acts, and in particular the duties of the regulators, may be interpreted as consistent with a formal aim of maximizing the present value of expected net benefits to consumers plus producers, subject to a minimum profit condition and to various constraints on the distribution of benefits to ensure Pareto efficiency (i.e. no major interest group is to be made worse off). The problem then faced by each regulator is to interpret this general criterion and make it operational. In particular, the regulator has to balance the interests of present and future consumers, both against each other and against the interests of present and future producers.

This chapter examines the experience of the United Kingdom with regulation of privatized monopolies. In particular, we consider: (1) whether the form of price control adopted is significantly different from US rate-of-return regulation and how far this constitutes an advantage; (2) how regulators have tackled their duty to promote competition and what mode of economic analysis is most appropriate for this; and (3) under what circumstances each of the two main regulatory duties is likely to be performed most effectively and what this implies for government policy.

PRICE CONTROL

Rate-of-return regulation is well established in the USA. There have been numerous variants across jurisdictions, across industries, and over time, but for present purposes the key features of 'traditional' rate-of-return regulation may be characterized as follows (see Phillips 1969).

The regulated company files a tariff when it wishes to revise its prices. For an agreed test period ('frequently the latest 12-month period for which complete data are available' (Phillips 1969)), the company calculates operating costs, capital employed and cost of capital. The regulator audits these calculations and determines a fair rate of return on capital employed. These data plus assumptions about demand are used to calculate the total revenue requirement. This determines the *level* of the tariff. The *structure* of the tariff has to avoid unfairness and unjust or unreasonable discrimination. The tariff therefore has to be approved on a line-by-line or service-by-service basis, which typically requires the allocation of common costs on the basis of, for example, output, direct costs, revenues, etc. An approved tariff generally stands until the company files to change it, usually on the grounds that the achieved rate of return has become inadequate.

When making its plans for privatizing British Telecom (BT), the Department of Industry's original intention was to adopt a modified rate-of-return regulation. After further discussion and investigation, however (Littlechild 1983), a control on prices, or price-cap, was finally adopted and variants of it have been used for the other privatized utilities.

The key features of this price control are that, for a pre-specified period of four to five years, the company can make any changes it wishes to prices, provided that the average price of a specified basket of its goods and services does not increase faster than RPI − X, where RPI is the retail price index (i.e. the rate of inflation) and X is a number specified by the government. At the end of the specified period, the level of X is reset by the regulator, and the process is repeated.

Rate of return versus RPI − X

The pros and cons of rate-of-return regulation versus RPI − X and other schemes have been frequently discussed (e.g. Littlechild 1983, Vickers and Yarrow 1988, Johnson 1989). Briefly, the main arguments for RPI − X, as originally spelled out in the context of privatizing BT and subsequently repeated in other cases, are threefold. First, RPI − X is less vulnerable to 'cost-plus' inefficiency and overcapitalization (the 'Averch–Johnson effect'). Because the company has the right to keep whatever profits it can earn during the specified period (and must also absorb any losses), this preserves the incentive to productive efficiency associated with unconstrained profit maximization. Part of this expected increased efficiency can be passed on to customers, via the level of X. Prices are therefore lower than they would be under rate-of-return control, without producers being worse off. Second, RPI − X allows the company greater flexibility to adjust the structure of prices within the basket, and in principle there is no constraint on prices outside the basket. This is of particular importance where, as with British Telecom, initial prices were thought to be considerably out of line with relative costs, yet 'optimal' prices could not be immediately determined and achieved because of inadequate knowledge of costs and demands, as well as political constraints on speed of adjustment. Third, RPI − X is simpler to operate by the regulator and the company. It is more transparent and better focused on the parameter(s) of greatest concern to customers, hence providing them with greater reassurance.

The main counterargument against the incentive and efficiency claim may be summarized as follows. The level of X must in practice be set, and repeatedly adjusted to secure a reasonable rate of return. If not, allocative inefficiencies will arise (from prices being out of line with costs), and there will be political pressures from company or consumers. If the criteria for revising X are left unclear, this will increase the cost of capital and/or discourage investment. Clear guidelines must therefore be laid down, or must emerge from precedent, for resetting X. These guidelines will have to embody an explicit feedback from cost reduction to (eventual) price reduction. This will negate the superior incentive effects claimed for RPI $- X$. Specifically, companies may believe that the short-term advantages of increased efficiency and lower costs will be more than offset by a tougher X and therefore lower prices in the next period, and may even induce an adverse change of X within the current period. In this view, RPI $- X$ is merely a special form of rate-of-return control, embodying no significant net advantage over the US approach on grounds of economic efficiency.

It is also questioned whether RPI $- X$ involves as much price flexibility and transparency as claimed. It is further suggested that greater price flexibility may be a disadvantage rather than an advantage, since it allows cross-subsidization which is allocatively inefficient and may be used anti-competitively.[3]

The key questions to pose in this section are thus whether in practice RPI $- X$ makes any difference to regulation and, if so, whether the differences are beneficial. Our aim is to assess how RPI $- X$ has actually operated in the United Kingdom. We make no attempt to assess its potential effectiveness in or appropriateness for the USA.

Setting and resetting X

In assessing these arguments, it is necessary to understand the procedures for setting and resetting X, and to appreciate the similarities and differences between them.

The RPI $- X$ constraint is one of many conditions in the regulated company's licence, all of which are initially set by the government. Unlike the other conditions, it has a limited duration, typically five years, and there is no formal constraint on the magnitude of X in any subsequent period. The regulator may modify any licence condition at any time by agreement with the licensee. If the licensee does not agree, the regulator may refer the matter to the Monopolies and Mergers Commission (MMC) and has the authority to modify the licence if and only if the MMC finds the licensees to be acting against the public interest. (With certain exceptions, the licensee has no power to refer possible licence modifications to the MMC.) Renewal of the RPI $- X$ constraint, whatever the level of X, is equivalent to a licence modification.

The initial level of X is set by the government at the time of privatization, *as part of the privatization process*, whereas X is reset by the regulator *as part of the continuing regulatory process*. This has three important implications.

First, the initial level of X is set as part of a whole package of measures, whose parameters affect the costs, revenues and risks of the regulated company. Some of these parameters pertain to the design of the price control itself, including the duration of the price constraint, its scope in terms of goods and services included, what costs (if any) are allowed to be 'passed through' into prices, and whether the constraint is calculated on the basis of historical or expected performance. All these parameters are embodied in licence conditions. Other parameters pertain to the wider regulatory framework, including what other non-commercial obligations or constraints are put on the company, what steps are taken to encourage or restrict competition, what policies are adopted towards suppliers, and so on. Both sets of parameters are fixed by the government more or less simultaneously in full acknowledgement of the interactions and trade-offs between them. They are gradually firmed up and made more precise in the run-up to privatization, culminating in the determination of certain key parameters, including X, prior to publication of the prospectus, a few weeks before flotation. (The striking price of the shares is determined later in this last period and will be heavily influenced by the anticipated changes in the stock-market level to the flotation date.)

In contrast, the resetting of X takes place in a context where these parameters have already been determined. Admittedly they could be changed, and in practice some have been, but to make substantial and unexpected changes would have potentially adverse effects on the company's cost of capital and hence on prices to customers. Moreover, in so far as any proposed changes pertain to the company's licence, if the company does not agree to the changes, the regulator may not wish to run the risk of an unsuccessful appeal to the MMC. There are thus fewer degrees of freedom in resetting X.

Second, the initial level of X is set by the government as owner of the company, whereas X is reset by a regulator who does not own the shares. The government as owner can choose, if it wishes, to take lower proceeds in return for, say, lower prices to customers. The regulator does not have that extra degree of freedom: any shift in favour of one interest group (such as customers) will be at the expense of another group (such as shareholders). The regulator is constrained by the expectations of shareholders and customers, which were established at privatization, and his or her discretion is limited to whatever range is deemed acceptable (or can be so presented).

The third difference between setting and resetting X, which reinforces the previous two, relates to the effect on the company's share price. In both cases the level of X will influence the share price via its effects on expected net revenue streams, so the stock market in fact decides the yield to shareholders. At the time that X is initially set, however, this effect has to be conjectured. It is not known with any certainty how potential investors will evaluate the company put before them. Nor is there any market valuation of the previous or alternative arrangements with which to compare it. After privatization, however, the views of investors are clearly reflected in the company's traded share price, with its accompanying dividend yield, price earnings ratio, relative risk factor β, etc. A *change* in the stock market's evaluation of the company, following any action by the regulator, in particular the revision of X, can be immediately observed in the change in share price. If the market regards the regulator's decision as favourable to the company (i.e. more favourable than expected), its share price is marked up and its cost of capital falls; the opposite happens if the decision is regarded unfavourably. The regulator cannot ignore this consideration in his or her decisions, and it reinforces the greater constraints on resetting X than on setting it initially.

To summarize, when setting X initially there are many degrees of freedom. X is just one of numerous parameters chosen simultaneously in the light of the political and economic trade-offs involved. There is nothing unique, optimal or mechanical about the initial choice of X. When X is reset, there are significantly fewer degrees of freedom. Nevertheless, there invariably *are* degrees of freedom open to the regulator.

The following two examples will illustrate the above procedures and provide further insights into the characteristics of the RPI $-$ X approach.

Setting X for Manchester Airport

The Airports Act of 1986 provides for economic regulation of 'designated' airports. At privatization, the Secretary of State designated BAA's three London airports and specified RPI $-$ X regulation with $X = 1$ per cent. He also designated Manchester Airport, but delegated to the Civil Aviation Authority (CAA), as regulator, the task of designing Manchester's regulatory constraint. The Airports Act required the CAA, in turn, to seek the advice of the MMC.

Since Manchester Airport was not to be privatized, but was to remain in the ownership of The Manchester City Council, in important respects the considerations involved were different from those where X is set or reset for a privatized company. None the less, there are useful insights to be obtained from the MMC report because it sets out in some detail its reasoning on RPI $-$ X. (Note that the MMC in this context is an 'advisor' to the regulator, not the regulator itself, and by convention the MMC's report is its only means of conveying that advice.)

The MMC recommended that RPI $-$ X be adopted rather than rate-of-return control, for the kinds of reasons given earlier. The Airports Act set the review period as five years, and the MMC was advised that the scope of price control had to comprise landing, parking and passenger charges, but not baggage handling charges. The MMC exercised judgement on four main parameters apart from the level of X. It recommended:

1 that there be a single basket for all three charges rather than (say) three separate baskets or additional subconstraints on prices;

2 that the formula be based on a 'tariff basket' (as used for British Telecom), with weights reflecting revenues in the previous year rather than on a 'revenue yield' (as used for BAA) involving predicted revenue per unit and a subsequent correction factor;
3 that no special allowance be made for passing-through costs associated with changes in (non-economic) government regulation, except for three-quarters of any additional airport security costs; and
4 that the present levels of airport charges (which some users claimed were too high) were the appropriate starting point for the formula.

In proposing a level for X, the MMC's procedure was first to examine four important issues: future traffic growth, the timing and financing of capital expenditure (particularly the construction of a second terminal), the development of (unregulated) commercial income, and the scope for cost reduction and productivity increases. After exploring a range of alternative assumptions, it adopted those used by the company itself (except on 100 per cent self-financing policy), albeit commenting that some of these assumptions were rather cautious. On the basis of the adopted assumptions, it used the company's financial model to make predictions, for each year over a five-year horizon, of four financial magnitudes (operating profit before and after interest and tax, net current assets, and shareholders' funds) and five financial ratios (gearing or debt–equity ratio, self-financing ratio, interest cover, dividend cover, and return on capital employed). The MMC then 'looked for a value of X which would give the necessary degree of protection to users of the airport while leaving the company in a financially sound position and able to carry through its capital expenditure plans' (see MMC 1987). It recommended that $X = 1$ per cent.

Note that the MMC approach was explicitly based on *future predictions*, and a central problem for the MMC was to decide what those predictions should be. It felt that Manchester's assumptions were often cautious, but had no firm basis for making alternative assumptions. (Over time, a regulator would aim to secure an independent source of information on these matters, and the CAA has begun to do so, as have the other regulators in their own areas. We discuss this point further on pp. 77–80.)

This forward-looking approach also applied to the financial calculations. The rate of return on (historic) book capital was only one of nine financial projections and ratios that the MMC looked at. It was projected to decline steadily from the present 18.8 per cent to 9.0 per cent at the end of five years. The MMC merely commented that these rates of return were considered 'consistent with our assessment of the company's financial soundness, which is also reflected in the other projections' (see MMC 1987). Thus, in order to assess the future yield to shareholders, the MMC found it necessary to go beyond a single historic cost ratio.

The CAA proposed to accept the MMC's recommendations. Manchester Airport then appealed to the CAA, arguing for $X = 2$ per cent (i.e.

RPI – 2) and a revenue yield approach. Other interested parties also made representations. The CAA upheld $X = 1$ per cent but granted Manchester Airport's request for revenue yield. The CAA report hints at the bargaining situation in which it found itself but, in giving its verdict, does not quantify (for example) the differential effect on future cash flows of revenue yield versus a tariff basket approach (see Civil Aviation Authority 1988).

Setting and resetting X for British Telecom

At a late stage in the privatization of British Telecom in 1984, three parameters remained to be determined: the contents of the 'basket' (i.e. the coverage of the price-cap), whether to allow unrestricted resale of BT's leased lines, and the level of X. The third parameter had clear implications for prices and proceeds, but so did the other two. Unrestricted resale would allow competitors to use low-priced BT circuits to undercut high-priced BT phone calls: this would mean lower prices, revenues and proceeds. Restricting the basket to local calls and connection charges, for which the monopoly was thought to be strongest, would leave little scope for price reductions. Indeed, British Telecom argued that local calls and connections were already underpriced. On the other hand, incorporating inland trunk calls – where competition was pending, prices were already considerably in excess of costs, and technological prospects were for yet lower costs – would give scope for greater average price reductions across the basket as a whole. (International calls, though known to be highly profitable, were not a serious candidate for inclusion at that time, perhaps reflecting the government's unwillingness to provoke issues of international liberalization at a time when only the USA was clearly pursuing similar policies.)

There was considerable negotiation, involving a wide range of Xs. (This has been repeated in subsequent privatizations.) The eventual outcome was a package comprising no resale, inland trunk calls in the basket, and $X = 3$ per cent. The detailed calculations on which this figure was based have not been published. (Nor, for that matter, have any of the calculations of other Xs by government departments.) The offer price for BT's shares was set to ensure that there would be demand from a large number of small shareholders and employees. After flotation, the share price was duly bid up by institutional shareholders, who had excess demand at the offer price.

As BT's profits increased, the question was raised whether they were excessive, even though its prices were within the RPI $- X$ constraint. The regulator published an assessment of the appropriate rate of return for BT to earn, concluding that the then observed level of 18 per cent on book value was about right (Director-General of Telecommunications 1986). (For a debate on the adequacy of this assessment, see Beesley *et al.* (1987)

and Carsberg (1987).) BT, in fact, held its prices below the permitted maximum for two years. The regulator also commented on BT's changing price structure, suggesting that rebalancing between inland trunk and local call prices had gone far enough. The regulator's staff published an analysis of price structure based on Ramsey pricing (Culham 1987), although this was viewed with caution by the regulator himself.

The resetting of X in 1989 was preceded by a consultative document (Director-General of Telecommunications 1988a) in which the regulator invited comments and suggestions for modification to the whole framework of BT's price control, such as substituting rate of return for RPI − X, using revenue yield instead of tariff basket, changing the coverage and duration of RPI − X, and so on. Each of these would have required a change in the licence, and therefore allowed the possibility of a challenge by BT and reference to the MMC. An agreement was reached. The regulator reduced the duration of the subsequent review period from five to four years (to reflect the uncertainties involved and BT's own investment planning horizon), slightly extended the coverage of the price-cap (to include directory services), and increased X from 3 per cent to 4.5 per cent. He rejected the options of including international calls in the basket, but indicated that he would keep this area under review. He gave no detailed explanation for his choice of X, beyond indicating that rate of return was the most important criterion, but not the only one. The other factor mentioned was the financing of investment. He stated that in determining X, he had considered the effect on growth in earnings and borrowing, as well as on rate of return (Director-General of Telecommunications 1988b).

The regulator noted that he had taken some account of current cost accounting results. Perhaps a decision based entirely on such a valuation would have indicated higher prices and therefore a lower X, which would have been favourable to BT. In explaining his position, however, the regulator stated that current cost accounting should not be used as the sole basis of regulation unless it was also used as the main basis of reporting to shareholders. BT was evidently unwilling to do this. Nor did BT think it advantageous to challenge the decision on X, which would have meant submitting to an MMC investigation. As it happens, BT's share price did not move significantly after the announcement, suggesting that changing X to 4.5 per cent did not alter the stock market's expectations of BT's future profit stream.

One may surmise that the regulator focused the issue of the future level of X on BT's prospective or possible gains in productivity. By making effective use of the degrees of freedom open to him in redefining the formula and of BT's unwillingness to challenge his decision, the regulator was able to get agreement to a higher X than would otherwise have been possible. He thus set a target for efficiency, which BT was constrained to follow; he did not base his judgement primarily on evidence of what had *previously* happened in the industry.

Incentives and efficiency

In light of these two examples, but also taking into account the experiences of the other industries, we may now address the argument on incentives and efficiency.

RPI $- X$ and rate-of-return regulation have certain common features. Both accept the need to secure an adequate return for the company's shareholders in order to induce them to continue to finance the business, without conceding unnecessarily high prices at the expense of customers. Nevertheless, there *are* significant differences between the two systems, which give RPI $- X$ a potential advantage with respect to incentives and efficiency.

First, RPI $- X$ embodies an exogenously determined risk period between appraisals of prices, whereas rate-of-return regulation makes the duration of this period endogenous. Admittedly, US regulatory commissions have tended not to intervene when profits are increasing, provided that prices are not increased (Joskow 1974), but the company can file for a new tariff whenever its performance diminishes, which may be quite frequently. This last is not possible in the UK. The regulator can propose a modification of X within the risk period. BT's regulator considered doing this, but he decided not to. Apart from the disincentive effects, there would have been a risk of not getting MMC support for a contested licence modification. BT's regulator also reinforced the concept of an exogenous risk period by reducing its duration from five to four years to limit the extent of uncertainty during the period and stressed that any mid-term review should be limited to major unexpected events outside the company's control (Director-General of Telecommunications 1988b).

Second, RPI $- X$ is more forward looking than rate-of-return regulation. The latter tends to be based on historic costs and demands, with adjustments for the future limited (at most) to an adjustment for inflation or the extrapolation of historic trends.[4] In contrast, RPI $- X$ embodies forecasts of what productivity improvements can be achieved and what future demands will be and is set on the basis of predicted future cash flows.

Third, there are more degrees of freedom in setting X than are involved in rate-of-return regulation. The latter system does allow flexibility (e.g. on the basis of asset valuation, the definition of the rate base, treatment of work in progress, etc.) but it would seem difficult to change these decisions repeatedly. X is initially set in the context of negotiations about the whole regulatory framework, including the coverage, duration and form of the price constraints, the extent of non-commercial obligations, the restrictions on competition, and the permissible rate of adjustment from inherited pricing policies. In resetting X, the regulator has fewer degrees of freedom, but none the less can modify (at least at the margins) any aspect of this framework and in practice has done so.

Fourth, in setting X the UK regulator has more discretion and less need to reveal the basis for decisions than does his or her US counterpart. The US tradition is to place all evidence and reasoning in the public record. In the UK, there is less pressure for due process. The UK regulator is deemed to be a person to whom public policy may be safely delegated, subject only to judicial review on the question of whether his actions are legitimate in terms of the Act. In the UK, neither governments nor regulators have given detailed reasons for their decisions on X. This reduces the basis for challenge (by company, competitors or customers).

The consequence of these four differences – exogenous risk period, forward-looking approach, degrees of freedom, and less requirement to explain – is that there is greater scope for *bargaining* in RPI – X than in rate-of-return regulation. The level of X can reflect negotiations with the company, not only about the scope for future productivity agreements, but also about other matters affecting the company's future, including the details of the price constraint formula, the rate at which competition is allowed to develop, the provision of information, and so on. In short, X may be thought of as one of several variables in a political and commercial bargaining process.

It is not suggested that UK regulation is conducted, or even perceived, primarily in terms of bargaining. Nor, on the other hand, is it claimed that there is *no* scope for bargaining in US rate-of-return regulation. Spulber (1989), for example, explicitly characterized US rate hearings as a bargaining process between consumers and the regulated firm. The hearings economize on the transaction costs of forming consumer coalitions and bargaining directly with the firms. The regulatory commission establishes rules for negotiation and mechanisms for the resolution of conflict, selects the issues that are open to debate, acts as arbiter and 'may select an outcome especially if bargaining does not yield a unique solution' (p. 270). Spulber also notes that 'rates are often set *indirectly* through decisions on methods of estimating costs, demand, and rates of return' (p. 272). These insights are not inconsistent with our own assessment. Our claim here is simply that the UK approach offers greater and more direct scope for bargaining, with a correspondingly more active role for the regulator.

There is an important implication for incentives and efficiency. The exogenous risk period and the forward-looking approach mean that the company is not deterred from making efficiency improvements either by fear of confiscation *within* the period or by the belief that allowed *future* prices will simply be an extrapolation of past costs. The regulator can take an independent view of the scope for productivity improvements and can use the discretion and degrees of freedom open to him or her including the absence of a requirement to justify decisions in detail, to negotiate a better deal than would otherwise be possible.

Whether the difference between RPI – X and rate-of-return regulation is significant depends on whether the regulator is able to use the additional bargaining power effectively. This depends upon the underlying scope for efficiency improvements and upon the extent and quality of the information available (see Vickers and Yarrow 1988). These factors will differ from one industry to another. We take up this issue in the final section of this chapter.

Price flexibility

Traditional US rate-of-return regulation requires each price to be individually approved. Changing a price requires filing a new tariff. In principle, RPI − X allows any price to be changed at any time, subject only to the price-cap on the average price within the basket. The coverage of the price-cap is approximately 37 per cent of BAA's total revenue, 57 per cent of BT's, 63 per cent of BG's, and probably 95 per cent or more of the water and electricity companies. Again, in principle, there is no constraint on prices outside the basket.

In practice, the regulated companies are typically more constrained than this. BAA has subconstraints on its two major airports; the public electricity suppliers will have separate constraints on their distribution and supply activities; and BT gave a written undertaking (outside the licence) to limit the rate of increase of residential line rentals to RPI +2. The regulator has since added an additional constraint for BT's private circuits and brought directory services into BT's basket; non-discrimination provisions have also been added for gas. There are also informal constraints: BT's regulator indicated that the rebalancing of trunk and local call prices had, in his view, gone far enough, with the threat of explicit control via modification of the licence. There is always an incentive for a regulator to increase control by refining and extending the basket.

On the other hand, the rebalancing problem was in part attributable to the definition of BT's basket (which included competitive as well as monopoly services) rather than to the RPI − X concept itself. As Johnson (1989) has suggested, a key task during each formal review is to redesign the basket(s) to reflect (changing) market conditions.[5] BT's regulator did not in fact press his concerns on relative prices and, in particular, did not adopt the Ramsey pricing philosophy examined by his staff. Any new contested constraint would, in any case, need MMC approval. In effect, the burden of proof is on the regulator to show cause why the rebalancing of prices should not occur. The opposite applies in US rate-of-return regulation, where the burden is on the company to justify the price changes it proposes. There seems no doubt that RPI − X allows greater pricing flexibility for the regulated company.

Whether this flexibility constitutes an advantage or a disadvantage depends upon how much need there is for price flexibility (e.g. to reflect changing conditions), how much information is available to the regulator for determining prices in detail, and what other instruments are available for dealing with anti-competitive pricing (e.g. non-discrimination provisions). Again, we return to these issues in the final section of the chapter.

Transparency: cost pass-through and the X formula

As privatization has been extended from BT to other utilities, questions have arisen as to whether the simple $RPI - X$ constraint is appropriate for industries with different cost and demand structures. For example, should certain costs be passed through into prices, and should the price-cap be based on historic or predicted parameters? Decisions on these questions have implications for profits and proceeds, consumer prices and economic efficiency, as well as having an effect on transparency.

Cost pass-through

An essential feature of any price-control scheme is the provision to be made for costs which are considered outside the control of the regulated company's management. Several options are available. A simple $RPI - X$ constraint, based on expected costs, would expose the company to greater risk, thereby increasing the cost of capital and reducing proceeds. Setting a lower (less stringent) value of X would provide a greater margin against risk, but would imply higher prices for customers. Shortening the review period would reduce risk, but also would reduce the scope and incentive for cost savings; the cost of review would also be incurred more frequently.

The fourth possibility is to allow increases in specified costs to be passed through to customers as they occur. This does not eliminate the risk, but simply transfers it from company to customer. It therefore reduces the incentive of the company to seek lower cost or less uncertain sources of supply – for example, by signing fixed-price contracts with suppliers – and increases that incentive for customers. To the extent that prices vary more directly with costs, there may be an increase in allocative efficiency at the expense of productive efficiency. There is a reduction in transparency because of the added complexity in the regulatory formula and the reduced predictability of prices.

UK practice has varied. Both BT and BAA have zero pass-through (except for three-quarters of the unforeseen additional cost of airport security). The price controls in the other three industries make significant provision for pass-through: for BG the costs of buying gas; for the water authorities, the costs of meeting any unforeseen government commitment such as new EC directives (subject to a minimum threshold set at 10 per cent of turnover); and for public electricity suppliers, the costs of purchasing electricity from the generating companies. In the latter case, a yardstick provision (relating a proportion of pass-through to the costs of the industry as a whole) is also envisaged.

Tariff basket versus revenue yield

Another feature of price control is the precise rule for determining allowed price changes. BT's rule is based on the concept of a 'tariff basket', whereby price changes must be such that the average price of the services in the basket, as weighted by *observed* usage in the *previous* year, does not increase by more than RPI − *X*. The water industry has a similar rule. In contrast, price regulation for BAA and BG (and prospectively for the privatized electricity companies) is based on a 'revenue yield' approach, whereby price changes must be such that the *forecasted* average revenue per unit of output (e.g. per passenger or per therm) in the *next* year does not increase by more than RPI − *X*. The necessary forecasts of output are made by the regulated company itself, and the formula involves an additional correction factor to repay or recoup any deviation between prediction and outcome.

The relative incentive effects of each type of formula have been debated and are not unambiguous, although it has been suggested that the revenue yield approach is more open to strategic behaviour by the regulated firm (see Cheong 1989). Revenue yield may be expected to reduce the risk to the regulated company in two ways: it smoothes, over time, the average revenue per unit and gives the company (via determination of the forecasts) greater control over the total level of revenue. As with cost pass-through, however, this simply transfers the risks to customers and may reduce the company's incentive to seek a less variable pattern of income. There is also less transparency as the regulatory formula becomes more complex and future price changes less predictable.

In sum, the record on transparency is somewhat mixed. BT's simple RPI − *X* constraint is still in place, but three of the other utilities make heavy use of cost pass-through, and three have revenue yield constraints based on expectations declared by the regulated companies themselves. Such features reduce transparency and efficiency, though they may protect profits and proceeds or may allow a tougher *X* on prices. In the absence of transparency, protection for customers has to depend upon faith in the regulatory process rather than upon an explicitly guaranteed outcome. In this respect, cost pass-through and revenue yield are similar to rate-of-return regulation.

THE PROMOTION OF COMPETITION

The promotion of competition is not traditionally associated with the regulation of utilities in the USA. The regulatory commissions have a long record of resisting entry, and it has been persuasively argued that the real purpose of regulation was to protect incumbents from competition (Stigler 1971, Jarrell 1978). Admittedly, competition issues have loomed increasingly large in telecommunications, especially since the 'above 890'[6] decision in 1969. The FCC has been concerned lately with protecting entrants from various forms of anti-competitive pricing. None the less (and in contrast to anti-trust policy), there is nothing in US utility regulation approaching a statutory duty to promote competition.[7]

The UK regulator's duty to promote competition reflects in part the fact that it is not possible to move from a nationalized monopoly to a competitive industry in a single step. The regulatory needs the authority and duty to complete the process of transition (as does the Secretary of State), otherwise obstacles to competition might remain in place.

The emphasis placed on this duty differs greatly between industries, depending upon the scope for entry afforded by the underlying technical and market conditions. At one extreme, potential competition is very limited in water supply, sewage disposal and airports.[8] The promotion of competition has a correspondingly small place in the Airports Act of 1986 and the Water Act of 1989. At the other extreme, the 1984 Telecommunications Act and the associated licences are, to an important extent, addressed to the pace at which competition in telecoms is permitted to develop. The regulator has a potential role in the licensing of entrants, specifying the terms on which rivals have access to BT's network and other facilities, and constraining BT's pricing policy (which might encourage or deter entry). Analogous provisions are embodied in the Electricity Act of 1989 and licences. To a lesser extent, this is true of the Gas Act of 1986 and licence, where the role of the regulator in promoting competition in gas supply has subsequently been strengthened as a result of the MMC report on that industry.

The duty to promote competition cannot be taken in isolation. The regulator needs to take into account a variety of other economic, social and political considerations. Specifically, he or she has duties to secure the financing of licensed activities and protect the interests of consumers. In most situations, different policies will be indicated, depending upon the weight given to each duty. We now give two examples of how regulators have in practice resolved this issue. We then consider the appropriate mode of economic analysis and suggest a direction for future research in order to improve the effectiveness of regulation to promote competition.

An illustration from telecommunications

When Mercury wished to interconnect with BT, it was unable to agree on terms, and the regulator, in accordance with BT's licence, was called upon to adjudicate.

One option, stemming primarily from the duty to protect the interests of customers and using traditional welfare economic concepts, was to attempt to calculate levels of interconnect charges which maximized allocative efficiency. This would have required a detailed calculation (for each possible level of interconnect charges) of Mercury's likely outputs in relevant markets, BT's consequent costs and losses in revenue, and the effect of these revenue losses on BT's prices and outputs. Mercury's market share would fall out as a residual from this exercise. However, the approach would beg the question of how to determine Mercury's output reaction function, and Mercury's implied strategy of entry and growth would not necessarily be consistent with promoting competition.

An alternative option was to begin with the duty to promote competition and therefore to examine the impact of the interconnect decision on Mercury's strategy. This would have meant looking at the situation from Mercury's perspective. The margins it could secure were central to its prospects for building up its voice (and other) telephony business. Favourable access to BT's local distribution system meant that Mercury's customers could get not only the benefits of lower prices for calls made over Mercury's long-distance system, but also discounts on virtually all calls delivered by BT. Furthermore, the prospects for future entrants could be expected to depend on the terms achieved for Mercury. Of course, the interconnect charges to be paid by Mercury and others were only part of the story about predicting entry. The effects on BT's costs, revenues, prices and outputs also needed to be taken into account. Nevertheless, the thrust of this approach is quite different from the allocative efficiency approach, and it would be surprising if its policy implications were the same.

Oftel's *Annual Report for 1985* simply noted that the Director-General 'established the prices, based on BT's costs, which should be paid by MCL (Mercury) to BT for use of its network'. No explanation of this cost basis was given, perhaps to avoid any statement that might evoke a test of the decision by the courts. It is widely felt that the phrase 'based on BT's costs' has to be taken with a pinch of salt. There was almost certainly no attempt to run a model of allocative efficiency. The essence of the matter was that the regulator either had to provide sufficient inducement for Mercury to enter the market, or his decision would put at risk a central point of the government's strategy – that Mercury should become a serious competitor. The regulator's decision does seem to have established a key condition for future effective competition. When it came to the crunch, therefore, the regulator did not let considerations of allocative efficiency stand in the way of a judgement about the promotion of competition, although the precise basis for this judgement was not given.

An illustration from gas

The second example is found in the MMC's 1988 report on gas. There had been numerous complaints against BG's policy of discriminating in price, according to whether its customers had access to an alternative fuel (typically oil). These customers, industrial consumers of substantial quantities of gas, lay outside the $RPI - X$ price-control basket, but were nevertheless within the regulator's general duty to enable competition. The privatization acts empower a regulator to refer any practice to the MMC. The regulated companies are also subject to general competition law, and it was in fact the Director-General of Fair Trading who referred BG to the MMC.

It is well known that, from an allocative point of view, price discrimination may have certain desirable properties. It can lead to greater output and aggregate value of output than a uniform monopoly price. Perfect discrimination yields an output and aggregate value of output precisely equal to that of perfect competition. Nevertheless, the MMC opposed BG's policy of price discrimination, primarily because it would deter new entry.[9] The MMC acknowledged that the prohibition of price discrimination was likely to make some customers worse off, and would limit BG's ability to compete against the oil companies. However, it believed that these disadvantages would be outweighed by the improved prospects for new entry which would be necessary to create 'gas-on-gas' competition, to which the MMC attached great importance.

This conclusion was consistent with the regulator's own view as given in evidence to the Commission. The MMC found BG's policy to be against the public interest and accepted the regulator's suggestion that BG should be required not to discriminate in price. It recommended specific provisions against discrimination to be incorporated in BG's licence. The regulator subsequently negotiated a licence modification of this kind. (Similar non-discrimination provisions have been incorporated into the draft licences of the electricity companies.)

Economic analysis of new entry

The two examples presented above indicate that regulators have taken seriously their duty to promote competition, and that in so doing they have implicitly gone beyond traditional welfare economics. We now consider what the problem of promoting competition involves, and what kinds of economic analysis might be most helpful in that task.

Promoting competition involves facilitating the entry of new competitors, including the entry of existing competitors into new parts of the market. To do this effectively involves three main steps. The first is to assess the likely pattern of entry over the foreseeable future. This will require a prediction of likely changes in technological and market conditions, since these will often provide the necessary opportunities for entry. The second step is to identify decisions that the regulators themselves can make in order to change the regulatory framework, and to assess the likely impact of these changes on the future pattern of entry. Examples of these regulatory decisions (in the British system) are the licensing of new entrants, identification and prohibition of anti-competitive practices, determination of interconnect or common carrier (use of system) charges, collection and publication of relevant information, and so on. The third step is to choose which regulatory changes to make. Other things being equal, the preferred changes are those likely to have the greatest positive impact on entry. This is not always an obvious calculation, however, particularly since the whole time path of entry must be considered. The telecommunications duopoly policy, for example, reflects in part the view that where an entrant has to make a large cost commitment it is more likely to enter, the less swiftly is a subsequent entrant able to attack the same market (Carsberg 1987).

In order to promote competition, the regulators' essential task is to assess the relation between their actions (which will include regulatory changes as well as determining disputes and constraining prices) and the probability that entry will actually occur. They will need to consider the scale and time path of entry and its impact on all the parties involved as well as on other potential entrants. It will prove impracticable to analyse all the possible avenues and problems of entry simultaneously, however, if only because the regulators' time and resources are necessarily limited. The regulators therefore have to be selective, that is to take a view about where entry might be most likely, if encouraged, and hence most effective in producing net benefits to consumers and producers, as they will be refined by the impact of entry.

What kind of economic model is most helpful in doing this? It is natural to begin with the same comparative static welfare economic approach that is conventionally used to analyse the problem of price control. This model takes as given (1) the relevant cost and demand functions, and (2) the extent of competition in the market, which essentially depends on the conditions of entry. These assumptions are used to trace the implications for (equilibrium) prices, outputs, profits, number and size of firms, and so on. It is then asked: what kinds of constraints on the regulated firm will maximize aggregate net surplus subject to securing adequate protection for various classes of consumers? Rate-of-return regulation is set firmly in this world. There is an extensive literature aimed at determining optimal pricing and investment rules that maximize allocative efficiency, taking costs and demands as given.

RPI − X requires the relaxation of the first assumption. It does *not* assume costs and demands are given or known: indeed, the problem is to provide adequate incentives for the company to discover them. The aim is to stimulate alertness to lower cost techniques and hitherto unmet demands. The emphasis is on productive rather than allocative efficiency (and even the RPI − X price-cap reflects distributional rather than allocative considerations). This is an Austrian world rather than a neo-classical one. (Austrian is here defined broadly to include both Leibenstein's familiar X-efficiency on the cost side and the corresponding Y-efficiency on the demand side proposed by Beesley (1973).)

The problem of promoting competition requires the relaxation of the second assumption. Here, the extent of competition and the conditions of entry are not given: the essential regulatory task is to ascertain what they are and how they might be changed. The object is to choose the regulatory policy which will maximize new entry, subject to adequate protection of the interests of producers and present consumers. Nor are costs and demands assumed given or known. Indeed, one of the means of promoting competition is precisely to *shift* potential entrants' assumptions about the costs and possibilities of serving new markets, and one of the expected benefits of entry is a shift in the incumbents' own assumptions about these parameters.

Substantial recent literature on potential competition and contestable markets analyse the relationship between conditions for entry and price. At least one textbook on regulation (Spulber 1989) is more concerned with entry and competition than with static welfare analysis of pricing for a protected monopoly. There have also been important developments in the economic analysis of strategic behaviour (Dixit 1982).

In practice, however, these models are of limited use for the task of promoting competition. Although they analyse the effects of any given entry conditions, they do not help to identify what the entry conditions *actually are* in any particular situation, nor what the entry conditions *would be* as a result of any particular regulatory change. Thus, they are of limited assistance to the regulators in assessing how much entry will take place, and where, when, and by whom, as a result of different regulatory policies.

Briefly, an alternative approach would run as follows. In order to identify the entry conditions obtaining at any time, and to predict the consequences of a change in policy, the regulators need to start from the question: where and when will entry be *profitable*? This in turn requires looking at the situation from the point of view of the potential entrant. Given its assets, knowledge, resources, its ability to buy at current input prices, and the pricing and product policy of the incumbent(s), what parts of the existing market can it profitably develop? What (if any) better contracts with respect to cost, including superior productivity, can it establish? Where have incumbents missed possibilities for adding value or been unable for various reasons to supply? How will incumbents react to its entry? Can it survive their response? In short, what advantages does it have over the incumbents, and how long will these advantages last? The answers to these kinds of questions determine the central calculation for an entrant: the equity that the entrant needs to ante-up in order to be a player in the game (i.e. its risk capital reflecting its potential sunk cost if unsuccessful), and its potential net revenue stream if successful (the reward for taking the risk).

Admittedly, the models referred to earlier assume profit maximization, but they do not ask where the profit is coming from. They deal with profit in a purely formal way which does not highlight the need for information about entry and gives little help to the regulators in identifying the relevant factors in practice. Future research might usefully reflect the Austrian insistence on profit as the engine of capitalism and, in particular, on the exploitation of hitherto unforeseen profit opportunities as central to the continuing market process (Schumpeter 1950; Kirzner 1973, 1985). Examination of actual rather than hypothetical situations is also necessary, as

Coase (1988) has long argued. Applications of the proposed approach (e.g. Beesley (1986) on airlines and Beesley and Laidlaw (1989) on telecommunications) suggest that there is more scope for promoting competition than has hitherto been recognized.

REGULATORY EFFECTIVENESS

We argued in the second section that the RPI $-$ X system offers more scope for bargaining, especially on productivity, than rate-of-return regulation. The importance of this depends upon the potential for productivity improvements and on the information available to the regulator to exploit this situation effectively. We also argued that RPI $-$ X offers the company more flexibility in pricing. Whether this is an advantage or disadvantage depends on the need for price changes, on the information available to the regulator, and on the existence of alternative instruments of policy. In the third section we noted the UK regulator's explicit duty to promote competition, which in practice has been taken very seriously. Regulatory effectiveness depends upon the scope for new entry and, again, on the information available to the regulator.

In order to carry out the twin tasks of controlling prices and promoting competition, the regulator thus needs to acquire adequate information concerning the scope for cost reductions and the extent and effects of new entry. The regulator will also need to transmit information to incumbents and potential entrants, in order to improve both efficiency and the prospects for entry. The generation and dissemination of information are therefore at the heart of regulatory effectiveness.[10]

Various devices intended to give companies the incentive to provide the regulator with relevant information have been suggested in the recent economic literature.[11] Typically these devices are set within the context of a given technology and product line: innovation and entry are not encompassed. Once the latter phenomena are admitted, it becomes apparent that the information which the regulator acquired is ephemeral: over time, it gradually becomes obsolete and needs to be replenished. Thus, if the regulator is to succeed in either of the two tasks – controlling prices or promoting competition – he or she needs to acquire information at a rate faster than that at which it decays. The feasibility of doing this depends on two main parameters.

First, there is the rate at which the underlying technological and market conditions change. The slower the change, the more likely the regulator will gradually come to acquire more relevant information and will be in a position to set realistic productivity targets (and, for that matter, performance standards) and determine allocatively efficient price structures for the regulated utility. The regulator will also be able to assess the effects of new entry more accurately. Where the underlying rate of change is slow, new entry is less attractive. In these circumstances, there is likely to be greater payoff to controlling prices than to promoting competition. Conversely, the faster the underlying rate of change in the industry, the more likely it is that the regulator's knowledge will decay faster than he or she can replenish it, and hence the less likely it is that he or she will be able to control prices efficiently.[12] However, rapid change provides the very circumstances in which new entry is feasible. Hence, in these circumstances, the regulator's priority should be to promote competition rather than control price. In the longer term, as the industry becomes more competitive, this will tend to reduce the need for price regulation.

The second main possibility of the regulator acquiring information faster than it decays is where there are multiple sources of information. Where there are many companies in an industry, even though they necessarily differ one from another, they may be sufficiently similar that the regulator can use the performance of one as an indication of what another could achieve. This yields a basis for setting efficiency targets in an RPI $-$ X price-control scheme. In these circumstances, the regulator's priority is to ensure that the laggards improve to match the (observed) performance of the leaders, while providing sufficient incentive for the leaders to stay ahead and blaze the way for the next round of target setting. The threat of takeover (if either the leaders or the laggards lapse into managerial slack) is an important aid in this endeavour. Conversely, where there is only one company in an industry, the regulator is more dependent upon that company for information, and his or her effectiveness in bargaining for productivity improvements is thereby reduced.

The prospects for generating information for regulatory purposes should therefore be an important argument in a government's decisions about the structure of the industry and the nature of the regulatory regime. Where the underlying rate of change is slow, there will be information advantages in creating and maintaining many similar firms for purposes of comparison.[13] Of course, it is economically efficient to do this only where the benefits of greater information are expected to outweigh any economies of scale or scope. This is more likely to be the case where a regulated industry is mainly an aggregate of several local monopolies (as with airports and local distribution networks for gas and electricity) than where the natural monopoly element is itself on a national scale (as with bulk transmission grids for gas or electricity).

An illustration from the United Kingdom

These ideas may be represented in a 2×2 matrix. In Tables 4.1 and 4.2, the columns represent the underlying rate of change in technology (and market conditions), classified as 'Low' or 'High', while the rows represent the number of regulated companies in the industry, classified as 'One' or 'Many'. Each regulated industry, or part thereof, can be located in one of the resulting four cells.

Table 4.1 Present position

	Rate of change of technology	
	Low	*High*
Number of regulated firms:		
Many	Water Electricity distribution	
One	Electricity transmission Gas transmission and distribution Airports	Telecoms Electricity generation Electricity supply Gas supply

Table 4.2 Potential position

	Rate of change of technology	
	Low	*High*
Number of regulated firms:		
Many	Water Electricity distribution Gas distribution Airports	Telecoms Electricity generation Electricity supply Gas supply
One	Electricity transmission Gas transmission	

Table 4.1 shows the matrix as it appears today for the five regulated utilities in the UK. The foregoing analysis indicates a policy of promoting competition in telecoms, gas supply, and electricity generation and supply. Water and electricity distribution provide the most promising conditions for price control. The difficulty of the single regulated utility presents itself in airports, electricity transmission, and gas transmission and distribution.

The structure of those industries characterized by a low rate of technological change could only be altered by government legislation (and clearly many other factors would need to be considered). Where there is a high underlying rate of change, however, the promotion of competition – at its simplest, by licensing new entry – would shift those industries in the one-firm cell into the many-firm cell. With the development of competition, specific industry regulation would become less necessary; whatever needed to be done to help keep competition active might well be performed by the anti-monopoly legislation common to all industries. In other words, deregulation might be indicated.

Table 4.2 shows the situation that could result in the United Kingdom if the policies discussed were put into effect. In telecoms, gas supply, and electricity generation and supply, the regulator's role of promoting competition would be paramount, perhaps via general competition policy rather than by specific regulation. In water, airports, and gas and electricity distribution, an emphasis on price control would be indicated, with prospects of success. The problematic areas would be national transmission grids for gas and electricity. Paradoxically, because transmission is so crucial to supply, regulatory attention in these natural monopolies would need to focus also on the promotion of competition in upstream and downstream markets via the terms to be set for the use of transmission facilities. So for electricity and gas transmission (and distribution too) the dual role of the regulator might be expected to continue in the foreseeable future.

RPI – X versus rate of return revisited

Future research might usefully assess US and UK regulatory systems in terms of the ideas suggested in this section, comparing their abilities to generate and use relevant information, depending upon rate of technological change and number of regulated firms. We may illustrate this by re-examining the initial question of the relative merits of RPI – X and rate-of-return regulation with respect to incentives and efficiency. We argued that RPI – X is indeed different because (*inter alia*) it incorporates a fixed risk period within which gains above the productivity bargain can be kept by the regulated firm(s). These productivity gains are potentially larger at the time of privatization than subsequently. They are also potentially larger the more rapidly technological conditions are changing, and where there are many different firms, with leaders blazing the way for laggards to follow.

Relating these considerations to the five regulated utilities, it follows that the case for RPI – X price control rather than rate-of-return regulation is strongest in telecoms, gas supply and electricity supply, where technology is indeed changing. If the aim is to 'hold the fort' until competition arrives, as Beesley and Littlechild (1986) put it, RPI – X will do this with greater potential productivity gains. At the other extreme, where there is less prospect of a shift in technology and only one firm in the industry, as with the electricity and gas transmission grids, there is less scope for bargaining about the potential for improvements in efficiency and no built-in mechanism to give the regulator scope for bargaining via directly relevant comparisons. Here, the grounds for preferring RPI – X are least strong.

In the remaining industries, notably water, gas, and electricity distribution, there is a strong reason for preferring RPI – X initially, given the potential productivity gains on privatization and the regulator's potential for generating superior information to that available to the companies taken separately. Admittedly, if there is indeed a low underlying rate of change in technology, both the scope for improvement and the discrepancies between companies may be expected to reduce over time, and in practice an RPI – X regime may gradually become indistinguishable from that of rate-of-return regulation. However, a permanently low underlying rate of change cannot be taken for granted. For the present, RPI – X seems to offer advantages.

NOTES

1 This chapter first appeared as an article in *RAND Journal of Economics* 20 (3), Autumn 1989, 454–72. We gratefully acknowledge helpful comments by Stanley Besen, Jan Acton, and a referee. It was written before the authors were associated with the Office of Electricity Regulation and does not necessarily represent the views of that office.
2 London Business School and University of Birmingham, respectively.
3 Other issues lie beyond the scope of this chapter. For example, it has been suggested that RPI – X may offer less incentive to maintain service quality (Vickers and Yarrow 1988; Besen 1989). The framework of regulation needs to be designed accordingly and the acts and licences do in fact reflect this consideration.
4 'Commissions base costs upon a test year due to the need for certainty – the need to avoid unresolvable factual disputes that threaten lengthy proceedings, arbitrary decisions, and court reversals. Although last year's prices will differ from likely future prices, at least they are known. One thereby avoids what would be an endless and unresolvable argument about what future costs will probably be' (Breyer 1982). 'The Commissions have been hesitant to make future forecasts of consumer demand, often preferring instead to assume that the test period demand conditions will hold in the immediate future' (Phillips 1969). Joskow (1974) noted that 'a few commissions have begun to cautiously use "projected" test year results, allowing companies to predict cost and demand conditions one or two years ahead', but this does not appear to have become standard practice. Automatic adjustment mechanisms are widely used, however (Joskow 1974, Spulber 1989).
5 The possibility of a company cross-subsidizing competitive uncapped services out of monopoly-capped services is frequently mentioned in the literature (e.g. Johnson 1989; Besen 1989; Spulber 1989) but to date this has not been a major issue in UK regulatory experience.
6 In 'Allocation of frequencies in the bands above 890 Mcs', 27 FCC 359 (1959), the Federal Communications Commission authorized the licensing of private communications systems to give large users an alternative to obtaining service from AT & T. Although this decision had little immediate effect, it set the stage for the introduction of Specialized Common Carriers, such as MCI, which eventually led to the competitive supply of ordinary long-distance telephone services.
7 The text by Phillips (1969) devotes just two and a half of its 774 pages to the then novel concept of strengthening the forces of market competition.
8 Competition *for* the market, via franchising, has been much discussed (see Vickers and Yarrow 1988; Spulber 1989), but is beyond the scope of this chapter.
9 'By relating prices to those of the alternatives available to each customer, it places BG in a position to selectively undercut potential competing gas suppliers; this may be expected to act as a deterrent to new entrants and to inhibit the development of competition in this market' (MMC 1988, paragraph 8.38 (b)).
10 Like the market participants, the regulator needs to be alert to hitherto undiscovered opportunities for profit, deriving from both the cost and demand sides. Kirzner (1985) has argued that 'nothing within the regulatory process seems able to stimulate, even remotely well, the discovery process that is so integral to the unregulated market'. Our argument is not that the regulatory process is more

effective than the competitive market process. (As indicated, the regulator has some advantages and some disadvantages compared to market participants.) Rather, our argument is that an effective regulator needs to be alert in order to promote greater alertness in markets that are not (yet) competitive.

11 See, for example, the surveys and references in Vickers and Yarrow (1988) and Spulber (1989).

12 Beesley and Glaister (1983) argued that this is the case in the taxicab industry. Wiseman (1957) has long argued that the very notion of an optimal price is untenable once uncertainty and change are admitted.

13 When dealing with mergers, the Water Act of 1989 embodies instructions to the MMC to this effect.

REFERENCES

Beesley, M.E. (1973) 'Mergers and economic welfare', in Arthur Selden (ed.) *Mergers, Takeovers and the Structure of Industry*, IEA Readings, no. 10, pp. 73–80.

—— (1986) 'Commitment, sunk costs and entry to the airline industry: reflections on experience', *Journal of Transport Economics and Policy* XX (2), May, 173–90.

—— and Glaister, S. (1983) 'Information for regulating: the case of taxis', *Economic Journal* 93: 594–615.

—— and Laidlaw, B. (1989) *The Future of Telecommunications: An Assessment of the Role of Competition in UK Policy*, Research Monograph no. 42, London Institute of Economic Affairs.

—— Gist, P. and Laidlaw, B.H. (1987) 'Prices and competition on voice telephony in the UK', *Telecommunications Policy* 11, 230–6.

—— and Littlechild, S. (1986) 'Privatization: principles, problems and priorities', In Lloyds Bank Review, July 1983.

Besen, S.M. (1989) *Statement Submitted by the National Cable Television Association*, in Federal Communications Commission CC Docket no. 87–313, 3 August.

Breyer, S. (1982) *Regulation and Its Reform*, Cambridge, Mass.: Harvard University Press.

Carsberg, B. (1987) 'Regulation of British Telecom', *Telecommunications Policy* 11, 237–42.

Cheong, K. (1989) 'The British experience with price cap (RPI − X) regulation', *Nera Topics*, London: NERA.

Civil Aviation Authority (1988) *Conditions as to Airport Charges in Relation to Manchester Airport under Section 40 (3) of the Act*, CAA Report, London, 25 February.

Coase, R.H. (1988) *The Firm, The Market and The Law*, Chicago: University of Chicago Press.

Culham, P.G. (1987) 'A method for determining the optimal balance of prices for telephone services', Oftel Working Paper, no. 1, March.

Director-General of Telecommunications (1986) *Review of British Telecom's Tariff Changes, November 1986*, London: Oftel.

—— (1988a) *The Regulation of British Telecom's Prices*, A Consultative Document, London: Oftel, January.

—— (1988b) *The Control of British Telecom's Prices*, London: Oftel, July.

Dixit, A.K. (1982) 'Recent developments in oligopoly theory', *American Economic Review* 72, 12–17.

Jarrell, G.A. (1978) 'The demand for state regulation of the electric utility industry', *Journal of Law and Economics* 21, 269–95.

Johnson, L.L. (1989) 'Price caps in telecommunications regulatory reforms', *RAND Note* N-2894-MF/RC, January.

Joskow, P.L. (1974) 'Inflation and environmental concern: structural change in the process of public utility price regulation', *Journal of Law and Economics* XVII (2), 291–328.

Kirzner, I.M. (1973) *Competition and Entrepreneurship*, Chicago: University of Chicago Press.

——(1985) 'The perils of regulation – a market process approach', in I.M. Kirzner (ed.) *Discovery and the Capitalist Process*, Chicago: University of Chicago Press.

Littlechild, S.C. (1983) *Regulation of British Telecommunications' Profitability*, London: Department of Industry.

Monopolies and Mergers Commission (1988) *Gas*, Cm 500, London: HMSO.

——(1987) *Manchester Airport p.l.c.: A Report on the Economic Regulation of the Airport*, Report MMC 1, Civil Aviation Authority, London, December.

Oftel (1986) *Report of the Director-General of Telecommunications (Annual Report 1985)*, London: HMSO, June.

Phillips, C.F. Jr (1969) *The Economics of Regulation*, Holmwood, III.: Irwin.

Schumpeter, J.A. (1950) *Capitalism, Socialism and Democracy*, 3rd edn, New York: Harper & Row.

Spulber, D.F. (1989) *Regulation and Markets*, Cambridge, Mass.: MIT Press.

Stigler, G.J. (1971) 'The theory of economic regulation', *The Bell Journal of Economics* 2, 3–21.

Vickers, J. and Yarrow, G. (1988) *Privatization: An Economic Analysis*, Cambridge, Mass.: MIT Press.

Wiseman, J. (1957) 'The theory of public utility price – an empty box', *Oxford Economic Papers* 9, 56–74.

5 Mergers and water regulation

M.E. Beesley

MANAGEMENT RIVALRY AND REGULATION

Because water is a natural monopoly in the product sense, it is widely agreed that, after privatization, competitive forces will chiefly consist of rivalry for the management of companies. Privatization will create a market for corporate control, in which less efficient management can be replaced by more efficient. Ministers have pointed to its importance on several occasions. A convincing case that this unique contribution of privatization will work well will blunt the inevitable criticism that 'private monopolies' are being created. This chapter sets down some thoughts on what policy in this area should be. Its main conclusion is that mergers having the effect of combining the ownership of more than one major water public limited company should be prohibited.

The overall strategy must be to create a regulatory system in which there are two complementary and reinforcing parts – general and continuous pressure for managements to seek more efficient ways to produce, and a price-control mechanism which ensures that the benefits of managements' efforts are passed on to consumers, in a manner consistent with maintaining incentives to seek improvements. The essence of the first element is potential rivalry between managements. An incumbent management must be capable of being supplanted by another management team. The mechanism for doing this is for the rival team to get the backing of the incumbent managers' shareholders to switch allegiance. The vehicle for activating the challenge will normally be the rival management team's own company. Of course, the basic driving force is the possibility of greater profits for shareholders. Hence the need for the complementary mechanism – the price-control system – for sharing out the benefits of greater efficiency.

Competition between managements will not only create continuous pressure towards efficiency, but will also be a support in the mechanism for setting prices. The regulator, in preparing for a periodic negotiation on the k^1 – perhaps every five years – will essentially proceed by constructing comparisons between the records of plcs and companies. The regulator will seek to distinguish between factors outside managements' control, such as those inherent in geographical variation, and those inside their control, such as managing capital inputs economically. In this, the extent of the cross-section of observations provided by the separate water interests in England and Wales is very important, because it gives the opportunity to build credible accounts of variations in performance. The regulator will also be able to explore engineering and other potential by seeking independent advice. The aim in a negotiation will be to establish the financial range over which the k might be varied, and to be assured that these are reasonably within the managements' control to influence.

The choice of the particular k within the range will then be settled by negotiation. The extent to which the regulator can press consumers' interests will depend on what managements could reasonably be expected to achieve. Challenge between managements, in its most fundamental sense of possible replacement, will set new standards of achievement within the industry. The regulator's hand in negotiations will be greatly strengthened by being able to appeal to these.

The question for policy therefore centres on competition between managements to acquire rights to manage water resources. How is it to be established, encouraged and preserved as a permanent feature of regulation?

CONDITIONS FOR EFFECTIVE COMPETITION BETWEEN MANAGEMENTS

Obstacles to be avoided

As the underlying objective is to make the control of assets subject to competitive forces, there is a general need not to discourage the transferability of activities to new ownerships. The water plcs will consist, in varying proportions, of saleable blocks of activities. The potential for such transfers of parts of the plcs' assets goes at least as far as the conventional divisions of water supply, sewage disposal, sewage treatment, and other non-water activities. For example, the transfer of assets could be facilitated by separate k for water supply and sewage for each company, but may prove difficult to establish and administer.

Obstacles to the takeover of the privatized companies should be minimized. Before privatization, the following potential inhibitions may require attention:

1 Limiting the potential number of bidders directly, for example by imposing bans, explicit and implied, on foreign ownership. Of all industries, water supply is the most universal. To inhibit foreign bids would be to miss an exceptionally favourable opportunity to establish competition.
2 Methods of flotation that will inhibit takeovers after privatization, for example, by maintaining a market, established at flotation, in bundles of rights to all water plcs.

Encouraging rivalry

The market for corporate control has two sides – the potential bidders for incumbent managements' plcs, and the number of incumbent target companies. As in any market, the more there are in each category the more effective is the competition likely to be. The need to encourage more bidders rather than fewer is self-evident. A first reason for keeping the number of potential targets high is that experience in one bid attempt can be transferred to other bids. The larger the number of targets, the more interest is stimulated, because the costs of learning about the industry and management time involved in setting up takeover proposals do not rise proportionately. The second and more important reason is that regulation will be a permanent feature of the UK water industry. To maintain the market discipline over time, we would wish to make the rivalry to bear as closely as possible on the individual undertakings. If this is to be achieved, the presumption is that they should remain in separate ownerships.

To keep the number of potential rivals to incumbent managements as high as possible is also important because, after flotation, the water plcs' attraction for bidders will vary. All incumbent managements are likely to be keen to exploit the new freedoms outside water, but start with different non-water bases. Interest in takeover will probably be correlated with the proportion of non-water activities, for two reasons. Non-water activities are not to be subject to control designed to share efficiency gains with consumers, as are water activities. Also, water plcs' managements are more likely to miss the profitable opportunities outside water which will open to them. A relatively 'pure' water plc will, like the others, be vulnerable if it fails to exploit the freedom to make profits inherent in the RPI – X type of control; a badly managed core business will be liable to takeover. But the 'pure' water companies will not have the added element of vulnerability implied by outside interests. The greater the overall interest, the less likely are these to escape the basic discipline.

WATER MERGER POLICY

In practice, policy designed to encourage competition for management control must work through merger rules. First, the fact that management rivalry depends on potential for replacement means that negotiated mergers or takeovers between management teams by definition lack the essential element of competition. They are suspect because of the following:

1 They do not necessarily signify that the aim is increased efficiency, which can be made the subject of the second part of the regulatory mechanism, designed to pass gains on to consumers (while leaving sufficient reward to producers, including managements). They may instead, for example, be intended to increase the potential for the managements to improve the rents they can abstract, via salaries higher than need to be paid,

and the many other forms in which rents can accrue, including the quieter life.
2 Any merger increases the scale of the (combined) firm. This makes possible future challenges by rival managements harder and more costly to mount. It may well be that one of the leading motives for agreed merger is to secure a greater immunity from hostile bids.

However, it will be impossible satisfactorily to distinguish between 'agreed' and other bids when merger proposals arise. Whether there is a real prospect of unseating incumbents can only be revealed by what happens when a bid is made. Moreover, the important rivalry is between top managements. At lower level there must be continuity in order to maintain the value of the target. But suitable merger rules can keep up the pressure. These are discussed next.

Merger rules in effect limit the takeovers which can be made. So they must to some extent conflict with the general presumption that restricting the potential set of bidders should be avoided. From this viewpoint, UK water plc alpha is welcome to bid for UK water plc beta so long as there is at least one rival bidder in the field to rule out the possibility of collusion between alpha's and beta's managements. But we cannot always or even usually be assured that such a contest will emerge. Avoiding collusive mergers is thus an additional reason for disallowing merger between them.

There may also be reasons on conventional grounds for limiting takeovers between UK water interests, even though entry into most of a given water plc's water-based activities is foreclosed. First, there is a small possibility of direct product competition at the borders of contiguous water plcs. This could be preserved by forbidding mergers among geographically contiguous plcs. Whether there should be a non-contiguity rule in mergers depends on (1) the possibilities of product competition at the borders, and (2) the economies necessarily associated with the merger. If the potential benefits of (2) outweigh losses from (1) then there is a presumption on conventional grounds for allowing the merger. If these benefits are large enough, they should logically also be allowed to challenge the argument that mergers are to be disallowed because of management collusion. How large are the net benefits likely to be?

It is true that little, in conventional terms, would usually be lost by permitting such a merger. Genuine rivalry for customers cannot be far pursued into each other's territory and the occasions where industrial customers open up opportunities for direct rivalry are few. But it seems very likely that, in the case of the authority's water plcs at least, economies associated with merger will also be small. Economies from combining the ownership of contiguous authorities must be distinguished from economies which can be secured without such combination. The two authorities will already be enjoying, separately, the available natural monopoly elements – the water distribution system, and the sewage disposal system. Merger will not affect these, favourably or otherwise. All other potential economies of merger, if present, could be realized by arrangements falling far short of merger. For example, billing systems and research and development may be cited, as yielding gains from merger. In so far as costs do fall with scale (a proposition to be treated with caution in these activities), they could equally well be realized through joint ownership of a free-standing company or contracting out to an independent organization. There is unlikely to be enough in these arguments to upset the presumption against merger.

There are further arguments in favour of limits on mergers. We have to consider the implications of the individual authorities' separate territorial monopolies. Successor water plcs may well wish to spread the influence of their basic natural monopolies into related markets. A movement into plumbing, for example, might have much in common with British Telecom's old control over maintenance, broken by privatization. There may well be a need to safeguard against this exploitation in downstream activities in water too.

In dealing with such monopoly powers which extend beyond the influence of price regulation, two lines of attack are possible. The first would be to leave the problem to the established 1973 Act procedures. A second might be to make a licence condition having the effect that any form of related water activity is permitted so long as it is not done in one's own territory. The argument would be: if a water plc indeed has superior water-based skills, let these be shown in the market of a neutral territory.

However this problem is tackled, sanctions would be less effective were contiguous authorities allowed to merge. And over time, any merger activity must decrease their effectiveness. The case on conventional grounds for prohibiting UK water mergers is thus strengthened.

To accept these limitations on who may bid is also to keep up the number of separate UK water industry targets. There are further important reasons for doing this. They concern the type, quality and the use of information by the regulator. As indicated earlier, yardstick comparisons will be prominent. Water privatization also creates a completely new opportunity – to derive information from a set of the stock-market quotations for what will be new water utilities. How this can be useful will be the subject of further study. But briefly, so long as the effects of the regulator's own action on stock price movements can be controlled, which I would argue is possible, we have in prospect very useful information about what drives the capital markets' relative assessment of the stocks, with strong implications, especially when combined with other data, for such issues as the 'required' or 'reasonable' rate of return. Without a rule prohibiting the merging of UK water interests, there is every possibility that such information will deteriorate over time. The information is quite distinct from comparisons between water operations which do not depend on ownership. If, for example, two water operations are found in a conglomerate, their separate operations can be compared with respect to common inputs and outputs. But to use stock-market information, we require quotations bearing on their separate ownership.

Stock-market quotations reflecting at least some underlying interests in UK water should increase over time, as water companies become plcs and/ or are taken over by outside quoted companies. But in the more important cases of the present Authorities, losses of independent quotations implied by merger between them is serious. We have only ten to start with. Even with a non-contiguity rule, there could in principle be a reduction to about three effective independent observations. Moreover, there is a prospect that each will become part of a larger set of assets outside water. It seems wise, with the prospect of a great reliance on comparisons, to keep the number of UK targets having independent quotations as large as possible.

The conclusion is that merger activity having the effect of combining UK water plcs under one ownership should not be allowed. Several important questions follow. They concern, respectively, the likely impact of such a rule on flotation; how shareholding falling short of outright ownership should be treated; how far the policy should be applied to what are now water companies; how the basic rule would fit with general UK and EEC merger policy; and whether there are grounds for intervening in the market for corporate control involving water interest beyond those already presented.

CONSEQUENTIAL QUESTIONS

We have yet to work out with the financial advisers the full implications for the *flotation* of alternative approaches to the consequential questions just posed, but Schroders have approved the basic thrust of the policy. Their reason is essentially that creating a more active after-market in the water plc shares, in which possibilities of bids are encouraged, is attractive to original investors.

What should our attitude be to the acquisition of *multiple minority shareholdings* in water plcs? The question is in part prompted by French activity in doing so for several water companies. The answer must depend on what we think the motives would be. If more than one minority stake is picked up as a preliminary to deciding on a full bid in one, the activity is not only permissible but welcome. The extent of the activity must of course be severely limited, the larger the targets are. A second motive would be to influence incumbent managements to adopt more efficient methods in order to secure exceptionally good returns from a water portfolio. This, too, is to be commended, not prevented. But perhaps the most likely longterm reason for such activity is to influence the incumbent managements towards everyday buying or selling activities favourable to the minority shareholder's interests. The corrective measures to be applied here lie in the proper domain of general UK control of monopoly procedures under the 1973 and 1980 Acts. It is up to the aggrieved rival suppliers to dispute the influence, and the Acts' procedures should take their course. The conclusion for minority shareholding in water is, therefore, that the only action required in water is to ensure that the Bill and licences do not hinder the application of the 1973 Act in this area.

For what are now the *water companies*, the case for preventing the merging of ownership is considerably less. The conventional product market arguments against merger are more likely to be offset by potential economies. We could envisage reverse takeovers of large water concerns, or water companies as the entry vehicle for non-UK interests, as a springboard for bids for large plcs, all of which increase the potential challenge to incumbent managements.

Agreed takeover activity involving the companies may have a beneficial effect on regulatory prospects, even though, again, this activity represents targets without going through the discipline of competition. Thus, there may well be a net increase of quoted companies having water interests when they occur. Their different position seems to indicate a need to draw a line between significant, larger cases and the rest. A rule analogous to that in general merger control, of an asset size below which no constraint on merger activity is needed, could be made. Or the rule could be formulated in terms of the numbers of independent undertakings remaining or the percentage of industry controlled. My own strong preference is for the first, because it is simple and introduces no principle new to merger control in the UK.

However these issues are settled for application in ongoing regulation, there is the very important fact that no UK water management has yet been tested in the market for corporate control. Opinions about management capabilities to deliver efficiency improvements will have to be formed, before setting the initial price control. These will be drawn, *inter alia*, from the efficiency studies. To some extent, the immediate stock-market reaction on flotation will show the degree to which its valuation of the water plcs' capabilities diverges from the government's. But the validation, or otherwise, of management capabilities will only emerge when the companies have had further exposure to the capital market. It might be wise, however, not to permit merger activity involving quoted companies for a period after flotation. One might argue that existing managements should not be distracted in the lead-up to flotation by possible immediate takeover threats. One year should suffice, allowing a good period for permitted takeover activity, within the other rules adopted, before changes in the price formula become possible, at five years. This formulation permits companies which would otherwise not reach water plc status to merge among themselves, and to do so before the flotation of the principal water plcs, so adding to the scope of the quoted water sector.

A rule forbidding the ownership of more than one major UK water interest would be an absolute rule, novel to UK and EEC monopoly policy. It implies that companies' takeover strategy cannot be planned to include such a combination, and that if, for example, a conglomerate already owns a UK water plc and wishes to acquire another, it must dispose of its original interest to do so. There should be no difficulty in mounting the case that water is indeed very 'different'. Aside from the economic issues, its fixity of market boundaries, its relative imperviousness to product competition, and its exceptional reliance on management rivalry in promoting efficiency as argued in this chapter, it is also arguably the most heavily regulated industry already in all countries, for the very good reason of its being the ultimate condition of survival.

GROUNDS FOR FURTHER TAKEOVER RULES

The policy so far spelt out is directed to increasing efficiency. But efficiency as judged by the corporate market place is not the whole content of announced water policy. Managers are expected, in addition, to pursue objectives which are designed to modify the single-minded pursuit of share-holders' interest. These objectives are exemplified in the quality conditions of the licence. The most obvious case of a potential conflict arises in one company's bid for another. The bid is an essential feature of competition between management, yet, if successful, it may result in the displacement of a management which, judged in terms of water policy's total objectives, is superior.

A trade-off situation will not often arise, because there is likely to be a strong correlation between management skills in meeting the various requirements, profit making or otherwise, imposed on them. However, in the period leading up to flotation, interest and concern will be shown about the fate of 'our local' water – will it fall into unsympathetic hands etc? The non-profit aspects of performance must also bulk large in the general public's and particular area consumers' minds after flotation. There is both a substantive and a presentational case for some further safeguard.

One possibility would be to establish some form of screening procedure for would-be acquirers of substantial UK water interests. There are many precedents for 'fitness tests' to be an operation in particular areas of economic activity, for example in airlines and banks. But much of this is centred on financial fitness. Here, our essential problem would be to screen for qualities other than financial ability. It seems to me quite impracticable to operate such a system, whoever might be responsible for it, in such a way as not to become an important deterrent to takeover activity in general. One should, instead, concentrate on the exceptional cases revealed by bid contests.

To do this, one can spell out the conditions in which there could be intervention to prevent a takeover, where that is objected to by the incumbent management. (Non-contested bids are permitted, and are therefore not in question, so long as they conform to the basic constraint about owner-ship. The presumption here is that agreed bids allow incumbent manage-ments still to survive, for the most part.) Relevant criteria should clearly be part of the yardstick comparisons on which regulation in general depends. The emphasis would be on incumbent managements' relative performance with respect to the financial targets set and relative performance in meeting service target levels. Other relevant evidence could be considered, external and internal to the company involved, but priority should be given to measurable elements in the yardstick comparisons which are progressively to be developed. 'Reasonable' grounds for intervention would be evidence of superior performance on the criteria. As most water managements cannot, *a fortiori*, be revealed superior, this possibility of aiding a takeover defence should not be a serious dampener on takeover interest.

NOTE

1 k refers to the percentage by which prices are allowed to deviate from RPI, the retail price index. Each water company was given its individual k in the lead-up to the flotations.

6 The required rate of return/cost of capital

M.E. Beesley

Clause 6 of the Bill (which became the Water Act 1989) imposes the duty to 'secure that undertakings can carry out their functions properly' and to finance the carrying out of these functions 'in particular by securing reasonable returns on their capital'. When water plc's shares are traded on the market, the market will determine what that 'reasonable' return is. In setting the k^1 now and to help form a view of how valuable the authorities' water assets will be when sold, we need to judge the likely rate. When the Director-General takes his or her view of the requirement, in future dealings with utilities, he or she will have the evidence of the market itself. In so far as we can now make an accurate estimate we can help to smooth the transition to the new status.

The 'cost of capital' to the plc and the required rate of return to the prospective provider of finance are not identical. Respective transactions costs and tax positions, for example, will create divergences. But the principal, indeed dominating, influence on both will be the stock market's assessment of how the water plcs and companies compare with other avenues for investment. Because no company can avoid this market discipline, it is appropriate to concentrate on the 'required rate of return'. Price regulation is intended to be strictly confined to companies' water interests, so we seek an estimate of the return required on the companies' water interests alone.

Investors' choices run from relatively risk-free government bonds to highly risky newcomers to the unlisted securities markets. The required return on their investment varies inversely with the different risks. The task essentially is to place water assets in this spectrum. In doing this, it is appropriate to focus in the first place on the required return on assets financed entirely by equity, since this best expresses the basic aim of computing the required return on a particular class of assets. When that rate is established, it is possible to consider the implications of gearing, that is splitting up the financing of the assets into equity and debt. (The principal effect of this is, of course, to raise the required return on equity as gearing is increased. However, the weighted average cost of capital, ignoring company tax considerations, remains the same.)

Investors have to be compensated according to the options available. The method of computing the final required return consists of recognizing these. First, nearly all risks can be avoided by investing in a government-backed bond which guarantees payouts independent of future inflation. Second, investors in equities must not only consider inflation, but also the fact that payoffs in the future will lack the certainty generated by the government's backing. They need not, however, shoulder more than the average risk of an equity market as a whole, because it is always open to them to take the option of diversifying their holdings. The second element is therefore the return, net of inflation, to be obtained in the UK equity market above that on the safe option.

The third element in the computation is the perceived risk of investment in water equity as compared with the average equity holding. Particular classes of equity may well be risky, or less risky, than the market as a whole. One would expect a markedly stable commodity like water to be regarded as much less risky than a holding in the motor industry, for example. The experience of changes in the return upon different stocks relative to the average is thus computed. The index ('beta') in essence computes the volatility of the return on a particular stock relative to that on the market as a whole. We would expect water to be considerably less volatile; hence applying the index should result in a lower required return than for the market average.

The first two elements – the return on risk-free assets and the required return on equities as a whole – are easily observable for whatever recent period is deemed to give a safe basis for projection. The best fix on the first element is index-linked bonds, which, however, are a relatively recent addition to investors' options. The redemption yields on indexed-linked government bonds which mature in the next century were as follows, as at January 1989. It seems reasonable to assess the first element at about 3.5– 3.7 per cent; the historical average real return on long-term gilts is less than this.

In computing the second element, a much wider choice of relevant period is available. LBS Risk Measurement Service notes (January–March 1989) that, in both the USA and the UK, the average annual risk premium 'over the years' has been close to 9 per cent, comparing equities with Treasury bills. Dr Dimson computes the average real returns on UK equities over 1955–87 as 10.6 per cent. Over the same period the real return on Treasury bills averaged 1.2 per cent, so the real risk premium over Treasury bills was 9.4 per cent. Morrison and Brealey computed 9 per cent real for the period 1919–56, and over a longer period, 1919–86, Frank Russell International computed the real difference between the return on equity and long gilts at 8.3 per cent. Ibbotson and Associates (1987), compute 8 per cent as the premium over long-term bonds for the period 1926–88 for the USA. So, whatever the definition of 'long term', estimates tend to be about the same for the UK (and for the USA, a market in which the water utilities now will

Table 6.1 Redemption yields on index-linked bonds, at January 1989

Maturity date	Redemption field (%)
2001	3.7
2003	3.7
2006	3.7
2009	3.7
2011	3.7
2013	3.7
2016	3.6
2020	3.6
2024	3.5

be traded on a considerable scale). A range of 8–9 per cent real seems reasonable as an estimate of the premium over indexed bond yields.

Relating UK water assets to the market average involves selecting analogies. Unfortunately, we do not have a set of UK utility stocks to which to refer. Two kinds of analogy seem close: the experiences of water utilities stocks traded in non-UK markets, and the experience of the large UK privatized plcs to date. Estimates of β are available for US water companies, and for the relevant UK plcs excluding British Steel. (This is too recently traded to yield a reliable estimate yet, but it is probably much more risky than water companies. The value of β for Bethlehem Steel in the USA, for example, is about 1.8.) Table 6.2 sets out the available observations.

Observations of β are for the shares of companies and reflect the debt/equity ratio (as computed by the market values as opposed to the formal balance sheet numbers). To assess the values of β of water *assets*, we have to allow for both of these. The US data are closest to the asset base with which we are dealing. The values of β are very low. Only twenty-one stocks of all the London market's listings as recorded in LBS data for the first quarter of 1989 record β as low as 0.32. A correction for gearing reduces these figures

Table 6.2 Estimates of β

US water companies		UK privatized plcs	
Beta computed as at October 1986 for sixty observations		LBS Risk Service β Last quarter 1988 issue	First quarter 1989 issue
Californian Water Service	0.15	British Airports	0.59	0.61
Consumers Water	0.26	British Gas	0.68	0.68
The Hydraulic Company	0.37	British Telecom	0.71	0.70
Philadelphia Suburban	0.55	British Petroleum	0.92	0.92
Southern Californian Water	0.43	British Aerospace	0.96	0.96
United Water Services	0.18	British Airways	1.15	1.15
Average (unweighted)	0.32			

even more, because the average percentage gearing of the quoted US water stocks ranges from 45 in the Californian case to 159 in the Philadelphia suburban case (gearing information here refers to long-term debt: the source is unclear on the precise definition). On the other hand, the American water industry is very tightly regulated by rate-of-return rules. I am not surprised that, over time, virtually all of the type of risk associated with equity holding appears to have been eliminated there. However, the figures in general remind us forcibly that water is indeed an extremely safe long-term bet.

Most observers would wish to give more weight to the UK 'privatized' experience. The plcs have been arranged in ascending order of β. Their placing in this order is wholly unsurprising. British Airports has the advantages of superior and virtually unchallengeable locations, together with a price-control regime which directly bears on only some 37 per cent of its revenue. At the other end of the scale, British Airways operates in a competitive environment, albeit modified by bilateral government agreements on licensing; accordingly it is rated as a greater than average risk. We should also note that there is little change in the individual values of β as new observations are made from quarter to quarter. This again is unsurprising, because computations of β are little affected by overall movements in the market. This is because the underlying relative riskiness of business itself changes basically only as the company concerned alters the production orientation of its asset base.

The plcs just quoted have varying degrees of gearing. 'True' underlying asset β (ungeared) will be lower, because the addition of loans has increased the recorded β. The correction for this effect involves estimates of the gearing. I have taken the March/April 1988 figures, estimating gearing as short- plus long-term loans as a ratio of market value of equity plus loans. The 'corrected' figures are as follows, taking β for the first quarter of the 1989 issue:

British Airports	0.55
British Gas	0.51
British Telecom	0.55
British Petroleum	0.68
British Aerospace	0.68
British Airways	0.66

This brings the observations closer, but still displays the expected distinctions between the less and the more risky operations. Using these 'corrected' figures, a defensible value of β for water would be a maximum of 0.5. On the one hand water utilities have the most secured market of all commercial activities; this view is supported by the US data. On the other hand, there are the risks associated with the future impact of regulation. There is no reason to suppose that the regulatory system will bear no more or less favourably on water utilities than it does on the regulated plcs in the list, namely Airports, Gas and Telecom.

Accepting an ungeared value of β of 0.5, the required real rate of return for water utilities works out as follows:

'Risk-free' element	3.5–3.7%
Required market premium	
$8–9.0 \times \beta(0.5) =$	4.0–4.5%
	7.5–8.2%

However, investors compare return on different assets on an after-tax basis. Because of the imputation tax system for corporation tax a further adjustment is appropriate. Payment of corporation tax discharges the share-holders' liability for income tax at the basic rate of 25 per cent. An adjust-ment has therefore to be made to the risk-free investment in government bonds, which is the starting point of our calculations. This reduces the overall required rate by up to 25 per cent of the range of 3.5–3.7 per cent, or by about 0.75 per cent. From the point of view of the prospective investor, the cash flows to which the appropriate discount rate may be applied are those after payment of corporation tax.

In practice we must try to foresee how the basic market risk premium will trend in the future. For example, many observers would expect some reduction in the yield on index-linked bonds. Taking this into account, a reasonable working basis for our approach would be that the required rate will be about 7 to 7.5 per cent and in any case is not likely to be more than 8 per cent. Many refinements are possible, and fresh data would be relevant, and should be added, but I doubt whether these will lead to a convincing case for a higher figure.

In modelling work we will also require a working assumption about the likely cost of borrowing. This can only be approximate, and therefore the selection of an optimal debt/equity ratio is doubtful, but also because all company borrowing must to some extent itself reflect a degree of risk; a plc cannot, for example, avoid the bankruptcy risk, so it never has the option of 100 per cent debt financing.

In practice, we have the following evidence, which points to a borrowing rate somewhat above the yield on corresponding 'risk-free' gilts.

1 Long-term water debentures are not frequently traded, and this, together with their small size, pushes up their yield to a level ranging from 1 to 1.5 per cent (Bristol) to 2 per cent (South Staffs) above the yield on corres-ponding gilts. The development of a more active market in larger issues should result in a lower yield basis.
2 Nationwide Anglia Building Society, which is probably of similar risk, has an indexed bond maturing in 2021 on a yield only 0.9 per cent above that on an indexed gilt of the same term.

3 A range of property companies, with equity β and variability of return about equal to the equity market, have long-term debentures with current yields about 1 per cent above that on long gilts.

So water plcs could, where deemed to be advantageous, raise long-term debt on a yield basis of 1–1.5 per cent above the yield on corresponding gilts.

NOTE

1 See note 1, Chapter 5 (p. 92).

7   The DGWS in operation[1]

M.E. Beesley

This note concentrates on the Director General of Water Services' (DG's) primary task of economic regulation and in particular on the needs of his first five years. It is written with the 10 'authority' PLCs mainly in mind; how companies will be fitted in must be dealt with in a later paper. It should be seen as a first contribution to the task of defining what the DG's central concerns will be, and how they are to be met.

TIMING OF REVIEWS

The effective organization of the DG's many tasks requires that there should be an express or implicit agreement with the industry that there will be a 5-yearly review of k for all PLCs simultaneously.[2] Such an understanding does not exist now, I believe. Rather, some expectations are that there will be a more sequential approach, with perhaps 3 tranches of PLCs coming forward at intervals. Concern is expressed that the DG's work load will be unmanageable if k's are settled at the same time. The short answer to this is that this is precisely what is happening now, with the added complication of flotation, and the DG could and should draft in expert help as required.

The more important point is probably that the authorities are not yet clear about the relationship between information flow and the DG's task of fixing k's. They are perhaps inclined to think of information given to the DG as a hostage to fortune at the next round of price fixing, or as encouraging time wasting pursuit of too much detail, e.g. about service levels. Given the Government's basic regulatory approach, these fears are not well founded – so long as the DG when appropriate reaffirms his adherence of it.

To recap, the policy consists of two main parts, price-fixing at intervals sufficient to enable PLCs to profit from their own efficiency, and the discipline of the market for corporate control, not directly influenced by the DG. In the intervals between price-fixing, the DG's task is primarily to monitor the licence conditions on prices and services. The new price-fixing opportunity is intended to be, and must be in practice, forward-looking. Any cost-pass-throughs that are triggered in the period are intended not to affect this principle. At a review the DG will be making judgements analogous to those being developed now, namely to fix prices so as prospectively to reward efficient management behaviour.

The issue for each PLC will be the permitted change from an already established k. The practical point for the DG is how far can he reasonably expect a given PLC to improve its performance in the next 5 years, which will itself of course imply effects stretching far beyond that limit. What is 'reasonable' must be bounded by best practice in the industry, again on a forward-looking basis. In this process of judgement the greatest risk to a PLC is that the DG is uninformed or unconvinced about key matters affecting future finances. A frank exchange will come to be seen as essential, I believe. As shown below, this in turn must imply a steady build up over the 5 years of relevant information, not a scrambled triggered off by the formal review process 15 months in advance.

The following arguments seem to point to the 'simultaneous' conclusion. First, it will be invidious to decide on a pecking order for companies to come forward. How will the public and the markets react when Alpha is picked in the first tranche and Beta in the last? (5 years probably allows at most 3 tranches of PLCs.) And the DG will surely have to announce and publicly justify his reason for distinctions. If we think of the first review, these reasons will have to be formulated without the benefit of the further information a simultaneous review would allow. Second, because at the limit there will be 39 PLCs, the likelihood that there will be appeals to MMC is quite high. True, if the process of frank exchange is established, they need not be many; it is in the interests of both the DG *and* the PLCs and Companies PLC that appeal should be avoided if possible, because among other things of the extra uncertainty generated. But there will always be the odd men out, who perceive advantage in appeal. If this happens, the appeal decision must be settled and digested by the parties well before the next round of price increases. Otherwise it will become dubious where the ultimate authority on price policies lies, the DG or MMC. And the risks of judicial review must increase in these circumstances. Moreover, it is imperative that MMC be consistent in response to appeals. The chance is much higher if they are simultaneous.

Very important to the DG's judgements and, by extension the whole credibility of the process, is use of comparative information. For this the argument for clear intervals seems overwhelming. The reference set must be *all* the UK water interests, and each has to be given its due weight at the point of decision. So the review must both be cross-sectional at a point in time, and so far as information over time is concerned, cover a similar period. Somewhat more subtly, as shown below, the DG's observation, e.g., about relative financial performance must as far as practicable discount regulations' effect on that performance. In other words, what the DG does affects the valuation of the companies; his aim must be to minimize these effects over as long a period as can be managed.

Because the water industry is not subject to the degree of market change met by other industries, and technology moves rather more slowly than in most, we can reasonably predict that the knowledge which can be held with fair certainty will grow over time. (The current upheavals in estimates are unlikely to be repeated on the same scale.) This implies that the 5-year intervals could get longer as regulation moves on in time. As the pool of information shared by the DG and the PLCs grows, as envisaged, so this prospect will be improved. To increase the intervals is an interest shared between the DG and the industry, and is one hall-mark of an overall regulatory policy which distinguishes RPI–k from rate of return control.

INFORMATION FLOWS

In approaching his task of deciding changes in the k's, the DG's economic framework should be that of cost–benefit analysis (CBA). The reasons for preferring this approach, rather than the main alternatives, are set out in the Appendix. It would, of course, not be quantified or formal CBA, but I argue that in the conditions faced in the water industry it is the correct reference set of economic ideas.

In making judgements, the central information in the DG's repertoire must be the anticipated cash flows for the companies. Partly because of the peculiar limitations on accounting evidence in water (both current cost and historic cost information leaves very big gaps) we have already made future cash flow the centre-piece of the DHS modelling effort. I have explained in an earlier paper how this could be developed for the current round of k-setting, in which the main policy trade offs are between consumers' interest in low k's on the one hand and flotation proceeds on the other. The DG will have the same need to look 20 years ahead from the point of decision and indeed should inherit and develop the model. The DG's principal concern will be the trade-off between consumers' and shareholders' interests, raising some further questions about information to be dealt with later.

If forward-looking cash flow is to be central then all major aspects of policy must have their reflection in it. In particular, consumers' interests in higher service levels and lower k's must be brought into relation with each other. For service standards already agreed, cash flow implications are now emerging, and will continue to be clarified under the DG. Further implications for cash flow will arise from the following:

(i)   changes in service standards, whether dealt with by statutory cost pass through or otherwise;

(ii) consequence or failure to meet standards, dealt with via the enforcement process;

(iii) changes in factor prices including labour, often affecting each company differently;

(iv) change in the cost-minimizing means of meeting standards, which requires technical specification of trade-offs between capital inputs and maintenance;

and, not least,

(v) changes in base revenues, mediated via estimates of customer numbers, and changes made to prices within the basket.

Building the necessary information to evaluate these will be an evolving process. It will depend for its effectiveness and pace of development on mutual trust between the DG and the industry. ('Mutual trust' does not mean 'capture', but a joint determination to lessen and crystallize the areas of disagreement, and therefore to enable some limits for the k (setting exercise to be anticipated.) We can, however, set out necessary technical conditions for the development of the information.

Most obvious is the translation of service standards via engineering standards and input prices into cash. Two aspects of this information will be important to the DG, the costs of a PLC's reaching higher individual standards, and, less obviously, the assessment of over-fulfilled standards. Providing increasing service levels is a way of inflating the cost base and therefore rasing the absolute level of profits. The DG needs to be able to distinguish between these and the cost of getting to agreed standards. He must use the comparative information across PLCs to decide on the quality/ cost trade-off when resetting k. To help him, he may well have to gather independent information on this trade-off from consumer panels. In conducting such inquiries, there is much useful precedent in marketing studies in other industries.

An overall view of the DG's task also includes safeguarding against 'undue discrimination', which most would probably interpret as 'avoiding unfairness to a particular class of customers'. In practical terms, it involves tracing the effects that changing methods of charging have on customers' bills, i.e. from the position they start in at flotation. For example, when rateable values are abandoned, the rate base changes. This does not directly complicate the k-setting issue, because once k has been established, proposed changes can always be related to the previous base if there is some common denominator. An underlying requirement, however, is that what the customer pays, the bill, can be mapped unequivocally to established k, to future k, and potential classes of customers, and of course ultimately to other aggregates now not systematically related, like 'principal services'. For the sake of control, information must be capable of being added up to correspond to total company experience. Even more important, perhaps, is the mapping of the customers bills, via 'classes', to the service standards. These now run, variously, in terms of, for example 'properties', and 'population' and other denominators ('Bills' appear only in the billing standards). The central point is that, ultimately, the customer can experience both a change in cash and a change in service level for any given decision on prices. 'Fairness' involves attention to both; the regulator needs to be able to attend to them side by side.

From the foregoing it is clear that information now being developed, such as that an asset plans and overground assets have to be continued, and if anything, intensified, at least in the early years, as the efficiency and fairness dimensions are explored. At 1994, say, the DG will seek to make judgements robust to public opinion, the stock market, and, not least, to MMC scrutiny. He will seek to complement his own professional expertise with others. Since, in the case of investment expenditures, for example, the formal process of certification will almost certainly not run to signing off on cash implications, the DG will be obliged further to consult independent but respected advice on the issue.

THE AMBITION VERSUS THE STARTING POINT

Several concerns about the present state of play on the licence emerge from attempting to compare the foregoing description with its provision. It may well be that the emphasis in what follows will be disputed by those more expert in the drafts than I am; and there may be straightforward difficulties in interpretation. But proceeding from 19 October and 17 October drafts of the Licence and the Bill, and following the earlier discussion, here they are:

First, as it affects the DG's needs, the model of information flow implicitly adopted too much emphasizes the confrontational aspect of setting k. An important distinction is made between 'Review information' and the rest of the information. Review information is clearly intended to be comprehensive and to go to the centre of business decisions. It is to be triggered off only with a lead time of just over a year for the DG, and less if an MMC referral is to be allowed for with the possible exception of procedures following a breach of duty on standards. Neither realism nor the interests of either side are secured by this compression.

If this were regulation of a single entity, or a duopoly, one might say that formal distinctions about what and when information can flow are not very important, because mutual needs will breed a sensible compromise. I do not think this is a viable line of argument with up to 39 separate interests. Hence, unfortunately, more depends on formality in water than in previous privatization.

Condition D makes it clear that the yearly reporting of accounts and accounting information are directed primarily to the issue of separation of the transactions between PLC subsidiaries. This is a very necessary step towards transparency and lessening possibilities of cross-subsidy; but its contribution towards the underlying financial issues in the core business is limited. In information terms it takes us little further than the input into starting point of the DHS model. The 'sequential' information, for example, provided for in clause (D5) adopts the divisions of operating costs reported now.

Second, the information requirements are geared to the task of providing an aggregate price control for a company's water and sewerage services. The regulatory requirement to keep open the challenge to management implies building the possibility that they should be capable of divestiture of parts of an original company (and of course, subject to merger rules, to take on another's separate activities). A principal practicable division is for example between water supply and sewerage provision. It may be that it makes good sense for a water company (say, after it becomes a PLC) to acquire some substantial sewerage operations, implying a transfer of assets which should be reflected in adjusting respective k's.

This kind of possibility is not directly addressed, so far as I am aware, in the Bill and Licence provisions, though doubtless they will have a complicated bearing on the issue. In principle, we would wish to see the information base to support divestiture and acquisition grow. Are, then, separate 'shadow' k's to be devised? Does a 'k' become a tradeable asset (or liability?). From the DG's point of view, in settling how these questions might be answered, it would be important not to confuse these implied changes in k for given PLCs with the trigger to set off a general review process, and to align them with the overall water merger policy in terms of control.

Third, it is necessary to clarify the meaning of 'chargeable supplies' now featuring as the denominator in k for unmeasured[3] water and sewerage. In particular, we need to know how it maps to 'bills', 'customers' and indeed any of the aggregates to be found in the licence or bill ('principal services', 'customers', 'classes', etc). Quite aside from the direct price control issue – we surely must not be the only privatization so far for which one cannot describe in detail what the price to be controlled is – the DG needs to be able to understand how all these categories work in terms of each other, not least because he has to keep an eye on how it all adds up.

Ofwat 3[4] also raised a question, yet to be settled, of how to deal with k setting when a water company, already in the control, decides to become a PLC.

NEW INFORMATION NEEDS

So far, what has been described carries forward into the DG's regime elements now being deployed in the current, first, k setting and judgement of standards. These elements – cash impacts, asset management statements of standards and efficiency studies, supplemented as described – will be the DG's continuing concern. I have also argued for a steady build-up in the 4 years to the start of the formal Review process. It may well be that the DG and the industry can agree to independent work on critical issues like the relationship between changes in standards and the technical means to deal with them; which it will be understood to be common ground before the price negotiation starts. But after the flotation, two new kinds of information will have to be developed, each very important to the DG's task, namely assessing the required return on future investments at the time of decision, and dealing with what is intended to be a capability for PLCs to switch from unmeasured to measured supply.

The required rate of return is one part of a two-fold task in a k-setting exercise. The other is the quantum of capital which will be needed in future, to which much of the work on assets is directed. The return question incorporates the following separable issues:

(a) to set conditions for needed capital flow in the future
(b) to bear on questions about whether the shareholder is or has been having a reasonable deal, and
(c) to help in the assessment of comparative performance between the water PLCs and companies.

For (a) one expects the DG to exploit stock market quotations for water PLCs and, perhaps, companies. There are well-rehearsed methods of extracting evidence on the market's evaluation of the average water risk premium with respect to the general market from time to series observations of market transactions. This is the most important line of evidence opened up uniquely by privatization and is part of the rationale of the plans to limit a possible decline in the set of quoted companies. Therefore, for (a) attention will be on experience in the set of PLCs and companies as a whole. For (c), the DG will need to use similar evidence to explore individual PLC's variance from the water industry average, and to relate this to the other dimensions of a given PLC's performance.

Inevitably, though the DG's economic task is always to predict, and the spirit of the RPI $- k$ is to let PLCs make their own financial decisions and stand by the consequences for 5 years at least, there may well be a need to set alongside the reporting of progress in standards, etc., some account of how the shareholders have done in a sense distinct from inferences about risks and returns of (a), hence category (b), the DG will face some difficult questions here. How does he encapsulate the 'shareholders interests'? Does he look at it as simply the amount shareholders put into the privatization in the first place? If so, he would trace, in the usual way, how £X invested in a Water portfolio in 1989 has fared in the interim compared to the market, to other utilities, or to whatever reference is deemed appropriate. But this kind of approach gets steadily out of date. Moreover, the implicit assumption is either that shareholders never change their original holdings, or that all shareholders have behaved randomly in their length of tenure of the stocks. The former assumption is fatally flawed, because, if it were true, no stock market quotation would be possible, because no one sells. Artificial as it is, the second approach is more sound in principle.

The second major need for new data concerns shifts to metering. The chief economic concern must be that the experiments now in hand should be structured so as to reveal the key point – when water is charged for at the margin, what is consumption response and how does it vary among different consumers, including those of different PLCs? Getting useful evidence is not an easy task when the starting price at the margin is zero, and there are unsettled questions about whether the experiments as now devised will be adequate to illuminate the elasticity question. However, the main point here is that DG's role in the studies is how far can he influence the method and profit by the information flow. We have yet to consider the proposals from this point of view.

The DG may well want to exercise his understanding of how PLC's and companies' price changes affect classes of consumers like the 'less well off' domestic users. For example, he might take a leaf from the Telecoms book, requiring the computation of an average residential bill, or even a representative median bill.

The DG will also be concerned with the specification of 'inset appointments'[5] and the arrangements for their competitive allocation. These have further implication for how the information interacts with the previously defined tasks, needing further consideration.

Also, we need to think more carefully about the relation between the mechanism for coping with customers representations and complaints and the control and evaluation of service standards. One important aspect of the elaborate system of customer consultation is that it will be a running critique of the adequacy of established standards. Among other things, for example, it will tend to illuminate the adequacy or otherwise of sampling procedures underlying the reporting on service standards. At the minimum, one of the DG's early tasks will be to align the information from the consultative side with established standards.

SUMMARY

This paper has not attempted a full description of what the DG will be doing in his first 5 years. One obvious point, not elaborated here, is that he will be busy with left over water company issues and implementation in his first years at least. Rather the paper has focused on economic information needs. Regulation is as good as information allows it to be, and strategic decisions about its gathering and who deploys it remain to be taken. I have basically argued that while it would be correct to aim for a simultaneous review of all companies to refix k at intervals not less than 5 years, the work leading up to this has to be continually developed from the DG's inheritance of the data base at vesting. The basic information strategy is to make effects on future cash flows the lynch pin. New lines of evidence have to be developed and integrated, principally to support and refine the trade-offs to be made, evaluated with respect to the central task of judgement in year 4+.

Regulation is at once a collaborative and adversarial process. I have argued that the adversarial has given too much weight in negotiations so far, and this is reflected in the licence and industry expectations. Had time not been so pressing, one would say that the likely possibility for improvement is to rely solely on condition J to provide the base for information flow, and to couple this with a clear statement of intention about how the Regulator would be asked to approach his task of combining the period of 'hands off' profits with a debate about finance after 4 years. As it is, probably the best that can be achieved is to clarify the position on the definitions of k, as argued above, and, when the DG is appointed, have an appropriate statement. It would help in getting industry consent if more emphasis could be given to the ways in which the DG can, while reserving his final judgements, feed back information useful *to* the industry.

In this general context, interim triggering of price reviews via the cost pass through will be confined as intended, to the narrow issue of impacts on costs up to the next Review, not to trigger wide questions of judgement at that point. Confidence that the cost pass through, once agreed, is intended to be financed by consumers must be preserved as part of the framework for developing trust between the DG and the industry. From this point of view, an early trigger of a cost-pass-through item is not to be deplored, because it will given an opportunity for the DG, while getting the steady build up of information he needs, to show his bona fides.

APPENDIX: THE ECONOMIC FRAMEWORK

The reasons for adopting a CBA approach to making economic judgements are as follows. First, the Government, in deciding to privatize water in essence conducted a cost–benefit analysis (CBA), though the decision was of course not formally expressed like this. Privatization was seen as a means to improve welfare, to be judged by its predicted future effects (technically on the prospective change in consumer and producer surpluses minus costs). We are now in the process of trying to realize these net benefits. Similarly, when reviewing k's the DG should consider the CBA merits of given change in k for the prospects, along dimensions. (Of course, this again would not be expressed in that formal way.)

The important underlying issue is the point of departure for judgement. The main alternative to adopting a CBA stance is to proceed from some ideal concept of output and prices, normally given by reference to a competitive industry. This is expressed, for example, as an aim to 'mimic' the effects of competition, or to adopt a substitute set of prices, e.g. 'Ramsey' or two part, which recognize a profit constraint. Even though the actual condition is one of natural monopoly, the industry and its members should be judged, it is often thought, by deviation from one of these standards. I would argue that they cannot sensibly be applied in water now, nor for a good while to come. If and when metering becomes the norm, and there is a direct relationship between price and quantities consumed, they will become more relevant standards. Meanwhile, I believe that, as well as being technically more correct, it will be far easier to base an understanding with the industry on the CBA approach.

NOTES

1 A paper written in 1988 as Adviser to the UK Government on Water Privatization.
2 For k, see note 1, Chapter 5 (p. 92).
3 Author's note: By far the largest number of customers' supplies were (and still are not) metered; hence 'unmeasured'.
4 An earlier paper.
5 Author's note: 'inset appointments' refers to new areas for supplying water or sewerage. Because all present customers are covered by the 39 companies, these would refer to new developments.

8 Competition and supply in London taxis[1]

M.E. Beesley

INTRODUCTION

In recent years, the growth in taxis and hire cars in the United Kingdom has been in remarkable contrast with other sectors of local passenger transport, particularly with the buses owned and operated by the large organizations characteristic of the bus industry. Very little, however, is known about the economics of these sectors; indeed for the hire cars, which till 1976 were completely unregulated and therefore unregistered, even the overall scale of activity is much in doubt. This chapter concentrates on the comparatively well-documented London taxi trade, and presents some results of research designed to improve our economic understanding of it.

We are concerned with several related issues. London's taxi trade is one of the very few in the developed world in which there is no quantity control over the entry or exit of cabs or drivers, and it is probably unique in combining this with significant quality controls – on the cab, producing a uniform special vehicle, and on the drivers, requiring high standards of previous conduct and specialized knowledge of London. The bearing of these features on the competition between the taxi trade and other modes, and on its capacity to adapt to changing economic circumstances, is of great interest in forming urban transport policy, an area which Denys Munby always considered of outstanding importance in the range of transport issues (1968: 173). We comment here on: reasons for the growth trends in the trade; taxi competition with hire cars; and, most important, changes in the real cost of taxi output, and the main apparent reason for these.

The history of London taxis shows a marked increase since the mid-1950s in the number of taxis and drivers licensed. As Table 8.1 shows, since 1960 this contrasts sharply with the fortunes of what are usually regarded as taxis' near public transport competitors, buses and underground. Taxis' nearest competitors are, however, hire cars. The shares of total public passenger transport held by these four modes is an important starting point for a discussion of the reasons for relative growth and decline. Unfortunately, we have relatively firm data only for 1969, when the Report of the Maxwell Stamp Committee (1970) provided figures for taxis and private car hire which, with much reservation, can be turned into yearly passenger miles. We can therefore directly estimate shares only for 1969.

The most doubtful figure is for hire cars. From figures in the report, we might suppose that the hire car trade performed roughly 752 million passenger miles in 1969.[2] Taxis can be set at about 197 million passenger miles.[3] Comparable figures for bus and underground in 1969 were 3,103 million and 3,105 million passenger miles respectively (London Transport Executive 1970). So private hire cars plus taxis performed some 13.3 per cent of total public passenger mileage of 7,157 million. *If* we can assume that private hire plus taxi passenger miles expanded, between 1963 and 1976, at the same rate as taxis in service, the comparable figures for 1963 and 1976 become 9.6 per cent and 19.4 per cent respectively. This probably underestimates private hire growth in the 1970s. *A fortiori*, we are fairly safe in assuming that private hire and taxis now provide one-fifth of (local) public passenger transport in London, measured in passenger miles. (In value terms, their shares are higher, of course. For example, in 1976, the price of a 2.5 mile taxi fare for one person was about 3.6 times the fare by bus.) Thus it can be concluded that, as taxis operate under similar economic conditions to private hire, we are considering phenomena of considerable importance to the development of public passenger transport as a whole.

GROWTH OF THE TAXI TRADE IN LONDON

Judgements about policies towards public transport modes, as for other industries, should be framed with the help of predictions about their likely growth and, as part of this, their likely competitive relations with each other. The predictions have largely to rest on interpretations of past events. Partly because of lack of data, accounts of the taxi trade, including official committees of inquiry such as that of Runciman in 1953 and Maxwell Stamp in 1970, have conspicuously failed to provide explanations. On the demand side, for example, R. G. D. Allen's estimate of 'near unit' price elasticity for the Runciman Committee in 1953 is still the sole quoted reference for London, and is indeed still often used for other taxi industries as well. (It was based on returns from five large proprietors, covering about 15 per cent of all cabs; there are reasons, to be dealt with later, for supposing the true estimate then to be considerably less than the quoted figure.)

The main reason for a paucity of explanations, however, is that very complex influences have been, and are, at work. On the supply side, to a degree perhaps not fully realized by past commentators, the London taxi trade consists of two independent parts: the suppliers of cabs, the proprietors, and those able to demand them, the drivers, with about half the trade supplied by owner-drivers, as measured by owners of one cab (see Table 8.1).

Cab proprietorship is a remarkably competitive trade. Entry is possible for any 'fit' person, as interpreted – very even-handedly – by the Public

Carriage Office. A scrutiny of several years' returns for the numbers of cabs owned by proprietors indicates not only much change in individual fleet sizes, but also very low concentration ratios, which have tended to decrease over time. Thus, for the latest year available (1976) the four-firm concentration ratio (i.e. the share of the four largest firms in total output, which is a conventional way of representing industrial concentration ratios) was as low as 7 per cent, measured by cab ownership. Cab company profits are greatly affected by how drivers decide to respond to economic opportunities. Fare and other changes first react on drivers, who (as we argue in more detail on pp. 126–31) must in the short run be regarded as a stock which is largely independent of the current state of recruitment. Drivers' hours and efforts – and their very presence in the market, for many are thought to be part-timers – can vary greatly.

On the demand side, apart from discovering trends in relevant underlying determinants such as the scale of visitors and the growth of real incomes, the identification of competitive variables is difficult. Taxis when 'plying for hire' in what is called the 'cruising market', and at other times, offer a relatively high-priced, convenient service. The service depends in a complicated way on the total number of taxis in a given market area and the ratio unengaged at a particular time, because the quality of service, and the likelihood of getting a taxi when one wants it, depend on the absolute number of unengaged taxis plying at the time. Fares charged affect demand too; and, of course, so do fares of near competitors and complementary services – and their service levels. So there is necessarily interdependence between supply conditions, which determine the terms on which taxis will make themselves available, and demand conditions. Identification of specific influences at work is complicated further in London (as elsewhere) by the fact that mandatory fare levels are set by regulators, not in response to economic analysis, but until 1975 in response to trade representations, and since then by reference to an index of motoring costs.[4] However, a start towards economic explanations has to start somewhere, and we can point to some main influences.

The most natural units for measuring passenger transport output – journeys or passenger miles – are denied to us in the case of taxis, except for the one estimate made in the introduction. However, Table 8.1 tabulates several series of interest to the present study which are used to attempt to pinpoint some influences over the years 1959–77. Among them are figures for taxis, and drivers, licensed at each year end. These are the only available proxies for output.

Taxis licensed provide probably the better measure of trends in taxi output over time, for these reasons. Taxis have a much shorter economic life than drivers, and are thus more subject to decisions to acquire new, or retire old, assets. Drivers, once licensed, have an investment for life as long as they care to incur the small cost of maintaining it. (The nature of this 'investment', the age of acquiring it, etc., are discussed on pp. 1126–31.)

Table 8.1 Taxi data, 1959–77

	1977	1976	1975	1974	1973	1972	1971	1970
Cabs								
No. cabs in service 31 Dec.	12,452	11,838	11,260	11,012	10,406	10,145	9,586	8,652
No. different owners	7,464	7,061	6,629	6,304	5,543	5,610	4,902	
No. different owners with one cab	6,971	6,556	6,129	5,746	4,992	5,068	4,323	3,764
No. cabs with two-way radio	2,577	2,291	2,223	1,797	1,347	1,085	1,048	963
Cabs licensed during year	12,895	12,137	11,718	11,492	10,839	10,589	10,038	8,990
New cabs licensed for first time	1,632	1,403	1,237	1,426	1,331	1,876	1,970	1,512
Cabs 4 years old of total licensed (%)		44	50	57	62	62	59	56
No. cabs reported unfit for service	3,454	2,976	3,562	3,247	3,405	3,498	3,667	3,846
No. taximeter tests per year	18,038	18,965	19,740	16,598	16,031	15,244	14,737	13,544
Rejections					189	201	151	151
Drivers								
No. licensed 31 Dec.	16,474	16,152	16,037	15,699	15,238	14,535	13,819	13,291
New licences issued[1]	5,559	5,645	5,497	5,348	5,392	5,145	4,977	4,878
Applications refused	158	172	116	132	122	185	138	112
Cab driving tests	842	728	1,067	1,151	1,493	1,441	1,230	1,170
Failures	168	167	250	259	358	324	270	251
Failure rate (%)	20	23	23	23	24	22.5	22	21
No. applying for knowledge first time	3,201	2,938	2,244	1,732	1,835	2,605	2,822	2,276
Attendances at oral exams	21,008	19,869	19,145	20,968	25,871	27,202	25,470	23,076
No. successful applicants (including suburban)	729	588	839	952	1,188	1,159	1,020	951
No. successful applicants (suburban)	123	121	147	115	134	166	152	151
No. successful applicants including transfers		570	801	899	1,125	1,122	982	909
Offences by cab drivers								
No. reported	511	683	261	299	322	308	405	516
Drivers/cabs 31 Dec.	1.32	1.36	1.42	1.42	1.46	1.43	1.44	1.54
London Transport journeys								
Bus passengers millions[3]		1,422	1,455	1,473	1,439	1,413	1,480	1,502
Underground passengers, millions		546	601	636	644	655	654	672

Source: Reports of the Commissioner of Police of the Metropolitan Area, 1959–77; London Transport Executive Annual Reports.

Notes:
1 Three-yearly renewals + first-time licences.
2 First full year with attendance by appointment.
3 Figures for 1960–4 including country buses and coaches; figures from 1963 onwards adjusted to exclude them.

1969	1968	1967	1966	1965	1964	1963	1962	1961	1960	1959
8,181	7,810	7,571	7,392	7,290	7,371	7,035	6,806	6,552	6,427	5,980
	3,913	4,004								
3,736	3,532	3,636		3,391	3,399	3,101	2,919	2,814	2,733	2,492
885	901	813	718		710	696	579	766	760	748
8,412	8,118	7,832	7,666	7,503	7,669	7,372	7,005	6,776	6,656	6,261
1,190	1,167	1,168	913	954						509
50	64.5				56	51	52			
3,625	3,827	3,681	3,825	3,387	3,324	3,314	3,052	2,898	3,308	2,270
12,763	11,323	11,078	10,354	10,462	11,588	10,712	10,136	10,800	10,658	
156	118	170	156	167	208	210	222	232	233	
12,770	12,348	12,140	11,872	11,534	11,071	10,744	10,404	10,203	9,936	9,608
4,392	4,430	4,489	3,755	4,438	4,199	3,422	3,855	3,884	3,112	3,465
99			108	116						
1,040	742	857	876	844	981	945	789	747	908	679
241	152	173	166	195	285	308	240	255	231	149
23			23							
2,119	1,627	1,446	1,254							
20,708				16,855	18,461[2]	16,448	12,380	11,095	14,289	14,079
871	613	721	715	671	666	648	498	594	625	539
112	109	102	97		105	114	65	65	30	75
834	595	684	689		646	628	478			
549	573	347	311	303	503	570	413	259	88	80
1.56	1.58	1.60	1.61	1.58	1.59	1.58	1.53	1.56	1.54	1.38
1,589	1,733	1,760	1,753	1,896	2,004	2,168				
					2,254	2,430	2,485	2,522	2,593	
676	655	661	667	657	674	673	668	675	674	

Changes in the stock of drivers are probably small relative to taxis. Drivers may well withdraw from the market permanently or temporarily, but are under no great pressure to yield up their licences if they do so. So, while *entry* to the set of drivers is a measured variable which responds to economic forces, there is no comparable statistic for 'withdrawal' of drivers. For these reasons, number of licensed cabs is the nearest equivalent to an output measure.

However, if one accepts numbers of cabs to measure taxi growth, one has in effect to explain trends in terms of motivations of one part of the trade – owners of cabs – only. As we shall see later, cab-related costs are the smaller part of total costs making up a fare. Cabs reflect total output changes in the trade in the long term, but decisions to invest in them must be seen in terms of proprietors' profits. In general, increases in demand are favourable, leading to greater perceived profits, and increases in costs are unfavourable, and vice versa. Changes in demand in London are a function chiefly of:

1 tourist demand, especially from foreign visitors, alleged to be the most important source of growth;
2 local demand, especially from those home customers typical of the greater area of London's taxi service, the central area;
3 the price of taxi journeys; and
4 the price of near competitors – bus and underground fares for like journeys.

Factors favourable to profits from the cost side would be principally those affecting labour supply, and in particular conditions of taxi labour supply, as seen in more detail below:

5 more unemployment in London at large would be favourable; and
6 less employment overall would also be favourable to the terms on which labour could be hired.

To a more or less satisfactory degree these influences may be captured in available data. For 1 the measures selected were visitors to Great Britain staying at least one night, most of whom take in London in their stay (independent measures of *London* overseas visitors are not available for our time series). Measure 2 presents the greatest difficulties. What is required is some measure of income available in Central London for spending on taxis. No such index exists, partly because so much of spending on taxis relates to business activity, not to households. Even for the households, no separate data for London are available. The best compromise seemed to be to use real household expenditure for the UK. Variables 3 and 4 were taken for the range of journeys between 2 and 2.5 miles. This covers the average taxi trip and an appropriate range of public transport fares. Employment and unemployment figures are for Greater London. The basic data are in Table 8.2, consisting of the relevant time series for 1960–76.

Table 8.2   Factors affecting taxi growth in London, 1960–76

	1960	1961	1962	1963	1964	1965	1966	1967	1968	1969	1970	1971	1972	1973	1974	1975	1976
Cabs, 31 December	6,427	6,552	6,806	7,035	7,371	7,290	7,392	7,571	7,810	8,181	8,652	9,586	10,145	10,406	11,012	11,260	11,838
Visitors to Great Britain, millions	1.7	1.9	2.0	2.1	2.5	2.7	3.0	3.2	3.6	4.4	5.0	5.2	5.4	5.8	6.0	6.7	7.6
Real expenditure of households p.w. (UK)*	21.1	20.6	20.4	19.5	19.1	22.8	23.0	19.8	22.8	23.8	23.2	22.9	25.8	24.4	22.6	24.2	24.7
Taxi fares* for 2.5 miles, pence	22.6	21.9	20.9	20.5	24.1	23.8	22.9	22.4	21.5	22.5	22.3	20.9	25.5	24.5	24.8	24.2	23.4
Underground fares* for 2.5 miles, pence	3.1	3.9	3.7	3.7	3.9	3.7	4.3	4.2	4.0	5.7	7.1	6.5	9.1	8.4	7.2	7.7	8.3
Bus fares* for 2.5 miles, pence	3.1	3.4	3.7	3.7	3.9	3.7	4.3	4.2	4.0	5.7	5.3	4.9	6.1	5.6	4.8	6.2	6.6
Employment, Greater London, millions	4.6	4.6	4.7	4.7	4.7	4.7	4.7	4.6	4.6	4.4	4.3	3.9	3.9	3.9	3.8	3.8	3.8
Unemployment, Greater London, %	0.7	0.84	1.25	1.15	0.75	0.7	0.95	1.50	1.45	1.30	1.35	1.65	1.55	1.20	1.30	2.2	2.4
Cost of motoring* 2.5 miles, pence	3.6	3.6	3.6	3.6	3.6	3.3	3.2	3.1	3.4	3.3	3.3	3.3	3.2	3.6	3.6	3.8	3.7

Sources:
Cabs: as for Table 8.1.
Visitors: English Tourist Office.
Real Expenditure: Family Expenditure Surveys.
Taxi fares: Police Commissioners' Reports.
Bus and underground fares: London Transport Executive.
Employment, unemployment: Annual Manual of Statistics.
Cost of motoring: Automobile Association estimates of running costs for 1,500–2,000 cc saloon; running costs include petrol, oils, tyres, servicing, repairs and renewals.
* Deflated by the retail prices index: all fares are weighted for the number of months a year the given fares ruled.

Some comment is perhaps needed on the reason for specifying taxi fares separately from competitors' fares. Normally one would think of a favourable demand experience as one in which others' prices had been raised relative to own price. Here, however, we have a regulated industry where prices are changed only periodically. In conditions of generally inelastic taxi demand, granting a fare increase would signal increased prospective revenues; increases in bus and underground fares would signal more customers (a shift outwards in total demand).

The preferable form of the model would be to specify a lag structure, so that, for example, this year's change in cabs is a function of last year's or other previous experience. But there is no independent evidence to lead to a preferred lag structure; and attempts to search for one by manipulating the data encountered little success. However, by pooling all the time series data, a model was estimated as follows:

$$C = 7,014 + 0.283V - 0.433RE + 0.264TF$$
$$(t = 6.93) \quad (6.33) \quad (-2.70) \quad (2.11)$$

$$-0.18BF + 0.094UF - 0.755EMP + 0.042UN$$
$$(-0.96) \quad (0.57) \quad (-3.64) \quad (1.44)$$

$$\bar{R}^2 0.987 D - W \text{ stat} = 1.63$$

where C = cabs; V = visitors; RE = real expenditure; TF = taxi fares; UF = underground fares; BF = bus fares; EMP =employment; UN = unemployment.

Two of the coefficients of the independents – real expenditure and bus fares had unexpected signs, with the latter very insignificant. Possibly the expenditure figure is a poor reflection of outlays for taxis in the relatively special, probably business-oriented, London market, but is, rather, correlated with unfavourable labour cost experience. Taxi fares behave as expected, and are significant, so confirming that taxis are indeed price inelastic. Employment and unemployment performed as expected, though unemployment is not very significant. Competitive fares explained little. Visitors, not surprisingly in view of their large and uninterrupted growth in the period, are highly significant.

The need to understand supply side changes alongside those of demand is confirmed by this limited evidence. What is perhaps somewhat surprising is the apparent lack of effect of the prices of two competitors – buses and underground. The nearest competitor – hire cars – is absent from the model, however, and is considered, necessarily quantitatively, in the next section. Moreover, the figures span a considerable period when, it may be argued, the competitors' markets moved closer together. Taxi fares between 1960 and 1976 rose only some 5 per cent in real terms, or, if the less favourable years 1962–72 are taken, 12 per cent, whereas the public transport rivals, underground and buses, rose together by an average of 140 per cent over

1960–76, measured for the model taxi trip of 2.0 to 2.5 miles. Private motoring costs, meanwhile, changed little in real terms (see Table 8.2).

Measuring the importance of visitors, home demand and other influences can be approached another way by assumptions about the share of the total trade now done for visitors. It has been alleged recently that about half of taxi custom, taken all the year round, now comes from the kind of (foreign) visitors represented in Table 8.2. There is no solid evidence for this, for expenditure on taxis was not, unfortunately, recorded separately when the English Tourist Board sampled the visitors. But it is possible, in view of London Transport's belief that 10 per cent of their total bus and under-ground fares come from the same source, and that the proportion in the taxis' main market, Central London, is much higher.

If visitors now account for 50 per cent of taxi output, they may well account for 4,500 of the total gain between 1960 and 1976 of 5,400 additional cabs in service, to judge from the increases recorded in Table 8.2. 'Home' demand, as exemplified by employees, has fallen over the period by 18 per cent. Real incomes of Londoners probably increased by about 40 per cent in the period, however. So we might guess that the net effect here was an increase of 15 per cent, giving an increase of 700 in the period. This would leave a gain of 200 or so to be accounted for by relative price or other changes. If visitors accounted for only 40 per cent of taxi activity in 1976, the 'visitor' gain would be 3,700, leaving about 1,000, rather than 200, to be accounted for by these price effects. A rather heroic estimate of this cross-price elasticity – the effect of the change in bus/underground fares on cab numbers, as measured over the whole period – would then be 0.19, using the 1,000 cabs as the quantity change. Even with this larger estimate of the effect, the indication is that there was little interrelation between bus and underground fares and cab demand over the period as a whole.

Now it may be that bus and underground markets on the one hand, and the taxi market on the other, which historically were probably largely independent because of differences of income among Londoners, were still so at the end of the period. But this is difficult to believe in the face of the relative fare changes just noted. Taxi fares on the one hand, and bus and underground fares on the other, were much closer by then. Moreover, though this is not a price effect, bus service levels in particular have fallen during the period; this must have reinforced and perhaps exceeded the price effects. Whatever might have been the case in 1960, by 1976 taxis may well have become important competitors to conventional public transport, especially in the central area, which accounts for much of taxi output. The competition nowadays focuses, we may be certain, to a much greater degree than fifteen years ago on the foreign visitor. In the home-based, non-visitor market, on the other hand, the more important developments may well have been in the competition between taxis and hire cars, to which we now turn.

TAXI AND HIRE CAR COMPETITION

One very important issue, yet to be resolved, is the development of competition between hire cars, and especially 'mini cabs', and taxis. Since the advent of two-way radio circuits, hire cars have become an important option for passenger movement. 'Mini cabs' are mass production car versions of hire cars, a category which also includes limousines, wedding cars, funeral cars, etc.

In the present context, the question is: to what extent has the taxi growth been due to penetration of the hire car market? This is perhaps an unusual way to pose the question. Normally it is suggested that, historically, the hire car trade has increased its custom at the expense of taxis, and drivers' resentments, expressed particularly in the early 1960s about mini cabs' activities, are cited as evidence. But what evidence we have might just as plausibly be seen differently.

First, it must be recognized that the taxi has an asymmetric relationship with the hire car. The taxi can ply for hire, the hire car cannot; but the taxi can also (if it has a radio) elect to perform as a hire car. So long as developments in the plying-for-hire market and the rest of the market favour the dual function, taxis will gain, and vice versa. The competition, as the Maxwell Stamp report emphasized in 1970, is at the margin between rather distinct markets, as evidenced in the very different average lengths of trips by taxis and hire cars.

Second, over the recent period of taxi growth there has been little or no change in the general rules governing competition between the two types of paratransit in London. The hire trade has, as it had in the 1960s when mini cabs appeared, completely free entry, unregistered and unregulated.[5] It may safely be assumed to conform to the requirements for competitive behaviour – prices will reflect costs, and the industry will have adjusted to the opportunities afforded by the idiosyncrasies in the rules of its nearest competitor. What has not been constant over the years is the relation of taxi fares to taxi costs; and there has been a shift in the structure relating fares to distances travelled.

The first of these effects – a tendency for fare regulation to proceed by discrete steps, thus producing shifts in relative fares as inflation proceeds – has probably not been very significant over the long term. In the long run, fare regulators are driven by cost changes, and the taxi trade is no exception. Moreover, in recent years, fare changes have become more and more frequent – and the levels of fares are now indexed, in effect, to cost changes.[6]

More significant in the present context is the fare structure point. As Sid Pearce points out (1977), there has been an increasing differentiation in the effective rate per mile taxis are compelled to charge, because of the tendency to weight the fixed proportions of the hire charge more heavily when acceding to claims for fare adjustments. His very valuable Figure 8 indicates

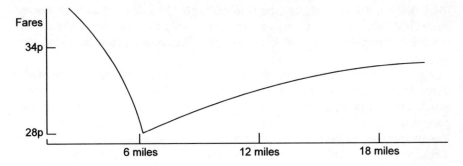

Figure 8.1   Fares per mile, 1975

clearly how, especially in the 1970s, the rate per mile has assumed a greater differentiation: (1) upwards for short distances within the 6 mile compellable limit; (2) to a lesser degree, upwards for trips over 6 miles. This produces the characteristic graph shown in Figure 8.1. The left side of this function has been getting steeper, after allowing for changes in real fares. From the point of view of taxi versus car hire competition, this has had the (probably quite unintended) effect of raising fares in the short-distance market comprising the bulk of the work of the taxi trade, where the plying exclusivity matters most, and of lowering fares in the area of greater competition – the longer-distance market. This effect is shown in Table 8.3.

Thus, irrespective of the merits or otherwise of this marked difference in fares per mile for differences in journey lengths (and Pearce makes a cogent argument for reversion to a flat rate per mile), the effect has probably been, over time, to induce a discrimination in pricing rather favourable to taxis competing at the margin for hire car work, for the following reasons.

If, at the relevant fare levels, elasticity of demand is not greater than unity (and, as we shall see later, this is a fair interpretation of the little evidence available), the effect of raising fares, *ceteris paribus*, is to generate greater net returns to the trade and to reduce output. Because of fare regulation, competition cannot bid down fares. There is then spare capacity. Profits can be increased further by using the spare capacity in the longer-distance

Table 8.3   London taxi fares for one person

	1 mile	2.5 miles	4.5 miles
21 March 1971	21p	39p	61p
1 April 1973	24p	42p	64p
7 April 1974	30p	55p	90p
31 July 1975	40p	70p	110p
13 December 1976	50p	80p	120p
22 December 1977	55p	90p	130p
Increase 1971–7	162%	131%	113%

market, even if the price per mile is lower there. The effect is as if cabs were controlled by a discriminating monopolist serving two markets – the lower-elasticity short-distance market, and the higher-elasticity long-distance market.

A symptom of this may be the history of radios fitted to cabs. One might argue that radios – which are a *sine qua non* of hire car operation – are a proxy for taxi penetration of the hire car market. Thus by 1976 taxis had picked up an important amount of hire car work.[7] In the early 1960s, the low proportion of cabs that were already fitted with radios was falling, as Table 8.1 shows. An absolute low was reached in 1962, when the 579 cabs fitted with radios comprised 8.5 per cent of the end-year fleet. Their numbers grew slowly till about 1972, when the proportion was 11 per cent. Radios then became more frequent – by 1976, 19.4 per cent of cabs had them.

This interpretation seems to be reinforced by the fact that, before the incursion of mini cabs in the early 1960s, there had already been a movement towards fitting radios to cabs: that is, some proprietors found it profitable then to subscribe to a radio service. When the cheaper form of hire car arrived (the mini cab was simply a standard small production car), it merely competed away much of the hire car part of the taxi trade. This would explain the absolute reduction in the number of radio-fitted cabs at the time. Perhaps it was this, just as much as alleged 'poaching' of the plying for hire trade, which provoked hostility among cab drivers.

Clearly, the terms of hire car and taxi competition are a very important factor in the interpretation of taxi trade development, precisely because taxis do represent a part of what may be a rapidly growing non-bus and non-private-car passenger (or 'paratransit') market. Taxis, because of their relative prominence and because they are regulated, generate attention and some data. Hire cars, and especially mini cabs, do not – a condition which is likely to continue. Arguments about the paratransit market will have to be pursued by analogy with taxis. But it can be argued that taxis are a much better indicator of this wider market sector than has been supposed hitherto, and certainly much that can be deduced about the economics of the taxi trade can be applied to the wider market.

SUPPLY SIDE DEVELOPMENTS

Changes in demand for taxis may be explained, we have seen, along familiar lines, if with different interpretations about their significance. Changes on the supply side are difficult to interpret, but are probably even more important in their implications for public transport as a whole than are taxis' responses to changing demand.

First is the apparently slow shift upwards in the real costs of taxi operation, as compared with those of London buses. When we seek to interpret the evidence of Table 8.2 on this, the vagaries of fare control on both sides cloud the picture. But overall, and over time, fares reflect costs unless subsidies are given. It can hardly be doubted that the general inference from Table 8.2 is that taxi fares have risen considerably less than have bus fares. Moreover, buses have enjoyed increasing direct subsidy over the years; taxis have not. (Taxis do not pay for all the costs that are incurred on their behalf, in particular the costs of most of the Public Carriage Office's services to the trade, including running the knowledge tests. But this does not affect the issue here.) Taxis in 1977, as in 1960, contained a single driver in one vehicle, and they carried about the same number of passengers per trip. If the cost of doing this rose in real terms considerably less than did the real costs of carrying passengers by bus over the same period, there is great interest in possible explanations. Some of these have to do with changes affecting buses (e.g. in their productivity); here, we confine attention to the taxi side of the comparison.

Changes in the real costs per unit of output in a given trade can arise from: changes in input prices; changes in productivity, given the available technology; and innovations, in the broad sense of new technology or new ways of organizing production in the trade. The following discussion will follow this division. However, an implicit assumption in proceeding in this way is that there is no change in the product.

Taxis have not changed their essential service much, although, if suggestions in the last section of increasing taxi penetration into the hire car trade are correct, there has been some tendency recently for the character of taxi output to change. (One indication, were it available, would be the average customer trip length. One would expect a slight increase in this average if the penetration has indeed happened.)[8] On the whole, however, we must look for sources other than change in output mix.

Input prices and their importance

The question of how input prices to taxi services have been changing raises the need to describe the costs involved. For this we have partly to rely on two sources – Maxwell Stamp (1970) and the later PCL Study (Doganis and Lowe 1976). Partly we have to construct new evidence – specifically to describe labour costs. As we have argued, drivers, whose input of time and effort is the main single cost, are a stock which will become available for taxi work so long as the returns from taxi driving are no less than their opportunity costs. If this is a correct view, the appropriate costs to assign to labour in taxi operation are earnings in alternative occupations, assuming drivers are free to enter or leave the trades in question. As we see later, (pp. 136–8) this seems likely.

We have been able to investigate this, thanks to a 5 per cent sample of information from the taxi drivers' records provided by the Public Carriage Office (PCO), taken in May–June 1977. This information included: the age of the driver; the date at which the driver applied to become licensed; the date the licence was received; the driver's occupation on application. This was useful in several ways; here, however, its significance was that we could classify drivers according to their likely alternative occupations and thus, via earnings survey data, estimate foregone earnings. The total sample was 800 drivers, of whom 769 were suitable for this purpose.

This approach to estimating costs is a new one. Previous attempts focused on costs associated with cab ownership and running, which are indeed important, but are a minor part of costs. In these studies drivers were dealt with by speculating about their remuneration from their taxi work. This is of course an inappropriate measure for our purposes.

The supply of taxi drivers' services is conditional upon each driver passing the knowledge test. To what extent does this barrier to entry affect interpretation of trends in drivers' costs? We tried to discover whether, over time, there was any connection between numbers of drivers embarking on the knowledge-learning process (the 'first applicants') and such factors as changes in this or last year's wages in bus driving, or changes in taxi fare levels or in visitors (which all might be supposed to hold out inducements to enter the trade). We found no systematic connection with these and other factors, with one major exception, namely the unemployment rate in London at the time of entry. This plays the dominant role in our models which visitors played in explaining the expansion of the industry.[9] Taxi driving thus appears to behave in a classical manner – when unemployment rises, the opportunity cost of acquiring the knowledge falls, and more would-be drivers come forward.

We discovered from the sample of PCO records that the average time taken to acquire the knowledge was 22.6 months, or just under 2 years, with a high standard deviation of 17.1 months, indicating a rather skewed distribution. We have been unable to discover any connection between time taken in this process and the variables which might be supposed to induce entrants to hurry or delay their training, such as upturns in visitors etc. It seems that, once embarked on the knowledge, the variation in personal circumstances and ability to absorb the knowledge (the average number of 'attendances' or examinations over the years 1960–76 is as large as eleven per entrant) swamp other sources of variation. The average time taken to pass the knowledge test and thus appear in the taxi labour market shows little systematic variation over the years. This probably indicates that the tests and their pace of administration have not altered much – though clearly, with entry subject to unemployment change, a large variation in candidates' numbers has implied a very variable workload for the PCO.[10] From time to time complaints are made about the delays in the Office. This is to be expected, since demand on its services is essentially uncontrollable and the standard of knowledge required does not vary.[11]

Since, as pointed out earlier, acquisition of the knowledge is a long-term investment (the average age in our sample at passing the test was 30), and as unemployment largely governs applicants in the short term, the best way to regard the supply of labour is probably as a pool from which, as the attractiveness of driving waxes and wanes, labour is offered. Of course, no one goes in for the knowledge test without a reasonably optimistic view of the London taxi trade, but the decision is akin to all such decisions to embark on qualifications – one hopes for long-run gains which will offset the immediate cost of acquiring them. After qualification, whether one practises the trade depends on the terms offered, which must be superior to one's alternative work opportunities. (A limited number of training grants has been available from time to time from charitable sources such as the British Legion, or from the Department of Employment.)

The relevant labour price change we have to consider is that of these alternatives. This is provided by classifying the sample of drivers into eighteen occupation groups recognized in the New Earnings Surveys and so computing a weighted earnings figure. It is assumed that the earnings data hold for the relevant dates used for our comparisons. This seems to be reasonable, because, although the data we have relate to drivers active in 1977, there is little sign in them that confining the measure to those active at certain dates would bring much variation in the occupational weights, although work on this is still in progress.[12]

Table 8.4 gives the distribution of drivers to the eighteen groups, the weekly earnings in London, and the more limited information, available for Great Britain only, about hours worked in the week. The figures apply to full-time male (over 21) employees. Table 8.5 applies the weights to Table 8.4 to give the alternative occupation wage per week at the different dates from 1973 onwards. For comparison, figures net income tax have also been calculated – a point referred to later p. 130.[13]

Two accounts of taxi costs are available, both intended to be comprehensive and both taking the cab as the unit of output: those of Maxwell Stamp (1970) for 1968 and of the PCL (Doganis and Lowe 1976) for 1975. They vary in the weights accorded to various items of costs. Table 7.6 sets out the items and the conclusions of the studies. PCL estimated for a range of 24,000–32,000 miles a year, Maxwell Stamp for 28,000. We have interpolated the PCL data for comparison.

The rise in the general retail price index between these dates was about 10 per cent. The difference in the totals recorded in Table 8.6 is 20 per cent. Obviously very different views about costs were being taken. Both depended on reported data from a very few taxi owners. Some of the items could be checked from independent sources and thus are clearly reliable. This is true of fuel and oil, and items 2 through 5. Other differences seem to be straightforward omissions, for example 6 and 7 for PCL and 10 for Maxwell Stamp. These are quite legitimate expenses for our purposes, so the estimates must be corrected for them.

Depreciation, maintenance and repairs, and the knowledge are debatable items. For the first two, the wide difference of views is underlined by the fact that Maxwell Stamp records £285 + 460 = £745 for them in 1968 prices

Table 8.4   Distribution of, and earnings in, previous occupations of London taxi drivers

Occupational group	Distribution of drivers %	Weekly earnings in London 1977 £	Hours worked in week GB
1 Managerial (a)	0.13	158.5	–
2 Professional (a)	0.78	117.6	–
3 Professional (b)	0.65	106.8	–
4 Literary etc.	1.69	100.2	–
5 Professional (c)	1.04	106.7	–
6 Managerial (b)	1.95	99.7	–
7 Clerical and related	8.45	74.1	40.1
8 Selling	11.83	78.8	40.1
9 Security etc.	2.86	91.4	45.8
10 Catering etc.	4.16	65.0	45.7
11 Farming etc.	0.00	63.1	45.5
12 Materials processing	1.69	73.8	45.8
13 Making and repairing	7.93	79.0	44.2
14 Processing	10.01	79.8	45.3
15 Painting etc.	1.69	70.8	44.3
16 Construction etc.	1.56	76.6	44.9
17 Transport operating	37.58	76.5	47.7
18 Miscellaneous	5.98	72.3	45.4
	99.98		

Source: New Earning Surveys 1973–7.

Notes:
1 Managerial (a) = Managerial (general management).
2 Professional (a) = Professional and related supporting management and administration.
3 Professional (b) = Professional and related in education, welfare and health.
5 Professional (c) = Professional and related in science, engineering, technology and similar fields.
6 Managerial (b) = Managerial (excluding general management).

and PCL records £456 + 130 = £586 in 1975 prices! PCL devoted much attention to these items. Its depreciation figure is derived from estimates of changes in prices for cabs of different ages plus the amount needed for the yearly overhaul to keep the cab on the road (i.e. to pass the annual test

Table 8.5   Earnings in alternative occupations, 1973–7, London area

	1973	1974	1975	1976	1977
Earnings	£41.5	£47.4	£61.6	£71.9	£78.4
Index: 1973 = 100	100	114	148	173	189
Earnings less tax*	£36.15	£40.6	£50.1	£58.2	£65.7
Index: 1973 = 100	100	112	139	161	182

* The calculations net of income tax assume: allowances, single or married according to the percentage of each in the population; child allowances for $1\frac{1}{2}$ children, half over and half under 16; and an allowance for a mortgage of £4,800.

Table 8.6 Taxi costs, 1968 and 1975: one year, 28,000 miles; current prices

	Maxwell Stamp	PCL
	1968	1975
	£	£
Standing charges		
1 Depreciation	285	456
2 Insurances		95
3 Meter rents		32
4 Licence	205	272
5 National insurance		20
Holiday pay		125
6 Garaging	70	
7 General overheads	120	
Running costs		
8 Fuel and oil	290	620
9 Maintenance, repairs	460	130
10 Tyres		52
Other		
11 Knowledge		193
Total, per year	£1,430	£1,723

inspection). The authors consider the trade-off between rising overhaul costs and purchase of new vehicles and work out, for example, that at 7 years old cabs are 'best' replaced by new vehicles. Maxwell Stamp includes 'return on capital' in its item (1). The figure given is a seven-year annuity whose present value after allowance for resale value is equivalent to the cost of a new taxi cab. The interest rate for the annuity is unstated. Presumably, the annual overhaul charge is included in 'maintenance' in the Maxwell Stamp figures.

There is no 'correct' figure for depreciation, or indeed for maintenance, independent of what happens on the demand side. For example, if demand falls sharply, so do the prices of second-hand taxis, and vice versa, particularly as taxis have limited alternative uses. The general trend for taxi activity over the period under review was quite strongly upward. Presumably this produced an upward tendency for second-hand prices, which would be reflected in the PCL approach. For our purposes, however, the relevant concept is the consumption of taxi services in a steady state at the level of activity at the times selected, 1968 and 1975. Thus all we need to know is what the taxi capital input would be in this steady state, plus, similarly, the maintenance, overhauls and servicing.

So far as taxi capital is concerned, we have figures for both the new taxis added to the fleet, and, by deduction, the withdrawals year by year (see Table 8.1). At a time of rising demand, as here, there must be a bias upward in the additions relative to constant demand, and a bias downward in the withdrawals (if the steady state were achieved these would balance). If

Table 8.7 New additions to, and deductions from, cab stock

	0–5.0	5.1–7.0	7.1–9.0	9.1–11.0	11.1–13.0	13.1–15.0	15.1–17.0	17.1–19.0	over 19.0%
Additions[1]–% of existing stock; observations for 1959, 1964–76			1	1	4	3	1	2	1
Withdrawals[2] + % of existing stock; observations for 1959, 1964–76	1	3	1	4	1	1	1		

Source: Table 8.1

Notes:
1 Cabs registered for the first time. Additions are current year's registrations over stock at beginning of the period, year 0.
2 Net withdrawals. Withdrawals are the difference between year 1 and year 0 as percentage of year 0's stock. There is necessarily one less observation for withdrawals.

we therefore compare the two sets of data we should be able to make some judgement about what the steady-state equivalent would be (see Table 8.7).

It seems reasonable, from this evidence, to set the steady-state input at the average of the additions and withdrawals shown in Table 8.7, or some 12 per cent, implying an average 'life' of 8.4 years. This is supported by the age of the cab fleet. From Table 8.1, we see that the average number of cabs more than 4 years old from 1962 onwards has ranged from 44 per cent (in 1976) to 64.5 per cent (in 1968), with an average of 55 per cent. These figures too are affected by the expansion of demand. (Cabs are increasingly likely to be withdrawn with age.) Translated into the inputs at 1968 and 1975, by applying the prices of a new Austin Diesel FX4 cab, the most popular version, we get £151 and £258 respectively.

Turning to maintenance, servicing and annual overhaul costs, we find that PCL allows for the first two £130 at 1975. One is rather sceptical about this figure. The Police Commissioners' reports show that consistently, over the years, about a quarter of all licensed taxis have stop notices served on them each year because of defects revealed in the frequent spot checks carried out (see Table 8.1). (Taxi licence plates are coded to months to make it easy to spot when a cab has passed its annual test and, by inference, when it may be more liable to show defects.) Putting the defects right quickly is essential to continuing service, and there are many advertisements by garages to provide this, presumably at some premium over scheduled maintenance.

PCL's total costs of overhaul for the 'most economic' policy is about £220. This, plus the £130 cited on the table for maintenance, equals £350 a year (at 1975 prices) or much *less* than Maxwell Stamp's 1968 figure at £460, which covers all three items. Pending further enquiry, we will average these two estimates, assuming that relevant input prices changed between

1968 and 1975 at motor vehicle fitter/mechanic earnings, namely at 141 per cent.[14]

Thus, given the following alternative accounts;

Maxwell Stamp   1968 £460 + 141 per cent = 1975 £1,109
PCL   1975 £350 ÷ 2.41   = 1968 £145

the averaging process gives us:

1968   1975
£303   £730

This is a drastic way of solving a problem of incompatible evidence. There is obviously great need to generate more reliable data on maintenance, servicing and overhaul costs, and, since availability of cabs is affected by the time needed for these processes, more evidence about the effects of the very high standard of reliability required by the public control processes.

The 'knowledge' is certainly a cost which has to be incurred in the conditions imposed on the London trade. Whether it is relevant for a particular issue concerning costs depends on what that issue is. In the short run, as we have seen, the number of entrants incurring the costs is a function principally of unemployment, and once they have acquired this knowledge, its costs are bygones and do not affect decisions to work more than the bare minimum necessary to protect the right to maintain a licence. For present purposes, however, the correct concept seems to be the costs which would be incurred to maintain, in the long run, the level of services which happened to be offered and sold in the years in question. This would include 'renewal' of drivers and thus knowledge inputs. Such costs which fall on the trade itself are the opportunity losses (wages forgone) during training.[15]

The rate of renewal of the driver 'stock' on a steady-state level depends on its ageing. We know the average age on entering is about 30, and, to judge from our sample, few care to carry on beyond 65. So perhaps most are active for about 30 years. The question is then, since many are part-timers nearly all their time, and probably most are part-timers at some stage in their careers, what is the number of years of service to apply? This cannot be known without sampling individual drivers. Maxwell Stamp reported that 20 per cent of drivers worked less than four shifts a week in 1968. We have no recent data.

We might estimate twenty years, which is plausible in the light of additions to the stock of drivers in the period for which we have figures, 1959–77. Since this was a period of expansion, additions to the stock must have been greater than would be needed simply to keep it in steady state. The yearly additions (the successful applicants for the test) have ranged from 3.6 per cent to 8.0 per cent, with an average of 6.1 per cent. See Table 8.8.

The 'required' knowledge input is then one-twentieth of the drivers' knowledge cost. That cost depends on the earnings forgone while acquiring

Table 8.8 Successful applicants as percentage of total drivers licensed, 1959–76: distribution by size

	Under 4.0	4.0– 4.9	5.0– 5.9	6.0– 6.9	7.0– 7.9	8.0	Total
Number of years	1	1	6	6	3	1	18

Source: As for Table 8.1

it. This again is not known directly. The average of twenty-two months conceals wide variations, though, as Table 8.9 shows, there is probably not much systematic variation with age at entry.

The problem is how far these months represent full-time work. The very speedy successes probably represent those having exceptional knowledge at the beginning. (There are a very few cases in our data of as little as one week being taken. These will include the occasional lapsed driver who is required to take the knowledge test again, and the very rare case such as an examiner turned examinee.) Equally, those who take four years to get through are most unlikely to have been working at the knowledge full time. Probably most find that full-time application to the training is the most efficient learning method. A reasonable guess from the data might be one and a quarter years' full-time equivalent work. Translating this via several further calculations, we get a knowledge cost per year of: 1968 £133, and 1975 £285.[16]

We can now itemize the revised cost structures for 1968 and 1975 in Table 8.10. The costs have been grouped in a manner which reflects the main relationships in the trade. As Pearce points out, two-thirds of the trade is essentially nowadays separated into two parts, what he calls the 'wholesaler' – the cab owner – and the 'retailer', or cab driver. The driver hires freely

Table 8.9 Driver's age on application and time taken to pass knowledge test (sub sample of 223 drivers)

Time Taken (months)	Age on Application							
	≤20	21–24	25–29	30–34	35–39	40–49	>50	Total
<6	0	2	2	6	2	3	2	17
7–12	1	11	4	6	1	4	2	29
13–18	5	17	18	8	9	7	2	66
19–24	2	10	15	5	6	8	0	46
25–30	1	7	5	9	3	6	0	31
31–36	1	2	2	2	0	2	0	9
37–42	0	6	2	2	1	0	0	11
43–48	0	1	0	1	1	0	0	3
>49	0	5	4	1	0	1	0	11
Total	10	61	52	40	23	31	6	223

Source: PCO sample.

from a large number of sellers; the owner equally has many alternative driver/customers. The remaining one-third of the trade combines both activities – the owner-drivers, a term indicating the fact that the cab owner and driver sets overlap.[17] Contracts between proprietor and driver can assume many forms, with responsibility for particular costs falling on either party. Table 8.10 thus first lists costs which proprietors normally always shoulder, then costs that drivers must bear, and then other costs which may be the concern of either. Owner-drivers combine all these responsibilities – to the extent that their cabs are hired for the assumed yearly output.

It will be seen that these costs are assessed very differently from those of Table 8.6. The general effect is to lower the Maxwell Stamp estimate (on costs recognized there, the Table 8.10 estimate is £1,080 compared with £1,430), and to raise the PCL estimate (£2,144 compared with £1,723). It is difficult to check the estimates against revenues – indeed, without new data, impossible. For 1975 we have Pearce's evidence of the distribution of cab rides (Pearce 1977: 23), which, together with his Figure 6 setting out fares per mile for August 1975, yields a rate per mile of about 28p, compared with 24.1p in Table 8.10 (£6,746 ÷ 28,000 miles).

Both figures need adjustments – for extra revenues (e.g. tips, extras on the clock and parcels carriage, etc.) on the one hand, and for the ratio of engaged to unengaged miles on the other. (Maxwell Stamp reported that the engaged was 60–65 per cent of the total mileage – as represented in the 28,000 miles (1970: 38).) We can include that the costs are not improbable and, certainly, a more plausible account than the partial estimates which they build on.

The effects of changes in input can now be seen. Overall, costs for a standard output rose 128 per cent between 1968 and 1975, compared with a rise of 107 per cent in the retail price index, or a rise in real terms of 19.6 per cent. Taxi fares rose 11 per cent in real terms in the same period. Driver-related costs rose by 24.5 per cent and proprietor-related by 11 per cent in real terms because of labour-intensive elements such as maintenance and overhaul.

The contrast between the 11 per cent rise in fares and the 24.5 per cent for driver-related costs, in particular, suggests that there must have been important factors offsetting input price increases over this period, assuming of course that the fares were not more than usually affected by fare controls at the specific dates concerned. Actually, there was an upward adjustment in fares in 1968, which lowers the observed price change in current terms, and thus will exaggerate the contrast between prices and costs then. Nevertheless, 1968–75 was probably not too untypical of the longer-term changes; it seems highly likely that prices of taxis have not matched input price changes. One possible explanation is that labour productivity has increased. We discuss this in the next section. It would have been interesting to

Table 8.10   Cost structures 1968 and 1975 based on a taxi running 28,000 miles in the year

(current prices)

		1968			1975	
	£	£	%	£	£	%
Proprietor related						
Cab purchase	151			285		
Insurance[1]	46			95		
Meter rents[1]	15			32		
Licence[1]	10			20		
Garaging[1]	70			145		
General overheads[1]	120			248		
		412	13.9		825	12.2
Maintenance, service and overhaul		303	10.2		730	10.8
Tyres		25	0.8		52	0.8
Driver related						
Driver opportunity costs[2]						
'DOC'	1,751			4,109		
'Knowledge'	133			285		
		1,884	63.6		4,394	65.1
Other costs						
National insurance, holiday pay[3]		50	1.7		125	1.9
Fuel and oil		290	9.8		620	9.2
		2,964			6,746	

Notes:
1 Assumed to change with retail price index.
2 Average weekly earnings of other occupations × Greater London uplift × 50 × multipliers: 1.22 for 1968, and 1.27 for 1975. The multipliers reflect changes in average hours worked, and are based on an assumed speed of 12 mph for 28,000 miles of travel. For 28,000 at 12 mph, the assumed average speed of Central London traffic = 2,333 hours. In 1968, the alternative occupations worked some 40 hours a week for 48 weeks = 1,920 hours and in 1975 40 hours × 46 weeks = 1,860 hours. So 2,333 and 1,840 respectively = 1.22 and 1.27.
3 Allows for increase in holiday entitlements between 1968 and 1975, which was substantial.

trace drivers' and other wages over the whole of the period covered by Table 8.10, which showed a long-term rise in taxi fares almost certainly much lower than in these wages. Unfortunately, the relevant earnings data do not permit this.

Our comparison also shows that rising wages were altering the cost structure. The changes noted are probably part of a longer-term trend, reflected in the slow change towards drivers in the negotiated division of commissions or 'on the clock' arrangements. In the post-war period to 1950 the division was 33.3 per cent driver, 66.6 per cent proprietor. After 1950, it was 37.5 to 62.5 per cent (Runciman 1953); by 1968 it was 40/60. In 1974 a night and day differential was introduced, yielding a night division of 50/50 and a day division of 45/55.

In the commission arrangements the proprietor would usually pay all but 'driver-related' costs of the table. As seen in Table 8.10, in the late 1960s and early 1970s the costs divided differently from the division in the commission arrangements. More than 60 per cent were driver related, and the proportion was growing. So it is possible that the very notable decline of the commission arrangement was at least partly due to its failure to adapt fast enough to reflect the changing cost structure. (Maxwell Stamp thought that two-thirds of work was done under this arrangement in 1968, yet Pearce doubts whether it was as much as 10 per cent in 1975.) Certainly, the number of variations on the commission arrangements – involving national insurance, fuel and oil exceptions, etc. – has been growing also. The commission arrangements are, of course, the remaining influence of traditional trade union negotiations in the taxi trade, so a further inference may be that trade union membership has been declining, partly because of a failure to keep up with wage movements elsewhere.

One further point on the trends of input prices should be made. Undoubtedly, the period under review was remarkable for the rise in the liability of wage earners in general to income tax. Taxi driving is an occupation offering an opportunity of tax minimization, and has always had that status. This, it may be argued, has had far more significance recently, as wage earners in other sectors have come under tax pressure. Also, the material underlying our 'DOC' estimates shows that drivers' alternative occupations are rather below average in earnings, again indicating a later, rather than earlier, inducement to modify a tax position. The suggestion is, therefore, that part of the explanation of taxi trade performance may well be due to lower real personal costs than appear on the surface, acting via other, alternative occupations.

Productivity changes

Taxis may have adjusted to rises in the real costs of inputs by increasing productivity. Table 8.10 indicates that this must mainly arise, if it does, from gains in labour productivity: such is the dominance of labour costs. These are of two kinds. By far the bigger is the drivers' own time, so the most important question is whether more output has been sold per labour hour. Quite important also, however, is maintenance, service and overhaul inputs, again heavily labour intensive, which, as we see from Table 8.10, have (on the rather arbitrary calculation involved) increased in importance since 1968. We know nothing of productivity trends in this sector of costs, but we comment in the next section on how changes in organization may have affected the issue.

The taxi is a standard vehicle, and demand presents itself in small groups which, so far as we know, are fairly stable over the years. (No potentially great savings in labour costs such as buses' one man operation (OMO) are available.) M. F. Talbot (1974) has suggested that, between 1962 and 1972, there could have been an increase in productivity. Comparing Greater London Traffic Survey data for 1972 with that for 1962, he notes that taxi journeys have increased by 134 per cent, whereas cabs and drivers had increased, as we also saw earlier, by much less (40 per cent and 49 per cent respectively). He is unfortunately also very sceptical of the trip figures, noting that these could have been underreported generally in 1962, and that by 1974, when the comparisons were made, it was doubtful whether a whole class of trips – those in a zonal area – had been included in the 1962 data. Nevertheless, to explain the seemingly higher trip making per driver and cab, he believes that there could have been more multiple shift working and improved servicing, enabling greater proportions of taxis to operate each day.

It is difficult to see how increased multiple shift working could help much, and even more efficient servicing would also not take us far to explain the difference. In any case, his explanation runs in terms of productivity per cab, whereas the real question is whether labour was actually producing more, as it would surely have had to do to produce the noted results. It seems that the difficulty Talbot faces in adopting this latter kind of explanation was that, on his figures, engaged trips as a ratio fell (he noted that the increase in engaged trips was 15 per cent less than total trips in his data).

Certainly, one might expect the ratio of engaged miles to increase if drivers were more successful in attracting custom. In fact, Talbot's study did not go directly to taxis for 1972 data, but instead (reasonably for the purpose at hand) concentrated on updating the quantities given by the Maxwell Stamp (1970) origin and destination data. The only reliable data on the ratio of unengaged to engaged mileage are direct reporting about what taxis are doing, because, while engaged trips are reported in other surveys (e.g. from household interviews), unengaged mileage, which includes dead heading, cruising, etc., cannot be. So Talbot's comparative data, which are based on trips reported in households are not conclusive. Indeed, an 'unengaged trip' is a very odd concept for a taxi plying for hire. So we cannot rule out the possibility that engaged mileage might have increased as a proportion of total mileage, more especially perhaps after the period concerning Talbot.

There have been changes, historically, in the ratio of engaged to unengaged mileage. Runciman in 1953 reported 58 per cent engaged as an average, and Maxwell Stamp (1970), as we have seen, reported 60–65 per cent for 1968. Could this 'trend', if it be such, have continued? Also, there might have been a favourable change so that drivers could perform more of all types of mileage per unit time.

Greater engaged mileage as a percentage of all mileage surely would chiefly come about through a favourable change in the places or times at which the demand appears. To do more engaged mileage the driver's probability of getting a fare has to rise. It will do so if, for example, the denser but less peaky traffic increases. It has also to rise in conditions which will not increase the time spent in serving customers. Perhaps, although this is again speculative, the net effect of the upsurge in 'visitors' traffic over the years has been, on balance, of this character. In this way also, the extra engaged mileage may have arisen in such a way as not to have an adverse effect, net, on cab availability (as might happen, *ceteris paribus*, as markets distant from the centre become more active). We need much more knowledge of how the various market sectors affect cab operation to get beyond speculation here.

Another possibility is that there has been more mileage of both kinds, engaged and unengaged, per driver hour. It is true that, on average, traffic speed in Central London has somewhat improved over the years in question, though how this specifically affects the condition of taxi output remains uncertain. We have also noted the possibility that taxis were taking on more hire-car-type work, and this would be at higher average speed.

Effective driver time can also be increased by better positioning of cabs *vis-à-vis* the labour supply, on the analogy of optimal siting of bus depots to recruit labour supplies more easily. There was, it seems, such a shift, of a rather fortuitous kind. Before about 1968, it was thought that cabs had to be garaged at proprietors' premises overnight. This was certainly a great convenience to inspectors of cabs bent on spot checks, and the notion was normally encouraged by their practices. However, it was then realized that nothing in the law prevented a driver from taking a proprietor's cab overnight and parking, perhaps, outside his or her own home. This resulted in a proliferation of appropriate deals between proprietors and drivers. In effect, such deals increase capital (the cab) to labour ratio. One could perhaps class them as a labour productivity gain, but they may well more properly be put under the label 'innovation', to which we now turn.

Innovations and productivity

All the significant innovations of the last fifteen years in London taxis have been organizational, and most of them have not been truly original, but merely more widespread. The cabs themselves have hardly changed in appearance or function, and production methods on the job have not changed either. Yet, cumulatively, organizational changes have wrought considerable modifications in the trade, and these may provide better explanations from the cab side of the apparent contrasts with trends in conventional bus costs than any of the factors so far explored. They have arisen not by incursion of large firms (as we have seen, concentration in cab proprietorship has been falling), but simply from the fact that, while the regulatory framework has been basically unchanged, its characteristic of free entry over specific barriers such as the cab and knowledge requirements has ensured that competitive adjustments are quickly and easily made to demand and to the state of factor supplies. There has been virtually nothing to impede the emergence of new ways of doing business, and the somewhat converging development of the larger hire car trade, itself completely unregulated, has provided a spur. This has two aspects. The nature of the labour supply may have changed, so that there may simply have emerged more drivers who wished to work longer hours and earn more. Nothing inhibited such a development. As we saw earlier, however, there is little evidence of systematic change in those labour characteristics we can measure. Second, and probably more important, is the contrast with the conditions governing labour contracts in public transport, which have not displayed so much flexibility.

Most remarkable is the way the cab trade has adjusted to changes in the real price of labour. One aspect of this is that technical changes in the cab itself have focused on the driver – for example, the closing of the driver's compartment, a movement of the partition to give drivers more room, adjustable seats for drivers, heaters operated by the drivers, and automatic gear shifts. The bus driver has shared comparable improvements. But by contrast, in the taxi case, there has been a proliferation of ways of forming labour contracts suitable for widely varying individual drivers' preferences. Writing in 1960, Ralph Turvey sought to explain why the almost universal system of sharing revenues (the commission system) had arisen. In 1973 I argued that his reasons for the disappearance of alternative systems were not sufficient (Beesley 1973). My argument went as follows:

> His explanation was that wage payments gave no incentives to drivers to earn fares and so were discarded (or never used). 'Flat' systems put the risk on to the driver, and lost ground against commission systems which 'shared risk and made the proprietor's receipts vary with engaged mileage', and which had the advantage that running costs, influenced by drivers, were also reflected in the deal. Also, with commission, there was an incentive to a driver to work hard.
>
> These explanations are not sufficient to demonstrate why only commission systems survived to that date. First, a wage system would in any case implicitly contain, in free competition, some bargain on the output expected from the driver. Drivers and proprietors would, by the working of the market, obtain satisfactory deals on this on each side. A more likely explanation of its rarity is that it was simply unnecessary: it was more convenient to pay a man from the takings at the end of each shift. There was no need to accumulate credits for a periodic payment.
>
> More seriously, however, the dominance of *one* form of labour contract could only have come about, in free competition, if workers were homogeneous in their desires and expectations of employment, and employers were also appropriately motivated. Specifically, there is no reason at all to suppose that, with competition on both sides of the market, a 'sharing' of risks and 'some' incentive to drivers would emerge as the dominant form. One would expect, instead, a variety of arrange-

ments to persist and to change over time in relative importance, depending on the changing distribution of attitudes to risk on each side. So an alternative explanation for the triumph of the commission system in the fifties must be sought, an explanation which must involve breaches in the conditions for competition. A more likely account starts from the point that union organisers had a crucial interest in the commission form. Essential to union organisation is of course control over the wage-payment system. This would occur only with the commission type system, for 'flat' systems at once discourage the growth of uniform attitudes and at the same time make the monitoring of wage bargains extremely difficult. Commission percentage could be argued about concretely with the 'average' man in mind. But this merely provided, it may be argued, the technical basis for organisation. Motive and economic opportunity must also have been present. These were most probably provided initially by chronic excess capacity in the 1930s and perhaps earlier (remarked on by post-war reports) and then by the renewed decline of the industry in the immediate post-war years. Unionism enjoyed growing support in these conditions, and with it grew the commission system. Employers organised for bargaining purposes correspondingly.

This became very relevant in the subsequent period of London's taxi expansion. Without control over supply on either side of the market, no union and employers' organisations could control the wage structure. And so it happened, contrary perhaps to expectation and certainly in complete reversal of history to that point, that after about 1960 or so the supposedly extinct 'flat' systems re-emerged – partly in more extreme form than before. In 1969–70 (Maxwell Stamp 1970: 38) as much as one-third of all hirings to journeymen were 'on the flat'.

Subsequent enquiries seem to confirm these interpretations. As seen earlier, commission arrangements now apparently account for as little as 10 per cent of the whole. Trade journals reveal an increasing variety of advertisements for contracts. There are full flat arrangements weekly or daily, half flat, 'night', 'long day' and 'day' contracts, in which differing times for cab hire can be purchased. Considerable variation in hiring prices for cabs of different ages has emerged. A variety of 'extras' (e.g. drive home service, take home, VAT and holiday pay arrangements, all extra services for the independent driver) can be purchased, according to the state of the market. Varieties of commission arrangements, to modify the basic division between proprietor and driver, have also emerged, and these, together with the mileage basis for hiring, have been coupled with particular 'extras' from time to time.

How does this proliferation of options represent a chance to discriminate between prospects? Are there possibilities for both proprietor and driver to choose among prospects offering different trade-offs between return and risk? To show this we must demonstrate how the different contracts vary with respect to expected return to each party and the risks involved. Pearce (1977) points out that there are four basic options – to be an owner-driver, to rent on a flat contract, to hire on mileage, and to offer or accept a commission ('on the clock') arrangement. There can be many subvariants. In particular, the owner-driver can enter the hiring market, and fuel purchase may fall, in hiring contracts, on either side, though it is usual for fuel to be paid for by the driver with 'flat' contracts.

Considering the main variants in which an owner deals with a driver, however, we can indeed discern different prospective returns and risks to the owner (or 'proprietor'). The owner can choose short period hires, at higher prices but with greater risks of failing to sell available capacity. Drivers, too, present opportunities for the trade-off. A reliable safe driver will get some extra inducement for loyalty.

For the driver, the options also vary both in committed outlays and in risks. 'Flat' arrangements involve less outlays than mileage arrangements, and so hold out a prospect of greater margins for given revenue. Table 8.10 demonstrates the relevant cost categories which proprietors must aim to cover in the long run when establishing contracts. These 'proprietor-related' costs in 1975 were estimated at £1,607, or 23.8 per cent of all costs.[18]

Fixed rate per mile contracts involve a further 9 per cent of Table 8.10 costs if fuel costs are borne by the proprietor, but in any case will consist mainly of proprietor-related costs. On the clock (commission) arrangements involve the driver in sharing all relevant costs other than his or her own time. As seen earlier, the division between driver and proprietor typically gives the proprietor a greater share of total costs than are accounted for by proprietor-related costs, even if fuel is included. Therefore, in terms of the prices represented by the contracts, it is likely that *most* will be paid by 'on the clock' drivers; less will on average be paid by mileage drivers, and least by 'flat' drivers. For given chances of getting fares, the prospective profit to the driver differs accordingly.

But the *risks* faced by drivers are also different. Most risk is associated with flat contracts, because the money has all to be paid in advance or contracted for. None has to be so paid by the 'on the clock' ('commission') driver; that is probably why so far as it exists nowadays this is the most popular contract, it is said, with the occasional part-timer, who does not wish to feel obliged to 'get back' a commitment by putting more time in than he or she had allowed for. Mileage risks fall in between; one has to lay out something, but can hedge as one gains knowledge of conditions in the hiring period.

Thus it is that these contracts, and their variants, can suit a great variety of hirers' and drivers' demands and attitudes. The old, near universal commission arrangement now suits relatively few. Sid Pearce (1977) personifies the 'flat' hirer as a youthful driver, eager for work and 'keeping on the go'; the mileage man is more 'passive', working from ranks; and the owner-driver is perhaps the 'most balanced'. Obviously, he is right in supposing that the conditions of contract will result in differing incentives to pursue particular business, and there may well be correlated personal attributes. But we probably should not go too far in such personification. The outstanding point about the system is that drivers can – and presumably do – move quite freely from one contract form to another as circumstances and their own needs for income, family obligations, etc., as well as short-term objectives, change.

The existence of this variety of contract forms has also probably had an indirect effect on the growth of owner-drivers as a proportion of the total, for which the numbers of owners of one cab only is usually taken as a proxy. In 1960, they owned 42 per cent of cabs; in 1976, 55.4 per cent. The relatively open opportunities represented by the taxi trade may well have attracted a more than average proportion of workers with entrepreneurial attitudes and ambitions, and it has always been held that the progression is typically from driver to owner-driver to multi-cab owner. (Whether this picture of the build-up of cab firms is still appropriate, however, needs investigation, for one also hears of much buying in and selling out of cab firms. It is alleged, for example, that some one-cab owners are publicans, and the entrants and exits of 'amateur' owners of cabs are often deplored.)

The extreme importance of these varieties of opportunity is underlined when we consider the characteristics of our sample of 800 drivers. As Table 8.9 shows, there is immense variety in the ages at which drivers decide to enter the trade. They take an equally great variety of times to undergo their knowledge training. Indeed, of all the non-zero cells in Table 8.9, the largest single cell holds only 8 per cent of observations. Requiring full-time attendances, or offering only one form of labour contract, would obviously have a greatly constraining effect on labour supply – and these are precisely the conditions under which much other public transport operates.

Equally remarkable is the variety of occupations from which taxi drivers emerge. Analysis of these indicates that 38 per cent of drivers come from the category of occupations 'Transport operating and Driving and Materials Storing and related' which includes professional drivers such as bus, other public service vehicle, and lorry drivers. This category includes other callings too, of course, and the proportion of those which can be identified as drivers is about 28 per cent. The rest cover a wide variety of (mainly manual and clerical) occupations. There can be little doubt of the importance of this variety in explaining another phenomenon – the growth of part-time drivers, often remarked (but still badly documented: the only solid evidence is quoted in Maxwell Stamp (1970) for 1952 and 1968).[19]

The dimension on which there is, so far, hardly any dispersion is sex, for it seems that only 3 of over 16,000 drivers are women. This scarcity is still a mystery, though it may have something to do with attitudes communicated particularly at the time of applying for or undertaking the knowledge test – the culture emphasizes such things as alleged danger to ladies which compellability entails (the vision is of the cab driver being instructed to drive to a remote spot and suffering, at minimum, the loss of the day's takings).

Nevertheless all these points about variety and opportunity are epitomized in an interview which a ladies' magazine (*Woman's Own* 1977) recently conducted with 'one of the trio, a delectable 28-year-old from Walthamstow'. She said: 'I find it [cruising the city streets] much more interesting than working in an office or shop. Also I can work the hours I like.' She also noted that husband Rusty is in the trade, and they use their new white cab ('It's white because we do a lot of weddings') in shifts – Joan works in the day, Rusty in the evenings. 'That way we have the afternoons together.' The five white cabs in the London trade have also formed themselves into a consortium for wedding parties. In such ways, the traditional distinctions between hire cars and taxis are declining in significance; competition in the trades is leading to product differentiation.

CONCLUSIONS

We have explored several hypotheses about reasons for the trends in total supply in the London taxi trade, reaching the broad conclusion that much of the apparent ability to keep real costs down in the face of rising real input prices has to do with adjustment in labour supply, itself a function of free entry, competition with the hire car trade, and, implicitly, the constraints which labour, wishing to improve its ability to reach a compromise between return and risk, meets elsewhere in the labour market. We are not concerned in these conclusions to draw the policy morals for public transport, but rather to focus on what the needs for further investigatory efforts seem to be. The justification for such effort is, of course, that, should such work turn out to support the often tentative evidence adduced here, the implications for public transport policy may be important.

By far the biggest gap is direct evidence on demand. As remarked earlier, for example, we are still stuck with R.G.D. Allen's estimate for the Runciman Committee of price elasticities of 1951–2, which on close inspection does not even strongly support the oft-quoted 'near unity' attribution.[20]

Until we have the necessary data, in a form which involves sampling firms' receipts etc., as Professor Allen did, we cannot attack questions like the importance of availability or fare in demand elasticity, the cross-elasticities with the hire trade in overlapping markets, and comparisons with other public transport demand and service elasticities. Undoubtedly, the best strategy will involve a combination of time series observations from firms and cross-sectional customer studies.

Second, at several points in this chapter the importance of the supplies of drivers has been remarked on. Nothing quantitatively is known in any precise way about what they do, how much, when, and under what conditions of contract. The taxi market is characterized by competitive cab proprietors and a heterogeneous labour supply, qualified for life by the knowledge, which moves relatively easily into proprietorship. Discussions have signally failed to recognize the implications of this structure, and in particular have ignored drivers' responses to changing demand and alternative opportunities. These defects can be made good by direct sampling of drivers.

At a number of crucial points, explanations advanced here have also made use of the idea of the taxi trade as a near competitor, on relatively advantageous terms, of the presumptively larger hire car trade. It makes less sense than ever it did to investigate taxis in isolation from this other manifestation of the 'paratransit' trades. Any further effort to improve data must recognize that with hire cars one starts with abysmal levels of knowledge, and far more potential difficulty with sampling frames, than one does with taxis. Nevertheless, the return to more information should be high.

NOTES

1 This chapter first appeared as a paper in the *Journal of Transport and Economics* XIII (1), January, 1979 pp. 102–31. Acknowledgement and thanks are due to the Rees Jeffreys Road Fund, whose funding made this work possible. The chapter benefited much from comments on an earlier draft from Peter Gist, Peter Kettle, Gilbert Ponsonby, Richard Butler, Stephen Glaister, Mr R. Ainsworth and his colleagues at the Public Carriage Office, and Mr M.J. Talbot. The remaining deficiencies are the author's.

2 On p. 58 of The Maxwell Stamp Report (1970), we are told that hire cars average 108 miles and six jobs per shift, and that the average duration of an engaged journey is 40 minutes. Elsewhere we learn that hire cars average 33,000 miles running a year, that there were probably 20,000 hire cars all told, and that the average job serves 1.9 passengers. Forty minutes at 15 mph = 10 miles per engaged journey (possibly rather more, as 15 mph is slow). Six jobs = 60 or so engaged miles per shift = 60 per cent engaged mileage; 60 per cent of 33,000 miles $\times 20,000 \times 1.9 = 752$ million miles.

3 On p. 47 of the Maxwell Stamp Report (1970), taxis were estimated to take 82 million passengers at an average trip length of 2.4 miles.

4 The regulatory authority is the Home Office. A formal model of this regulatory problem is to be found in Chapter 9 of this book.

5 The Local Government (Miscellaneous Provisions) Act 1976 gave permissive powers to authorities to regulate hire cars, but not with respect to quantity or fares. London was excluded from this Act.

6 In responding to requests for fare increases, the Home Office refers to an index of motoring costs.

7 Since hire cars are unregulated, they have little opportunity to protest as a body at these developments. This, and taxis' success in gaining markets, might account for the relative lack of adverse taxi comment of late on the 'mini cab' issue.

8 Since this was drafted the 1978 Price Commission report has estimated the London taxi average trip as 2.7 miles, an increase over the Maxwell Stamp finding.

9 We regressed applications, *inter alia*, as a function of unemployment, real wages of bus drivers, and taxi fares related to taxi, bus and underground fares in various models. Unemployment was always highly significant. In some model forms real wages were significant but of wrong sign, and the fare terms were

insignificant. Lagged models performed similarly. The 'best' model regressed applications on experience in the previous year; the result was that first applications are a function of

a constant; real taxi fares, $t-_1$; unemployment, $t-_1$; + real bus wages, $t-_1$.
−252.4   − 33.0   + 1, 104.5   + 66.81
$(t = -0.252)$ $(t = -0.670)$ $(t = +4.592)$ $(t = +1.658)$

The 'wrong' effect of bus wages is interesting. It is tempting to argue that increasing bus wages increases applications because money to finance the knowledge is more available! But this depends on the importance of bus drivers or like sources as a source of taxi labour. It turns out (see p. 137) that this is not likely to be a very significant factor.

10 In the period 1959–76, the highest number of attendances for oral exams in a year was 27,202 in 1972, and the lowest 11,095 in 1961.

11 We had some hope of using the average length of time taken for the knowledge test as a proxy for the proportion of part-time drivers entering the workforce, on the argument that those who had part-time jobs already would keep them going, thus taking a part-time 'course' as it were, and so continuing part-time operation as taxi drivers. We also tried to discover whether the numbers of drivers entering the 'course' from particularly part-time types of work were changing over time. We did not succeed in establishing these points, or disproving them either. There is no substitute, it seems, for observing directly whether taxi drivers are, or are not, part-time operators.

12 A chi-squared test on a partition of the sample for earlier and later years indicated differences in the occupational structure only at the 0.20+ significance level.

13 It is also possible to estimate a labour supply elasticity from the distribution of alternative occupations and earnings. Since at any one point in time, say 1977, the stock of drivers is an accumulation over many years, in response to varying experiences of demand for taxi work, and contains a variety of full, part and non-participating drivers, one can regard the distribution as representing the varying amounts necessary to induce labour to be supplied. As Table 8.4 shows, about 90 per cent of the total labour lies in the range of earnings between £70 and £80 a week. Over this range, the average proportional increase in earnings related to this corresponding proportional increase in numbers available indicates an elasticity of 14.5. Unsurprisingly, the elasticity of supply turns out, on this evidence, to be high over a big range of outputs.

14 New Earnings Survey data for 1968 and 1975.

15 Where alternative employment is not available, these losses are nil, and the cost falls on the community in the shape of unemployment pay. We noted earlier the importance of the rate of unemployment in inducing entrants to the trade.

16 For 1968, we take the estimated weekly earnings of drivers' previous occupations (£24.80) for GB. We uplift this by 1.157, the estimated Greater London differential. We assume 62 weeks' acquisition time, giving £1,779 per man. The 1968 ratio of drivers to cabs was 1.50, giving a per cab basis of £2,668 (PCL seem to have overlooked this point); dividing by 20 gives us £133. The equivalent 1975 calculation is

$$\frac{£56.47 \times 1.146 \times 62 \times 1.42}{20} = £285.$$

17 From the available data (of Table 8.1) we cannot tell whether the owners of one cab are owner-drivers. About half of all cabs are owned singly. Some of these will be owned by non-drivers.

18 That these were in the right ballpark at least is perhaps confirmed by examples of advertisements for flat hiring arrangements in 1975. For weekly hire for days,

prices advertised ranged from £18 to £32, depending on the age of the cab. Other advertisements indicate that half flat arrangements range from 62 to 88 per cent of weekly contracts. Presumably shorter day contracts were higher for an equivalent number of hours. What mix of hirings a proprietor accepts will determine the actual receipts. To cover the costs, we calculate a proprietor would have to get 50 week hirings of about £32 or their equivalent. As one would expect, where there are opportunities for night lettings rates are lower, in order to encourage off-peak use. Using these and other opportunities, the average proprietor might well have reached our 'target'.

19 In 1952 6.5 per cent of drivers worked less than four shifts a week, in 1968 20 per cent (Maxwell Stamp 1970: 35).

20 Professor Allen had to measure over quarters in 1951 and 1952 for five large cab companies. He noted a decrease of 6 per cent in jobs and engaged mileage, and his table indicates (not his text, which is silent on this) an increase in receipts per job of 20 per cent, measured against the lower price. From this, he remarks 'It is tempting to conclude that demand is slightly (*sic*) inelastic', and then goes on to give reasons why the 'conclusion is not warranted', namely that the fare actually increased for part of the earlier period, and that 'the sampled firms may have increased their shares at the expense of other companies'. These are not compelling reasons, and, as he remarks, the oft-quoted conclusion 'needs to be supported by more evidence than is presently available' (Runciman 1953: p. 32). Moreover, there was a quality shift, because engaged miles fell, from 62 to 58 per cent. The improvement in availability was in effect a shift in demand to the right. This indeed may have made the apparent elasticity less than the true figure, but Professor Allen does not rely on this explanation. In all, however, the base crude observation of an elasticity of -0.35, namely,

$$\frac{Q_0 - Q_1}{1/2(Q_0 + Q_1)} \div \frac{P_0 - P_1}{1/2(P_0 + P_1)} \text{ or } \frac{6.553}{18.36}$$

which was Professor Allen's actual observation, needs a great deal more explanation to raise it to -1.00.

REFERENCES

Beesley, M.E. (1973) *Urban Transport: Studies in Economic Policy*, London: Butterworth.

Doganis, R.S. and Lowe, S.R. (1976) *Alternative Taxicab Systems: A London Case Study*, Polytechnic of Central London, April.

London Transport Executive (1970) *Annual Report*.

The Maxwell Stamp Report (1970) *Report of the Departmental Committee on the London Taxicab Trade*, Cmnd. 4483, London: HMSO.

Munby, D.L. (1968) 'Mrs. Castle's transport policy', *Journal of Transport Economics and Policy* II (2), May.

Pearce, Sid (1977) *The Case for Tariff Reform in the London Cab Trade*, Owner-Drivers' Society and the Licensed Taxi Drivers' Association, March.

The Runciman Report (1953) *Report of the Committee on the Taxicab Service*, Cmnd. 8804, London: HMSO.

Talbot, M.F. (1974) *A Study of Taxi Tips*, Greater London Council, RM307.

Turvey, Ralph (1960) 'Some economic features of the London cab trade', *Economic Journal* LXX (May).

Woman's Own (1977), 10 December.

9   Information for regulating

The case of taxis[1]

M.E. Beesley and S. Glaister[2]

We are concerned with the problem of intervention in markets where service levels, as well as prices charged, are important. We show that intervention in such markets could, in principle, improve welfare. However, effective intervention depends on generating and using suitable information. In markets in which demand cannot be kept analytically separate from supply, this is not easy. This difficulty characterizes the markets with which we are concerned, and so we suggest methods of inferring parameters relevant to particular interventionary acts. We thus contribute to discussion of a basic question – whether or not to intervene. This, following Demsetz (1968), should involve a comparison of outcomes with intervention with those expected without it, in which one argument must be the prospect of suitable regulatory information.

We concentrate on taxi industries and, more specifically, on the cruising taxi markets characteristic of large cities. These have a simple economic structure allowing us to concentrate on essential relationships and we know what information is likely in practice to be available to interventionary agencies. In the western world, taxi industries are almost everywhere regulated; if regulated, prices (fares) are fixed and a variety of other restrictions are often imposed, most notably on the number of taxis licensed to operate. (See Beesley (1973) for a review of types of regulation in taxis.)

The problems of intervention can be most conveniently shown in Figure 9.1 which incorporates some known conditions in the London taxi market in 1978.[3] Quantity demanded (trips) depends on prices (fares) and service quality. Service quality, in a cruising taxi market, depends on the number of empty (cruising) taxis available when a customer wishes to make a trip. The diagram is drawn with four downward-sloping curves representing response to fares at different levels of service. These are labelled respectively $2\frac{1}{2}$ min. 2 min. etc., indicating the expected time to encounter an unengaged cab. They are spaced so as to reflect various implied service elasticities – at first large, and decreasing as 1 min. is approached. (These service levels were assumed for illustration since service elasticities in the London market have not been measured.) The first essential part of the problem, then, is that demand depends upon service and service depends on both supply and demand.

The second essential part of the problem emerges when we consider the supply side. As argued in Beesley (1979), in a trade with unrestricted entry we can plausibly think of taxi hours (the cabs and their drivers) as being infinitely elastically supplied at a given rate of remuneration per hour: the supply price. Both engaged and unengaged time has to be paid for. The fare is given only for an accomplished trip; but prices must also reflect service levels, which depend on unengaged cabs.

Figure 9.1 supposes three alternative levels of supply price, £4.00, £2.92 (an estimate for London (Price Commission 1978) and £2.00 per hour. Each corresponds to a dashed line representing a locus of industry equilibria at various fare levels. (The Appendix on pp. 160–3 details the calculations.) At each point that one of these lines encounters a constant service level demand curve, the diagram shows the total number of cabs operating, both engaged and unengaged, and the relation between these, represented by the engaged ratio. Taking a given service level, for example the highest or 1 min. level, it can be seen that as the supply price and hence the equilibrium price per trip falls, trip numbers increase. (The price elasticity assumed in the diagram for all service levels is −1. There is some evidence of

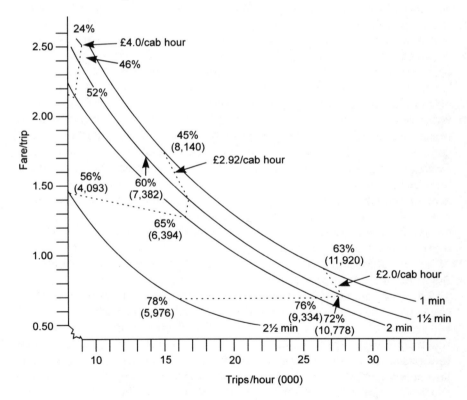

Figure 9.1 A market for taxi services. Percentages represent engaged ratios. Numbers in parentheses are the number of cabs operating.

a 'price elasticity' of −1 in previous London studies, but this is suspect, as argued in Beesley (1979).) However, the total number of cabs operating does not increase proportionately. For example, between £1.82 per trip and £0.89, 8,140 cabs increase only to 11,920 even though the price fall has increased trips demanded from about 13,000 to 26,000. The reason for this is that the absolute number of unengaged cabs required to sustain a given service level does not increase as more trips are made; this is reflected in an increase in the engaged ratios as one moves down each service level curve. (See, for example, columns (a) to (b) of the table in the Appendix, for a given service level.)

Thus the second element in the problem is that for given service levels there is an economy of resources as trip numbers increase.[4] This suggests the possibility that intervention could improve welfare. For instance, consider a proposal to subsidize the taxi industry. Suppose the industry to be operating, without intervention, at the highest service level. (We shall show later that one would expect this to be characteristic of unregulated competition in the industry.) Suppose also that the supply price is £2.92 per hour. A subsidy of £0.92 per hour is proposed, to be paid to cab operators. Fares per trip fall from £1.82 to £0.89. Under the usual cost–benefit conventions, society gains from this subsidy.[5]

But matters must usually be more complicated than this. Normally there is pre-existing regulation and therefore there is some other, historically determined, starting point at which regulatory decisions must be made. Moreover, subsidies for taxi industries are rarely proposed, and still less often specifically instituted. The situation is usually one of changing service levels in the context of regulation of the number of taxis, in addition to price. Once we also have this problem, the chances of demonstrating social gain or loss are greatly reduced. If subsidy is ruled out, the alternatives available for policy involve a given supply price. In Figure 9.1, at £2.00 per hour, is the 1 min. or the 1 min. service level to be preferred? The answer, in general, requires evaluation of areas under the curves, that is intramarginal users' valuations become relevant. Without such information, which cannot be derived with information generally available, a conclusion cannot be drawn because the value of the extra service level which involves fewer trips of higher value cannot be calculated, as would be needed, to set it against the increase in resources represented by the increase of cabs from 10,778 to 11,920. Non-intervention – in this case a market structure characterized by competition – can well produce such a trade-off. Left to itself, the industry will tend towards the highest service level consistent with the appropriate remuneration per hour (the point where the dashed line becomes tangential to a service level curve), simply because that is always associated with the largest number of cabs. So long as the required hourly remuneration is available, supplies will be forthcoming. If less is available, there will be no effective supply; and if more, excess supply will drive the remuneration levels down. (See the record section, pp. 156–9.)

The argument for non-intervention is of course never confined to the welfare arguments illustrated here. It could well be argued that free entry is itself desirable because of effects of experimentation, development of market differentiation, new services and prevention of producer-side exploitation.[6] However, regulation is likely to remain a reality in this trade; hence it is important to generate information on both price and service elasticities relevant to a given taxi industry. What can be observed is the number of cabs operating, the ratio of engaged to engaged plus unengaged cabs, trips made and waiting times. These four quantities have been prominent in discussions of the trade. Evidence on profits is confined to data, sometimes of doubtful authenticity, of premiums paid when there is control on entry. It is useful to consider what regulators may or may not be justified in inferring from the limited data likely to be available to them. To do this, a model capable of analysing the problem in the neighbourhood of any given starting point is needed. This 'local' model is presented next. We then turn to a discussion of whether regulation is likely to be successful in practice in the following sections.

LOCAL ANALYSIS

Variation of fare with free entry to the trade

The demand for trips per unit time (say, per hour) is expressed in terms of the fare per trip, p, and the level of service, w, as $f(p, w)$. By the level of service we mean that component of overall service quality represented by the time that an individual would expect to have to wait for service on the average, whether by direct hailing in the street, telephoning or searching out at ranks. We could have used the probability that the individual will be served within a given time period as an alternative. We shall argue in terms of the average price for a trip of average length and we assume that the latter is constant. We are thus abstracting from the complications posed by the structure of fare scales and the fact that average trip lengths may vary with circumstances.[7] If λ is the time taken per average trip then the demand for engaged cab hours per hour, E, will be given by

$$E = \lambda f(p, w). \tag{1}$$

The remaining relationships concern the industry supply.

Beesley (1979) has shown that whilst drivers must pass stringent tests to obtain a licence to ply in London, there is a 'pool' of qualified drivers who, under normal conditions, are currently engaged in alternative occupations.[8] From an analysis of alternative occupations of drivers he has estimated that over a large range the elasticity of supply is of the order of 14.5 in the case of London. We assume an infinitely elastic supply of drivers with vehicles, wishing to work at the going supply price. Regulations specifying minimum safety standards for vehicles and 'suitability' standards for drivers will affect the level of the supply price, but not the supply elasticity. (De Vany (1975a) discusses this assumption in more detail.) The component of costs which has traditionally attracted the attention of regulators, the trade and others (see Maxwell Stamp 1970, Doganis and Lowe 1976, Transport and General Workers' Union 1978), namely the costs associated with the vehicle and its garaging, only account for about one-third of the total. The remaining two-thirds is the opportunity cost of the labour provided by the driver himself (Beesley 1979).

In London fares are fixed but there is no overall limit on the numbers of cabs or drivers permitted to operate and we begin with an analysis of this case. It follows that the size of the trade will adjust to the point at which the total revenue per cab hour (engaged + vacant) just matches the supply price (including normal profits) per cab hour:

$$nc = Ep/\lambda \text{ or } nc = pf(p, w), \tag{2}$$

where n is the number of cabs operating and c is the hourly supply price.

The number of cabs operating is the same thing as the number of cab hours supplied per hour and this must be the same as the sum of the number of hours engaged and the number vacant, V:

$$n = E + V. \tag{3}$$

For any given pattern of searching behaviour on the part of the customer, average waiting time will be determined by the number of vacant cabs available. Various formulations give similar results and we here choose the simplest:

$$w = g/V \text{ or equivalently } w = g/[n - \lambda f(p, w)], \tag{4}$$

where g is a constant of inverse proportionality. This might be appropriate, for instance, if vacant cabs search for fares by moving at random in the street network. It implies that a 1 per cent increase in vacant cabs will cause a 1 per cent fall in mean waiting times.

For a given value of the price, p, relations (1) to (4) determine values for E, V, n and w, assuming a solution to exist. Without specifying an exact form for the demand function $f(p, w)$ it is not possible to write these solutions explicitly. However, a great deal of information may be obtained without giving an explicit form.

From (1) and (2) the engaged ratio, R, is given by

$$R = \frac{E}{E + V} = \frac{\lambda c}{p}. \tag{5}$$

Hence for a given trip time, λ, and supply price, c, the engaged ratio is simply inversely proportional to the regulated fare. Typically, a regulator has to act when there has been a reduction in real fare levels. Assuming that there have been no shifts in trip times or costs, the regulator would expect to observe a rise in the engaged ratio. But he or she cannot use this observation to assist in inferences about other quantities of interest, for example the price and waiting time elasticities or service levels. Neither can it be used to monitor exogenous changes in total demand due, say, to income or tourism changes, because they will leave the ratio unchanged, with free entry to the trade. So one of the quantities easily available to regulators and often quoted turns out to be of very limited use.

Now, let

$$\eta = \frac{\lambda p}{E} \frac{\partial f}{\partial p} (p, w), \omega = \frac{\lambda w}{E} \frac{\partial f}{\partial \omega} (p, w) \tag{6}$$

be respectively the price and waiting time elasticities of demand for trips. Both will be negative.

The elasticities of response to a fares change of engaged hours, cab numbers and waiting times are given by

$$\frac{p}{E} \frac{dE}{dp} = \frac{1}{(1+\omega)} \left[\eta - \omega \left(1 + \frac{E}{V} \right) \right], \tag{7}$$

$$\frac{p}{n} \frac{dn}{dp} = \frac{1}{(1+\omega)} \left[(1+\eta) - \omega \frac{E}{V} \right], \tag{8}$$

$$\frac{\omega}{p} \frac{d\omega}{dp} = \frac{1}{(1+\omega)} \left[(1+\eta) + \frac{E}{V} \right]. \tag{9}$$

Our aim is now to use (7), (8) and (9) together with assumptions on the sizes of the elasticities to predict the impact of a fare reduction on the numbers of engaged cabs (and hence trips), total cab numbers and waiting times. We also wish to indicate the converse: how historical observations of these movements might be used to infer likely ranges for the elasticities, information which would then be useful for statistical estimation, prediction and evaluation.

Predictions of the impact of a fare reduction with free entry

With three quantities available to be observed, there are eight possible patterns of direction of change in response to, say, a price fall. In the absence of exogenous shifts in the demand or supply conditions, four of these patterns are ruled out *a priori*. These are those involving either an observed increase in cabs with a decrease in trips, whether waiting times (*a*) decrease or (*b*) increase, or a decrease in cabs and a decrease in waiting time, whether trips (*c*) decrease or (*d*) increase. (*a*) and (*b*) cannot occur because aggregate revenues would have fallen, which under free entry and exit could not result in more cabs being in the trade. (*c*) is impossible because then all three quantities would fall simultaneously: service would then be improved when price has fallen; therefore trips must increase, on the usual assumption about demand. (*d*) is ruled out because if waiting times fall and engaged cabs (equivalent to trips on our assumptions) rise then both vacant and engaged cabs have risen, so the total of cabs could not have fallen. The remaining four possible patterns are the subject of the following analysis, resulting in Table 9.1 (increases are denoted + and decreases −). The outcomes depend on price and waiting time elasticities. Cases A and B are illustrated by the initial positions correspondingly marked on the dashed curves on Figure 9.1. Numerical examples of all the cases are given in Glaister (1982).

We first rule out the possibility that equilibrium could be stable with free entry if the service elasticity were greater than unity in absolute value. If so, then a 1 per cent increase in the number of cabs would cause a 1 per cent increase in the number of vacant (and of engaged) cabs and hence a 1 per cent fall in waiting times. This in turn would generate more than a 1 per cent increase in revenue implying an increase in the profit per cab. Thus more cabs would be attracted into the industry, and so expansion would continue until the service elasticity fell below unity (cf. De Vany 1975b: 333). A formal proof of this instability is given below.[9] We assume in what follows that the service elasticity is less than unity, that is $-1 < \omega < 0$.

Suppose that demand is price inelastic. Then (8) and (9) show that a fare reduction will definitely reduce the number of cabs and increase waiting times. The effect on the number of trips is ambiguous. But by combining (7) and (9),

Table 9.1 Feasible outcomes from a price fall

	Observed quantities' direction of change					Relation of price elasticity to other variables	
Case	Cabs	Trips eng.cabs	Waiting time				
A	−	−	+	Price inelastic		Price elasticity small relative to waiting time effect	
B	−	+	+			Price elasticity large relative to waiting time effect	
C	−	−	+	Price elastic	As A	Price elasticity above 1 but fairly close to it	$1 - \dfrac{1}{|\eta|} < R$
D	−	+	+		As B	Price elasticity well above 1	
E	+	+	+				
F	+	+	−			Very high price elasticity	$1 - \dfrac{1}{|\eta|} > R$

$$\frac{p}{E}\frac{\mathrm{d}E}{\mathrm{d}p} = \omega\frac{p}{\omega}\frac{\mathrm{d}\omega}{\mathrm{d}p} + \eta. \tag{10}$$

In other words, for a 1 per cent price fall,[10]

$$\begin{aligned}\% \text{ change in trips} &= |\text{price elasticity}| \\ &- (|\text{service elasticity}| \times \% \text{ change in waiting time}).\end{aligned} \tag{11}$$

Hence, if the price response is small and/or the overall service effect is relatively large, then trips (and engaged cabs) will fall because then there will be insufficient trips generated by the price fall to compensate for the service deterioration. This ambiguity accounts for the two rows of Table 9.1, labelled A and B, under the price inelastic umbrella.

In the price elastic case the situation is more complicated, as rows C to F of Table 9.1 indicate. Suppose first that

$$1 - \frac{1}{|\text{price elasticity}|} > R, \tag{11}$$

or equivalently,

$$|\text{price elasticity}| - 1 > \frac{\text{engaged cabs}}{\text{vacant cabs}}. \tag{12}$$

(With an engaged ratio of 0.65, a typical value for London, this would require an absolute price elasticity in excess of 2.9.) If (12) is satisfied then (9) shows that a price fall must cause a waiting time fall. In these circumstances it is clear that trips (engaged cabs) must increase. So must the total number of cabs, since vacant cabs must also have increased to allow the waiting time fall. This accounts for row F of Table 8.1.

The explanation of this case is that price elasticity is so high that the price fall generates sufficient extra industry revenue for the trade to expand more than enough to supply the extra demand, so that service quality can be improved.

The remaining rows of Table 9.1 occur if the price elasticity is above one, but not sufficiently large to satisfy (12). The arguments leading to C and D are identical to those already given for rows A and B; the absolute price elasticity is sufficiently close to unity for the negative term $(1 + \eta)$ in (8) to be dominated by the positive term, $-\omega(E/V)$. This means that the signs of the right-hand sides of (7) and (8) remain as they would be if price elasticity were less than one. However, if the absolute price elasticity becomes sufficiently large the sign of (8) will be reversed and the number of cabs will increase as in row E. Here, since we assume that (12) is not satisfied we know that waiting times will increase.

It remains to determine the direction of the effect on trips (and engaged cabs) in case E. By combining (8) and (9)

$$\frac{p}{n}\frac{\mathrm{d}n}{\mathrm{d}p} = 1 + \eta + \omega\frac{p}{w}\frac{\mathrm{d}w}{\mathrm{d}p}, \tag{13}$$

or in other words, for a 1 per cent price fall,

$$\% \text{ change in cabs} = (|\text{price elasticity}| - 1)$$
$$- (|\text{service elasticity}| \times \% \text{ change in waiting time}). \tag{14}$$

Thus, taking (10) and (13) together,

$$\frac{p}{E}\frac{\mathrm{d}E}{\mathrm{d}p} = \frac{p}{n}\frac{\mathrm{d}n}{\mathrm{d}p} - 1. \tag{15}$$

Equivalently,

$$\% \text{ change in trips} = \% \text{ change in cabs} + 1 \tag{16}$$

for a 1 per cent price fall. It follows immediately that if cabs increase, as they do in case E then trips must also increase, although the converse is not necessarily the case. Thus case E is one where the price elasticity is sufficiently large for the price fall to generate enough revenue for the trade to expand. Unlike case F, it does not expand enough to reduce waiting times because all the new capacity is absorbed by the new trips.

This completes our construction of Table 9.1, which we present as our basic analytical device for the use of a regulator wishing to consider the effects of a moderate change in fare levels, abstracting from exogenous changes in demands and costs. If there is reliable evidence on the magnitude of the service and price elasticities, then it is a simple matter to identify which of the rows A to F of the table is the appropriate one and qualitative predictions can be made directly from it. Further, given some extra simple information on the levels of the relevant variables (7) to (9) may be used to make quantitative estimates.

Inference from experience

However, there is typically very little reliable information on service and price effects and it is rare that suitable data have been recorded to enable them to be estimated with any precision. Therefore, it would be useful to use the table 'in reverse', to draw inferences about the likely range of the elasticities and the relationships between them implied by the general directions of changes which are known to have occurred in the past. This would be useful for future predictions and policy evaluation. For instance, suppose fares have fallen in real terms over the recent past whilst waiting times have fallen and both engaged and vacant cabs have increased. That would unambiguously indicate case F; and if the engaged ratio has been in the region of, say, 0.65 then the price elasticity must be something in excess of 2.9. Case E is similarly uniquely identified.

In order to distinguish between cases A and C and between B and D one extra piece of information is required: whether the price elasticity is greater than or less than one. It may be acceptable in particular cases to make an assumption about this, or there may be some suitable evidence available.

Given this it would be possible to make the indicated deductions about the relationships between price and waiting time elasticities, and percentage waiting time effects (these are drawn from (10), (13) and (15)).

It is worth noting that the very common practice of increasing regulated fares in proportion to measured increases in material inputs is unlikely to be neutral in the way that regulators intend it should be. This is because the larger component of the supply price, labour input costs, will probably be changing quite differently. Even if the ratio of real fares to real supply price is successfully maintained the policy will only be neutral if users' money incomes are growing at the same rate as the incomes of the alternative occupations which determine the supply price, and if all consumer valuations of taxi service levels are remaining constant. The latter will generally change over time because of changes in the conditions in competing transport modes.

Finally, exogenous demand shifts due to changes in real incomes or growth in business activity and tourism, such as has occurred in London recently, will distort the picture. If there is an exogenous increase in demand so that (1) becomes

$$E = \lambda f(p, w)(1 + \delta),$$

then if fare is held constant, with free entry

$$\frac{\mathrm{d}E}{E} = \frac{\mathrm{d}n}{n} = \frac{\delta}{(1 + \omega)},$$

and

$$\frac{\mathrm{d}\omega}{\omega} = \frac{-\delta}{(1 + \omega)}.$$

Thus the demand increase will cause a more than proportionate growth in the trade, and a fall in waiting times. This is a manifestation of the beneficial scale effect that we have already noted.

The practical application of this analysis would require considerable skill, not least because things are likely to be made more complicated by such exogenous changes. In our model some important possibilities are as follows: first a change in average trip time due possibly to a change in road speeds or a change in average trip distances (perhaps because of changes in other public transport fares or changes in the competing mini cab trade); second, a change in the supply price because of changes in real costs of material inputs like vehicles or in relative labour costs (it has been claimed that some quite dramatic falls in real fares in the British trades have been sustainable because of substantial increases in driver productivity due to flexible methods of working, part-time working, job duplication, etc. (Price Commission 1978, Pearce 1977)).

We have demonstrated that even with the many simplifying assumptions we have made the market is more complicated and harder to understand than a simplistic demand and supply approach would indicate. Since the majority of the world's taxi trades have limitations on the number of vehicles allowed to ply we now add this complication to our analysis.

Limitation of the number of cabs

Suppose that the number of cabs operating at any time is restricted to $\bar{n}$ by the concession of a fixed number of licences. Then the profit per cab hour will be given by

$$\pi = \frac{Ep}{\bar{n}\lambda} - c. \tag{17}$$

The market value of a licence will then be the value of an investment of equivalent risk, yielding $\pounds\pi$ per working hour in perpetuity. Therefore if τ is the appropriate hourly interest rate, the value of a licence will be $\pounds\pi/\tau$.[11]

Invariably it is the number of licences or vehicles allowed to operate that is controlled rather than the number of vehicle hours actually supplied. In practice there will therefore be some elasticity in the number of cabs on the road at any one time as the intensity of use of the permitted stock of vehicles responds to the profitability of operation. In our text, we shall assume that this elasticity is zero. Hence the control of vehicle numbers translates into a direct control on $\bar{n}$. However, variations in the intensity of use may be important. Incorporating them complicates the analysis without greatly changing the qualitative results. In general the directions of the effects will be the same but the magnitudes will be reduced. There are in principle some exceptions to this. We show how the results are changed in note 12 and in note 14.

In this case the supply of engaged hours, E^s is given by

$$E^s = \bar{n} - \frac{g}{w}.$$

Thus, in Figure 9.2 E^s is represented by a vertical line which moves to the right as waiting times are increased because less vacant cabs necessarily mean more engaged ones ($w_2 > w_1$ in Figure 9.2). The locus of solutions is again shown as a dashed line. In contrast to the free entry case, a fall in fares will always cause an increase in the number of trips. However, it must also cause an increase in waiting times. If, on the other hand, cab numbers are increased at a fixed price then trips must rise and waiting times decrease.

The effect of a change in fare on profitability

By differentiating (1), (3) and (4) with n held constant

$$\frac{d\pi}{dp} = \frac{E}{\bar{n}\lambda}\left[\frac{\eta}{1 - \omega(E/V)} + 1\right]. \tag{18}$$

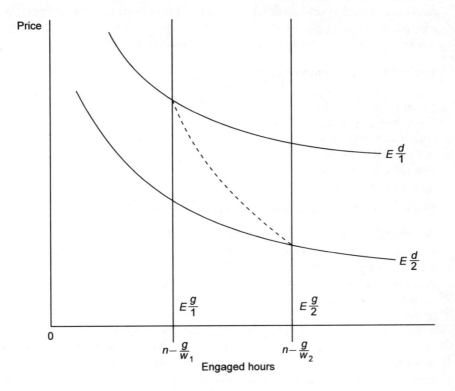

Figure 9.2   The market with restricted entry

This will be positive if and only if

$$1 + \eta > \frac{\omega E}{V} = w\,\frac{R}{1-R}$$

or

$$|\text{price elasticity}| - 1 < |\text{service elasticity}|\,\frac{\text{engaged cabs}}{\text{vacant cabs}}, \qquad (19)$$

where R is the engaged ratio. This condition (which may be compared with (12)) shows that a price fall will certainly reduce profit per cab if the price elasticity is less than one. However, if demand is elastic ($\eta < -1$) this may or may not be so. We have argued that in the case of free entry with a high elasticity of supply, we would expect a change in fare levels to have little effect on earnings per cab in the long run. We have now shown that even when numbers are fixed by licensing, it does not necessarily follow that fares reduction will bring about decreased earnings per cab. It is not surprising that a price elasticity of less than one is sufficient to guarantee reduced earnings under a price fall. What is less obvious is that it is not necessary, and that the condition involves the waiting time elasticity and the engaged ratio.

The response of trips to a price fall is, from (1), (3) and (4),

$$\frac{p}{E} \frac{dE}{dp} = \frac{\eta}{[1 - \omega(E/V)]}, \tag{20}$$

which is always negative as Figure 9.2 shows. Note that the proportionate price change will exceed the proportionate engaged cab change if and only if (19) is satisfied; that is, if and only if a price fall would cause a fall in profit per cab. Waiting time must move in an opposite direction to engaged cabs and the engaged ratio is directly proportional to it.

The effect of a change in permitted numbers on profitability

Where there is a fixed number of licences there is almost always opposition from the trade to any proposal to increase the number issued, presumably on the assumption that this will reduce the net earnings of existing licence holders and hence the market value of the licences themselves. But this is so if and only if the service elasticity is less than one. (This is seen by reinterpreting the asterisked values in note 9 as limited entry values rather than free entry equilibrium values.) Although we have argued that a stable free entry equilibrium can only occur if the service elasticity is less than one, it is perfectly possible that a heavily restricted trade could exhibit a service elasticity in excess of one. In such a case licence values would be increased by issuing more licences, because the improved service would generate so much more trade.[13, 14]

Inferences from licence values and engaged ratio

In trades with restricted entry regulators may have the possibility of observing profits, which, depending on the organization of the trade, will accrue to either cab owners or drivers. Some regulators operate on the principle of using these profits to indicate the need for greater or lesser restriction. Our arguments show that a change in numbers is not unambiguously related to profits or to the other variables of common interest to the regulator. In parallel with our discussion of the free entry case we now consider the deductions concerning the price and service elasticities which may be made from historical information on the movements of licence values and the engaged ratios (or trip numbers or waiting times) in response to changes in fare levels and in the number of licences available.

The first step is to consider the service elasticity. We know that the value of a licence will fall when the number of licences issued is increased (holding real fares constant) if and only if the service elasticity is less than one. However, the prices at which licences change hands are notoriously difficult to estimate, especially if, as is often the case, trading is officially frowned upon or even illegal. It is therefore unlikely that a reliable estimate of the direction of *change* of capital values will be available. A better approach would be to look at the behaviour of the engaged ratio in response to a change in permitted numbers. Let ϱ be the elasticity of the engaged ratio, R, with respect to numbers. Then some manipulation shows that

$$\omega = \frac{1 - R}{R - [1/(1 + \rho)]}.$$

Then if the *ceteris paribus* effect of a historical numbers change on the engaged ratio can be estimated, this expression will give a direct estimate of the service elasticity.

Consider now a *ceteris paribus* fare change. Taking (17), (18) and (20) together gives

$$\frac{\partial \pi}{\partial p} = \frac{R}{\lambda} \left(\frac{p}{E} \frac{\partial E}{\partial p} + 1 \right)$$

or

$$\frac{\partial \pi}{\partial p} = \frac{R}{\lambda} \left(\frac{p}{R} \frac{\partial R}{\partial p} + 1 \right).$$

Hence, whatever the price elasticity, a price fall will cause a fall in licence values if and only if the percentage increase in trips (or in the engaged ratio) exceeds the percentage price fall. This provides an indirect way of assessing the likely historical movement of licence values if no direct evidence on this has been recorded.

However, for the purpose of prediction, this begs the question of what the percentage increase in trips will in fact be and hence whether licence values will increase or decrease. As (20) shows this requires information of the relationship between the price elasticity of demand, the service elasticity and the engaged ratio. If the service elasticity can be estimated from historical experience when permitted numbers have changed as described above, if the engaged ratio is known, and if it is known that licence values have fallen when real fares have fallen, then (19) provides an upper bound for the absolute price elasticity of demand:

$$|\text{price elasticity}| < |\text{service elasticity}| \left(\frac{R}{1 - R} + 1 \right).$$

OPTIMAL INTERVENTION

Having analysed the properties of the market we now return to the question of the case for intervention. There are two distinct concepts. One is that of the competitive market: the outcome of free competition with free entry. The other is the efficient market: where fares and service levels are determined, as if by a central planner, or regulator, so as to achieve economic efficiency. Will the two coincide?

Because of the extreme difficulty in obtaining general results previous authors have all resorted to one strong assumption or another in order to be able to make firm statements about intervention in free markets.[15] In his famous 1924 paper, Knight was able to show that the private owner of a single road providing a superior quality of service would charge the socially optimum toll. But this relied on the assumption of an infinite supply of uncongested but inferior roads. This constrained the toll chargeable on the better road to the difference between the cost experienced by the marginal user of the better road and the cost that would be experienced on the other roads. He was also one of the first to observe that the essential problem of competition between independent road users for scarce road space, giving rise to an externality requiring intervention by taxation or other means, would disappear were one to contrive integrated operation by road provider and road user.

In the taxi context Orr uses a notion of a 'normal' relationship between passenger miles demanded and service hours supplied which he hypothesized to occur 'when there is no pressure (generated by excessive waiting, say) on either side of the market to change the fare or the output of service hours' (Orr 1969: 144).

These studies employed means of judging issues of intervention by simplifying the relation between service and demand. In the same vein, our welfare calculation in the introductory section abolished the problem of different service levels by supposing trips at £1.82 each and £0.89 each had identical service valuations. These are perfectly legitimate procedures in principle, which may be justified by the need to make progress on the issue at hand.

Regulation when time values are uniform

By far the most common assumption is that all consumers have the same value of time and that the 'full' or 'generalized cost' formulation of consumer behaviour is valid, whereby the consumer views the cost of his or her trip as the arithmetic sum of the money fare and the product of the common value of time and the time taken in obtaining service. This is true of De Vany (1975a) on taxis, De Vany (1975b) and Panzar (1979) on airline regulation, Mohring (1972) on optimum subsidies to service levels of urban bus services (he additionally assumes that the number of trips is constant so that the problem reduces to one of system cost minimization).

In a very general treatment Kay (1979) derives rules for efficient pricing and capacity when service quality depends upon both the number of users and the level of capacity, as in our case. He shows that the efficiency conditions might be satisfied in a competitive market, but only under restrictive assumptions on consumer behaviour, the leading example being, once again, that all consumers have a common time valuation. But there is a further difficulty. The efficient solution is only consistent with zero profit if the service quality measure is homogeneous of degree zero in usage and capacity – that is, if doubling both leaves quality unchanged. If, as in our case, doubling both improves quality then the efficient solution implies a loss and the competitive solution could not be sustained without a subsidy. In the particular case of our simple waiting time function (4), which is homogeneous of degree -1, the efficient price would be given by $p = \lambda c$, that is the fare should just cover the cost of supplying the time the trip takes. Vacant time must therefore be funded from elsewhere. It exists for the equal benefit of all customers and it has some of the characteristics of a public good.

Though one might think of ways in which such a subsidy might be administered it would be unrealistic to suggest it would be introduced. There have been experiments with subsidizing particular sets of consumers (e.g. the aged and infirm) to take cabs, but no case of general subsidy has come to our notice. It may seem more useful therefore to investigate the properties of efficient prices subject to the additional constraint that zero profit be made. (Dixit and Stiglitz (1977: 300) refer to this as 'a more appropriate notion of optimality'. Their analysis concentrates on the case of many diverse products and one consumer, whereas ours has many diverse consumers and one undifferential product.) In other words, should regulators concentrate on fare fixing alone, leaving entry free, or should they not intervene at all?

This is a problem of the second best and it suggests an elaboration of Kay's method. Let θ be the shadow price on the profit constraint, that is the marginal social disbenefit of not being able to provide subsidy. Let η^c be the compensated price elasticity. Then the efficient price should satisfy

$$p\left[1 + \frac{\theta}{(1+\theta)}\frac{1}{\eta^c}\right] = \frac{1}{(1+\theta)}\frac{\lambda w}{(n-\lambda f)}\left(\sum_h MV^h + \frac{p\theta}{\eta^c}\sum_h \frac{\partial f^h}{\partial y^h}MV^h\right), \quad (21)$$

where $\partial f^h/\partial y^h$ is the change in demand for trips by individual h in response to a change in his or her income, and MV^h is the marginal valuation of a unit reduction in waiting time for each trip made. If all consumers have the same value of time, τ, then $\sum MV^h = \sum \tau f^h = \tau f$. In that case (21) can be rearranged to

$$p\left[1 + \frac{\theta}{(1+\theta)}\frac{1}{\eta^c}\right]\left[1 - \frac{\theta}{(1+\theta)}\frac{\eta}{\eta^c}\right]^{-1} = \frac{E}{V}\tau w. \quad (22)$$

This will only be the same as the free entry, competitive solution in the very special case that $\eta = -1$ under all circumstances, in which case (22) reduces to Kay's result. Otherwise the free market will produce a price satisfying

$$p = \frac{w\tau}{(1 - R)} = w\tau\left(1 + \frac{E}{V}\right). \tag{23}$$

Note that on the assumption of common, constant time values service and price elasticities are related by

$$\omega = \eta\frac{\tau W}{p}, \tag{24}$$

and using (23) and (24) with (9) gives

$$\frac{dw}{dp} = -\frac{1}{\tau}. \tag{25}$$

This states that at the equilibrium the rate at which the market is offering waiting time savings in exchange for fares increases must equal the rate of exchange implied by the common value of time. This will have the property of minimizing the total generalized cost faced by each consumer, and hence maximizing the total demand for trips, as we claimed earlier (cf. De Vany 1975a: 93).

In principle (22) gives a formula for the setting of an efficient price, with free entry and no subsidy. However, we would note that it is only valid on the restrictive assumption that time values are uniform. Further, the prosecution of such a policy would require estimates of compensated and uncompensated price elasticities and, perhaps the most difficult item, the social return to subsidy at the margin.

As an alternative system of regulation, suppose that

$$k = \left[1 + \frac{\theta}{(1 + \theta)}\frac{1}{\eta^c}\right]\left[1 - \frac{\theta}{(1 + \theta)}\frac{\eta}{\eta^c}\right]^{-1} - \frac{1}{\eta} \tag{26}$$

can be treated as a constant. A monopoly is created with capacity fixed by licensing, subject to a tax such that if p is the consumer price then $p^{1/k}$ is received. Then providing that an appropriate number of licences are issued, profit maximization will lead the monopolist to set the efficient price in (22), for a predetermined ('fair') level of profit in the industry (which could be zero or positive). This method of 'successful' regulation is of little practical interest, but it illustrates that efficient pricing might be achieved through the creation of a monopoly protected by licensing. This is a result of the second-best nature of the problem which is further illustrated by the following numerical example.

In the London case, where the zero profit condition does hold because there is free entry, one can compare the alternative policies of restricting numbers or lowering the regulated fares assuming consumers have uniform time values. For instance, in 1978, the industry was operating with a fare £1.26 for an average trip and there were 6,400 cabs on average on the roads. A 20 per cent enforced reduction on the cab numbers would have yielded a profit per cab hour of about £0.58, but caused a net welfare loss of £1,960 an hour. On the other hand, a net gain of £515 an hour would have been achieved by reducing the regulated fare by 10 per cent whilst still allowing free entry. (These calculations are explained at the end of the Appendix.) In this case, restricting numbers is the inferior policy, as one would normally expect economists to argue. However, this is not necessarily the case. If the value of users' time were very low, then it is possible to construct examples where the value of the production resources saved by restricting the cab numbers outweigh losses due to deteriorating service quality.

The non-uniformity of time values

We think that to assume uniform time values is fundamentally unsatisfactory in the taxi context. Taxis typically compete closely with several alternative modes of transport and they are used by a wide range of differing individuals for a multitude of trip purposes. Response of demand to changing service quality must therefore have at least as much to do with particular individuals being on the margin of being willing to pay for better service under particular circumstances, as with a set of identical individuals making the same marginal change in the same number of trips. We would therefore agree with Turvey and Mohring's statement that 'we have to recognise that it is a lack of uniformity, that is to say a dispersion round the average, which partly generates the problem in the first place!', which they make before going on to assume uniformity on pragmatic grounds (Turvey and Mohring 1975: 283). We have shown that given the assumption of uniform time values efficient regulation would be possible in principle, but extremely difficult in practice. Rejecting the assumption, the calculation of either competitive or efficient solutions would require far more information than the regulator can usually be expected to have.

CONCLUSION

Our main theme has been to consider the regulators' problems of inferring relevant evidence. We have shown how, using an appropriate model, some relevant inferences can be made. In general, and unsurprisingly, it proves easier where price alone is regulated. Under conditions of free entry, service elasticities of greater than unity can be ruled out. With free entry, engaged ratios yield little information, but certain combinations of the other variables can yield much more. For example, it is helpful if a price elasticity of less than unity can be plausibly established, for then deductions about the numerical range of other variables can be made. In the case of entry (numbers) regulation, profits earned are also relevant; but profits cannot be used alone to indicate a desirable direction for a change in cab numbers. And profits are difficult to observe. The behaviour of the engaged ratio and numbers of cabs operating can be of help in inferences about them. But for

inference about price elasticity, for example, the chain of required observations is long.

In the light of the complex reasoning involved, a natural question arises
about the feasibility of improving welfare by regulatory action. Regulators
are dependent on restricted information; they cannot in practice alter prices
and cab numbers in order to satisfy the requirements of experimental
design. Not only does the required model depend on rather simplified
assumptions – notably, service at a given point, a single fare, uniform trip
lengths and infinitely elastic supply – but also fitting it requires controlling
for changes in several additional variables. The bias towards time series in
evidence commonly available could be countered by more cross-sectional
observations, but controlling for area variance would be difficult.

Supposing the econometric needs to be met, interpreting past experience
on a trade or trades, while necessary for prediction of welfare effects in
establishing relevant parameters, would not be sufficient. Cruising taxi
trades operate in such a way as to make necessary explicit valuations of
the welfare of those who are potentially consumers but excluded from
consumption. For example, welfare may be improved by bringing into the
market those with high valuations of time saved and deterred by low service
levels, or vice versa. Moreover, regulation has direct costs of operation and
indirect costs of mistakes. In practice there is always a tendency to follow
rules of thumb when faced with complexities. These can be misleading, as
we showed in the cases of regulating numbers with respect to profits, or
regarding fixing prices with respect to an index of costs as neutral in welfare
terms. As the choice between regulation and competition is so difficult to
make in terms of the arguments analysed, we think that other arguments
about free entry, indicated in the introductory section, should be prominent
in such a decision.

APPENDIX: CONSTRUCTION OF FIGURE 9.1

As noted in the text, Figure 9.1 shows four curves, each of which is assumed
to have a unit price elasticity. They are drawn at constant average waiting
times of $2\frac{1}{2}$, 2, $1\frac{1}{2}$ and 1 min. respectively. We assume that vacant cabs are
searching at random for fares and are therefore passing at a 'typical' point
in the area under consideration at a rate of 24, 30, 40 or 60 per hour
respectively. These arrival rates correspond to probabilities of 0.55, 0.63,
0.74 and 0.86 of an individual who arrives at random at a point being
served by a vacant cab within 2 min. (0.86, 0.92, 0.96 and 0.99 within 5
min.). The spacing between the curves is determined by the waiting time
elasticity; between the $2\frac{1}{2}$ and 2 min. curves it is -2, between the 2 min. and
$1\frac{1}{2}$ min. curves it is $-\frac{1}{2}$, and in moving to the 1 min. curve it drops to $-\frac{1}{4}$.
Table A9.1 contains the calculations.

Refer to the fourth line of block B of Table A9.1. In this block it is
assumed that average waiting time is 2 min. and so the flow rate of vacant

cabs is 30 per hour (column *a*). This can be provided by a total of 2,236 vacant cabs (column *b*) moving at random in the area under consideration. With a fare of £1 per trip (column *c*) 18,668 trips per hour will be demanded (column *d*) and this will yield a revenue of £18,668 per hour (column *e*). Since a trip takes 16.8 min. or 0.28 h, 5,227 engaged cabs are required (column *f*). Thus 70 per cent of all cabs are engaged (column *g*) and the revenue per cab hour is £2.50 (column *h*).

Consider the row immediately above. The fare is raised to £1.26 and the demand falls to 14,816 trips per hour. However, service quality is assumed to be unchanged and so the unitary price elasticity implies that industry revenue is unchanged. The remaining columns of this row are calculated as before, yielding a lower engaged ratio at 65 per cent and a higher revenue at £2.92 per cab hour. The remaining rows are constructed in the same way.

The other three blocks of the table are constructed similarly, assuming the stated waiting times. In moving from block A to block B the waiting time elasticity is -2, from B to C it is $-\frac{1}{2}$, and from C to D it is $-\frac{1}{4}$.

This completes the description of the demand side of the market. Equilibria are identified as follows. Suppose that the supply price is £2.00 per cab hour. Then block A shows this to be consistent with a fare of £0.80 and a waiting time of $2\frac{1}{2}$ min., block B gives the fare to be £0.74 at 2 min., C gives £0.77 at $1\frac{1}{2}$ min. and D gives £0.89 at 1 min. The four equilibrium points are joined on Figure 9.1 to give a locus of possible equilibria at a supply price of £2.00. The line thus identifies fare and output combinations which would be consistent with equilibrium at this operating cost. We show in the text that if entry is free the first part of the locus would represent unstable equilibrium because the waiting time elasticity is greater than one.

It will be noted that in moving from block B to C to D, a relatively small increase in fare from £0.74 to £0.77 to £0.89 creates an improvement in service quality and a fall in engaged ratio, and it also involves an increase in the number of cabs (from 9,334 to 10,778 to 11,920) and an initial rise in trips with a final fall (25,350 to 27,850 to 26,636).

Similar equilibrium loci are drawn for supply prices of £2.92 and £4.00. In these cases the directions of changes induced by price changes are the same, but their relative magnitudes are very different. In the £4.00 case equilibrium demand is almost independent of fare, the increase in revenue being almost entirely absorbed by the additional taxis required to improve the service quality. It will be noted that the equilibrium locus can 'bend backwards' for low waiting time elasticity as cases B and D of local analysis in the text confirms.

The cost–benefit calculation referred to in the introduction is carried out as follows. The equation of this 1 min. curve is

$$q = (13, 107)(1.82)p^{-1}.$$

The area between the prices 0.89 and 1.82 is therefore 23,854.7 $(\log 1.82 - \log 0.89) = £17,065$ per hour. The extra resources used in the

Table A9.1 Construction of Figure 9.1

	No. of unengaged cabs past typical point per hour (a)	No. of unengaged cabs operating (a)×74.5 (b)	Fare per trip £ (c)	Trips sold per hour (d)
(A) Waiting time 2½ min.	24	1,788	2.79	4,286
	24	1,788	1.45	8,233
	24	1,788	1.26	9,508
	24	1,788	1.00	11,952
	24	1,788	0.80	14,957
	24	1,788	0.54	22,071
	24	1,788	0.31	38,558
(B) Waiting time 2 min.	30	2,236	2.15	8,682
	30	2,236	1.50	12,445
	30	2,236	1.26	14,816
	30	2,236	1.00	18,668
	30	2,236	0.74	25,350
	30	2,236	0.51	36,462
	30	2,236	0.31	58,686
(C) Waiting time 1½ min.	40	2,980	2.42	8,925
	40	2,980	1.37	15,721
	40	2,980	1.26	17,148
	40	2,980	1.00	21,556
	40	2,980	0.77	27,850
	40	2,980	0.53	40,680
	40	2,980	0.32	66,343
(D) Waiting time 1 min.	60	4,470	4.57	5,336
	60	4,470	1.82	13,107
	60	4,470	1.26	18,933
	60	4,470	1.00	23,856
	60	4,470	0.89	26,636
	60	4,470	0.58	40,836
	60	4,470	0.34	69,236

industry are 0.92 $(11, 920 - 8, 140)$ assuming a £ for £ opportunity cost. The net benefits are therefore £13,587 per hour.

The cost–benefit analysis in the second section also assumes a price elasticity of -1. The uniform value of waiting time is assumed to be £8 an hour on the basis of Family Expenditure Survey data on taxi users in the London area, and other information. The waiting time elasticity is assumed to be -0.21 which is the value implied by (24). The evaluation is performed by numerical solution of the equations (1) to (4) or (1), (3) and (4) as appropriate, and numerical approximation of the appropriate areas under the curves. Glaister (1982) gives details of several examples of this kind.

Revenue per hour £ (e)	Engaged cabs (d)×0.28 (f)	Per cent engaged 100 × (f) (f) + (b) (g)	Revenue per cab hour (e) (f) × (b) (h)	Total no. of cabs operating (b) + (f) (i)
11,952	1,200	40	4.00	2,988
11,952	2,305	56	2.92	4,093
11,952	2,662	60	2.68	4,450
11,952	3,347	65	2.32	5,135
11,952	4,188	70	2.00	5,976
11,952	6,180	78	1.50	7,968
11,952	10,795	86	0.95	12,583
18,668	2,431	52	4.00	4,667
18,668	3,485	61	3.26	5,721
18,668	4,158	65	2.92	6,394
18,668	5,227	70	2.50	7,463
18,668	7,098	76	2.00	9,334
18,668	10,209	82	1.50	12,445
18,668	16,432	88	1.00	18,668
21,556	2,499	46	4.00	5,479
21,556	4,402	60	2.92	7,382
21,556	4,802	62	2.77	7,782
21,556	6,036	66	2.39	9,016
21,556	7,798	72	2.00	10,778
21,556	11,391	79	1.50	14,371
21,556	18,576	86	1.00	21,556
23,856	1,494	25	4.00	5,964
23,856	3,670	45	2.92	8,140
23,856	5,300	54	2.44	9,770
23,856	6,680	60	2.14	11,150
23,856	7,450	63	2.00	11,920
23,856	11,434	71	1.50	15,904
23,856	19,386	81	1.00	23,856

NOTES

1 This chapter first appeared as a paper in the *Economic Journal* (1983) 93, 594–615. We are indebted to Charles Baden-Fuller, Alan Walters, Stephen Littlechild, John Kay, two referees and the editors for helpful comments.

2 London Business School and London School of Economics, respectively.

3 In London entry to the trade is open to any qualified driver who has passed the 'Knowledge' test and who buys, hires or is employed to drive a vehicle that meets a set of specifications. In 1978 waiting times were about 2 min. at major intersections, and the fare was about £1.26 per average trip which took about 17 min. About 15,000 trips were being provided by about 6,400 cabs in a typical hour. These were engaged about 65 per cent of the time. The supply price was

estimated at £1.92 an hour. The total number of cabs registered in London in the Metropolitan Police District was 12,080 at December 1977. Thus, about half plied at any one time in the centre (Price Commission 1978, Beesley 1979). The surveys for the Price Commission revealed enormous variations in firm sizes in London and between conurbations. In London there has been a substantial growth in owner-driven cabs to 56 per cent of the total. Proprietor ownership patterns have remained stable. There are 500 proprietors with 2 or more cabs, 31 with 40 or more, 9 with 100 or more and 2 with more than 200. (Beesley (1979) analyses the changes in predominant arrangements between proprietors and drivers.) The picture is similar in Liverpool, but in Manchester there are no large fleets and in Glasgow nearly all taxis are owner driven.

4 Many other service-oriented industries have the added complexity of lumpiness in supplying capacity. This means that congestion (i.e. lowered service levels with higher demand) must also be considered, as in providing aircraft. In these industries there are at least two factors of possible concern on the supply side: the relation between the total scale of the industry and service provided, as in our case, and economies of scale in plants, which are negligible in our case. Underlying factors like these, though elementary, are not in general well specified in the relevant literature, yet it is essential to do so if analysis is to be applied. A notable exception is work on supplying roads, following Walters (1968).

5 The detailed calculations are in the Appendix. The net benefit is £13,587 per hour.

6 Compare the discussion in Beesley (1973). The reasons for regulation may well include other judgements, for example that without fare-control exploitations of the ignorant consumer would occur, or that there are external effects – such as congestion – which are ameliorated by reducing cab numbers. We are not concerned with the merits of these arguments here, though we are rather sceptical about their importance. Our analysis therefore only concerns part of the issues facing regulators in practice.

7 There is evidence that average trip lengths in London have increased from 2.4 to 2.7 miles since 1969. This may be because of the substantial shift in the fare structure caused by the tendency to load tariff increases entirely on to the initial hiring charge, thus making longer trips relatively cheaper (Beesley 1979, Pearce 1977).

8 The Price Commission (1978) reports that 15 per cent of drivers licensed for London were currently in an alternative full-time occupation, and one-quarter of those doing some driving were part-timers.

9 To prove instability, suppose that an equilibrium has been established at the values E^*, V^*, n^*, w^* and p^*, and suppose that there is a small perturbation in n, dn. Then the effect on profitability per cab will be given by

$$d\pi = \frac{d}{dn}\left(\frac{E^*p^*}{\lambda n^*} - c\right)dn = \frac{p^*}{\lambda n^{*2}}\left(n^*\frac{dE^*}{dn} - E^*\right)dn.$$

But from (1), (3) and (4) $E^* = \lambda f[p^*, g/(n^* - E)]$. Differentiating this and rearranging,

$$\frac{dE^*}{dn} = \frac{1}{1 - (V^*/E^*\omega)}.$$

Substituting,

$$\frac{d\pi}{dn} = \frac{p^*}{\lambda n^{*2}}\left[\frac{n^*}{1 - (V^*/E^*\omega)} - E^*\right],$$

and this will be positive if and only if $\omega < -1$. In that case an increase in cab numbers will increase profitability per cab and hence the equilibrium cannot be stable.

10 It should be noted that whilst (10), (13) and (15) are valid for a small price change in either direction, the corresponding interpretations in (11), (14) and (16) are worded on the assumption of a 1 per cent price fall.

11 One estimate put licence values in England and Wales in the range of £4,000 to £12,000 (Price Commission 1978).

12 Suppose that the number of cab hours supplied responds to the rate of profit per cab hour, π, as well as the number of licences, $\bar{n}$; $s(\bar{n}, \pi)$. Let σ represent the elasticity of the supply of hours with respect to profit. Then it may be shown that (18) should be amended by dividing the right-hand side by the expression

$$1 + \left(\frac{\pi + c}{\pi}\right) \frac{(1 + \omega)}{(1 - \omega E/V)} \sigma.$$

So long as $\omega > -1$ this must be a positive number greater than one. The conclusion sion drawn from (19) in the text is then unaffected, except that the magnitude of the response of profit to fare change is reduced – the more so the higher the elasticity of the intensity of use, σ.

It is a theoretical possibility that the above expression be negative, if the service quality elasticity were larger than unity (which might occur in a heavily restricted situation) and if the intensity of use elasticity were sufficiently large. This would reverse all the previous conclusions. This situation is unlikely to occur, however, because one would not expect much scope for improving utilization in response to increased profitability to remain if the numbers of licences were sufficiently restricted to be consistent with such a high service elasticity.

13 This observation may explain why licence values reportedly did increase in 1978 in Hong Kong when the intention to issue more licences was announced (private communication with the Deputy Secretary of the Environment, Hong Kong Government).

14 If, as in note 12, we assume that there is some elasticity in the intensity of use of licences with respect to the returns to operation, then the expression for the change in profit with respect to a change in permitted numbers in note 9 must be modified to

$$\frac{\partial \pi}{\partial n} = \frac{p}{\lambda s^2} \left[\frac{s}{(1 - V/E\omega)} - E \right] \left\{ 1 - \left(\frac{\pi + c}{\pi}\right) \left[\frac{s}{(1 - V/E\omega)} - E \right] \frac{\sigma}{E} \right\}^{-1}.$$

This expression is the same as that in note 9 (with s written for n), except for the division by the final term. If the unmodified effect is negative, so that an increase in licences would cause a fall in profit, then the last term in braces will be a positive number greater than one. In this case therefore the modified effect will still be negative but reduced in absolute magnitude. If the unmodified effect is positive and the intensity elasticity, σ, is small then this modified effect will again be positive but increased in magnitude. It is, in principle, possible for a positive unmodified effect to be converted into a negative modified effect if the intensity of use elasticity were sufficiently large.

15 Douglas (1972) gives an analysis of the free entry case which is similar to our own. We do not, however, share his reservations concerning the ability of the competitive mechanism to find an equilibrium and our characterization of the competitive equilibrium is different. We think that Shreiber's (1975) analysis is deficient in its failure to treat service quality effects adequately. Further, he argues that even the regular, informed customer, when in the plying for hire

market, will be presented with available cabs one at a time and will be obliged to cede to what is at least a temporary monopoly power. This seems implausible; an 'informed' customer is also informed about probabilities of getting taxis and the cab driver no doubt has expectations about the frequency of available customers. Opportunities to 'exploit' then apply to both sides of the market. At the most all that is required is protection for the 'uninformed' which could be secured by a simple requirement for a driver to announce the terms of dealing before the vehicle is entered. Like Coffman (1977) we feel that there is ample evidence against his worries that competitive forces are absent. Walters (1979) provides some useful new evidence on this issue. We also agree with Coffman's (1977) view of the underlying reasons for the existence and motivation of regulation. None of these authors considers the arguments for competition in taxis that depend on stimulating innovation.

REFERENCES

Beesley, Michael E. (1973) 'Regulation of taxis', *Economic Journal* 83, 150–73.
——(1979) 'Competition and supply in London taxis', *Journal of Transport Economics and Policy* 13 (1), 10–131.
Caves, Richard (1962) *Air Transport and Its Regulators*, Cambridge, Mass.: Harvard University Press.
Coffman, Richard B. (1977) 'The economic reasons for price and entry regulation of taxicabs, a comment', *Journal of Transport Economics and Policy* 3, 288–97.
Demsetz, Harold (1968) 'Why regulate utilities?', *Journal of Law and Economics*, April.
De Vany, A.S. (1975a) 'Capacity utilization under alternative regulatory restraints: an analysis of taxi markets', *Journal of Political Economy* 83 (1), 83–94.
——(1975b) 'The effect of price and entry regulations on airline output', *Bell Journal of Economics*, spring.
Dixit, A.K. and Stiglitz, J.E. (1977) 'Monopolistic competition and optimum product diversity', *American Economic Review* 67, 297–308.
Doganis, R.S. and Lowe, S.R. (1976) *Alternative Taxicab Systems: A London Case Study*, Polytechnic of Central London, April.
Douglas, George W. (1972) 'Price regulation and optimal service standards', *Journal of Transport Economics and Policy* 4 (2), 116–27.
Glaister, S. (1982). 'Some proposals on the de-regulation of transport services in London', *Zeitschrift für Nationalökonomie*, suppl. 2.
Kay, J.A. (1979) 'Uncertainty, congestion and peak load pricing', *Review of Economic Studies* 46, 601–11.
Knight, F.H. (1924) 'Some fallacies in the interpretation of social cost', *Quarterly Journal of Economics* 38, 528–606.
Maxwell Stamp, The Hon. S. (Chairman) (1970) *Report of the Departmental Committee on the London Taxicab Trade*, Cmnd. 4483, London: HMSO.
Mohring, H. (1972) 'Optimization and scale economics in urban bus transportation', *American Economic Review* 62, 591–604.
Orr, Daniel (1969) 'The "taxicab problem": a proposed solution', *Journal of Political Economy* 77 (1), 141–7.
Panzar, J.C. (1979) 'Equilibrium and welfare in unregulated airline markets', *American Economic Review*, May.
Pearce, Sid (1977) *The Case for Tariff Reform in the London Cab Trade*, Licensed Taxi Drivers' Association Ltd, March.
Price Commission (1978) 'Prices, costs and margins in the provision of taxicabs and private hire car services', HC 655.

Shreiber, Chanock (1975) 'The economic reasons for price and entry regulation of taxicabs', *Journal of Transport Economics and Policy* 9 (3), 268–79.

Transport and General Workers' Union (1978) *Cost Index for the London Taxi Trade*, April, London.

Turvey, R. and Mohring, H. (1975) 'Optimal bus fares', *Journal of Transport Economics and Policy* IX (3), 280.

Walters, Alan A. (1968) 'The economies of road user changes', *World Bank Occasional Paper*, no. 5.

—— (1979) 'Economics and subsidies in bus business', manuscript, December.

Williams, D.J. (1980) 'The economic reason for price and entry regulation of taxicabs: a comment', *Journal of Transport Economics and Policy* 14 (1), 105–12.

10 Bus deregulation[1]

M.E. Beesley

SUMMARY

Bus deregulation involves free entry and creates a competitive bus industry. It will principally affect the large conurbations. The chief benefits are: a lowering of labour input costs and a gain in productivity quite probably sufficient in aggregate to sustain bus outputs equivalent on average to those now associated with subsidized provision; a continuation of these gains over time; a substantial reorientation of bus outputs in urban areas, particularly towards those having better financial ratios. These will generate further gains, so correcting a major failing of cross-subsidization. The change, on the whole, will have benign distributional effects; and a great variety of potential innovatory gains in services offered will emerge. External effects on road congestion will be favourable.

Consequences for present organizations, the incumbent bus operators, will be severe, involving shrinkage of assets and changes in subsidy provision. When the transition to free competition is effected, local authority subsidy could be more efficient than it is now. To help overcome transitional problems and to speed them, collateral policies are proposed – on potential entry barriers, subsidy, and disposal of assets.

There is little room for compromise to achieve the benefits of competitive supply without the organizational and other consequences. Deregulation is they key move to *create* effective competition. It may well be judged to have fewer presentational difficulties than alternative ways forward.

INTRODUCTION

This chapter argues the case for deregulating buses. In effect, this means abolishing the present lower limit to free entry, standing at 30 miles. In terms of people's opportunity to travel, by far the biggest impacts will be felt in urban areas, where most shorter-distance travel is done. Thus the chapter concentrates on stage services in the major conurbations. The message is stark: potential economic and social gains from deregulation are large; but the consequent organizational upheaval will also be large; and compromises designed to get the benefits of the policy without its drawbacks look distinctly unpromising.

Deregulation means substituting a competitive bus industry for the present regime because the present large-scale conurbation bus organizations are the product of legislation, not of economic forces. But the chapter does not proceed by way of contrasting the welfare advantages of competition versus some scheme of regulatory intervention, as is most often done in the literature. It is, in fact, quite impractical to demonstrate the superiority either of competition or of regulation once the real-world question is raised of how regulators, as well as competitors, behave. Instead, we ask the question of how deregulation is likely to affect costs, output and adaptation to market change given the present conditions of urban bus supply. This is necessarily speculative; amongst other things, the limited experience so far with deregulation in the UK is relevant only in a peripheral way.

The main fears arising from deregulation about impacts on the general welfare seem to be as follows:

1 There would be damage to the price and quality of services; or in other words, aggregate output would be lower and inferior.
2 Cross-subsidization between services, now deemed to favour the less well off, would be undermined; or, in other words, the distributional effects of deregulation would be adverse.
3 It would normally be conceded, perhaps, that innovation in service types and methods of production would be enhanced, but held that these possible benefits are too small to outweigh the detriments.

This chapter argues that both 1 and 2 are mistaken, and hence the conclusion in 3 also.

IMPACTS ON COSTS AND PRODUCTIVITY

A leading characteristic of urban bus operations is subsidy. In the seven conurbations, on 1982/3 estimates, average revenue support will be 32 per cent of total costs. A stringent test of deregulation, therefore, is whether the present output (and quality) of bus services in the average conurbation could be expected to be attained *without* such subsidy. We can consider this in two parts: free competition's effects on bus costs and the impact on the kinds of services being offered.

On bus costs, the straightforward implication of deregulation is a demise of union influence in many important areas. That deregulation is fatal to labour constraints is quite clear not only from analogy abroad, but from experience in London's own backyard – as witness the remarkable decline of union influence in the taxi trade in the last thirty years.[2] The important point here is that even with an otherwise highly controlled trade (with respect to quality requirements, high costs of entry including the 'knowledge', and fare control) freedom to enter produces an immense variety of labour contracts and a highly elastic labour supply with varying part-time operation, co-operation of ownership, integration of cab operations, etc.

With labour monopsony removed, what is the likely impact on cost per hour of labour, and its productivity? Estimates vary considerably, and there are great problems in applying analogies to our conurbations. However, Webster[3] and others' work make it quite reasonable to expect unit labour costs (including perks etc.) to fall by, say, 10 per cent. Far more important would be effects on recruitment and deployment of labour: peak operation would have a much larger part-time element; the degree of integration of organizations supplying bus services would fall (more outside contracting etc.); and so on. These effects are generally held to outweigh direct effects on unit labour costs, so, again, a reasonable expectation would be a reduction in overall labour costs of a quarter. This would not be affected greatly if proficiency tests were required of drivers. So long as quantity restrictions are avoided, the benefits can be obtained, as they are in the case of London taxi drivers who are subject to rigorous tests.

This is by no means the end of the story. Deregulation would affect other parts of the cost structure too, and not in one direction only. Buying power now enjoyed by Public Transport Executives (PTEs) etc. would probably diminish as scale of operation fell. On the other hand, capital costs (e.g. of buses) would fall, partly because it would be impossible to insist on present constraints on sourcing, and partly because the bus fleet used would in aggregate probably include more smaller buses, more cheaply produced. Moreover, free entry would ensure that, over time, wages for drivers would tend to diminish relative to their likely course under the present regime, for two main reasons: driving is a skill continuously spreading to those whose alternative occupations yield wages at the lower end of the spectrum (including notably women); and there would be no obstacle to the adaptation of labour-saving devices, new kinds of labour contract, etc. Work on subsidization of urban transport strongly suggests that, under typical present arrangements, subsidy seeps back in part to wages as subsidy levels are increased.[4] Deregulation makes subsidy possible without these effects of labour monopsony.

SERVICE PROVISION

Hence it is not fanciful to suppose that, on average, the current levels of output could be achieved at or near zero subsidy. However, this is an aggregate effect. What would be the effect on service provision within conurbations? Here we come to the main neglected area of discussion – the immense variance across bus routes within urban areas of their service output, their calls on subsidy, and their relative social worth. Discussions of subsidy, where these are rationalized at all, tend to run in terms of global increases or decreases for conurbations as a whole; fares and services provision are considered at a very high level of aggregation, for example bus fares in London, as contrasted, say, to tube fares. This is probably inevitable given the nature of the bargaining for funds now involved. Its main consequence is to miss a salient point: namely that the main deleterious effect of cross-subsidization is that relatively 'good' services are too small; they are not producing large enough quantities of services to passengers.

That there is considerable variance is hardly disputable. Revenue/cost ratios in non-conurbation town services range from 0.52 to 1.38. In conurbations the range is very probably much greater. (From 0 to over 145 in one PTE's case.) The point is important because whatever is done about subsidy under a deregulated regime, entry by private operators to present services or markets is bound to be biased towards the 'better' routes. Its main effect on present routes would indeed be to reduce the 'poor' service outputs, that is those with poor revenue/cost ratios, and expand the better. What might be the consequence can be illustrated by the above-quoted PTE figures.

If there were to be in the PTE a switching of resources from the 'worst' routes, for example those where the revenue/cost ratios were below 65, to those where they were above, or, even more clearly, to those with ratios of 95 or better, gross revenues would increase by 11 to 25 per cent. In this particular PTE's case, the latter increase would be sufficient to cover total cost.

One hastens to add caveats. The calculation assumes that the 'costs' recorded are in fact able to be redeployed. The expanded services are deemed in the calculation equally to be able to gain revenues from the corresponding increases in resources. Actually, the costs could be more favourably disposed to incremental charges in 'better' routes and the abandonment of the worse ones, that is possible favourable net changes in avoidable cost terms could be understated. But the most important concern here will of course be the question: what are the relative values of output lost versus output gained? On this, again, evidence is scarce, but work done for the London Transport Executive (LTE) is very relevant. This study looked carefully at the impact of changing service levels on individual LTE services, both for buses and tubes, to measure passenger miles lost or gained and the social 'impacts' of such passenger changes, as measured by consumer–producer surplus changes plus external effects on road users.[5]

The evidence was, again, of considerable variance in different services. Three individual bus services were studied in detail, selected for their varying financial performance. In terms of passenger miles lost or gained by a small change in subsidy, the 'best' service in financial terms showed more sensitivity than the others. A switch of subsidy and thus resources to it from the others would have shown passenger gains far outweighing those lost. That there could be such gains from expanding the relatively good services financially is hardly surprising. They tend to be the more dense and older routes and have higher elasticities. Despite this, they have been particularly vulnerable to neglect; they do not occasion special concern. One of the major effects of fifty years of licensing has been first to encourage the development of the less financially rewarding routes, and then, in adverse circumstances in more recent years, to encourage their bolstering. When total resources available fall, the temptation – and internal and external pressures – has been to conserve, not reallocate drastically across services.

IMPACTS ON DISTRIBUTION OF INCOMES AND EXTERNAL INTERESTS

The predicted effect of deregulation on expansion and contraction of existing routes is favourable to existing and potential passengers. A very respectable case could be made out that the distributional effects of this are favourable too. Both existing users and potential bus users as a whole are characterized by lower incomes. Within urban areas, incomes are strongly differentiated by location. Except in Central London, with its high income areas and tourist market, and the 'gentrified' inner areas of outer conurbations, the general rule is that incomes rise with distance from the centre. The distribution of financially good and bad routes is the inverse to this; the worst are in the suburbs. Thus, in general, expansion of 'good' and contraction of 'bad' will distribute income downwards, that is in the generally approved-of manner. In particular, 'deprived' inner city areas will benefit strongly. The question also arises of whether the collapse of labour monopsony, and consequently freer recruitment, tends the same way. It seems quite plausible that it does so, for example one expects inner city centres such as Brixton to provide more than proportionately the driver recruits to firms entering the market. So also for the other labour inputs. In other words, less well-off workers' gains will tend to offset the losses from losing monopsonistic labour advantages.

This may not dispose of one worry – namely the consequences of complete withdrawal of particular services or, even more so, routes. Clearly it is possible for losses in consumer welfare to rise as zero output of services is approached. Whether this will be significant depends on service location and the collateral effects of deregulation. Total service losses are most likely in suburbs, and much more unlikely nearer the centre. Deregulation will also alter the type and pattern of service offered, which moves the argument to innovation. However, working from present service offerings, and assuming no subsidy is given to offset effects, one must accept that there will be some welfare losses. Most obviously affected are lower-income groups in suburbs without car access. Nevertheless, it would be difficult to assert that these will outweigh the distributional gains. There will, of course, *ceteris paribus*, be more subsidy funds available because of resource savings. If these are used in a way consonant with the changed opportunities, much could be done to compensate the prospective losers.

The final point to be noticed in this argument about removing existing inefficiencies, and providing positive distributional effects, inherent in the present variety of returns by routes is the effect on externalities. The LTE study clearly showed that increasing passengers per £ of resources spent (supported in that case by subsidy) was highly correlated across all LTE services with social benefits. Externalities – net changes in road congestion – were not, overall, a very important part of social benefits, but the bus services constituted an exception. Drawing passengers on to bus public transport, and thus reducing road congestion, created road user benefits nearly as large as the other major source of social gain – namely that to LTE's own customers – and were comparable to the change in its own resource costs. *A fortiori*, successful reorientation of bus services to attract passengers, particularly in bus routes in more congested central areas, will yield net gains externally.

INNOVATION AND DEREGULATION

Let us now turn to innovation – development of new urban bus markets, and new ways of serving them. It seems to me that the presumption in favour of deregulation here is overwhelming, and this for several reasons. 'Presumption' it must remain, because direct tests of the proposition for the UK are lacking. (There is plenty of indirect evidence in the shape of contrasts between countries with respect to regulated and unregulated bus industries.) First, there is the fact that existing rival producers, largely confined to urban fringes, have been nurtured in years of restriction. Their motive must be to preserve existing niches in the market, not to confront large established organizations. Such opportunities as are now, since the 1980 Act, available to mount some challenge, have to take place with the danger of retaliatory and predatory competition from established organizations. The failure of the Monopolies and Mergers Commission to recommend adversely on this in its July 1982 report on Stage Carriage Services is, for a body judging commercial matters, beyond comprehension. Such behaviour, announced by the incumbent as an explicit intention and discussed in Chapter 11 of the report, would in similar circumstances merit and get triple-damages suits under US law, and a round condemnation together with a substantial fine under EEC law, if indulged in by dominant private enterprise companies.[6]

More important is the fact that deregulation, as it would be quite general, would severely limit the payoff to specific predatory behaviour on the part of established organizations, even if, as of course is not necessarily the case, they wished to indulge in it. One cannot plug all the leaking holes at once! There is an instructive parallel with developments following the move to 30-mile deregulation here. This of course was applied to the whole long-distance market. Competition was, and is, vigorous, but is not, so far as I am aware, predatory (at least as between bus operators!). In the longer run the development of this, as in any other industry, depends on entry conditions, governing the emergence of new firms and expansion of old. One expects urban entry to be more widespread with general deregulation largely because entry into terminal provision is not likely to be so difficult as it is in interurban competition. However, we develop this argument further at a later point (see p. 177).

Innovation can therefore be confidently predicted to be feasible. It will be many-sided. As Professor Walters has argued, one would expect considerable change in methods of operation and bus frequencies on established routes.[7] In particular, given free choice of methods, smaller buses would be used, implying higher frequencies and hence consumer benefits. Because of proliferation of types of labour contracts, as opposed to the rigid specifications now characterizing labour bargains, one could expect far more attention on average by operators to returns per bus. There is also a large literature which suggests that, in conditions of free entry, the large gap in the market spectrum, now characteristic of conurbation bus offerings, will be filled.

Efforts in recent years to provide services to fill this gap (e.g. minibus services) with flexible or novel routings have had, so far as I am aware, very limited success. Wage costs, dominated by years of substitution of capital for labour in ordinary bus operation (e.g. OMO), and the exigencies of wage bargaining, are too adverse. The emergence of paratransit is strongly associated with deregulation conditions, as shown by the Urban Institute's work over several years, and Roth and Wynne's book.[8] A natural corollary of deregulation of buses is, of course, freedom for entry into taxi operation in conurbations outside London, and the maintaining of the presently relatively unfettered state of the hire car trade. Thus, with deregulation, the 'gap' can be expected to be attacked from both ends. Many more admixtures of pick-up, line-haul and distribution activities will emerge.

Indeed, the likely scale of successful entry is such as to raise legitimate questions about added street congestion. As just seen, the overall effects of far more effective competition to the private car (and for London particularly, to non-shared-ride taxis) is to lower the vehicle/traveller ratio to the benefit of road congestion. However, competition for favourable stopping places will become keener. But as in other parts of the world (e.g. Hong Kong) enforcement of local traffic rules will deal with the (exceptional) added spots of congestion. As far as old-fashioned worries about 'pirates' and 'cutting in to get passengers' are concerned, one must riposte that nowadays, in competition with the car, the more 'pirates' the better. The successful 'cutter' is a fully loaded cutter, and it is by no means clear that more stopping will in fact result, partly because all kinds of express or limited-stop services can also be expected to emerge.

One further consequence of deregulation will be that present methods of foreseeing, and providing for, new urban bus market opportunities will largely be superseded by less intellectual, trial and error, methods of testing markets; by more evaluation from other areas and from abroad; and by professionals entirely new to buses. If one arrays the likely entrants, they constitute a very large and diverse set. There will be a great deal of experimentation with subcontracting by those now operating their own services, often at high cost. Good examples of the latter are provided by Health Authorities, whose arrangements for patient movement would probably benefit greatly.

It seems reasonable that these market tests are likely to be more effective than present arrangements. In conurbations especially, formal market-building efforts tend to such moves as changing the global pricing strategy, applying improved service standards uniformly, etc. True, PTEs differ in their reputation for innovation. Ever present, however, must be the question of the consequences, pro and con, to the system as a whole of proposed change. One advantage of free entry is that innovation in one market does not set up a presumption for or against its adoption elsewhere. If the market endorses it, it will be copied, and there is no obstacle to diffusion aside from prospective lack of net profit. Equally, mistaken enthusiasms are ruthlessly eliminated.

IMPACTS ON ORGANIZATIONS

The argument so far is that deregulation, implying free entry to bus provision, will provide gains from lowering costs; these gains may well be sufficient to offset present average revenue subsidy levels; output in existing sources will be higher and more valuable; distributional effects, on a reasonable view, are not adverse; gains will tend to grow in future; and innovatory potential is high. The organizational consequences would be quite drastic. Union power will be undermined. Present large-scale bus organizations, PTEs and LTE, would be unlikely to be able to sustain the present scale of operations. They too would gain, in principle, from favourable cost changes. But they would be extremely vulnerable to market change and innovation. Their chief *raison d'être* – centralized decision making – would disappear. Even the National Bus Company, less vulnerable to stage carriage entry because of less reliance on subsidy, would have great difficulty in retaining its present scale. It would be beset in both long-distance and stage service markets; its ability to use bargaining power in one of these markets to increase ability to manoeuvre competitively in the other would be sharply diminished. No one can doubt that, at the very least, these prospects present difficulties in advocating a highly beneficial policy.

However, besides the benefits described, deregulation opens the way to far more effective use by local authorities of subsidy, and, by extension, by government. Transitional problems are discussed on pp. 176–7. But when the effects of free entry are fully worked through, local authorities will be presented with much clearer indications of the limits of free-market provision, that is what can be provided without subsidy. If a policy of direct local subsidy is followed, contracting for specified services in supplementation to market offerings would then be simple, presenting no difference from contracting for other local authority supplies. Competition for contracts will be keen and costs per passenger carried will be lower in real terms than their equivalents now. There is some limit, true, to the scale this activity can assume without becoming an important independent market influence, but given freedom to enter all bus and near-bus markets, this is not likely to be worrisome. (Much will depend here on the level at which subsidy decisions are effectively taken. At the level of the average London borough, for example, it is highly unlikely that bus supply will be affected.) Alternatively, as often advocated as being more logical, authorities could apply a policy of user-side subsidies. In this case too, users will have a far richer set of alternatives to suit their particular needs than they now have.

TRANSITIONAL PROBLEMS AND COLLATERAL POLICIES

But what is involved in the transition from present arrangements to the deregulated markets? Suppose deregulation were declared henceforth; how might events unfurl? What could or should be done to speed the process? Obviously a full analysis is outside this chapter's scope, but some comments may be useful. One would not expect adjustments to happen quickly, if only because ownership of most relevant and potential assets in bus supply are held by PTEs, LTE and NBC. Entry early on would necessarily consist principally of independent coach properties, new minibus operations, private companies or co-operatives, etc. As with any industry opened up to competition, the eventual market structure will depend on disclosed barriers to entry – if any – which might replace the major and dominant present barrier, regulation. The problem here is to spot in advance what these might chiefly be. A plausible scenario might be as described in the following paragraphs.

But the pace (and pains) of transition depend also on whether sensible collateral policies are pursued. For example, it seems most unwise to drop levels of subsidy to present operators, the incumbents, suddenly. On the other hand, to continue to raise subsidy levels to them is to defeat the policy objective of encouraging entry. So clearly gradual withdrawal of support from present operators (in real terms) is envisaged. Clearly this is much easier to manage if at the same time some of the subsidies released are fed back to the markets in a different way, for example by user-side subsidies. With the steady withdrawal of direct producer subsidies, and simultaneous free entry, one would expect, following the earlier arguments, that competition would first develop mainly on existing relatively dense routes and at peak times. This is because entrants would operate where their margins were most favourable, where demand is good and where advantages of flexible labour supplies, small vehicles, etc. would give their most relative advantage – in 'good' routes at peak times. The incumbents would be faced with loss of market share. Their logical reaction would be to cut down costs where least favourable, that is on the poorer routes and on 'good' routes at peaks. (Cutting extremely expensive peak output would greatly relieve costs.) Competition would also induce, but at predictably slower pace, lower wage costs and greater labour flexibility for incumbents, limiting their need to cut back output. Assets (e.g. buses) thus released would be sold and could of course be purchased by intending entrants, amongst others.

Developing innovation and increasing range of bus sizes would spread competition to other routes, continuing the process of incumbent contraction. How far this would go principally depends on the 'disclosed' entry barriers. The only obvious barrier to emerge would be garage capacity, in which to house buses and to perform routine maintenance. These would be increasingly important to newcomers as their markets are developed. Undoubtedly, as for coach terminals in the corresponding long-distance trade, there would be great planning and other resistance to conversion of sites for this purpose. Intervention to clear the barrier might be required. Planning constraints would selectively be relaxed, or, probably with less difficulty, the sale or leasing of capacity surplus to incumbents' requirements would be required.

To speed the transition along, other collateral moves could be envisaged. For example, a favourite free-market form of bus operation is co-operation by drivers and other workers in buses. These could be encouraged by supporting loan operations. Incumbent operators would no doubt wish, and be encouraged, to sell off outlying assets to independents, and these might well be a favourable background to the formation of cooperatives.

When direct subsidy to incumbents is eventually withdrawn, one would expect to see some surviving incumbent operations, depending on the speed with which they initially adjust to the changed market conditions and are willing to retreat in order to survive. The consensus that there are no economies of scale in bus operation would indicate that a range of surviving firm sizes are possible. Once a considerable contraction of the incumbents has taken place, they could well survive. However, if the owners of these remaining operations, PTE and LTE, are also to be required to be a vehicle for subsidy, conflicts of interest will emerge. Subsidy mechanisms would then be better managed as a separate system. Alternatively there could be divestiture of the remaining operations.

Thus there will be difficulties in transition, as in any major change. Sensible collateral policies can speed it along. Methods of giving subsidies have to be modified. Given the quite large upheaval, particularly of existing institutions, the question naturally arises whether the chief advantages of deregulation could be gained without such upheavals. In particular, could not competitive supply be combined with a basic PTE/LTE planning of services and granting of subsidies? I conclude with some observations on this issue.

IS THERE A VIABLE COMPROMISE?

In some ways, the advantages and disadvantages of a system in which a PTE or LTE decided on what bus service provision would be, and then conducted subcontracting operations to competitive suppliers, are clear. Most of the benefits of free-market testing and search would have to be forgone; basic services would no doubt be defined from transport planning precepts and models, with a strong dose of protection of traditional routes; experimentation and innovation would be PTE inspired, not entrepreneurially led. On the other hand, a monopsony purchaser (e.g. a PTE) could use its market power to ensure that what is supplied by the competitive industry is done very efficiently. It might well have two kinds of difficulty in sustaining this over a longish period, though. It has, in effect, to decide units of supply which can be bid for, and defining these requires considerable and sustained judgement. Also, devising an optimal rebidding system, involving shifting contract periods, arranging for fresh sets of bidders, changing route bidding blocks, etc., may well not be easy. However, to advance the argument, let us grant the professionalism and ingenuity to do this.

The principal doubt concerns how in practice to get from the present structure to one of effective competition *without* first having deregulated. Existing potential independent bidders have little presence in urban areas – they have few assets with which effectively to run the large quantity of services involved. They are steeped in traditions of gaining from regulation, not profiting from free competition. The one major potential entrant to London, NBC, would hardly be calculated to bid on even terms with others, and it has very little opposition elsewhere. It would have neither an important carrot nor a stick driving it on. Fringe urban operations could no doubt be effectively bid for, as could much of small-town routes. One cannot, however, see the progression from there to more serious competition without some large change imposed from outside.

The obvious alternative to deregulation, and thus to following a path like that described earlier, is to privatize existing local authority urban bus operations, and to require NBC to be split to constituent companies. However, even here one is very dubious about how effective such a policy could be without a substantial period of deregulation first. Quite aside from the problem of interesting the capital markets in what they will regard as a non-growth area, there is the difficulty that prospective purchasers will be buying what amounts to a gamble on local authority's future policies – to say nothing of government's attitudes. Furthermore, the presentational difficulties of announcing an intention to privatize are surely more formidable than the ostensibly less radical one of extending deregulation from its 30-mile limit. The precise implications of deregulation are difficult to pin down, and therefore to organize opposition around, in contrast to the obvious target presented by privatization.

In short, there seems no real possibility that one can get the main benefits without going through the difficult transitional period which would follow deregulation. Policy should concentrate instead on the collateral policies needed to make this easier. Deregulation is the key move to develop a viably competitive and responsive urban bus industry.

NOTES

1 Presented to the Department of Transport, December 1982.
2 As documented in Beesley, M.E. (1979) 'Competition and supply in London taxis', *Journal of Transport Economics and Policy* 13 (1), 10–131.
3 As reported in 'The importance of cost minimisation on public transport operations' (unpublished paper).
4 Bly, P.H., Webster, F.V., and Pounds, S. (1980) 'Subsidisation of urban public transport', *TRRL Supplementary Report* 541.
5 Beesley, M.E., Glaiser, S., and Gist, P. (1983) 'Social cost–benefit analysis: application to London Transport policies', *Progress and Planning* 19 (3). A main purpose of the study was also to compare the effects of global change in fares and service levels, for example bus services as a whole, with more disaggregated case studies.
6 To be fair, the MMC felt obliged to identify supposed benefits from cross-subsidization as a defence. Predatory behaviour supports services elsewhere, so is condoned, producing a conflict in public interest. But one expected a very critical look at this supposed trade-off, and a robust statement to the effect that subsidy policy should be rethought. The implications of this MMC report for controlling the dominant behaviour of any organization are not good, to say the least.
7 Walters, A. (1982) *Externalities in Urban Buses*, Institute of Urban Economics, vol. II, pp. 60–72.
8 Roth, G. and Wynne, G.G. (1982) *Free Enterprise/Urban Transportation*, Washington DC: Transaction Books.

11 Collusion, predation and merger in the UK bus industry[1]

M.E. Beesley

UK COMPETITION AUTHORITIES AND THE BUS INDUSTRY

When local ('stage') bus services outside London were deregulated by the 1985 Transport Act the intention was to promote competition. So it was logical to accompany deregulation with removal of the industry's long-standing exemption from the UK laws promoting competition, principally those to govern agreements in restraint of trade, first enacted in 1956; to control mergers, as codified in the 1973 Fair Trading Act; and to control dominant large firm behaviour, first tackled in the Competition Act 1980.

The final arbiter in deciding upon the public interest in restrictive practices agreed to and registered by many firms is the Restrictive Practices Court, to which the Director General of Fair Trading must refer for determination. Mergers are referred to the Monopolies and Mergers Commission (MMC) when this course is decided upon by the Secretary of State for Trade and Industry, on advice from the Office of Fair Trading (OFT). Anti-competitive behaviour by individual firms is dealt with in the first instance by OFT, which publishes its investigations and their outcomes. In this area, OFT may (and often does) negotiate with the 'guilty' party to modify its conduct. If that party refuses to agree to OFT's modification, the case is referred to MMC, which makes its own investigation.

After 50 years of regulated local monopolies, exposure to competition policy represented a significant change in the context of local bus operation. It was also a substantial addition to the portfolio of work facing the UK competition authorities. In particular, the office of Fair Trading, as the principal trigger for dealing with anti-competitive behaviour, had to build up its information about restrictive practices, possible anti-competitive action by individual firms, and merger proposals. In the first area, it was helped by the rules on registration of agreements. On the second, it had to wait for complaints to emerge from aggrieved parties. On the third, effective action had to await the outcome of an opposite process, the break-up of NCB, finally accomplished only in 1988. The later 1980s was also a period when the UK's anti-monopoly legislation had increasingly to define its position in relation to EEC competition law and practice. For example, it had to be decided whether highly local markets like buses were 'significant' in UK and EEC competition terms.

Principally for these reasons, the UK competition bodies have been slow to take action on possible anti-competitive moves in the bus industry, but the outline of the attitudes they are taking is now becoming clearer. The focus has been upon collusion, as represented in restrictive practice agreements; combating the power of single firms, and particularly their predatory behaviour; and defining rules for mergers.

By late 1988, 239 agreements in restraint of trade had been submitted to OFT. Of these, 115 were found to include clauses, restricting the parties' freedom to make decisions on fares and services, which the Director General found to be objectionable. By September 1989 OFT had investigated three cases involving alleged predation (West Yorkshire Road Car Company Ltd. (August 1989), Highland Scottish Omnibuses Ltd. (September 1989) and South Yorkshire Transport Ltd (October 1989)), and one (Southern Vectris Omnibus Co. Ltd. (February 1988)) involving refusal to allow access to a bus station. West Yorkshire's conduct was found not to be anti-competitive; that of Highland Scottish and of South Yorkshire was found to be predatory. The Southern Vectris case effectively confirmed the intention of the 1985 Transport Act to prevent ownership of bus stations from being used to restrict access to them.

In March 1989 the Monopolies and Mergers Commission, in its first bus merger case, established that the two geographically contiguous companies involved were a 'substantial part' of the UK within the meaning of the 1973 Act, and, while finding this particular merger not to be against the public interest, gave notice that it would be particularly concerned about proposed mergers of contiguous companies.[2] The MMC was given occasion to follow this up by the references to it in February 1990 of Stagecoach Holdings and Portsmouth City, and in March 1990 of South Yorkshire's acquisition of three local companies. On referring the former, the Secretary of State pointed to the 'possible effects on competition in the market for commercial and contracted bus services in Portsmouth and Havant and this surrounding area'.[3] By implication, mergers not involving contiguous bus companies are regarded of little concern *per se*; though several have occurred none has been referred.

Though judgements are thus in the course of being shaped, there remain to be answered questions on the effectiveness of action, the remedies proposed and the enforcement of decisions which may follow them. In fact, this present uncertainty is inherent in the UK's competition policy processes. In restrictive practices, the attitude of the Court to the economic consequences of restrictive agreements is no longer in doubt; scarcely any have survived its scrutiny since 1956. Once an agreement is registered and determined by the court, severe penalties attach to subsequently reviving a like agreement: hence a tendency, over the years, to seek to avoid registration or to find substitutes for restrictions.

So the OFT has referred selected agreements to the Restrictive Trade Practices Court, with a view to underpinning enforcement.[4] In two cases, Plymouth City Bus and Western National (September 1989) and Midland Fox and G.K. Kinch (August 1989), agreements were not furnished to the office within the permitted time limits. This action against non-registration of agreements reflects what is recognized to be a principal weakness in the present legislation identified on page 1 of the 1988 Review of Restrictive Trade Practices Policy (OFT 1988). Part of its proposals for reform include clearing the way for private actions in the courts to reinforce OFT's actions. 'In addition to the Court action being taken by the Director General, any person adversely affected by the operator of the agreement may have grounds for seeking damages in the Courts.'

When there is anti-competitive behaviour by an individual company, the practice is for OFT to negotiate with the 'guilty' party to abandon it. In the West Yorkshire case it succeeded in doing so, but in that of Highland it did not. Consequently, the MMC is considering the Highland case at the time of writing. The second and third merger cases are still pending MMC's judgement; and all cases so far have been *post hoc* enquiries. This implies that remedies, if they are judged to be necessary, will tend to be constrained by the costs of reversing an accomplished commercial process. MMC will attach more significance to these costs than it would in the more usual case of referral before a merger is accomplished.

But, apart from the time taken to gear up the pro-competition mechanisms and the doubts about how the authorities will act, effectiveness of remedies primarily depends on the aptness of the analysis applied and the evidence brought to bear. I shall argue that there should be both a significant extension of the analysis typically made and a different approach to the search for, and use of, evidence. In what follows I first attempt to show how the approach advocated diverges from more conventional analysis, and then consider the evidence used so far in the competition authorities' analyses of the (stage) bus industry. These have concentrated principally on the issues of predation and, to a lesser extent, merger. I indicate my preferred line of development of evidence.

ANALYSIS TO UNDERPIN PRO-COMPETITIVE ACTION

Collusion, predation and merger have in common that they are moves designed to improve a firm's profit. Pro-competitive action by regulators is feasible to the extent that its effects on the prospective profits of incumbents and possible entrants is understood. A profit-oriented view of deregulation and the other changes wrought by the 1985 Act begins by considering what effect, if any, the Act had on incumbents' profits, and from that explains their motives in adopting particular moves in response.

Deregulation removed what was, after 50 years of operation, the currently binding constraint on entry. What entry would then occur would depend, first, on the remaining constraints on entry which now would become binding. This would simultaneously define the likelihood of entry and the incumbents' potential exposure to it. Second, the Act was multi-purpose. In particular, changes in subsidy would alter revenue prospects, and thus would affect ability and willingness to enter. A pro-competitive authority affects the emergence of competitors if by its actions it can alter the contemporary constraints on entry. To do this, it of course needs to know what they are. Further, entrants are motivated by profit, too. A competition authority must analyse their potential sources of profit. These might well imply that the entrant foresees shelter from further entry, for example, by an innovation in service. In practice, by the time an authority is in a position to act, entry conditions will have changed, either pro or con entry, and this will have to be taken into account. Also, the means to tackle some restraints on entry may lie outside a given authority's sphere of influence, so that it will have to consider whether action can be taken by other authorities.

In effect, therefore, the model of the pro-competition authority presented here is of managing a transition to more competitive conditions in an industry. I would argue that this is a correct view of how such authorities discharge their obligations. Of course, one could argue that the correct aim is simply to seek out and remove all barriers forthwith. Entry would then principally depend on the profits foreseen to be obtainable from innovations: for example, supplying new routes, using new means to increase labour productivity and so lowering costs, etc. But the authorities cannot achieve all this at once. In choosing what to do, they have to perform what is fundamentally a cost–benefit test, asking: what will be the effect of a proposed change on the welfare of the parties involved, including producers, consumers, and other third parties? Pro-competition authorities do, in practice, apply such criteria, at least implicitly. The arguments in the present paper are directed at the analytical requirements to predict outcomes of pro-competitive policy; they do not try to evaluate the outcomes of that policy. An analysis of the likelihood of entry is a necessary guide in choosing the reform or reforms to be undertaken.

Analysis must start with the White Paper (Department of Transport 1984). This announced the policy enacted in 1985. It was an unexpectedly radical document, even to those charged at the time with the task of writing policy alternatives. I would argue that those events must have reduced the value of incumbent firms, on average, both through prospective competition and through the greater uncertainty attaching to revenue streams in particular. But one would expect the extent of the reduction to vary widely, depending on the underlying remaining barriers to entry.

Conspicuous among the possible emerging constraints on entry were property rights over existing factors of production; for example, garage locations in areas where conversions of property to garage use are prevented or difficult. I have argued elsewhere (Beesley 1989a: 33–4) that not only were the underlying barriers to entry underestimated at the time of deregulation, but also concomitant changes in the 1985 policy, notably the changes in the scale of subsidy and its redistribution towards subsidizing fares, actually increased the barriers. Subsidy was decreased, as intended, overall, and became more dependent on fare discounts, travel passes, etc., organized by local authorities. These changes in subventions to 'commercial' operators have, I maintained, the effect of making more uncertain the prospective revenues which could be secured by entrants. Potential entrants also face, at the same time, obligations to run services for six weeks; this substantially increases the risk that the required revenue will be insufficient.

To the extent that the incumbents were exposed by deregulation, their logical response would be to seek to restore profits by appropriate action. The possible options facing a particular incumbent, after deregulation, for raising the firm's value were:

(a) contract bus output, and switch management and resources to other non-bus opportunities;
(b) innovate within the bus industry – that is, provide new services in the market and/or take advantage of new financial and organizational moves to reduce costs;
(c) act as a predator: for example, keep existing output levels at the same level until entry occurs, then react to eliminate competition by price cutting or other means, aiming to raise prices later sufficiently to compensate for the losses incurred;
(d) collude with other incumbents to raise the costs facing possible entrants or to reduce their revenue expectations, again in order to restore previous values;
(e) merge with other incumbents to create like effects.

The key feature of the analysis of options (c), (d) and (e) would be to show how profits were improved by that choice. Action to restore the effect of deregulation would then depend on dealing with the substitutive support for profit. In this framework, the moves must first be understood in terms of the disclosed barriers to entry, and secondly as providing the means to restore profits. Because the need to make a 'move' comes only from adverse shifts in barriers, one expects the emergence of a particular move to be related systematically to those shifts.

Agreements in restraint of trade are an explicit, organized manifestation of collusion. Collusion does not have to be enshrined in a formal agreement if discipline can be maintained without it. A formal agreement can be expected to pay off most in situations where the agreement itself constitutes the principal barrier (there is no better way of preventing competition). We would therefore expect restrictive practice agreements to emerge where the experience of competition after deregulation is most intense. There is a cost to firms in pursuing registration, and the agreement might well in the end be condemned and removed, but meanwhile there would be a gain to the participants. There is also the chance that, against most expectations, the Restrictive Trade Practices Court might condone the agreement. In this case, a secure barrier to entry would have been established.

Where predation occurs, one expects to find that there has been very little weakening of existing underlying barriers. A well-judged predation strategy means that entrants, in the end, can then always be repulsed, because incumbents' underlying grip on entry barriers has not been changed, and pre-deregulation profit is not much affected. Entry is, on this view, a mistaken judgement about the incumbents' sustainable position. Further, as the conditions emerging after deregulation come to be better appreciated by all parties, the evidence of predation can be expected to decrease, other things being equal.

Typically, the issues raised by a merger are viewed by the competition authorities as a trade-off between benefits of economies of scale and the detriments to competition from increased concentration. Deregulation in itself probably did little directly to promote divestiture of ownership. Privatization involved dramatic divestiture. It is understandable that re-merger, particularly with companies run by selected ex-colleagues, should be contemplated, and it is mergers between ex-NBC subsidiaries which have attracted most attention. But, whereas collusion and predation, if found, can be understood to have a fairly direct relationship to restoring profits, merger is a good deal more difficult to interpret.

The regulatory system has normally been assumed to have been a power-ful force in increasing the size of firms, because it paid to be big in bargaining with regulators, particularly about new and profitable routes, and it gave countervailing power in dealings with local authorities respons-ible for block subsidies. Increased firm size was reinforced by nationaliza-tion in 1968. Deregulation has removed that reason for firm scale, and block subsidies have also been removed; so the reasons for increasing firm scope now are elusive, unless it is a necessary condition for acquiring new property rights conferring shelter from entry. If an incumbent possesses an asset useful for restraining entry, he does not necessarily have to retain its initial scale in order to exploit it. For example, exploiting ownership of a favourably placed bus depot, in a town where planning restrictions discour-age conversions to bus depots, does not imply downstream ownership of bus operations. The most profitable course, other things being equal, will be to auction the scarce bus slots to rival bus companies. True, after the Act, there are still regulatory forces setting lower limits on firm scale. Routes still have to be organized for registration with authorities. Ownership of suffi-cient buses to serve the whole service proposed is still expected, and leasing facilities are as yet limited. There are constraints on contracting independ-ent drivers, which frustrate a devolved form of organization such as that found in the taxi and minibus trade, where firm sizes are very small indeed.[5] But all this hardly explains how profits are increased by mergers on the scale caught by the 1973 Act. A profit-oriented view would carefully scrutinize both the necessary relation between substituting administrative relations for market relations (that is, increasing firm scope) and possible economies, *and* the sources, if any, of increased deterrence to entry.

CONTRASTS WITH PREVIOUS ANALYSIS

Since the White Paper (Department of Transport 1984) economists have shown great interest in the welfare implications of the structure of the local bus industry. Their analyses have, in a neo-classical vein, examined the forms of competition, either expected (for example, Dodgson and Katsoulacos 1989), or observed (for example, Evans 1988). They have assumed that the nature of entry barriers in the new situation is known. My position is that they must be explored. The difference is well illustrated by Evans: 'We can expect large incumbents to defeat small challengers unless they are simultaneously challenged on too many routes' (p. 300). The thrust of the analysis advocated here is precisely to distinguish the entry conditions which will lead to many, not few, entrants, and thus to analyse the vulnerability of the 'large incumbents'. Again, Dodgson and Katsoulacos, in reviewing the period after 1986, say (on page 13): 'Of course, entry is by no means always deterred. The question is what form competition takes when it does occur.' Here the question is why it is or is not deterred.

This leads to a considerable difference in the views taken of the starting structure of the industry at deregulation. Incumbents entered the deregulated era with a 100 per cent market share, and many were large in relation to the local markets served. To many observers, size necessarily conveyed market power which would be used. The ability to exercise it has been seen (for example, by Gwilliam 1989) as the basis of the need for action by pro-competitive authorities. The present paper argues that the supposed power must be demonstrated, and not assumed.

But my principal difference from these approaches emerges in what is assumed about information. This paper is more Austrian in spirit than neo-classical. My view is that market developments reveal information. At any one time firms have inherited information, but they also generate it both by paying for it and by action in the market place. Very often, testing in the market is the only way in which supposed 'information' can be validated. A forthcoming event like deregulation changes the information set which underpins profit seeking. Specifically, in the case at hand, one has to keep an open mind about the appropriateness of incumbents' and potential entrants' stocks of information. There is no *a priori* reason to suppose that relevant information is necessarily biased towards incumbents in all aspects; entry may well be a function of disagreement about the 'facts' presented by the market place, and successful entry (in the sense of either sustained operation or selling out at a profit, for example, to an incumbent) may be a sign that the entrant was, in the event, in some sense better informed.[6]

Like the work already cited, the viewpoint adopted in this paper does depend on a firm's having a systematic preference for more profitable options. This makes the analysis vulnerable to assertions about motivation, particularly of incumbents. There are many reasons to believe that the profit motive before 1985 was weak, with cross-subsidy not only possible but a tacit condition of licences. For publicly owned operators, preserving market share may logically be preferred to profit. Experience of long-distance bus operations in the period after they were deregulated by the 1981 Act strongly points to NBC's pursuing a policy of market share maximization, with at best a low profit constraint (Beesley 1989). Non-profit motives may well have persisted after the 1985 Act, too, particularly among the larger municipals. But there have been recent moves to privatize further, as in the buyout of Yorkshire Rider and in the announcement of the plans for divestiture and privatization of the Scottish Bus Group, which justify the view that profit seeking is becoming more prevalent, and analysis based on it more apt. Moreover, the predictions which pro-competition agencies have to make are much simplified (and I would say more reliable) if profit-seeking behaviour is assumed. Any other assumption leads to impossibly complicated alternative possibilities for action by these agencies.

WHAT EVIDENCE SHOULD BE LOOKED FOR?

I have suggested that the appropriate framework in which to devise pro-competitive action is analysis of disclosure of, and changes in, entry barriers, and the logic of profit-restoring market moves by incumbents and profit seeking by entrants. Particular 'moves' such as collusion, predation and merger must be regarded as highly conditioned by entry barriers and prospective changes in them. Pro-competition authorities have to understand these implications and act accordingly, so far as their remit allows. The authorities' actions, however, are normally related to particular events – cases of alleged predation, discovery of collusion, or an individual merger. The need for evidence is therefore two-fold – to learn about changes in entry barriers in general, and to gather particular evidence about behaviour in individual cases, to be interpreted in the framework set out.

The natural approach to learning more about the nature and incidence of disclosed entry barriers is to explain the variance of actual experience of entry. That is possible. The stage bus industry was the subject of an intense information-gathering exercise by government during and after deregulation. This yields, *inter alia*, details of registration and deregistration of routes and their operating characteristics and the operators providing them. (The data are held at the Transport and Road Research Laboratory.) The details of operation have since been used in studies of the processes of competition, but not in the way proposed here. Unfortunately, the data had certain drawbacks (for example, there was no direct measurement of passenger miles) and their collection had to be abandoned, as too expensive, in

May 1988, leaving a relatively short period of 18 months in which post-deregulation markets could be observed. But the great advantage was the comprehensive locational detail, with local market areas separately observed. Indeed, the local bus industry approaches the ideal for cross-section study of contrasting firms' experiences – separate markets, but subject to very similar or controllable conditions in factor price inputs and production possibilities.

Surprisingly, no attempt appears to have been made to establish what light the evidence throws on differential entry conditions until recent work at the London Business School, from which some preliminary results are available. In the following paragraphs I report findings based on the data at the 63 counties level, which show the approach adopted and are sufficiently interesting to suggest that it is worth following up.[7]

The measure of variation in entry is necessarily crude. The available measure of output quantity was annualized mileage performed by 'entrants' as compared with 'incumbents' at May 1988. 'Entrants' are those appearing at May 1988, but not in the list at October 1986. The rest were deemed 'incumbents'. 'Entrants' thus include new firm formations and established firms entering from outside the county. 'Incumbents' are those surviving till 1988 in the county. Our measure of relative entry is the ratio (estimated by TRRL) of annualized mileage of 'entrants' to that of 'incumbents'. The weighted average ratio for all the 63 counties was 6.0 per cent. Annualized mileage included both 'commercial' and 'tendered' services. The way in which the records are kept makes it difficult to compare entries separately under these heads over time. The analysis could also be refined by analysis of 'turbulence' – from movement into and out of the lists at the four quarterly market dates between October 1986 and May 1987.

Table 11.1 lists counties with greater than average 'entry', and presents for them two further country-wide variables which are proxies for factors believed to have effects on entry: namely, population density and the initial concentration ratio enjoyed by incumbents at October 1986. The former could tend to pick up the factors that I suggested earlier may well inhibit entry in urban areas; and the latter picks up the notion of incumbent power to deter entrants. Population density is measured by population at 1985 divided by area in square kilometres. Concentration is measured, again crudely, as the percentage of the total annualized mileage performed in the county by the top three firms in October 1986. The grand average population density is 0.43, and average concentration was 76.0 per cent.

Of the 21 counties, 17 have less than average densities, and 5 have higher than average concentration. So the crude figures suggest that neither hypothesis can be rejected. There is support for the 'differentially high barriers to entry in urban areas' hypothesis. That high initial concentration damped down entry (or the reverse, that low concentration 'encouraged' entry) is also quite possible. So far, then, we cannot say how far these ideas may be opposed. The high initial concentration may be affecting the outcomes directly, or through an association of high concentration with high underlying barriers to entry, which have tended to persist since deregulation. The search for systematic explanations should go on; and in this respect it is very important that further observations should be made and should be directed to the basic idea of learning from variance of entry.

The figures also throw some light on the notion, canvassed earlier, that collusion, as manifested in registered agreements, is mainly to be thought of as representing a relative lack of incumbent control over entry barriers. We may first examine the 115 agreements registered with OFT, described above. The listings[8] include 113 companies in total. All but three of these are bilateral, involving only two companies; the three involve three companies each. Tracing the agreements between companies, however, discloses that most are to be found as clusters of agreements; that is, groups of companies have agreements in common. The distribution of agreements in these clusters, and the number of companies involved in each, is shown in Table 11.2.

Thus nearly two-thirds of registered agreements are found in three clusters; one accounts for 36 per cent. There is a low incidence of isolated agreements involving just two companies and no others (eight agreements).

Table 11.1 Counties experiencing greater than average entry 1986–8

	Annualized mileage: entrants as % of incumbents 1988	*Population density: persons per square kilometre*	*Concentration of initial incumbents: % of annualized mileage held by 3 largest operators, 1986*
Cleveland	12.4	0.96	90.7
Durham	10.7	0.25	66.8
North Yorkshire	7.0	0.08	70.6
Buckinghamshire	6.4	0.32	70.9
Essex	53.9	0.41	64.4
Hampshire	14.7	0.40	52.2
Isle of Wight	6.1	0.32	97.6
Kent	8.5	0.40	62.2
Oxfordshire	17.2	0.22	71.4
Surrey	6.5	0.60	70.1
West Sussex	6.5	0.35	75.1
Cornwall	9.5	0.12	74.3
Dorset	9.6	0.24	80.7
Somerset	6.9	0.13	78.4
Shropshire	6.7	0.11	69.8
Greater Manchester	16.0	2.01	69.8
Lancashire	11.8	0.45	51.0
Dyfed	8.6	0.06	50.8
Dumfries and Galloway	11.3	0.02	69.7
Highland	10.3	0.01	77.1
Islands	11.5	0.01	36.2

Table 11.2 115 agreements registered with OFT: distribution to clusters

29 companies have 41 agreements in one cluster
13 companies have 17 agreements in one cluster
15 companies have 17 agreements in one cluster
5 companies have 5 agreements in one cluster
6 companies have 5 agreements in one cluster
5 companies have 4 agreements in one cluster
3 companies have 3 agreements in one cluster
12 companies in 3 clusters have 3 in each cluster (9 agreements)
9 companies in 3 clusters have 2 in each cluster (6 agreements)
16 companies in 8 clusters have 1 in each cluster (8 agreements)
Total companies, 113; total agreements 115

Source: OFT: Agreements as at 1988.

While there can be other explanations of the clusters, such as persistence of arrangements existing before deregulation, this distribution lends support to the view that collusion must be systematic, involving mutual reinforcement, if it is to be useful as a means of supporting profits. It is also noticeable that the largest cluster is concentrated in the south east of the country (involving principally companies in the home counties near London). As Table 11.1 shows, seven of the counties with relatively extensive entry are in that area. The second cluster is concentrated in Lancashire, and the third in Wales, which may well also have experienced above average entry.

OFT AND MMC ANALYSIS

Pro-competition authorities have, however, so far proceeded without analysis along the lines suggested. This is in part because their action has to follow specific complaints or references. We have, so far, the analysis presented by OFT in considering predation cases, and that by MMC in one merger case. Let us consider what has emerged. For predation, it is useful to take the Highlands case, since the analysis in it is characteristic of OFT's procedures, and this is the case before the MMC, which will therefore have to make its own reappraisal of the arguments.

OFT explains that, in assessing whether a firm's behaviour is predatory, the Office considers three factors:

(a) whether the structure and characteristics of the market are such as to make predation feasible;
(b) the relationship between revenues and costs; and
(c) evidence on the motives and intention at the time, including relevant evidence about its behaviour in other markets.[9]

OFT states first that predation must be profit-oriented. It

involves the deliberate acceptance of losses in the short run, so that enhanced profits can be earned in the long term by raising prices above

the competitive level. Several conditions are necessary if predatory behaviour is to be feasible. The predator must have market power and the
ability to finance losses for the time necessary, whether through cash
reserves, better financing or cross-subsidy from other markets or products. There must also be barriers to entry in the market so that, once
competition is eliminated, prices can be raised above the competitive
level so as to more than compensate for the period of losses, without
attracting new entrants. (p. 37)

The first basic problem with this view, from the viewpoint adopted in this
paper, is that it is unclear what is deemed to be happening to barriers in
the subject market. Unless something has shifted in favour of entrants in the
first place, they will only enter because of different views on relevant
information, or simply because they are mistaken. But if something *has*
happened to barriers to encourage entry, how can predation (or any other
behaviour) restore the barriers to yield the previously enjoyed levels of
profit? In other words, the notion of 'satisfactory' or 'restored' profit levels
requires an examination of whether barriers have been shifted or not. The
uncertainty on the issue of barriers is shown in the discussion at 5.10 (p. 38)
where no decision is made on what, if any, 'barriers to entry remain'.

The Office shows that the incumbents' behaviour indicates exploitation
of monopoly power (elasticity in the market is observed at greater than -1).
The question what, if anything, deregulation did to entry barriers is
bypassed, in favour of assuming that information is distributed asymmetric-
ally in favour of the incumbent, Highland. 'Asymmetry is likely to be very
important in the bus industry where 50 years of regulation have conditioned
operators to accept a lack of direct competition, so that new entrants are
likely to be unsure about how existing operators will respond to new
competition' (p. 38). In fact, however, entry did occur; and, as explained
earlier, 50 years of regulation also can create asymmetry in favour of newcomers. Also 'existing operators have an incentive to build up a reputation
for toughness in the face of competition to deter new entrants'. Again one
must, on this view, have entry (unexplained) to be able to take predatory
action to deter further entrants; and whether this is a feasible tactic depends
on how many and how widespread threats of entry are, which again
depends on showing what entry barriers exist.

The remaining argument on feasibility basically concerns Highland's
access to funds to finance the presumptive losses, and raises very reasonably
the question whether this availability was a part of the Scottish Bus Group's
tactics leading up to privatization. In any case, reserves might well be
allocated to it at privatization. (Why prospective shareholders would toler-
ate funds being used in this way is not explained; but there certainly are
arguments that high, preserved market share is comforting to backers.) But
these considerations are peripheral; we can grant that *any* 'predatory'
behaviour must be fundable.

OFT's further arguments concern the second and third of its criteria. But before we tackle those it must be noted that, having finally nailed its colours (correctly) to the 'improvement of profit' mast, OFT has simply not produced the evidence to show that there *was* compensating profit. To do so is inherently difficult, of course, and this raises the whole question how 'monopoly profit' is demonstrated. Conventional measures of rates of profit on book assets are highly contentious, but defensible measures from the economist's standpoint require observations in which the firm itself is valued by market processes.[10] These are probably not practicable in many bus company cases; and in the case at hand there was no mechanism for valuation, because at the relevant time Highland was part of a nationalized industry.

This means that all the usable evidence concerns revenue/cost margins and the wider question of 'predatory intent'. OFT's position on the first is the reasonable one that, whereas pricing below relevant (avoidable) costs is evidence of predatory intent because establishing the acceptance of losses, that intent may still be consistent with pricing above such costs. In the Highland case, the evidence was that the first condition could not be demonstrated unequivocally, so the argument shifted to evidence of predatory intent. On this, OFT did find evidence: of undercutting rather than matching fares, of increasing total mileage, and of systematic running of duplicates as responses to entry.[11] The conduct is also shown to be exceptional. Highland did not pursue similar tactics elsewhere; so a concentration on a single competitor was intended.

The case, alongside the proceeding ones, has helped to define what will henceforth be regarded as predatory behaviour. The upshot is strongly reminiscent of US legal attitudes to predation: that there must be shown to be an intent to monopolize, recognized by a set of different market tactics including pricing directed at a particular competitor; this amounts to conduct in breach of the Sherman Act. However, remedies and enforcement in the UK are quite different from those in the US. If MMC concurs with OFT, no doubt MMC will require as its remedy an undertaking from the 'guilty' party to desist. The subsequent enforcement mechanism is not regarded as particularly effective; that is one of the reasons why the procedures under the Competition Act 1980 are being reviewed. Though 'objectionable' behaviour is unclear, it is not certain that the signals thrown up by the mechanism will be much heeded. I suggest below what should be a more effective remedy and enforcement procedure. However, the basic criticism of both analysis and implied remedy remain: effective remedies require more attention to possible change in barriers and prospective profitability for entrants.

At the time of writing, an appraisal of MMC's analysis of bus merger has to refer to the Badgerline Holdings case (MMC 1989). It took the normal form of search for detriments from loss of competitive rivalry to be set against benefits (chiefly cost savings) attending the merger. The conclusions (pp. 34–41) were that there was 'no material loss of competition' in commercial services in the relevant area, the County of Avon and part of surrounding counties, but that on contract services the majority report found that there were 'serious detriments' to competition, sufficient to outweigh the benefits (chiefly joint procurement and administrative cost savings of £500,000 a year). A minority disagreed with the judgement on contract services, holding that at a time of significantly changing ownership, competition and regulation, and when competition from other bus services seemed to be sharpening, the direct loss of independent contractors would not offset the benefits (pp. 43–4). Undertakings in accordance with the majority opinion were accepted by the company; they were chiefly on maintenance of tendering by the two subsidiaries and restrictions on registering a service after a deregistration had led the local authority to ask for tendered contracts for a route (Appendix 7.2).

The Commission was thus unable to reconcile two different views held by members of its panel about the future prospects for competition. If the required analysis of entry barriers and their shifts had been done, it might have been possible to resolve the differences. There is, in fact, some evidence in the report which bears on entry. Thus, though the possible significance of geographical variation in entry was not canvassed, the report notes very few attempts at entry in the Midland West (City line) territory, covering Bristol at its centre, whereas in Badgerline's territory outside Bristol, the urban sector, the company 'faced competition in all or part of 52 of its routes' (p. 9). Apparently, too, the Commission did not consider the implication for entry control of ownership of bus depots. City line owned four depots for maintenance and storage of vehicles, three of them under licence from Bristol City Council. BL owned one such site in central Bristol. A major reason for merging, carrying by far the greatest tangible cash benefit, was to realize the value of this and other sites. 'Ways of realising this potential are being investigated (by the companies) and may include the merger of BL Bristol and City line engineering workshops on to a single site.'[12] This was not therefore an analysis based on tracing profitable moves and their likely effect on entry. Because entry prospects were not analysed one also cannot judge how far the 'undertakings' were or were not necessary.[13]

CONCLUSIONS

The title of this paper is perhaps a rather portentous one, since the incidence of the phenomena described is quantitatively uncertain. But they properly concern pro-competitive authorities. The paper has suggested that collusion, predation and merger should be analysed in a common framework, in which entry barrier change and its implications for profit seeking by incumbents and entrants are central. If pro-competition authorities wish to encourage competition, entry barriers have to be revealed, and entrants' likely reactions predicted. Official analysis so far has shown reluctance to adopt this framework. I have suggested several kinds of barriers which deregulation has disclosed or collateral policies have encouraged: for example, garage locations and other property rights, requirements to enter for at least six weeks, operation of subsidy, and restrictions on sub-contracting to drivers. Systematic work on reasons for differential entry by location would doubtless produce more.

The case for a profit-oriented approach which emphasizes prediction of those conditions under which entry will occur is at its strongest during the remedy and enforcement phases of pro-competitive control. Enforcement is the more effective if based on ideas about what profitable moves are open to incumbents, particularly if they substitute one kind of response to increased competitive pressure for another. Remedies must be directed at entry barriers; this may well lie outside the direct competence of the pro-competition authorities. If so, the appropriate remedies to remove a barrier must be devised. Legislative change may also be needed. For example, to attack the constraint on entry implied by the requirements to register routes would require reform of the 1985 Act.

With respect to the three types of 'move' considered here, particular conclusions about their importance, and for enforcement, follow from the earlier arguments. Collusion is significant because it is a barrier in itself. Present legislation is quite capable of removing known cases, and indeed will do so. Interest passes to increasing the penalties for failure to register, as envisaged in current legislative proposals. There remain considerable doubts about the incidence of predation, since the conditions for it cannot be firmly demonstrated. However, if, as I argue, improvement of profit is a key issue, it seems to me that the current focus on the incumbent's experience is misplaced. The more important issue is the effect on entrants' profits – does the behaviour held to be typical of predation cause losses such as to prevent competition by any interest from recurring? (In reality, new competitors, whether the original interest or not, have usually been remarkably persistent in maintaining their presence even in the most clear-cut cases of predatory behaviour.) For enforcement, this means giving the injured party the right to have profits restored. Moreover, to demonstrate relevant effects on profits is much more feasible in the case of the small entrant than in that of the presumptively larger incumbent. To make enforcement more vigorous, one could borrow from the US book and allow triple damages if, on the balance of evidence, losses are shown. The mechanism would then not act while alleged 'predation' was occurring, but afterwards. In other words, relief for individual losers would be postponed; but the strategy of intending predators would become prospectively very much more costly than it is now; thus the incidence of predation would fall. This kind of reform, again, must await the outcome of the current review of UK procedures under the Competition Act.

As we have seen earlier, MMC is now returning to the merger issue with the Portsmouth and South Yorkshire cases. The fact that no non-contiguous mergers have been referred, and that these are contiguous mergers, may well indicate that an anti-monoploy rule of thumb is emerging, intended to draw the line at contiguous mergers where the interests involved are substantial. In the UK each case is decided afresh, on its merits, so the prospects for establishing the rule of thumb permanently are doubtful. Because, as also argued earlier, in the absence of entry constraints the profit-oriented reasons for merger are in any case negligible, establishing such a rule of thumb would do no harm. It might well catch cases in which the merger is a necessary condition for establishing new barriers through the joint acquisition of property rights.

With merger, I would expect the current mechanisms to be adequate, if the lack of advance notification of mergers can be overcome. As we saw earlier, MMC's actions on a reference after merging are in practice more constrained than on a proposed merger. OFT, like any other observer, has to pick up intelligence about proposed mergers from trade sources. Bus companies are relatively small, and substantial merger activity can take place without the need for Stock Exchange permission. However, the main requirement is the reorientation of analysis argued for earlier when cases are referred. With proper attention to, and removal of, critical barriers to entry in buses, the pay-off to divestiture rather than merger will substantially increase. As we saw, this will often require action outside the present scope of the pro-competitive agencies. But unless the pay-offs to merger are analysed, no effective action can be expected.

NOTES

1 *Journal of Transport Economics and Policy*, 26(3), September 1990.
2 Badgerline Holdings and Midland Red West Holdings. MMC, March 1989.
3 Press release, DTI, February 1990.
4 Statement in two press releases, 24 August and 8 September.
5 Probably less than one cab's output in the London taxi trade.
6 As I have pointed out elsewhere (Beesley 1989), interpretation of events since 1985 has been highly coloured by the basic position taken by authors about markets on the one hand, and planning on the other; and there is little sign of either side shifting its position. To commentators of my persuasion, the central aim of deregulation was to substitute freer market tests for planning decisions; that is, a heavy emphasis was placed on the view that planners' information (and that of their allies, the incumbents) was faulty or seriously incomplete. Many other commentators would dispute this.
7 Some 400 areas are distinguished in the data bank, but the short length of time for observation, some 18 months in total only, had to be traded off against subdivision to market areas. Hence our adoption of the 63 county level. It is a great pity that at least aggregate data such as are used here were not continued beyond May 1988!
8 Kindly supplied by OFT, to whom thanks are due.
9 OFT 1989; the analysis covers pages 37–43.
10 As for example in Tobin's 'q', in which the presence of monopoly rents is detected by comparing the value of a company as valued on stock markets with measures of the reproducible cost of its assets.

11 A fourth, curious ground is added. The (Highland) 'business plan suggests a willingness to sustain losses providing competition is not expected to continue for too much longer' (p. 42). This indeed sounds as if the incumbent was very unsure that his tactics would succeed, and throws doubt on his supposed abilities and intent!

12 Page 18. The property stood at £3 m in the balance sheet. We are not told what the market valuation was, or whether it was different from the book values.

13 The analysis in this paragraph follows my paper to the Thredbo Conference (Beesley 1989b).

REFERENCES

Beesley, M. E. (1989a) *UK Experience with Freight and Passenger Deregulation*, ECMT Round Table, no. 83, Paris.

——— (1989b) 'Bus deregulation: lessons from the UK', *International Conference on Competition and Ownership of Bus and Coach Services*, Thredbo, NSW.

Department of Transport (1984) *Buses*, CMND 9300, H.M. Stationery Office.

Dodgson, J. S. and Y. Katsoulacos (1989): 'Competition, contestability and predation: the economics of competition in deregulated bus markets', *International Conference on Competition and Ownership of Bus and Coach Services*. Thredbo, NSW.

Evans, A. (1988) 'Hereford: A case study of bus deregulation', *Journal of Transport Economics and Policy*, vol. 22, no. 3, September.

Gwilliam, K. M. (1989) 'Setting the market free. Deregulation of the bus industry', *Journal of Transport Economics and Policy*, vol. 23, no. 1, January.

Monopolies and Mergers Commission (1989) *Badgerline Holdings Ltd. and Midland Red West Holdings Ltd.*, CM 595, H.M. Stationery Office.

Office of Fair Trading (1988) *Review of Restrictive Trade Practices Policy*, CM 331, H.M. Stationery Office.

——— (1989) *Highland Scottish Omnibuses Ltd.*

12 Commitment, sunk costs, and entry to the airline industry[1]

Reflections on experience

M.E. Beesley

INTRODUCTION

Industrial economics has enjoyed a new popularity since the mid-1970s. Primarily because of practical issues raised by deregulation in the USA, notably of telecommunications, airlines and road haulage, academic minds have become engaged in more rigorous statements about the welfare implications of changes in rules affecting these industries. Dixit (1982) found that 'Research in oligopoly theory has grown so rapidly that ... I can highlight only one or two important new developments.' Two developments were, indeed, in issues central to regulation. One was 'strategic behaviour yielding credible threats of entry deterrence'; the other was 'the strategic specification of conditions under which all such threats are empty'. A special case of this was the conditions for 'contestable markets' specified in the work of Baumol *et al.* (1981).

These developments pursued further the logic of interaction between firms in a given industry under neo-classical assumptions, including free access to unchanging technology and known demand. Because the policy issues spurring the discussion also had to deal with regulatory bodies, there was a revival and further development of older ideas incorporating views on regulators' regulations with firms and the franchising of (particularly 'natural') monopoly. Prominent contributors were Williamson and Demsetz. Demsetz, apart from doing much to further the idea of competition *for* a monopoly, also focused attention on the shortcomings of entry barriers, as conventionally treated, as indicators of costs relevant in welfare analyses. Focusing on the costs of producing the physical output of an existing firm or industry is 'much too narrow a view', tending to treat as 'unproductive costs that will be incurred to create and maintain a good reputation, to bear risks of innovation, and to build a scale of operations appropriate to the economical servicing of consumer demands; and it tends to neglect the incentives that will face future decision makers as a result of today's policy.' (Demsetz 1982: 56).

It is generally agreed that this upswell of theorizing breeds a great scepticism about, and at the same time a desire for, empirical work which might underpin it, and which would help to fill a gap described by Demsetz: 'There exist neither cost benefit analyses nor market given prices by which to weight (the implied) tradeoffs.' Dixit concludes that: 'In practice careful empirical work in a specific context will have to be undertaken before we can say whether an industry is contestable and sustainable, and decide whether and what regulatory attention it deserves' (Dixit 1982: 16). This chapter aims to contribute some empirical work: its concentration on one case is perhaps justified by the complexity of the ideas needing illumination. One of the favourite examples put forward by contestable market theorists is airlines, so it is appropriate that the case concerns entry of a newly formed airline, London Express Aviation Ltd, to the United Kingdom charter market. The author is currently chairman, and has been involved in its activities since the very early days of conception. It turns out that the experience is particularly useful for considering three problems: the definition of what are often referred to as 'committed' or 'sunk costs', the specification of empirical work on the relation between revealed profits and industry structure, and some important aspects of a regulator's task in intervention.

Much of the new work centres on the challenge an entrant offers to an incumbent operator. Gilbert Ponsonby showed his interest in this relationship as early as 1935, when he was concerned with the impact of road haulage on railway financing. He was profoundly sceptical about claims that railway's assets such as tunnels, embankments, rolling stock and so on are, under the stress of competition, abandoned 'wastefully' (Ponsonby 1935: 449); he detected the danger of waste rather in protection from competition. A re-reading of this article, fifty years on, makes one cautious about claiming progress for economic insights in this area. Gilbert showed by example how to further economic arguments by a knowledge of the operations of industry. This chapter tries to follow his practice.

THE IDEAS NEEDING ILLUMINATION

It is convenient to follow Dixit's survey of 'Recent developments in oligopoly theory' (Dixit 1982: 12) in dividing this work into two lines: (1) strategic behaviour yielding credible threats to deter entry and (2) specification of conditions in which all threats are empty, so that the prospect of entry disciplines any incumbent or incumbents.

Credible threats to deter

The first line, associated with Eaton and Lipsey (1979), Schelling (1960), Salop (1979) and others, involves the 'commitment' of costs, of which 'sunk capacity' is the most frequently cited example (Dixit 1982: 13). The essential characteristics of this committed/sunk capacity are:

It has to be 'known (and made known)' to all 'prior to an entrant's decision' (ibid., p. 13).

It is irreversible: 'sunk capacity only serves the purpose of deterrence if it *cannot* be costlessly liquidated' (p. 13) – that is, turned back into cash. Because the commitment is costly, to the extent that the costs exist they lower the prospective profit of the incumbent below the monopoly level (ibid., pp. 13, 14).

Concrete examples of the costs are not given; they are to be recognized by these characteristics, and by some that they *cannot* have: for example, costs for which an 'efficient resale market' exists cannot be 'sunk' or 'committed' (ibid., p. 13).

In this family of models, firms are supposed to look forward to a series of moves in a sequential game, in which they foresee alternative sequences of moves which affect the profits to be made. Being an entrant firm, or being an incumbent firm, is a position in the game. The game tree is 'solved', that is worked out in a manner to yield an equilibrium solution by, as Dixit puts it, 'solving the game backwards' (Dixit 1982: 12), namely foreseeing the moves and rolling them back to the point of decision. This yields a view, *ex ante*, of what is required for rational profit-seeking behaviour. Commitment, associated with the incumbent, is shown to be favourable in terms of the value of the game.

When all threats are empty

The second line, particularly associated with the work of Baumol and Willig, concentrates on *ex post* entry conditions, working back to constraints on the behaviour of a monopolistic incumbent. How sunk costs are defined in this work is not stated in Dixit. We can, however, turn to Baumol and Willig (1981). They distinguish the following:

> Such costs depend on the passage of time: 'In the long run all sunk costs are zero' (ibid., p. 405); that is, they are positive for a period, then do not have to be incurred afterwards.
>
> They 'cannot be eliminated, even by total cessation of production' (ibid., p. 406). If production is to be started, they have to be incurred. Thereafter, as with the first line of argument, they cannot be liquidated.

Here also, concrete examples are sparse. They are not the same as 'fixed costs', which might be avoidable, for example, by renting assets from another market on short contracts, though they might well be embodied in items of equipment to the extent that the market supplying (renting) the equipment itself reflected 'sunk costs' of commitment to *that* market. This gives relevance to the state of markets other than that which is the immediate focus of analysis. Airlines are cited as an example of possible low 'sunk' costs on a particular route (i.e., a city-pair market) where there are fixed costs which 'may considerably exceed their sunk costs', because aircraft, for example, may be used in other city-pair markets (Baumol and Willig 1981: 407).

This line of argument concludes that, in the absence of 'sunk costs', incumbency does not confer advantage. The implication is that if 'sunk costs' are present, a rational firm prefers the position of incumbent to that of entrant. This is again to state the proposition in the way required for rational profit making – as applying to a decision taken *ex ante*.

Commitment and time

It is important to note that in both these lines of thought there are two essential ideas, namely the commitment of outlays (costs) *and* the passage of time. Time converts an *ex ante* commitment of outlays to an *ex post* irrelevance. Both elements, however, are foreseen by potential participants.

Perhaps the term 'commitment' is the better description, largely because of the confusion likely to be generated by simply using the term 'sunk costs'. Economics students have long been taught to regard 'sunk costs' as identical with 'bygones', and of no account. An example of a standard textbook treatment is Call and Holahan (1983: 148): 'Historical cost ... is irrelevant to an economist. It is a sunk cost and does not measure an opportunity cost.' This is the first and last appearance of the term in a book which devotes 150 pages to competition, monopoly and oligopoly. Sunk costs are certainly not irrelevant in Baumol and Willig (1981): indeed their presence or absence determines whether deviations from competitive outcomes are predicted. In particular, single occupation of a market by a firm, even when it enjoys scale economies, is not sufficient to give supernormal profits if sunk costs are absent.

In the work we are concerned with commitment, and its place in a sequence of postulated events also distinguishes an 'incumbent', I, from an 'entrant', E, or would-be entrant. An incumbent is a firm which commits first. What is committed is seen as non-repeatable and non-recoverable; that is, it does not have to be committed again, even in the long run, and it cannot be recouped.

Incumbent rights are marketable

A difficulty emerges at this point, because users of the models wish, apart from the distinction between I and E just noted, to keep all the normal neoclassical assumptions in place – including known technology, demand and factor prices which all firms are deemed to face. The difficulty is that the postulated relationship between I and E introduces a distinction between firms, and there is, in principle, no good reason to eliminate the working of another market, namely, that for the sale of the distinction – the right to commit – uniquely identified with I. As we noted, the work cited certainly appeals to the markets in which I and E hire their factors, to help to explain limits on 'sunk' or 'committed' costs. Looking to the capital market in particular, clearly a profitable opportunity will command its price. Is it useful, one might wonder, so to limit one's reference to market forces?

It seems to me that the sensible answer is 'no', in the kinds of problems which industrial economists have to face. Indeed, the postulated relation between I and E is akin to any other factor which gives an advantage to an ownership interest – for example, property rights of various forms. In classical discussions of barriers to entry, it would be an example of what Bain (1956) termed an 'absolute' barrier to entry, one unique to the interest possessing it. An implication of such an implicit property right is that the committed costs in question can always be liquidated (i.e. turned back into cash), so long as they convey an equivalent value realizable by selling the right, or the firm owning it, and there is competition for that right or firm. An incumbent can always sell out, perhaps to a would-be entrant, and get at least the value put in, so long as nothing else changes in the mean-time. Since most discussions *assume* no distinction between the incumbent and 'entrant' or other firms except the 'property right', a competitive bid is always possible, and is reflected in the value of the incumbent. This is the equivalent, of course, to Demsetz's competitive bids for a monopoly franchise. So one condition named above for recognition of sunk costs – the inability to liquidate – is a consequence of *assuming* a restricted role for markets.[2]

In models which emphasize competitive moves in the market, committed costs are essential to the argument because they constitute the basis of the credible threat posed by the incumbent. After commitment, it is always rational (i.e. tending to greatest profit) for the incumbent to ignore committed costs, whereas an entrant, not having committed, cannot ignore them. The precise amount of the costs is important. For example, in a solution with equilibrium in which firms do not enter, Dixit (1982: 13) derives this condition:

$$Pm - Pd > c > Pd - Pw,$$

where
   Pm = prospective monopoly profits (to the incumbent);
   Pd = profits split with an entrant, that is with duopoly agreement;
    c = committed costs; and
   Pw = profits with war between the firms.

On the other hand, as we have seen, markets are contestable in the Baumol and Willig line of argument when committed costs are absent, or at least (though this is not explicit) 'small'. (If *any* element of committed costs would suffice to make a market non-contestable, the theory is surely empty, as Shepherd (1984) points out.) For reasons such as this, it seems useful to nail down 'committed costs' in a real case.

Generation and protection of profit

The brief review will have sufficed also to indicate the connection to ideas about how profits are initially generated, and then realized and protected. One can hardly get far without considering how the incumbent comes to have the privilege, and he or she is most easily thought of as a potential or possible monopolist. Since time is also necessarily involved, we must be concerned with such issues as 'first mover advantages' (Williamson 1975) and, more broadly, with the Schumpeterian line of thought about profits as the return on innovation. The practical question to ask is: what is the relative importance of committed costs compared with other possible sources of profit generation and shelter from competition? This is the more important because the new industrial economics has sharply reduced the importance of costs, other than committed ones, in explaining outcomes. But the older ideas about what constitutes a firm's access to competitive shelters (e.g. various means of acquiring rights denied to others) have not been abolished. Thus the interest here is in the role of committed costs in creating a new market in what we have termed a 'property right', as emphasized by Austrian thought, and the related problem of the characteristics of that market, once established – the problem emphasized by Demsetz (1982).

At this point, the reader will see that we have already collected a number of points which will prove onerous in empirical work. 'Committed' (sunk) costs, if to be relevant, strictly concern *both* and *ex ante* and an *ex post* concept. I and E are presumably to be thought of as members of an industry, the usual unit for empirical work, which by definition is conducted after the event. Reconstruction of the relevant aspects of the costs may be difficult. We also have to define the relation in time of the critical costs. Further, if it is viewed as a property right, the commitment is only one of a number of possibilities in the category of 'absolute' cost advantage. Other examples are possession of unique natural resources and uncopiable techniques. These have been notoriously difficult to pin down in empirical work. This work has, instead, concentrated on what have been taken to be measurable independent items like scale, underpinned by technology assumed to be commonly available to all members of the industry.

A final preliminary remark: empirical work on revealed profit rates in industries has traditionally relied, as we saw, on defining an exogenous set of variables (e.g. scale economies) which could be set up as independent variables, to explain profit arising from ensuing monopolistic or oligopolistic behaviour. The new industrial economics stresses the interactions between firms and regards the 'game' as an essential part of the explanation. As Eaton and Lipsey put it:

> Bain observed that we cannot meaningfully analyse oligopoly problems without explicit attention to the possibility of entry. Dixit (1980) and Eaton and Lipsey (1979) observe that as long as we insist on commit-

ment and not threat, we cannot analyse entry deterrence without an underlying model of oligopoly.

(Eaton and Lipsey 1981: 594)

However, those who use tests of hypotheses that centre on commitment would wish, presumably, to substitute measures of 'committed cost' as independent discriminators. Is this a move from the frying pan into the fire? Will it prove difficult, even perhaps impossible, to be sure, *ex post*, what they (the sunk or committed costs) really were at the relevant times? No doubt the answer will vary from industry to industry, but one must begin somewhere.

THE ENTRY OF LONDON EXPRESS AVIATION ('LEX')

London Express Aviation Ltd owed its origin principally to overinvestment in Singapore hotels. About the end of 1983, a need to generate more tourist flights to Singapore was becoming an urgent concern of the Singapore Tourist Board. The national airline, Singapore International Airways (SIA), was preoccupied in seeking to develop in other directions, notably in the business market (it had the youngest 747 fleet in the world and was taking delivery of its stretched upper-deck 747s), and on the UK route it was looking for more permissions for scheduled flights.[3] But Changi Airport, Singapore, had a close connection with Schipol, Amsterdam, and it was suggested that a recent director of Schipol might attempt to set up a fresh UK–Singapore operation. Intending to move to the UK in any event, he duly did so, and the idea of LEX was started in January 1984.

This was a very risky venture. Its success required several key moves to fall into place. Finance had to be sought; the 'happy band of brothers', as I christened the original group, had little more to give than their own time and small outlays. So, from the beginning, the LEX idea depended on a market test – would the capital be invested? Prospective investors had to work out for themselves the basic questions – how and why should LEX generate satisfactory profits? What profit would be satisfactory? How and over what period could the resources be assembled to get into the air? What would be competitors' reactions? Similar questions preoccupied the 'happy band'.

London/Singapore is a highly regulated city-pair air market, in which the authorities of both countries work within an understanding of how much scheduled capacity is appropriate, and applications, with appropriate hearings, must be made for any increases in capacity. British Airways, SIA and British Caledonian supplied most UK–Singapore flights. The key authority for LEX was the Civil Aviation Authority (CAA) at its home base, London. The CAA had just entered what most observers thought of as a new, liberal phase in regulation. Its July 1984 statement of policy on airline competition, while retaining a traditional concern for favouring British airline development, put a new stress on flexibility, 'competition as a valuable mechanism', the benefits of potential substitution, wider choice, innovation and a determination to counter 'abuse of a dominant position' (CAA 1984: 28). LEX would have to apply formally to operate a long-distance regular charter business. Its financial fitness to do so had to be shown, as well as its economic justification.

Scope in the charter market

The LEX 'concept', from an early stage, was to carve a niche in the charter market – that is, selling to inclusive tour operators selling package holidays – by offering a specialist long-distance operation, with emphasis on the quality of the passenger's experience in starting and completing his or her holiday. No such service existed on the London–Singapore route. LEX decided, also early on, that it would enter with one 747 aircraft, which would make two round trips a week to Singapore. At prices to tour operators likely to be achievable, as noted below, this would be insufficient use of an aircraft. A second route was needed. So a once-a-week flight to Hong Kong was, prospectively, added. Existing competition for the tour operators' custom was the rear cabin economy seats of the scheduled airlines. The best estimate was that the numbers of package tours sold in each market was small: to Singapore it was only about 11,000 in 1984, but LEX would be aiming to sell about 44,000 seats a year to tour operators. Package tours from UK to Hong Kong were about 60–70,000 in 1984. There, LEX would be selling 22,000 a year.

Tour operators would be wooed with the following arguments. The tour market is ripe for a growth in longer-distance packages, particularly to South-East Asia. It is worth while to cultivate this on a year-round basis. LEX will offer – as no other airline can – a contract in which an unchanging number of seats over the year can be purchased at a price more suitable for a longer-term continuous commitment than has been available hitherto. LEX will be innovative in its concentration on the holiday-maker, as opposed to the mixed clientele of the scheduled carriers.[4] It was deemed necessary, early on, to announce the range of seat prices at which LEX was aiming, some £100 or so below going prices paid by the tour operators. Schedule operators, it was realized, had a strict hierarchy of selling to their several client groups; selling to tour operators yielded a smaller margin than a sale of the same seat to non-package tour travellers, so they needed to vary the quantities made available to tour operators.

Hopes and fears

LEX revenues were foreseen as arising from seat sales, from drinks and duty-free sales to passengers en route, and from entertainments.[5] Costs would depend principally on the type of 747 used, the fuel consumed, the need to ensure back-up in a one-plane operation, and maintenance. If things went well, investors could, it was thought, make profits in the first full year of operation; this is most unusual for an airline start-up. One essential reason for this optimism was the expected nature of the contract with the tour operators. This would call for down payments, and in charter operations for cash for seats in advance, as the ultimate UK holiday-maker pays in advance. After a successful start, the airline would have a negative working capital, because the main bills, such as those for fuel, would be payable in arrears.

So the airline's 'happy band' and prospective investors had the possibility of high returns if successful. The main doubts concerned the willingness of tour operators to take a new form of contract for a specialist operation, the granting of permission to fly, and how the costs would in fact compare with budget. The prospect was sufficiently attractive to arouse a great deal of interest among venture capital sources; after some false starts, investors were found. At the time of writing, a CAA licence to Singapore and Hong Kong has been granted, conditional on satisfactory financial prospects being shown at the time of takeoff (this will mean principally that the tour operators are signed up as expected). Singapore's permission has likewise been granted; and Hong Kong's is in process of consideration. The expected takeoff date is mid-1986.

THE ROLE OF COMMITTED COSTS

We are not essentially concerned here with the foolhardiness or wisdom of this venture. Suffice it to say that it justified its risks to the capital market, and considerable sums have already been spent. The narrative just given concentrates on the points most germane to the issue of assessing the role of 'committed' costs. First, what are the candidates in LEX's expected cost stream?

Equity funds needed

It is worth noting at the outset that time is indeed of the essence, and that calculations are inseparable from considerations of risk. To make its expected profit levels, LEX has to generate in the first year of operation about £28 million of revenue. When airborne, its profits (we hope) begin to flow. Until then, cash is expended in anticipation of takeoff. Total equity funds needed are estimated at about £1.2 million at minimum. Whatever they turn out to be, they are regarded as the funds at risk – the sum needed to satisfy creditors in the unhappy event of a failure. The picturesque term for this, among venture capitalists, is 'the hole'. But at the beginning all costs were prospective. What was the rationalization for the 'hole'?

Essentially, the exercise was one of imagining not success, which causes the outflow concerned either to disappear or to be covered by inflow, but of imagining failure. The difficulty was that failure could, in principle, happen at any time in the future with, of course, differing probabilities. But one could not persuade anyone, whether an investor or the CAA, with an infinitude of possible calculations. So everyone concerned agreed (with remarkably little dissension) that there were, in anticipation, really three critical phases.

The first would be up to the point when permissions were granted. Then it would be practicable to get the principal resources in place – the plane, the seven aircrew needed, and the support staff. A second point of measurement was therefore at the point of maximum outlay before takeoff, or, strictly, at the point at which the revenues were expected to begin.

If LEX got to that point, tour operator contracts must necessarily, by then, be in place, so cash inflow would be positive thereafter. A third point of measurement had to cover the possibility that tour operators had, after all, themselves mistaken the market and wished to abort the contracts. The consensus view was that this would occur, if it did at all, about three or four months after commencement of operations. Then the cash inflows would have to be assumed zero, since, though the defections of the tour operators would not necessarily mean the end for LEX, as other work might be substituted and tour operators would have cancellation penalties, these cash flows would possibly not be realizable in time. So the calculation focused on the unavoidable outlays which would then be faced by LEX. These would depend on LEX's contracts for payments. Prominent items would be inescapable payments for the plane, which would depend on the deal originally struck, and severance pay for crew.

Our first estimates of these, sequential, quantities were: for the first phase £50,000 for the second £350,000, and for the third £800,000, totalling £1.2 million. These, and other cost estimates, were part of the approved financial plans put to CAA, whose principal test of 'financial fitness' is ability to fund losses on failure. In total they were the centrepiece of efforts to raise capital: and, though CAA were willing to consider part in the form of subordinated loan, they were, for all intents and purposes, the risk capital. Which, if any, of these outlays qualifies for the description 'committed costs', and with what qualifications were they 'committed'?

Costs of LEX and of a competitor

Most of the items in LEX's expected cash outflows would be faced by any competitor to LEX. Ideas about the relative importance of different items varied as time went on, but certainly some of the first two sums would undoubtedly be incurred, as a necessary part of a start-up contemplated by any entrant. Would they necessarily not be repeated, however? Not entirely, because, while much of the first tranche of £50,000 was spent in the process of getting licence permissions (lawyers' fees being prominent), the licences themselves were for a limited period. (It is unusual for charter operators to receive more than one year's licence.) Some small proportion (say one-fifth) would recur in the renewed licences for further operation.

LEX is a new airline. If a potential entrant/competitor were to be established, its costs of a start-up would conceivably be less than the costs facing LEX if it employed aircrew who were familiar with the routes and who had low or zero opportunity cost. Or its opportunity costs might equal or even exceed those of LEX. Indeed, any points about the state of an entrant's contracts, markets, etc. would be pertinent. This bears in particular on the second tranche of LEX outlay, the £350,000. However, to postulate asymmetry between the incumbent (LEX) and a newcomer is to breach the simplified assumptions of the formal reasoning. Hence there is a need, if models are to be richer, to think in terms of a range of would-be entrants, ranged in order of potential committed costs.

But for a start-up competitor, the LEX costs are, certainly, a reasonable estimate. In sum, therefore, in the LEX case, £40–50,000 plus £350,000 is a reasonable first estimate of the non-repeatable costs. Whether LEX will liquidate them depends on its success. Investors think of that set of problems – as do the 'happy band' – under the head of risks incurred to obtain revenue. But £800,000 is a wholly contingent sum regarded as an integral part of the money at risk.

Experienced venturers

A considerable period of interchange with possible investors shows clearly why this merging of outlays, actual and contingent, occurs. The more experienced a venture capitalist is, the more he or she will be thinking in terms of a portfolio of ventures. The only practicable way to manage these on a forward-looking basis seems to be to decide on a total budget to be made up of ventures, so the quantity to be devoted at maximum to a given venture has to be decided after consideration of its possible return. The judgement includes, as a leading argument, the management time likely to be incurred if a venture is funded, because the scarce resource is the ability to assess the many ventures for possible inclusion.

The £800,000, indeed, poses quite a difficult problem of interpretation. There is no doubt that its availability is essential to the prospective incumbent LEX. CAA insists on it; under UK regulations it is an unavoidable condition of entry. But CAA's rules merely reflect experience of airline financing. It is very probable that such a sum would have been deemed necessary by any experienced supplier of capital (i.e. one with knowledge of this industry). Of course, there *may* be capital suppliers who are ignorant: but, even if there are, the 'happy band' could not have dealt with them. An interesting speculation is whether, without CAA's constraints, an entrant such as LEX might have found uninformed supplies of capital.

However, if we assume the given state of information to include the same considerations for all potential suppliers, does the possibility of losing

£800,000 exist for both LEX and a future entrant? Unless we assume another difference between LEX and an entrant – that LEX has better management and foresight – LEX's failure would not be due to an entrant's action; it would show that LEX was wrong in its assessment of profit. If LEX succeeds, the £800,000 is not paid out.

A new entry might, of course, in the event cause losses to LEX. But 'committed costs' are defined as being independent of entrants' actions; specifically, they are the items that make war between LEX and an entrant illogical. So it emerges that the biggest element in the capital at risk cannot be fitted into the received idea of 'committed' costs. It is, in reality, a hedge against a defect in knowledge of the market: that tour operators are mistaken in their assessment of demand. CAA's permission to LEX was, indeed, based principally on their willingness to let the market be tested by production of tour operators' contracts with LEX.

The scale of 'committed' costs

We have, therefore, some costs in LEX which fit the requirements of 'committed' cost. Many other costs are known with fair certainty, though their scale has varied from time to time, as experience has been gained. To set them against the identified 'commitments', one needs, in principle, some discounted present value equivalent, because they fall for payment at various points in time. This raises another problem. What discount rate should be used? In fact, I estimate that the average offer of finance to LEX was the equivalent of about 60–70 per cent per annum on the sums to be advanced. In view of the risk/return profile, this seemed reasonable; but, in any case, one cannot avoid the market opinion.[6]

Because of the extremely high discount rates, it is a fair approximation to ignore discounting by considering 'committed' costs in relation to the first year outlays. Proportionate outlays in the first year were broken down as shown in Table 12.1 in earlier (end 1984) and later (autumn 1985) estimates.

On the basis of the autumn 1985 figures, our first estimate of £400,000 to £450,000 of non-renewable committed costs would represent about 1.6 per cent. Were there perhaps other parts of the costs in Table 12.1 which incorporated the essential elements of 'committal'? Since these costs represented potential contracts with a finite life, rarely more than one year, they would cease if production ceased. At any one time they would, however, have different contract lengths, and, because LEX was a newcomer, there could in principle have been start-up elements in them. If the contracts were not as favourable to LEX as they might have been, because of reflected ignorance on LEX's part, or a premium for risks in dealing with LEX, the extra costs are not legitimate 'committed costs', since they must be regarded as denoting a possible difference between LEX's ability to hire factors and those of an entrant. It is impossible to guess what start-up elements there

Table 12.1 LEX: estimates of outlays in first year

	End 1984 %	Autumn 1985 %
Fuel	49.5	42.8
Aircraft leasing costs	12.1	11.6
Insurance	1.7	4.2
Maintenance	11.3	20.8
Other aircraft running costs	7.7	3.0
Personnel costs (crew)	6.9	5.7
Passenger costs (catering etc.)	4.9	6.2
Other, mainly administrative, costs	5.9	5.8
	100.0	100.1

might have been in all the ongoing contracts, but it is very possible that they are negligible. There were, in any case, other reasons for discerning some elements giving LEX a windfall advantage. This was particularly true of fuel costs, which were negotiated on favourable terms.

The basic reason for this was that LEX proposed to operate from Stansted, the underused third London airport. This proposal was of no particular consequence to LEX's customers, the tour operators; but it was significant for fuel companies, because, by happy accident, LEX represented the first prospective 747 operation from Stansted. Fuel companies had invested in anticipation of expansion in air traffic there, encouraged by bullish government policy statements and no doubt wishing to get first-mover advantage of their own. LEX represented a useful potential customer, and the final contract reflected this.

We may also usefully note that the proposition, advanced earlier, that 'committed' costs can always be liquidated if circumstances affecting profitability do not change, was confirmed by LEX's experience in obtaining substitute investors as time went on. Each successive newcomer paid more for his or her equity interest. Those retiring recouped their risked money to that point. Meanwhile LEX's prospects were essentially unaltered. It was simply that the stages of entry were being accomplished.

LEX'S 'COMMITTED COSTS' AND ENTRY CONDITIONS

The two tranches of cost we have most clearly identified as approximating to 'committed' costs are essentially concerned with assembling the operation and commissioning the start-up. These outlays were almost wholly for personal services. The 1.6 per cent of first-year outlays is, by any reckoning, a small relative cost to contemplate as a major determinant of market structure. In one sense, this confirms the intuition that the airline business is easily entered. It is true, for example, that the very important physical plant – the 747 – is represented by a small cost element – about 11 or 12 per cent of a year's costs. Much more important are straightforward avoidable variable costs such as fuel and maintenance. But contemplation of the relation of these items gives a misleading view of the problems of entry as seen by all those concerned.

For one thing, as we have already seen, investors must be more concerned with the amount potentially at risk. For another, the committed cash flows in the pre-flying period do not exhaust the possible impact on timing of outlays. The outstanding example in LEX's case is the lease-or-buy decision on the aircraft. The essential distinction, to simplify drastically, is the trade-off between the later cash outlays and the assumption of risk of fluctuation in the resale value of the asset. 'Leasing' does not involve this risk, 'buying' does. The investors had options to proceed in either fashion. Leasing would, it appeared, be quite likely to produce a large front-end outlay for LEX before the take-off date; buying, a smaller one. One might regard the hypothetical loss involved in aborting a contract, if adopted, as a 'committed' cost, its size and incidence again depending on the investors' attitude to taking the risks of ownership.

Degrees of risk

That the investors had this option also underlines a problem in defining the amount of 'capital' involved in LEX's entry. We have seen that the equity was clearly identified at £1.2 million. But standing alongside this, and viewed quite separately, were a possible ownership commitment (by the investors in a plane) and other guarantees prospectively required by those who might become LEX's creditors. For example, the Singapore authorities required a substantial bond to cover repatriation of passengers in the event of LEX's failure.

But these items were subject to a quite different order of risk from that associated with LEX equity. A 747 is saleable, largely because of the exceptional efforts airlines make (also reflected in LEX's cash flows) to keep aircraft capable of generating a constant flow of service, and because of expected world growth in air traffic. On the bond, the postulated circumstances would coincide with the very contingency foreseen by the required £800,000 element, and LEX argued (unsuccessfully) to the Singapore authorities that the bond was redundant. However, what matters most in costs is not the size of the licensing authorities' requirements, but how the relevant markets view the risk. It was expected that this particular 'risk' could be covered at quite low financing cost.

Note, however, that the ability to negotiate this had to be present. In effect, the investors were making a *series* of investments relevant to LEX, one of which (the £1.2 million) was conspicuously a high-risk/high-return prospect, while others, equally essential but not appearing in LEX's capital accounts, involved low-risk and low net financing cost.

Defences against competition

We classified a postulated *relationship* between committed costs faced by
the incumbent and not by the entrant as an 'absolute' advantage akin to a
unique property right. How did this aspect compare with other sources of
potential shelter from competition for LEX? In posing this question we are,
again, making the account of entry richer than that contemplated by the
formal models outlined earlier, in which no difference between I and E was
permitted beyond I's commitment. LEX was certainly proposing to compete in a market already, to an undefined degree, inhabited by competition.
The competitors also sold to tour operators, in quantities described earlier.
However, scheduled operators had, in effect, a hierarchy of markets in
which they sold seats, from business travel to the 'bucket shops' – though
it was generally thought that on the Singapore and Hong Kong routes
relatively few seats were remaindered in that lower-price market.

The result was that the scheduled airlines offered tour operators a highly
variable supply through the year, with relatively small lead time on quantities, at prices varying widely according to the season – that is, in response to
scheduled airlines' perceptions of the chances of selling in the higher-priced
markets.[7] LEX by contrast offered a new form of contract – fixed capacity
for a year and a stable, lower price. It aimed, in effect, to become a base-load
plant for the tour operators to use; but at the same time it offered, as
remarked earlier, substantial product differentiation through specialization.

There was little doubt in anyone's mind – CAA's, investors' or the 'happy
band's' – that profit principally depended on persuading tour operators
themselves to make, in effect, a small innovation. Nevertheless, the possibility of retaliation by scheduled airlines was also seen as important. One
scheduled operator at least thought it worthwhile to try to prevent LEX
from entering by using the regulatory process; this perhaps indicates that a
certain threat was perceived. British Airways opposed LEX's CAA application. Their principal grounds for doing so were said to be the danger, as
they saw it, of LEX's being a 'bucket shop' operator. They were not
convinced by, or chose not to respond to, LEX's counterargument that it
was a potential base-load carrier for tour operators and therefore, if bucket
shop sales did emerge, it would be others, not LEX, who would wish to
'remainder' in that market. CAA responded by making it a condition of
LEX's operation that its capacity be devoted exclusively to inclusive tour
operators.

LEX and its investors thought the risk of effective retaliation quite small,
for these reasons: because of the nature of its prospective contracts with
tour operators, because it was not big enough (yet) to warrant a serious
price-cutting move by the majors, and for the time-honoured reason of the
difficulty of limiting a price cut to LEX's customers only. Perhaps it would
be truer to say that *this* risk, though clearly present, weighed far less in
LEX's strategy than the risks that regulatory permissions would not be

secured or would come late, the unforeseeable difficulties of actually getting a plane to UK register standard at the time wanted and at an acceptable price, and many other matters inseparable from the start-up. It would, in sum, be correct to say that the *monetary* outlays in the form of recognizable 'committed' costs were negligible, but the problems of which they were symptoms certainly were not. On the contrary, behind relatively small amounts there lurked many of the main perceived risks. This must surely be true in practice of most entries. Entrants *hope* to be able to accumulate as many items of 'shelter' from competition as they can, but much of their risk is in the sheer complexity of 'getting the act together', and this is common to all entries.

Prospects if LEX succeeds

Suppose LEX is successful, and creates its looked-for profits. It certainly will aim to grow, for reasons both of cost and revenue. Costs per seat delivered to tour operators will fall with the addition of a second plane, and again – though less certainly – with a third. The chief reason will probably be lower payment to hedge the risk of breakdown, obviously great for a single-plane operation. (That risk also helps to account for the change in the insurance costs recorded in Table 12.1. As options were explored, it became clear that it had to be covered in essence by sharing in other airlines' cover for a fee.) On the revenue side, LEX would seek to build on its expertise in serving the inclusive tour market to add new long-distance charter routes. It would repeat its initial strategy of offering a new form of contract and generating entirely new charter destination markets on routes already served by scheduled airlines, remaining a competitor for customers for a small part only of their capacity.

Imitators will certainly arise if LEX succeeds. Its established business then will depend on retaining first-mover advantage with tour operators. But airplane capacity can serve many markets, including freight; LEX will doubtless diversify. Retaliation by specific competitors will be similarly diverse. The logic of firm-on-firm commitment and threat must, to be useful to LEX's strategy, be applied to several possible confrontations, more or less simultaneously. In fact, though recognized, these issues occupy the thoughts of LEX's Board much less often than the many other considerations affecting the profit stream. It should, however, be added that the basic economic messages about factors likely to affect that stream, and in particular the reflections on the nature of profit, on avoiding losing it by unwise deals, and on its protection against competition, have proved not only useful, but critical, particularly in the acid test of ability to attract risk capital.

COMMITTED COSTS, EMPIRICAL WORK, AND REGULATION

How far can we use estimates of 'committed' costs as an independent explanation in empirical work on different profit experience in industries?

Our findings about their scale in LEX's case is of less importance than their closer definition. Contestable market theorists were, so far as our evidence goes, right to think of the airline market as 'contestable' in their terms. That LEX's move is an entry by a whole firm, rather than an extension by an established airline into a new route, makes it an even better example. (In the case of an established airline, observed ease of entry to a particular route rather begs important questions about the ability of airline firms to maintain operations in a set of markets.)

But LEX's experience emphasizes the importance of recognizing the 'property right' element in the notion of 'committed' costs. For LEX, to be able to be the incumbent was crucial. The cost of getting to this position was one of a set of factors of which it was intending to take advantage in order to make the considerable risks of entry tolerable – that is, attractive to risk capital. Those risks included retaliation of established operators, but mostly, on the cost side, concerned the sheer logistical problems of production which must be overcome in time to take advantage of the shelters in prospect.

Capital at risk, *ex ante*, includes but greatly exceeds 'committed' costs. The shelters derived partly from entry to regulated scheduled markets and partly from innovation of service and, more important, of type of contract offered to tour operators. The moral for empirical work on profits is that the idea of 'committed' costs as critical would be very difficult to pin down in quantitative terms, and even more so in retrospect. It is highly unlikely that they can be treated as an exogenous factor affecting all relevant firms, but of themselves they may well be of less moment than a class of factors to which they also belong, the family of 'absolute' barriers to entry.

One-sided disclosure forced by regulation

Finally, we may comment on the significance of the LEX experience for regulation. All regulators must be concerned to predict the effect of entry on consumer welfare, and usually on other interests within the industry. As Stephen Glaister and I have shown (Beesley and Glaister 1983) in the context of taxis – an industry with a structure highly favourable to competition – the regulator's empirical task is formidably difficult. To say the least, the problems of taxis seem far less complex than those of airlines. It is very hard to see how an attempt to measure, and analyse the consequences of, 'committed' costs is likely to make the task more tractable.

The particular British context of LEX's case is, however, of a more general interest. British airline regulation is notably 'liberal' when compared with its European counterparts; indeed, it might well claim to be next to the United States. It certainly embraces the idea of using entry to improve welfare, as the July 1984 statement shows (CAA 1984). This was shown in its willingness to let LEX's application for entry be tested by LEX's ability to persuade tour operators to agree forward contracts to fill the plane. But one aspect of the procedure, quite unavoidable in any regulatory system, which allows challenge by interests in the industry to an intending entrant, did have possibly serious implications.

CAA procedure allows any airline holding relevant licences (not just anyone) to object to a proposed entry. In LEX's case, British Airways did so, but no other scheduled airline incumbents. An objector is entitled to a formal hearing to contest the case. As we saw earlier, in fact the objection by British Airways was narrowly based, and it was not pursued with great vigour (BA did not appeal against the CAA's decision in LEX's favour). From LEX's point of view, the potentially harmful point of the formal procedures was not its cost or any likelihood of failure, because most people who were well informed on CAA's past performance thought that LEX would get its permissions in some form.

Rather, the point was the enforced disclosure, early in LEX's career, of its plan to enter. At a relatively trifling cost, any incumbent could by objecting gain a great deal of information about the intentions of a potential competitor. Once the objection was entered, public disclosure – that is, disclosure to all incumbents – was inevitable. This opens up to incumbents defensive strategies that would be difficult to come by otherwise. The general context of potential threats is known to air operators, of course, but disclosure of a specific proposition gives knowledge of quite a different order, and in principle makes it possible to mount many kinds of pre-emptive strategies and to aim them with reasonable accuracy. Whether it would be worth while for the scheduled operators to do so, one cannot of course say, without equal knowledge about them; and the inquiry process gave no help at all to LEX towards gaining this. So that process appeared to LEX to be anti-competitive in two related ways – it helped scheduled operators to formulate precise responses, and it leaked knowledge too early, from LEX's point of view, without compensatory gains.

At LEX, we felt very strongly the discrepancy between the effects of the objections process and the extremely helpful attitude of the CAA officials. CAA operates its financial fitness screening, for example, in a way which we found scrupulously fair and, indeed, helpful in our own plans. Best of all, it was quite private, with safeguards to prevent leaks to scheduled incumbents. As a result of our experience, it seems to me that it is quite practicable to operate a check on would-be entrants which would not seriously deter entry, but quite impossible to have an objections procedure which would not weaken the main weapon possessed by a new entrant or potential incumbent – a monopoly of knowledge of its own intentions. An important part of a movement from an illiberal to a 'liberal' regulatory system should be to drop procedures changing the state of information in a way harmful to would-be entrants.

NOTES

1 This chapter first appeared as a paper in the *Journal of Transport Economics and Policy*, May, 1986, 173–90. I am indebted to Peter Gist and Simon Domberger for very helpful comments.
2 The market may of course be 'thin', subject to various limitations affecting liquidation. But to assume the absence of *any* market seems implausible.
3 It succeeded in getting three flights a week into Manchester in 1985.
4 Product innovations originally proposed included a casino operator on the top deck, fruit machines and banking aboard.
5 Freight to Singapore was later added.
6 The offers came in several differently structured packages, some involving long-term equity holdings, some emphasizing a quick return of principal. The 60–70 per cent relates to those for which the calculation of an overall discount rate is feasible, that is those on which the original sum advanced was returned.
7 One typical tour operator was known to have paid, in the 1984/5 season, prices to a scheduled operator for seats involving a difference of 40 per cent between low season and peak.

REFERENCES

Bain, J.S. (1956) *Barriers to New Competition*, Cambridge, Mass.: Harvard University Press.
Baumol, W.J. and Willig, R.D. (1981) *Contestable Markets and the Theory of Industry Structure*, San Diego: Harcourt Brace Jovanovich.
Beesley, M.E. and Glaister, S. (1983) 'Information for regulating: the case of taxis', *Economic Journal* 93, 594–615.
Call, S.T. and Holahan, W.L. (1983) *Microeconomics*, 2nd edn, Belmont: Wadsworth.
Civil Aviation Authority (1984) *Airline Competition Policy. Final Report*, London: HMSO.
Demsetz, H. (1982) 'Barriers to entry', *American Economic Review* 72 (1), March, 47–57.
Dixit, A. (1980) 'The role of investment in entry deterrence', *Economic Journal* 90, March, 95–106.
——(1982) 'Recent developments in oligopoly theory', *American Economic Review* 72 (1), May, 12–18.
Eaton, B and Lipsey R. (1979) 'The theory of market preemption: the persistence of excess capacity and monopoly in growing spatial markets', *Economica* XC, March, 149–58.
——(1981) 'Capital, commitment and entry equilibrium', *Bell Journal of Economics* 12, autumn, 593–604.
Ponsonby, Gilbert J. (1935) 'An aspect of competition in transport', *Economica* II, new series, November.
Salop, S. (1979) 'Strategic entry deterrence', *American Economic Review Proceedings*, 69, May, 335–8.
Schelling, Thomas (1960) *The Strategy of Conflict*, Cambridge, Mass.: Harvard University Press.
Shepherd, W.G. (1984) 'Contestability versus competition', *American Economic Review* 74 (4), September, 572–87.
Williamson, O.E. (1975) *Markets and Hierarchies; Analysis and Antitrust Implications: A Study of the Economics of Internal Organization*, New York: Free Press.

13 UK experience with freight and passenger regulation[1]

M.E. Beesley

INTRODUCTION

The UK formally deregulated road freight transport in the Act of 1968, long-distance road passenger transport in the Act of 1981 and short-distance passenger operations, outside London, in the Act of 1985. The economic connotation of 'deregulation' in these Acts was to lift pre-existing restraints on the quantity of service offered, that is to drop governmental control on the entry of new capacity, whether by incumbent operators or newcomers, and on the exit of capacity. Regulation of the quality of operations, for example with respect to obligations concerning safety, were retained and indeed, in some respects, enhanced. Entry, expansion and contraction were thus to be left to the market, with some (relatively minor) increase in costs of operation.

The UK has gained the reputation of being a pioneer of deregulation in these industries. It is natural to pose the basic question – is this a model other countries should follow? At base, this is a policy-oriented cost–benefit (CBA) problem. Have the measures resulted in gains to UK consumers and producers? How have resource costs changed? This chapter does not set out a formal answer to these questions; it does, however, attempt to draw conclusions of use to those contemplating similar policy changes.

No one, indeed, has been able to satisfactorily answer the cost–benefit question so far, for three principal reasons. First, the problem requires specifying the base case, namely, what would have happened, without deregulation, over the period needed to parallel the adjustment to the new conditions? This is difficult in itself but, more importantly, requires the passage of sufficient time for the expected effects of deregulation to work out. As we shall see, this is particularly relevant for assessing the 1985 Act's reform of short-distance passenger transport. Second, the anticipated benefits from freeing market entry and exit via deregulation are importantly those of innovation in services offered and in ways of reorganizing the means of, and inputs to, production. This requires analysis involving redefining both the demand and supply conditions to be associated with deregulation, always a formidably difficult technical problem to handle. Third, there will in practice be gainers and losers from the change, requiring quite complicated tracing of effects on particular groups. Certainly, the UK's policy changes were not the result of economists' calculations. As elsewhere, they were political moves, in response to beliefs in the inherent superiority of free markets.

But the particular difficulties in assessing UK experience are of rather more interest than economists' problems of CBA measurement. Deregulation was in no case a single policy move. In freight, the 1968 Act, passed by a Labour government at that time focusing on efficiency in the UK economy, had been preceded by policies which greatly affected its impact. In 1953, a Conservative government had started the process of denationalizing its inherited freight interests (we would today call this 'privatization'). To sell the vehicles, it had to offer them with no effective constraints on how they could be used, that is with the most liberal form of licence to operate then available: an A licence. Despite this, by 1956 they were left with 16,000 vehicles from the original 46,000 they hoped to dispose of.

From the point of view of a potential entrant, in the years 1953–6 the formal quantity licensing system, though in operation, had relatively little significance. The entrant's purchase of a government right (a sustainable permission to operate the licence) was of little independent value when he or she knew that thousands of such rights were potentially available to others. After 1956, the government stopped sales and retained the remaining vehicles in three public sector concerns. These were born of failing the acid test of the market value of their assets. They were to be weak sellers overhanging large parts of the total freight market for many years to come. Indeed, not until 1982, when the Conservative government sold the remaining freight interests in the form of a management buy-out, was this position to be radically altered. Judging the impact of the 1968 Act is, accordingly, made more difficult.

Passenger transport, as we shall see, illustrates another difficulty in pinning down the independent effect of deregulation. This concerns Sherlock Holmes-like questions about 'the dog that did not bark in the night'. The 1980 Act, while lifting quantity restrictions on long-distance passenger transport, did not address the question of the entry barriers which might be disclosed when the formerly binding constraint – the quantity control – was relaxed. Also, analysis would normally proceed on the assumption that the firms concerned would be concerned to maximize the gain to the owners. As I argue later (see p. 202), that would have been an inaccurate description of the motivation of the dominant firm, the National Bus Company (NBC), which was left at that time intact to carry on as a public enterprise.

Moreover, in the case of the 1985 Act, three government policies were, in fact, being pursued simultaneously – deregulation, reduction of government subsidy to the industry and privatization of NBC, following the perceived success of the National Freight Company's privatization. In this case also, as we shall see, the question of disclosed constraints on entry is significant. Any account of UK deregulation must inevitably take on board these collateral events, or omissions, in policy making.

ROAD FREIGHT TRANSPORT

The regime between 1953 and 1968

The period between 1953 and 1968 is interesting because of the light it throws on the unintended consequences of licensing, arising from its structure; and the bias to development of an industry which can be imparted by a licensing system. As the subsequent history shows, it took a considerable time for the newly 'freed' industry to modify these influences.

In the UK system, operated on a quasi-judicial basis, with calling of evidence before a commissioner and a judgement appeal mechanism, a great deal turned on where the burden of proof lay. If a would-be entrant applied for a licence, did he or she have to prove 'need' positively or was it the incumbents who had to show cause for refusal? The original 1953 Act, setting up quantity controls, had not been couched in a way meant to be highly restrictive, but the onus of proof was placed on the would-be entrant. In practice, the regulation system, focusing on the evidence for need and working by case law, built up to be a formidable barrier to entry in the period to 1953. The principal reason given for refusals of applications for licences was their prospective abstraction of traffic from rail. It was, of course, inherently easier for railways to bring evidence of 'abstraction' than for applicants to argue that they would be innovators in market services. The requirement to show 'need' for extra capacity was, however, easier for incumbent road operators to meet than for newcomers, imparting a systematic bias in favour of growth of firm size in haulage. One unintended consequence of this protection for incumbents was a build-up of financially unviable capacity in the nationalized road freight concern, no doubt aided by the *realpolitik* of public ownership, as shown by the relative failure to find buyers after 1953.

However, the 1953 Act, in providing for denationalization of long-distance haulage, also shifted the burden of proof to the incumbents. The first-level regulators, the Area Traffic Commissioners, accordingly granted many more licences. Though the appellate mechanism reversed over 60 per cent of the cases which were taken up, there is little doubt that capacity substantially increased, while still biasing the outcomes in favour of larger road haulage incumbents. (I recall that a cynical view at the time was that reversals on appeal were needed for the regulatory system to ensure its own survival!) But the more significant effect was the bias imparted to the organization of road haulage.

Brian Bayliss's 1971 study, to which all observers of UK freight haulage are indebted, showed the following changes in licences granted between

1953 and 1968. The meaning of the respective licence classes in organizational terms is as follows: A licences allowed carriage for hire and reward, necessary to build an independent multi-customer haulage operation; B licences allowed unrestricted carriage of one's own goods, plus a highly restricted operation in the hire and reward mode. The A contract licence applied to stand-alone haulage operators who contracted their capacity to a single customer for at least one year. A contract licences were the operationally disintegrated versions of the biggest licence category, C, which allowed haulage of one's own goods exclusively in one's own vehicles. Table 13.1 adapts Bayliss's Table 29.

Haulage on own account in one's own vehicle was always exempt from licensing constraints (licences were given as of right) and was the principal means to avoid the restrictions imposed on the professional haulier. C licences included vehicles of all sizes, including vans; hence the discrepancy between per cent of vehicles and per cent of ton mileage performed in these categories. B contract, A contract and A licence categories had higher proportions of big vehicles, in that order, with a marked gap between C, B and the A types (compare columns (iii) and (vi) of Table 13.1). Thus the device to evade licensing, the C licence, still increased slightly in the more liberal post-1953 conditions. Increasing use was also made of the device to put independent hauliers under contract to carry one's goods, as shown in the rapid growth of A contract licences. Own-account carriage was presumably made less costly by these means.

A further way to reduce the cost of own-account carriage was to carry for others. This was also increasing over the period, as indicated by the B licence growth. However, the possible development of this mode of operation to become a specialized haulier for others involved a transition from B to (unrestricted) A licences. This was blocked by Tribunal decisions (compare p. 37 and Table 31 of Bayliss 1971). After 1956, A licences remained

Table 13.1 Types of licence held by goods vehicles, Great Britain

Licence class	1953 %	1968 %	Numbers held	% changes numbers	% ton mileage in GB performed by road
(i)	(ii)	(iii)	(iv)	(v) 1953–68	(vi) 1968
A	9.3	7.1	104,000	+16	35.2
B	6.1	6.5	96,000	+63	13.2
A Contract	1.0	2.6	38,000	+300	11.8
C	83.5	83.8	1,236,000	+55	60.2
		Total	1,474,000		

Source: Bayliss, Brian T. (1971) *The Small Firm in the Road Haulage Industry*, London: HMSO, pp. 24 and 38. (*Note*: Table 29 appears to have an error in total vehicles recorded for 1968.)

hard to get directly, too. Organizationally, therefore, the influence of the system was to encourage the adaptation and rationalization of haulage of one's own goods in an integrated operation, which could, to a limited extent, take advantage of licensing loopholes to reduce costs. The carriage of goods for any customers as an unintegrated operation was markedly inhibited, as the small increase in A licences shows. As one would expect in these conditions, A licence vehicles commanded a scarcity premium, estimated in 1965 as £300 per ton unladen by the 1965 Geddes Report on *Carriers Licenscing*.[2]

Licensing authorities also showed their propensity to prefer more control to less during this period. B licences could be granted solely for hire and reward. Granting this type of licence rather than an A licence for hire and reward allowed the authorities to impose constraints on operations, in respect of distance or type of goods carried, for example. In the early years of the regulatory system, no such specialist hire and reward category had been evolved. Its use after 1953 was probably a reaction to the shift in the basic burden of proof: regulators felt that change in this industry should not be too precipitate. Evidence of this was that dealing with B licence appeals also occupied far more time in the appellate system than did A licences, it appears. Bayliss reports 1,049 B cases in the period from 1953 to 1968 as opposed to 622 A licence cases (cf. pp. 38–9), far more in proportion to their respective total number.

By the time formal controls on quantity were abolished in 1968, replacing the A, B and C licences with a single operator's licence concerning fitness to own vehicles, the industry had taken many opportunities to evade or adapt to the rules. The principal effects of the quantity control were, it was thought, to encourage integrated operation involving the carriage of one's own goods and, on the public haulier side, an increase in firm size. The former was much encouraged by exogenous factors also. The 1960s had seen the beginning of greater concern with packaging and distribution, of the notion of a manufacturer's responsibilities reaching to the customer's warehouse or retail outlet, with appropriate control and high service levels. Specialism of vehicles to fit particular distribution needs was growing fast also. A natural reaction was to identify control with the need to own vehicles.

On the other hand, the specialist haulier's concern was with building a business on negotiable property rights, particularly the scarce A licence. Haulage had developed as a local business, and the right to carry anywhere in the UK represented an important requisite for extending into national markets. The first UK motorway was opened in 1958, followed by the M1 London–Birmingham motorway in 1959. The prime question while licensing lasted was to combine the property rights to best advantage. Increasing firm size was one apparent result, though public haulage retained very large numbers of small operators, no doubt because small A licence holders retained the option to operate profitably without yielding ownership.

The effects of 1968 deregulation

It was widely expected that the 1968 Act would have considerable impacts on the industry, and that these would be apparent soon after the Act's provisions came fully into force in March 1970. The Act removed quantity control on the previously controlled vehicles of over 3.5 tons gross weight, and established an operator's licence, to be held by all who ran vehicles over that weight, whether operating for hire or reward or on own account. The operator's licence was principally directed to backing up the Act's quality control provisions, for example those concerning proper maintenance. Operators had to show their competence either by experience or formal qualifications by nominated examining bodies.

Reviewing this positive side of licensing in 1978, the Foster Report on Road Haulage Operators' Licensing[3] found that licensing authorities had interpreted the rules concerning quality in the following ways: the operator had to be a 'fit person', of 'good repute'. Although intended to be wide enough to include inquiring into the applicant operator's wider legal standing, in fact only direct breaches of the 1968 Act's own provisions were taken into account and even this varied by regulator. Drivers' hours and records had to be kept: 'all that a licensing authority can do here is to ensure that a suitable system has been devised'. But on overloading, the Committee could see no way in which evidence could then be brought to bear. There were, however, fairly effective ways in which the authority could ensure that maintenance provisions were adequate, and that there was a suitable operating centre in which to keep or park vehicles not in use. The Act also included a mandatory requirement to investigate an applicant's financial standing: the authorities had, however, found it 'impossible to check this meaningfully'. Some authorities did, however, hold inquisitions about applicants' forecasts of costs, rates, workloads, etc. which, the Committee concluded, in a few areas 'comes close to requiring an applicant to show proof of need – rather as in the old regime' (Foster Report 1979: 23). However, the Committee apparently did not regard this as a major surviving constraint on entry.

Curiously, the Committee did not speculate directly about the impact of the 1968 Act's quality provisions on the industry's behaviour. However, from its relatively mild proposals to make more effective the authorities' knowledge of operators' competences, and its concern that 'quality licensing should [not] become a means of protecting existing operators through the back door' (Foster Report 1979: 93), we can at least infer that the quality dimension had not been adversely affected by the Act's other changes, and may well have been improved by the positive measures. Thus the Geddes Committee's original judgement, when recommending the abolition of quantity licensing in 1965, that there was no causal link between quantity licensing and such parameters of quality as greater safety, was confirmed; the two types of control could be expected to function adequately side by side.

Expectations about the impact of abolishing quantity licensing on the economic dimensions of the industries' performance were much firmer. The Geddes Committee focused on its effect on raising the price of goods transport and, in particular, on the distinction between hire or reward, subject to licensing, and own-account operations, which were not. This induced inefficiency, it argued, because of inhibitions on gathering back-loads.[3] It was widely feared, it noted, that there would be adverse economic effects from removing quantity licensing, in particular that greater bank-ruptcies would contribute, alongside increased entry, to create greater 'instability' in the industry. Profit would fall; investment would be discouraged. Since, as noted above, licensing had caused sizes of haulage firms to increase, deregulation would reverse this trend.

In the event, the two principal inquests held after the change basically failed to demonstrate that there had been *any* such effects. (These inquests were, respectively, B.T. Bayliss's 'The road haulage industry since 1968', published in 1973,[4] and the Foster Committee's work already quoted.) On the principal alleged inefficiency – restrictions on own-account operations – the expectation was both that hire and reward operation would be widely substituted for own-account, that is firms having such operations would either disintegrate their in-house haulage or, alternatively, take on substantially more outside work, using the clearing-house mechanism to get back-loads (clearing houses, which had been a feature of the unregulated industry, had been severely curtailed afterwards, partly also because of nationalization of long-distance road haulage in 1947). It was also expected that the setting of a lower limit to the vehicle size requiring an operator's permit for operation would lead to evasion by substituting smaller lorries.

On the basis of careful sampling of public hauliers, former own-account (C licence) holders, and licence records to establish entry and exit over the period 1968 to 1971, Bayliss concluded the following:

1 A very small increase in tonnage was carried for others by mainly own-account operators. This amounted to less than 2 per cent of the total tonnage carried for others in 1971.
2 No evidence of a substantial number of exits of professional hauliers from the industry was found.
3 No measurable impact of deregulation was shown in profit margins, costs and charges and investment. If expectations of 'instability' were unfounded, so were the other assumed economic effects of regulation. There was no measurable reduction in firm size, and no evidence of behaviour to evade the impact of the weight limit on operators' licensing.

The later Foster Report did not dissent from these findings. Indeed, it confirmed some of them. 'Though, as in any healthy industry, some failures must occur, the impression we formed was that the industry was surprisingly stable' (Foster Report 1979: 34). Low or negative profits experienced in the mid-1970s were a function of the 'depressed national economy'

(Foster Report 1979: 36). The report's Table A 22 had shown that liquidation and bankruptcies had fluctuated between 1969 and 1976, reaching their lowest point in 1973, just before the first oil crisis. The report confirmed the very low incidence in own-account operators' total output of work done for others. The report's Table 4.3 records a percentage of turnover derived from hire and reward work which varied with fleet size, from 4.0 for 2–5 vehicles, to 6.5 for 21–100 vehicles, and 3.7 for a fleet of more than 100 vehicles. J.C. Cooper also confirmed Bayliss's earlier tonnage figures for hire and reward work, in a 1978 study.[5]

In part, these failures to detect any, or very little, measurable impact from deregulation were to be expected because of the previous history, recounted earlier, of the impact of 'privatization' and the growth of means of modifying the effect of quantity control. At the aggregate level, effects on costs, charges and profitability, if any, could not be disentangled from other factors governing the growth of demand and the supply of factors. But the failure to detect distortions on incentives within the industry is, at first sight, more puzzling. Specifically, there should have been a reversal of firm size in professional haulage if the leading incentive had been acquisition of licensed capacity; and there certainly should have been an observable correction of the preverse incentives to reject hire and reward in favour of own-account operations.

Contractual and organizational change

These judgements would, I think, be echoed by most economic commentators. My own interpretation of this lack of evidence runs along rather different lines, however. First, there is a tendency to expect the impacts of any major change such as deregulation to appear quite quickly. In fact, it is more realistic to expect a considerable period to pass before they do. Freight transport is a derived demand. Deregulation gives the opportunity to change modes of doing business. This is a necessary condition for changes, but sufficient conditions are found in changes of profitability as seen by those who require transport services. For example, whether a large food chain wishes to disturb its existing freight supply depends on the perceived need to change its warehousing and distribution strategy. This, in turn, depends on retail competition, the development of retail sites, etc. There is no necessary reason why this kind of opportunity should arise with a particular event, such as quantity deregulation, in the supplying industry.

Second, expectations about a change are largely based on historical organizational arrangements. These may not be appropriate to the changed circumstances at the time the actual change occurs. A good example of this is probably the expectations about clearing houses. In road freight transport's early days, in the 1920s and 1930s, clearing houses were important market-makers. They brought together, often physically, loads which had been consigned for potential carriers. These carriers were often back-loading to their point of departure, not having made arrangements to get a back-load. As explained earlier, clearing houses were expected strongly to revive on deregulation. Yet the Foster Committee, in 1978,[6] reported that 'we have been unable to obtain any quantitative information about the number and type of clearing houses, or their significance in the market for transport'. This did not prevent 'abundant testimony', hostile to clearing houses, being given to the Committee. But 'no clearing house came forward to give evidence' to the Committee. What, in fact, was being described was a function, not a specialized institution as it had been in the past. The function by that time was already shared among hauliers' associations, freight forwarders and indeed own-account operators, among many other parties. 'Clearing houses', I suspect, were then – and even more later – rather like the yeti, an animal whose footprints are well known, but who is never reliably sighted. The 'footprints' were, of course, the unprofitable deals often done in a highly competitive industry, causing the 'man' to get a bad reputation.

Third, if, as I have argued, deregulation makes possible new contractual arrangements, this does not mean that other brakes on competition will not appear. Not mentioned by the Foster Committee, but undoubtedly important for the time being reviewed (1969–78), was the impact of governmental price control, applied in practice to carriage for hire and reward. (Own-account operation, in the sense of owning and manning vehicles, was affected by price control only indirectly by effects on input prices, especially wage settlements.) Price control was reinstated in 1973, and was thereafter an important policy instrument until the advent of the Thatcher government in 1979, which formally removed it in 1980. The effect of price control was to create an umbrella to modify competition.

Dr Bernard Warner describes this period as follows: 'Price increases were limited to what was required to recover increased production (or operating) costs and profits to the average of the best two years of the last five.' This legitimized price increases to customers. It 'allows NFC and other hauliers to cover costs plus a margin'.[7] 'The [price] Commission would tell us [the NFC] they had no objection and we would tell our customers the Commission had agreed it.' 'These prices were accepted with little or no negotiation, because they in turn could pass it on to their customers. There was no reference in the submission to the scope or the reward for better production – and no incentive to achieve it.'[8] This was, of course, a time of unprecedented inflation; and it was also the last period in which road haulage unions could feel able to mount, and win, large-scale strikes. So this was not a propitious time for firms involved in haulage to take advantage of the contractual potential opened up by deregulation.

Contractual and organizational changes are difficult to capture in a statistical series. The longest running relevant UK statistic we have for the whole period since 1968 is the division of the total market between

Table 13.2 Shares of 'mainly for public hire' and 'mainly for own account' in total road freight, Great Britain 1968–87

	1968	1971	1974	1977 old basis	1977 new basis	1980	1983	1987
Tonnes lifted								
Public hire %	46	50	54	54	57	50	50	59
Own account %	54	50	56	46	43	50	50	41
Tonne km lifted								
Public hire %	60	59	64	66	68	61	64	71
Own account %	40	41	36	34	32	39	36	29

Sources: *Transport Statistics in Great Britain, 1968–78*, Tables 76, 77; *Transport Statistics in Great Britain, 1977–87*, Tables 2.31, 2.32.

Note: The computerization of records occasioned a change of base for 1977 figures and afterwards.

'public haulage' and 'own account'. The development from 1968 to 1987 is illustrated in Table 13.2.

As the table shows, there was in fact a long-run shift from own-account operation, more marked in the measure of total work performed, tonne kilometres. But this did not become very prominent until the later 1980s. The description 'own account' and 'public hire' are inadequate descriptions of the more important changes in contractual relationships which were actually taking place. 'Public hire' conventionally included the business of hiring one's vehicles to a single buyer. This was a form which combined the advantages of control over the carriage of one's own goods with using the market to supply the haulage. As we saw in Table 13.1, this form (A contract hire) was growing rapidly in the 1953–68 period, but from a very low base. After the final withdrawal of government influence on the haulage market around 1980, this form of arrangement seems to have blossomed.

A striking testimony to this change is found in the remarkable success story of the National Freight Corporation (NFC), from the time of the management buy-out in 1982 to its flotation in 1988. In a turnover increasing from £493 million in 1983 to £911 million in 1987, over half its turnover in 1987 was accounted for by contract hire, described as a 'rapidly growing sector of the UK transport market', in which NFC had an 8 per cent market share (phasing out of UK capital allowances had helped this shift). Contract hire covered a variety of contractual relationships, from supplying vehicles and maintenance only to supplying drivers, organizing licences, insurance, etc. NFC described it as a part of the market in which large operators could gain at the expense of smaller ones 'because of the scale of operation required and the emphasis on high service standards'. Large multiples such as Gateway and the Cooperative Wholesale Society (CWS)

Table 13.3 Distribution of operators by fleet size, Great Britain, 1980 and 1973

Fleet size (vehicles)	1980 (000)	%	1973 (000)	%
1	67.7	53.6	70.1	53.5
2	22.0		22.7	
3	10.5		10.9	
4	6.1	33.6	6.3	33.4
5	3.8		3.9	
6–10	8.6		8.9	
11–20	4.3	10.2	4.7	10.4
21–30	1.4		1.5	
31–40	0.6		0.7	
41–50	0.4		0.4	
51–100	0.6	2.5	0.7	2.7
101–200	0.2		0.2	
Over 200	0.1		0.1	
	126.3		131.1	

Source: (1980) *Returns for Heavy Goods Vehicles Operators Licences*, Department of Transport, 1973; Foster Report, September 1980, Table A5.

used NFC in this way. Truck rental was another important development. By 1988 NFC had 'relatively little contracted general haulage activities'. It had, however, extended rapidly into distribution, offering services varying from 'identifying sites for regional distribution to providing a fully integrated warehousing and delivery operation'.[9]

This development of contract hire into services, allowing a large customer to offload its integrated distribution system to an independent supplier, was not confined to the UK's largest haulage firm. It is quite common now for custom-designed systems, which may well include the provision of new trailer types, to be put out to tender, and the competition for those contracts between the larger haulage-based firms is increasing. The device of using management buy-outs to float off freight companies has also been used after recent major takeovers – for example, United Parcels, spun off from Bunz, and Lowfield Transport, from Imperial Tobacco. The outstanding characteristic of the industry in the 1980s has been differentiation and specialization, in which the industry structure, superficially little changed over the years, has in fact developed a large variety of contractual relationships.

Interest in the trend of firm size in haulage has greatly diminished since the 1970s, and there are no up-to-date figures from which to draw conclusions, but it is highly probable that the size structure – high proportions of operators concentrated in small fleet sizes – persists. In the last year for which statistics were taken, 1980, the distribution of vehicles subject to operators' licensing by fleet size was as shown in Table 13.3.

Subsequent road goods surveys have indicated that this distribution has not substantially changed since. The smaller the firm size, the more likely it is to be a subcontractor for other operators. Service differentiation, the principal concern of the larger operators, is reflected in the activities of smaller operators also. But these are probably the principal suppliers of the spot market for haulage, whose precise dimensions remain unknown.

I would argue that the full effects of deregulation, which, to repeat, is a necessary but not sufficient condition for contractual change in the industry, did not become fully apparent until after 1980. By that time, other impediments, notably price control, had disappeared. There is little doubt that a large change in productivity and other economic indicators did occur in the 1980s. Warner describes the significant changes, compared with the 1970s, as follows:

1 The annual distance driven per vehicle declined slowly between 1973 and 1979, but over the 1980s (from 1981 to 1986) steadily increased from 60,000 km to 75,000 km (measured for articulated vehicles of more than 32 tonnes).
2 Annual tonne km carried per vehicle declined from 1973 to 1979, but increased steadily and rapidly after 1980, due in small part only to the introduction of 38 tonne vehicles in 1983.
3 Road haulage rates for the heaviest vehicles, for a given mileage, increased by more than operating costs over 1976–9. From 1980 to 1986, rates have increased by less than costs.[10]

Warner concludes that, after 1979, productivity of heavy articulated vehicles in the UK rose by an average of 4 per cent a year; less than a third of this is due to the 38 tonne lorry. Real operating costs decreased by an average of 2.5 per cent per year, followed closely by rates.

One cannot assign productivity charges to separate causes. Other concurrent factors, such as an expanding motorway network and changes in permitted driving hours, helped the productivity gains. But the change in direction of productivity measured since 1980, the turning point, is difficult to explain without according the abandonment of the last obstacle to free contracting – price control – an important part. At all events, the UK road freight industry today epitomizes flexibility and adaptability to changing demands. The long period of reforms, intended to promote competition, which included formal deregulation in 1968, may now be said to be complete.

BUS DEREGULATION OF LONG-DISTANCE OPERATIONS

The quantity deregulation of long-distance (more than thirty miles) bus operations in 1980 is of interest to economists particularly because of its unusual context. The long-distance coaching trade's major incumbents before 1980 were nationalized industries, the National Bus Company, covering England and Wales, and the Scottish Bus Company. These offered the only network of services, based on ownership of key terminal sites in big cities, notably Victoria Station in London. These sites were typically the only permitted passenger exchange points in those cities. Private sector independents occupied about 20 per cent of the total market, but few routes were served by more than one operator. British Rail was the only effective network competitor.

The unusual element in the 1980 deregulation was that it was a deliberate attempt by the Conservative government to introduce competition to a nationalized industry. The move belonged to the relatively short period in the Thatcher government when attention was focused on making public enterprises more efficient, short of privatizing them. (Privatization was the preferred policy, pursued for the big public utilities in particular, from 1982 onwards.) The 1980 Act case therefore presents the only recent UK example of a policy category much advocated by the critics of privatization. The argument of these critics is that liberalization, as embodied in deregulation, is the key to substantial consumer gains, not privatization. The latter has, they think, conceded far too much market power to the incumbents being privatized. The period of the NBC's operation in a nationalized industry subjected to competition was short: the 1985 Act not only privatized NBC (but not the Scottish Bus Company), as noticed earlier, but also added liberalization to virtually all of their bus markets by deregulating bus operations of less than thirty miles outside London. But the experience during the period 1980–5 or so is generally regarded as indicating the effectiveness of deregulation in producing benefits for the consumer.

The nationalized industry period

The standard account, following Vickers and Yarrow[11] (1988: 372–7), which draws extensively on Davis,[12] is as follows. Immediately after deregulation, attempted entry by rival network operators at prices roughly half those of the incumbent, NBC's National Express (NE) subsidiary, was met by NBC. The quality offered sharply improved; there were more direct services between large towns, at higher speed, though smaller towns suffered some loss of service. Demand expanded on main routes by as much as 200 per cent. After the withdrawal of the main new entrant in 1983, prices rose but NBC retained its policy of aggressive price competition, preserving and enhancing its market share. Rivals tended to develop niche markets such as luxury coaches serving specific intertown routes, neglected by NE commuter services to large towns, and summer tour business. The main rivalry to NE came from British Rail, which targeted off-peak travellers and offered lower fares whenever their Inter-City trains' spare capacity indicated, at various times of the day and week. In short, all the classic responses expected from competition were found – lower fares, higher frequencies, concentration on profitable routes and a variety of innovatory moves.

That National Express should increase its market share was not expected but, with hindsight, the commentators are clear that it used its incumbent advantages ruthlessly. These were, first, its head start in national marketing, as a back-up to its national network. This was quickly reinforced by computerized booking systems. Most important was the use of its control over terminals or hubs such as Victoria Station, where as many as 24 per cent of arriving passengers interchanged. NBC pursued an active policy to hinder competition. It not only refused entry to newcomers to those hubs and terminals but also, when their activity was deemed competitive, ejected independent operators who had used them before 1980. NBC went so far in at least one case as to exclude an operator from a terminal even when its proposed competitive service did not use the terminal concerned.[13] This was a clear example of using monopoly power in one location as a lever to harass competition in another.

So, to the critics, liberalization had failed to disturb the principal constraint on entry underlying quantity control. The lesson was partly absorbed by the government when it drew up the 1985 Bill. Control of Victoria Station was vested in a separate company among NBC's successors and transferred to London Regional Transport. Provisions to prevent anticompetitive exploitation of bus stations were included (the words 'partly absorbed' are used because, as seen later, further questions about other properties, important in local bus operations, remained unresolved outside the 1985 Act). There can be little doubt that, in long-distance operations, access to bus terminals was indeed an extremely important constraint on entry. But the question remains – why did NBC elect to behave as if it were in perfectly contestable markets, by raising output and increasing quality while reducing prices, so producing a result very akin to what one would expect from such markets, namely an incumbent with a very high share, constrained to act as if it were in full competition? It did not need to do so, because of its control of key entry conditions.

The evidence does not allow us to give a very good answer to the problem. Vickers and Yarrow's comment on NBC's behaviour is as follows.

> Given the nature of its incumbent advantages, it is not surprising that National Express responded aggressively... before its rivals could build up goodwill and customer awareness. The entrants' pockets could not withstand the effects of the incumbents' sharp price cutting strategy for very long and National Express had good reason to believe that short-run revenue losses would soon be recouped by the return of its market dominance. National Express's policy bears some sign of a campaign of predatory pricing but, whether or not this is so, the competition authorities stood by and did nothing.[14]

Actually, the 'authorities' were in a poor position to do anything at the time: the Competition Act of 1980, aimed at strengthening the UK's control of individual company market power to cover predation amongst other matters, was focused on private industry. Nationalized concerns were merely to be subject to scrutiny which could *not* call into question their attempts to meet their financial targets, thus eliminating any serious inquisition of their pricing. Moreover, the bus industry enjoyed a general immunity from the provision of the UK's principal anti-trust law, the Fair Trading Act of 1973. This immunity was repealed only in the 1985 Act.

So NBC's *ability* after 1980 to harass competition (through National Express) was even greater than the commentators appreciated. In pursuing what would be judged by most anti-trust standards as 'competitive dubious practices', its nationalized status was a help. But, of course, predatory tactics are only rational if greater profits are made later, which more than compensate for immediate losses. And even if NBC's tactics were not predatory, their pursuit of increasing market share via lower prices and increased output should, in principle, have been their best option for increasing profits. If we are to maintain the notion of NBC as a nationalized concern, seeking optimum profit strategies, we would seek for evidence that – with all their incumbent advantages – there were not other, more profitable, options available. (One might have been to extract the potential rents from their key hubs, leaving actual operation of buses to other companies.)

Unfortunately, the record on profit is extremely obscure. Davis does indeed report that National Express 'increased its profits...from £3.1 million to £5.4 million between 1980 and 1982.' NBC's last annual report before privatization, for the year 1985, records that the year was one of 'consolidation' in the express coach business. Competition had been strong. There had been more concentration on using network advantages, including computerized booking. There was emphasis on cultivating an improved quality of service, and an investment in 143 high-grade coaches for the principal inter-city service, Rapide. 'Contribution to profit', on a turnover of £71.4 million, increased by 20 per cent on the year to £7.9 million. One might think an increase from £3.1 to £7.9 million 'profit' a modest achievement for all that frenetic competitive activity!

But the important question is, of course, what 'profit' meant in the actual corporate context. NBC's total turnover was £873 million in 1985. The vast bulk of its business was in local bus services; and its local bus subsidiaries dealt with National Express as carriers for them. How common costs were allocated among the seventy-two subsidiaries is not stated. The real test of profitability of National Express was as a stand-alone operation, a question not aired before privatization. (National Express was regarded as a prime part of NBC at privatization, but the valuations and other deals made at that time to float it off have not, at least in public, been related back to the accounts of the 1980–5 period.) So whether the £7.9 million reflected truly profitable business or not will probably now never be revealed.

My own judgement of NBC's policy for National Express in that period is that it is inappropriate to postulate a model of private, profit-maximizing behaviour. Instead, a much more plausible model is that of a sales maximizer, subject to a (low) profit constraint, which might in fact have been negative, to allow some help for National Express from the more profitable sectors of the business which, I suspect, were the still-regulated, moderately publicly subsidized local bus operations. This seems to me a fairer description of the likely motives and actions of nationalized industries as I have known them. The extent of the nationalized industry operations, the industry's protection and enlargement, is a prime consideration for a nationalized Board, sandwiched as it is between political expectations from above and union power from below. (This Board's instinct to preserve territory was vividly expressed in the attitudes of nationalized industry chairmen when facing privatization. They have all fought hard to achieve privatization as one unit. In NBC's case, the proposed break-up into seventy-two companies was presided over by a new chairman, brought in for the purpose.) If we accept the alternative hypothesis on aims, the apparent contradiction between incumbent strength and observed contestable market behaviour disappears. So does the problem of reaping the benefits from possible 'predatory' behaviour. Output had to be kept up and increased if possible; maximizing profit was not the aim.

The post-privatization period

The process of privatizing National Express continued from the time of the Act to its final sale in March 1988. Of course, it is too early to make an evaluation of the impact on industry performance of this event but one would expect that with most, at least, of the structural requisites for competition in place, what was a spirited defence of a nationalized industry in the face of deregulation might well be transformed into a textbook case of a contestable market. Entry foreclosure using station ownership is now inhibited. The industry is subject to normal UK anti-trust rules (and, of course, the EEC's).

There are many signs in National Express's post-March 1988 behaviour that the market is indeed fiercely contested and displaying innovation in services. For example, on pricing, NE introduced differential time-of-day pricing over much of its network on Tuesdays and Saturdays in October 1988. It cut off-peak prices in January 1989 for a season until April, at a time when a major external competitor, BR, raised theirs. On competitive tactics, NBC launched its first TV advertising campaign for two years in May 1988. At about the same time, many more towns were included in the network, and extra stopping services introduced; later in the year, networks were being extended to include smaller towns, and were being speeded up. Quality of service, focused on the Rapide, was being boosted.

But if the market conditions have indeed eliminated the old incumbent advantages, or modified them significantly, one would expect the incumbent to shift to more profitable modes of doing business. There are, in fact, some strong indications of this. The privatization deal which launched NE is reported to have included coach station properties at Birmingham, Leeds and Manchester. With the inhibitions to deny competitive access on them, these important inherited properties will doubtless be viewed as means of creating profit by serving operations, not necessarily from operating itself. The art will be to maximize passenger throughput, as in the parallel case of airports.

Similarly, NE inherited only a small number of vehicles at privatization. Most of the 950 coaches in use each day are now provided by other bus companies on contracts. This pushes much further the movement towards contracting out noticed in the 1985 NBC accounts, when twenty-four non-NBC operators were used as subcontractors. In other words, NE is moving towards a form of franchising operation, as a part of developing its Rapide brand. Further alliances with foreign operators, to provide integrated services and to maximize the use of computerized booking, are being formed. (These arrangements have at least the short-term advantage of freedom from close anti-trust surveillance.) Finally, more permanent alliances can be sought, not imposed from above, as in NBC days. Thus, NE bid £6 million for another ex-NBC property, Crosville Wales, in 1988.

In summary, the case of the UK's long-distance bus operations has further lessons for the analyst of deregulation. In road freight, we saw that if quantity constraints are not binding, little change in behaviour can be expected. In long-distance passenger operations, the quantity restrictions were indeed inhibiting the development of the market, but their removal did not lead to a successful challenge to the incumbent. On my interpretation, the incumbent used other, underlying impediments to entry to maximize sales, with scarce attention to profit making. What would have happened had their removal been combined with a persistence with ownership, instead of privatization? Very probably, the combination would have led to a rapid shrinkage of the public sector operations.

As it was, the collateral 1985 policy of privatization persuaded all players to become more profit oriented. NE was deprived of the protection of its much larger parent, itself not a single-minded pursuer of profit. Entry now being eased, profit seeking moved to where the above-normal profit might now be, upstream and downstream of bus operation itself. The market is now as close to a fully contestable market as one is likely to encounter in the real world, but the lowering of barriers is, to profit seekers, the occasion to find ways in which new ones may be created. This involves redefining the service and altering the approach both to the consumer and in the organization of production. In both freight and long-distance passenger transport the search for profit has meant substantial change, after deregulation, in the relation between integrated production and ownership.

DEREGULATION OF LOCAL (STAGE) BUS SERVICES

The 1985 Act

Deregulation of local bus services in the 1985 Act was seen by the industry itself, government and commentators as a far greater upheaval for the industry than the 1981 measure had been. It reversed a 50-year-old policy of route licensing which had applied both to incumbents wishing to offer new routes and to entrants. Thenceforward, any operator wishing to provide a public service was obliged simply to register the route with the Area Traffic Commission. Forty-two days' notice to commence, to make a significant modification, or to withdraw is required.

The Act's other principal policy innovations were to privatize NBC, the bulk of whose revenue was derived from local services; to switch public financial support for services from general payments to operators to support specific services, which would be put out to competitive tender; and to require that Metropolitan and Public Transport Executive bus fleets, the main suppliers of bus services in the UK conurbations outside London, should be put at arm's length from local authorities as newly formed Passenger Transport Companies. These were to be treated, in principle, as any other transport suppliers with respect to subsidized services and to other policies such as concessionary fares for old-age pensioners.

The conditions under which licences for local services were given had, in fact, been changed as part of the previous 1981 Act. At that time, the burden of proof for a licence was changed, as nearly thirty years before in the freight industry. Instead of the newcomer having to show that it *would* be in the public interest to be allowed a route, an existing operator, normally an incumbent, had now to show that this would *not* be in the public interest. An appeal against a traffic commissioner's decision was allowed, to the (Conservative) Secretary of State for Transport, known to favour competition. This shift, however, was not sufficient to persuade significant numbers of newcomers to take on the risks of attempted entry. Presumably, the cost of application and the uncertain outcome were deterrents. Traffic Commissions could not be expected to revise their basic opinions about what was or was not in the public interest simply because the burden of proof had been formally shifted. The same phenomenon was observed in London after a 1984 Act had, among other provisions, similarly changed the burden of proof. In effect, under this Act's provisions, London Transport was obliged progressively to put its own routes out to tender, but the Act retained licensing for new entry, subject to appeal to the Secretary of State. Not until late 1988, when Devon General applied for and received a licence (unopposed by London Transport) to operate minibuses in East London, including the Docklands, has substantial independent commercial entry occurred there.

Contrasting expectations about deregulation

Amongst economists, expectations about the effect of deregulation (to take effect fully from February 1987) varied widely. These are perhaps best epitomized by the exchange between Gwilliam *et al.* on the one hand, and Beesley and Glaister on the other, in *Transportation Reviews on the Government's White Paper of 1984*[15] which preceded the 1985 Act.[16] The first authors described the government policy as set out in the White Paper as essentially putting forward four propositions:

1 Deregulation will produce a competitive market.
2 Competition will substantially reduce costs.
3 A competitive market will improve resource allocation.
4 Such a market will not cause any significant undesirable spin-off effect.

The authors rejected all these propositions except number 2, about which they, in any case, had severe reservations. 'If there is any competition at all on bus routes, it will tend to be small-group rather than large-group. Neither will produce efficient results except under extreme assumptions concerning contestability of markets, which we reject.' 'Competition would not produce an efficient allocation of resources. . . . Entry of new services like mini-buses into dense urban markets would be unlikely to succeed, except by creaming off the best traffic.' This would be undesirable 'because of the resulting dilution of conventional bus frequencies and the congestion effects'. 'If improvements in cost efficiency are available, most of them would be captured by competitive tendering, which should be extended to all routes.' 'Competition of the market would avoid many of the costs of on-the-road competition.'[17]

The reply saw these authors' paper as, in reality, defending the proposition that planning for buses is good for the industry, bus consumers and society at large. The assumption of fully knowledgeable, all-wise planners was false. The authors had not dealt with the White Paper's central proposition that deregulation would encourage much-needed innovation. The authors' notion of competition 'for the market' meant that competition 'when allied with planning wisdom' is a good thing after all. But what was to be supplied should be decided by operators' own choice, not by planners'. Deregulation was in any case a pre-condition of competition and hence of effective tendering. The authors' scepticism about cost savings (the White Paper had predicted a 30 per cent reduction) was misplaced.

The fundamental division between the two sets of authors was clearly about the relative roles of market forces and planning. It was inherently unlikely, in the nature of things, that what happened after deregulation would convince either side of the falsity of its basic view. The Act was accompanied by a strenuous government effort to set up monitoring procedures; for the first time, for example, it sought to distinguish clearly what was being provided by operators in local bus operations (now defined as less than 15-mile trips). Assessments of the impacts of the Act quickly burgeoned, using the newly available data. However, the data unfortunately left important elements unsurveyed, including measurement of trip length (so that total output, passenger miles, was not directly observed). Nor were the changes in contractual relationships in the industry which might be expected to follow deregulation monitored. Interpretations to confirm one's own prejudices were thus only too easy to make.

But with that warning, one may present a cross-section of the interpretations of the experience so far. The first set, from the largest number of commentators, basically represents the views of the pro-interventionists in markets. The second, opposed, interpretation draws heavily on my own paper delivered at the Thredbo Conference in May 1989, and may perhaps be said to represent a free-market view, probably a minority one among UK transport economists.[18] The reason that there is unlikely to be an independent technical test of the rival views is essentially that touched on earlier. Both sides agree that evaluation of this policy change, like any other, is in principle susceptible to a CBA treatment, comparing 'after' with 'before'. Unfortunately, in addition to the difficulties stated earlier, over the two years available for comparison there have been very large changes in important parameters, which stretch credulity in the applicability of conventional measurements (e.g. of price elasticity). Moreover, important new services, changes in service levels and abandonments of routes have occurred, and have been experienced very differently by different groups.

Reported results

W.J. Tyson,[19] having considered the likely effects of changing population and unemployment, concluded that over the first year of deregulation

> there is little doubt that in total, fewer people are using buses in the Metropolitan areas and in Strathclyde than before deregulation. An upper limit may be around 10 per cent. There has been a high degree of competition and potential competition for both commercial and tendered services.

Fares increased substantially in real terms. There has been reduction in operating costs, from various sources – labour redundancies, lower pay increases and lower pay for minibus operators. Reviewing also the 1988 experience, he reports[20] that 'the high degree of competition has on the whole been sustained. Service levels have continued to fluctuate. The rapid rate of change of services has not abated and this itself must be having an adverse effect on passengers'.

Professor Peter Hills reports the results of the monitoring programme (to November 1987) in eight areas of Scotland, ranging from the thinly populated Highland Region to the densely populated Glasgow area (Strathclyde). He points to the 'high rate of change that here prevailed' and echoes Tyson's concern about 'instability'. However, 'the evidence so far is that many of the adverse predictions [about deregulation] have not yet come to pass' and 'some aims of the Government have been achieved. For example, competition has arisen in places, [and] unit costs of operation have fallen.'[21] In all study areas, bus kilometre operation has increased, especially in urban areas. On the road, competition has been extensive in the urban study areas. New independent operators were, however, few. Experiences of fare changes were mixed. More buses were carrying fewer passengers. On the quality of service, favourable impressions were reported in more areas than not.

Dr Peter White and Dr Roy Turner most usefully summarize relevant statistics from the Department of Transport's first monitoring report of December 1988. From these, the changes in relevant parameters can be deduced for the period 1985/6, before deregulation, to 1987/8, after it. Several areas are reported, including London, in which tendering, not deregulation, was progressing. Table 13.4 sets out the percentage changes in vehicle kilometres, in passenger trips, fares and operating costs per bus kilometre.

Table 13.4 Changes in local bus services, 1985/6 to 1987/8

| | Percentage changes by area | | | | |
	Metropolitan counties	English shires	Scotland	Wales	London
Passengers trips	−16.2	−3.8	−3.3	−0.6	+10.2
Bus km performed	+7.5	+17.8	+15.4	+8.4	−1.8
Fares	+28.6	+1.4	+9.2	NA	+3.6
Operating costs	−26	−21	−14	−14	−11

Source: White, P. and Turner, R. (1989) 'Overall impacts of local bus deregulation in Britain', *International Conference on Competition and Ownership of Bus and Coach Services, Thredbo, NSW, 1–4 May 1989.*

White and Turner derive a pessimistic view of deregulation's impact from arguments based on, and developing these figures. 'Though deregulation had produced some impressive savings in cost per local bus-kilometre, these have been offset by falling loads to produce only marginal reductions in operating cost per passenger trip outside London.' Many other comment-ators have remarked on the increase in minibus operations associated with deregulation; indeed, it is viewed as the principal innovatory move so far. White and Turner (1989: 19) say: 'Where some useful innovations have appeared during the phase of competition, they may be retained.' But they are principally impressed with 'instability' in the network of services, which they think must account for most of the passenger losses reported. This, in effect, labels the residual, unaccounted-for falls in passenger trips when exogenous trend factors, fare rises (with an imputed elasticity of −0.3) and increased service levels (evaluation at a service elasticity of $+0.4$) have been accounted for. The main lesson they draw from the London experience is that there would be 'no clear benefit in extending regulation to the capital – if anything, the opposite', but 'further scope may exist for reducing cost for bus-km, and for minibus introduction, especially in suburban areas' (1989: 19).

Professor Gwilliam, at the same conference, restated his belief that the 'market is not perfectly contestable and hence an effective control against predation is required'. This would be necessary, but not sufficient, to control 'dimensions of competitive activity, which reduce welfare'. Competition pressure reduced costs, but 'competition for the market (as in London) is at least as effective and immediate in this respect as competition in the market'.[22]

Clearly, the experience so far has not quelled the doubters' fears. Gomez-Ibanez and Meyer sum up in this way:

> neither the advocates nor the opponents of reform have been completely vindicated by subsequent events. However, as to whether or not competition would emerge, which was central in the prior debate, the advocates appear to have the better of the argument.[23]

Perhaps it would also be fair to say that regulation's impact on costs has, in effect, been conceded. So has the positive impact of deregulation on innovations. Yet the fundamental difference of view about markets versus planning remains. What, to the free-market advocate, is the market learning with difficulty to slough off fifty years of constraints, is to opponents an unnecessary cost in disturbance and 'instability'. The latter will say that the combination of planners deciding what is to be consumed plus competitive tendering is preferable; their opponents will still distrust planners.

In London, the enthusiasts would point out that the threat of deregulation is implicit in the 1985 Act. Although, when the government was discussing that possibility in 1987, the Act was deemed to be technically unsound for its purpose of extending deregulation to London and thus would require a further Act, the government's intention has not been abandoned.[24] More significantly, London Regional Transport itself formally embraced a policy of welcoming deregulation in 1987, undoubtedly with the hearty agreement of the Chairman of London Buses Ltd, who has made no bones about its importance in helping his drive towards greater labour productivity and the need to reorganize London Buses into independent management units.[25]

But I would argue that the experience of deregulation in freight and long-distance passenger transport reminds us that the influence of collateral policies is very important, and that deregulation is merely one step in what might be a series of relevant reforms which have impacts on an industry. Doubters of, and enthusiasts for, deregulation would both agree (and have repeatedly said) that it is too early yet to judge fully the UK experience. I shall, in effect, argue in the next section that 'doubters' fail to appreciate the implications of the fact that deregulation is, at best, a necessary and sufficient condition for competition. Further, it is more relevant analytically to enquire how entry conditions might be changing as the result (in part) of deregulation, and to understand how profits are generated and protected, than to *assume* entry conditions and derive propositions from the assumptions. The chief problem with the latter approach is one can too easily slip from a demonstration that, for example, the conditions for contestability are not fully met, to the prediction that incumbents are unlikely to be attackable.

The relevant policy changes

The simultaneous and sweeping changes accompanying the 1985 Act make it very hazardous to try to answer the question: what does the record show, so far, about the impact of deregulation? The Act did not say so, but government policy at the time was not only to change subsidy payment methods, but also to save on subsidy, which had grown alarmingly over the previous decade. From the point of view of saving public money *and* preserving bus output, deregulation was seen as a key move, because it would, it was hoped, both discipline wage rates and encourage productivity bargains. Also, as seen earlier, only one underlying constraint had been identified at the time – the possible anti-competitive potential of bus station ownership. This was dealt with in the Act, but there was no attempt to define a policy for whatever impediments to entry there might be once what was assumed to be the binding constraint – the licensing system – was removed. Some of us responsible for providing the policy guidance at the time knew this well, but the point was too subtle and difficult to answer in time to affect the policy process.

The UK *Bus and Coach Statistics* (B&CS) now tell us much more about local (stage) bus services than they did. A proper statistical design to use these data would proceed as follows.

The principal policy elements would be nominated. In this case, they are deregulation, subsidy and privatization. We would then try to distinguish geographical areas displaying the required variance with respect to the policy element. The aims would vary with respect to: deregulation/no deregulation; areas where subsidy changed much and where it changed little; and areas which experienced privatization or did not. These contrasts would yield $2 \times 2 \times 2 = 8$ possible combinations. The area observations would show these combinations.

But certain combinations in the eight refuse to emerge in practice. The most useful comparisons are possible between operations in English Shire Counties (ES) and English Metropolitan Counties (EM). ES represented 41 per cent of all local bus service kilometres in Great Britain in 1985/6 and 47 per cent outside London. EC covered 28 per cent and 32 per cent respectively. Limited comparisons are possible also with Scotland, for which the comparative figures are 14 per cent and 16 per cent. We can take 1985/6 as the best available representation of the 'before the Act' situation, and the latest representation two years later, 1987/8, as have other commentators.

The areas' common experience of deregulation was tempered by different starting points and collateral changes. As between ES and EM, there was a very differing level of initial subsidy for policy attack. On the other hand, ES was the scene of most privatization; the EM organizational change here was meant at the time to facilitate change in subsidy methods, and as a possible precursor only to privatization later. So, here we have the two policy measures affecting each other differently. A comparison between EM and Scotland focuses more on the privatization issue, though Scotland had a markedly higher level of initial subsidy.

From B&CS we can build up the following picture of passenger experience and impact on operator finances over the two years. Table 13.5 presents changes in numbers of journeys made; a quality variable, namely the quantity of services offered in vehicle km; and average fares. The figures in Table 13.5 are drawn from the revised version of the data published in June 1989, so do not match the figures of Table 13.4. The revised data omit some important details used in the calculations which follow Table 13.5. I have, therefore, retained the computation based on the preliminary data for further computations. A close inspection of the sources reveals that it is highly unlikely that the conclusions would be affected; the reported revisions are very small indeed.

Alongside these changes were important shifts in operators' finances. These elements are involved – the change in fare box money collected via: direct charging; changes in costs; and, changes in subsidy received.

B&CS allows estimates to be made as follows: passenger journeys (T2.1) are multiplied by the real fares index (T3.1). For costs, vehicle km (T1.1) are multiplied by relevant costs per km (T4.1), using the proxies mentioned earlier. Subsidy comprises four elements for ES and Scotland: public transport support (T5.5); concessionary fares (T5.3); fuel duty rebate (T5.1); and rural bus grant. These are estimated by the proportion of vehicle km operated in Great Britain outside London, the basis for T5.1 (references are to the December 1988 source). Table 13.6 presents these changes,

Table 13.5 Passenger experience over 1985/6 to 1987/8

| | Percentage changes | | |
	ES	EM	Scotland
Journeys[26]	−3.0	−16.2	−3.4
Quality of service[27] (vehicle km supplied)	+19.5	+7.3	+15.8
Real fares (average)[28]	+1.6	+29.0	+0.3

Source: Bus and Coach Statistics, Department of Transport, UK, June 1989.

together with changes in costs per vehicle km (T4.1) and the calculated incidence of subsidy per passenger journey.

A plausible scenario for the EM sector is that the authorities' companies raised fares sharply, in response to a drastic cut in subsidy, but were much helped by deregulation, whose effect on costs was drastic. Deregulation, it seems, represented a credible threat to rents enjoyed by labour under regulation. The appropriate adjustments were quickly achieved. That the bargaining position of local authority bus operators versus organized labour shifted sharply in the former's favour is well brought out by Table 7.3 of B&CS, reprinted here as the Appendix. Here the shift in the types of staff employed over the two years is tracked among different types of operators. Arguably, the most formidable strongholds of union power were in maintenance and in the urban areas. Yet, in two years, the Metropolitan PTCs shed 41 per cent of their maintenance staff, easily the highest among all the operator categories (National Bus followed with 23 per cent). Presumably, maintenance was contracted out instead. The shift in platform staff, by contrast, though generally downwards, had more to do with achieving required output change. In Scotland, where subsidy was hardly changed, the reduction in overall costs per vehicle kilometre was much less but, again, it did not experience privatization. As Table 13.6 shows, costs per vehicle kilometre fell over 20 per cent in ES. But this sector was also that most affected by shifts in the operator's vehicle size. Table 6.3 of B&CS (1988) makes it possible to infer that the seats supplied in smaller (less than

Table 13.6   Changes in bus operating costs and finances, 1985/6 to 1987/8

% Fare box	ES −2.5		% Change	EM −7.7		% Change	Scotland −2.9		% Change
Subsidy	£m real			£m real			£m real		
	85/6	87/8		85/6	87/8		85/6	87/8	
Public transport support	94	67		218	117		29	22	
Concessionary fares	69	68		115	124		40	43	
Fuel duty rebate	57	58		39	36		19	19	
Rural bus grant	–	–		–	–		–	4	
Totals	220	203		372	277		88	88	
			−7.3			−25.5			+0
Total costs			−8.4			−19.4			+2.6
Subsidy per vehicle kilometre	0.259	0.204		0.647	0.448		0.309	0.267	
			−21.2			−30.7			−13.4
Subsidy per vehicle passenger journey	0.139	0.134		0.179	0.160		0.131	0.136	
			−3.8			−10.7			+3.5
Representative costs per vehicle km	0.9	0.7		1.3	0.9		0.9	0.8	
			−22.2			−30.8			−11.1
Ratio % of total subsidy to total vehicle costs	28.8	29.1		49.8	49.8		34.3	33.4	

thirty-five seat) vehicles, including so-called 'minibuses', may have shifted from about 2 per cent to over 10 per cent during the two years.[29] No other type of operator was affected nearly so greatly.

Subsidy change also clearly affects the 'passenger experience' indicated in Table 13.5. One could not expect EM, losing subsidy heavily, to expand service quality as much as did Scotland or ES, and so it happens. Yet, all did increase service. Scotland's very small change in subsidy, when seen against all others' experience, permits the generalization that quality of service was probably positively affected by deregulation. As Table 13.6 figures on the ratio of subsidy to vehicle costs per km show, the UK stage bus industry remains a heavily subsidized one.

Effects on entry

In practice, to predict entry, one does one's best to imagine the underlying barriers, to reason by analogy from other, freer industries, and to understand how those placed upstream and downstream of the activity under scrutiny could themselves profit by organizing entry, not necessarily by themselves. As seen earlier, the Act's framers did spot the importance of one potential barrier. But access to bus stations is of much less importance in running local stage services, and little else was actively anticipated. Two years of experience of deregulation suggest possible disclosed barriers to entry.

It is generally agreed that actual entry into established incumbents' service areas has been very patchy so far. TRRL's study of deregulation's first year reports that '400 more private operators are running local bus services'.[30] The total number of private operators in Great Britain is about 5,000. From a very low base, private operators' stage service provision outside London nearly doubled between 1985/6 and 1987/8 (B&CS, Table 1.4). Much of this new work was probably from successful bids for contracted subsidized services. Private operators supplied 29 per cent of these services outside London in 1987/8 (B&CS, Table 1.4). The entrants have contributed substantially to what most observers would judge to be active competition for the new-style, specifically subsidized services contracted by local authorities.

One might have expected that the new style of individual route tendering, oriented explicitly to social purposes, would be the basis for a new kind of specialist enterprise. It would become expert both in perceiving and justifying the needs for specific subsidies, and in organizing supply to meet the needs. It would be capable of bidding in several geographical areas simultaneously, rather in the style already found in subsidized food catering work, where large companies have been created. Part of the attraction of this postulated new enterprise would be skill in defining bases and rationalizations for specific subsidies, a much underdeveloped expertise. The ability to use independent local supply, rather than own it, would be crucial.

However, there are few signs that changing to this new form of subsidy has provided important profit-making opportunities for new styles of operation. Unfortunately, the kind of scale of this form of subsidy has fallen substantially. As Table 13.6 shows, in ES and EM and Scotland, public transport support declined in real terms from £341 million to £206 million over the two years. This is hardly conducive to innovatory effort! Also, there were inhibitions to forms of organization which would require great flexibility in hiring factors of production, as seen below.

Private and other operators have, instead, probably regarded the subsidized work as a fringe activity. A very wide dispersion of bids has been observed and, as Glaister and Beesley have shown, this has been a repeated pattern over a considerable period.[31] Bidding is opportunistic, dictated essentially by the state of a company's work in other areas at the time of bidding, which will mostly be non-stage work. The search for profit then produces bids ranging from those reflecting attempts to fund new vehicles and men, to those filling up spare capacity.

Organizational innovation is much dampened by the survival of barriers to entry from pre-1985 days. Specifically, vertical disintegration of bus ownership and operation appears to be very difficult because of rules on operators' licences which are, of course, still required to offer a service. Some of these do not seriously inhibit entry and are desirable on other grounds, for example the requirement to be of 'good repute'. But to get a standard licence, 'You or your transport manager must satisfy the requirement of professional competence', meaning either a grandfather right, or examination by various competent professional bodies.[32] 'Financial fitness' and adequate maintenance arrangements have also to be shown. The significance of these barriers to vertical integration is, in particular, underlined by a recent case concerning the question of whether a licence holder could franchise drivers without the qualifications to run buses on his or her behalf. That is, could drivers, holding only PSV licences entitling them simply to drive buses, be hired as self-employed persons? The answer was 'no'. This reinforced the need for drivers to be wage earners and blocked off what, for many, might be an attractive way to get independence, with attendant risks and returns (and tax advantages).

The consequences of this for entry are clearly adverse, and go further than imposing a cost of entry for any driver-employee who wishes to compete independently. (Until deregulation, the almost universal norm was for bus companies to own, not lease, vehicles, as part of a fully integrated operation through to the drivers.) Franchising, or, more widely, the divorce of ownership of vehicles from their use by individual drivers, is an important support for the growth of the bus-leasing business, which at present is slow. In the London taxi trade, where leasing is common and there are no bounds on disintegrated forms of production, drivers can, and do, surmount substantial personal entry costs, to create very elastic labour supply. We can, perhaps, expect disintegrated forms of production in the stage carriage buses eventually to emerge, after the set-back just described. But we cannot be certain that there are not other inhibitions to such organizational innovation, yet to be disclosed.

In the 'commercial' operations (defined as those not specifically tendered) which comprise over 80 per cent of stage carriage work, substantial incumbents have not, so far, apparently had to yield much market share. As explained earlier, an immediate effect of deregulation was to loosen the labour market. This was probably a differential bonus to the larger incumbents, especially those in urban areas, because the rents enjoyed before deregulation were higher there. Their position was strengthened relative to potential competitors, whose initial labour rents were probably lower. Again, NBC successor companies, in particular, anticipated innovatory moves by investing heavily in minibuses before deregulation and then running them during the changeover. It is possible to interpret events so far in a way which would be in line with ideas about contestable markets, namely, that incumbents have been constrained to act as if in competition. But are incumbents sustained in other ways? Two leading candidates to consider are the impact of subsidy and its operation; and access to location for operating.

Subsidy and other entry barriers

We have seen that, largely as a result of falling unit costs, subsidy in total is as important to finances now as it was before deregulation, and has switched towards concessionary fares. Methods of giving concessional fares vary, and have different consequences for calculations about entry. Concessionary fares are an important element of receipts in 'commercial' routes (i.e. those not directly subsidized and subject to tender). An entrant who wishes to establish a service of whatever size must be able to anticipate cash flow from this source. What risk does he or she face?

Local authorities are formally forbidden to operate schemes which favour the incumbents. Whatever scheme is devised must be open to all comers. (Most were focused on 'elderly persons', the blind, and those with limited mobility at the time of deregulation.[33]) From the present viewpoint, the important distinction is between those schemes which generate trips through putting the cost for a marginal trip, albeit within stated times etc., at zero, and those which do not. The principal form of the latter is the token, entitling a fixed recompense to an operator getting one from a customer. Apart from the transaction costs the operator faces to do so (and incumbents cannot escape these either), tokens pose no special problem for the entrant in terms of predicting quantity of travel. Token schemes are far more frequent than we realized in 1985. But they are mostly found outside the big conurbations and have a disproportionate share of large incumbents, often municipal operators.

The principal problem for a would-be entrant is judging what his or her revenue will be. In considering 'commercial' operations the potential entrant, particularly in urban areas, has a very difficult task in computing what the take (the contribution from subsidy) will be. The entrant will be recompensed for the carriage, say, of an old-age pensioner on a half-fare pass, but how many times can he or she hope to pick up pensioners, and with what certainty? What is known about trip-makers' responses to half-price or, even more, free-pass travel is of little comfort. The TRRL report on bus trip-generating fares – concessionary fare schemes in six towns – makes the uncertainty very clear.[34] Further, there is the problem of the subsidy authority's cost of validating claims. These must be backed up by enforcement procedures, involving some form of spot checking. This is disproportionately costly the smaller the entrant, and it would not be surprising if the subsidy authority operates the system in practice so as to discourage the small operator.

An entrant's most simple way of judging demand is by practical trials. This was always the most effective form of market research in the bus industry. But it is severely discouraged where there is a substantial quantity of concessionary fare travel. Moreover, an experiment, if the entrant attempts it, must also be defined, in effect announced, to the incumbents six weeks in advance and be carried out for six weeks before it can be withdrawn. In order to reduce the uncertainty of payouts from subsidy, the scale of entry must be raised. (If it was large enough, presumably the entrant's expectation of payout would be the same as the incumbents'.) So, in present conditions, a substantial barrier to entry arises.

In metropolitan areas with alternative public transport modes, for ex-ample some form of rail operation, the potential entrant's difficulty in assessing payout is compounded by the operation of cross-mode passes. Buses represent an important short-trip complement in such cases. The problem of getting proper recompense from these here is important for London Buses, even though LBL is in the same ownership as London Underground; the method of computing the cash due to LBL from trips made by such pass-holders has been very contentious.

All forms of fare passes, whether offering free trips at the point of use or not, offer user convenience. Were a specialist form of agent to arise dealing in such passes, a would-be entrant's difficulty in overcoming incumbents' advantages would be eased. (An incumbent has, for example, always the right to refuse to recognize another company's pass, and would always do so unless adequately compensated.) So far as I am aware, there has been little sign of agency activity of this sort. It is hardly surprising, since would-be agents too must judge the chances of entrants' establishing worthwhile business. Thus the problems generated by subsidy are compounded.

These arguments strongly suggest that entry into urban core areas is differentially impeded. The Monopolies and Mergers Commission report, on the Badger Line (BL) and City Line (CL) merger does, by implication, add another probable constraint: the ownership of bus depots.[35] CL owned four bus depots for maintenance and storage of vehicles, three of these under licence from Bristol City Council. BL owned one such site in Central Bristol. A major reason for merging – indeed, easily the most substantial tangible cash benefit – was realizing the value of this and other sites. 'Ways of realizing this potential are being investigated and may include the merger of BL Bristol and City Line engineering workshops onto a single site.' The property covered stood at over £3 million in the balance sheet.[36]

Many incumbents in central urban areas have inherited sites such as these, whose scarcity value in bus operations is sustained by town planning rules. Conversion of rival premises for operations by existing users probably, at best, involves a protracted planning negotiation. Incumbents owning these service sites have the option of profiting from their sale, but then have to substitute premises if they also wish to continue in bus operations. If they can find a suitable partner with well-placed excess capacity, they can both sell and continue bus operations without incurring the costs of search, conversion of a new location, etc. (This seems to have been a basis for the BL and CL merger. BL had the freehold, CL the licensed depots from which bus operations could be sustained by BL.)

A further deterrent to entry has been brought to my attention by Mr Harry Blundred, whose company has become a major provider of minibus services since 1986 (including entry into East London, noted earlier). The market for leasing buses is relatively underdeveloped, he believes, putting a brake on bus firms' expansion. In principle, this denotes imperfection in the capital market, rather than a barrier in bus operation *per se*. But it well illuminates the point that appropriate supply responses will take a considerable time, perhaps some years, before the opportunities opened up by deregulation are converted to profitable operation.

If we put together the suspected entry constraints which have been revealed by the withdrawal of the primary constraint, the pre-1986 restrictions, we have the hypothesis that entry has been both quantitatively greater and more likely to have been sustained, the less densely populated the area of operation. The relative incidence of subsidy, its constitution, its administration and the impact of locations for operations all point in the same direction. Also, negatively, the inhibition on organizational innovation, which is basically more favourable where labour supplies are plentiful, has yet to be realized.

CONCLUSIONS

Though separated by many years, the UK's experiences of freight and passenger deregulation display important and common lessons. First, a point implicit in the account given above: deregulation of quantity licensing is a separable issue from ensuring safe operation, that is from the issue of the quality of professional standards to be applied. No critic of quantity deregulation has seriously sought to maintain that there has been an adverse relationship between these after the fact of quantity deregulation, though much misgiving before the event was displayed. Second, the economic effects of quantity deregulation are rarely seen in isolation. Collateral policies can make the intended constraint on entry and expansion of little consequence. At other times and places, the effect can be considerable. Third, the evaluation of deregulation calls for contrasting modes of economic analysis.

Formally, the question is one of applying a cost–benefit analysis to a policy change. This is an exercise in application of well-known neo-classical principles. There are formidable difficulties in doing this successfully. But apart from this, the important economic insight about the influence of deregulation must proceed from a different analytical standpoint, one which emphasizes its impacts on how and why opportunities to make profit are changed. The first proceeds *from* assumed entry conditions; the second considers how these conditions may be altered in future, and views deregulation as a necessary but not sufficient condition for changing the economic relationships in the industry.

Critics of and enthusiasts for deregulation have accordingly shaped their expectations and interpretations. Perhaps the greatest contrast has emerged in the preparation for and the aftermath of the 1985 Act. The one side interprets the ambiguous evidence, so far, as throwing the burden of proof more strongly on measures to deregulate. The other side did not, and does not, expect adjustments to competitive opportunities in a complex industry to be as short as two years and, in any case, sees any shortcomings in competitive vigour as likely to be caused by the failure to anticipate adequately what entry barriers lay behind the quantity restriction. I would also add that the history recounted in this chapter tends to show that the issue of public ownership or private ownership *does* have an important impact on competition. This was, I believe, true in freight and in long-distance passenger services, and may also well prove to be so in local bus operation, where the privatization of municipally owned bus companies, now in process, will increase the contestability of the markets.[37]

Anti-trust issues

In buses, there is an additional item of underdeveloped, and certainly not finished, business. This is the application of UK anti-trust laws in regulating competition. As pointed out earlier, being subject to UK anti-trust was an innovation for the industry in 1985. The two arms of UK competition policy – that concerning restrictive trade practices and that concerned with control of monopoly and merger – are beginning to show their hands. Early in 1989, the Office of Fair Trading (OFT) declared certain agreements between operators about timetabling and fare arrangements to appear to contravene the Restrictive Trade Practices Act, 1973. At the time of writing, discussions with the trade are proceeding to try to eliminate the restrictions implicit in these agreements. This is a normal way to begin

OFT's activity when entering a new field. The crunch will come if and when OFT decides that remaining agreements are restrictive, and proceeds to their determination by the Restrictive Trade Practices Court. OFT is known to be investigating many claims about anti-competitive practices, but has yet to make up its mind publicly about what is actionable.

The other arm of UK anti-trust, the Monopolies and Mergers Commission, made an important clarification of the permissible scope of merger in its report on Badger Line.[38] This was one of several post-1985 Act mergers of companies which had been sold separately after the 1985 Act. The Commission (in the course of declaring the merger to be expected to operate against the public interest, and suggesting conditions on the merged company's future conduct in tendering[39] clarified its geographical remit with respect to buses. The two companies, occupying most of the County of Avon in their confined territories, were deemed to be a 'substantial part' of the United Kingdom, and thus within their jurisdiction under the 1973 Act. No doubt there were exchanges of views between the MMC and EEC in arriving at this decision, which means that virtually all proposed mergers of substantial bus companies will be open to reference to the MMC.

Moreover, the MMC, though it did not require divestment in this case, effectively gave notice that it would be particularly vigilant about proposed mergers by contiguous bus companies. To those who accord great weight to bus company size in predicting competition outcomes, this is a significant implicit constraint. MMC does not frown on links in separate geographical areas, but may preserve local independence. To those who emphasize the underlying barriers to entry, and who think in terms of capital markets as the discipline of managements, merger is of consequence only if it indicates the need for action on those barriers. They will note that in the freely entered freight industry, large firms can and do exist, but merger is not a particularly interesting commercial strategy. It is also true that OFT has (in public at least) never had a serious problem of possible breaches of the 1973 Act with respect to freight.

The final item on the 'unfinished' agenda is the significance of 1992 for the UK freight and bus industries. Looked at in comparative terms with respect to other UK industries, the judgement must be that, as they are remarkably competitive, thanks in part to deregulation, they must prosper, probably at the expense of their European counterparts. But this would be perhaps too much of a concession to the method of analysis *not* preferred in this chapter. The question should be: what will 1992 open up in the way of suitable opportunities to get more profit – that is, for a time at least to *escape* competitive rigours? Perhaps this is a good point at which to leave the analysis to experts on EEC freight and bus regulation and, equally important, on industry structure and prospects outside the UK.

But I can add a semi-serious closing remark. There is at least one important potential barrier to 'efficient' UK road transport industries gaining substantial market shares in Europe. This is the UK's comparative disadvantage in not speaking foreign languages. These are service industries, and service means the intensive use of language skills at low levels in an organization. One can imagine, therefore, that the extreme flexibility in contractual arrangements, which I have argued is characteristic of the UK industries, may offer the 'best' opportunities to enterprising, English-speaking EEC firms, who will be able to apply the UK lessons on liberalization in their own countries!

APPENDIX

Table A 13.1 Changes in staff by type of employment and operator (thousands)

		Platform staff	Maintenance staff	Other staff	All staff
London Buses Ltd	1985/6	17.9	3.7	4.2	25.7
	1986/7	16.1	3.5	3.8	23.4
	1987/8 (p)	13.4	3.2	3.1	19.8
Metropolitan PTCs	1985/6	19.2	10.3	6.5	36.0
	1986/7	17.1	8.0	5.4	30.4
	1987/8 (p)	16.0	6.1	4.4	26.5
Municipal PTCs	1985/6	9.6	3.9	2.6	16.1
	1986/7	9.0	3.3	2.3	14.7
	1987/8 (p)	9.4	3.2	2.2	14.7
Scottish Bus Group	1985/6	5.6	2.1	1.5	9.2
	1986/7	5.8	2.0	1.6	9.4
	1987/8 (p)	5.6	1.9	1.5	8.9
National Bus Company (and ex-NBC)	1985/6	28.0	10.3	8.8	47.0
	1986/7	29.0	9.4	8.5	46.9
	1987/8 (p)	28.5	7.9	7.2	43.5
Other private companies	1985/6	25.1	6.9	8.1	40.1
	1986/7	26.7	6.8	8.2	41.7
	1987/8 (p)	30.4	7.5	7.5	45.4
All operators	1985/6	105.4	37.3	31.6	174.3
	1986/7	103.7	32.9	29.9	166.5
	1987/8 (p)	103.3	29.7	25.8	158.8

Source: Reports in *Bus and Coach Statistics*, December 1988 (Table 7.3), Department of Transport.

Note: (p) = provisional figures.

NOTES

1 ECMT Round Table, August 1989.
2 *Carriers Licencing*, The Report of the Geddes Committee, 1965.
3 Cf. The Geddes Report (1965) *Carriers Licencing*, ch.8.
4 Bayliss, B.T. (1973) 'The road haulage industry since 1968', Department of the Environment, London: HMSO.

5 Cooper, J.C. (1978) 'Carrying for others: the role of the own account operator', Polytechnic of Central London, Transport Studies Group, paper no. 7.
6 The Foster Report (1979) *Report of Independent Committee of Inquiry*, November 1978, p.32, London: HMSO.
7 NFC was the National Freight Corporation, inheritor of the 1953 Act's unsold vehicles and subsequently the largest UK operator.
8 The Response of Road Haulage; 'Marketing rail freight in a deregulated market; the challenge of 1992', *UIC Freight Symposium, 17–18 May 1988*.
9 National Freight Corporation–UBS–Phillips and Drew Research Group Study, 1988.
10 ibid., pp. 3–4.
11 This is, I think, a fair summary of perhaps most economic comment since 1983. A good example is found in Vickers, J. and Yarrow, G. (1988) *Privatisation and Economic Analysis*, Cambridge, Mass.: MIT Press.
12 Davis, Evan (1984) 'Express coaching since 1980; liberalisation in practice', *Journal of Fiscal Studies*, vol. 5.1: 76–86.
13 ibid., p. 154.
14 Vickers and Yarrow, op. cit., p. 374.
15 Buses Cmnd, 9300, 1984.
16 Gwilliam, K., Nash, C.A., and Mackie, P.J. (1985) 'Deregulating the bus industry in Great Britain: (B) The case against', *Transport Reviews 1985* 5 (2), 105–32; and '(C) A response', by M.E. Beesley and S. Glaister, pp. 133–42.
17 ibid., p. 132.
18 Beesley, M.E. (1989) 'Bus deregulation: lesson from UK', International Conference on Competition and Ownership of Buses and Coach Services, Thredbo, NSW, 1–4 May 1989.
19 Tyson, W.J. (1989) 'TBM deregulation in the UK', *UTIP Review* 38–2/89, May–June.
20 ibid., p. 50.
21 Hills, P. (1989) 'Early consequence of the deregulation of bus services in Scotland', International Conference on Competition and Ownership of Buses and Coach Services, op. cit., p. 3.
22 Gwilliam, K. (1989) 'Contestability, competition practice and control', International Conference on Competition and Ownership of Buses and Coach Services, op. cit.
23 Gomez-Ibanez, J.A. and Meyer, J.R. (1989) 'Privatising and deregulating local bus services: lessons from Britain's buses', *Transportation Research Board Annual Meeting*, Washington, DC, January 1989.
24 The technicality concerned the implicit contradictions with the 1984 Act as giving London Regional Transport a duty to be responsible for and to co-ordinate passenger transport services in London.
25 Compare London Regional Transport Statement of Strategy, 1988.
26 Calculated from B&CS.
27 Calculated from B&CS.
28 Calculated from B&CS, using the retail price index deflator presented.
29 Attributing 14 seats to the up-to-16 seats category, 25 seats to the 17–35, 10 seats to the 36-plus category and 70 to double-deckers.
30 Balcomb, R.J., Hopkins, J.M., and Penet, K.E. (1989) 'Bus deregulation in Great Britain: a review of the first year', *TRRL Research Report* 161, p. 23.
31 Glaister, S. and Beesley, M.E. (1989) 'Bidding for tendered bus routes in London', *International Conference on Competition and Ownership of Buses and Coach Services*, op. cit.
32 *PSV Operator Licensing*, London: HMSO, November 1986, para. 8 and Appendix 5.

33 Compare Table 1 in O'Reilly, D.M. (1988) 'Concessionary fare schemes in Great Britain', *TRRL Report* 165, Department of Transport.
34 Goodison, P.B., Hopkins, J.M., and McKenzie, R.P. (1988) 'Bus trip generation from concessionary fares schemes: a study of six towns', *TRRL Report* 127, Department of Transport.
35 'Badger Line Holdings and Midland West Holdings', *Report of the Monopolies and Mergers Commission*, March 1989.
36 ibid., p. 18. We are not told what the market valuation was or if different from the book value.
37 Legislation to privatize the Scottish Bus Group in eleven units is currently proceeding through Parliament. Several ITA and municipally owned companies have now (1989) been sold and others are up for sale. Ministers are considering how far the very large ITA-owned companies should be split up for sale. These points were made in June 1989 by A.J. Goldman of the Department of Transport, at a Leeds seminar on the bus industry: 'The bus industry: where now? A government view'.
38 'Badger Line Holdings and Midland West Holdings, op. cit.
39 Action on these, by OFT, is pending.

14 Liberalization of the use of British Telecommunications' network[1]

M.E. Beesley

INTRODUCTION

On 21 July 1980, the Secretary of State for Industry, Sir Keith Joseph, announced to Parliament the government's proposals for relaxing British Telecommunications' monopoly. During his statement he said,

> We are going to allow people more freedom to use British Telecommunications' circuits to offer services to third parties which are not currently provided by British Telecommunications, for example in the data processing field. I expect this change to lead to a significant growth in information, data transmission, educational and entertainment services provided over telephone circuits and to the emergence of new business. I have also decided to commission an independent economic assessment of the implications of allowing complete liberalisation for what are commonly referred to as value added network services.

In September 1980 the Department of Industry commissioned me to undertake a study into the economic implications of allowing complete freedom to offer services to third parties over British Telecommunications' circuits. My terms of reference were:

> to examine the scope for, and means of realizing, profitable leasing of the network to users who would have unrestricted use of the capacity to provide services, taking account of:
> (a) the need for such arrangements to operate to the benefit of the consumer;
> (b) the effect of such arrangements on BT's present pricing structure and profitability.

I would like to thank all those who submitted evidence and gave information. In particular, I pay warm tribute to officers of British Telecommunications itself, who were open and unstinting in responding to my requests. I also owe a particular debt to Mr Peter Gist who assisted me throughout the study. Most of what follows is the result of our many discussions.

The study was of necessity essentially confined to three months. There are in consequence interested parties whose views have not been in time for incorporation. Nevertheless we did get a considerable number of submissions which I believe adequately cover the spectrum of opinion.

BACKGROUND

The Secretary of State's announcement of an independent economic study was associated with the question of how far the provisions that were called 'VANS' ('value-added network services') should be open to supply independent of British Telecommunications (BT). It was also envisaged that BT should conduct its operations in the area through a separately accountable subsidiary. This separation, and the suggestion that commercial relations affecting the supply of VANS might be subject to the scrutiny of the Director-General of Fair Trading, were thought to meet the difficulties which might ensue from the BT's continued monopoly of the network, which would mean a dependence of new entrants on a competitor for essential elements of supply. In the event, my terms of reference do not refer specifically to VANS, or to the conditions of trading that were mooted at the time of the announcement. The reasons for this follow.

As seen in the terms of reference, I was asked to consider the question of resale of BT's capacity by BT's customers who would not be restricted in the use made of that capacity, taking account in particular of effects on consumers and BT's finances. This is partly a question of assessing the attractions of such activity to newcomers, that is the scope for profitable development of services, in turn involving questions of technical feasibility and prospective payoff to companies considering entering the field. 'Consumers' I take to be in the first instance these (largely new) commercial interests and, ultimately, all consumers of new and existing telecommunications services. In so far as BT's finances and its commercial practices might be affected by the resale activity, constraints on it, and/or fresh rules to provide a framework for competition, might well be required, but it seemed premature to specify in advance of investigation what these might be; I duly consider them later. The absence of reference to VANS arises from the fact that to concentrate on them, whilst a reasonable starting point for discussion, quickly turns out to be an unsatisfactory way of attacking the underlying issues.

'Value added' betokens the idea that basic services are to be enhanced by superimposing extra activities. When one considers the nature of actual services that might be offered, however, the underlying division of labour that is postulated between basic and other services becomes hazy. The provision of such services by independents poses questions of reservation of functions to BT. More significantly, perhaps, questions of commercial opportunity and financial impact arise. Should services provided by outsiders be viewed as restricting BT's opportunities to expand, that is loss of potential sales and profit? Or should they be judged as possibly involving BT in reduction in current sales and surplus – that is, leading to an erosion of BT's current position? The last interpretation seems to have given rise to a refined VANS concept, namely 'genuine VANS', services which will not adversely affect BT's net revenues. These considerations are given added point by the fact that capacity, once in the hands of an outsider, can be used not only for activities normally in the VANS category – such as accessing, processing and then transmitting data – but also for transmitting the voice. Voice transmission is still the overwhelmingly largest part of telecommunication activity, at home and abroad. To define the scope of this inquiry by reference to such a criterion as effect on BT's revenue would have been to beg the essential questions of where the balance of advantage between consumers' and producers' gains and losses lies.

In fact, services often referred to as 'value added' can operate at several technical levels in the telecommunications system. A brief excursion into systems analysis is necessary here. In a highly simplified way, and subject to much detailed technical argument, one can envisage a telecommunications system as in Figure 14.1. It consists of two end points A and B, each consisting of a subsystem. A subsystem comprises layers of activity, the lower levels providing the transportation system of the message, and the upper the substance of the message to be transported from A to B. In between A and B, in any complicated system, comprising a network, will be a means of switching through the network, as indicated in the figure.

The system works through three elements: the physical basis – the cables, radio, apparatus, etc. making the connections; the signals, or electromagnetic variables comprising the signals transported; and the protocols, the procedures for using the system. These last essentially are rules of procedure which ensure co-operation between the various components (of the network and users). As one requests the system to take on more sophisticated end uses, so in general do protocols get more complex. A data network, for example, requires facilities for storage, multi-addressing and processing of various levels, all expressed in an appropriate protocol. This means that in constructing systems the principles of 'isolation' and 'transparency' are important. 'Isolation' means that when operating at a given level, one can consider that level on its own, without going into how other levels work. 'Transparency' means that any level can deal with a message sent by a higher level without distortion of significance.

In the figure, level 1 represents the physical currents, impedances, etc. which are put through the physical connectors. Level 2 represents the message signals and formats to be used on this link. Levels 3 and upwards represent the protocols involved. Level 3 comprises the routeing and network control functions; level 4 the end-to-end control function for transportation; levels 7 down to 5 respectively initiate the activity, present it in an acceptable form, and process it in a manner suitable for transport. Examples of 'value-added' services which operate at these several levels are: computer bureaux, data banks, and message recording, which operate at level 4 and above. Multiplexing and/or local switching to concentrate many

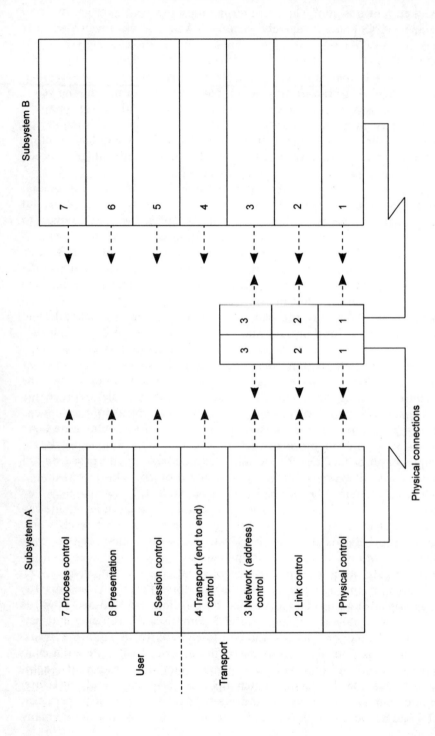

Figure 14.1 A simplified description of a telecommunications system (based on ISO system protocols)

users on to a smaller number of transport lines operates at levels 3 or 4, depending on the point of view. Essentially this activity involves a subsidiary network, grafted on to the main network. From the point of view of the owner of the main network, this is a level 4 activity; from the subsidiary network owner's point of view, level 3 activity is involved. Other examples can involve lower levels. Thus, where local switches or multiplexers are linked by the main network, levels 3 or 2 are involved.

From this description, it is clear that even the conventional telephone market, transmitting the voice, can legitimately be considered a 'value-added' service once one attempts to describe the concept in protocol terms. Ordinary telephone service operates up to level 4, at which point dialling on the instrument occurs, and, where aids to telephoning are involved (e.g. instructions for dialling, storing messages, etc.), higher levels are involved. Attempts to define boundaries of a public service carrier as a transporter or transmitter of messages distinct from further operations have failed where attempts to do so have been made in practice, as in the FCC's efforts to define a 'common carrier' as having exclusively transmitting functions. As Matheson, for example, remarks, a common carrier offering a packet network service could furnish, as part of a terminal interface protocol, the ability to 'edit' terminal input data. Should this function be defined as data processing, and excluded totally from the carrier's service offering?[2] Such a question may require an answer in regulatory practice, but a decision one way or the other cannot be defended in technical terms.

In effect, the idea of a BT 'monopoly' of the network is not a watertight one. Even if, as some US commentators hold with respect to their own system, public monopoly were to be confined to levels 1–3, boundary questions would still arise. On the other hand, it would be logically possible to declare a monopoly of the system as a whole. This, however, would involve a quite absurd incursion into areas traditionally reserved to users, and is at odds with the impact of recent technological development, which has of course seen a remarkable proliferation in applications involving particularly data transmission.

The position taken here is, therefore, to consider the benefits and costs of a specific proposal to alter the conditions which govern BT's transactions with its existing and potential customers, recognizing that there is varying degree of monopoly power as one moves up the hierarchy, which may be shifted in the future. BT will necessarily be in the position of conducting its transactions with a varying power to influence market outcomes, and it is its dual position as supplier and competitor which raises important questions of public interest in its conduct. It is also perhaps fair to say that the Post Office has operated in the past with relatively little pressure to explain and justify its commercial conduct; whatever its merits, it is certain that the need for accountability in this sense will grow, as elsewhere in public corporations' experience.

BT defines VANS as

those in which lines are leased from a common carrier by a private operator who then adds special terminal equipment or 'conditions' the lines so that they can sustain a specialised service, such as high speed facsimile or data which he then offers to the public.

The present study in effect terminates the sentence at 'operator'. The rest of the sentence seems to express two relevant ideas: first the notion of something different from BT's own services, and therefore not threatening to BT's revenues, and second the confining of the lessee to selling his own output, that is excluding resale of the capacity. The latter is crucially tied up with the possibility of sharing of lines and establishing switching capacity outside the 'common carrier' (BT's) ownership. These are seen to be undesirable not so much because of any formal breach of 'monopoly' ideas but because first, there would be a loss of net revenue involved, particularly from the long-distance voice market. Capacity to switch is important here because it greatly increases the potential opportunities to BT's voice customers to divert to private operators' services. Hence, for example, the current international 'recommendations' governing the lease of international private leased circuits in which it is provided, *inter alia*, that access to the public telephone network at each terminal of a circuit can be provided, but not in both simultaneously; and that leased circuits connecting users with a data processing centre may not be used for exchange of information between terminals directly or on a store or forward basis. In sum 'the customer shall not be permitted to operate in the manner of an Administration by providing Telecommunications services to others'.[3]

Given that substantial diversion of net revenue would be in prospect, several further disadvantages are seen. In recent years in particular public sector borrowing requirements have effectively put severe constraints on the rate of development of BT's system. To some extent constraints in borrowing can be made up by self-financing via increasing prices to consumers, particularly in an industry like telecommunications in which low elasticities of demand and substantial trend growth are experienced. A responsible nationalized industry must, it is in effect argued, not push this possibility too far, however; and indeed only in international markets, not directly of concern to this inquiry, are elasticities high enough to suggest that monopoly power is in fact exercised as it might be.[4] Real price increases are considered to be difficult to justify in public terms. Loss of net revenue therefore is seen as a direct brake on developing the system; and certainly it is not hard to imagine that, even given self-imposed constraints on pricing – such as is practised for example by AT & T in the USA – BT could very easily expand its resources for development by direct recourse to the capital markets.[5] Reduction in the rate of expansion would lessen future prospective net cash inflows, reflect adversely on staff morale, and dampen innovation.

Other immediate and strategic disadvantages are seen: loss of net revenue implies a lessening of the capacity to cross-subsidize. The Post Office's traditional protection of the right of all customers to be connected to the network, irrespective of geographical location, at no penalty, and, similarly, the provision of universally high standards would be compromised. The threat would be the worse because the concession of the right to resell without constraint would ultimately tend to undermine a lucrative international market (the UK would be alone among CCITT members in this concession). Currently, surpluses ('business profits') on international services accounted for £165.6 million of a total of £236.1 million, with inland services at −£36.5 million (the balance being made up of 'exceptional items') (1979/80).

Aside from possible threats to net revenue, BT would be generally uneasy about what would amount to a lessening of its present degree of monopoly of supply. This stems from, on the one hand, a belief in the 'natural monopoly' argument, and on the other from considerations of optimal technical development of the network. The 'natural monopoly' argument has been put to us in terms of the economies of scale in transmission and switching: the belief is that sharing development of the network inevitably means higher real costs to consumers. This argument is in one sense peripheral to our main interest in that its full force would only become apparent were direct entry by one or more competing common carriers in question. However, in so far as unrestricted leasing leads to the building of private switched networks, the point stands. As seen later, the evidence is rather controversial and bears only indirectly on the central question of the future costs in an expanding network. A more relevant worry is the question of how far breaching of the monopoly supply is consistent with what is regarded as the best technical development of the network. BT puts the point in the following way:

> BT does not wish to see any reduction in its capacity to develop a disciplined telecommunications infrastructure (technical and administrative arrangements which support interconnection both nationally and internationally...which can be undermined by incompatible services and products).... It thus needs to form a view on the extent to which a proposed new service...would lead to the proliferation of specialised incompatible networks, and would thus harm exploitation of information technology.

We understand this worry to arise from the needs of system architecture. It is convenient to deal with it at this point, for it seems to be rather a red herring. In designing large networks, only a partitioning into modules and levels makes a workable design possible. Partitioning means functional modules such as terminal links and subsystems for switching, control, etc. at nodal centres. Modern telephone systems developed around the modular principle, and BT is no exception. The digital System X, towards which the development of its exchange system is directed, is modular in concept. On the other hand, the protocol level concept outlined earlier arose in the field of computer networks. It seems to be accepted that both concepts are now essential. Their juxtaposition enhances the need for defining the concepts of isolation and transparency, also noticed earlier. Particularly is this so with developments involving levels 3–5 in protocol terms; and the proliferation of the kind of services under review here would certainly increase the task of standardization. However, standardization does not imply veto by BT or restriction of other producers' efforts; relevant agreements can be reached via normal professional channels. Design freedom implies specifications of a more functional nature than would otherwise be the case, which would in turn imply a willingness to generate such specifications. There is no reason to suppose that these would not be forthcoming in the existing arrangements or suitable developments of them. We should also note that the likelihood that the System X plus a public packet switched network, when fully developed, could cope with all substantial user needs is not in itself a technical reason for BT's control of developing specifications. It may be, of course, that the costs of developing specifications will be affected, but this can hardly be a significant element in the investment involved.

CURRENT POSITIONS ON RESALE

For several reasons, then, BT would prefer not to see an untrammelled development of leased capacity. In its evidence to us, it 'accepts that it is unrealistic and inadvisable to provide all new services with a significant telecom element on a monopoly basis'. It also

> accepts that a case can be made for the provision of services to third parties using private circuits from BT whenever these services provide added value to the end user, are significantly different from those provided or planned by BT, and in the effective national exploitation of information technology.

The Post Office Engineering Union, though it would ideally like to carry the idea of a supply monopoly further, takes essentially a similar position. Should there be further liberalization, however, BT would like to see various safeguards, in particular that there should be 'positive evidence that there is a national net benefit to the use of resources', and that

> there is no net financial disbenefit to BT, and that ... there is no inhibition to the development of enhanced telecommunications systems, e.g. by introducing systems which will not be capable of interconnection with wider services which may be provided. The system should also conform to relevant standards.

(BT's evidence also proposes other measures concerning the oversight and functioning of the arrangements, which fall to be considered when the substantive change has been evaluated.) The essence of their submission is therefore that service differentiation should be ensured, and no financial loss be in prospect.

On the other hand, we received many examples designed to illustrate the proposition that BT's monopoly had slowed down the development of new services. Delays were cited in providing advertised services, including installing private circuits, telephone extensions and PBXs. An outcome of the monopoly was also held to be slowness in developing technology and introducing new services. Examples quoted were the long gestation period for the stored programme control PABX 'Monarch', still not at the time of writing available in London; of development of digital technology, which has, it is said, restricted the provision of the range of services already available in the USA, for example the more extensive packet switching available (though not through AT & T) and push-button phones with memory for telephone numbers, etc. There were those, much fewer but not confined to BT or POEU, who thought well of BT's achievements; for example, a high proportion of direct dialling internationally, and the uses which could now be made of Prestel, BT's viewdata service.

These submissions, pro and con, do not amount to much more than illustrations of an already articulated position for or against a BT monopoly. The general relations between that monopoly and the likely emergence and rate of growth of new services are indeed relevant, but require a more systematic treatment, and we return to the subject later. More to the immediate point is the question of restraints on what may be done with BT's private leased circuits; and we received several examples of developments which the resale restriction inhibits. These include: a large company who wished to access another large company's computer service for storing and forwarding of messages; direct debit arrangements between customers and banks; extension of professional services to related financial and other institutions; and radio paging services who also wished to extend their existing business to store and forward messages. The common characteristic of these is the sharing of leased circuits with other businesses thus obviating the need for the second or third parties to have their own direct BT lines. The function is essentially that of retailing BT's capacity.

BT licenses a large number of services consistent with its principal policies, namely: not allowing private switching between independent parties; permitting services in which it has no commercial interest; and product or service differentiation. These can be run under general licences, as with indoor speaking telephones, alarm systems in old people's dwellings,[6] or message-conveying computers relating solely and exclusively to the business affairs of either the operator or the addressee of the message. Individual licences have been granted, for example, for outside broadcast links; cable television and communal aerial systems; private automatic exchanges allowing a company and its subsidiaries or public service organizations to share a network run over BT's circuits; private mobile radio systems, including radio paging systems; North Sea microwave links; and music by wire, for the distribution of recorded music to business premises or restaurants.

There has been a tendency to grant licences more freely, we are told; an example quoted is in mobile radios, where for some years it was PO policy to insist that wherever practicable PO circuits must be used for the remote control links. Recently this was relaxed to allow operators to run their own remote control links.

On the other hand, the limits have been confirmed in refusals of 'firm proposals' for: a competitive public telephone system; tone-only paging in London (an example of a direct competitor to PO's own service, a decision now under review); privately maintained equipment deemed an integral part of the public network; and message-switching facilities where the private equipment was run outside the terms of the general licence (just noted) and offering third-party switching between unrelated organizations. BT thus takes a general stand on its principles but is willing to consider exceptions to the rules which it judges to have commercial advantages to it.

We have received relatively few representations of proposals frustrated by present BT policies on leasing and these are not always concrete. Those that we listed above tend to centre on ideas breaching the essential BT criteria for licensing, for example a radio pager who would like to incorporate message switching, and a public sector body operating its own network on leased lines who would like to explore the possibilities of storing voice messages for transmission.

One reason for this comparative paucity is that those who formulate concrete proposals have an interest not so much in innovation in general but their own prospective position in particular. A licence from BT under present conditions essentially grants a limited extension of the BT's own monopoly; the prospects for profit are enhanced by applications which do *not* open the door for further competition. In some cases, negotiations with BT are in progress.

Second, innovation awaits upon legislation. We were told, quite frequently, that concrete proposals would have to await the passage of the Bill. This accords with US experience: innovative activity has tended to accelerate after key decisions favouring liberalization. Third, much innovation can be expected to be simply a replication of existing services enjoyed by those firms large enough to lease their own private circuits, for one effect of allowing freer resale would be to encourage middlemen, providing for smaller firms on a sharing basis what is now enjoyed by larger. Fourth, taking advantage of switching capability would encourage the emergence of consortia, for example to establish credit checking and cash transfer facilities via co-operation between banks and retailers. Until such possibilities are seen concretely to exist, consortia have little chance to become effective. Much depends on trial and error, and potential surprise is high. A striking example of this, quoted to us by MCI Communications Corporation,[7] was MCI's recent foray into the residential call market in Denver. The approach to the potential residential market was based, for the first time in MCI's marketing plans, on TV advertising. An unexpected by-product was a considerable response by small firms interested not in residential service, but in MCI's regular 'Execunet' services, of which the customers were previously unaware.

So for various reasons we cannot rely on current development to gauge potential with free resale. Free resale would radically alter the way in which relevant business would assess the possibilities of developing new services. Many of the opportunities will centre around the use of concentrators to economize on the number of lines needed to conduct services. Efficiency will often require the sharing of capacity by independent enterprises. This is a question of not only giving to smaller clients what can already be given to, or developed themselves by, larger clients, but also being an important additional element in larger organizations planning to access data banks, store and forward messages by operators or machines, etc. on the same network. The principles involved are not new to BT; it is simply a question of opening the door to a much wider set of potential users. It is therefore useful to consider whether there is any more general evidence bearing on the question of development of the non-voice markets and liberalization. The next section reviews some relevant data.

LOSS OF BT REVENUE AND PROFIT

BT has estimated for the Department of Industry what the losses of revenue from inland calls would be were unconstrained reselling of its capacity allowed, focusing on 1984/5 out-turns. It assumes that: international resale services will not be permitted; there will be no entry into network provision; and impacts on revenue from private circuits will be small, because 'private circuits tend to be used to capacity'. It also assumes a neutral effect so far as market expansion in 'value-added' services is concerned; any loss of business from existing or potential BT services 'will be offset by revenue from stimulation of the market as a result of innovation, in which BT will share'. (This seems to imply that the effect of liberalization must be to expand the total market, confirming earlier arguments in this report.) In working out the impacts on trunk revenue diverted, BT makes a number of assumptions which lead to a loss of (somewhat less than) £39 million (1984/5 prices). This would be offset by gains in revenue from local calls to give access to the leased lines, of £9 million. The net loss of revenue would therefore be £30 million.

For various reasons, BT thinks this estimate of what is usually referred to as 'cream skimming' is a likely underestimate. Partly basing itself on US experience, it points to the following factors favouring a greater expansion: cash consciousness of companies; increasing sophistication by customers in their use of information handling, and its growing significance for management; the probability of US companies' entry to the market, with an eye on future extension of the principles to international markets, and the UK's compactness, making it easier to move beyond the main towns. On assumptions reflecting these factors, BT estimates a revenue loss of £140 million, offset by £30 million in local calls, making £110 million. So the range between the lower and upper estimates, assuming there are no offsetting changes in costs due to diversion of traffic, assesses the prospective loss of that revenue at between 0.4 per cent and 1.5 per cent of gross revenue; between 3.2 per cent and 12 per cent of profits; and between 1 per cent and 4 per cent of capital outlays.

The upper estimates postulate a fairly large business for the newcomers in aggregate, probably about the same as was achieved by US independents in 1979 (at $367 million), if one takes into account the extra non-voice service revenues. BT's analysis notes that, in 1979, the five major US capacity resale companies using AT & T facilities, as opposed to the other independents, had a revenue of $47 million. These are mainly sales of non-voice services. Compared with the larger independents, whose business is chiefly voice (we were told that it was up to 93 per cent), it is clear that resale *without* voice is indeed likely to be a relatively minor activity. Both voice and non-voice markets are growing fast, of course: MCI for example increased its total revenue by 45 per cent between 1979 and 1980;[8] and the President of SP Communications reports a current 4 per cent *monthly* growth rate to us in November 1980. However, both voice and non-voice markets are growing roughly in step. This again reinforces the perception of 'non-voice' markets as an issue, secondary in business development terms, to the voice business. But there is reason to think that the threat of diversion is somewhat exaggerated by the higher estimate, more especially in the time period assumed.

Indeed, the estimates seem very vulnerable when put in a business development context. They approach the problem by calculating what part of BT's revenues are at risk. This is natural, but it does not deal specifically with what would be involved in entry to the market via leasing. For one thing, the estimates depend heavily on penetration of the small business market (which we may identify as those having one line only). Over half of the loss of calls in the upper estimate is deemed to be in this market. (The two-five-line market accounts for a further fifth.) US experience is against this. The independents have developed by concentrating on larger-scale businesses in specific city-pair markets, for obvious reasons of costs of serving customers and the possibility of offering more than a competitive voice option (data transmission needs are correlated with size of business). The plausibility of BT's estimate can to some extent be checked.

After some years of growth, and three years after reaching the point of positive profits, MCI in 1980 had an average billing of $3,500 per customer. This was lower than the figure of $5,000 for 1979, which was before MCI had entered the residential market.[9] BT's assumption of 45.5 per cent of lines vulnerable to attack means that the 'attacker' would be dealing with much smaller customers on average – there were, for example, 1,916,000 business single-line customers in 1979; there would presumably be more in 1984/5. If, as the assumptions imply, about 30 per cent of these customers would be induced to shift partly to the 'attacker', there would be perhaps some 600,000 such customers in 1984/5, with an average 'attacker's' billing for the voice market of under £200 a year each (at 1984/5 prices). Considering that price rises of more than 10 per cent a year between now and then are widely anticipated, the projective average billing looks far too small to tempt the 'attacker'. On the other hand, it is quite plausible to suppose that nearly all large businesses, those having eleven or more lines, would opt to include new services. There were 10,000 of these at 1979; but they account for only £17 million of the postulated £140 million loss, of £1,700 a year each – much more in line with current US billings.

Furthermore, we have to consider the changes a would-be 'attacker', the private operator, has to face. A crucial assumption is the persistence of BT's present pricing structure by which trunk calls are priced above cost and the revenues contribute to subsidizing local calls and private circuit rentals (which have been recently subject to price revision, but still, we understand, are below what BT would regard as a rental which would be in line with BT's ambitions 'to balance returns correctly' between sectors of its business.) We have to assess the likely impact of BT's price changes.

The extent to which a private operator can divert calls is, in the limit, determined by the capacity of the leases he takes. We can assume as a first approximation that there is no restriction on leasing, assumed to be governed simply by the demand forthcoming at the announced prices for private circuits. (The latter prices could be changed, as argued later, but the likelihood of this depends on the scope of the business involved, the power of BT to discriminate between lessees with different uses in mind, and, ultimately, any rules governing competitive relationships which might be established.) We have continued BT's own conjectures on the revenue vulnerability issue by calculating what inducements face the private operator.

We first illustrate this in the following example. We suppose a private operator who leases a circuit at a fixed annual rental between two of his or her offices over which customers' telephone calls are routed. This pattern of operation, a likely arrangement, though simplified for the example, is that the calls to the office are switched on to the leased circuit, transmitted to the second office, and then switched back to the local telephone network.[10] The customer using the private operator thus faces the price of two local calls (one at each end) and the price charged by the operator. The latter must, to compete effectively, offer a price reduction; this price must be less than the STD price for a call *less* the price of two local phone calls. (We assume, as is realistic, that the customer will keep his BT connection going. Therefore, the relevant BT price avoided is the STD call for the distance and time of day involved.)

With BT prices at November 1980, and reckoning on a five-minute peak rate call, when call prices are at their highest for business callers, and alternatively for up to and over 56 km (the principal distinction now made for inland STD calls), we arrive at the following margins for effective competition:

			£	£
Up to 56 kmm	Price of local calls	$0.10 \times 2 =$		0.2
	STD price			0.4
	Margin			0.2
56 km and over	Price of local calls	$0.10 \times 2 =$		0.2
	STD price			1.2
	Margin			1.0

These represent the present chance of 'cream skimming' on trunk routes.

However, as we have noted, BT has a clearly enumerated policy, irrespective of the leasing issue, of revising charges to correct for present shortcomings, seen as a failure to reflect costs of provision closely enough. We have not investigated the cost position thoroughly enough to pronounce on the correctness of this view from the perspective of what is conducive to a better allocation of resources. But the basis of costing in BT has been explained, and we recognize it as a form of fully allocated costing which, whatever its formal distance from the incremental costing normally associated with economic argument, will probably be adequate for the problem we are concerned with, namely the pricing appropriate for an expanding industry over a reasonable time period ahead.

It is in any case common economic wisdom in telecommunications that prices for long-distance phone calls give larger margins than for short. In the USA in particular, this perception is a major reason given by regulators in justifying reform of tariffs. It is relevant to remark here that eleven years of costing exercises designed to 'allocate' costs acceptable under FCC aegis were described to us as a complete failure. What is inspiring the reform of tariffs in the USA is not a result of delving into AT & T's realized costs, but the facts of potential entry. It is quite clear that, whereas entry into long-distance carrying is subject particularly to new forms of technique, leading to marked anticipated falls in real costs, local distribution is not so greatly affected. Hence, whatever these historic relationships, future prospects strongly indicate that local prices will have to rise relative to long distance if costs are to be the dominant basis. We may therefore accept this price change as at least moving in the correct direction from the point of view of allocating resources. BT gave us some figures to illustrate what these price changes could be.

Under these notional prices, the margins would be changed:

			£	£
Up to 56 km	Price of local calls	$0.13 \times 2 =$		0.26
	STD price			0.27
	Margin			0.01
	Price of local calls	$0.13 \times 2 =$		0.26
Over 56 km	STD price			0.67
	Margin			0.41

Price 'corrections', justified by BT on cost grounds, would then virtually wipe out the margin up to 56 km, and reduce it by over 50 per cent for 56 km and over. But adjustments to BT rental charges to reflect costs more closely would also involve changes for private circuits. We now have to allow for this in our calculations. Rises required would be sharp up to about 50 km, but would not be substantial at greater distances. We have accordingly calculated the lessee's position under these price changes.

Obviously most interest centres in the longer-distance markets – because of the relationships just noted, because much higher rentals would more than eliminate the 'cream', and because of the nature of the potential market, concentrated on city pairs at 56 km and upwards. It is one of the curiosities of corporate planning in BT that we could not base our analysis, as we would have wished, on city-pair, origin and destination volumes of calls, still less on the major customers' own origin and destination call patterns. Planning is content to estimate volumes at points on the networks, undoubtedly useful when considering volume-related investments, but inadequate to confront specific competitive threats.

We assume that a private operator would fill his or her capacity by diverting 4,000 calls a year for a line, involving some multiplexing, which gives a reasonable expectation of maintaining a quality of service comparable to BT's. For 64 km and 112 km, current annual rentals are £1,000 and £1,520 respectively, and would notionally rise by 2 per cent and 0.5 per cent. Before the adjustment, at 64 km and under current conditions, the lessee would make £3,000 a year; and with a 112 km circuit £2,480. In the postulated 'cost-adjusted' situation, these figures would fall to £620 and £112 respectively, decreases of some 80 per cent or more. The examples are sufficient to show that 'cream skimming' is extremely vulnerable to price changes quite justified in terms of BT's costs. Cost-based pricing is a general ambition for nationalized industries. That there is doubt about the speed with which these aims may be achieved simply adds to prospective lessees' uncertainty.

The argument so far is that much of the fear of 'cream skimming' is a function of the present BT price structure, correctable in principle and indicating an uncertain prospect in home markets for the lessees. There are also possibilities for bringing BT's tariffs closer to costs than have been assumed in the foregoing discussion. An important example for the diversion issue is a tariff for trunk calls with more recognition of distance than can be accommodated in the present two-band distinction. More distance bands would at once make tariffs reflect costs better and reduce the margins which attract competition. We have yet to consider possibilities of specific BT price retaliation, the question of whether BT and lessees might gain by bargaining together, and the question of possible quality change. We should note, however, some implicit ambiguity in the views of entry inducements just discussed. BT assumes some adjustment of prices at least towards equalizing returns from sectors. It is not clear how far the diversion calculations just examined did so, perhaps implicitly; we think they probably did not, since the approach taken was quite different. It is clear that material used by the department on diversion assumed no such change, because part of its enumeration of 'action open to BT to preserve its revenue', which the BT paper has indicated was at risk to the degree just described, was equalizing returns on charges. The most relevant 'balancing' is for us in the business market, which, together with the headroom given by the changing RPI in an industry like telecommunications, should be sufficient to enable the price adjustments we have indicated.

BT gave us a separate estimate of the effects of compensating for trunk call revenue losses by residential rental increases. From this it emerges that, at 1981/2 forecast levels, each 1 per cent loss of trunk call revenue, whether due to the activities of alternate carriers or to introducing a more correlated tariff, requires for recoupment a 2 per cent increase in residential rentals. The base trunk call revenue assumed was £1,600 million; so for each £16 million in lost revenue, the hypothesized residential rental of £60 per annum would have to rise by £1.20. Using the index of deflation consistent with BT's own estimates, to translate the outside BT estimate, given earlier, of £110 million loss in 1984/5 to £85.7 million, at 1981/2 prices, we reach the conclusion that the compensating rental rise for residential consumers would be £6.40.[11] This, for reasons given earlier, is the maximum estimate and gives a far less alarming view of the likely impact of required impositions than it appears at first sight. It is not, however, a negligible sacrifice to require of residential consumers, and we must enquire whether the prospective losses would be altered by the further factors just mentioned.[12] As BT points out, the loss of residential system size due to rental increases will emerge as a persistent depression in net demand. Each 10 per cent increase in rentals results in a loss in new residential demand, and thus installation work, of about 2.5 per cent. Elasticities might, they say, increase from 0.1 at higher tariff levels, indicating further price increases to compensate. Nevertheless, the estimate looks reasonable; and losses of system size of course have implications for lessening required capital outlay also not specifically considered in this calculation.

So far, the implicit view of effects of competition by lessees is that there is a zero-sum game: lessees' gains will be BT's losses. This ignores first the possibility that there would be a response to the lower average prices which must, if lessees are to undercut BT, occur. Estimates of elasticity of telephone demand are not wholly convincing. As Appendix 1 shows, a large variance is found between studies. One of the most unsatisfactory features is the tendency to work in terms of calls, rather than the more relevant account of the total time demanded. Sellers of telephone capacity are presumably interested in the time sold, not only the individual call. This is certainly true for pricing systems based on time, as in BT's case. The analogy with transport is apt – public carriers sell seat miles, not simply seats. BT, for most of its work, assumes a (call) elasticity of -0.1, at the low end of the range of estimates. (As we have seen it recognizes higher elasticities for the decision to join or leave the network, but these are still influenced by the -0.1 call assumption, and are well below unity. BT also believes in a much higher elasticity for international calls, approaching unity.) However, we accept that even if true elasticities are higher than assumed, it is highly unlikely that they will exceed unity at the going prices, as is necessary to derive extra revenue from a price fall. Other things being equal, then, the lower average price will increase use of the network, somewhat depress total revenue, and, more so, to the extent that there are extra costs associated with more use, reduce the joint profits available to BT plus competition. (Consumers of course gain directly from this.)

'Other things' may not be equal. In particular, it may be the case that private operators, diligently chasing business, and deploying the well-chosen marketing and advertising methods seemingly characteristic of American entrepreneurship in this field, could discover additional sources of revenue. In other words, were BT to be effectively constrained from such activities, for whatever reason, the private operator could add to benefits. It is unlikely, however, that the private operator will be able to do so without cutting prices. A possible position is that BT cannot or will not discriminate between customers, but the private operator could do so. This could create a situation more profitable to BT. Let us imagine, for example, a private operator who has already leased a 64 km circuit from BT which has to be filled by diverting the 4,000 calls a year assumed earlier. The operator then leases an additional 64 km circuit. If this is to stimulate further traffic it has to be by price concessions coupled with an elasticity of more than unity. A price concession could either be given to all or some customers. We therefore suppose either a single price conceded to all customers, including the diverted customers or a series confined to customer groups. In both cases, we assume, for purposes of illustration, a very high elasticity of -2.5. Then the outcomes will vary according to the price concessions made. The following table, 14.1, shows the possibilities and refers to 'cost-adjusted' prices described earlier.

This example ignores costs associated with changing number of calls, and indeed the private operator's costs of conducting business, which have to come out of the gross margin, but it does serve to show that:

1 The extent of the profit the private operator makes is never as great as that which can be made with one circuit, unless he or she can discriminate. The operator would indeed need a discriminatory cut of more than 20 per cent to achieve this ((b) in Table 14.1);
2 It will pay BT to allow price discrimination which it itself forswears. BT gains whether the private operator gives a single or multiple price concession; it sells more capacity, and gains from local calls.

Thus it is likely that possibilities of discrimination would lessen the prospective loss via diversion. The offset will be much smaller than that of the illustration, for reasons of lower realized elasticities and other costs. The inducement to hire capacity for this purpose is therefore limited.

The discussion so far has also assumed that customers are given the same quality of service. The standards worked to by BT are high but arbitrary. Clearly another basis for discrimination, which might again be practised by the private operator only, is to offer lower quality but at a lower price, pack the circuits more effectively and thus increase net revenue. It is indeed highly probable that the availability of options involving different price and quality combinations would yield higher revenues and consumer benefits. Supposing, as we do at this point of the argument, that BT maintains its own standards, and merely permits lower quality to be supplied by the private operators, free to choose their own standards, it is likely that a better mix would actually emerge – as it has done, we are told, in the USA. (It would be unwise to impose minimum call quality standard on all

Table 14.1　Margins made on two circuits with and without price discrimination

Price charged by private operator £	Price concession	Number of calls		Call revenue		Private operator's rental costs £
		(a) Same price to all	(b) Different prices	(a) £	(b) £	
0.41	0	4,000	4,000	1,640	1,640	1,020
0.34	10%	5,140	4,000 at 0.41 plus 1,140 at £0.34	1,748	2,028	2,040
0.28	20%	6,667	Above plus 1,527 at £0.28	1,867	2,456	2,040

Private operator's gross margin		BT's diversion loss £	BT's gain from local calls £	BT's revenue circuit rental £	BT's margin £
(a) £	(b) £				
+620	+620	2,680	1,040	1,020	−620
−292	−12	2,680	1,336	2,040	+696
−173	+416	2,680	1,733	2,040	+1,093

competitors, BT and competitors alike. This would reduce possibilities of profit and consumer satisfaction. Moreover, private operators would then complain that they would be at a disadvantage because of the deterioration in call quality inherent in transmitting through local exchanges in tandem. This would complicate the problem of ensuring 'fair' competitive conditions and give rise, as it has in the USA, to demands for private operators to be connected directly to higher levels of the network, e.g. on the trunk side of local exchanges.) It would be a simple and practical thing for BT to allow; and it is, in any case, difficult to see how private operators' choice in the matter could be prevented.

We are unable to speculate very far about how private operators' costs are likely to behave, for the work they do either in substitution for, or in addition to, BT's own service. In so far as they can show some improvement in costs compared to BT's alternative of in-house production, so will their prospective profits be improved. Given that competition is active in the resale markets, so also will the position of the consumer improve. Evidence on economies of scale in the most relevant activity, multiplexing and switching, is not particularly consistent. We have been told by BT of 'substantial' economies in switching. Other authorities (e.g. Charles River Associates) downpoint its importance.

> In summary, engineering studies conclude that large economies of scale are present in long distance terrestrial transmission. Investment costs typically focus on only one component of such costs (basic transmission), excluding all related equipment such as multiplexing (and switching when needed) and related operating costs. When these other cost elements are included, overall economies of scale appear lower.[13]

It is in any case highly doubtful whether economies of scale, viewed as a question of expanding a total system, are directly relevant to the issue considered here (they obviously are germane to issues of entry into transmission and associated activities). Strictly, we should compare additions to BT's activities with like additions conducted by independents including *all* differences in options open to the respective parties to affect their costs. We suspect that whereas losses in scale-related economies are inevitable in the context of dividing a given amount of work between two or more parties, the outcome is not only less clear if there is a question of additional total market size connected with outsiders' activities, but it also misses important potential sources of cost saving in practice. To name one obvious difference: other things being equal, the independents would have a much less constrained choice of suppliers of equipment than will BT as a nationalized industry. They will have greater freedom to redraw labour contracts or create resources. There are doubtless economies of specialization to markets in other ways too. It would, in sum, be very risky to assume a cost penalty in independent operations.[14]

Leaving the issue of relative costs on one side, then, it remains possible that the private operators and BT could, jointly, gain from resale activities. True, these depend to an extent on special assumptions about BT's own self-denying, or imposed, inhibitions. Such inhibitions are characteristic not only of nationalized industries, but also of many very large and publicly exposed telephone operations. The question that naturally arises is, therefore, whether BT's prospective loss of profits can be lessened, or its gains increased, by altering another assumption, namely that BT sells to private operators on terms common for leasing and available to all comers. Could BT not raise rentals to operators, or in some other way increase charges to them? There are two possible sources of such an increase: the first is in the prospects just discussed, and the second is by trying to capture some of the rewards the private operator gets from his non-voice business. BT could capture a share of the prospective extra surplus in several ways – by charging resellers a higher rental, by negotiating a royalty payment reflecting the higher anticipated revenues, or by auctioning its capacity.

The last we may perhaps discount as too alien a procedure. However, it is attractive in principle. If BT were to announce that a certain number of city-pair lines would be made available for use for unrestricted resale purposes, and that rights to use these would be permanent and transferable at will, it could auction the capacity and sell all rights to the successful bidders. Probably the rule would have to be that sealed bids would be called for, all transactions being then fixed at the lowest successful bid, that is the bid which, when all are ranked, is just sufficient to secure the last unit of capacity. (BT could extract more individual surplus by more discriminatory procedures, but would probably have to be content to see the minimum successful price at a lower level, because the chance of picking up capacity at less than one is prepared to pay at the limit is itself an inducement to enter the auction.) So long as the 'successful' bid level exceeded BT's expected return from not leasing the capacity in the resale market it would gain. It could in any case set a lower limit for bids, namely the usual lease price without the belief that resale is profitable. No doubt, BT would proceed cautiously, letting out relatively little to begin with and, with favourable results, could expand. The information arising would be useful too for whatever monitoring or regulatory process BT might be subject to. Indeed, market tests of the value of capacity are precisely the most difficult kind of information for monitors or regulators to acquire.

A similar process could be performed with more limited rights than permanency, and free resale of rights to others, but with less likelihood of net gains to BT, because of the extra uncertainties implied. Similarly, the value of the rights in prospective customers' eyes would be lessened by prospects of extra capacity being made available in a second and subsequent auction. BT would have a further incentive to proceed with caution. The auction idea may seem odd, but it merely proceeds from the alternative of working with quantity rather than price: the more normal way of thinking about the possibilities is to formulate a price, either nominated for the capacity in advance, as in effect assumed in our examples, or arrived at between BT and prospective customers. When the approach is via price, the quantity settles itself. When it is by the quantity, the price is the free variable. Prediction of outcomes is a common problem to both. With the auction procedure, there would be a basic need for the Department to monitor the question of whether sufficient capacity is provided, that is to check on the profits made by lessees and the values at which the rights change hands. The procedures described later for monitoring would there-fore apply.

If BT were to proceed by adhering to its traditional practice of announ-cing prices for leased lines irrespective of the (permitted) purposes to which they were to be put, but simply altering the present ban on resale, then it would only reap net benefits from the resale relaxation were the average price of leased circuits to rise. It is unlikely to affect BT's desired price for leasing circuits very much, for the simple reason that by far the majority of transactions governing leased circuits would not involve resale operators. As argued earlier, resale operators would offer to most customers an altern-ative, or complement as they would see it, to BT's services. Few companies would be content to rely on resale operators' capacity alone, and the practical market scope, as we said, must for a long time ahead consist chiefly of the larger users who, though they may have individually specta-cularly high bills,[15] do not dominate the private leased set.

The third alternative is for BT to charge the resale operators according to some measure of the value they set upon the opportunity, presumably in the form of a leasing charge at the normal circuit rentals, with the appropriate quantity discounts for groups, etc., together with a royalty payment accord-ing to use. Both BT and POEU would wish to see this safeguard to BT's revenue were resale allowed. The normal monitoring agreed to in contracts associated with royalty deals is difficult in the case of telecommunications, as it would require special measures to check by time of day, extent of use in the network concerned, etc. This could be achieved, at some cost, but it would probably be unnecessary, in that revenues of the private operator could be a base. This is already proposed in the case of Reuters, we under-stand, and payment by use made of circuits has precedents in international markets.[16] True, BT would have, to some extent, to trust reporting by customers. But there are normally independent sources for checking com-pany revenues, and rights of inspection could be granted, if necessary. It is quite a different matter if some attempt were made to allow resale subject to avoidance of the voice market. Here there would be every incentive to conceal those revenues attributable to the leased capacity, and it is extre-mely difficult to imagine the content of messages being discriminated, that is to sort the 'legitimate' from the 'illegitimate' use of the capacity. Here again, however, it could be achieved, albeit at much higher costs than merely surveying total quantity of use. We understand also that discrimination based solely on the use of leased capacity would also encounter objections in terms of EEC competition rules.[17] The real point is that neither party in the transaction would deem it a tolerable state of affairs to anticipate. Everyone accepts that if resale is to be allowed, one must expect and allow for the fact that voices will be part of the messages sent.

Leased circuit charges plus a royalty seem, therefore, the most appropriate form for charging to reflect customers' prospective benefits. Other bases have been suggested, but these seem to be inferior and therefore unnecessary if royalties are indeed as feasible as they appear to be. Examples of alternatives are access charges to the local network, that is in effect raising the circuit charges, and basing circuit charges on the traffic-handling capacity of equipment. Both are partial in effect. The first increases the risk faced by prospective operators by increasing the lump sum payments to be faced. The second ignores the fact that some uses are more profitable to operators than others. One wants the incentives to lessor and lessee to run as closely together as possible; and royalties share risks. Also, traffic-handling capacity is a doubtful quantity, hard to fix in advance of market experiment and liable to technological slippage.

BT could strike individual bargains on the basis of royalties and achieve a high degree of discrimination between resale operators – in fact, it would have to do so, because it would be impossible to squeeze all conceivable operators into one fixed royalty payment. Different potential operators would vary considerably in the value they proposed to add to leased capacity. Codification of opportunities to types of resale activities seems very far-fetched in a field of complex and rapid technical development; and bargains would have to reflect the degree which each side anticipated that these activities would result in diversion of voice revenues from BT. Individual bargains for royalties would have to be struck.

To this there could well arise objections of principle. Bargaining power would seem, and in reality probably would be, unequal. *De facto* discrimination would seem 'unfair' as between prospective private operators. BT could be deemed to be dragging its feet in concluding transactions. Unsuccessful bargaining would be labelled wilful refusal to treat. There could well be difficulty with meeting competition rules. But for the present argument about effects on BT's financial outcomes these points are immaterial. BT could, undoubtedly, reduce its prospective losses of net revenue by striking bargains reflecting the prospective gain by resellers. It represents the most attractive way to assuage the effects of reselling which is in principle open to BT. Of our options, auctioning is far too explicit, and is essentially irreversible. Royalties of unrelated payments offer the most flexible, least risky, and at the same time possible financially advantageous option – as seen from BT's viewpoint.

From the consumer's viewpoint, the issue is less clear. Discrimination tends to increase output, and to that extent is a benefit. However, the consumer has an interest in conditions generally favourable to innovative activity. It may well be that here the interest lies in conditions reducing prospective uncertainty for those wishing to establish new business. The known and predictable terms for acquiring capacity (i.e. the price announced in advance and similar for all comers) are probably superior for this. Having discarded the auction option as unacceptable for reasons of unfamiliarity and radicalness, this points to freedom for BT to set the level of prices of private circuits, but equally to non-discriminatory access to that capacity.

The price charged by BT would be for renting a circuit. It would not include royalty payments. It has been put to us that a royalty might be paid which is the same for all comers, thus avoiding the objections just raised, and at the same time doing something to recoup for BT the losses it might otherwise face. We do not think such a standard royalty would be desirable, for these main reasons. First, a standard mark-up on turnover is difficult to defend in terms of its effect on the allocation of resources. It neither reflects prospective profits made by lessees (which would be more defensible) nor, more important, BT's own costs of supplying circuits. It would also act as a tax on innovation, undesirable in itself. Second, in practical terms, the standard has to be picked and, in the end, justified, in terms of its effects. This would inevitably involve the Department in judgements which, as we argue later, there are good reasons to avoid. Also, in practice, and given their generally pessimistic view of elasticities in the voice market, which we have argued will be aligned with the development of non-voice services, BT would press for higher rather than lower royalties in order to discourage competition. Third, any royalty system must involve the specification of those who resell and those who do not. This, in contrast with the rule for which we have argued, sets up a basis on which non-price discrimination could be effected. Without a royalty, it becomes much more difficult to distinguish potential competitors from allies, which is one intention of the non-discriminatory rule.

A final assumption made in these arguments is that BT would not retaliate to attempt to restore its 'losses', if any, as a result of the lessee's operations. Retaliation could take the form of direct price cutting to limit operators' voice returns, predatory competition with like services of its own in the non-voice markets, and lowering of service qualities. None of these, we think, would be a particularly attractive course of action when compared with that of seeking to share in the gains made by private operators. Price cutting in the voice market presupposes effective counter-offers to private operators' customers, which we argue will be large organizations and concentrating on particular city-pair message flows. Price cuts, to be effective, would have to refer to a large customer's total calls. This would deprive BT of revenue on its remaining business with these individual customers who, as we have argued, will normally wish to maintain the BT option in any event. There could be a tendency for concessions to spread to the users' other markets. Costs of billing etc. would rise and, to what would be a vocal and influential set of customers, the marketing and pricing stance would be less easily defensible. Demands for cost-based, publicly monitored pricing would increase, with an eventual loss of overall flexibility. If the returns get big enough, large customers in particular have considerable resource in switching the formal responsibilities for contract among subsidiaries and in passing on favourable possibilities within the company. Would the company not be justified in calling for equal treatment of all its subsidiaries? Selective price cutting would also, no doubt, attract its undue share of attention by anti-trust authorities, both British and European.

Retaliatory competition in the non-voice market would be a poor return for the ingenuity put into developing such services. The payoff to product differentiation and indirect competition is likely to be higher. BT would not underrate the ingenuity of opponents, either, who could also alter their product mix, and with greater alacrity than BT itself. BT's strategy here would be based on its scale, ubiquity and the particular advantages of its developing digital network. Other suppliers could presumably avoid these advantages, and BT would be loath to sacrifice them.

Lowering of general voice service quality, by packing circuits as we have described for private operators, would, on the other hand, be much more feasible technically. Again, however, BT would be in the difficulty of having to use a steam hammer to crack a nut. BT makes a virtue of, and can publicly defend, a given standard. In its anti-competitive moves it would presumably seek to avoid catching the innocent, that is those not patronizing the competition. Far more likely is explicit or implicit failure to give comparable service facilities to competitors, that is using its position as supplier of the network to fail to meet the logistical needs of the competitors. This is indeed an aspect of monopoly power which would require attention in any event. In general, however, we may assume that the balance of advantage will be seen not to pursue market-oriented retaliation.

FURTHER IMPLICATIONS OF RESALE

Throughout our enquiries, we were made aware that more was seen to be at stake than a prospective diversion of, at most, £110 million a year from BT's coffers by 1984–5. Freedom to resell is, we have concluded, worth while in itself. But the prospective difference made by changing the rules in terms either of the long-run change of non-voice provision, or of BT's net revenues, even taken at BT's own evaluation, seems a small hook on which to raise fears about such issues as whether there is a threat to BT as the 'natural provider of telecommunications networks and network services and facilities' or 'the capacity of the country to develop strong electronics and information process industries (and the supporting basic technologies)' or a 'reduction in BT's capacity to develop a disciplined telecommunications infrastructure', to quote BT's evidence. The change, in itself, would encourage ingenuity in meeting customers' demands which would, we judge, have favourable spin-off in supplying industries and therefore export markets. No doubt entry by foreign firms, notably American, having track records in product development, would be encouraged, to the general enrichment of UK's stock of entrepreneurship in this field.

The minds of the protagonists were often not focused on the somewhat narrow issues of VANS – like services and diversion. They felt that we were, rather, considering a test case of the change towards modifying the PO monopoly in telecommunications. How this was dealt with would be the possible harbinger of more far-reaching changes. Submissions clearly showed awareness of possible implications of this identified shift, most clearly the POEU. Also, in a sense more directly relevant to our starting point, whatever happens on the larger stage has implications for the value of prospective leases. If, for example, the freedom to resell were to extend to the international market, or there were possible options in alternative suppliers of transmission facilities, the attractions to investing in non-voice (and voice!) market development would, other things being equal, be greater, and probably much greater.

Equally, for the Department, in trying to decide how to define and use its power under the Bill, it makes a considerable difference whether the context is merely one of licensing VANS or like services in the UK, or, instead, of wishing to exercise a much wider discretion. Regulation is less efficiently performed, the greater the number of variables to be considered. (This is one of the cogent reasons for preferring not to allow BT to contract with resellers on a royalty basis. The amount of information needed to oversee a system allowing discrimination is more than the alternative argued for, which would avoid the complex problems associated with assessing rival payoffs.) We should therefore specify where we stand on these issues, seen by many to be very important to the development of the industry. The purpose is not to pronounce upon them in any sense definitively, but rather to ensure that our arguments can be subsequently related to what may well be a very far-reaching debate.

We consider first some international issues. BT is clear that it does not regard our remit as extending to international circuits. We for our part have made it clear that while we are not directly considering resale in this context, we cannot ignore the bearing of international matters on the principle of allowing resale. Certainly, the international stakes are high for BT. In 1979/80 BT's international income's share of the total was 18 per cent (it is expected to be 17 per cent in 1980/1). About two-thirds of it was telephone service; the rest was mainly telex, telegrams and leased circuits. Thus, though the total business is much smaller than domestic, there is a high business content. Predicted five year growth of international paid minutes is expected to exceed that of inland trunk calls over the period 1980–5 by 18 per cent as opposed to 8.6 per cent. More importantly, and in great contrast to the absolute size of the international business, 'business profits' from international services in 1979/80 compared as follows with other principal sources of profits:

	£m
Inland	−36.5
International	+165.6
Exceptional items	+117.0
Total, net	+246.1

This indicates that the international market is very significant as a source of profit to BT.[18]

In terms of the attraction to would-be 'creamers' of traffic, international markets are more attractive than home. Some idea of the possible order of magnitude can be gleaned from one US correspondent's assertion that with current prices charged by PTTs, and using best available technology, it costs five and a half times as much to set up a useful service to transmit data across the Atlantic than it does to send them across the USA itself. This estimate was not challenged when put to other knowledgeable people. The difference lies chiefly in the cost of hiring the relevant circuits, which might well each be via satellite. The incentive to share circuits and to perform the wholesaling function is higher than at home.

BT's own pricing policy internationally is strongly influenced by the need to raise cash to underpin investment. In November 1980 prices would not have been raised had it not been for this, we were told. BT described its international pricing and service policy as follows. By 1985, BT expects that international capacity will have increased considerably. Between 1980 and 1985 available circuits will double; the share of satellite circuits will increase from 21 per cent to 31 per cent, and microwave from 21 to 24 per cent. Costs are thus becoming less distance sensitive, and BT intends to reduce the five distance-based charge bands now used to three. Because of reducing cost differentiation with distance, BT expects to progress towards 'equalizing' the return on capital within charge bands, but notes that there may still be cross-subsidization within a band, for example between the USA, a high profit earner, compared with Haiti and Guadeloupe. So it will maintain the service policy to provide the same quality of service to all countries within a charge band at a standard tariff, partly in hope of encouraging traffic in the less wealthy areas.

Some of the same themes run through a discussion on the international markets as they do for the home market. There is seen a need to protect an important net revenue-earning section of the business. Traditional service standards will be maintained, and there is an intention to change tariffs more towards costs. There are some significant differences in the situation, however, apart from the manifest extra attractions to the would-be-entrant. Price increases are constrained by two factors: the much greater elasticity of demand for international than home calls in general, and BT's prices compared with its rivals among the national systems. As Appendix 1 shows, for the important USA–UK route, a mean expected elasticity of −0.936 is estimated for three-minute calls. For UK–New Zealand, it is −0.816, and for France, −0.378. If these examples are representative, the long-distance international elasticities are getting close to unity (they have had some tendency to increase as time has elapsed, due no doubt in part to the greater ease with which calls can now be made). Outgoing calls to the USA have an elasticity of −1.094.

In these circumstances there is no great revenue to pay off to BT in a shift of price arising from international agreement. Competition in the international voice market, however, clearly has a far better chance of discovering generated traffic than in the home market where the basic elasticity is deemed to be −0.1. Were resale to be allowed, the prospective payoff to a strategy of lowering prices, offering lower quality and packing the circuits, is much greater. So that part of the analysis of the home market which canvassed the possibility of BT's remaining a high-quality, relatively high-price competitor, whilst leasing to others willing and able to offer different price quality mixes, would appear even more applicable in the international context. It may be that BT could find a way out of the present constraints in this direction. To wish to do this, it must also believe that potential resellers will be more adept at creating some markets than it is itself, and it would prefer to see a control on the quantity of resale activity. Too much resale activity would probably be seen to undermine the highly profitable price structure. But at a time of sharply increasing demand, predicted to outstrip the prospective increase in circuit capacity, even this caution may well be unwise.[19] BT could gain, we think, from leasing on a royalty basis.

The relations between prices charged by the different telecommunications authorities are also very relevant. Despite exchange rate strength, in late 1980 BT still had low charges relative to most Europeans. In the transatlantic market to the USA, in a range of eleven European countries, prices for a one-minute telephone call ranged from 92p (UK) to £1.93 (Belgium), with Sweden being the nearest to UK at 99p.

European systems are in competition in so far as calls may be routed via their systems rather than others. CEPT, the cartel governing their pricing activities, has, we understand, effectively preserved the countries' price relativities. Competition by non-price (service-quality) means is presumably left open. BT, and the UK, enjoy a considerable trade advantage because of its favourable price position. This is more significant for business than for residential demand, and particularly for business in non-European countries, which can (sometimes with the help of brokers) take advantage of cheap routes. More specifically, we understand that a relatively large and well-sustained share of the telex market is enjoyed by BT. This is a reflection of its relative telex charges. For a one-minute call, France took the lowest position in late 1980 at 77p. The UK was next lowest at 86p, to be reduced in 1981 to 69p. The ten other countries ranged up to £1.93 for Belgium, with an average of £1.33.[20]

In terms of rentals for leased international circuits, the UK also generally maintains lower prices outwards than do other nations to the UK. The important exception here is to the USA, where the leases for USA to UK are considerably cheaper (over one-quarter in 1980). In the Europe to USA market, the UK has cheap calls, but its outgoing leased circuit charges to the USA are not so markedly below the European average. (Of ten European countries including the UK, UK rentals are about 10 per cent below the average.[21]) So the UK is, in general, a most favourable place from which to conduct international business, as well as being a favourable location through which to route international calls from locations elsewhere. Within the framework of international agreements, the UK has a favourable commercial position, its greatest rival obviously being France, in which the France–USA route in particular has not only lower charges for calls, but also very much cheaper leased circuits (two-thirds of the average European–US price and 72 per cent of the UK's, at end 1980).

The further significant difference between the home and international markets as it affects BT (and its sponsor department, of course) is that the international market structure is one of partially competing organizations having very high degrees of monopoly power at home. Whereas the UK can conduct its internal affairs in such a way as to require its monopoly to stimulate competitive outcomes, or indeed any other feasible policy, when it comes up against external competition the context must be realistically viewed as how to ensure favourable outcomes for the UK in a cartel, CEPT, whose base is rooted in bilateral agreements between governments, as is the case with IATA in the airline industry. One can be fairly certain that international agreement will in effect keep the capacity available on international routes relatively scarce. BT has characterized the profits which arise as 'rents of scarcity'. The ultimate desirability of this is much open to question, but we must assume that, for the foreseeable future, BT and the department will be expected to place first emphasis on expanding the UK's returns from international activity, which means pursuing an optimal strategy for the UK in the cartel context. The European administrations already perceive the international industry to be increasingly subject to competitive forces. We noticed earlier some administrations' actions designed to counter these. There is no reason why other administrations should not press for a different line.

It seems at least very possible that the UK's own strategy to increase its international profits would be helped by domestic resale. To the extent that the UK encouraged the developments of the kind outlined earlier, so will the UK tend to become a relatively more attractive location, both for customers and for the developers of new services, with consequential beneficial spin-offs. There is nothing in the international agreements which would prevent such a domestic policy, and it has not been put to us that international embarrassment would ensue. Neither has it been said that there would be a danger of direct leakage from international markets if resale were permitted in national markets. This would be physically possible but the commercial dangers would be great. Obviously, it would be a relatively simple technical matter to link resale use to, say, leased international lines, but BT has presumably ample ability to discipline its international lessees. No one who has built a business on international leased lines would wish to have this business threatened by being detected in cheating, and BT would be supported in disciplinary action by custom and common sense. But the longer-term strategic point about admitting resale as a principle is whether it will hasten the day when resale emerges on the international scene.

If this is the effect, we think that far from being undesirable, it represents possibilities of clear advantages to the UK and, subject to the form resale takes, to BT as well. We envisage that it would be a specifically UK policy at least for a period, for we understand that the European administrations are not now contemplating liberalization. The advantages would lie in preparing for its adoption ahead of other cartel members, thus prolonging the UK's favourable current relative position. In the longer term, accrual of internationally mobile service companies and presenting a favourable home for company headquarters, with associated research and development, is a rather more secure base for maintaining or increasing the UK international market than is the initial lower price structure, which is itself open to modification and, doubtless, some tendency to arbitrariness amongst the partial competitors. This is particularly true, it seems, on the North Atlantic routes to the USA, where, as we have seen, current UK price advantages compared with its rivals are not so great.[22] There seems little doubt that were the UK to take this line, it would become a very favoured location from which to conduct the relevant kinds of business; the argument of the effects of home resale or stimulation of innovation would also be reinforced were resale to be extended.

Liberalization in this form would of course mean changing the relevant international agreements. Pressures for changes, one way or another, are endemic in cartels. The most solidly based agreements can wilt under external pressures towards competition, as IATA's recent history demonstrates. But we are acutely aware that the complexities of increasing the number, or rationing the existing capacity of, satellites, and many other points cannot be taken on board in this study. We would not presume finally to judge the issue of how to conduct a UK strategy. We simply point out that resale at home, if it is part of a general trend, can be seen to have potential advantages. What the gains to BT itself might be, if any, depend mostly on the form resale might take.

In the international context as described, the argument for putting resale in the form of royalty payments to BT seems to us much stronger than is the case for the home market. For one thing, there is, as we have argued, a much more certain prospect that extra traffic will be generated by independents. This would be reinforced by the anticipated locational shifts. There is bound to be a greater interaction between the resale market internationally and the existing leased circuits in it, because of the much smaller scale of the international leased line business. The underlying rationale of having leases available on the same terms to all comers is that a competitive market would so operate. While it is feasible to require a monopolist at home to behave in this fashion, the presence of (often recalcitrant) other national monopolies in the international market makes it less so there. In circumstances of capacity constrained to lag market developments, there is economic merit in allowing discrimination according to what the market will bear where this can be achieved. Capacity will then tend to be used by those making the greatest potential gains. BT has indicated that it would prefer a royalty basis at home; presumably it would also prefer it for international business, were resale there to come. A royalty basis would, realistically, also be more attractive to other partners in potential bilateral deals. Again there would be less pressure to justify specific bargains than there would be in the home market. Because at least two national systems would be involved, the arguments for equal treatment would be the less easy for the discontented to make. Nevertheless, there would be a need for measures for regulation and control.

LONGER-TERM ISSUES

We have explained that the main underlying objection to resale is that it makes more easy future erosion of BT's monopoly. In the USA, development of value-added services was tied up with developing entry into transmission. The original motive of entrants was not to meet AT & T head on in the voice market, but that is how it has turned out. We take the point, urged on us many times, that US experience is peculiar in several ways. The consent decree effectively forbidding AT & T to provide value-added services in 1956 was itself a stimulus to external suppliers. The rival common carriers first won the right to provide transmission service to individual customers. Then they were able to enter the extremely lucrative long-distance voice market serving one to many, and then many to many, customers by a series of decisions which could not be said to have formed part of a rational plan for stimulating competition. Indeed, the story of American regulation throws into doubt the feasibility of a forward-looking regulatory policy consistently pursuing stated goals. This adds colour to the argument that once competition is introduced, unforeseeable forces build up which accumulate to further competition, and entry to the network and transmissions, the lowest three of the layers of Figure 14.1. The apprehensions are the more acute because of the inherent impossibility of drawing a hard and fast line between the several functions, as explained earlier. The first telephone on the premises is the line at which BT supply monopoly is now drawn; but it has no immutable logic as a boundary. An argument has therefore to be faced; it may be that resale is, even with the best of intentions to the contrary, conductive to more fundamental competition.

There is another reason for considering the question of further entry to transmission and switching. This is the question of the operation, legitimacy and justification of the regulatory process itself as it must apply in the UK. The Secretary of State has assumed powers in the Bill giving discretion to license new capacity. These will be used more freely, or less; either way the uses will have ultimately to be rationalized to outsiders' satisfaction. Moreover, the separation of the two arms of the Post Office has meant that a more visible, highly important and clearly profitable nationalized industry has emerged, in which the burden of discharging conceptions of the public interest have become more sharply focused on what it does. Until recently, at least, and probably still now, though the Post Office was quite often subject to public inquiries and outside scrutiny, it was able to conduct its affairs as an enlightened monopolist in which it very largely shouldered its own problems of social justification of policies. This is bound to become an increasing concern of a department which manifestly will influence how the relevant markets will develop, and which has already carried liberalization of instrument supply a considerable way.

In view of US experience in particular, the department quite rightly wishes to avoid discharging these duties in a way which will lead to spiralling costs, of staff and public argument. It seeks to have the least paraphernalia consistent with discharging its duty. This view finds support in the opinions of US officials who have reflected on the course regulation has taken in the USA. Both NTIA and the respondents we talked to in FCC stressed that, in their view, attempts to approach the regulatory task by making rules encouraging innovation by the monopolist, or otherwise modifying its behaviour, had on the whole failed. (Inadvertently they had sometimes paved the way for entry, of course.) But the question was not only of avoiding unproductive effort. Their positive view was that the regulatory task is the easier, the greater the number of reference points competition makes available. This view was arrived at by the following arguments.

Trying to mark out separate spheres for the operation of 'basic' services and others has not succeeded. Promotion of more effective competition seemed a more promising line of attack, including a relaxation of constraints on AT & T's behaviour. This strategy was given added point by recent and pending technological developments. Three major technological challenges to the traditional wire, namely radio, satellite and optical fibre, together with rival wire development, as in cable TV, had transformed the possibility of relying on competition to secure the public interest, or would do so shortly. Indeed regulation's task was now not to regulate established monopoly, but to unlock impediments to the emergence of competition. This was already well developed in long-distance markets. But there were increasing possibilities of encouraging competition in local distribution. A good example cited was the encouragement of AT & T and local companies to raise short-distance charges, in part by adopting payment by time used, and to lower longer-distance tariffs.[23] This would have the effect of increasing the chances of direct entry to local distribution of telephone services, by existing or new devices, and hence introducing competition to the most entrenched monopoly position: that in local distribution. It is argued that a major influence of competition by independents has been to stimulate AT & T to offer many new services, and that the comparatively very minor share of the total market taken by such entrants as MCI and SPC has had effects belying their size. The AT & T officials to whom we spoke were undoubtedly sincere in their appreciation of the effect of entry in creating the 'new realism' about active competition in AT & T.

Debate centres on how far to enable AT & T to increase its competitive response. If competition is indeed now effective, at least in long-distance markets, logic requires that AT & T should not be debarred from direct competition in areas now denied it. Enough doubt remains, however, about the potential strengths of AT & T, to say nothing of its existing dominant position, to foster ideas that it should compete in all but 'basic' services via 'stand-off' subsidiaries. (Scepticism of such bodies as truly operating at arm's length is expressed by anti-trust experts.)

We do not think that enough work has yet been done to form the basis of a resolution of the question whether it would be on balance economically advantageous to encourage entry in the UK into transmission and switching. BT, POEU and others are convinced that it would be deleterious. Their essential arguments involve economies of scale, presented by BT in particular. Monopoly, they argue, is a natural outcome of economies of scale. We therefore considered whether there might be objections to a policy of increasing competition which could be based on these economies. Appendix 2 reviews relevant contributions.

Argument on 'natural monopoly' by economists has recently been thrown into some disarray by careful examination of the basis of asserting that monopoly, or competition, is 'sustainable'. Continuously falling costs with scale create the conditions, it is traditionally argued, in which only one firm or organization can survive, given that the plant involved must belong to one interest. Recent work has stressed that, on the other hand, economies of scale are neither necessary nor sufficient for monopoly.[24] The key to the paradox is that economies also can arise from producing more than one product simultaneously. Traditional arguments concentrate on the one-product (or service) case. Obviously there is considerable scope here for debate on what constitutes one or more service, but the economist would tend to judge this, in principle, by the cross-elasticities observed in the marketplace (though these are not frequently observed in telecommunications work, as Appendix 1 discloses). At all events, arguments assume that products or services are distinguishable in market terms. Then the cross-product effects of joint costs can lead to situations where either monopoly in a given product market is not sustainable (i.e. can be attacked success-fully by another enjoying different economies of joint production) or com-petition is not sustainable (where the chief effects of scale economies are individual products). However, those advocating the idea of a natural monopoly for BT did not seek to characterize typical potential rivals as enjoying economies of scale across products which would threaten BT. Rather the argument is confined to the traditional grounds, which therefore must concern us here. The position adopted by BT is thus essentially that were BT free to compete without constraint, no other producers in the relevant markets could survive. (How the resultant monopoly power is used is another matter, as we have already seen.) If this is not true, then the pricing or other policies characteristic of the actual pattern of ownership rights – which is one of exclusive supply of certain services – cannot be justified in underlying cost terms.[25]

BT's specific evidence on economies of scale is based on general demon-strations of falling costs with scale in transmission and switching. For a 100 km link, whether the technique used is cable, radio or optical fibre, cost penalties for failure to achieve a given scale tend to be high at lower levels but become small after the 5,000 circuit level is reached. With exchanges, penalties similarly are high for smaller numbers of connections, but tend to fade when one considers the differences at high numbers of connections. As seen earlier other expert evidence is sceptical.

The great difficulty with the evidence as it stands is that system design is itself a variable. How many circuits to build from A to B depends on the size of the market *and* alternative routeing possibilities, what one has already built, etc. There is probably demand between large centres of population like Philadelphia and New York for 80,000 circuits; but whether one should provide these in one lump is debatable. Similarly, whether one has a large or small exchange is a matter of choice, depending, among other things, on expected busy hour demand. Moreover, if instead of basing oneself on *ex ante* engineering estimates, one looked to what BT's freedom to design has produced, one can see an immense variety of scales of groups of connections in transmission and of exchanges. By implication, many of these have been built or at least perpetuated in the face of incurring cost penalties, so there must be many other factors to be explained. The obvious response, that BT is obliged to maintain 'non-economic' service in some areas, will not, we think, wholly explain the point away.

Meyer *et al.* calculate in 1980 how much higher system costs in the USA might be if, by 1985, new entrants have secured (an 'optimistic') 2 per cent of the total US telecom market. Basing their estimates on available evidence of scale economies, they concluded that the cost penalty might be that system costs would be $500 million or 1 per cent higher than they would otherwise have been. They hasten to add that this estimate is almost certainly 'on the high side', and that substantial economies of scale were assumed in the calculation. BT's approach to calculating scale economies, though not as thorough as Meyer *et al.*'s, is not, so far as we can judge, inconsistent with this kind of estimate. Meyer *et al.* say 'For every dollar of revenue gained by the independents 33 per cent may represent increased costs.' (The authors point out that, in the US case, there are almost certainly equivalent costs to be saved by dismantling regulation, which perhaps should serve as an awful warning against allowing regulation to grow![26]) If these kinds of costs have to be contemplated, there would indeed be posed a dilemma for public policy, namely the benefits of added competition against higher costs. It must be remembered, of course, that entry even in the US case is very limited, and that benefits of allowing entry are claimed to extend far beyond the 2 per cent of the market just quoted.

But in any case, debate about the constructs involved in computing economies of scale in the abstract is only peripheral to the main issue, which partly stems from the agreed fact of telecommunications being a rapidly growing industry. The question is not what would happen to costs if scale were halved, or doubled, in the kinds of study quoted, but what are the costs of adding capacity to the system as it stands? If this were added by newcomers, would avoidable costs rise? To answer this, one must have a concrete notion of who the entrants might be, and their command over the necessary resources and the extra costs, if any, of providing connections from BT to their operations. No independent observer has, apparently, made the obvious comparisons for the USA, namely to compare actual entrants' costs with AT & T's in similar circumstances. Since, when we commenced our study, no one had begun seriously to contemplate entry in the UK, these questions cannot be definitively answered here (though they are quite susceptible of calculation, given time). It is relevant perhaps in this connection that British Rail, which has a large inter-city network of conventional construction for the most part, reports that in 1980 its total annual costs of telecommunications, including depreciation and interest, was about £23 million. Using charge rates ruling up to November 1980, it calculates that, had its telephone calls been made on the PO network, call charges alone would have been £32 million a year – that is, without considering rentals.[27]

We strongly suspect that there may be favourably placed potential entrants. Partly this is an inference from US developments. There, entrants via radio, using their own or acquired wayleaves, claim to have no less favourable costs for developing links than AT & T. Indeed, they seem confident enough of their cost position to predict that, even when restructuring of prices produces the anticipated squeeze in their long-distance voice business, they will survive chiefly because of their lean cost structure. (The usual 'small is beautiful' points about avoiding 'goldplating' of equipment, keen cost control, sharper sourcing for inputs, and, most of all, being able to maintain a higher average throughout on the plant that is built are claimed too.) There would be misgivings about entry into the longer-distance UK market by radio because of congestion. But we are told that these problems can quite readily be solved by using existing frequencies more intensively and moving to higher ones when the incentives are great enough. Technical change is constantly reducing the cost of doing this. Even in the short-distance, local distribution market, we have been told of tentative plans to supplement existing private networks with radio links.

Entry by satellite is, we are informed, much more problematical than in the USA in view of the shorter distances involved, and is specially difficult with local distribution. However, even here, it would be a foolhardy person who wholly discounted the possibilities of technical developments making the essential breakthroughs, notably in the cost of sending as well as receiving transmission. Optical fibre technology, by contrast, is deemed a very active possibility for newcomers to adopt. Its leading characteristic for our problem is the fact that it can be adopted by anyone with the necessary wayleaves, largely irrespective of what is being done with them now, because of its property of non-interference in use. Owners of surface way-leaves are in an especially favourable position, particularly if they connect the large centres of population on which demand concentrates. This may give them some cost advantage compared with BT – or at least lessen a cost disadvantage – for most BT wayleaves (i.e. ducts) are buried, often deeply to avoid interference, and optical fibres would replace existing cable. Favourable costs, in turn, would be a useful basis on which to justify entry irrespective of the nature of the entrant. (Objections to entrants on grounds of their ownership – e.g. one nationalized industry's encroaching on another's territory – would be the less compelling were it demonstrated that lower overall costs of expansion would result.)

Effective entry requires connection to a local distribution system. Though some owners of wayleaves have within-city distribution possibilities, and connection to radio distribution is an active possibility, BT would, one supposes, have to be involved. There would arise many analogues to the question now being fought out in the USA about the correct terms on which bargains between the new common carriers and AT & T should be struck. We note that the recent settlement between AT & T and MCI, albeit arbitrary, and not as favourable as MCI would have liked, has none the less been accepted as a sufficient basis on which MCI has been able to launch a foray into the domestic phone market. There would be a corresponding need to monitor the terms on which BT offered local connections.

If entry is feasible, in these ways, even at some overall cost penalty, there would be a possibility, indeed a necessity, to rethink present policies in several important directions. Clearly a most compelling additional reason to encourage entry would be a predictably favourable effect on suppliers, who would have additional customers (though not to judge by the USA very large ones by the standards of the main carrier). Entry would undoubtedly concentrate on BT's main city pairs. Though provision would be expanding, prices would tend to be driven towards costs. The margins for BT would still be healthy, one would suppose, because the number of favourably placed potential entrants is limited. Nevertheless, policy would clearly have to recognize that BT's revenues would have to rise in other areas, which will be much less prone to entry. The government might deem the consequent price rises unpalatable. In that case, to maintain commercial incentives in the industry, some form of explicit subsidies should be devised, to allow lower prices to be charged in particular cases. Also, the points made earlier about removing illogical constraints on BT's freedom to act commercially would be reinforced in a regime in which entry to transmission is allowed.

All this is highly speculative, in the sense that it lacks important pieces of evidence. Nevertheless, we conclude that it is entirely possible to base policy on the presumption that a greater degree of competition will emerge. We think that the apprehensions of those who see resale of leased circuits as one step along a continuing road are justified in their implicit predictions. We believe that it would be correct, on balance, to encourage such a development, but our direct concern is with the leasing issue. Entry into transmission would substantially improve the position of those wishing to offer new services via leased circuits, and to that extent the beneficial effects for which we have argued would be reinforced. Moreover, if one can look forward to progressive extension of the freedom to compete, it would give a clear direction to policy towards the industry which would ease the tasks of those who most influence its development, namely the department.

SUMMARY OF CONCLUSIONS

On the specific terms of reference, we find that:

1 In the home market there should be no restriction on the freedom to offer services to third parties over BT's network, because
2 the prospective benefits to consumers outweigh the prospective loss of net revenues by BT.
3 We think this is the case even were the present constraints on BT's pricing policy and investment budget maintained. However,
4 it is illogical to maintain these constraints in a regime of freer competition. In particular, the existing trend towards moving tariffs towards costs should be taken further.
5 Prices at which BT offers leased circuits should continue to be announced. Customers should be able to lease these at the appropriate price irrespective of the use made of them. BT should be free to determine its level.
6 There will be needs, not often manifest, to safeguard customers' interests with respect to conditions of supply. Different aspects of this should be undertaken by the department and by the Director-General of Fair Trading.
7 BT should be free to engage in competition in the non-voice markets. To require this to be done via a separately accounting subsidiary is useful,

but of less importance than the rules governing transactions, for which the department and the Director-General should share a monitoring role.

We consider also the implications for our remit of resale in the international market and possibilities of future new entry into transmission and switching. We argued that:

8 Free resale at home would be consistent with extending the principle to the lease of international circuits. With respect to increasing the share, and profitability, of BT's, and thus the UK's, international business in telecoms, we see advantages in aiming towards this greater freedom.
9 If international resale comes about, BT should be free to negotiate leases based on royalty payments, a form we do not consider appropriate for the home market.
10 Possible entry into transmission and switching is important as bearing on the options open to lessees of BT's circuits and on the basic direction of policy towards the regulation of BT's monopoly. Economic evidence is poor, but we see no merit in resisting such entry on the score of possibilities of increased costs; and a context of increasing competition in this sphere makes more tractable the task of regulation.

APPENDIX 1: PRICE ELASTICITIES OF DEMAND FOR TELEPHONE CALLS

International evidence on price elasticities of demand for telephone calls which we have collected, and which is summarized in Tables A14.1 to A14.4 indicates the following:

1 The demand for business calls is less price elastic than residential call demand.
2 Price elasticities for both business and residential calls increase with distance of call.
3 For the UK all available estimates indicated that price elasticity for inland calls is less than unity, but that international calls are considerably more price sensitive and in one estimate (for UK–USA calls) exceeded unity.

Consideration of the estimates must note the following:
The estimates we have collected are derived from econometric models of time series on numbers of calls related to selected explanatory variables. In making comparisons between the results it should be noted that explanatory variables other than price are not necessarily the same, and, where possible, differences have been indicated.

In considering the absolute size of the elasticity estimate reported it must also be noted that the dependent variable chosen by the studies has been numbers of calls, rather than some measure of call volume which would

Table A14.1 Price elasticity coefficients in various UK inland trunk call studies

Study reference	Data analysed	Elasticity coefficient	95% confidence limits	Other variables in model	Remarks
GPO Chief Statisticians Division Report 41 (February 1965) – Model 1	Annual time series of full rate trunk calls[1] 1947–63	0.52	N/A	Constant real consumers' expenditure, business connections, STD availability	Model in % growth terms so shows approximately constant price elasticity. Major definition change in series – treatment uncertain
SBRD Report 2 (September 1963) – Model 1	Annual time series of cheap rate[1] trunk calls 1946–66	0.77	N/A	Constant real consumers' expenditure rental and connection charge, STD availability	Model in % growth terms so shows approximately constant price elasticity. Major definition change in series – treatment uncertain
SBRD General Report 12 (June 1971)	Annual time series of total trunk calls 1956/7–1969/70	0.17	0.07 to 0.27	Real total final expenditure, residential connections, STD availability	Model in % growth terms so shows approximately constant price elasticity
SBRD Report 27 (April 1973)	Annual time series of total trunk calls 1958/9–1971/2	0.18	0.06 to 0.30	Real total final expenditure, residential connections, STD availability	Updated version of Model described above
SBRD Report 61 (July 1975)	Annual time series of total trunk calls 1959/60–1974/5	0.089	−0.050 to 0.228	Real total final expenditure, residential connections, STD availability	Updated version of Model described above. Price elasticity not significant at 5% level
	Annual time series of full rate trunk calls 1961/2–1974/5	0.112	−0.008 to 0.232	Real total final expenditure, total connections, STD availability, working days	Model in % growth terms. Price elasticity not significant at 5% level
SBRD Report 66 (December 1975)	Monthly time series of full rate trunk calls August 1965–June 1975	0.55	−0.083 to 0.194	Box-Jenkins noise process	Price elasticity not significant at 5% level

Study reference	Data analysed	Elasticity coefficient	95% confidence limits	Other variables in model	Remarks
	Monthly time series of cheap rate trunk calls August 1965–October 1975	0.115	−0.052 to 0.282	Box-Jenkins noise process	Price elasticity not significant at 5% level
SBRD Report 73 (November 1976)	Quarterly time series of cheap rate trunk calls 1961/II–1976/I	0.096	0.052 to 0.140	Real consumers expenditure residential connections, STD availability	Model in log – differenced form so shows constant price elasticity
SBRD Report 89 (April 1977)	Quarterly time series of full rate trunk calls 1961/II–1976/IV	0.114	0.066 to 0.162	Real service, sector output, business stations, STD availability, working days	Model in log – differenced form so shows constant price elasticity
Current forecasting models	Quarterly time series of full rate trunk calls 1961/II–1980/II	0.131	0.089 to 0.173	Real output, variable business stations, STD availability, working days	Model in log – differenced form so shows constant price elasticity
	Quarterly time series of cheap rate trunk calls 1961/II–1980/II	0.115	0.053 to 0.177	Real consumers expenditure, residential connections, coinbox telephones, STD availability	Model in log – differenced form so shows constant price elasticity

Source: Post Office Central Headquarters Statistics and Business Research Department.

Note: [1] Full rate calls: trunk calls made on weekdays between 8 a.m. and 6 p.m. Cheap rate calls: trunk calls made at all other times.

also take account of duration of calls, e.g. Erlangs. For purposes of estimating the revenue effects of tariff changes, where tariffs in most countries for trunk calls at least are related to duration (as well as distance), one would expect the volume related measure to be the more relevant. *A priori*, an elasticity which reflected the effect on both numbers of calls and duration would be higher than the elasticity measuring numbers of calls only.[28]

In making comparisons between US and UK based estimates, especially, it must be borne in mind that the studies (or rather reports of them, since we have had to rely in many instances on reports rather than the studies themselves) are not explicit about how cross-elasticity effects have been

Table A14.2   Price elasticity studies reported by Littlechild

Author	Country	Dependent variable	Elasticity with respect to price
Turner (unpublished)	UK	Local calls	−0.06
Waverman (1974)	UK	Inland trunk calls per telephone	−0.63
Waverman (1974)	Canada	Residential revenue per telephone	−1.20
Waverman (1974)	Sweden	Trunk calls per telephone	−0.29
Davis *et al.* (1973)	USA	Local	−0.21
		Toll	−0.88
		Private line	−0.74
		WATS	−0.14
Lago (1970)	International	International calls	−1.25
Nace (1974)	Japan	International calls	−2.28
Drew (1973)	UK	International messages (calls and letters)	−0.86

Source: S.C. Littlechild, *Elements of Telecommunications Economics* (1979), London and New York: Institution of Electrical Engineers.

Table A14.3   'Net' price elasticity[1] in the US for customer dialled station-to-station calls by mileage band

Mileage band (miles)	Business	Residence
1–30	−0.28 to −0.44	−0.26 to −0.51
31–85	+0.02 to −0.66	−0.10 to −0.36
86–196	−0.28 to −0.60	−0.33 to −0.87
197–430	−0.48 to −0.94	−0.38 to −1.18
431–3000	−0.47 to −0.94	−0.66 to −1.12

Source: Robert R. Auray, (1978), 'Consumer response to changes in interstate MTS rates' in Trebing, H.M. (ed), Assessing New Pricing Concepts in Public Utilities, MSU Public Utilities, pp. 47–82.

Note: [1] The net price elasticity for a given market sector is the sum of the own-price and cross-price coefficients.

considered, or to put it another way, have not clearly defined the extent of the market (by product type) for which elasticity is being measured. As an example of a possible consequence of this consider the change in demand for off-peak calls resulting from a fall in tariffs. Part of the increase in calls which could be expected would be due to calls transferring from peak to off-peak times. The elasticity measure of changes in numbers of off-peak calls (only) with respect to the changed tariff would thus be higher than the measure of the change in the number of telephone calls throughout the day with respect to the change in off-peak tariffs. Evidence for this can be

Table A14.4 Price elasticity coefficients in various international telephone demand studies

Study reference	Data analysed	Elasticity coefficient	95% confidence limits	Remarks
SBRD Report 28 (October 1973)	UK international telephone calls	0.117	0.099–0.135	Elasticities derived from telephone share model and 1971/72 traffic volume – somewhat out of date
CPRD study of UK-USA calls (September 1979)	UK–USA[1] Telephone calls Quarterly data 1965/II to 1978/I	0.936	0.507–1.365	
ATT international demand analysis presentation US–UK Craver & Neckowitz (September 1979)	UK–USA	0.515	0.295–0.735	Estimate considered unreliable – probable mis-specification of model and incorrect price index
ATT international demand analysis presentation US–UK Craver & Neckowitz (September 1979)	USA–UK Billed minutes	0.325	0.155–0.495	Model mis-specification likely but estimate consistent with elasticities computed using other (rather crude) methods
CPRD study of UK–France calls (September 1979)	UK–France Telephone calls	0.211 (Short run elasticity) 0.378 (Long run elasticity)	0.095–0.327 0.229–0.534	Response to tariff increases still not fully analysed
CPRD study of UK–New Zealand calls (September 1979)	UK–New Zealand calls	0.816	0.343–1.289	Timing of the response to tariff changes not yet fully investigated
Overseas telephone Demand: an econometric analysis by R. Khadem (March 1977) (Paper presented at Windermere Public Utility Forecasting Conference)	Canadian international telephone calls	1.00 (Short run elasticity) 1.50 (Long run elasticity)	0.48–1.52 N/A	Model specified in levels rather than differences, so elasticity estimate likely to be unreliable
Management services contractor study of future INTERSAT user requirements (November 1976)	Traffic on various international routes	0.4	N/A	Same elasticity estimate used for all routes – no information on the origin of this figure provided
Determinants of demand for international telecommunication by G. Yatrakis (1972)	Cross sectional data on total originating calls in 46 nations during 1967	1.030	0.35–1.71	Elasticity estimate likely to be out of date and heavily influenced by the range of countries examined

Table A14.4 (cont.)

Study reference	Data analysed	Elasticity coefficient	95% confidence limits	Remarks
Forecasting techniques: applications to the telecommunications industry by Bernstein, Corbo and Pindyck (March 1977) (Paper presented at Windermere Public Utilities Forecasting Conference)	Canadian International Telephone Traffic	1.391	0.083–2.699	Elasticity estimate unreliable as model is in levels form and includes too many variables, but seems to agree with that established by Khadem

Source: D. Cracknell and L.E. Payne 'Price elasticities on international telephone calls' British Telecoms Corporate Planning and Research Department (CPRD) September 1979.
Note: [1] An alternative estimate of price elasticity of outgoing calls to the USA by Cracknell and Payne is 1.094 ('An econometric model of UK–USA telephone calls' CPRD research note no. 50). In this note they report: 'The price elasticity estimate of 1.094 is much greater than similar estimates obtained on inland trunk calls. It is largely based on the response to the most recent tariff charges. Using data covering 1965–72, a period when real price fell consistently, no significant relationship between calls and price could be established. The response to tariff changes since 1973 seems, however, to have been remarkably consistent, and the price elasticity estimate when these increases are added to the data series, very stable.'

deduced from the UK Post Office estimates reported in Table A14.1. There, elasticity estimates for total calls (full rate and cheap) is approximately half the size of elasticity estimates for full rate or cheap calls only. This confusion may well be one reason why reported measures of elasticity in the US are higher than comparable UK measures (effects of distance aside). The variety of ways in which a telephone call can be made in the US (tariff structures available) and the range of operators to whom to subscribe, must increase the chances of overestimating total market elasticities for telephone calls by including what are strictly speaking cross-price effects. (The US evidence reported in Table A14.3 attempts to take explicit account of this by adding own price and cross-price elasticities for toll calls to produce a 'net price elasticity'.)

APPENDIX 2: NATURAL MONOPOLY AND ECONOMIES OF SCALE IN TELECOMMUNICATIONS

The assertion is often made that telecommunications is an industry which exhibits characteristics of natural monopoly, that is

> an industry in which economies of scale[29] are so great, compared with the size of the market, that it is inefficient to have more than one firm producing the industry's output, and in fact, only one firm would be able to survive in such an industry.[30]

In the debate on regulation of telecommunications in the USA much evidence has been produced to support or refute the proposition that the telecommunications industry, either as a whole or parts of it, exhibits characteristics of increasing returns to scale. That this is the case is used as the basis for asserting that entry into provision of telecommunications should be restricted, and the monopoly of AT & T retained. Whether the existence of economies of scale is a necessary attribute of natural monopoly has, however, been questioned recently in economic literature, as has the basis of the studies of economies of scale.

That there is *in some sense* a 'natural monopoly' in the provision of telecommunications in the UK was often asserted in the submissions we received, although none explicitly described the criterion by which 'natural monopoly' was defined. Also views differed on whether 'natural monopoly' applied to (1) the provision of the entire network and package of services on it, (2) the transmission of basic telephone services only (either on the entire network or parts of it, i.e. trunk services as opposed to services on local networks) or (3) the provision of the basic network, distinct from the uses to which it would be put. Thus one submission asserted that there was a natural monopoly in 'basic telephone service' whilst others regarded natural monopoly to exist in the provision of 'the public switched telecommunications network' or 'basic transmission facility'. One submission asserted, however, that in order that any privately supplied transmission facility met 'a real need' it would be 'unrealistic' for it to attempt to provide the trunk network (for which it should negotiate with BT) but should confine itself to the provision of the 'peripheral microwave links required' (i.e. the local connections). However, many expressed the view that if any part of the network exhibited characteristics of natural monopoly it was the local network and not the trunk sections.

The submission from BT on the question of natural monopoly based its argument explicitly upon demonstrating the existence of economies of scale in the provision of various parts of the telecommunications network (the junction network, the main network transmission systems, and switching mechanisms themselves). In local transmission (junction network) costs per circuit are shown to decline dramatically up to about 200 circuits and then level off. Digital technology (as opposed to analogue) is shown to reduce costs at all levels of output but for costs to decline in the same manner as output increases. This is also shown to be the case with main network transmission systems, with costs declining dramatically with provision of up to 2,000 circuits. Costs per connection for analogue and digital exchanges also decline as the number of connections are increased with constant levels of traffic (measured in Erlangs).

Criticism of the manner in which studies of economies of scale have been conducted has centred on the way in which 'output' has been defined. In most US studies output is defined as revenues from particular services (e.g. AT & T long lines or individual operating companies, i.e. local networks), or from the operation of the system as a whole. (Inputs are similarly defined in financial terms.[31]) Since time series data are often the basis of these studies, the financial measures of output and input must be corrected for price changes. This raises a difficult indexing problem, since the output (and inputs) of whole telecommunications organizations comprise many different services and resources, the prices of which may be changing at different rates. Ideally, these studies should have used volume measures of output, but this raises the question of whether different telecommunications services can then be aggregated. It is interesting to note that the BT submission defines 'output' as provision of the telecommunications network itself (with the exception of the study of economies of scale in switching equipment), rather than some measure of service offerings (either physical such as Erlangs or financial). In doing so, it avoids the criticism levelled at the American studies.

An extension of the criticisms about the definitions of output commonly used by studies of economies of scale is the purpose to which the results are put. The common argument is that demonstration of economies of scale is sufficient to support the view that the telecommunications industry is a 'natural monopoly', that is an industry in which multi-firm production is more costly than production by a monopoly. Baumol demonstrates that only in the case of a single output or where bundles of goods or services are produced in *fixed proportions* is the existence of economies of scale sufficient to demonstrate subadditivity of costs.[32] Even in this case the reverse is not true; if subadditivity of costs exists (i.e. natural monopoly) it is not necessarily so that the producer therefore experiences economies of scale.

This throws us back upon the definition of output which studies of economies of scale have used. Time series data of aggregate measures for system output (revenues) must have incorporated by definition all the services which the organizations produce. It is highly unlikely that the proportion of revenue contributed by each service remained constant during the periods studied.[33]

When one moves to consider variable multi-product output explicitly, however, the importance of economies of scale for the natural monopoly argument diminishes considerably; indeed with many outputs produced in variable proportions the existence of scale economies is neither necessary nor sufficient to prove natural monopoly. (Thus even if the result is accepted that economies of scale exist in whole systems its relevance to the argument that the industry is a natural monopoly is now questioned.) Figures A14.1 (a) and (b), taken from Baumol's article, illustrate this proposition. The diagrams illustrate the total costs associated with production of two goods or services (labelled Y_1 and Y_2).

In both cases production of Y_1 and Y_2 in conjunction exhibits increasing returns to scale (average costs decline as output increases). However in case (a) average costs of production are least where Y_1 and Y_2 are produced, *completely separately* (e.g. at points C and C'), whereas in case (b) average

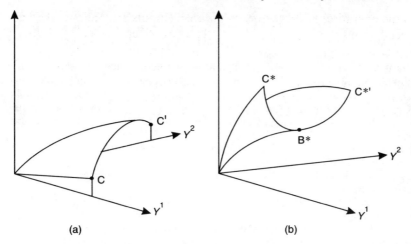

(a)   (b)

Figure A14.1 Total costs associated with production of two goods or services

costs of production are least where Y_1 and Y_2 are produced *in conjunction* (e.g. at point B*).

The explanation lies in the shape of the surface whose edge is CC' in (a) and C*C*' in (b). In the former this is concave to the origin, but in the latter convex. Typically, the production of goods which involved considerable joint costs would imply a cost surface shaped as in (b), where 'joint costs' could be described as costs common to the production of more than one good or service. Producing these goods together thus enables joint costs to be spread between the two products.

The question of whether the telecommunications industry, or parts of it, is a natural monopoly has therefore not yet been established, strictly speaking. Studies of sections of the industry in the USA could be accused of confusing the definition of output considered, and even accepting the result that economies of scale exist in systems as a whole appears insufficient to prove natural monopoly. What will be required are studies to establish economies of scale in the production of individual telecommunications services, or, for systems as a whole, the demonstration that considerable joint costs exist in the provision of different services together. As the text of our study points out, policy will often be concerned with a somewhat different issue, namely the costs of expansion achievable by the (existing) monopolist and alternatively by a potential entrant.

NOTES

1 *Report to the Secretary of State*, London: HMSO, January, 1981.
2 Matheson, S.L. (1978) 'Commercial, legal and international aspects of packet communications', *Proc. IEEE* 66 (11), 1533.
3 See sections 6 and 7, *Recommendations for General Application*, CCITT Recommendation D1.

4 As seen in Appendix 1, elasticity measurements are scarce and often suspect. However, domestic markets are thought to approximate to 0.1, whereas for the North Atlantic market, elasticities approach unity – that is, much nearer to the expected profit-maximizing point.

5 In 1979/80, capital investment in BT was funded to the extent of about 79 per cent by internally generated funds. A very striking, and clear, example of recent shifts in funding of telephone services is in Hull, the (single) independent public UK phone operation. In the year to March 1974, 3.3 per cent of capital expenditure for the year was provided from revenue account; in 1979/80 this was 88 per cent.

6 BT have told us that 'Communication between old people is not permitted, nor is connection to any PO circuit or equipment.'

7 MCI provides long-distance telecommunications services on the company's own microwave network.

8 *Annual Report 1980*, MCI Communications Company. Total revenue in 1980 was $144 million.

9 Calculated from *Annual Report 1980*, MCI Communications Company.

10 The lessee may also lease shorter lines from his or her offices to the local exchange, for which rental would also be paid under existing arrangements. BT may also wish to charge a connection fee to attach the lessee's private circuits to the local exchange. These additions to this lessee's costs would make no essential difference to the argument advanced in the example.

11 The calculation is (£85.7 million $\div$ £16 million) $\times$ £1.20 = £6.40 million.

12 The calculations of residential rental levels assumed that there would be 15 million connections, an elasticity of gross residential cessations with respect to a total bill index of $+0.29$, and an elasticity of residential new demand with respect to the index of -0.6. The index is a weighted index of rental and call charges, the former having a weight of 40 per cent. Hence a weight of 60 per cent was given to the call elasticity of 0.1. This seems a very reasonable way to describe the expected reaction, setting the decision of the consumer in the context of expected flow of services to be gained or forgone. The 0.1 net revenue is reached after allowing for the loss of rental and call income due to cessation and lost new demand. Loss of call revenue is equalled with the average bill, assumed to be £100. Other changes are expected to balance.

13 Meyer, J. R. *et al.* (1980) *The Economics of Competition in the Telecommunications Industry*, p. 143, Cambridge, Mass.: Oelgeschlager, Gunn and Hain Inc.

14 Meyer *et al.*, ibid., p. 143, also add to the previous quotation the following: 'whatever scale economies there may be, moreover, do not preclude the offering by value added common carriers of non-contractual and innovative long distance services if cost-saving techniques or valuable new features are made available to customers'. In the USA 'value added' refers exclusively to services built on leased lines, so the comment is particularly apt for the case under review.

15 The biggest to come to our notice is the £190 million a year paid to BT by the government's own phone services, which make substantial use of a network of leased lines. As a government concern, they do not foresee resale as a possibility.

16 Reuters intend to introduce an international service for dealing in currency and commodities early in 1981. This will use lines leased from PTTs for which fixed rentals and volume-related tariffs will be paid. Reuters themselves will measure the quantity of information which each subscriber transmits (for their own billing purposes) and declare volumes to the PITs. Royalties will be paid on a simple per volume basis.

17 It has been explained to us that EEC competition rules (which take precedence over the UK's in circumstances of contradiction) would imply the following: (1) in relations between BT and licensees there must be no guaranteed exclusivity by

BT to a licensee, and that BT must not exploit a dominant position *vis-à-vis* licensees in discriminating between them; (2) in relations between licensees and their customers, no licensee similarly should exploit a dominant market position. Dominance in the sense of market share held is not confined to very large shares of a given market.

18 The 'loss' in inland services will be noted. This throws some doubt upon the starting point for the earlier calculations of potential loss from inland diversion of calls. There, it was implicitly assumed that there was already a profitable point to start from. If in fact 'losses' were made, the (extra) 'loss' due to diversion is overestimated, conversely the importance of price corrections.

19 In the large UK–USA market, BT predicts calls to grow by an average of 22 per cent a year between 1981/2 and 1986/7, more than doubling over a four-year period. Recently, calls have been growing at a rate of over 30 per cent compound a year!

20 The countries involved in these comparisons are Austria, Belgium, France, FRG, Italy, the Netherlands, Norway, Spain, Sweden, Switzerland and the UK.

21 Calculated for an AVD circuit of normal quality. The list of countries is as for the last note, except that data for the Netherlands were not available.

22 The UK has rather less to fear from diversion of calls from its public network in the European to US market than most of its rivals. It has lower call prices but not such an inducement to rent lines.

23 Local calls in the USA are usually free of charge. The areas over which this holds are, however, much smaller that the UK's local telephone areas.

24 Littlechild, S.C. (1979) *Elements of Telecommunications Economics*, p. 201, London and New York: Institution of Electrical Engineers.

25 It was also put to us by others that the fact that the telephone users prefer more, rather than less, people connected to the network also is a basis for supply monopoly. This, however, tends to boil down to an argument about the cost of connection between rival networks. In any case, it is not disputed that some geographical differentiation of ownership in a given country (e.g. the UK) is not particularly costly – if it does raise costs at all. For example, no one, to our knowledge, has argued that the presence of Hull in the UK system severely raises costs; and Hull would strenuously dispute such an assertion.

26 Meyer *et al.* op. cit., p. 45.

27 The calculation involves apportionment of staff costs between telecommunication and other purposes.

28 Littlechild (*Elements of Telecommunications Economics*, 1979) reports two studies bearing on this: (i) a US study by Gale, W.A. (1976) Bell Telephone Laboratories Memorandum: Petition by Pacific North West Bell Telephone Company to State of Washington concerning Intrastate Message Toll Service: Cause U-75-40, Exhibit 66: witness L.K. Baumgartner, 12 Jan, 1976 estimated an elasticity of duration with respect to price of -0.14 for intrastate toll calls (up to 124 miles) based on cross section data. The study also found elasticity higher for business than for residential. (ii) Waverman (1974) found price elasticities of residential revenue per telephone in Canada to be -1.20 (see Table A14.2).

29 Economies of scale are said to exist when a given increase in all inputs in a production process gives a greater proportionate increase in output. Given constant prices for inputs, this implies that the average cost of producing individual units of output declines as the level of output rises.

30 Littlechild, op. cit.

31 Examples of such studies are: (1) Mantell, Leroy H. (1975) *Returns to scale in telecommunications*, Office of Telecommunications, Department of Commerce, Executive Office of the President, mimeograph. This found an elasticity coefficient for the system as a whole of approximately 1.16 (where a coefficient greater

than 1.0 indicates economies of scale), but for long lines, and the operating companies separately, 1.26 and 1.10 respectively. (2) Dobell, A.R., Taylor, L.D., Waverman, L., Liv, T.H., and Copeland, M.D.G. (1972) 'Telephone communications in Canada: demand production and investment decisions', *Bell Journal of Economics and Management Science*, 3 (1) Spring, pp. 175–219. This study found that between 1952 and 1967 Bell Canada exhibited a scale coefficient of 1.19.

32 See Baumol, W.J. (1977) 'On the proper cost tests for natural monopoly in a multiproduct industry', *American Economic Review*. Baumol defines an industry with natural monopoly characteristics as one in which the cost function is 'strictly and globally subadditive', that is an industry in which multi-firm production is more costly than production by a monopoly. Formally, a cost function is strictly and globally subadditive in the set of commodities $N = 1, \cdots, m$, if: $C(Y_1 + \cdots + Y_m) < C(Y_1) + \cdots + C(Y_m)$. It is possible that for some output vectors an industry will be a natural monopoly while for others it will not.

33 BT's submission acknowledges this point but attempts to counter it by asserting 'In an idealized system, telecommunications can be thought of as producing switching and transmission in constant proportion.' This seems highly unlikely actually to occur given system changes required by changing population distribution, and the effects of technological change upon the switching/transmission mix required.

15 The British Telecom/Mercury interconnect determination[1]

An exposition and commentary

M.E. Beesley and B. Laidlaw

THE CONTEXT

Our subject is 'Determination of terms and conditions for the purposes of an agreement on the interconnection of the British Telecommunications Telephone System and the Mercury Communications Ltd System under Condition 13 of the licence granted to British Telecommunications under section 7 of the Telecommunications Act 1984', issued by the Office of Telecommunications in October 1985. No short title is given. That forty-four words are used well illustrates one need for this paper. The determination is a document to which court actions may refer in the future. One issue might be how well Bryan Carsberg, the Director-General of Telecommunications, has discharged his duties under the 1984 Act; hence the extreme care to present a fastidious document in legal language. In contrast with its custom on other issues, Oftel cannot wisely provide a layman's interpretation or explanatory comment, for the same reason.

Following the determination, BT and Mercury signed an agreement on interconnection on 18 March 1986. The agreement has not been made public. The intrinsic importance of interconnect in the development of telecommunications business and policy calls for exposition and interpretation. Our purpose is to provide the economic and business background to the determination as we see it, to explain individual paragraphs, and to say how we think customers' options and opportunities for future market entrants will be affected. The commentary is not in any sense officially inspired. Although the principal parties have been consulted, the views expressed are our own. It is offered as a contribution to what must surely be a continuing debate on how telecommunications policy in the UK should evolve.

The importance of interconnection

Interconnection of public networks has been a leading issue in UK telecommunications policy since the 1970s, as it has been in the USA. A movement towards liberalization, such as that begun in the UK with the

British Telecommunications Act 1981, posed the central question: at what speed should competition in voice telephony be allowed to develop? It was recognized that other basic services, for example telex and data transmission, would also be in contention, but that manoeuvring for markets with respect to them would always be heavily influenced by their implication for the development of the core market of voice telephony. In UK terms, any new competitor, whether owning independent capacity or leasing from BT, would at some stage need access to the BT customer base, or face relatively narrow markets.

When liberalization began, the chief opportunity to make profits in voice telephony was the prospective margins opened up by existing BT pricing of telephone calls. Essentially, prices were high for long-distance calls, low for short. The use of capacity leased from BT to exploit this opportunity was not permitted. Instead, Mercury was licensed as a 'newcomer' in February 1982. The prospective market opportunity for a competitor with independent capacity consisted of using digital technology to get favourable costs, especially over longer distances, and using the headroom created by BT's traditional pricing to offer low prices. The feasibility of doing so depended chiefly on three factors:

1 Permission to interconnect;
2 Mercury's costs;
3 BT's own future price policy.

Mercury's costs would depend on the price from BT for the interconnect service and the cost of other outlays. What could be charged to customers depended on how BT would realign its prices, for long-distance calls especially. The interconnect issue thus has two important dimensions: first, how the terms of interconnect permit or limit access to the market for voice; and, second, as conditioning one element in the costs faced by BT's competitors. As is also quite evident, competitive possibilities depend on other elements, in particular charges for leased lines, any cost advantage of digital equipment, and BT's own charges to customers. The last have already been substantially realigned with the effect of lowering the target prices for competitors. Even if such realignments by BT proceeded further, however, the question of a viable margin to get substantial business would still be open because, for example, newcomers might have favourable costs.

For its part, and fulfilling its side of the agreements which accompanied the flotation of BT, government strategy remains to preserve obstacles to competitors other than Mercury at least till 1990. From BT's standpoint, this gives time for cost reduction and pre-emptive moves. But the context for government policy must be of advancing competition. Therefore, in so far as competitors do achieve interconnect, it would be expected that their business would be channelled as far as possible to long-distance services, where capacity and costs are relatively favourable. Mercury's main requirement from the determination stems from its necessarily limited network. To build markets, it needs increased ability to distribute calls, connection of good quality, and to use its advanced technology. The advantages of this technology chiefly consist in:

1 Flexibility in network configuration;
2 Combining the voice and data demands of customers; and
3 Provision of ancillary services.

We review later (see pp. 307–9) the commercial implications of BT's and Mercury's very different starting points in vying for custom. As explained there, the policy of duopoly leads to an expectation that BT and Mercury must consider the outcome not only of rivalry, but also of co-operation.

The determination reflects Oftel's principal regulatory remit, to oversee the licences for BT and Mercury arising from the 1984 Act. It was, and remains, declared government policy to concentrate on liberalizing the domestic market, leaving international matters to follow, if at all, from home market developments. The licences, however, cover all activity, and Oftel's determination has to include international business. The determination provides for access by Mercury to BT's international network. However, at the time of writing, Oftel was still preparing the code of practice on accounting arrangements for international services provided by BT and Mercury. In consequence, the full implications of international interconnection cannot be considered here. We must consider also a final element in the background – Mercury's transition to 100 per cent Cable and Wireless ownership. The effect of this development is to establish a UK base for an international telecommunications business. We explore the business logic of this later.

In summary, our consideration of key issues highlights the following areas:

1 How far is permission to interconnect taken; what kinds of business will now become possible, or difficult?
2 In particular, how will it affect the development of competition in voice telephony in the UK, now formally limited by policy commitments until at least 1990?
3 As part of competitive entry and market development, how will ability to enter and relative margins in short and long-distance traffic in the UK be affected?
4 What are the implications for international business conducted from the UK?

The background to the determination

A new framework for the licensing and regulation of public networks was constructed under the Telecommunications Act 1984. In BT's case, the licence granted under the 1984 Act replaced the previous 'exclusive privilege' under which BT and its predecessor the Post Office had run public telephone services as a monopoly. For Mercury, the new licence replaced the earlier limited authorization granted in 1982. The terms and conditions of the BT and Mercury licences are broadly equivalent, although Mercury escaped from several aspects of the universal service obligation placed on BT. The operators of public networks were designated public telecommunication operators (PTOs). BT and Mercury were licensed as the only two PTOs able to provide national and international services. In the language of their licences, BT and Mercury are 'Long Line PTOs', that is they are authorized to provide services over fixed links greater than 50 km in length. As such, BT and Mercury are distinguished from the cellular radio and broadband cable networks, which have also been designated PTOs. The distinction is important in the implementation of the principles of network interconnection contained in the Long Line PTO licences, namely the principles of 'any-to-any' and 'customer choice'.

In regard to interconnection, the two PTO licences were symmetrical in placing on BT and Mercury a requirement to connect other networks authorized to connect to them. In drafting the interconnection conditions for BT, whose licence was written first, it was accepted that rival public networks should be connected so that a subscriber to one network could call any subscriber of another network. This has become known as the 'any-to-any' principle. The 'any-to-any' principle applies to all networks run by BT under its licence, not just the telephone network.

For 'Long Line PTOs', that is BT and Mercury, a second principle was laid down, namely that subscribers should be able to exercise a separate choice of network for the trunk element of a call (the 'customer choice' principle). Customer choice of network routeing was perceived to be essential if competition in long-distance services was to develop, as distinct from rival end-to-end services. The principle is particularly significant for Mercury in enabling it to compete on trunk calls without constructing extensive local facilities.

The practical form that interconnection should take in order to implement these principles was not specified in the licences. Nor did the government indicate in any detail its preferred approach, although there had been extensive discussions among the parties at the drafting stage. The licence condition (13 in the BT licence) merely required that there should be negotiations between BT and Mercury with the aim of reaching an agreement on interconnection. Such an agreement can cover only matters directly relating to network interconnection. This limitation was intended to prevent BT linking the offer of interconnection to other commercial matters, that is to limit the scope for pre-emptive market tactics.

If an agreement were not reached after a reasonable period, the terms of interconnection could be determined by the Director-General of Telecommunications if requested by either party. In the event, BT held up the discussions on its licence until it had concluded Heads of Agreement on interconnection with Mercury. At the time of the coming into effect of the new regulatory regime, therefore, there was a good understanding among the parties of the form that interconnection might take.

Once negotiations on the full interconnection agreement got under way, in accordance with the conditions in their licences, BT and Mercury took radically different views of the status of these Heads of Agreement. BT believed that, as the licences had been drawn up on the basis of the interconnection arrangements foreshadowed in the Heads of Agreement, the Heads should form the agenda for negotiations. Mercury took the view that the Heads of Agreement could not constrain the negotiations. In January 1985, after four months of discussion, Mercury put the issue to the Director-General. In the face of BT's assertion that the Heads of Agreement were legally binding and so prevented intervention by Oftel, Mercury successfully sought a ruling in the High Court. Subsequent negotiations between BT and Mercury proved inconclusive and the Director-General and his staff began work on the terms of interconnection in April 1985. The text of his determination was published on 11 October 1985.

THE DETERMINATION

Scope of the determination

The determination applies to interconnection between the BT Telephone System and the MCL System. The capital initial letters signify defined terms. The BT Telephone System is the national network of exchanges and lines connected to them used primarily for voice telephone. This network is commonly referred to as the public switched telephone network or PSTN. Excluded from the scope of the determination are specialized networks such as the telex and PSS networks and mobile radio services run by BT. Where these are connected to BT's PSTN, Mercury could access them indirectly. The MCL System is defined to include all networks operated by Mercury under its licence.

This asymmetry in scope is potentially of great significance. As Mercury introduces network services, voice or non-voice, it will be able to offer access to them via the PSTN run by BT. Access to Mercury's services will not extend to BT's other networks. For example, it is understood that Mercury intends to introduce a telex service in the near future. Mercury will be able, under the determination, to connect its telex network to customers via the PSTN. However, to connect its telex network to BT's telex network or to PSS, Mercury will require to negotiate a separate interconnection agreement (or, if not successful in securing an agreement, seek a fresh determination from the Director-General). The terms on which Mercury will be able to enter non-voice markets have not yet been settled.

The determination applies only to the direct interconnection of BT and Mercury networks. It does not apply to networks run by other PTOs, although it does apply to calls that are routed successively over BT's, Mercury's and a third network and vice versa. BT has separate interconnection agreements with mobile and cellular radio networks that have PTO status and may in future sign agreements covering telephony services with broadband cable networks. Mercury has already done so. Paragraph 21 contains an explicit exclusion of any obligation on BT to convey messages to other systems with which it has no interconnect agreement. These provisions ensure that residential customers and business customers with their own private networks can access Mercury via BT and vice versa.

The determination does not itself constitute an agreement or contract for the provision of interconnection between BT and Mercury. Rather, it stipulates the contents of such an agreement, which the two parties are required to conclude. Continuing points of disagreement, if not resolved by the parties, would be a matter for civil action through the courts. Certain specific issues are to be referred by either side to a committee, comprising one representative each from BT and Mercury and a chairman acceptable to both sides. There are detailed arrangements for the costs of the committee to be borne by the party whose case is not upheld.

The form interconnection will take

In his determination, the Director-General has specified two forms of public network interconnection to be implemented between BT and Mercury. Following the language of the Heads of Agreement, these are termed Levels 3L and 3J. Level 3L is

>   the connection of a BT Exchange Line served from a Local Exchange to the MCL System at a point of connection within the exchange area served by that Exchange;

Level 3L therefore provides Mercury with the normal form of access to the BT network available to any BT subscriber. That is, it would enable a BT subscriber to access Mercury by means of an ordinary directory number. To then reach a customer of the Mercury network, in accordance with the 'any-to-any' principle, further dialling would be required. Additional hardware to simplify this task can be acquired.

Level 3J is described as:

>   the connection of the MCL System to the BT Telephone System at the junction side of a Trunk Exchange.

Level 3J therefore provides Mercury with a means of direct access to the BT trunk network, bypassing the BT local exchange network. The junction side of a trunk exchange is the side to which lines from local exchanges are connected to the trunk network. Junction switches are tandem, forming the link in BT's network between a set of local exchanges within a local call charge area as well as between BT's local and trunk networks. In consequence, interconnection at Level 3J provides Mercury with potential access to an entire call charge area served by the trunk exchange as well as access to the trunk network. In major cities, of which London is the prime example, the trunk exchanges each serve only a sector within the local call charging area. In London, the determination specifies eleven such sectors to which Mercury can connect. Elsewhere, a single trunk exchange may serve several local call charge areas.

In respect of Level 3L interconnection, the connection of BT exchange lines must be accomplished within three months of a request from Mercury. In respect of Level 3J interconnection, BT is directed to connect Mercury lines to trunk exchanges in twenty-four towns and cities listed in an Annex to the determination by 30 March 1986, if Mercury so requests. These locations match the expected geographical spread of the Mercury network at the present time.[2] Mercury had to make its request for connection at these locations by 1 November 1985, stating the capacity required. Thereafter, BT must provide Level 3J connections or additional capacity at existing connections at a trunk exchange in any locality within six months of a request from Mercury.

Figure 15.1 provides a highly simplified representation of the BT network, for the purpose of illustrating 3L and 3J interconnection. For clarity, the transit exchanges which route traffic between some trunk exchanges within the BT trunk network have been omitted. The classical network configuration illustrated is undergoing change as the result of the conversion from analogue to digital technology. Modern switching systems are inherently more flexible as regards routeing of traffic. More important, the attenuation of signal strength experienced during transmission, or each time a call passes through an exchange, that is characteristic of the analogue network, will be eliminated. BT's plans for its national network are still evolving and may well undergo some modification in the light of the determination. As digitalization of BT's network proceeds, the distinction between Levels 3J and 3L will become less significant, as they perform similar technical functions. As we shall see, however, market strategies have first to recognize what is possible in the near future. Our exposition takes this starting point.

The definition of Level 3J interconnection in the determination refers essentially to the existing mixed analogue/digital world, not to the future. Mercury would wish to connect to any feasible point of BT's network and presumably was not seeking a determination that would be bounded by the current state of BT's network. The wording of the determination gives room for debate between the parties about the points at which Mercury can connect. This may, in the end, have to be resolved by a further ruling.

Meanwhile, the importance of the 3L/3J definitions lies mainly in their effect on transmission quality. It would be quite feasible technically for Mercury to use 3L to reach any point in BT's network. However, the attenuation would very often be such as to breach the CCITT Recommen-

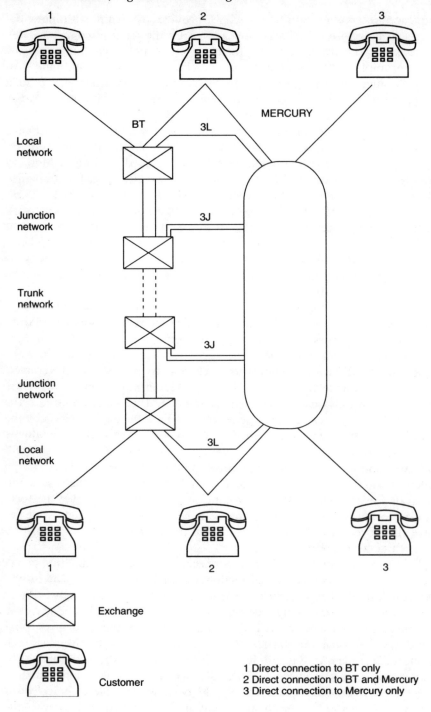

Figure 15.1 Interconnection at levels 3L and 3J

dation on attenuation which has been incorporated in the determination. As things are, quality is better by having 3J connections.

Whereas BT is constrained by the need for a smooth transition from an analogue to a digital network, exchange by exchange, Mercury is building a network from scratch. It has the freedom to exploit the capabilities of digital technology to the full. The network deployed by Mercury need not copy in form or capability that of BT. Figure 15.1 shows the Mercury network as a chrysalis, with its final form indeterminate. In principle, and subject only to practical constraints imposed by numbering, transmission losses and other technical factors, Mercury can build its network so as to connect any local area to any other local area within the UK by means of interconnection with BT.

A consequence of the technological change in telephone exchanges and network design is that the determination could not be very precise in its references to local and trunk exchanges. In turn, this imprecision has created room for continuing debate between the parties. In the determination, a local exchange is defined as an exchange to which customers are directly connected by an exchange line. An exchange line is simply a line connecting an exchange to a customer's premises (Schedule 1 of the BT Licence). While the ordinary meaning is clear, it is not unusual for trunk exchanges (Group Switching Centres) to provide exchange connections for customers in addition to their other functions. Moreover, there is, potentially, no technical or regulatory bar on customers being directly connected to a trunk exchange. As discussed below, a consequence of the determination is likely to be that both BT and Mercury will introduce such a service for major customers (local bypass).

The position with trunk exchanges is even more ambiguous. The determination states where trunk exchanges are to be found, by listing in an Annex all the towns in the UK that contain them. However, it does not specify their function. In the Annex on technical principles, it is stated 'For the purposes of "3J" connections, a BT Trunk Exchange is a Group Switching Centre (GSC), or its functional successor as digitalization of the BT Telephone System progresses.' However, it is understood that the functions of a GSC will, after conversion to digital working, be divided between the principal trunk exchanges, the Digital Main Switching Units (DMSUs) and the principal trunk exchanges, the Digital Central Call Exchanges (DCCEs). The interconnection determination is intended to apply to both situations where BT retains for the time being analogue switches and where it is has already installed digital switches. It is not apparent on the face of the document how the latter is to be accomplished. There may well have to be a further determination if agreement is not reached between the parties.

When the BT network is converted to digital working, the advantage of having a connection on the equivalent of what is now the trunk side of a GSC would be limited to a set of transit exchanges relatively unimportant to Mercury. That the determination is couched in terms of analogue/digital requirements means that Mercury must be interested in whether 3J connections can be made at the DMSU level now. The determination is unclear on this.

Where a digital Mercury exchange is to be connected to an analogue BT exchange at Level 3J, so that analogue-to-digital conversion of calls being handed over is necessary, the determination requires any conversion to and from analogue to be undertaken within the BT network at BT's expense. During BT's transition to digital working there will be a requirement for such conversion within the BT network in any event.

As regards numbering, the determination provides for Mercury to be allocated national number groups and other numbers necessary to implement interconnection 'as soon as possible'. In practice the options are limited unless the existing allocation of numbers is disturbed. Only national number groups in the 07XX series and individual numbers in the 1XX operator services series are available to Mercury. The allocation of a restricted range of national number groups to Mercury will limit the degree of geographical differentiation that Mercury can introduce into its network and the number of subscribers in each area. It seems unlikely that this approach will survive in the long term, as the allocation of national number groups is insufficient to secure equal treatment of the BT and Mercury networks. Nor would it enable additional networks to be accommodated within the national numbering plan (see explanatory note to paragraph 7 of the determination). Meanwhile, the temporary arrangement of allocating Mercury the 131 access code will not give to a Mercury customer the access available to a BT customer. To achieve parity, there would have to be a means for a BT customer to have access to a customer directly connected only to Mercury. This is not provided for. BT would have to request it as a separate matter, and, so far as we are aware, has not yet done so.

Before describing, in the next section, the charging arrangements for interconnection, the implications of the forms of interconnection laid down by the determination for the choices available to customers of BT and Mercury are considered. There are three cases:

1 The subscriber to the BT network;
2 The subscriber to both networks;
3 The subscriber to the Mercury network;

where a subscriber is a customer with a direct exchange connection (direct service line in Mercury's terms).

Case 1: Customers directly connected to BT

The largest category will be existing BT subscribers who wish to become customers of Mercury. If a BT subscriber obtains a direct connection to Mercury's network then, of course, he or she becomes a Mercury subscriber (see cases 2 and 3 below). In all other circumstances, a BT subscriber using the Mercury network would need first to make a call over the BT network. There are three possible ways of so obtaining access to the Mercury network (sometimes termed 'ingress'):

1 A local call;
2 A network access call;
3 A trunk call.

In each case, the BT subscriber would need to dial not only the necessary digits to obtain access to Mercury, but also the further digits of the personal authorization code used to identify the subscriber for billing purposes.

Where Mercury has a Level 3L interconnection, the BT subscriber would access the Mercury network by dialing Mercury's local number. It would not normally be worthwhile to do so to make a local call. To make a trunk call would involve dialling also the national number of the called party. With Level 3J interconnection, the BT subscriber could select the Mercury network by dialling a special access code (for example, 131) and then the number of the destination customer. From the customer's point of view, access at 3J involves less dialling and, usually, less attenuation. It would be possible for a BT subscriber to access Mercury by means of a trunk call. To do so might be economic, since the trunk call would be paid for by Mercury in accordance with the scale of payments for interconnected calls rather than at the full BT tariff.

Once the BT subscriber had accessed Mercury, the following things could happen. If Mercury directly served the called party, it could take the call all the way. If it were connected to the local exchange serving the called party, Mercury could hand over the call at the distant end for final delivery by BT (Level 3L). If it was not connected to the local exchange but was connected to a BT trunk exchange serving the local call charge area in which the called party was located, it would hand over the call to BT at Level 3J for delivery. If Mercury did not have a connection to a trunk exchange serving the destination area, it would hand over the call to BT in the originating local exchange area or at some intermediate point, depending on the extent of development of the Mercury network and anticipated attenuation over each route. The intermediate point could be a trunk exchange within 56 km (35 miles) of the destination, thereby converting a long national call over the BT network into a short national call for which a lower interconnection charge would be payable (see the section on payments on pp. 311–16).

Case 2: Subscribers to both networks

Subscribers to the BT network that have appropriate call connection equipment will be able to connect directly to both networks. Connection to the Mercury network could take the form of either a line provided by BT (a private circuit connection of the kind described in previous interconnect discussions as Level 2) or a direct service line provided by Mercury. The use of either form of connection would enable the subscriber to route calls over the Mercury network without extended dialling. Direct connection to the Mercury would make use of the connection for local calls feasible. Whether Mercury would be willing to accept such use would depend on its costs, including the interconnection charges payable to BT (see the section below on charges). As before, Mercury could deliver trunk calls received by it to the final destination, if also a Mercury subscriber, hand over the call at the local BT exchange to which the called party is connected (3L) or hand over the call to a BT trunk exchange in the originating customer's area or at the limit of the Mercury network (3J).

Case 3: The Mercury-only subscriber

It is not yet known in detail how calls between Mercury subscribers will be handled by the Mercury network. However, a Mercury subscriber would, when the necessary numbering groups had been allocated, have the equivalent choice of network routeing, using Mercury or accessing the BT network en route to another Mercury subscriber (the temporary 131 allocation will not permit this freedom). If BT were selected to convey a trunk call to a Mercury subscriber, then BT would need to hand over the call to Mercury at the distant end. The handover would be either at the trunk exchange serving the local call charge area in which the called party was located (3J) or at the local exchange nearest to the called party (3L).

In addition, the Mercury subscriber would wish to access the BT network to reach BT subscribers in the same local call charge area. If the local exchange to which the called BT subscriber is connected is one to which the Mercury network is directly connected (Level 3L), Mercury could hand over the local call to BT for final delivery at that exchange. If not, then Mercury would hand over the call to a BT trunk exchange (3J) for delivery.

Forms of interconnection excluded from the determination

In determining that network interconnection should take place at Levels 3L and 3J, the Director-General has set aside other forms of interconnection. In addition, at both 3L and 3J, there are limitations on the use that Mercury can make of the right of interconnection granted.

In the current state of development of BT's network, the most significant technical omission is direct interconnection between Mercury trunk lines and the trunk side of BT trunk exchanges. This could also include access by Mercury to exchanges at higher levels in the hierarchy of exchanges. By comparison with 3J, such interconnection (often termed 'Level 4') would have enabled Mercury to engage in long-distance operations by collecting and distributing calls through the BT network.

Direct trunk interconnection would also have enabled Mercury to use the BT trunk network as an extension of its own trunk lines with less transmission loss. This extension is given with interconnection at Level 3J, since Mercury can feed in calls to the BT trunk network by means of a 3J interconnection in an area intermediate between the originating and destination area. But the penalty of doing so is a more complex network routing for Mercury and a higher transmission loss arising from the greater number of switching points that such calls pass through. Transmission losses will be significant so long as the BT network contains analogue equipment.

The technical principles of the determination require that interconnecting calls are not conveyed if the expected transmission losses exceed internationally agreed norms (the relevant CCITT Recommendations). This is more likely to occur with 3L interconnection. Local 3L interconnection is limited to the local exchange area in question. Connection to a BT local exchange in another call charge area is a facility available to the generality of BT customers. It is termed an out-of-area exchange line. Moreover, BT is not obliged to connect parts of the Mercury network isolated from the rest of the Mercury network. In consequence, Mercury cannot provide a line connecting its subscribers direct to a BT exchange.

The determination does not cover two forms of interconnection that figured in the 1982 interconnection agreement between BT and Mercury (termed Levels 1 and 2). Level 1 interconnection was described as the connection of a BT subscriber's apparatus (such as a PABX) to the Mercury network by means of a Mercury line. Level 2 interconnection was described as the direct connection of a subscriber to the Mercury network by means of a BT leased line. The 1982 agreement still stands, but Levels 1 and 2 have not been considered within the scope of the Director-General's determination because, within the framework of regulation established under the 1984 Act, they do not constitute forms of network interconnection. Levels 1 and 2 simply describe the connection of subscribers' apparatus to the Mercury network. In the case of Level 1, the connection is made by Mercury in circumstances where the subscriber is also connected to the BT network. In the case of Level 2, the connection is made by a private circuit leased from BT.

Payments under the determination

Charges for interconnection

BT exchange lines connected at Level 3L to the Mercury network are to be charged for at the quarterly rental for an exclusive business exchange line. For Level 3J connection, Mercury will provide the line up to the point of connection with the BT exchange, and will pay BT for work done to make the connection. In addition to these charges, Mercury is to pay 50 per cent of the cost of increasing capacity in order to accommodate Mercury's lines. This charge is payable even if BT has excess capacity at its exchanges. In that case, the charge is to be based on the notional cost that BT would have incurred in increasing the capacity of an exchange. It is understood that these additional payments apply only to the exchange to which a connection is made and not to wider effects on the BT network.

As part of the arrangement, Mercury must supply BT with annual forecasts of the number and location of points of connection required at Level 3J. If Mercury's actual traffic volume over the point of connection exceeds, in any twelve-month period, the capacity requested by Mercury, Mercury will pay an additional 20 per cent per annum of the cost to BT of providing the capacity used.

The effect of these charges is that Mercury will have to pay BT 50 per cent or more of the capital cost of the exchange equipment in the BT network used by Mercury for interconnecting calls. The higher sums are payable if Mercury is more successful than it predicts. The running costs incurred in handling interconnecting calls are to be covered by the payments described in the next section.

On the assumption that the initial connections at Level 3J, required to be made by 30 March 1986, will be to analogue trunk exchanges, Mercury will effectively contribute to the cost of the analogue-to-digital conversion carried out by BT. As BT progressively changes to digital technology, it will have substantial excess capacity at the exchanges to which Mercury is connected in the form of redundant analogue exchange equipment. It is not clear from the determination whether the capital charge to Mercury, where it is based on a notional cost to BT, will relate to the higher cost levels of analogue exchange equipment (plus conversion equipment) or to the lower cost levels of digital equipment.

Payments for interconnected calls

In establishing the basis of payments for interconnected calls, the Director-General was required by Condition 13 of the BT licence to 'take account of the overall pattern of the Licensee's costs'. He is further required to ensure that the payment for 'anything done pursuant to or in connection with the agreement' in implementing his determination meets the cost 'including fully allocated costs attributable to the services to be provided and taking into account relevant overheads and a reasonable rate of return on attributable assets'. That is to say, the Director-General was required to fix the scale of payments for interconnected calls by reference to costs, rather than tariffs or any other yardstick. Moreover, the costs that are deemed relevant are average costs rather than incremental or marginal costs.

For several reasons, we think that the determination has had to recognize that these obligations provide virtually no practical base. First, in terms of business strategy, what matters are costs which are avoidable now and in the future. As seen earlier, BT is in the process of changing technologies for both switching (electromechanical to electronic, analogue to digital) and transmission (copper to optical fibre). Thus, it is providing services at markedly different avoidable costs at different times and places. In the nature of expanding its network while changing technologies, BT will experience points where capacity is constrained and those where there is, for the time being, substantial excess capacity. For BT, average costs over its whole system may, therefore, be significantly above or below costs over a particular route or to or from a particular destination.

Mercury, by contrast, as it builds its network in advance of demand, will have for some time a substantially lower proportion of capacity in use than BT. In consequence, Mercury will almost certainly have avoidable costs per call lower than BT's over most, if not all, of its routes for a considerable period ahead.

In making his determination, the Director-General has fixed one set of payments to apply to all parts of the country and to both the BT and the Mercury networks. Even within the constraints of the licence condition governing his actions, the Director-General has abstracted from the details of costs and produced highly averaged numbers. Attempting to establish costs per call on any basis would be very difficult. The basic telephone service is divided between services covered by rental payments and services covered by call charges using essentially arbitrary, historical methods. To fully allocate costs to services would require the application of broad accounting principles that are acknowledged to be remote from any empirical foundation. On top of these analytical deficiencies, the cost data generated by BT at present are known to be of poor quality.

On the other hand, Mercury has yet to place substantial orders for its national network of exchanges. The Director-General will have had access to cost data from overseas, particularly the United States, which may have provided some guidance on expected levels of costs. None the less, the determined payments probably mostly reflect the Director-General's judgement of Mercury's requirement to be given the opportunity to trade profitably. This, we think, included the judgement that Mercury's approach, in targeting markets, would be to focus on the difference between BT's tariff for particular calls and Mercury's possible payments for carrying interconnecting calls. For Mercury to have a competitive opportunity, the payment to BT for interconnecting calls should allow enough margin to finance development and required profits. In practice, the payment to BT ought, in Mercury's eyes, to be low enough to allow Mercury to offer its customers a discount on its tariff relative to BT's tariff. Mercury's delighted response to the determination would seem to indicate that the Director-General's ruling on payments was consistent with Mercury's approach.

In the event, the system of payments for interconnected calls is based on charging for each segment of a call carried by one network on behalf of the other. A 'segment' is that fraction of a call from the point where the call is received from a subscriber or handed over to a network to the point where the network hands the call on again or delivers it to a subscriber.

Four segments are distinguished:

1 *Local 3L segment* where connection is at Level 3L and the call is carried within a BT local call charge area.
2 *Local 3J segment* where connection is at Level 3J and the call is carried within a BT local call charge area.
3 *Short national segment* where the call is carried outside a local call charge area (i.e. over a trunk network) between points of connection less than 56 kilometres apart.
4 *Long national segment* where the call is carried over a trunk network between points of connection more than 56 kilometres apart.

As an illustration, a trunk call by a BT subscriber that is handed over by BT to Mercury for conveyance over its trunk network and then handed back to BT for delivery to its destination would consist of three segments, typically a local 3L or 3J segment provided by BT at the originating end, or long national segment provided by Mercury and a local 3L or 3J segment at the destination end.

However, the segments as defined will not, in all cases, correspond to that part of a call carried over the trunk network or over the local network. For example, if a call is handed over by Mercury to BT for conveyance over its trunk network and is also delivered by BT to its destination over the local network, conveyance from the point of handover to destination would comprise one segment only for the purposes of payment (a short or long national segment). In consequence, there would normally be a maximum of only two segments for which an interconnect payment must be made in respect of any call.

The network which collects payment from the customer originating the call is to pay the other network for the segments of the call that it provides. Which network collects payment from the calling customer depends on how a call is originated. If an interconnected call has been originated by the subscriber to one network without exercising a choice of network routeing, that network will charge its subscriber for the call and pay the other network for carrying the call after it has been handed over. If the subscriber had exercised a choice of network routeing then the chosen network would charge its customer and pay the network which first handled the call for the segment of the call it provided. If the chosen network subsequently handed the call back to the first network for delivery, it would pay also for the final segment of the call provided by that network. Under these arrangements, if the call is not answered the chosen network would pay only for the first segment of the call.

Table 15.1 sets out the payments determined by the Director-General for the period until 1 November 1986 (when BT's tariff is expected to be revised). For each segment over which a call is carried, a different payment is incurred at cheap, standard and peak periods (defined in accordance with BT's tariff). Where the customer exercises a choice of network routeing,

Table 15.1 Payments for interconnected calls, (pence per minute)

Segment	Period		
	Cheap	Standard	Peak
Local 3L	1.0	2.3	2.6
Local 3J	1.0	2.0	2.3
Short national A	2.2	4.4	6.0
B	1.1	3.1	4.6
Long national A	2.4	5.0	6.5
B	1.4	3.5	4.8

payments are reduced if the call is handed back to the other network for final delivery (rows labelled B in the table). The reductions in the payment per minute for national segments reflect the fact that, in cases where calls are handed back for final delivery, the national segment will normally include conveyance over the trunk network only.

To illustrate the variety of ways in which interconnection could work in practice and what payments for interconnected calls would result, we consider a trunk call by a customer choosing to use Mercury. It is assumed that, made by the BT network, this call would be 'low cost' and so the 'bl' tariff would apply. In the peak period, such a call lasting 200 seconds would cost 45p at the current BT tariff. As already indicated, there are many ways in which Mercury could handle all or part of the call. These are summarized in Table 15.2 in terms of the five possible methods of access to the Mercury network (ingress) and means of final delivery of the call (egress). In principle, these are equivalent, although the means of final delivery is selected by Mercury.

The table shows the charge in pence by BT to Mercury for the same call for each combination of method of access to the Mercury network and means of final delivery. For example, if the call illustrated were made by accessing the Mercury network at Level 3J (row 3 in Table 15.2) and the call was delivered by means of a short national segment (column 4), the

Table 15.2 Interconnection arrangements and payments: an illustration

A peak period 'low cost' long national call that lasts 200 seconds (BT tariff 45p)

Method of access to Mercury network (ingress)	Interconnection payments by means of final delivery (egress)				
	1	2	3	4	5
1 Directly connected Mercury subscriber	0	8.8	7.8	20.4	22.1
2 Local call (3L)	8.8	17.6	16.6	24.4	25.1
3 Network access code (3J)	7.8	16.6	15.6	23.4	24.1
4 Trunk call (short national)	20.4	24.4	23.4	31.3	32.0
5 Trunk call (long national)	22.1	25.1	24.1	32.0	32.6

interconnection charge by BT to Mercury would be 23.4p. As already noted, Mercury cannot yet provide a switched service between directly connected customers.

IMPLICATIONS FOR COMPETITIVE DEVELOPMENTS

Having described the main elements in the determination, we now turn to comment. Competitive relationships in telecommunications have been drastically changed by the combined impact of liberalization and privatization. They are best understood as emerging from the longer-term aims of the incumbents in, and potential entrants to, the market, as modified by the decisions of the licensor and the regulator. We describe the likely emerging strategies in this section, starting with the two main incumbents, BT and Mercury. We then analyse the effects of the determination on their competitive relations, dealing with its impact on their markets' scope and the impact of the determination's charges on Mercury's need to build its markets. Duopoly necessarily implies that both co-operative and rivalrous strategies are considered. This is also important when the position of potential entrants is considered, which is the subject of our final paragraphs.

BT's strategy *vis-à-vis* Mercury

BT's strategy for meeting growing competition is conditioned greatly by its starting point, namely, its existing plans to digitalize its capacity. This calls for progressive conversion, starting with the highest capacity links and nodes. Technical problems still to be solved influence this; a notable example is the difficulty experienced by System X suppliers of developing a large local exchange. Speeding up conversion means that trunk capacity in particular will be available ahead of peripheral, because this is where the major competitive impact is foreseen. This imparts a new dimension to competition, from BT's viewpoint. Costs will fall rapidly in trunks, less so in local distribution.

As explained earlier, government strategy remains to preserve obstacles to potential competitors at least till 1990. From BT's standpoint, this gives time for cost reduction and for pre-emptive moves. But the context, meanwhile, must also be of advancing competition. Thus, now that *some* accommodation to newcomers is inevitable, one might expect BT's charges to customers to favour long-distance use of BT's network, and to discourage short-distance use.

Mercury's prime need has been, and still is, to get prospective customers for a high-capacity digital network. The network's planning and construction have coincided with a time of changing licensing and regulatory requirements. These may explain Mercury's varying attitude to resale of leased transmission capacity as time has elapsed. Concern that resale would be a competitive threat has given way to acknowledgement that it can improve Mercury's access to small customers and degree of capacity utilization. Small customers would typically have a high proportion of local to long-distance calls. The local element could be dealt with by Mercury's contracting with local distributors (such as broadband cable networks) to increase its own service scope, and the long-distance element by contracting with resellers, who would provide the same function for long-distance calls. Its principal market opportunity, we would argue, lies in combining serving substantial businesses directly, with resale of its capacity to other wholesalers and distributors of data and voice services. For both these market opportunities, it needs to increase its possible local pick-up points.

Mercury's best opportunity to achieve local pick-up with favourable margins is in London, and the London telephone area itself represents a considerable potential for interchange. By extension, the same arguments apply, with somewhat less force, to the other conurbations served by Mercury's figure-of-eight network. Mercury's relative market strength therefore lies in building on London and adding conurbation markets, with high emphasis on local pick-up. Delivery to distant markets is, of course, still important, but not so critical as appeared the case early on.

International business from the UK is a potential duopoly (aside from private leased networks) and a much more secure one because the rest of the world lags behind the UK, USA and Japanese liberalization. Therefore, we expect there to be at least implicit market sharing between BT and Mercury. The principal concern of the two parties must be to discourage international bypass, especially by large customers. Whereas, at home, we expect Mercury and BT to temper competition between them to meet common competitive threats, for example from large users, we expect co-operation to dominate in international matters. Also, there must be a mutual interest in, and the potential to deal with, the commercial implications of substitute technology, specifically the emergence of satellite capacity. As we shall see, the determination bears importantly on these points.

The determination and BT/Mercury competition

The determination aims principally at defining the ways in which Mercury may use BT's network to build its markets. Implicit in our descriptions in earlier sections are limitations on Mercury's scope to do this. We comment on the more important of these, as we see it, in this section. But Mercury has always the potential advantage that its network's configuration and size can be adapted to the determination, whereas BT's room for manoeuvre in this respect is much conditioned by its huge inherited investment. Mercury, as the pygmy, must be as agile as it can be in the face of the giant's defensive moves. It has some allies in its efforts, chiefly the predisposition of the government towards effective alternatives to BT, and the support this gives to a pro-competitive Oftel, whose main discipline on BT must always be the implied threat to encourage competition to emerge at a rate faster than that preferred by BT.

Nevertheless, Mercury faces important obstacles. Our explanation of the interconnect determination points to several, which we will take in the order dealt with earlier. Mercury will have to seek separate interconnect agreements with BT if it wishes to connect directly to BT's telex network or to PSS. The existing agreement may yet encounter disputes in interpretation which will require a favourable opinion from the committee, the Director-General or the courts. There are some uncertainties about how interconnect will be accomplished technically, as the determination applies to both analogue and digital situations and does not specify how change from one to the other is to be dealt with. There is, we pointed out, a potential limitation in the allocation of the range of national numbering groups. Current arrangements underline the asymmetry of the determination. Mercury-only customers will be disadvantaged unless or until BT seeks access to them, or the numbering arrangements are changed.

The obligation to declare oneself a subscriber to BT, to both, or to Mercury only, will of course be mainly significant for the savings in prospect on the telephone bill, and we deal with the implications of the charging provisions later. But the 3J and 3L distinction will also bear on the choice a customer makes, 3J saving dialled digits for a BT customer wanting to use Mercury. Quality of calls on average will be better over Mercury's network the more it invests in local nodes.

The more significant limitations on market scope arise from omissions in the determination. In particular, the lack of an immediate trunk side connection of BT's trunk exchanges has prevented a very attractive market-building tactic. With such connection, Mercury could have concentrated at first on filling its basic figure-of-eight network with long-distance connections. Mercury, proceeding from a prospective all-digital base, would naturally seek connection at any feasible BT point. The determination, running in terms appropriate to an analogue/digital transition phase, lays the basis for a restricted interpretation of Mercury's points of connection. This obliges Mercury to increase markets by extending the network into the local areas it intends to secure. Further, 3L's limitation to the local exchange area excludes Mercury from emulating BT's out-of-area exchange lines. This facility would have enabled Mercury to target on particular traffic routes with immediate profit potential and to meet the demands of particular customers in advance of the construction of its full network. Mercury is obliged to locate nodes of its network in those local exchange areas to which its customers want access.

Unless it is content to accept a slower market penetration, dependence on 3L and 3J interconnect rather than direct trunk connection will be an additional spur to Mercury to extend its network, because of the obligation to keep within the limits set by CCITT Recommendations for transmission loss. But the other side of the CCITT coin is its relevance in sustaining any agreement which BT and Mercury may find advantageous in dealing with international opportunities. For this, agreement to adopt CCITT Recommendations is necessary. The implication is that customers' options to accept a lower-price, lower-quality service, which is perfectly feasible with current technology, will have, it seems, to await internationally agreed modifications.

Perhaps customers' most important expectation of UK's liberalization was, and still is, its impact on the company and domestic telephone bill. As US experience shows, competition in voice telephony starts in earnest when large-scale users see the opportunity to make major cost savings. Smaller customers quickly follow suit. The interconnect agreement's potential for Mercury in this area is dealt with next.

Charges and margins for competition

The interconnect agreement establishes a firm base for competitive strategy in pricing of services. As explained earlier, there are provisions to alter the charges established in the determination, but these can be relatively easily foreseen. We may expect Mercury's plans – including implied effects on investment choice – to be laid accordingly. The charges provide one element of a decision to attack particular markets, namely the margin between BT's price to customers for a particular type of call, and what Mercury has to pay to BT to effect the calls as set out in Table 15.1 above.

To illustrate the effect of these payments on the margins available to Mercury, consider the examples of interconnected calls listed in Table 15.3. The examples have been selected as the most likely types of interconnected calls that Mercury is expected to offer and all relate to situations in which the interconnection payments are to be made by Mercury to BT. Table 15.4 sets out, for each example, the charge that would be made by BT for carrying the call from end to end, and the payment that Mercury must make to BT for the segments of the call that BT actually provides in each case. The calls are assumed to last for five minutes (300 seconds). The difference gives an indication of the amount available to Mercury to cover its costs, including profit, and to offer a tariff to customers discounted relative to BT's. These margins do not take into account payments by Mercury to BT for unsuccessful call attempts. At the peak period, such payments may reduce Mercury's margins by up to 10 per cent.

Table 15.5 expresses for each call the difference as a percentage of the BT tariff for the same call. The examples indicate that the differences potentially available to Mercury are significantly weighted towards calls at peak hours and towards trunk calls. Without knowledge of Mercury's costs, it is not possible to say which calls will be good business, although, as already noted, excess capacity in early years will provide a strong incentive to take any traffic yielding a significant revenue.

Table 15.3 Examples of interconnected calls

Local calls

Example 1   A directly connected Mercury subscriber to a BT subscriber handed over at the local exchange to which the BT subscriber is connected, so that a 3L charge is payable (3L)

Example 2   A directly connected Mercury subscriber to a BT subscriber handed over at the junction side of the trunk exchange serving the BT subscriber (Local 3J)

Short national calls

Example 3   A directly connected Mercury subscriber to a BT subscriber handed over at the trunk exchange serving the area in which the Mercury subscriber is located (Short national A)

Example 4   A directly connected Mercury subscriber to a BT subscriber handed over at the trunk exchange serving the area in which the BT subscriber is located (Local 3J)

Example 5   A BT subscriber to another BT subscriber with Mercury's network selected: the call is handed over to Mercury at the trunk network in the originating area and handed back by Mercury in the destination area (Local 3J at both ends)

Long national calls

Example 6   A directly connected Mercury subscriber to a BT subscriber handed over at the trunk exchange serving the originating area (Long national A)

Example 7   A BT subscriber to another BT subscriber with Mercury's network selected: the call is handed over at the trunk exchange in the originating area and handed back by Mercury in the destination area (Local 3J at both ends).

Example 8   A BT subscriber to another BT subscriber with Mercury's network selected: the call is handed over at the trunk in the originating area and handed back by Mercury to a BT trunk exchange to be carried on to the destination area (Local 3J plus short national B).

As Table 15.5 shows, the concentration of high 'differences' during business hours is marked. The determination provides an incentive to Mercury to pursue the business rather than the residential customer. It is unlikely that this incentive represents a deliberate act of policy by the Director-General. Given his stated aims (and statutory duty) of encouraging competition, the payments laid down appear perverse in narrowing the market that Mercury will find it most profitable to supply. Mercury has already indicated that its own costs are most favourable in relation to supplying high capacity to major businesses.

The Mercury tariff issued in April 1986 distinguishes customers directly connected to the Mercury network from customers who access Mercury via the BT network. Switched telephone service is now available only for directly connected customers (Mercury 2100); the Mercury 2200 switched service for access to Mercury via BT is to be introduced later in the year.

Both the 2100 and 2200 services offer outgoing calls only (i.e. they are point-to-multipoint). Directly connected (2100) customers will have a

Table 15.4 The differences available to Mercury for interconnected calls (pence)

	Cheap	Standard	Peak
Local calls			
1 BT tariff (local)	5	15	20
Interconnection charge	5	11.5	13
Difference	0	3.5	7
2 BT tariff (local)	5	15	20
Interconnection charge	5	10	11.5
Difference	0	5	8.5
Short national calls			
3 BT tariff (a)	15	40	50
Interconnection charge	11	22	30
Difference	4	18	20
4 BT tariff (a)	15	40	50
Interconnection charge	5	10	11.5
Difference	10	30	38.5
5 BT tariff (a)	15	40	50
Interconnection charge	10	20	23
Difference	5	20	27
Long national calls			
6 BT tariff (b1)	25	50	70
Interconnection charge	12	25	32.5
Difference	13	25	37.5
7 BT tariff (b1)	25	50	70
Interconnection charge	10	20	23
Difference	15	30	47
8 BT tariff (b)	35	70	90
Interconnection charge	10.5	25.5	34.5
Difference	24.5	44.5	55.5

Note: BT tariff and interconnection charges calculated for a call of 300 seconds duration.

Table 15.5 Difference available to Mercury as a percentage of the BT tariff

	Cheap	Standard	Peak
Local calls			
Example 1	0	23	35
Example 2	0	23	42
Short national calls			
Example 3	27	45	40
Example 4	67	75	77
Example 5	33	50	54
Long national calls			
Example 6	52	50	53
Example 7	60	60	67
Example 8	70	63	62

Note: For descriptions of the examples selected, see Table 15.3.

PABX and be subscribers to both networks. Connection to Mercury will be by direct service line, either microwave radio or, in the City of London, by optical fibre cable. Calls can be routed to Mercury either by least-cost routeing software incorporated in the PABX or users can select Mercury by dialling a prefix different from that usually dialled to gain a BT outside line.

Customers of the 2200 service will be supplied with equipment providing accelerated dialling, authorization code and conversion from loop disconnect signalling to multi-frequency signalling used by Mercury for this service. This equipment can be connected to a PABX or fitted into a special telephone instrument. In the latter case, the user presses a button marked 'M' and then dials the number required.

The tariff published for switched services covers local, trunk and international calls. The charges for trunk calls are divided at 56 km and split between prime, standard and economy periods in the same way as BT's charges. In addition, calls with a destination in BT call charge areas where Mercury does not have a distribution node (and hence local interconnection) are charged at a higher rate. This means that Mercury has four levels (called Tiers) of trunk call charges, depending on distance and relation to the installed Mercury network.

For the Mercury 2100 service, a comparison with BT's trunk tariff indicates that the unweighted average discount offered by Mercury is 19 per cent, varying between 0 and 40 per cent. This comparison refers to a call of 200 seconds duration. Local calls tend to be longer and for a local call in the cheap or economy period lasting longer than 263 seconds, Mercury's charge is higher than BT's. For local calls during business hours, however, Mercury's charges are lower by about 20 per cent. Mercury charges per second for calls; call charges are rounded to the nearest penny with a minimum charge of 3p per call. BT have a 5p unit fee and vary charges by changing the number of seconds per unit. As BT charge in full unit steps, the Mercury discount will vary slightly for calls of different durations.

For a typical call made by a directly connected Mercury customer, Figure 15.2 shows the BT and Mercury call charges in relation to the interconnect charges for different means of final delivery of the call. Figure 15.2 brings out the fact that for call destinations where Mercury does not have local interconnection arrangements the discounts to customers can be very low. This would occur if Mercury did not have local interconnection at either end of a route designated 'low cost' by BT and so charged at the 'b1' tariff. Detailed comparison of 'b1' and Tier 1 routes reveals that such low discount routes are relatively few. Indeed, for customers outside London directly connected to the Mercury network, there are likely to be significantly more Tier 1 routes than 'b1'.

The first Mercury tariff has a number of interesting features. Most strikingly, Mercury is offering a full range of switched services to a selected group of customers. The high minimum rental for direct connection should deter most smaller customers. In general, the limitation of service to large, directly connected customers should eliminate virtually all unprofitable calls. When the 2200 service becomes available for customers connected via BT, Mercury will need to control customers' use of the service to ensure that excessive interconnect charges are not incurred. This could be done by geographical variation in authorization and network access codes.

The average discount for trunk calls appears to provide a significant incentive to BT subscribers to consider becoming Mercury customers, although little is known about the price sensitivity of business users. Given the proportion of trunk calls in telephone bills (less than 50 per cent on average) and, for indirectly connected customers, the number of destinations Mercury cannot yet reach because of attenuation problems, the effect on the total bill of using Mercury could be much smaller, perhaps less than 5 per cent.

The proportion of trunk calls is particularly low for businesses in London, because of the size of the London call charge area. This characteristic, combined with the concentration of b1 routes to and from London, would have the result of making 2,100 customers outside London more attractive to Mercury than customers in London unless Mercury had a competitive local call charge. However, at first, Mercury will handle local calls to adjacent call charge areas only, not calls within the London area.

Apart from these considerations, the structure of the Mercury tariff is similar to BT's. This may reflect natural caution in the absence of good information on the likely response of customers to a competitive alternative to BT. However, it is not obvious, to take one example, why Mercury needs to have a peak period when its network is bound to have excess capacity over a considerable period. As very few Mercury customers yet have least cost routeing equipment in place, few businesses could take advantage of detailed differences in tariffs between BT and Mercury. As it is, least cost routeing only appears to have a function in handling overflow traffic or in selecting BT or Mercury on a geographical basis.

The similarity in structure of the two tariffs will simplify BT's response. There is limited value in speculating about the immediate tactical interaction of BT and Mercury since the latter's service offerings and tariff can change rapidly. However, the broad outlines of BT's incentives are clear. First, BT can be expected to continue to reduce trunk call charges during business hours relative to other call charges. For this shift to be reflected in interconnection charges BT must demonstrate that it is cost justified. Second, BT can be expected to offer to large customers improved forms of network access as a means of offering volume discounts. For example, large customers could be offered the equivalent of connection at Level 3J. Calls sent over such connections would bypass local exchanges and so, in accordance with the charging principles of the interconnect determination, could be charged for at a lower rate.

As Mercury is starting with very few directly connected customers, BT does not have to adjust its tariff immediately to protect its market share. The indications are that BT will need time to prepare the ground for a preferential tariff for large customers, including securing the assent of Oftel.

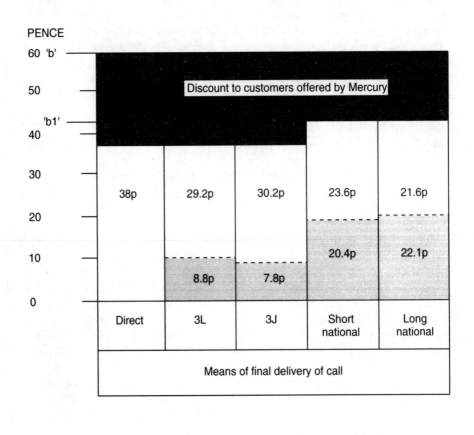

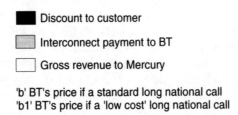

KEY

■ Discount to customer

▨ Interconnect payment to BT

□ Gross revenue to Mercury

'b' BT's price if a standard long national call
'b1' BT's price if a 'low cost' long national call

Figure 15.2 Analysis of BT and Mercury charges for a peak period long national call lasting 200 seconds by a directly connected Mercury customer

BT should not be able to sustain the argument that large customers can receive volume discounts simply because they make large numbers of calls. Beyond the exchange connection, the costs of which are in principle covered by connection and rental charges, reductions in costs per call with increased volume produce benefits for all customers, not just those who make or receive the largest number of them.

New market entrants

In the debates leading up to the 1984 Act, and in the drafting of regulatory instruments following it, there appears to have been a belief that the leading issue in establishing commercial opportunity for would-be competitors would be BT's role in influencing their costs. Moreover, there seems to have been a belief that it would be possible to establish a 'correct' price for transactions between BT and competitors based on costs. These views are reflected in Oftel's duties with respect to the determination. We have already commented on the way in which we think the charges for interconnection were derived and their lack of precise relationship to costs. We now point up the consequences for new competition.

First, as we have just argued, there is no exclusive relation between the charges sanctioned in the determination and the market prospects for the competitors. What is charged will affect, but not determine, prospective margins. Though the determination gives a set of charges made by *both* BT and Mercury, those of the dominant supplier, BT, are far more relevant. Second, in the context of the development of competition policy in telecommunications, the important point is the effect of the determination as a whole on competitors' abilities to enter and grow. We have indicated that, despite a favourable ruling on interconnection charges, Mercury faces significant technical and commercial problems in attacking BT's market.

The interconnect determination must also be seen as embodying the understanding and pledges between government and telephone interests, especially BT. Given these pledges, BT's own strategy can be summed up as a race against time – to replace outmoded analogue equipment in a very large system and, as far as possible, outmoded contracts with labour and suppliers, before competition is able to make, or is positioned to make, considerable inroads. The critical horizon is 1990.

Both BT and Mercury are aware that the most formidable potential competition on voice telephony is to be expected from private networks. Very large leased line users may well see advantage in using their big internal switching and transmission capacity to expand into serving others, including of course each other, possibly by merging their respective telecommunications interests. They also have the strongest interest in what is now high margin, and rapidly growing, international traffic. One might speculate that one of the difficulties which prevented BT and Mercury reaching their own agreement without determination by the Director-General was the question of treatment of the large-customer markets. However that might be, private networks represent a substantial competitive threat to both parties for several reasons.

First, and most obviously, private network operators have considerable bargaining power *vis-à-vis* public network operators and are biased heavily towards long-distance domestic and international calls. Digital capacity caters for both voice and data, so adding to the prospective opportunity to lower costs, through their ability to load their own systems. Developments in other areas of policy, more especially in the data network area, are encouraging to large users. The current proposals on value-added and data services opens the prospect of applications for licences combining elements of voice and data. The substitution of one's own network also offers attractive 'bypass' possibilities – of avoiding local as well as long-distance PTO charges. Collaboration with others would add to short-distance bypass business as well as to long. Once established with a good in-house base load, a policy of adding on smaller companies' demands, again possible with local bypass, would be attractive. In short, PTOs face a problem which more 'normal' industries have long recognized as extremely powerful – namely, the option for large customers to integrate back to their own supply, and, if necessary, to collaborate in doing so and, where favourably placed, to take on outside business.

Mercury's position in these developments has been difficult. It commenced its entry to the market by emphasizing, as was natural at the time, its attraction to large customers as a second source, lessening dependence on BT. Hence its original main interest in interconnect was to secure local distribution, by BT, so it could present a plausible service to these customers. It would, in effect, provide cheap bypass to BT's trunk service.

But subsequent changes in BT's pricing policy have, we would argue, shifted the balance of advantage towards another form of bypass – local. Because of the prospects for large potential customers just analysed, those customers are now more likely to see their option in terms of using the bargaining power coming from their possibilities of integration to cut more favourable deals with BT. Mercury must therefore consider the composition of its target customer base to have changed towards smaller customers. It may be expected to look more favourably on resale, as time goes on, because of its need to use middlemen to aggregate traffic from such smaller customers.

NOTES

1 This chapter was originally published by Spicer and Pegler Associates.
2 List of exchanges – The places at which BT trunk exchanges were connected to the Mercury network by 30 March 1986 were:

Central London (Centre, City, North Central and South Central Sectors)
Outer London (East, North, North West, South, South East, South West and West Sectors).

Birmingham	Milton Keynes
Bradford	Nottingham
Bristol	Reading
Coventry	Sheffield
Derby	Slough
Gloucester	Stoke-on-Trent
Hemel Hempstead	Swindon
Leeds	Uxbridge
Leicester	Walsall
Liverpool	Warrington
Luton	Weybridge
Manchester	Wolverhampton

16 The liberalization of telephone services in the UK[1]

M.E. Beesley and B. Laidlaw

INTRODUCTION

This chapter shows how the telecommunications market in the United Kingdom has been progressively opened over the eleven years from 1981 to the end of 1992. By analysing the development of the regulatory framework over a decade we hope to show that further substantial modification is still required and, more important, to indicate what kind of reforms are needed. During this period, a principal aim of the Government's policy has been to promote effective competition in the provision of telecommunication services. We focus on competition in voice telephony, which accounts for over 80 per cent of the market, measured by revenues.

One innovation in applying policy over this period has been to set up a sector-specific regulatory body, Oftel, with two main tasks:

- to regulate British Telecom's prices and profits and
- to manage the development of competition.

To understand UK policy now, one must trace its formative influences at least from 1981, when the first substantial change occurred, the separation of the nationalized industry, BT, from the rest of postal services. External influences on UK policy have been very muted. At the start of the decade, US developments indicated what was possible but held few specific lessons. Subsequently, the EC developed and began to apply its own telecommunications policy; this drew from rather than influenced the British experience.

STATE OF THE TELECOMMUNICATIONS MARKET IN 1981

The Government's aim of opening the voice telephony market was a response to the condition of the industry in the UK at the end of the 1970s. Three aspects in particular were the focus of concern:

(1) the poor quality of telephone service;
(2) delays in the modernization of the national network;

(3) the difficulty customers had in obtaining the most recent types of equipment.

We describe each of these briefly.

Poor service

Although the technical performance of the national telephone network had steadily improved in the years up to 1981, the volume of complaints from users about the service provided continued to rise. The explanation probably lies in the financial and institutional constraints on the adjustment of supply to increasing demand. Telecommunications was subject to Treasury rules on borrowing to finance investment. The severity of this constraint varied from year to year, with the overall effect of reducing the rate of investment.

As an institution, moreover, BT inherited from the Telecommunications Business of the Post Office deficient marketing and customer relations. The deficiency went beyond the arrogance towards customers to be expected of an assured monopoly. The organization was production-orientated and focused on the universal availability of a standard and basic service. Demand for non-standard services or equipment, even for items as simple as a telephone answering machine, was neglected or suppressed.

System X

Up to 1981, the Telecommunications Business of the Post Office and the main British manufacturers co-ordinated the development and supply of equipment. The Post Office was the dominant partner in the cartel; it undertook or funded most of the development work, set the technical specifications and, most important, placed the orders that determined which products were made. Apart from the relatively small-scale production of handsets, the Post Office was not permitted to manufacture itself. The Post Office naturally gave priority to its own plans; its specifications and orders took little account of implications for exports. This organization had not produced a successful industrial policy; the export performance of the manufacturing industry had declined steadily for many years.

The development of digital switching technology crystallized several of the difficulties inherent in the relationship with the manufacturing sector. System X, the British design of digital telephone exchange sponsored by the Post Office, was heralded in the mid-1970s as a project of national importance that would produce a spectacular improvement in the performance of the national network and in the range of services it could provide to customers. However, installation of the new technology in the national telephone network was delayed for several years, partly because of delays in development and partly because of the financial and institutional constraints already referred to. In the meantime (indeed, up till 1987), BT invested heavily in an electronic, but non-digital exchange design, TXE4. This had a better performance and much lower operating costs than earlier designs, but could not be sold overseas.

In the event, System X has turned out to be a standard product, not noticeably better or worse than a dozen other designs produced overseas. The anticipated gains from digitalization on quality of service and overall productivity were, at best, postponed and have not been as dramatic as hoped for. The manufacturing cartel was reorganized after the withdrawal of BT's sponsorship in 1981–2 and the industry further concentrated. BT bought a second exchange design from overseas, subject only to requiring assembly in the UK. By so doing, BT secured much lower prices for its procurement of digital exchanges. For the manufacturers, therefore, the domestic market remains protected to some degree but has probably ceased to be significantly more profitable than exports.

Equipment standards

The clearest indication of poor service was the difficulty many customers found in obtaining permission to use new types of equipment, such as answering machines. As the variety of equipment available on the world market increased, and both manufacturers and retailers joined the criticism of BT's policies, it quickly became clear that piecemeal opening of the UK market would not suffice. A formal arrangement based on national technical standards was considered necessary.

The early involvement with the standards issue and the experience with System X were the main factors that led to a shift of policy priority from sponsoring manufacturing to promoting new services in the UK telecommunications industry. For the Government, promoting telecommunication services had many attractions:

- It enabled the sector to be linked to the computer revolution, even though the application of the same technical developments in telecommunications was bogged down.
- It enabled support to be given to small and new firms as well as the traditional recipients of sponsorship.
- Exhortation, awareness programmes and pilot projects were relatively cheap forms of Government activity.

This shift in policy led naturally to the narrowing in the scope of BT's monopoly and an espousal of liberalization.[2]

THE 1981 ACT

The primary purpose of the British Telecommunications Act 1981 was to complete the separation of telecommunication from postal services. BT came into existence as a public corporation independent of the Post Office in October 1981. It preserved in formal terms BT's 'exclusive privilege' as a provider of public telecommunication services and hence with the power to license others. Nevertheless, the Government, acting through the Secretary of State for Industry (now Trade and Industry), was empowered to license competitive network operators and service providers. The Act also established the authority of the Secretary of State to approve the supply of apparatus. The Secretary of State was to be advised by the British Approvals Board for Telecommunications (BABT), whose committees provided an avenue for British manufacturers to influence the approvals process. While this new system of approvals got under way, BT continued for some years to act as a standard body.

The regulatory framework was hybrid, therefore, with the Government and BT having overlapping powers. While it was safe to assume that BT would not encourage competitive entry, it was not at first clear what use the Secretary of State might make of his licensing powers. The policy debate had crystallized around three distinct sectors:

- equipment owned and operated by users (subscribers' apparatus)
- value-added network services (VANS)
- basic network services, both voice and data.

Value-added network services were defined as comprising the use of computer equipment to enhance messages in the course of transmission. It was thought that this characteristic would permit the liberalization of VANS to proceed without necessarily disturbing the monopoly of basic network services.

Network competition

What use could be made of the public telephone network first arose as a practical policy question in 1980, as the Bill was going through the Commons. The issue was the terms on which commercial value-added services would be permitted to be provided by firms other than BT itself. The implicit assumption was that a technical distinction could be drawn between value-added services and voice telephony and used as the basis for regulation. The Secretary of State for Industry, Sir Keith Joseph, asked Professor Michael Beesley[3] to hold a public inquiry into the matter. Having his doubts about this distinction, he asked for his terms of reference to be widened to include consideration of the effects of any third party use of public networks, that is, of resale as a principle.

The Beesley Report's main findings were that a sustainable regulatory distinction between value-added services and telephone calls could not be found. As the USA in particular had shown, commercial developments in the UK could and should take place in the context of growing network competition. As part of that, there should be no restriction on the resale of capacity on BT's network; the effect on BT's net revenues would not be severe, largely because of the probability of rebalancing tariffs to reduce the profitability of long-distance services. Regulation should concentrate on ensuring that BT's conduct, in pricing as in other matters, did not discriminate against newcomers.

The Government appeared to be surprised by the recommendations of the Beesley Report, which amounted to freedom to enter the voice telephony markets on all fronts. Although the 1981 legislation (the Bill became an Act in July) gave the Government the powers to follow the Beesley line, it was not prepared to go that far. The choice for network competition was seen as being between freeing resale and allowing entry by a new national network operator; the Government opted for the latter. The decisive consideration was the expected effect of resale on the structure of the voice telephony tariff. A rapid fall in long-distance charges offset by rising rental and local call charges would benefit most business users, but adversely affect the average residential user. In July 1981, Mr Kenneth Baker, announcing the decision, welcomed the 'tone' of the Beesley Report but in effect deferred resale, while welcoming an initiative by Cable & Wireless, BP and Barclays Merchant Bank to lay an optical fibre network along the railway lines linking major business centres in England (the Mercury Project).

BT as a nationalized industry

For the next year, policy concentrated on defining more precisely the scope of competition permitted on BT's network. BT's line of argument against permitting voice resale was in effect condoned. This argument had less to do with the absolute effect on its profits than with the effect on the pricing structure for voice telephony. It was assumed that competition would focus on long-distance services which were highly profitable (international services were even more profitable, but it was assumed that entry at that level was not practically possible). If BT reduced long-distance charges in response to entry, local charges and rental charges would rise. This 'tariff rebalancing' would undo the traditional subsidy of residential telephone services which was considered to be essential to the achievement of universal service.

The policy debate about network competition and its implications for BT as a nationalized industry was neither intense nor long lasting. The practical question was who would enter, what precisely would they do and on what terms. The Mercury Project was the only proposition in front of Ministers in 1981; naturally, it was accepted in principle, even though at this point it was unclear how important Mercury would become. The statement by Mr Kenneth Baker in July 1981 was encouraging but vague.

Here, however, events conspired to undermine BT's defence of its monopoly. In October 1981, BT had managed to get permission for a significant increase in prices, above the rate of inflation. It had done so mainly because the Government was determined to hold down public sector borrowing, while acknowledging that BT had to be allowed to invest in network modernization. Higher prices would enable this investment to be largely self-financed; only £200 million needed to be borrowed (termed the external financing limit or EFL) in 1981–2 to meet BT's planned investments. By April 1982, it was clear that BT's management had failed to meet its targets for investment; the shortfall in spending was greater than the EFL agreed by the Treasury and cast doubt on the scale of the price increase agreed by the Department of Industry the previous autumn. Thus, a direct consequence of BT's failure to spend the money was that it was obliged to reduce its prices immediately. In May 1982, BT introduced 50 per cent reductions in charges on 'low cost' trunk routes. These were effectively the routes considered vulnerable to entry, whether by resellers or by Mercury. So, in the event, tariff rebalancing was begun without a storm of complaint from consumers.

BT's failure to invest sums so painfully extracted from Government had even more drastic implications. Throughout 1981, the Government had sought a way out of the financing dilemma by permitting BT to raise funds in the City rather than borrowing from the Government. The idea was somehow to divorce the Government from underwriting the risks of investing in operations which it owned and controlled. Inevitably, the attempts failed. The financial instrument devised in 1981, termed the 'Busby Bond' after a cartoon character featured in BT's advertisements of the time, was ultimately abandoned and privatization came into focus as a more fundamentally sound option for attracting private sector funds into the expansion of BT's network.

PRIVATIZATION

Privatization of the large nationalized industries had not been part of the governing Conservative Party's manifesto at the last election in 1979. Rather, it now developed, with BT as the first example, as a result of the perceived failure of the Government's first attempts to reshape and galvanize the nationalized industries. Part of these attempts was the Competition Act, 1980, Section 11 of which created powers for the detailed investigation of the efficiency of nationalized industries. Such investigations could not stray into questions of pricing and finance, which were effectively reserved to the Treasury. In effect, therefore, the 1980 vision of influencing nationalized industry conduct was to be strongly distinguished from that of industry in general. Privatization marked a sharp decline in the faith accorded that policy.

The decision to privatize BT had far-reaching consequences both for attitudes to network competition and for the regulatory framework for the sector. However, these aspects were not given much consideration at the time the decision was taken. As the announcement to Parliament on 19 July 1982 by the Secretary of State, Mr Patrick Jenkin, made clear, the decision to privatize was intended to resolve the problem of how to reconcile BT's investment programme with the Government's tight limits on borrowing. He said,

> Unless something is done radically to change the capital structure and ownership of BT and to provide a direct spur to efficiency, higher investment could mean still higher charges for the customer.

As has been noted, the price increases already granted had been more than sufficient to meet the level of investment achieved in the 1981–2 financial year. The privatization decision was not, therefore, simply a response to a short-term crisis. Rather it was the culmination of a two-year debate over the financing of investment. BT's modernization programme was expected to take at least ten years and cost some £20 billion.

The Government accepted the rather exaggerated views of the strategic national importance of network modernization then prevalent. Simply refusing BT permission to increase its investment programme (as had been done in the past) was therefore not an option. Increasing prices would not only be unpopular with customers, but inconsistent with counter-inflation policy and with promoting network competition.

A further factor in the decision, implicit in Mr Jenkin's remarks, was dissatisfaction with the quality of BT's management. Failing to spend an agreed annual budget is a cardinal sin in the public sector. Beyond that, BT appeared to be dithering over technical choices and failing to improve productivity as fast as was expected. The Government were convinced that a transfer of ownership to the private sector would shake up internal decision making and improve management quality in BT.

Privatization on such a scale was understood to require a long gestation period and anyway could not be successful if there was a risk of the Government changing, so Ministers could safely undertake not to execute their decision until after the next General Election. Even so, Parliamentary time for the enabling legislation was found in the 1982–3 session. The 1983 election was called a matter of weeks before the legislation would have been ready for Royal Assent; the Bill was reintroduced in the Autumn of 1983 and finally became the Telecommunications Act in July 1984.

Divestiture

Although regulatory reform was not central to the privatization policy, it quickly became the focus of debate. A logical approach to the question of how to restrain the exercise of BT's monopoly power would have been to borrow from contemporary US developments; AT&T was divested of its local network operations as a result of the 1982 Modified Final Judgment, settling an anti-trust case brought by the Department of Justice. The issue was debated in relation to BT but BT's management was strongly opposed. Merchant bank advice was that trading records for component parts of BT would need to be established. As the internal accounts would have taken time to be developed, divestiture would therefore have meant postponing privatization for years, a delay Ministers were unwilling to contemplate.

The issue of the divestiture is still implicit in policy debates. In the USA, it enabled competition in long-distance services to develop rapidly and produced seven financially strong regional companies. Several of these (termed 'Baby Bells' or 'RBOCs'[4]) have subsequently invested in the UK and other markets around the world. They are, however, increasingly irked at their exclusion from competitive voice telephony markets in the USA, generating a long series of regulatory disputes for the US authorities. It seems inevitable that, in due course, some or all of the restrictions on the RBOCs will be removed. That is, divestiture appears to be a feasible long-term method of generating network competition as well as a short-term way of restraining the abuse of monopoly. Since privatization, BT has been careful not to organize its operations on a geographical basis, so that, although its internal accounting and management systems have greatly improved, divestiture would still be difficult in practice.

Mercury

Privatization of BT also brought conflicting policy requirements, having very important implications for the development of competition in telecoms. The main problem was how to ensure success in the flotation of BT, in the sense of raising cash for the Treasury, while retaining a credible defence against accusations of unleashing a powerful private monopoly. At first, concern was expressed that the sale of shares was on so great a scale that it would be difficult to obtain good value for BT's assets. It was realized, quite late in the day, that a second political objective could be secured by pricing the issue so as to attract a large number of private shareholders. Giving millions of BT's customers a stake in the company would then to a degree forestall criticism of rising profits. On competition, the way to stiffen the challenge to BT without putting BT's profitability at risk was to upgrade the existing network competitor.

The licence granted to Cable & Wireless in February 1982 to operate the Mercury network required it to build a digital network connecting thirty specified cities. Mercury's activities in voice telephony was limited in the licence to 3 per cent of BT's revenues. All of this was intended to reassure BT's management and customers that network competition would not endanger the modernization programme or mean higher prices, but was merely consistent with Mercury's business plans at that time. However, Mercury was not allowed to offer international services. This was a significant restriction but, again, it had been dictated by concern not to reduce BT's ability to finance network modernization.

The Government agreed to remove virtually all the restrictions on Mercury's business (a prohibition on Mercury's providing public call boxes lasted until 1988). Mercury would henceforth not be merely a limited domestic rival to BT for business customers but a fully-fledged public service provider. Mercury's parents, particularly Cable & Wireless, would need to be persuaded to commit to a much larger investment. In return for this commitment, assurance was sought from Ministers that other entrants would not be licensed. At this stage, Mercury was also against permitting resale. Out of the extended negotiation came the Fixed Links Duopoly policy, finally agreed between the Government, BT and Mercury in November 1983. Mr Baker's statement describing how BT and Mercury would operate and saying that there would be no further entry into public network operation at least until November 1990 settled the main lines of telecom policy until the Duopoly Review.

Cable television

The Fixed Links Duopoly cut across the Government's previous promotion of cable television networks as providing the basis for advanced telecommunication services at local level as well as delivering TV programmes to homes. Under the new policy, cable TV networks were licensed as local telecommunication networks but were not allowed to connect to each other. That is, they could connect outside their franchise area only via BT or Mercury, effectively removing their competitive potential. These restrictions have now been removed, but the national total of telephone lines installed by the cable companies had at December 1992 barely reached 50,000.

Mobile radio

The licensing of cellular and other mobile radio services was exempt from the restrictions of the Duopoly policy. At this point, the potential of radio telephony to offer a competitive telephone service was considered no more than a remote possibility for the future. No provision was made in licensing the cellular networks to cover this possibility. In the event, cellular radio became a spectacular commercial success without having any wider implications for sector policy. Other mobile services to be licensed during the Duopoly, such as Band III and Telepoint,[5] have not repeated that success.

OFTEL

Part of the political solution to controlling private monopoly power was to establish a separate body to take over BT's residual regulatory functions and be a quasi-independent player in the interchanges between industry and Government. The Office of Fair Trading (OFT) was the model for the Office of Telecommunications (Oftel). OFT had felt unable to take on the task of detailed sector regulation itself, but Oftel was designed so that it could easily be merged with OFT at a future date.[6]

It was recognized that the problem of controlling single, large-firm power had only lately been tackled in the Competition Act 1980, which was an uncertain instrument for controlling BT. Hence BT's licence was furnished with intended guarantees of acceptable conduct. These were based on what might have arisen if BT had already been found to have acted against the public interest on a 1973 Act monopolies reference. Subsequently, these conditions were introduced into all PTO[7] licences; thereby, they became a general framework for competition in network operators rather than rules explicitly designed to constrain BT.

OFT can also evoke a general monopoly reference of BT if need be, though it is scarcely conceivable that it would not co-ordinate such action with Oftel. The Monopolies and Mergers Commission (MMC) can enter as a referee in two ways: on appeal when changes in licence conditions are disputed between BT and Oftel and as a consequence of a general referral on monopoly. This background is essential to understanding OFTEL's remit. Like OFT, Oftel works in conjunction with the MMC and DTI; it has relatively little independent authority. Its primary tasks are to enforce the conditions in licences, to resolve commercial disputes and to advise the Government. The Secretary of State retains the power to license new operators. If Oftel is unable to resolve disputes with licensees, the issue can be referred to the MMC.

OFTEL's actual influence has exceeded its formal powers, partly because it alone among the regulatory agencies has the resources to deal with a wide range of detailed issues and partly because of the success of the first Director-General of Telecommunications, Sir Bryan Carsberg, in carving out a pivotal role in policy debates.

Price control

Since 1984, the system of price control applied to BT[8] has become widely recognized as a workable, and probably superior, alternative to US-style rate of return regulation. Its essence is a periodic settlement of a cap on the permitted rate of increase of prices[9] for voice telephony services, based on a mix of financial projections and bargaining between Oftel and BT. Oftel must take a view on prospective profits, taking into account achievable productivity gains and the likely consequences of tariff rebalancing. The DG's duty to ensure BT's ability to finance its operations effectively sets the company's cost of capital as a lower limit to the impact that the price control could have on profits. While precise measurement of the cost of capital is difficult, in practice BT's reported profits appear to have remained well above that limit.

The initial level of the price cap was set by the Government taking into account the implications for the price of BT shares. In 1988, the value of X was redetermined by Professor Carsberg (the DG). His method was essentially to project BT's financial performance and calculate the rate of reduction of prices that would bring profits down over four or five years to the company's cost of capital. If BT can do better than the DG believes, it can retain the extra profits until the next price review. The incentive to improve efficiency marks the most important difference from rate of return control applied year by year in response to applications by operators for price increases.[10]

The starting level of the price control was set at RPI−3 for five years in 1984 and tightened to RPI−4.5 in 1988 to apply for the four years from 1989. However, in 1990, the DG intervened to include international call charges in the basket of controlled prices. As it was expected that these would fall by 10 per cent a year, the control was redefined as RPI−6.25. The intervention was intended to be neutral in its effect on efficiency incentives, being a response to public concern about the high returns BT was earning on international calls (estimated by Oftel as over 80 per cent on capital employed). In 1992, the value of X was further increased from 6.25 to 7.5 per cent for four years from 1993. The continued ratcheting up of X reflected BT's steadily rising rate of return on capital employed.

The inclusion of international call charges (and international private circuits from 1991) continued a trend to broaden the coverage of price controls to cover a higher proportion of BT's telephone services. The original control covered 55 per cent of BT's total revenues. By 1991, 73.5 per cent of total revenues and 90 per cent of telephone service revenue were covered. The broadening scope of controls has been in response to concern that BT was increasing the profitability of unregulated services.

Additional constraints on prices are also in place, intended to curtail tariff rebalancing. At the outset, the annual rate of change of residential rental charges was limited to RPI + 2; later a similar control on business rental charges was set at RPI + 5. From 1989, a RPI−0 control on the median residential consumer's bill has been applied.

Bargaining between Oftel and BT on price controls intensified after 1988, partly as a preliminary skirmish in relation to the Duopoly Review, without leading to a break down. In the negotiations, the DG could threaten that he would recommend an acceleration of market entry; BT could exploit its information advantage. Both sides seem to have decided it was in their best interests to avoid a reference of the issues to the MMC.

Clearly, large business customers have gained more than customers overall. The dictates of competitive developments, strongly focused on recruiting substantial customers, ensured that this would happen. But it is impossible to show that the price level of telephone service has fallen faster in real terms that it would have done in the absence of privatization, principally because a plausible model of the alternative pricing regime is absent. BT's management have given the impression that the financial targets implicitly given to them are demanding, while their efforts to contain costs have taken a long time to show results.

Network competition in the Duopoly era

In one sense, the period since 1984 represents a continuation of the pre-privatization policy of goading the nationalized industry to be more efficient, with different means being employed. More far-reaching liberalization of network operation was put off until the outcome of the twin experiments with privatization and network competition was known.

By the start of the Duopoly era, the supply of telecommunication equipment had been liberalized and BT's operating monopoly had been moved behind the first point of connection of such equipment to the network. Having relieved BT of responsibility for shaping, or at least paying for, the UK's manufacturing strategy in telecommunications, reliance was now placed on the profit incentive within an increasingly open market. Liberalizing moves in VANS, mobile radio, etc., forced BT to concentrate more on its basic business of real-time voice telephony.

In this regard, Oftel's first task was to ensure that Mercury could indeed survive and grow. Because any entrant required full access to customers, Oftel's principal instrument was the interconnection agreement which it dictated in 1985. With this agreement, Mercury was enabled to invest sufficiently to meet its licence obligations. In 1987, when Mercury was able to show that the agreement did not enable it to make profits on many international calls handed over to BT for delivery overseas, Oftel adjusted the charges to ensure that it could.

With its interconnection agreement secured, Mercury was able to offer a discount of 15 to 25 per cent on calls compared to BT, depending on the precise mix of local, long-distance and international calls made by each customer. Whether this was a sufficiently attractive saving to induce a customer to switch from BT depended on the cost and convenience of connection to Mercury. By charging more than BT for an equivalent connection, Mercury was able to focus its appeal on businesses with high volumes of telecommunication traffic. Even so, most potential customers and Mercury's own marketing staff appeared to find it difficult to evaluate whether their business would benefit from Mercury service and to solve the technical problems of connection.

Even with the protection of the Duopoly and the assistance of favourable interconnection terms, Mercury did not become the 'second national network' envisaged by the Government's policy. Rather, it concentrated on serving customers in the City of London, particularly those making many international calls. At first, some 90 per cent of its business was accounted for by firms in City locations. Mercury found that, to meet the demands of its selected customer group, it had to offer good local, long-distance and international services. It therefore built a local fibre-optic network in the City of London and five other business districts to complement the intercity figure-of-eight optical fibre network laid along railway lines which had figured in its original proposal. Mercury also sought direct international transmission capacity, across the Atlantic in particular.

Mercury's interconnect business – that is, calls conveyed for customers that remained directly connected to BT's local network – did not prosper. The number of single exchange line customers with a 'blue button' telephone that could dial the codes to reach the Mercury network via a BT exchange line grew very slowly; by 1991, less than 5 per cent of Mercury's revenues came from this customer group.

The only exception to the generalization that Mercury concentrated on directly connected customers in central business districts was Hull, where Kingston Communications, the independent, municipally-owned, local telephone network, introduced a form of equal access[11] that enabled its customers to nominate BT or Mercury as their preferred long-distance and international operator. Under this arrangement, Mercury's share of outgoing calls from Hull quickly rose to more than 50 per cent.

As a result of these factors, although narrowly focused in terms of customers served, Mercury's network has turned out to be rather more diverse than had been anticipated. BT's initial response consisted mainly of concentrating investment on network modernization on services and areas where there appeared to be a challenge from Mercury and by a gradual rebalancing of tariffs. For example, BT decided to accelerate the conversion of its trunk network to digital working and to delay conversion of local networks. Tariff rebalancing lowered trunk tariffs and raised rental and connection charges. As it became clear that Mercury's challenge was having a significant impact on only a small percentage of BT's customers, albeit high-volume users, BT unsuccessfully sought permission to introduce volume discounts for calls.

The conclusion to be drawn from the competitive interchange between BT and Mercury during the Duopoly era is that BT was able to accommodate itself to the newcomer without difficulty. Mercury grew fast (sustaining a growth rate of about 40 per cent a year) but did not prevent the growth of BT's revenues or profits. BT was obliged to re-examine its commercial policies, but competition from Mercury has evidently not been the external shock that could induce BT's managers to make exceptional efforts to improve productivity. BT remains greatly overmanned by the best standards obtaining in overseas markets.[12]

International satellite services

Satellite communications have the technical characteristic of being able to by-pass entirely complex public telephone networks, enabling transmissions to take place directly between users within the coverage area ('footprint') of a satellite. This characteristic permitted a gradual liberalization of satellite communications that form part of private networks and are not interconnected with public networks.

The 1983 Duopoly Policy expressly allowed for this exception. Even so, not until 1988 were licences granted, and then only six were awarded to a diverse selection of applicants. The successful bids appeared to have been chosen on the basis that they intended to occupy noncompeting niche markets within the UK (international links were prohibited). After much argument, a proposal from PanAmSat to offer a private network service by means of international satellite communications across the North Atlantic was also authorized in 1988 (PanAmSat did not require a UK licence, merely confirmation of the right to be connected to its customers by means of circuits leased from BT).

The surviving domestic satellite licensees, not presenting a challenge on voice telephony, were later given permission to operate internationally. So, during the Duopoly, satellite communications were liberalized reluctantly and in a way that limited and deferred their competitive potential.

THE DUOPOLY REVIEW

Writing in early 1989 with the intention of opening debate about the scope for market entry when the Fixed Links Duopoly ended, we set out a programme designed to address the central issue of increasing effective competition in voice telephony. It called for the following steps (taken from Beeslay and Laidlaw 1989)[13]:

Recommended liberalization moves in voice telephony

Immediately
1 Relax restrictions on the use of domestic bilateral private circuits.

At July 1989
2 License public resale service providers.
3 Relax 200 metre rule to permit interconnection of privately constructed transmission facilities with public and other private networks within local call charge areas.

Before April 1990
4 Develop interconnection rules for public networks.
5 Accelerate implementation of new national numbering plan.

At November 1990
6 Remove restrictions on provision of voice telephony by local broadband cable networks, including direct interconnection with other such networks.
7 License additional public networks.
8 Remove remaining restrictions on domestic own-account operations.

After November 1990
9 Permit resale of international private circuits.

These steps would, we[13] thought, encourage competition from large users acting on their own account, new public networks, cable networks and resellers – in that order of relative policy significance. Our proposals on timing have proved optimistic, but all the steps were among the options considered between November 1990 and July 1991, when the Review was substantially completed.[14] Which steps have in the event been taken? What, so far as can be deduced, are the reasons for omissions or limitations? And how has competition between BT and Mercury been affected?

Private networks and resale

Steps 1, 3 and 8 were directed particularly at allowing large consumers of telephone services to develop their domestic private networks in any way they wish. In practice, such users would have to make a judicious selection among possible contracts for control and use of capacity, ranging from outright ownership and internal management to short-term leasing and devolution to network managers. The Review has produced movement on steps 1 and 3, but the most critical freedom – to mix leased and owned capacity for conveying calls in the UK on behalf of whomever wishes to pay for it – remains forbidden. Thus a potentially very effective form of resale entry is still inhibited. No explicit rationalization for this inhibition has appeared.

However, it is now possible for private network operators to make a rational choice between leasing transmission capacity from a public network or installing links for their own use. The economics of such choice have been clear for many years: own account operation pays if on a large scale and over long distances. The significance of this development is two-fold. First, it provides a stronger constraint on prices of leased circuits, tending to hold them closer to costs. Second, it provides a stimulus to the relatively small number of large-scale private networks already in existence. These are almost entirely operated by current and former nationalized industries. These networks are to a large extent still dependent on micro-wave technologies; access to radio spectrum for this purpose has not been liberalized.

Steps 2 and 9 were directed at promoting resale entry. The July 1989 removal of restrictions on simple resale (that is, the use of leased circuits to by-pass public switched telephone networks) was foreshadowed in licences issued under the Duopoly regime; positive action to prevent it would have been required. The date passed without such action being taken. In this way, all domestic restrictions on resale were finally removed in 1989, but only a few entrants emerged in the UK, offering shared use of leased lines rather than competition with switched voice services.

At first, potential resellers were caught by the application of apparatus approval regulations: no equipment that could operate a resale service was approved before the Duopoly Review began. Within the UK, margins for resellers have been squeezed by increases in price of leased lines (which nonetheless remain cheap by European standards) and local call charges, and reductions in long-distance charges, as we anticipated in predicting little competitive effect from the 1989 liberalization. The main reason for the lack of commercial interest appears to be inaction on step 9. International restrictions on resale have largely remained in place and the strongest demand for resale came from businesses with widely dispersed international operations. A handful of American resellers have opened for business, offering cheaper international calls to North America; for most businesses, this represents too small a market to produce worthwhile savings. Regulatory authorities in other countries will not permit resale from their jurisdictions.

Steps 4 (developing interconnection rules), 6 (helping cable-based entry), 7 (licensing additional public networks) and 5 (formulating a new national numbering plan) were, we argued, necessary means to hold out prospects for profitable rival networks. We examine progress on each of these steps in turn.

Interconnection

Once the Government and Oftel had decided to encourage market entry, the question of its effect on BT's prospective profits and thus its capacity to finance its service obligations had to be dealt with. However, much to the surprise of other participants in the Review, Oftel decided to settle this question before announcing which forms of market entry would be permitted. Its proposals could therefore only be discussed with BT and Mercury before being published with the White Paper in March 1991.

In the Review, BT's financing of its service obligations was largely identified with preserving cross-subsidies from call revenue to charges for 'access' to the network.[15] Arguments about the need to identify the specific costs of service obligations (that is, their impact on BT's net cash flow) and to consider alternative ways of funding them, which were current when the Duopoly was being devised, dropped out of sight and still do not feature in Oftel's strategy.

Early in the Review process, Mercury drew a considerable red herring across the path by advocating 'equal access', by which it appeared to mean reproducing in the rest of the country the situation in Hull, where the independent local telephone company has chosen to deal on equal terms with BT and Mercury as trunk operators while effectively excluding them from the Hull area. In the absence of divestiture by BT of its local operations, it is unrealistic to imagine equal access on Hull terms being projected nationwide. Mercury had second thoughts once it became clear that equal access would be offered to allcomers and so would remove its advantage as the main challenger to BT. The outcome of the debate was for Oftel to propose a complex procedure for considering equal access which postponed a decision for at least two more years, during which the terms for competitive network interconnection could be sorted out.

As the Review proceeded, Oftel at first gave great weight to BT's argument on the cross-subsidy of residential exchange lines. Oftel responded by proposing two changes in the way interconnection charges are assessed:

- Charges for interconnected calls (the conveyance charge) to be based on BT's fully allocated costs plus a reasonable return on capital employed.
- An additional charge per call to share out the cross-subsidy among all interconnected networks (a Contribution).

BT would determine its own cost allocation, within the limits set by auditing of its accounts. The outcry by Mercury and potential entrants led Oftel to change tack on the Contribution element and to give itself powers to check the cost allocations that underlay estimates of the cross-subsidy.

Access Deficit Contributions (ADCs) would still be payable but would be delayed and subject to possible waivers if certain criteria were met. The likelihood of an entrant's encountering such a liability appears now to depend on a market share trigger (commonly 25 per cent); the capital intensiveness of its planned investment; and how far the service to be provided competes directly with incumbents' offerings or is innovative. For example, an international simple resale operation in POTS based entirely on leased lines would be likely to be required to pay ADCs. While revised interconnect changes have not yet been determined by Oftel, managing entry has clearly shifted from rationing licence take-up towards differentiating the commercial terms on which entry is attempted.

Rebalancing and price controls

The Review also examined how BT's tariff structure had changed during the Duopoly period (see Table 16.1). Broadly, the direction in which prices for voice telephony service have moved has been determined by the initial margins between prices and costs, while the pace of rebalancing has been set by the competitive pressure from Mercury and the restraint exercised by price controls. There have been two waves of tariff rebalancing so far: the first, under the RPI−3 regime, showed a relatively faster rate of reduction on trunk prices, presumably in anticipation of the entry by Mercury, while the second, under RPI−4.5, showed a relatively faster rate of increase in rental charges. In this second period, BT has taken full advantage of the headroom given by the RPI+2 limit on increases in residential rentals.

The further tightening of price controls from 1993 and the prospect of entry by trunk operators are expected to induce more rapid falls in long-distance and international call charges. BT will have little room to increase rental charges within the price cap.

Table 16.1 British Telecom's voice telephony service: price changes 1984–91

	1984	1985	1986	1987	1988	1989	1990	1991
Rate of inflation	5.1	7.0	2.5	4.2	4.6	8.3	9.8	5.8
Permitted change	+2.1	+4.0	−0.5	+1.2	+1.6	+3.8	+5.3	−0.4
Actual change	+2.0	+3.7	−0.3	–	–	+3.5	+5.3	−1.0
Residential rental	+7.1	+8.5	+3.7	–	–	+10.0	+11.6	+7.8
Business rental	+6.8	+8.8	+3.9	–	–	+10.1	+11.8	+7.7
Calls:								
Local*	+6.8	+6.4	+6.4	–	–	+4.3	−4.5	+4.7
Trunk*	−10.2	−13.8	−12.0	–	–	–	−10.0	–

*Calls in standard period only; trunk calls b1 only.
Source: Oftel, January 1992.

The White Paper acknowledged the link between the pace of rebalancing and entry prospects. In particular, a faster rate of increase in rental charges should enhance the profitability of entry at local level and diminish that of entry by trunk operators. Oftel has frequently expressed concern that the pattern of market entry should not be distorted by incorrect price signals (meaning prices out of line with costs). In Oftel's terms, 'inefficient entry'. This concern is largely misplaced. The distortion in BT's price structure is common to virtually all telephone companies worldwide. Since all are aware that, in the UK at least, rebalancing is expected to carry on apace, prospective entrants are most unlikely to be misled by it. In any event, in making the decision to enter, companies are likely to be more concerned about how their own costs and their own perceptions of the market differ from BT's.

Cable-based telephony

It has seemed for several years that cable-based telephony offered the best hope in the long run for effective competition with BT's local network. In turn, this is the area where competition offered the best hope of benefits to users once the restrictions of the Duopoly had ended. Cable TV interests appear to have got what they asked for out of the Duopoly Review, namely independence from Mercury, the prospect of standardized interconnection arrangements and the ability to combine operations. The question remains whether they have yet reached a position from which they can mount an effective challenge to BT in local telephone services. BT's desire for a faster rate of tariff rebalancing would suggest that it does not think this is imminent. Moreover, since the Duopoly Review, BT has reversed its position of discouraging cable companies from seeking to interconnect with it. It is now competing with Mercury to offer them terms for access to its national network.

Additional licensees: trunk and international telephony

BT's arguments during the Review implied that it expected an intensification of competition in long-distance services. Several companies, in association with owners of rights of way, have submitted applications to enter the long-distance market. Licences have not yet been granted by the Secretary of State. It is not clear from the limited information in the public domain whether these proposals are for the kind of regional networks we advocated in 1989, which would combine limited trunk services with direct connections to customers, or would depend upon the introduction of equal access. We are inclined to doubt that extensive entry will occur in the long-distance market, for much the same reasons as resale has turned out to be a damp squib, and because of our scepticism about equal access, unless the entrants can identify and retain specific customer groups. The Duopoly Review has not significantly improved the prospects in the near term.

We predicted that proposals to offer international services only would not be welcomed by Oftel and DTI. There seems no reason yet to amend this view.

As at August 1992, four PTO licences had been drafted and published for comment. These cover a variety of services: National Network is an existing reseller, Millicom and Ionica L3 have ideas for innovative radio applications, and Worldcom appears to be a specialist business network. In addition, two international simple resale licences have been awarded to ACC and IISS) and Australia, Canada and Sweden have been authorized as international destinations for simple resale services. The significance of this announcement is, of course, the non-appearance of USA on the list of authorized destinations. Its exclusion is presumed to be linked to wider trade issues which have yet to be resolved.

The first fruits of the post-Duopoly policy are not very revealing of Ministerial thinking. The impression is that the Government is willing to license any entrant unless there are compelling reasons not to. The draft licences are also devoid of any specific service obligations. That is, all those who have applied for a licence can expect to obtain what they have asked for in due course unless they sought to avoid any commitment to invest in the provision of domestic services entirely.

Numbering

The planning of telephone numbers is significant for this discussion because of its potential to act as a barrier to entry.[16] Users will be less inclined to change from one PTO to another, or one type of service (fixed, cellular, etc.) to another, if to do so involves a change of number. Oftel has been considering the issues for several years; its current plans are to extend the 'portability' of numbers as far as is technically possible and to introduce a separate prefix for each type of service, though no timetable has been set for these changes. Entrants would be assisted by early decisions, even if these are to do nothing.

BT/Mercury Competition

As we argued in 1989, the Duopoly Review was strongly conditioned by the need to ensure Mercury's continued growth as the principal instrument of increasing the competitive challenge in voice telephony. How has Mercury's position been affected by the Review? There are two principal aspects to consider:

- Mercury's position *vis-à-vis* new entrants, where the chief implication of the Review is that competitive entry would be adverse for Mercury but complementary entry favourable; and
- Mercury's direct competition with BT, where its costs are affected by the changes in the rules governing interconnection and its prospects are affected by BT's ability to counter its lower tariffs.

We have already concluded that entry to the voice telephony market will in general not develop swiftly following the Review. Insofar as it does, we expect that it will tend to be complementary. The most important potential help to Mercury (as to the trunk entrants) would be entry into local network provision. The use of radio for this purpose awaits both technical developments and spectrum allocation decisions, so cable-based telephone operations remain Mercury's natural allies in offering users in general discounts to BT's prices.

So far as Mercury's interconnection charges are concerned, doubtless BT had hoped at the start of the Review to raise the amounts it received as well as to lay the basis for extracting more favourable interconnection terms from potential entrants. Its strategy of reallocating costs from local calls to access, and then calling for contributions from other PTOs to the access deficit thereby created, was only partially successful. Mercury's access deficit payments, if they occur at all, will be considerably delayed; in the meantime, the reallocation of costs should mean that charges for the conveyance of local calls should be limited to close to their present level. Standardization of interconnection payments, which could erode Mercury's position *vis-à-vis* trunk operators, has yet to emerge. Securing interconnection with BT is still an uncertain process, so Mercury retains much of its first mover advantages; thereby, it has a useful base for alliances.

BT has at last obtained permission to use volume discounts targeted to the same set of large customers on which Mercury has concentrated its efforts. Since 1986, BT had been trying to produce an acceptable 'optional call plan'[17]; in August 1991, the first to be accepted was introduced. Discounting can take either a weaker or a stronger form. The weaker is to grant all customers of a given size a quantity discount; this lessens the incentive to route traffic via Mercury because of the loss of volume going to BT (most Mercury customers retain at least some BT lines). The stronger form is to focus discounts as closely as possible on the particular set of customers Mercury now has, or is likely to acquire. BT is also now allowed to offer different call charges to groups of customers to whom it is providing other services.

This permission may be of some significance when BT's virtual private network[18] service becomes established.

We have yet to see how the new licence condition governing this will affect BT's trade-off – loss of revenue by giving discounts where Mercury is not involved versus gains by attracting specific Mercury customers. The volume discounts announced to date are all variants of the original 'option call plan'. But the new rules, if difficult to interpret, do seem to be moving towards BT having to justify price discrimination between customers on the basis of avoidable, incremental cost differences. This, and the fact that the burden of proof to show such cost differences rests with BT, will continue to limit the tactical effectiveness to its weaker form and within stringent margins.

In any case, Mercury can (and has) responded to BT's discount offers. The question now is how far it pays BT and Mercury to indulge in duopolistic rivalry and how far it pays to live and let live. Since Mercury's general position has been little, if at all, weakened relative to BT or other potential players, it seems most unlikely that war will break out. The growing market will make a continuing accommodation likely.

THE REGULATORY PROCESS

The Duopoly Review, by opening up many competitive options, should have a bigger impact on BT if these options are realized. But this is likely to take some time and, partly as a result, most of the options are likely not to be pursued to the point of producing a competitive challenge to BT.

The regulatory authorities themselves began the Review with a predisposition towards openness in the telecommunications market coupled with an aversion to unpicking the results of past decisions. The regulatory options were not clear at the outset: Cable & Wireless is now well established in the UK but the potential for network competition to improve BT's delivery of its services has not yet been realized. The experience of the BT/Mercury duopoly yielded clues as to the scope for future competitive entry, but careful analysis was required to discern the likely future structure of the market. The authorities did not have much taste for quantitative analysis of the options.[19] Rather, the regulatory authorities largely relied on commercial interests to indicate which areas of the market they wished to enter.

The position after the Review is that entrants have, as before, to negotiate interconnection terms with BT, with Oftel making a determination when they fail to agree. The discussions with BT must centre on conveyance charges, unaffected by the furore over Contributions. Views on Oftel's likely determination will of course greatly influence negotiations and continued uncertainty on this point make reference to Oftel inevitable, further delaying the arrival of effective competition. However, Oftel did suggest that it might, at some point, make a standard determination covering a class of entrants. The DG has clearly recognized the impracticability of maintaining the 1984 approach in which interconnection was to be dealt with as a commercial negotiation within a loose framework of rules. While this remains the formal position, the reality is that Oftel will manage the evolution of interconnection arrangements in future.

When the opportunity to enter the market is determined by the decision of the regulatory authorities, the regulatory process itself must be subject to scrutiny. The willingness of companies, particularly the North American interests, to invest in competitive opportunities depends on both policy priorities and the specifics of the regulatory framework. These still remain uncertain; in consequence the negotiations between the regulatory authorities and commercial interests have run on and look likely to continue for another year or two before producing a new settlement, and into 1994 before the shape of the new competitive challenge becomes evident.

We believe that the experience with liberalization has revealed significant weaknesses in regulation that should be addressed. Over the period, there has been a fundamental change in the regulatory process. Until 1984, regulation was exercised informally by DTI and BT, with few other commercial interests that needed to be taken into account. This very informality allowed Ministers to take radical decisions to change the structure of the sector. Now, there is a complex regulatory framework of rules and institutions and a multiplicity of interests. As the Duopoly Review has shown, the regulatory process can best be characterized as successive rounds of negotiation in which the regulatory authorities have sought to accommodate the expressed demands of incumbents, potential investors and consumers. This inevitably constrains radicalism.

Encouraging local entry

The DG has signalled on a number of occasions his preference for encouraging competition at local level, as being most likely to produce the greatest benefits for users. This preference has not been carried through, probably because the DG has relatively little leverage on the licensing decisions which determine market structure. At the present time, there are two options for promoting local network entry: to release cable TV networks from present regulatory restraints and to encourage innovative applications of radio technologies. Neither has been dealt with very satisfactorily in the Review.

Willingness to invest in local telephony, whether via cable TV or otherwise, is constrained by the residual regulatory requirement for universal service. The White Paper has little to say on this topic, but it is evident that universal service is still considered an appropriate principle for local entrants as well as incumbent PTOs. As applied to entrants, universal service entails an obligation to invest on a sufficient scale to serve all customers within a defined area. Thereby, flexibility in marketing is reduced and the risks of entry are significantly increased. As there is little practical benefit for users from imposing a universal requirement on entrants, it should be abolished rather than left to wither.

The feasibility of local entry should gradually improve as BT's rebalancing of its tariff for voice telephony continues. However, the end result to be expected from rebalancing remains entirely obscure; Oftel has given no sign of what the limit will be, nor has it published the data on which commercial interests could reach their own conclusions. The effect of this uncertainty will be to delay rather than to encourage entry.

Cable TV

Some basic constraints on cable-based telephony remain in place. First, there are simply far too many franchisees to mount an effective challenge to BT on the regulatory front. Second, franchise areas are too small to be run as independent local networks. Third, the television distribution business, to which the cable companies' local telephone businesses are tied, is making slow progress, even after a substantial inflow of North American investment.

The permission to interconnect freely with neighbouring franchises which have been secured may not be adequate compensation for the basic mistakes made in first tying franchise areas to local authority boundaries in urban areas and then arbitrarily limiting their linear extent to 50 km. The result is inevitably a patchwork of franchises which make little commercial sense if considered as potential rivals to BT. Of course, the problem can be sorted out by the companies themselves; the rationalization of the industry is already underway. It seems likely that the number of participants will be reduced to between six and ten within a few years.

To be viable competitors, the surviving participants will certainly need to link their franchises in different parts of the country; that is, they will be long-distance as well as local operators. Given the option of trunk network operation, the North American telephone companies that now own the majority of franchises must await the final outcome of the interconnection debate before deciding whether the returns on investment in local telephony will be sufficiently attractive.

Radio applications

The Duopoly Review has also failed to shed much light on the future competitive balance between fixed and mobile voice telephony services. With mobile radio, there are two distinct market entry questions:

(1) whether PCN services will appear on the market as cellular radio like services but without the capacity constraint on radio frequencies (and hence without the duopoly power that underpins cellular's high call charges) or whether PCN and other radio applications will develop price/performance characteristics that enable it to rival fixed link telephony services;

(2) whether radio links can be generally mixed in with the fixed network or remain, like Telepoint to date, a specialist device.

Both of these are longer term developments, but it is already evident that the regulatory process is unable to deal with them satisfactorily. The commercial failure of Telepoint to date has its origins in the mistaken regulatory requirement that network operators commit to nationwide service while technical standards were still being debated. The Review has not resolved this problem which lies somewhere in between telecommunication and radiocommunication policies. The co-ordination between Oftel, the agency for fixed telephony services, and the Radiocommunications Agency, which handles spectrum management, is the responsibility of DTI; in reality, nobody is clearly in charge.

One important arena, in which this failure so far to deal with mobile radio satisfactorily, is interconnection. The logic of basing interconnection charges on BT's fully allocated costs is that all networks interconnecting with BT should pay the same, since BT's costs in handling a call from A to B are the same irrespective of which network handed it over for conveyance. However, the cellular radio networks have interconnection agreements with BT that are really quite different from that between BT and Mercury. The DG now has the scope for making standard determinations; but he seems unlikely to use it for this purpose.

In summary, a competitive market structure may eventually emerge at local level, but as yet the regulatory process has not given a clear sign of the intention to assist such a development.

Oftel and licensing powers

The imbalance in Oftel's powers can also be seen in its dealings with BT. Regulatory pressure on BT to improve its performance could be applied either by tightening controls such as RPI $-X$ or by intensifying the competitive threat. Oftel can do the first, and has done so, but cannot exercise the second option. We suggested in 1989 that the DG should have the power to license entry, with the Secretary of State retaining the right to review refusals of licences on appeal. Reform along these lines has now become urgent.

The principal reason for concentrating licensing powers with the Secretary of State was concern to preserve universal service in the face of developing competition. As things have turned out, however, the issue of universal service has surfaced almost exclusively in the contexts of price controls on BT and the terms of interconnection with BT. These are matters that should be determined by Oftel, not the Secretary of State. The regulatory process would be improved and simplified if Oftel were to be given powers to issue PTO licences. As radio applications multiply, Oftel should also be given powers to issue wireless telegraphy licences, with the Radiocommunications Agency providing technical advice.

Oftel could not take on extra responsibilities without an overhaul of its internal organization; it is unable to carry out its present functions without repeated delays in decision making. Oftel's effectiveness as a regulatory body could be further strengthened if it was able to recruit more staff from outside the civil service. The present arrangements appear to have been dictated by the desire to align Oftel and the agencies in other sectors closely with OFT and MMC. In the event, co-ordination with these more senior bodies has proved to be a relatively minor issue. Oftel's major problem has been how to manage its relations with BT, Cable & Wireless and other commercial interests. Civil servants need to recruit external expertise to make the kind of technical and commercial assessments that are now Oftel's stock in trade.

In summary, since 1981 telecommunications policy in the UK has moved from a position of merely experimenting with competition in voice telephony to regarding it as the principal method of ensuring continued improvements in the service provided to users and of implementing innovation in services. Competitive developments have been closely allied to the evolution of the regulatory process. We have concluded that this evolution should continue, in particular directions, to produce arrangements capable of managing the growth of competition.

NOTES

1 *International Review of Comparative Public Policy* (ed. Nicholas Mercuro), Vol. 5, 1993.
2 The Carter Report (*Report of the Post Office Review Committee*, Cmnd 6850, July 1977) had first suggested the liberalization of equipment supply as part of a strategy to promote manufacturing but its recommendations had been largely ignored.
3 M.E. Beesley, *Liberalisation of the Use of British Telecommunications' Network*, London, HMSO, 1981.
4 Regional Bell Operating Companies: the acronym is pronounced 'arbok'.
5 Band III is a spectrum-efficient method of providing private mobile radio services; Telepoint is a dual service, operating at home as a digital cordless telephone and in public places as a mobile radio service.
6 In the event, Oftel's long-term future looks assured and its first Director-General Professor Sir Bryan Carsberg has been appointed to head OFT.
7 Public telecommunication operator is the UK term for a business licensed to run a public telephone network.
8 The price cap system is based on recommendations in a report by Professor Stephen Littlechild, *The Regulation of British Telecommunications' Profitability*, Department of Industry, 1983.

9 The price cap is termed RPI−X, indicating that controlled prices may rise by X per cent less than the rate of inflation, as measured by the Retail Price Index.

10 See M.E. Beesley and S.C. Littlechild, 'The regulation of privatized monopolies in the United Kingdom', *Rand Journal of Economics*, 1989, vol. 20, no. 3, pp. 454–72, for further comparisons.

11 Equal access is an arrangement whereby local network operators deal on equal terms with a number of competing long-distance operators. It exists in the USA, where equal access was stipulated as part of the grand settlement of industry structure known as the MFJ. In the USA, customers nominate (pre-select) a particular long-distance network that they wish to use.

12 The standard measure favoured by the World Bank for comparing manning levels is the ratio of staff per thousand direct exchange lines (DELs). The best telephone companies in the USA have reduced this ratio to about 4.6 (1990 figures); for BT, the ratio of staff per thousand DELs is about 8.9.

13 M.E. Beesley and B. Laidlaw, *The Future of Telecommunications*, IEA 1989. We were afraid that the duration of the Fixed Links Duopoly would be extended by delays in decision making; in the event, the duopoly has lasted at least eighteen months longer than originally intended.

14 The main policy decisions were announced in the White Paper, *Competition and Choice: Telecommunications Policy for the 1990s*, Cm 1461, London: HMSO, 1991.

15 'Access' is a term used to cover the installation and maintenance of a direct exchange line.

16 Revision of numbering plans also results in substantial costs for users and for PTOs. The costs have been estimated at about £200m for the UK. For this reason, changes in numbering should be few and far between. It remains a matter of controversy whether another change is needed in the near future, or whether the initiative for change should be taken at national or European level.

17 Optional call plan is the term used to describe a tariff for voice telephony services incorporating a volume discount.

18 A virtual private network (VPN) enables circuits to be redefined as PSTN access lines or private circuits through software controls.

19 *The Infrastructure for Tomorrow* (HMSO 1988) was the only relevant official study published before the Review.

17 Price regulation and competition[1]

M.E. Beesley

INTRODUCTION

In this lecture I want to draw out further implications of a line of argument about privatized utility regulation in the UK which Stephen Littlechild and I developed in our *Rand Journal* paper eighteen months ago (Beesley and Littlechild 1989). By 'privatized utilities' was (and is) meant airports, electricity, gas, telecoms and water.

We argued there that the Regulator's tasks that have emerged from the process of privatization are essentially two: the control of prices, and the promotion of competition. We recognized that the emphasis to be given to these two tasks is, to a great extent, determined by the utilities' economic characteristics. And all have in common a very high market share on privatization. Whether, given appropriate policies, competition could directly remove that dominance depended mostly, we thought, on underlying technological change. Hence the basic scope for competition varied, and indeed would affect different parts of the utilities dissimilarly. In telecoms, electricity generation and supply and gas supply, competition prospects were favourable. In water, airports and gas and electricity transmission and distribution, they were not. The weight given by Regulator to the two tasks should in principle differ accordingly. In the 'non-competitive' cases, there would still of course be a task of promoting competition, but it would focus on the competition problems upstream and downstream of the regulated services.

PRICE CONTROL AND PROMOTING COMPETITION

The most compelling reason why it is important to be explicit about the two tasks is, I would argue, the very difficult analytic traditions that each must draw upon. As we shall see, they can conflict. The price control task is principally served by neo-classical comparative statics. In this, relevant cost and demand functions are given, as are entry conditions, which determine the extent of competition in the market. In the UK tradition, the indications about prices and outputs that this kind of analysis yield are used to conduct what is essentially a cost–benefit analysis. A governing Act directs the regulator to consider returns to the regulated firm and to provide adequate protection for classes of consumers. That is, proposals for price changes are judged by the prospective changes in respective parties' surpluses. A large literature advises on rules that maximize allocative efficiency, taking costs and demand as given, and which indicate appropriate decisions where constraints are imposed on the surplus to be enjoyed by parties, e.g. where the incumbent is to earn no more than an adequate return.

In the problem of promoting competition, and especially from a starting position of dominance by the regulated firm, neither prop of the neo-classical approach is an appropriate starting point. Demands and costs are not given; they have to be discovered, to a greater or lesser degree. Neither are the conditions of entry given: it is the regulator's task to find out what they actually are and how they might be changed. This means focusing on potential profits available to would-be entrants, and how they may be affected by incumbent reaction and regulatory action itself. As we argued in the *Rand Journal* article, one of the means of promoting competition is precisely to shift potential entrants' assumptions about the costs and possibilities serving existing and new markets. And one of the expected benefits of entry is a shift in the incumbents' own assumptions about these parameters. Entry is seen as a necessary instrument to goad the incumbent into appropriate action.

The contrast in the modes of thought – neo-classicism and what may be more aptly labelled Austrian – is most striking in their view of entry. In the former, the method proceeds from assumptions which tend to minimize potential differences between incumbents and entrants. Relaxing symmetry conditions will yield many interesting predictions about new equilibrium prices and output, some involving entry. But this is a poor substitute for making the central issue that of whether, in the face of a given regulatory change, entry will occur. For this, one needs to start from the perception that entry is much more likely to be a function of differences between incumbents and entrants, differences which, despite the dominance of incumbents, will profitably support the risk of entry. So profit seeking is at the centre of the analysis; the sources of profit are highly likely to be Schumpeterian – that is, innovation, very widely interpreted to mean all the ways in which entrants can improve on what incumbents do.

Does the presence of two contrasting approaches to analysis in regulatory conduct matter? Only if relevant questions simply fail to be recognized and acted upon or if they lead to different specific indications for regulatory decisions, i.e. if the regulator (or the Government) may take the wrong decision. Of course, some indicated decisions will be common whichever line of analysis is taken. Also the pressure on the regulator to stick to the same line of argument differs. In our system of limited concern for due process the pressure for consistent argument is less. In the American system, by contrast, one expects the existing dominance of neo-classical reasoning to persist, because it is the common currency of what is a very open debate. Regulatory decisions have to be basically justified with respect to that paradigm. (Hence a great deal of the ingenuity expert witnesses display in expanding that paradigm to embrace variations on the basic assumptions.) Here, the regulator has a greater degree of freedom in what he argues.

It is in the area of price discrimination that the different objectives of regulation (control of monopoly prices versus promotion of competition) and the different corresponding economic arguments most obviously have potential for conflict. The most common expression of a British regulator's duty here is to prevent 'undue' discrimination.

What is 'undue' discrimination? If there is permanent monopoly power, public utility pricing principles should rule. Price discrimination between customers is virtuous so long as there is a suitable constraint on the enterprise as a whole concerning the costs, including the required profit. Consumers should be grouped into similar demand classes, and offered terms calculated to minimize their loss of consumer surplus, subject to their paying at least the avoidable costs of consumption. It is likely that the cost condition underpinning the monopoly will indicate that a fair degree of sophistication in offering two-part tariffs is justified.

By contrast, in the world of encouraging competitive entry, differential prices offered by an incumbent are regarded very differently, and with great scepticism. The likely indicated policy stems from the fact that the problem is specifically to move from a near 100 per cent market share. What is needed is to head off incumbent forestalling tactics. Entry, if it comes, will be partial and, hopefully, increasing over time. In these circumstances the regulator is able to raise the cost of forestalling by requiring non-discrimination by the incumbent, at whatever level in the supply chain is relevant. The simplest rule is that the incumbent may choose to price as he likes, but must offer similar terms to all-comers, whether involving new entrants or not. In these circumstances, the incumbent will find the cost of picking on potential or actual entrants prohibitive because particular price differences must be generalized.

In regulatory moves to promote competition the question of the burden of proof is critical. If the incumbent has it, he will predictably have great trouble in justifying anything more than avoidable costs. For example, in the overall cost conditions facing BT, a strict avoidable cost test will not support much differential (because the incidence of common costs, economies of scope, etc., are big and have to be recouped by mark-up over costs). If the regulator has the burden of proof, he will find it very difficult to get enough data to reject assertions by the incumbent, or to avoid putting up hostages to fortune as a sequence of decisions about discrimination is made. Fortunately for telecom entrants so far, the burden of proof has been on BT. I will come to the Duopoly Review exchange later, but I hope that this strategic regulatory advantage has been maintained.

Telecoms also provides a good example where the indicated policy points in the same direction whichever analysis is used. I refer to the recent rather public debate about BT's expressed need further to 'rebalance' its tariffs. BT relied strongly on the argument that rentals and call charges, the principal elements in customers bills, should be 'rebalanced' so that rentals rose relatively to call charges. The argument was the classical case that this would align prices more nearly to costs, and some very eminent economists were brought in to support it.

The trouble here is that 'rental' constitutes not only one service, but a bundle of services, including such items as billing, maintenance, directory production, installation and (until very recently) directory enquiries. If a high level of bundling is to be persisted in, it probably makes more sense to think in terms of rentals and calls as being the fixed and variable parts of a two-part tariff system, and apply economic reasoning accordingly. But there is in this case no reason at all not to recognize the very different production conditions underlying the rental bundle. The neo-classical argument requires that different types of production should be recognized, as a foundation of ideas on allocation. Here indicated neo-classical policy is pointing in a direction compatible with promoting entry. The more consumers regard telephone services as separable, the more likely profitable entry possibilities will be discerned. So the appropriate precondition for mounting the neo-classical argument, *and* the practical prescription for entry, is that services be unbundled for pricing. It is, incidentally, a great pity that the most important issue of unbundling did not get a specific airing in the Duopoly Review Consultation Document.

I would like now to use the points I have made to comment on some major issues in three of the utilities: water, gas, and telecoms. That there are three, not five, is partly due to time constraints, but also for a particular reason. As adviser to Offer, I am naturally wary of sticking my neck out in Electricity (but I do not seek to inhibit audience choice when the time comes on this, or for that matter, on Airport issues).

PRICING IN WATER

In water, the prevention of 'undue' discrimination between customers is central to Ofwat's influence on the structure of prices, which fall within the overall RPI + *k* price caps. Within the price basket, each undertaking is empowered to fix charges, subject to this proviso. What constitutes proper water pricing was tested in the Courts well before privatization, and companies enjoyed a wide scope. As a result, they mostly chose the rates as a basis. What impels the need for discussion is the Water Act's ban on rating valuation as a basis for charging after 1 April 2000. Ofwat's recent Consultative Paper (Ofwat 1991) set off a discussion on principles of charging.

Ofwat is keen to reform water pricing, and the paper offers four bases: 'tariffs could reflect the costs imposed by customers; or ability to pay; or the value of the service to the individual consumer; or all customers could be charged equally, irrespective of their use of potential use of water and sewage services' (Ofwat 1991: 9–10). Little is heard of the last option, equal pricing. I would say, quite rightly, because it would falsely apply the analogue of the perfectly competitive industry. Ofwat clearly thinks the choice lies in some combination of the cost related, ability to pay, or value of service principles.

Now, no one expects serious competition to emerge in water. So we might have thought that neo-classical public utility pricing principles would have been dominant in the discussion. These would have called for starting from a clear front-runner, namely a two-part tariff to be applied to customer classes having like values for water and sewerage services, where the variable charge relates to their attributable costs. The rest of the costs would be recovered on the principle of minimizing loss of consumer surplus, or inverse to the respective marginal valuations of water. In this respect the paper is somewhat disappointing. I detect, for example, a tendency in it to avoid the important distinction between having charges reflect consumption *per se* (as, for example, by a proxy measure such as rateable value (*op. cit.*: 18) with the question of disciplining the consumer (and thus the producer) by charges to which they can and will adjust behaviour. Charges which 'reflect' but do not actually discipline consumption have no particular virtue for resource allocation. It is disconcerting to see that Ofwat follows its discussion of meters with what it describes as 'alternatives' which are related to use, such as numbers of rooms, without hoisting the health warning that these do not carry the implications of disciplining consumption (*op. cit.*: 22–3).

Of course, the real problem is that the only practicable discipline is metering. But this will cost £3–4 billion at today's prices, which probably makes any cost–benefit analysis of adopting it universally come out negative now. It may well be so even as we look ahead to rising real water prices. And Ofwat is cautious about the water companies' adopting meters voluntarily. Partial adoption has its own difficulties in defending oneself against a charge of 'discrimination'.

Even if market discipline is so difficult to promote, we should still be concerned with 'fairness and equity' and regard 'simplicity' as a desirable property, as indeed Ofwat does. However, the notion of 'value' and how it might be determined is given remarkably little discussion, considering its connection with the desirable aim of minimizing losses of consumer surplus. Perhaps this was because value was seen primarily as relevant to justifying higher prices for industrial users. One can see why the question – why not base charges on the value domestic consumers place on their water consumption? – was difficult to attack directly. For example, one might well imagine that the best way to achieve simplicity in charges is to diverge as little as possible from what is there already. But this would have raised the awkward question of how reteable values perform as proxies for the value consumers set on water. In fact, we are told only about the rateable value base as a proxy (and not a very good one, it turns out) for consumption.

In any event, I think there is much more to be said for pursuing the value base. I think it might be quite practicable to give value a firmer foundation than we have now. Among candidates for exploration there might be the following:

(a) Direct experiments to establish elasticities. Perhaps someone from Ofwat can tell us what the prospects are for measuring relevant elasticities from the current metering trials?
(b) Discovering relative valuations by hypothetical choice studies which essentially are laboratory experiments in consumer choices.

A longer shot in getting a line on relative valuation might be:

(c) Implicit values of water derived from house price comparisons.

And:

(d) Can anything be gleaned from willingness to pay for complements to water use?

In short, I do think a lot more effort might usefully be put into the valuation problem. Rateable values might turn out to be a reasonable proxy. Unfortunately, the push for the poll tax meant that, in 1988/89, rateable values were front line political targets. One might suppose this no longer to be an imperative. The intriguing possibility opens up that the Water Acts' ban will, by implication, soon look at least faintly ridiculous. A good maxim for both governments and regulators conducting their affairs is 'if it ain't broke, don't fix it'. I suspect that this advice perhaps should be followed in water – and a way found to drop the ban, if necessary by a mending legislation.

PRICING GAS

Now let us turn to gas. It will be recalled that to make progress in countering British Gas's near monopoly Ofgas called upon OFT to make a monopoly reference to MMC resulting in the report of 1988 (MMC 1988). The recommendations have since been the principal basis of moves by Ofgas to increase competition. As they are covered by price control procedures in the Gas Act 1986, tariff customers were excluded from MMC's remit. Hence MMC concentrated on industrial customers. Its principal recommendations were, first, for new published tariffs to be constructed by British Gas on the basis of considerations of 'cost, volume and load factors of supply, which might also be index linked' (MMC 1988: 85). They replaced British Gas's previously negotiated tariffs which were in effect loosely based on an inverse elasticity rule – higher charges for less elastic demands and vice versa. British Gas's scope to refuse supply to interruptible gas customers, including those with gas turbine combined Heat and Power schemes, was to be curbed. In buying to take advantage of the schedule, customers could aggregate multiple sites. Moving to British Gas's grid and transmission systems, it called for transparency, in principle, of carriage charges, so as to put a potential customer in a position to make a reasonable estimate of what they would be. Further upstream, because of British Gas's purchasing dominance, it proposed the 90/10 rule, limiting British Gas acquisition of new gas to 90 per cent.

Neither the Gas Act nor the licence has a general prescription on 'undue discrimination' in the non-tariff market. It was open to MMC to suggest such a rule, but it preferred the route of British Gas's publishing a tariff schedule. This was to leave British Gas free to choose the average level of gas prices, but to constrain it to the approved discriminators, cost, volume and load factors. MMC thought that prohibiting discrimination should be confined to *deviations* from the schedule intended to give individual customer special discounts or premia (MMC 1988: 106). Thus the route of simply requiring non-discrimination except where avoidable cost differences could be shown, with the burden of proof on the incumbent, was rejected.

From the point of view of promoting competition I think this package deficient in several ways. The important possibilities for entry concern upstream conditions – getting independent supplies of gas, and not being picked off in getting it to potential customers. The problem of British Gas's dominance was recognized by the 90/10 rule. The problem of ensuring non-discrimination in conveyance was not adequately tackled. Nothing was said in the MMC report – and I can find no reference in subsequent Ofgas annual reports – about a further necessary condition to promote competition, namely the critical question of unbundling British Gas's present charges for services. When attempting to wrest a customer from British Gas, an entrant needs both to know what is the carriage element in the present (British Gas) customer charge, against which he has to bid, *and* to have a reassurance that the total price offered will not be subject to a forestalling revision. All MMC's, and subsequent Ofgas's, attention has been on the question of the entrant's getting a reliable, reasonable quotation for carriage, not on what that element is in British Gas's own total price to customers. There have been reductions in British Gas quotations for carriage, even to the point that it may be that independent gas pipe-lines are being discouraged (Ofgas 1990: 23). But for this problem, the essence is for British Gas to unbundle carriage charges from the rest in all its transactions, and for a non-discrimination rule in carriage, with burden of proof (justified by cost differences if deemed desirable) on British Gas.[2]

Further, neither the MMC nor subsequently Ofgas, so far as I am aware, have considered the importance in dealing with promoting competition of requiring the incumbent to provide an appropriate background accounting system. What is required is a disaggregation by relevant activities, recognizing the different horizontal markets that British Gas occupies. These may be defined, for instance, as buying gas, transport by the principal high-pressure gas grids, local distribution and the retailing function (selling and billing to final customers). These are activities for which one can conceive of quite separate free-standing organizations between which transactions could take place. MMC thought of a 'structural solution', namely a separate transmission company, as a probably necessary condition of competition (MMC 1988: 111) but did not recommend this course 'at present'. Ofgas has referred to this passage as a possible fall back position in the 1990 Annual Report (Ofgas 1990: 7).

Actual separation would clearly require new legislation. The chances of this are perhaps remote. But it would be logical and useful to seek the evidence for the shadow structure, so that, for example, the basis of transparent transfer pricing is established. The indications are that Ofgas is pursuing its British Gas costing studies in another way, namely by trying to get a satisfactory division by end market sectors – the tariff market, the firm contract market and the interruptible market. One can understand the reasons for this, but one can only hope that this cost apportionment exercise, as it is described, will not get in the way of developing the more fundamental information.

As a final comment on the influence of the MMC's contribution, perhaps it was my colleagues' starting point that persuaded them to concentrate on the pricing schedule. This was that one should try to produce the results one expects from competition rather than to analyse entry prospects in depth. Had they put the two regulatory tasks in the foreground, they might well have concluded that substantial entry was still 5 years away at best. So they might have considered – which apparently they did not – the option of recommending extending the price control to the non-tariff sector; perhaps with an underlying structure in which the leading principle would be discrimination based on an inverse elasticity rule. In practice, this would have meant doing very little about the existing price structure, because prices clearly were already based on roughly the correct principle. That would, in turn, have largely avoided the discontents which have since accompanied the new price structure. As Ofgas says in its 1990 Annual Report: 'the schedule has become irksome for gas users. The customer had anticipated (there would be) choice of supplier as a trade-off against the rigidity of the schedules (which they now believe) impose a more stringent regime than the one which existed pre-privatization' (Ofgas 1990: 9). Furthermore, the ability to aggregate separate points of consumption in order to benefit from quantity discounts has led to deliberate waste (gas 'flaring') (*op. cit.*: 14) More important for the present argument, it indicates that MMC's hopes that the schedule would be based on costs were not well founded – there surely can be no justifiable transaction or other cost basis for getting discounts where one's take-off points are geographically widely dispersed!

In sum, given concerns that *something* had to be done about the industrial market it might well have been better to have allowed neo-classical reasoning to have guided policy for the near future, while beginning to prepare the ground straight away for an effective switch to promoting competition, which would in fact occur at a later point. On the way one should have made full use of the common ground (in this case unbundling and more transparent transfer pricing). While we cannot rewrite history, it seems clear that there is much to be done to promote competition based on the alternative view of the conditions for encouraging entry. In saying all this, I am conscious not only of Ofgas's commitment to more competition, but also of its reliance on other regulators, especially MMC, to pioneer new developments. The translation of regulatory strategy into tactics, even if the strategy were to be agreed, is exceptionally difficult in gas, given the basic framework of the 1966 Act.

TELECOMS: AFTER THE DUOPOLY WHITE PAPER

In terms of my earlier analysis, telecoms is the utility for which we can confidently predict a highly competitive future in most types of service, and in particular in the market underpinning the finances of present incumbent, the real-time voice market. After 7 years the two tasks of regulation – price control and promoting competition – have a clear relationship in principle. Price control of a 100 per cent dominant incumbent has to decline as competition, mediated by the regulator, increases. The strategic regulatory question is the relationships between, and the speed of, each development as this happens. The publication in March of the outcome of the Duopoly Review makes this a good time at which to comment.

Most commentators have remarked on the imminence of vigorous competition. I admit happily that in some important respects the White Paper fulfils the agenda for liberalization which Bruce Laidlaw and I set out two years ago in our IEA Monograph (Beesley and Laidlaw 1989), perhaps the first salvo in the ensuing duopoly debate. Restrictions on Cable TV's choice of telephone operator have been removed; additional public networks will be licensed; general interconnect rules will in part replace *ad hoc* discussions; and there has been a start towards international simple resale. But Sir Bryan will not be surprised to hear me say that on both aspects of the task more could and should have been done.

The most puzzling timidity in pushing forward competition in the White Paper is in what Bruce Laidlaw and I called 'own account operation' – the freedom for what would in practice be the big business customer in particular to develop its own mixture of leased and owned capacity. Big telephone users' needs have driven most of telecom liberalization, in whatever country. The White Paper allows more freedom to interconnect with public switched systems, but no resale of capacity. The restriction cuts off possibly the most vigorous development of resale, and seems a most unwelcome potential restriction on the development of sophisticated network management. There are, for example, many small operators of value-added services over leased lines who would benefit from merger with big own-account telephone operators, as would the latter from the stimulus of innovators.

The White Paper should be regarded not so much as the end of the duopoly policy on fixed link voice telephony but its extension to embrace a new set of approved entrants, including of course, Mercury. The others are Cable TV companies and Personal Communication Networks (PCN) licensees. Their status is indicated by the relief they are given from prospects of further entry in their particular markets.

Mercury is to keep, at least for a considerable tranche of its anticipated growth, better interconnect terms than new entrants (including Cable TV and PCN licensees) will have. Cable TV is encouraged to invest by holding off possible responses by BT in its basic priority of carrying entertainment. The 10 (or perhaps 7) year period of grace is generous. PCN licensees' ambitions are helped by the decision not to encourage yet the nearest competitor, to increase its range. This is now called 'neighbourhood telepoint' – in other words two-way voice services by radio to fixed points. The White Paper points to no significant steps here before January 1994 (:22). The technical problems cited in support of this delay – spectrum availability, the required power levels and the implications for standards – are old restrictive standbys, and are no more convincing than ever they were. One implication of adopting the appropriate (Austrian) analytical base for the task of promoting competition is that such decisions about ordering entry, and arranging contingent shelter for entrants, has to be taken, so I cannot complain about staging entry in principle. However, I would be far happier if there was evidence in the White Paper and the preceding documents that this analytical framework had been applied.

I do not think it had. I think this partly because there are clear signs of trying to fit the analysis of entry into a neo-classical strait-jacket. For example, losses of 'economies of scale' from allowing entry are feared, to my mind the least of worries in telecoms now. We are not concerned with comparison between rival scales of possible entry, relevant for evaluating economies of scale, but rather possible entry against an incumbent who, if entry is successful, may have to contract. Too much implicit symmetry between incumbents and entrants is postulated. The fact that an incumbent can and will price down to his avoidable costs to avert entry if it pays him to do so is seen as a general condition requiring intervention from the regulator if entry is to occur. Instead it should be seen as a particular problem in preventing discrimination against the partial entry actually to be expected.

Partly my misgivings arise because, had there been a profit-orientated analysis of entry prospects as they bear on local telephone competition, I think it doubtful whether a PCN operation would have been preferred ahead of a neighbourhood telepoint operation. Perhaps such analysis were indeed done, but the November 1990 Consultative Document (:29)[8] in referring to the preliminary studies of the economics of local telephone, indicates that the focus was different. The results suggest the costs associated with further telecommunications operators using their own way leaves and ducts would be greater than the theoretical average cost of provision by an efficient monopoly provider.

The most important single element affecting an entrant's prospects is his interconnect payments. This means paying BT in particular to collect and deliver calls. While Mercury was the duopolist with BT, the thoroughly sensibly *ad hoc* position was taken to set payments, the details of which have not been publicly disclosed, at levels allowing it to expand. Now that other players are relevant, practical considerations dictate a standardized, more open approach. I do not know, of course, what will emerge from the consultations under review as this is written. In the exchange leading up to the White Paper's announced basic structure there was a good deal of neo-classical argument, which was rather difficult to follow, about the proper basis to be adopted. However these economic arguments did not include what I would regard as the leading candidate, namely an attempt to define the price, in forward looking fully remunerated cash flow terms, at which an *efficient* operator (not a particular incumbent) would require to carry the traffic offered by an entrant. One could readily imagine BT as a series of local delivery and collection areas, which any entrant lacking this must patronize. The question would then be at what price could each handle calls, given the efficiency levels to which BT could reasonably aspire? Hull, the longest running independent local operation, would be a useful piece of evidence in this exercise, one supposes. Costs, and therefore prices, for the services would inevitably be revealed as varying considerably in different locations, as befits their underlying layout, density, differing factor costs, etc. Interconnect prices based on this kind of exercise would have the desirable property of spurring BT to achieve the accompanying cost levels.

As things are, interconnect charges are to have two components, a basic charge for conveyance reflecting the previous year's fully allocated costs, plus an applicable rate of return, which I assume will be close to the old arrangement, plus a new component, a 'contribution'. This is intended to compensate BT for the accounting losses it incurs in access – which includes principally rentals. What the relative weights for these two components are to be we do not yet know.

The 'contribution' element's impact may not be large enough in practice in entrants' costs to put them off, but the underlying principle is surely wrong. BT is not allowed to rebalance – that is, raise rentals – because this, it is argued, would be to exploit BT's monopoly power. The effect of preventing rebalancing is to prevent prices faced by entrants from rising or falling. The new rule in effect seeks to limit this effect by raising entrants' costs. This seems to me most unlikely to be either effective or efficient. Moreover, the calculation is based on the very accounting allocations Oftel has recently found so dubious. And, perhaps most important, the route being pursued involves abandoning the defensible basis for a contribution by entrants, namely the damage done to BT's ability to fund the specific social obligations it faces, and which incumbents do not. The line of attack – involving 'access payments' – was mooted in the Review, but finally left in the limbo it has occupied since 1984.

Despite the uncertainty about what the contribution will be, I do not think, however, that the White Paper will change an entrant's view about the overall prospects of rebalancing. Any prudent entrant will expect this to occur; the long-term trend will continue. An entrant may well be more worried by what the incumbents are allowed to do by way of price retaliation. On this, the White Paper is not very explicit. Given that costs have to enter the argument, my preferred position would be to ensure that such retaliation is constrained by differences in the avoidable costs of supplying different classes of customers. One subtle shift from the White Paper to the subsequent Notice of amendment to BT's and Mercury's licences makes me hopeful. Whereas the former referred to a position of 'proportionality to incremental costs of serving customers', the latter drops 'proportionality'. Instead, it refers directly to the incremental costs of serving different classes of customers.

However, the apparent retreat from enquiring, on the one hand, about impacts on BT's future net revenues as a basis for contribution to social obligations and, on the other, acceptance of fully allocated costs from historic records, makes me uneasy from another viewpoint. Effective regulation must have an emphasis on the cash-flow implications of incumbents' (as well as entrants') moves. In telecoms, this inevitably leads to far-reaching questions about an incumbent's profits or losses in serving different geographical areas. This in turn conjures up the possibility of free-standing local operations or at least profit centres Speculations like this could have been construed as precursors of an actual reorganization for BT. The Duopoly Review's remit did not include this, but there is no reason why outsiders should be so inhibited!

I believe that sooner or later, and preferably sooner, BT will have to consider the possibility of free-standing local operation, and a corresponding free-standing core network. Local distribution and collection is well suited, for example, to a stand-off franchising operation. A corresponding concentration on the core business would certainly be conducive to furthering international network management and similar operations, which BT sees as its major line for the future. As it is, it seems that the White Paper is pressing for a development in BT's financial reporting which is based on a different approach, namely that of accounting for categories of service: exchange lines, local calls, long-distance and international calls. All costs and returns are to be absorbed in these categories. The alternative I have suggested – simulating free-standing local and core businesses – is not I suppose in principle inconsistent with Sir Bryan's intentions about developing information expressed at p. 47 of the White Paper, but I would expect my formulation to require a very different top management view in BT on what growing competition demands. On the contrary, the signs are that regional and local managerial independence is seen as a hangover from the bad old days, to be combated.

The second, corresponding, regulatory task is to manage the retreat of price controls. Most people would probably judge that, far from this, the White Paper marks a further movement away from the original ideas of price capping to more detailed concern with extending the basket and controlling particular items in it. It can be argued that there has been a strong shift away from the policy of RPI − X rate capping to rate of return regulation. In support would be cited the future effective shortening of the review periods (a decline of 5 to 4 has now become 2). There are to be more side constraints (e.g. RPI + 5 on business leases), low user discounts, a side constraint on international lines at (RPI − 0); and more emphasis on achieved rates of return. It is indeed difficult to see regulation getting 'lighter' as competition advances, as the grand strategy at privatization dictated.

By contrast, my arguments suggest that there should now be a retreat to price control where substantial monopoly is likely to be longest lasting. The rest should be an exercise in unblocking entry, and preventing forestalling tactics by incumbents by non-discrimination rules. Much of the White Paper's paraphernalia of constraints is dictated not by curbing monopoly profit but by concern about the smaller consumer. In this respect I am sorry to see that a control based on the median residential bill has not been made a central influence on price control. I lobbied hard for this version of price control of incumbent power in the lead-up to the Act of 1984, but unsuccessfully. The White Paper (p. 65) says that Sir Bryan 'expects that limitation of increases in the median residential bill to the same rate as increases in the Retail Price Index should be the main constraint on rebalancing after that time' (mid 1993 when the current RPI − X arrangements have ended). But this is far from making it the central feature of price control. In the form I advocated, BT could select any combination of prices in all services so long as the total bill paid by the median residential consumer did not exceed a given relation with RPI. It was intended to be the least constraining of price controls in that sense. My original point was that the median residential consumer was, I thought, the proper object of concern about the distributional impact of BT's monopoly power, and should be dissociated as far as possible from issues of competition, including rebalancing.

This argument is even more apt now, I think. And in practice, with a weight of about 40 per cent in the median residential basket, there would be an important constraining effect on raising rentals. As competition develops in long-distance markets the weight given to rentals and local calls increase. There could also be a powerful effect on BT's room for manoeuvre if BT had to justify differences in the prices of all forms of running lines from exchanges to customer premises in terms of differences in incremental costs.

With the exception of international prices, we have surely reached the point when (always given effective policies on discrimination) non-residential consumers can be left to fend for themselves. Rebalancing can be left to market forces. I would hope, therefore, that on the next round of price cap negotiations the median residential bill will emerge as the only RPI − X control. The aim would be the abolition of price control after a further, relatively short period. An international price constraint, reflecting longer lasting monopoly power might well remain. In this, it would in effect become a specific price control instrument familiar as an option in general competition policy. Its longevity would depend on the development of a substantial liberalization of international telecoms.

In summary, my principal criticism of the Duopoly Review is that it has lacked a clear commitment, and a reasoned path, to the lightening, and ultimate abandonment, of price controls. This should have been explicitly recognized as a logical accompaniment to managing more entry. I have suggested a way forward which I hope will be vigorously debated. But I must say in conclusion how much I admire Sir Bryan's skill in picking a pro-competitive path among the political thickets. I suspect that many of my criticisms really should not be laid at his door. Long may he continue to provide the lead!

NOTES

1 *Lectures on Regulation 1991* (ed, M.E. Beesley), Centre for Business Strategy, London Business School, 1991.
2 Interestingly, British Gas did propose to MMC a solution to anticipated predation in its conveyance charges, namely a floor on the (bundled) price of gas (MMC 1988: 92), thus by implication indicating its concern to retain bundling as a tactic. There was no implication that British Gas was prepared to unbundle in principle.

REFERENCES

Beesley, M.E. and Littlechild, S.C. (1989) 'The regulation of privatised monopolies in the United Kingdom', *Rand Journal of Economics*, **20** (3): 454–72.
Beesley, M.E. and Laidlaw, B (1989), *The Future of Telecommunications*, Institute of Economic Affairs, Research Monograph 42.
Duopoly Review White Paper (1991) *Competition and Choice: Telecommunications Policy for the 1990s* Cm 1461, London: HMSO.
MMC (1988)...Gas, CM 500, Monopolies and Mergers Commission, London: HMSO.
Ofgas (1990), Annual Report.
Ofwat (1991), *Paying for Water*.

18 The conditions for effective utility regulation[1]

M.E. Beesley

INTRODUCTION

This paper's objective is to derive from UK experience of regulating privatized utilities the conditions most conducive to effective regulation. The particular UK context has referred both to a particular form of price control, RPI − X, and to privately owned utilities. My aim is to emphasize the basic elements in this experience which apply whatever the precise form of control or ownership adopted. I also address the fact that a regulator's tasks are, as in ACCC's case, basically two-fold, the control of charges which stem from a utility's position as supplier of services not subject to serious competitive challenge (the pipes and wires) and control of competitive conduct using those services (competition to sell over the pipes and wires). I will call these the 'non-contestable' and the 'contestable' activities respectively.

Within the approach to the regulator's task thus indicated, you were particularly interested to understand how it would apply to underpinning the prices allowed to be charged to different consumers by the owner of the pipes and wires, or in other words the price/charging structure, and how this related to the question of controlling competitive conduct over the pipes and wires. (There are various ways of expressing the latter concept – in UK we speak of electricity 'supply', you often speak of 'retailing' or 'whole-saling' or 'marketing'.) A significant part both of setting the overall price control and, is, as you noted, how the valuation of the assets is dealt with, and I commented on this also.

As will emerge, what I am putting forward is in a sense an ideal paradigm for regulatory activity in these areas. In the UK, regulation in the several utilities started from very different positions handed to each by the Government, and have themselves learned much from experience since. I believe that, over time, there has been a movement in general towards setting up a more logical and consistent approach to the tasks, reflected in my description that follows. The three UK utilities of most immediate concern for you – Electricity, Gas and Telecoms – still now present varying pictures when judged with respect to the desirable conditions. But all have made progress, as I hope to show briefly during the course of this paper.

THE CONDITIONS FOR REGULATORY EFFECTIVENESS

Contestable and non-contestable separation

The first essential is that the collection of men and assets comprising the non-contestable activities should be clearly distinguishable from those comprising the contestable ones. This principle lends itself to much lip-service and evasion of difficult issues. The regulatory ideal is to be confronted with separately owned interest in each of these types of activities. The difficulty arises essentially because the starting point for the regulator is almost invariably one of ownership of both the pipes and wires and the means of selling over them, i.e. a near 100 per cent market share of activities which are, at that point, only *potentially* contestable. The incumbent starts with both interests. Short of divestiture as a preliminary to regulation, the separation must be achieved by 'ring fencing'. This is a flexible term, and easily exploitable by incumbents. From UK experience, the required ring-fencing standard is stringent – namely, reporting in terms of subsidiary companies, or shadow subsidiary companies, in terms of profit and loss account, balance sheet, reconciliation to cash flow, and detailed cash accounting for intra-company dealing. The balance sheets should incorporate a shadow capital structure.[2]

The reasons for reportage to this level are: (a) to support the method for determining the future allowable revenues in cash terms, to be outlined below; (b) to lasso in attempts to 'shift costs' from contestable to non-contestable activities or vice versa in an uncontrolled way; (c) to enable the regulator to form a view about the financial implications of proposed price controls; and, as part of this, (d) to recognize that non-contestable activities are normally markedly less risky than the rest of this incumbent's activities and so requiring a lower rate of return and/or permitting higher gearing. The regulator, that is, should be able to (e) construct a model of what would be an efficient manner of financing the non-contestable activities.

How close practice is to this specification of course also depends on the state of information within a regulated company at any one time. Good management practice will require recognition by the company of activities which call for very different skills and other resources, but it is rare indeed for this to be accomplished before the onset of regulation. One of the misconceptions common in dealing with UK regulation in particular is that on privatization, the utility has itself the information it needs to play games of deception with the regulator to its financial advantage. There is no doubt of the utility's determination to get favourable price reviews, but its capacity for understanding its business in this sophisticated way has to be developed. Regulators learn alongside them. Ultimately, it is probable that incumbent management will create for itself a structure of men and assets which will reflect regulatory realities. Regulators can achieve the distinctions they require only in so far as internal company practice itself moves; but they are themselves an independent spur to such movement. Hence, for example, the 'wise' regulator will keep track of the development of management accounts as well as financial, and will learn much from them.[3]

The basic distinction between the non-contestable and potentially contestable parts of the incumbent's business calls for judgements both about how long the non-contestable conditions will persist and how long it will be before entry to the contestable activities actually occurs. The first judgement is relatively easy in the case of electricity and gas: the condition will last at least for several price control periods. True, there will be fringe competitive entry, e.g. in high-pressure gas pipes, but it will not seriously affect the very large inherited network which is the principal subject of the control. In practice, the fringe competition can be dealt with *ad hoc*, e.g. by distinguishing the treatment of major new connections to the system.

In telecoms, the position is more subtle. The non-contestable activities for the incumbent nowadays refers to the need for telecoms entrants to offer a full delivery service to customers. As in UK experience, entrants can and do offer customers access to the network, in competition with the incumbent, but cannot offer universal delivery, an ability confined to the incumbent. In telecoms, therefore, recognition of non-contestable activities means that the two network functions – access and delivery – have to be distinguished. The incumbent's assets and men in the network are used for both, so the regulatory task is both to define their total scope, and to apply rules about charging for delivery over the network. This, in effect, calls for the simultaneous consideration of the total amount of funding required by the network and the justification of the structure of prices to be charged for differential use of the networks services by the newcomers and by the incumbent's own retailing activities.

Assessing allowed total revenues

Having defined the activities to which the price control refers, and thus secure the necessary basis for the information flow, the next necessary condition is to define, for the period of the forthcoming price control, the total revenue which will suffice to meet the need for the regulator to ensure that an incumbent operator of pipes or wires will be financially viable. The latter regulatory obligation is universally found in relevant Acts governing the arrangements; it appropriately reflects the fact that competition cannot perform its normal job of both limiting the power of exploitation via price and by service quality *and* ensuring, through free entry, that the market is supplied.

In terms of the total information flow required from the incumbent, the typical situation will be a division of the total entity into three areas: the non-contestable activities, as just described; the potentially contestable activities involving the incumbent's use of its own networks; and the rest of activities, not subject to specific regulatory measures. The regulator thus needs related models as a means of settling the price control as it bears on the pipes and wires business, and as a means of tracing the effects of price control decisions in the pipes and wires business on the finances of the group as a whole. The basic reason for the wider financial model is, of course, major decisions affecting the shareholders' interests (whether actual shareholders or the respective state treasurers as proxy 'shareholders') bear at total company level. Strictly, a regulator could confine attention to the non-contestable actual or shadow company, which should be subject to its own balance sheet and capital structure. Such isolation of focus would make the regulator rather ineffective in practical affairs so long as ownership straddles wider interests. As we shall see later, potentially contestable set of activities also need to be regarded as a whole in expenditure terms, and will appear in the financial model. I shall first concentrate on the biggest question – the treatment of the separated pipes or wires business in the price control.

Deriving the 'control total' of outlays[4]

The aim of an RPI/CPI $- X$ regime is to set up a total allowed revenue stream for a period of years ahead, with the intention to create an incentive to beat the productivity gains built into that allowed revenue. For reasons explained in Chapter 19, this should run basically in terms of a forward-looking cash flow, in effect viewing the wires or pipes business as a financial project, evaluated at the discount rate implied by the required cost of capital at the time of decision. The following control period (say, 5 years) should be set within a longer view of needs for outlays, a view long enough to settle the most important economic trade-offs which occur in these types of business, namely those in timing of capital expenditure and between its substitutes in current expenditure such as maintenance and its relation to different service levels which could be offered. An adequate asset replacement model is essential, and the subject of much concern in UK in both electricity and gas now.

As explained in Chapter 19, there are two principal elements in the required future cash flows: that representing outlays of all kinds needed to produce the service levels specified, and some allowance for the shareholders' established interest and other outside parties with financial claims. The first element, viewed as a financial project at NPV = 0, suffices (just) to fund all future outlays at the required rate of return. The second recognizes both the inherited 'rights' of shareholders and the need to recognize that while, for the economist bygones are bygones, in the real world incentives always have a backward-looking dimension also. These two elements may be expressed in accounting, not forward-looking terms; but the underlying reasons for the forward-looking approach, related to cash, is that the regulator's position as judge of what is practical in productivity terms depends on reviewing the corporate plans put to him and subjecting them to expert evaluation. Such evaluation must be in concrete, cash outlay terms; the regulator can never take book values like 'depreciation' to be equivalent to real outlays in the future, and still less to permit them to drive the required revenue.

Chapter 19 hopefully contains answers to some of the question which this line of attack encounters. For the present purposes, I will assume that we have reached a position where the sum of the two elements have been defined, so that we are now working within an established 'control total' for the wires/pipes business, in which future outlays of whatever kind will appear (what is known as the 'asset valuation' problem in effect is a large element in the debate about how to determine the second element in the required cash flow, the shareholder's interest.)

To establish the 'control total' in the way described is crucial for several reasons: (a) it ensures that, in subsequent derivations and inferences from the data, there are no 'black holes' (unaccounted for outlays or double accounting of outlays) (a favourite dodge to get more out of a regulator); (b) it provides the basis for deriving prices to be charged to different customer sets which can be summed to the total revenue allowed; (c) it ensures that all policy concerns can, when articulated, be related to consistent information on allowed revenue; (d) because it is forward looking, it can be used to illuminate economic arguments about 'costs' (only possible with forward-looking estimates and, as seen later, 'mark-ups'); (e) it matches real-life concerns of the company finance officers, especially those facing capital markets (or Treasurers, who are normally concerned with the taxable capacity the utilities represent).

As noted earlier, there is a need to establish a similar control total for the potentially contestable side of the incumbent's business. This arises from the need to monitor competitive behaviour. Prospects for entry actually being realized against the incumbent depend, *inter alia*, on the way in which services for the pipes and wires are charged, *and* the pricing practices of the incumbent as trader over the wires or pipes. Separating the two activities enables one necessary condition be fulfilled, namely, to ensure that the charging system for the former can manifestly treat both the incumbent as trader and newcomers on equal terms. Entry can be accomplished, in principle, within a widely ranging set of prices for services used, so long as the terms are the same for the (separate) incumbent and newcomer alike. In practice, regulators are never indifferent to the levels of these charges, even if formally non-discriminatory. They may suspect (probably rightly) that charges could well be biased in a way which will only be revealed when entry is attempted and fails. Hence the perceived need for rationalized levels of charges[5] to face both incumbent and newcomer. There are, of course, other practical reasons to enquire into the relative levels of such charges – e.g. to underpin predictions about distributional issues affecting different customers (poor versus rich, for example) and to consider what might be the contribution of network charging to preserving and/or modifying the end-consumer's initial position after the onset of competition. So there will be a need for manipulation of the control total to yield defensible relative prices as they impinge on the user of the network.

With respect to the incumbent's initial contestable business, the principal concern will be exercise of initial dominance to deter entry, should that appear profitable. The purpose of deriving material bearing on relative prices for the different consumers served is to lay the basis for monitoring or action in response to defensive moves by the incumbent. Broadly, there are two types of solutions to this problem, both acquiring the same under-lying information: either to mandate a set of permissible prices for the incumbent to charge, or, to rely upon a complaint mechanism to which the regulator will react. A later section comments further on the use of the information in competition rules as applied to the entry problem. Thus the fourth condition for effective regulatory is a capacity to derive appropriate information about price structures. This is the subject of the next main section.

DERIVING THE PREFERRED PRICE STRUCTURE[6]

To illustrate the process, I shall take up the example of the pipes and wires business both because of its intrinsic importance and because, as we shall see, it poses the trickier problems of dealing with the 'mark-up' issue. The 'control total' for the non-contestable business is, as noted, the starting point. The basic data will be in the form of dated cash flows. It may well be convenient, when following the steps to be described, to think first in terms of the control total as an aggregate present value of future outlays. The process involved is essentially one of filling a matrix consisting of columns representing the different classes of customers the business serves, and of rows representing the business activities required to serve them. It is highly unlikely that a regulator will discover the company has a ready-made matrix. The required information has to be developed from what the company has. One will have to accept considerable approximations and iterations to start the process off. It is probable, for example, that the existing costing systems used by the company will require modification and reinterpretation, because they will have been set up in response to different perceived needs. This reinforces the need to be able to sum to the control total; unless the regulator can systematically relate rate the basic allowed revenue to how it emerges in charges, he or she is extremely vulnerable to special pleading and unforeseen outcomes. A further moral is that it is wise to begin the task of setting up the required approach to reporting information early on in the regulatory regime (there is normally a considerable period before the regulator is called upon to make major price control decisions).

The aim of the process is to bring economic arguments to bear on the question of charging. The matrix reflects the two sides of the economic argument: demand, represented in the columns, and costs, represented in the rows. The aim is to attribute the forward-looking outlays the cash flow, as described above, to particular customer sets, as required in good economic (and business) practice.[7] In pipes and wires networks, one expects considerable influence of non-attributable outlays because mainly of the economies of scope – joint use by customers of network services. These are not taken as given, however, in the work being described here. Rather, their extent is to be revealed as part of the process. The basic test for attribution is reaction of outlays to output change, i.e. of change in activity levels. Because we are working with the sum of all future outlays in which all future capex, etc., is accounted for, many elements often associated with 'fixity' of costs, and thus deemed unattributable, become subject to attribution. There will inevitably be an unattributable remainder, measured by the extent to which the sum of the attributed costs falls short of the control total. (As an example, an exercise for British Telecoms in 1992 found around 30 per cent of all outlays unattributable and 70 per cent attributable.) This brings up the second economic (and business) problem – how to fund that shortfall. By definition, the problem cannot be solved by attempting to attribute 'costs'. The argument must turn on what is added to attributed costs to form the total prices set for the consumers – the 'mark-up' problem. I briefly review options here later.

In outline, the matrix will shape up as in Figure 18.1. The cells are filled in $ terms. Particular cells within the matrix may well have 0 entries. In the cases of both of customer sets and activities, the purpose is to describe completely the constituents making up the control total. The box labelled 'outlays subject to mark-up', is arrived at by deduction from the control total of the sum of the attributed outlays, which are established in the manner to be described.

How are the 'customer sets' and 'activities' to be defined? As far as customers are concerned, one will always start with the conventions employed in the past, e.g. 'residential' or 'domestic', 'commercial' and 'industrial' customers, and various subsets representing past charging practices. A shift to charging more in line with cost attribution, normally agreed on all sides to be a desirable change, will necessarily require some revision of the sets. This will be a considerable part of the exchanges to be expected between regulator and regulated. Two points are worth particular note in deciding the regulator's approach to revision. First, the focus must be on the final price charged to the customer. The matrix does not deal with the particular 'structure' of prices now typically making up a customer's bill – e.g. the 'fixed' and 'variable' divisions of the typical charge. Hence, adopt

BUSINESS ACTIVITIES		CUSTOMER CLASSES/SETS							
		$ millions							
		A	B	C	D	Rest of Customer classes	Total outlays	Total attributed outlays	Residual
	1								
	2								
	3								
	4								
Rest of Activities	:								
	:								
	:								
ATTRIBUTED OUTLAYS									
CONTROL TOTAL									
OUTLAYS SUBJECT TO MARK-UP									

Figure 18.1 An activity/customer matrix

ing the approach described here is usually a challenge to the way in which 'costs' have recognized in the past, and so will implicitly suggest revision of practice. The way in which indicators for subdividing bills to customers will, on the present approach, arise is from the revealed division between attri- butable costs and the outcome of a separate decision on how mark-ups are to be settled. The function of the matrix is to give the regulator a sound basis for assessment of the prices now charged.

The second point relates to what should drive revision of the classes from the regulator's viewpoint. The point of distinguishing 'classes' is that they sort out the alike from the unalike when viewed in terms of cost- causation. The good reason for distinguishing, say, residential from com- mercial customers is that the former will use more of the network which delivers their gas or electricity or in making 'phone calls. This suggests that the classes should be defined to reflect major cost drivers. In practice, it turns out that by far the most important distinction here lies in the yearly take of gas, electricity, etc., i.e. the size of the yearly consumption as it relates to a particular take-off point. It may be relevant – because costs tend to fall that way – to add location as a descriptor; and it may be that size of 'take-off' criterion needs to be refined better to reflect the time pattern of consumption over the year or day. In other words, one needs to consider the consumption habits of the various proposed classes before deciding which particular customers are alike and which are sufficiently different in cost causation terms to justify separate treatment. The process of definition will be part of the refinement of the information over time as the regulator-regulated exchanges proceed.

Because we are assuming that there has been an effective separation of the pipes/wires business, the consumer sets will not only be the final consumers familiar in integrated operations. They will be potentially rivalous retailers, for example, in competition with the incumbent retail operation. This is why take-off – or use – of the system is the basic classification; whoever sells to the final customer must be charged according to their call on the system. This implies that the bills these intermediaries pay will be an amalgam of the types of customers they in turn serve. Because dealing with them itself implies outlays, aside from the impact of the customers they serve, the columns will include types of retailers, etc., suitably distinguished by the different outlays in transacting with them. For them, entries will appear on the matrix for the activities concerned.[8]

Turning to the rows in the matrix in Figure 18.1: they represent a complete description of the production processes involved in serving customers. In gas and electricity, a natural division into the activities is to follow the progress of the input (gas at the beach or electricity generation connectors) down through the network levels to the take-off points, using the pressures or voltage levels as the guide. Each level is recognized to require its inputs of men materials and capex items. A set of transaction activities will also be recognized, such as metering and billing of customers. The set will be completed by the service functions to the enterprise – personnel, finance, etc., down to and including top management. In telephones, the study mentioned earlier recognized some 32 activities in total, including installation, maintenance, local exchanges and other lines, operators services, marketing, finance and billing. (In what was a preliminary study, we had to accept whatever divisions were to hand, but it still proved possible to derive robust results for purposes of attribution to the components of final bills then at issue – namely, business access, residential access, local, network, and international calls.) The study of incremental costs in BT is now in process of much greater elaboration, involving the recognition of many more subdivisions. In telecoms, this whole area is undergoing great change currently, as the concept of what are called 'incremental' costs has only recently been recognized as a fundamental underpinning of policy. As Oftel think further about 'incremental costs' they seem to be getting closer to what are called 'attributed' costs here.[9]

The essential starting point to determining costs related to output change in these activities is to consider each of these rows individually. The central question is what happens to the expenditure on men and materials, and other expenditure relating to that activity, when its volume change by a given percentage. The advice on that is basically a matter for the managers concerned. (Hence the importance of aligning the enquiries as far as possible with the actual practice in, especially, the management accounts.)

Managers will find it conceptually easier to think in terms of a reasonably large change in 'their' activity (e.g. 20 per cent), not the very small change beloved of economists. I mentioned in the lecture the willingness of managers on the ground to enter the spirit of the exercise when pursuing this same broad line of attack with the Post Office some years ago. However, it is quite possible for the regulator with suitable advice to construct his own estimates, given basic reportage of the total sums associated with each row from those with experience in running the kind of business in question.

It is the change in total outlays associated with the change in the activity which is relevant. One would quite often expect a 20 per cent change multiplied by 5 to fail to sum to the total expenditures on that activity, because of the incidence of economies which are derived from serving different customers, with their different demands on the activity, simultaneously. Shortfalls of this kind are picked up in the residual in summing the attributable amounts, as described above. The selection of the unit of activity in which to express the output change is a matter of convenience, suitable to the individual activity concerned. Thus, in, gas, a natural unit in the network function may be the volume of gas dealt with. In the support services, other units, such as customer numbers, may be more appropriate. There is no need for the different activities to use the same output change measure. The degree to which each kind of customer uses the activity is dealt with as a separate matter, to reflect the fact that different customers consume more or less of given activities. In other words, the process just described establishes a per unit attributable cost, then considers how customers 'take' the units.

Those readers with economic training will doubtless have a number of questions in their mind at this point. Chief among them, I suspect, will be – how much does it matter whether we take the 20 per cent change to mean plus or minus 20 per cent? And what is the pay-off, if any, to considering alternative changes, like 5 per cent or 10 per cent? The first question bears on the point that, in any system which is not in long-run equilibrium in respect of capacity/demand relationships, it will make a difference as to the sign of the change which is taken. If – as is typical of the over-engineered systems regulators are usually confronted with – there is excess capacity, an addition of 20 per cent may be accommodated on the system and with a rise in attributed cost not much different from a reduction of 20 per cent. By contrast, if there is considerable congestion on the system, it is possible that an increase of 20 per cent will be far more costly than the parallel release of resources associated with a reduction of 20 per cent. Many variations on this theme are possible. The broad answer to the question is that the more acute possibilities of inconsistency arise only if the present system is considered fixed. By contrast, if one takes as one's base, as here, the present value of costs including capex, stretching into the future, the question of 'fixed capacity' does not arise. The control total will itself, and consequent to the starting points of the individual rows, refer to an adjustment process to meet foreseen demands which will usually be different from today's. This greatly reduces the impact of the problem. In practice it has not proved difficult.

The point of testing for different activity changes, e.g. the 5 per cent or 10 per cent, is essentially to check on the short cuts of assuming that dividing the derived total cost changes by 20 represents a correct view of the unit attributable outlay change over the range of output likely to come into question. It could be said that failure to test for other output levels may lead to inaccurate representation of the residual, which then in turn will appear, incorrectly, in the subsequent stage of the exercise, i.e. the attribution of mark-ups to account for the unattributed outlays. Again, the answer is that with the inclusive view of costs being taken here, a complication such as this probably is unlikely to be worth the candle, at least to start with. Of course, one can always make exceptions for particular activities where one has reason to suspect important effects. My own experience, having posed the question in the form of alternative percentage changes in practice, is that it makes little difference to the unit attribution which results.

A more important question will be how to incorporate the incidence of time of consumption within the year in the outlays to be attributed. This issue will, of course, affect some activities more than others. (Billing or metering, for example, are not dependent on weather fluctuations which cause demand differences over the year.) For those which are clearly affected, such as providing different network levels, an additional testing of cost sensitivities is desirable. One obvious approach in pursuing, for example, the point that 'network scale depends on peak use', is to consider the impact on total activity costs of the notional withdrawal of demands at different times. These can then form a set of potential weights to be attached to the attributed costs according to the demand characteristics in time, of the different customers sets. The actual attribution of the weights will depend on what is known about the average characteristics of the customers within the set. Those who argue for 'peak use' as a dominant cost driver often ignore what consumers actually do. The consumer who confines his/her consumption to particular periods of time such as the peak winter period is a rather rare person. The best approach is to start with greatest attention to the yearly quantity consumed and its significance, and then refine the estimates as more evidence comes forward.

Having thus divided the outlays recognized in the separate activities into attributable unit costs, and a residual, the next step is to consider the degree which each customer set (each column) draws on the respective activities. This will vary considerably, depending on the customer. In gas and electricity, for example, big (industrial) users will typically take their loads off the system higher in the network than will the smaller user. The former will have a zero entry for the lowest network level activity, the local net. With respect to the higher levels in the hierarchy, each consumer set will be attributed his unit attributable cost according to the respective volume of use at that level. A particularly important example of this recognition of drawing on activity differentially is for interconnecting operators in telecoms. Here there will be (if UK is a guide) great variance in the use of the incumbent's network, which has to be recognized. Indeed, the front-line 'customer sets' to be recognized in telecoms are basically the incumbent's own retail operation, which will call on virtually all the activities, and competitive sellers using only parts of the network. In order to keep tally of the nature of these front-line customers demands, the characteristics of the final consumers they serve will have to be preserved in the cost attribution system.

In this way relevant cells of the matrix will be populated with data. The column totals will give the attributable costs to customer sets, and the activity rows total attributable costs in that activity, and the residual costs to be dealt with separately. Using a very simplified matrix, one can envisage the result shown in Figure 18.2 (taking 4 rows and columns only from Figure 18.1 above).

DEALING WITH THE MARK-UPS

Giving the incumbent reasonable prospects of remaining viable implies that the non-attributed outlays must be recovered. They have to be faced, even if not attributable. If we rule out applying a subsidy from outside, they must be recovered in prices charged.[10] I briefly referred in my lecture to the main rival principles for such recovery in prices charged. I shall confine myself now also to a sketch; there are, of course, decades of economic literature on the subject. Here, I look at the options with the practical regulatory task to the forefront.

Briefly, then, virtually all 'solutions' have in common the perception that there must be a lower limit on prices charged. This, of course, is the attributable outlays that customers occasion by their usage; hence the need to proceed along the lines just discussed, to establish what these are. (I fear that you will find the literature remarkably short both on clarity about what is meant by attributable outlay – or whatever like term is used – and, even more, on how to do it in practice. I should also note that what I have defined and labelled as 'attributable outlays' goes by a large number of other terms, more or less pointing in the same direction, but fuzzy on inspection – e.g. 'incremental costs', 'avoidable costs', 'marginal costs', often with various adjectives.) The underlying business rationale of this lower limit – that to price lower than this is to lose money – is widely accepted in policy terms. Such obviously 'inefficient' behaviour, it is thought, should be avoided, and when pricing reform is on the agenda, a very wide consensus in favour of applying at least this minimum will be found. The question, then, is what should be added – in such a way to generate (just) enough cash to cover the non-attributed outlays?

BUSINESS ACTIVITIES		CUSTOMER CLASSES/SETS						
		$ millions						
		A	B	C	D	Total outlays	Total attributed outlays	Residual
		(i)	(ii)	(iii)	(iv)	(v)	(vi)	(v)–(vi)
	1	40	120	160	100	640	420	220
	2	30	150	100	200	560	480	80
	3	60	30	120	–	400	210	190
	4	–	70	130	100	400	300	100
ATTRIBUTED OUTLAYS		130	370	510	400		1410	
CONTROL TOTAL						2000		
OUTLAYS SUBJECT TO MARK-UP								590

Figure 18.2 A simplified activity/customer matrix

Perhaps the most widely practised method is to divide the required sum through some output measure and allocate accordingly. Since this lacks a foundation in terms of its effects on prices, it is normally rejected by economists, who nevertheless find difficulty in getting agreement to alternatives which are well founded. The economists' front runner is Ramsey pricing – i.e. mark-ups on attributed costs inversely proportional to customers' demand elasticities. The underlying rationale here is to minimize the loss of consumers' surplus when applying the different mark-ups. If applied to operators of wires or pipes, this would, it is argued, feed through to final prices downstream. Apart from practical difficulties in fixing such mark-ups, chiefly of getting reliable, believable estimates of the elasticities, and the unfortunate fact that the changes from present prices which would be implied much exaggerates the effects on important sets of existing consumers – who at the start often will not be paying even their attributable costs – the fundamental objection from the regulator's point of view is that Ramsey pricing does not address the problem with which he is faced. This is the likely advance of competition in the contestable part of the incumbent's business. In such circumstances, the final prices actually faced by consumers will be affected by how far competition provides options. One has to include this effect in any realistic view of what elasticities different customers will face, which undermines the whole point of Ramsey pricing, which was, and is, to prescribe a second best solution to a problem of monopoly.

In reality, the regulator's usual position is as one who is enjoined to pursue two fundamentally incompatible objectives – to ensure viability of the incumbent, yet to encourage competition in a large part of his business. He is also expected to promote efficient behaviour in general. The solution must be a compromise. The outstanding fact about the situation is normally that competition has not yet arrived – it will arise, perhaps in fairly predictable ways in general, but with a particular incidence which cannot be foreseen. My own 'solution' is to propose that the required mark-ups be proportional to the attributed costs, i.e. the required sum be raised by selecting that common percentage which will just yield the sum needed.

With this rule the regulator can show that he is fulfilling his remit to ensure viability in the face of unknown competitive effects, and is keeping the influence of attributable costs, giving useful safeguards against uneconomic behaviour in the final markets, because all competitors (in the potentially contestable markets) will face, and be obliged to pay, the appropriate charge from the non-contestable supplier. The rule will also tend to safeguard against the incumbent who might wish to reflect the competition he believes he faces in the final markets in particular cases. Also, though the pipes and wires businesses in gas and electricity are, and will be, basically unassailable for a long period, there is always fringe competition. Final suppliers can build their own rival means to supply when conditions are exceptionally favourable. The 'rule' will give useful signals in this connection also. In telecoms, of course, entry into networks is proceeding fast in the UK, and the rule has great significance there. I have advocated the principle in discussions on telecoms pricing for some time now. It is perhaps no accident that, after a lot of wavering, Oftel appears to have decided to adopt mark-ups proportionate to what they call 'incremental' costs as the principle to follow in their December 1995 Consultative Document *Pricing of Telecommunications Services from 1997*.

PROGRESS TOWARDS ADOPTION IN THE UK

This paper has devoted considerable space to the question of how the forward-looking 'control total' for revenue should be translated into a pricing structure. As in the presentation this is a response to your request to pursue the basic approach to setting the overall price control into the charging system which should result. As Chapter 19 stresses, the history of UK regulation is of progress towards realizing the necessary conditions for effective regulation; the start in each utility was in its own way imperfect. On the most important pricing issues – of separation and the forward-looking cash flow approach – gas has made the most obvious progress (as I would see it) since 1993. On the second condition British Gas is fighting a rear-guard action to have capex driven by depreciation provisions rather than justified future outlays in the current price control. You may be interested to learn how that battle goes. In Electricity, the influence of the forward-looking cash-based approach has grown over successive price control fixing episodes. It has not been helped by the initial governmental mistake of decreeing separate review dates for 'transmission' (NGC's grid), supply as part of the REC's business, and distribution, also part of the REC's business. After $1\frac{1}{2}$ cycles of these price-fixing episodes, the regulatory drawbacks of doing this are only too clear. However, the prospect in 1998 of opening the small consumer markets to competition has focused minds on the separation issue, and, in the current NGC price review, the influence of the forward cash-based approach will, I judge, be seen to have grown. As I stress in the Appendix, the approach is necessary to mount an effective critique of company plans. There is little doubt that Offer's effectiveness here is growing.

In telecoms, there never has been a serious direct attack on the separation issue, despite the divisions canvassed before privatization. BT has always resisted the notion that they could be ring-fencing to the standard I set out in paragraph 3. It has continuously stressed the integrated nature of its business. It regards digitalization as reinforcing this; and has recently been able, as a reinforcement, to enlist arguments about an emerging national high-capacity digital 'highway'. Indeed, some view the current price control exchanges as an episode in a longer term BT strategy to concede ground on the price regulation front in order to gain the right to enter the business of TV programming and dissemination, in part to counter cable companies, and in part to position itself as the prime mover in the 'highway' provision.

However, the problems of entry into, and over, network provision, long subject to *ad hoc* regulatory proposals and actions, have prompted what seem to be important movements on the price structure front. In keeping with Oftel practice, this has been promoted in effect separately from the question of justifying the validity of BT's investment plans, and other future cash outlays. Hence there is currently an attempt to set up an 'incremental' cost approach (as in the consultative paper) without revisiting the foundations of the price control. This remains, effectively, as Sir Bryan Carsberg left it – an exercise in critiquing BT's achieved returns on capital. It is an open question how far this apparent attempt to maintain the divorce between the control total and what should be derived prices can be sustained. Oftel's first period of consultation on the structure has been completed; there will be a second period of consultation in March to May this year in which the 'value of X' – i.e. how much revenue is allowed overall, will be the focus. I would expect there to be vigorous arguments to integrate the two in the final decisions.

Though it is still unclear whether there will be a clearly separated retailing function for BT for its still dominant share of the final market, alongside its function of supplier of delivery services to all comers (including itself as retailer), there is much less doubt in the case of electricity and gas. This enables a clearer focus on the nature of the competitive problem over the pipes and wires; how to manage the transition from 100 per cent market share to a share determined by competitive forces. In gas and electricity, this has been approached by successively opening the market overtime to large concerns and then to those of lesser size. So far, again, the movement has been accomplished without special attention to the ultimate regulatory requirements for information to bear on competitive conduct. Now that for both gas and electricity the highly populated markets of small consumers are to be opened, the issue is being addressed. There are of course a large number of strands in the whole web of competitive policy as it affects the utilities, and I cannot attempt a rounded picture here. It will be useful, however, to pick up the options for the control of conduct which are presented by the analysis of the basis for the structure of prices just made.

COMPETITIVE CONDUCT RULES

The regulator is faced with a considerable period of development of competition. Because of the incumbent's choice, denied to newcomers, of how and when to meet competitors' offers, using his established consumer base, and whether to do so at all, the question will arise of how to put limits on the incumbent's competitive responses. Looked at in the broad, the options are two-fold as noted earlier: the incumbent's prices can be prescribed; or the market can be left to develop with sanctions available in the anti-monopoly rules which apply to the rest of the economy. In practice, there will be a need to decide when to move from one mode of influence to another, and this will greatly depend on one's view of the operation of the normal anti-monopoly rules. I cannot, of course, pursue this here as it applies in the Australian context (much as I would wish to!), but this is where the information from the price structure arguments bear.

Given that both for the pipes and wires business and the incumbent's retailing business the underlying attributable cost calculations have been developed, the focus at this point is on the latter business. (I assume all players will be faced with the same charges for pipes and wires services, and I have given my preferred solution to their content for this purpose.) This will have much reduced the room for anti-competition manoeuvre by the incumbent, but he still has a choice as to where he takes his margins with respect to the retail business. The two options are then, to mandate that the incumbent follows prescribed outlay attribution and mark-up procedure for that business as the basis for prices which he has to publish and adhere to, or to allow freedom to formulate margins, and to defer action on conduct until complaints from consumers or rival producers are made.

The second course of action is clearly more in line with the control of conduct in the general anti-monopoly mode. In the latter case, the same information will provide the basis for the standard pricing test for allegations of unfair competitive conduct (e.g. predation against entrants). In anti-monopoly control this is the attributable cost or, as interpreted here, attributable outlay test. This is a test for the deliberate intention to lose money in order to get an enhanced market advantage at a later stage, compared to what would be possible in the absence of such behaviour.

There is also need for the companion test – that of pricing 'too highly' to customers not (yet) subject to competition, in order to finance the losses. This is the 'stand-alone' test – what price competitors could hypothetically produce for if they were to serve these other customers. The mark-up rule preferred earlier will also provide a first marker to alert the regulator to possible 'excess' mark-ups. However, the stand-alone test will require independent evidence as well. Hence the regulator's armoury must include in effect a model of shadow competition for all customer sets. This is a tough assignment, so the incumbent's set of properly attributed and marked-up outlays will in practice be a key input for the regulator.

The decision of whether, and when, to rely on normal control of competitive conduct will, on UK experience in gas and telephones, be a difficult one. Once entry occurs, there will be immediate pressure from the incumbent to allow retaliation (with appropriate rhetoric about 'level playing fields', 'competing with one hand tied', etc.). In gas in the markets now open to competition (over 2,500 therms), Ofgas are in the process of charging from a mandated publishing of prices and terms – from which no deviation by British Gas was allowed – set out to cope with allowing entry initially, to reliance on monitoring competitive behaviour, backed by new non-discriminatory provisions. These are under negotiation. Ofgas also intends strengthening its position on cost information related to structure. In the under-2,500 therm markets, to be opened progressively from the south-west of England this year, it is intended to hold the existing price control in some form at least till 1997 and perhaps beyond. The problem which then presents itself is how to operate a price control in a situation where the customers concerned can be attracted to competitors. Possible solutions to this within a price control mechanism are canvassed in a current consultation paper. They present many practical difficulties. I would expect Ofgas to prefer to move as quickly as it can to the reactive anti-monopoly style of conduct control in the under-2,500 therm market also.

In telecoms, possible ways to cope with widespread entry in parts of BT's market are likewise currently being canvassed and are out to consultation. Oftel appears to be leaning in the direction of setting up criteria for judging when a given market sector has become competitive enough for the service concerned to be dropped from the price control. Oftel earlier appeared to go through a phase in which it preferred to elaborate rules of conduct tailored to individual markets. BT's response was, *inter alia*, to seek protection against competitors who proposed service innovation which could be anticipated to be unfair to it. Less seems now to be made of these ideas, but they are still on the table.

These efforts by the individual offices to run their own versions of control of anti-competitive behaviour must seem odd to outsiders who value known and stable conditions for monitoring conduct which are the same for all sections of economic activity. The basic problem in the UK is the weakness of UK general competition law, in particular the 1980 Competition Act, which has been revealed to be wanting in sectors in other than dealing with utilities in its ability to address the abuse of single firm power, and in particular in cases of predation.[11] In the longer run the remedy lies in strengthening the disincentives to the use of such power in the UK law as a whole. If this is done (and there is little sign of it yet) the specialist regulators will be providers of evidence needed to enforce such laws.[12]

ASSET VALUATION ISSUES

The final topic I addressed in the seminar was issues in asset valuation, presented in Australia as a key issue in price control matters. The reason for its prominence appears to me to arise from its connection with the question of preserving or enhancing the return State Treasuries have traditionally enjoyed from their publicly owned utilities. Last year's agreement between the States and the Federal Government about the post-Hilmer treatment of these in the national competition framework has not, so I am told, removed the Treasurer's financial concerns in this area. Given the required rate of return, the asset values selected strongly influence the total 'dividend' flow received by the State. Indeed, since the utilities largely offer services sold in uncontestable markets, a treasurer can in effect mandate the 'return' as an input rather than – as is the case of private sector having to leave dividends as an output – a residual resulting from realized outlays and revenues. Treasuries have an understandable wish to justify what are essentially taxes on consumers by reference to the circumstances of the particular industries. Hence the search for a valuation rationalized in terms of replacement of the physical assets used in the business. I understand that the favoured version of this is 'optimized depreciation replacement cost', to which 'deprival value' is closely related. Because the utilities in some cases have already been privatized – and there is an active prospect of privatization in others, and regulation must in principle cover all utilities regardless of ownership – there is concern that similar asset valuation should be employed in both cases.

It would not be appropriate here to go into the details, or relative merits, of the alternative versions of valuations on offer, which are derivations of an older idea, modern equivalent asset valuation. Suffice it to say that any such attempt to create an objective 'value' is doomed to logical failure. 'Valuation' by reference to this will always be found to imply choice between irrelevant options, which ignore what actually faces the regulator. The reason is simply that, in general, there is no market – that is, competitive – test of the worth of the 'assets' (these are uncontestable activities). Moreover, the actual worth of 'assets' is formally *derived* from the net cash flow available when the terms of price control, etc., have been settled. A utility subject to price control which is meant to avoid the unconstrained search after market values must encounter circularity – the 'assets' are, finally, worth what the regulator decides they *are* worth. The constructive way to look at this problem is to consider how reasonable limits can be placed on the regulator's range of solutions to the final outcome, as explained in Chapter 19.

One of the merits of the forward-looking approach is that of addressing directly what is otherwise implicit in the asset valuation methods. The big issue in utility funding is of what speed and with what alternatives the current system will have to be modified, replaced, etc. To bury this issue in the assumptions made in the asset valuation procedures is to risk ignoring the need actually to enquire into the real options now facing utility managements. The recent and, indeed current, *cause célèbre* in gas regulation in UK is precisely this conflict – British Gas wishes the cash allowed in the new price control to reflect the depreciation provisions implicit in the current asset values. Ofgas is determined to make future capex, etc., expenditure subject to scrutiny.

To be clear, I am not asserting that the comparisons underlying the asset valuation methods are not useful as inputs to the real tasks. Insofar as they help address the major problems posed by the forward-looking approach, they help to narrow down the range of outcomes the regulator has to consider. They also have value in helping governments and their advisers to set up aims for realizations when privatizing utilities. In Treasury terms, a privatization capitalizes expected future 'dividends' from a utility. The hope will be that the shift of ownership in itself will generate extra sources of gain not open in public control – notably efficiencies to be derived by managements driven by the capital market, and that the privatization process itself will generate competition among bidders to ensure that the prospective gains from this prospect are imputed to the Treasury. All this, however, again does not remove circularity from the *ex-ante* 'valuation' process. In realizing values, much will turn on the regulatory conditions proposed; in effect the Treasury has to go through the forward-looking process as best as it can, leaving the privatization bidding process actually to settle how valuable the businesses are at the start of the regulation regime.

In the broader context of regulation, focusing on *asset* valuation is something of a red herring – it is the ability to generate net cash flows which is central. This becomes only too clear when the question is the price control to be applied for the protected parts of the market – e.g. small customers, served by potentially contestable means, but not yet open to rivalry. These businesses, with their large retail element, do not have much in the way of the concrete assets so obvious in networks and pipes, and so any attempt to judge allowed returns on assets has immediately to be abandoned.

The central regulatory task in this problem of narrowing down the arbitrary character of the regulator's necessary effect on company values is to use as many means as he can to reduce the perception of regulatory risk. By this I mean recognizing that the actual values of the companies are an outcome of a bargaining exchange between regulation and regulated, but putting in place believable limits to the range of outcomes to be expected from a price control episode. Confidence that *future* capex, etc., will be funded at the required rate of return is of major importance, since it reduces prospects of bankruptcy because of regulatory intervention virtually to vanishing point. Respect for such market valuation as have been manifest is also important. In all UK price-fixing episodes, the terms for which the punters put up their money on privatization has been influential. The latest example, I am confident, will be in the current NGC (Grid) price review; the regulator will pay due heed to the market valuations established in December 1995.

There are two further elements in establishing confidence in the regulatory regime from the company's (and if relevant the stock market's) viewpoint. First the basic aim of CPI$-X$ control is to establish a base from which anticipated management efficiency will be rewarded. This implies that there will be no 'claw-back' of achieved unforeseen profits due to this performance, when the price falls to be reset at the end of the period. Partly, this can be met by establishing, and making public, the extent which the original decision on the X, because based on a forward look which extends beyond the forthcoming price period, has implied assent to capex, etc., spend in the subsequent periods. No regulator can sensibly bind himself to a very long price guarantee, and it is understood that, at a subsequent refix, proposals for expenditure will be reviewed on their merits, in the light of circumstances at the time. But the public acknowledgement of the implications of the bases of the original deal sets limits to what, in the event, can be deemed reasonable regulatory behaviour. (You will notice that this implies that there must be a means of independent appeal from the regulator's price decision – the role played in the UK by MMC.) A further important element is an understanding about the speed at which any revealed extra efficiency gains will be subsequently passed on to consumers. A common attitude in the UK is that such gains should pass the consumer over the up-coming price review period. This whole area is currently the subject of debate in the UK, and Chapter 19 was part of that debate in the case of gas.

In summary, to focus on 'asset valuation' in an ongoing price control is inessence not to address the questions which will concern the consumer: the scale of funding to be allowed – a much larger question than the issue of what the return to shareholders should be – and the setting of an incentive system which will work to the consumers' advantage over the long run. In Australia the concern is quite largely a reflection of the interest of safeguarding what is in effect a tax flow to the respective Treasuries. If the utilities are to remain in the public sector the correct context is one of arguing about alternatives for raising tax and their consequences, of which taxing State utilities is one.

APPENDIX

Ring-fencing standards

The circumstances warranting 'such a detailed ring-fencing standard' are that the difficulties of attempting price and competition regulation without it have been increasingly revealed. In gas, this is now admitted on all sides; British Gas is committed, competition to divide itself formally along the critical line of distinguishing sales over the pipes from the pipes themselves. In electricity the original 'regulatory accounts' eagerly dropped out of the real negotiations with the Regional Electricity Companies, and similarly in NGC's (National Grid's) case. The key additional information concerns the generation of cash (where?), the complex re-charging provisions among activities ('cost shifting') and what is done to fund common activities. As I imply in the paper, all this mirrors what a sensibly managed company would do for itself via its management accounts; the regulators' needs reflect the same concerns. The reason for pushing through to separate profits and losses and balance sheets with a shadow capital structure is principally to recognize the very different risks and ability to generate cash flow the two types of business represent – quite apart from its significance for the contrasting competitive situations.

The next big issue in electricity is the post-1998 competition for the millions of small accounts. This is a highly complex story but I think it very doubtful if competition in these markets can be effective without a formal separation of the REC's distribution and 'supply' businesses.

In telecoms also, I think the lack of attention to lassoing in lasting monopoly activities from others in focusing price controls is fast coming home to roost. In all the current flurry of consultation papers, Oftel has been silent about how it is getting on with accounting separation – not surprising when the original six-fold division was set up to recognize notional activities like 'Access'. No doubt a massive exercise in notional re-charging is going on.

Is there a 'hierarchy' in the above categories of accounts? No, they are all essential; they hang together. They will, however, meet with increasing resistance as one includes 'shadow capital structure' and intra-company dealing material – for two reasons: companies usually have to *create* the information; and their degrees of freedom to swing expenses onto the controlled price areas narrow.

You raised the question of a distinction between 'routine' and 'one off' reporting of information to the regulator. I do not think that *routine* reporting of information, of whatever level, has proved to be useful to the regulator. Price fixing is episodic, and every occasion will bring its new needs for information. On the other hand, one can never safely leave it to the firm to define 'broad categories' such as attributable and unattributable costs. One can only define these operationally with respect to a concrete case at hand. So in effect one uses the price-fixing 'episode' to construct the model, which must be as detailed as the firm's own information at that point allows. This may well be confined to less detailed definition of activities, etc., at the outset than will be possible later. Between 'episodes' one keeps the dialogue going towards understanding more of the firm's business and makes sure principles are argued (as openly as possible). One important thing is to keep an eye on how management accounts are being developed over time – this tells you a great deal about what will be feasible. So far as adjudicating competitive issues are concerned, these too must arise essentially as a response to complaints about incumbents' pricing, etc. Hopefully, spade-work on attributable costs, etc., along the lines I suggested will have been done; more detailed *ad hoc* investigations will be needed which will concentrate on adaptations of the basic expectations as derived from the spade-work.

'Splitting assets': Provided that one has tackled the problem of the total company worth on the correct principles (I will not repeat that debate here) one should have no particular difficulty in using proportions based on book values. You will find it necessary to complement this where there are in fact few concrete assets, as in supplying over networks, essentially a retailing operation. There the principal 'asset' is likely to be working capital.

'Potentially contestable activities' and 'ring fencing': This is a most interesting point. 'Continuous reviewing' will lead to insurmountable regulatory difficulties, and be highly unsatisfactory for incumbents and newcomers alike. I think the problem must be stood on its head. Regulators should seek to define at one time in what an incumbent's persisting market strength is, stabilize this boundary for a set period ahead, to set up the relevant price control, attribution and mark up information, in that set of ring-fenced activities. There will always be the possibility of *ad hoc* inquiry outside that area to deal with particular complaints. I suspect this is a Telecom-inspired question; it is certainly a live issue now in the UK. In practical terms, my advice means creating a 'stand-alone' company from British Telecom's activities – men and assets – concerned with local distribution and pick-up. British Telecom's essential market power, as I said in the paper, now lies in its ability to provide near-universal delivery (not so much pick-up) which all newcomers must be able to offer. This will mean solving a tricky cost attribution and mark-up problem with respect to that stand-alone company, because a lot of costs will prove to be joint. The regulator should seek to narrow down price controls to that 'company' and rely upon competitive conduct rules, when necessary, to safeguard customers in other respects. Needless to say, such a solution is radical for UK Telecoms, as elsewhere in the world.

'Control total'

An adequate replacement model is one which incorporates latest information about technical and purchasing options in asset replacement. In practice, thanks to developments in these, replacement is getting less costly in real terms, but company accounting practice lags behind; the company financial interest *vis-à-vis* the regulator is to be conservative. The specific concerns in gas were highlighted in the MMC 1993 Gas inquiry as a contrast between CCA depreciation and actual replacement expenditure. This concern has risen again in the current TransCo review – it turns out that TransCo has not essentially altered its position since. (Ofgas's proposals, published on 13 May 1996, take up these points.) In electricity, this problem of the level, and timing of funding for future capex arises in RECs and NGC also. But with respect to the latter, NGC have, since 1992 shifted their replacement strategy markedly against automatic renewal in favour of detailed asset monitoring. This raises the interesting question of whether this can be deemed to be an improvement already to be expected, given the state of the art, or whether it must be deemed an outcome of unexpected gains from managerial efficiency. The distinction is a crucial one in settling the 'regulatory contract' between the regulator and regulated. You will be interested to know that in Gas there is an intention to draft a formal 'regulatory contract' in the 13 May Consultation Document.

'Rationalized levels of charges'

This means charges which have been through the mill of attribution and mark-up. 'Perceived' means by potential competitors the customers and the world at large. As I said, though it is possible to be content with non-discriminatory prices as such, whether 'properly' reflecting attributable costs and mark-ups or not, in the competitive context experience teaches us that this economist's point will never be terribly convincing to real world players.

Deriving the preferred price structure

You enquired about the so-called 'light-handed approach' to the regulation in the UK. This really requires an essay on the development of regulation from its Telecoms beginnings. 'Light handed' was a description of the UK incentive approach via $RPI-X$ as opposed to a bogey called US-style regulation. The broad position now is that the evolution of price control has been towards a greater separation between the incumbents' inherent, and lasting, monopoly strength and the rest of activities. Within the former set, price control has become more detailed (it has also become far more transparent and open to critical input too). In the latter set, regulators are becoming specialist general competition agents (because of the continuing failure in UK to move on the 'abuse of monopoly power' in the general law). So, in dealing with vertical integration, the important point is not so much a matter of how to recognize the degree of vertical integration in comprehensive regulation, but of separation of what must be regulated by a price control and what to deal with under competition rules. Detailed scrutiny is inevitable – and getting more expert – in the former area; in the latter the tendency is to set oneself up to react to competitive problems as they arise. As explained in the test, to understand the nature of the attribution and mark-up problems one must start with the 'control total' – the firm as a whole, whatever its degree of integration. The different activities essentially define the areas of concern for monopoly power, and that for competitive concerns, which has involved additional involvement for the regulator, in the UK, at least.

The role of activity-based costing

You asked how activity-based costing maps on to the attribution process. I described in the text: Activity-based costing will normally provide a useful contribution to setting up the kind of system I described. I am sceptical about 'casual factors' as they are usually interpreted. (I speak here on the basis of analyses done for Ofgas involving the Public Gas supply business.) It may turn out that there is a confusion between customer categories and the behaviour of costs for the activities (the columns and rows in my exposition). There is a tendency to short-circuit this by, for example, constraining effects on costs to 'numbers of customers' as the driver. On inspection, it turns out that it all hinges on what is meant by 'customers'. I advocate regarding each row or activity, as being subject to a hypothetical change of output measured in whatever account of output is convenient. It is a quite separate question how much of the activity a customer set defined in a particular way is deemed to take. This way, one can cope with any definition of customer sets which exhaust revenue sources. So the catch is in 'well developed', 'reasonable basis' and 'true' joint costs. These last have to be discovered; they are highly unlikely to be acceptable, given my starting point, from a ready-made costing system, and, though providing useful information will require considerable re-vamping.

NOTES

1 Text of a presentation given to the Australian Competition and Consumer Commission, 2 February 1996. Commission members raised several points which I dealt with subsequently in correspondence. These are attached in, and referred in the text to, the Appendix.
2 See Appendix: ring-fencing standards.
3 This raises questions about the rights of regulators to demand information. Only in later privatizations was the importance of this fully appreciated. It is conceivable, of course, that management accounts can be 'cooked' for negotiating purposes. Such a danger seems exaggerated; it argues yet a further level of internal knowledge and control which I find very implausible.
4 See Appendix: 'Control total'.
5 See Appendix: Rationalized levels of charges.
6 See Appendix, page 391: 'Deriving the preferred price structure'.

7 The forward-looking cash flows in question comprise both outlays which economists would normally term 'avoidable', because the subject of options and choice; and the cash added because of the element which recognizes past commitments. Of course, the former greatly outweighs the latter. But because of this additional element, I shall not use the term 'avoidable costs'. It would be expected, of course, that the attribution process to be described will affect the 'avoidable' elements only. The second element will appear as an unattributable item.

8 This approach is a useful way to look at the interconnect problem in telecoms. Interconnecting operators are assigned charges reflecting their customers' use of the underlying network. The complications caused by the differential impact of competition over the network, noted earlier, are referred to below.

9 See Appendix: 'The role of activity-based costing'.

10 The current effort in UK telecoms to free BT's pricing from the inherited bias in favour of small consumers includes the proposition that subsidy be justified and made the subject of an explicit fund, to be funded from all the competitors, including BT. This may replace the highly dubious and erratic means of protecting BT by exacting 'Access Deficit Contributions' from competitors. Excess subsidy leaves the way clearer for a more logical approach to recovery of non-attributable costs.

11 Hence the incumbent's licence provisions, bearing on competitive conduct, were formulated. It is now also the practice to operate a concordat between the specialist officials and the DGFT in matters (e.g. monopoly references) which transcend the scope of the individual Acts. The question has already arisen of when is the potential contestability realized sufficient to drop the special provisions? So far, the answer has been 'not yet'; and indeed licence provisions are expanding as markets previously treated as franchises are formally open to rival supply (e.g. the under-2,500 therm gas market).

12 My 1994 London Business School Regulation lecture dealt with this need for reform in the UK law at large. It is to be hoped the Australian competition laws are, or can be made, more robust than the UK's in this area!

19 RPI−X principles and their application to gas[1,2]

M.E. Beesley

INTRODUCTION

As one of those who helped to put the RPI−X system into place, what strikes me about the current debate is the unwillingness to see it as a major change in the modes of influencing utilities. Technically, RPI−X is an incentive system for motivating utility managements. Its essence is in the forward-looking targeting of prices for a period ahead sufficient to give inducements for companies to better their targets. Privatization's essential contribution was the break from old forces shaping the motivations of incumbent managements. Exposure to capital markets and potential competition among managements for control plus the personal gains in prospect no doubt has tended, over time, to replace the incumbent management culture.

But the fundamental shift, in my opinion, is in *ex-post* and *ex-ante* influences on incumbent conduct. By this, I mean that before privatization conduct was bounded by the very limited forward-look permitted by Treasury control, and, much more, by criticism *ex-post*, via House of Commons committee, MMC 1980 Act inquiries and the like. To attempt to set price limits in advance, leaving room for unexpected efficiency gains, was a very big undertaking indeed. I notice that critics do not wish to give up the incentive properties of RPI−X. The problem is that they sharply underestimate what was and is *still* involved in the change.

My plan for the lecture is first to remind ourselves of what the regulatory task of creating the necessary conditions to mount a successful incentive system was on privatization; to review progress in the essential tasks to date and to draw some perhaps not fully appreciated consequences of adopting the required approach to deriving relevant information. I shall then comment on the current problem of fixing British Gas's TransCo prices. Finally, I shall reflect briefly on the implications for proposed reforms of RPI−X such as profit sharing.

THE INHERITANCE

Regulators inherited a poor information base for their emerging tasks. The nationalized industries simply did not need, or have, commercially driven information systems. Evidence on this is necessarily anecdotal, but those of us actually engaged in the process were acutely aware of the deficiencies. My experience includes the following: when conducting my original telecoms inquiry on competition in 1980, one main issue was prospective damage to BT's net cash flow that resale on leased BT lines would involve. (Even then, a central issue was BT's ability in the future to sustain the large elements of cross-subsidy implicit in continued response to social obligations.) I expected, naturally, that this would be approached by BT's considering what large business accounts were in danger, since obviously large businesses with substantial telephone bills would be first in line. To my asking, 'What was your total business with ICI last year?', BT's response was one of astonishment. To paraphrase their response, this was a wholly unreasonable request. ICI could be any of at least 4,000 local accounts, and, even if these could be totalled for a customer, which they never had been, there were many other ways (e.g. leasing itself) in which BT collected revenue from ICI. Of course, BT said, it would be possible to do this when local exchanges were fully digitalized, then expected at about 2003. There I learnt the first lesson – that the information for regulation meant very great changes *in the subject firms*, not likely to be achieved overnight.

The second memory is the widely fluctuating estimates from companies of the capex consequences of adhering, belatedly, to European water standards, suddenly required because Brussels could now refuse to sign off on the Water Bill. At one point, X's of up to 12 per cent or more a year looked quite possible. Of course, some order was brought to this, and the wilder estimates revised. The moral here, however, was that ten years' planning of options for meeting standards had to be initiated virtually from scratch. Again, as late as the MMC inquiry in 92/93, MMC were told that it was impossible for British Gas to estimate, even very crudely, what the cash likely to be needed or generated would be beyond the 4 years then remaining in the price control. (This did not prevent MMC from making its own estimates.) So the history since privatization is the companies' development towards relevant commercial information and the regulators' increasing ability to use it. But we should not overestimate the speed that was, and is still, possible.

Information has to be interpreted, indeed defined, in some conceptual framework. At privatization this was weak also. I recall that, in contemplating floating BT in 1983, solemn advice from the Merchant Bank advisers was that if 100 per cent of shares were to be floated at once, the Gilt market would be affected for six months! So much, then, for the influence of business school finance departments at that time. CAPM and perfect capital markets did not command the respect they do now. Today, something like a consensus is emerging on the intellectual issues in this area – for example, the approach to the required cost of capital – to no little extent prompted by regulators' needs when price controls loom up.

My first point is, then, that the basis for laying practical incentive system of control, expressed in RPI−X as a particular form, takes time and mutual effort on each side of the regulatory relationship. The general opinion now is that the Government imposed too lax X's in the respective first periods of price control, for several imputed motives. However that might be, my own experience suggests that the basis for anything which would remotely satisfy present critics was simply not there. In effect, the present methods of supporting an *ex-ante* view of prices – a critique of company plans based on comparators and/or simulation of what is judged to be an efficient company's cash needs – have had to evolve, and the pace has not been even across utilities. I would claim that the principal focus of this forward-looking effort has to be expenditure, or, in other words, cash-flow oriented, for reasons I shall spell out shortly.

However, another necessary building block has had to be formed from the initial hand the regulators were dealt. This stems from the fact that effective regulation, UK style, depends on separation of contestable from non-contestable activities (or potentially competitive or natural monopoly elements, if you prefer). Unless price controls can be effectively confined to the latter, regulators have difficulty in clarifying what the RPI−X 'bargain' – the target efficiency level – is, to say nothing of the tactical advantage to incumbents in bargaining when the frontiers for inter-company transactions are fuzzy. This is a quite general requirement, whatever the form incentive pricing takes. The ideal standard of separation and reportage this implies is, in effect, a ring-fenced natural monopoly where there is at least a shadow stand-alone company, with its balance sheet, capital structure, and reporting within the company to cash reconciliation level.

Often, with very hesitant steps, the utilities have progressed differentially towards this ideal. In telecoms, the ideal seems, still, remote. In later privatizations, the Government did indeed pursue separation, but perhaps with more concern to meet critics on implications for competition, rather than to pay closer attention to price regulation needs. In electricity, having 12–14 'comparators' is and was useful, and should be preserved; but there is still Scottish integration, and no structural separation of REC's businesses in supply and distribution. Even in water, where the issues were more clearly seen, there is still regulatory mileage in separating water supply from sewage in big companies. In gas, most progress has arguably been made, thanks to the restructuring after the MMC report. But it took until 1993 for this to happen, well into the second price control period.

So far, then, I have in effect been addressing the case for saying – 'do not expect a regulatory system to perform well until it has been given the time needed to construct the tools'. One corollary is, of course, that it is foolish to attempt a sophisticated incentive tango before one has learned, and is able to perform, the basic steps.

THE FORWARD-LOOKING EXPENDITURE APPROACH

I wish to turn next to supporting my assertion that the centre-piece of effective incentive regulation is the forward-looking expenditure as seen in future cash flow. As is apt for an incentive mechanism, it fixes the target. It is the necessary focus for appraisals for these reasons:

First for a practical reason. Outputs for model, however derived, of what needs to be spent have to focus on evidence about actual past cash outlays, then consider how they may trend in the future. The issues involved in assessment are largely economic. The application of economic reasoning to costs must be forward looking. In economics, by-gones are by-gones. Economists' conclusions here are always to do with options *now* available; however fancy the econometric work on past data has been, the application has to be translated to future conditions; hence an emphasis on 'avoidable' costs. In practice, this means forecasting cash flows.

Second, in practical regulatory affairs, there is a need to underpin principles for price structures with appropriate cash estimates. The principles should involve attribution of costs and, with joint costs, mark-ups. This need is common to both sides of regulation work, price controls and encouraging competition. In the natural monopoly areas, the influence of price fixing goes through to final prices, and the incidence of costs in consumption for various consumer groups have to be recognized. In competitive areas, rules for competition and dealing with conflict will have to incorporate views of costs, for example, as triggers for detecting 'too low' or 'too high' prices offered by incumbents and entrants. (In practice this centres on 'predation', for which both attributable avoidable costs and 'stand-alone' costs are relevant – again necessarily forward looking.) A consistency in the measurement of costs between the two areas of regulatory work is essential if regulators are to be effective. In other words, the forward-looking expenditure approach in both is required. Moreover, the main incumbent is typically a conglomerate. Insofar as it is necessary to predict effects of regulatory decisions on total company welfare, the adding-up process can only feasibly be done if all sub-businesses are looked at in a common currency. This is the cash flow which will be involved.

Third, whatever method is used to establish the target trend in productivity underlying 'X', the tests have to be translated to actual prospective expenditure. The principal need at a price review is to set the scene sufficiently far ahead to make sense of the main trade-offs occurring in utilities, namely the timing of capex and its substitution by opex. Hypotheses about their effects must be formulated in response to economic views of costs, though it will typically be engineers who propose feasible technical means to explore options.

Cash flows should, therefore, be the chief organizing principle of a regulator's activities. There has been a need for parallel development, internally, in companies since privatization. Businesses newly exposed to capital markets and other market forces have to develop their own information systems, various forms of management accounts and testing for commercial change. As the company gets better informed, so the potential relevant information for regulators is increased.

But the corollaries of a forward-looking expenditure approach do not fall comfortably on certain ears. First, the approach down-points distinctions between different forms of outlays. In a forward-looking context, lumpy outlays (capex) are just a dated cash outflow. The consequence is that 'assets' (embodied capex) have no special significance either. Assets in balance sheets are necessary, of course, to translate the effects of cash flow movements into financial accounts for company reporting, etc. But the tendency to identify 'assets' with the 'shareholders' interest' has not been happy in the regulatory context. Accountants are extremely uncomfortable with the notion that the shareholders' payout is not necessarily connected with what the books happen to say about 'assets'. Fundamentally, what shareholders subscribed to on privatization was to own a company which had rights to generate net income in a utility; they did not invest in 'assets'. The capital markets assess companies on their future capabilities to throw off dividends (cash) and add to the share price, convertible into cash by shareholders via the market. Trying to stuff shareholders' interests into the 'assets' strait-jacket has caused much diversion, but little enlightenment. This strait-jacket is particularly unhelpful in situations where 'assets' are in any case of much less importance, compared to operating expenditure, as in supply price controls.

The implication is that a price control-fixing episode is an exercise in forming and assessing a financial project, just as is the assessment of any business opportunity. So long as a compatible set of prices is selected to match PV of outlays, the company can be said to be 'financially viable', as required by all privatization Acts. But this is insufficient, for several reasons. First, it ignores what shareholders have already put up. From their perspective, mere ability to finance future flows implies that they are going to commit sums in future (the outlays) which will earn at the required rate. They will justifiably argue that they have money already committed up to the present. Moreover, punters rarely invest in a financial project simply to get their opportunity cost of capital, duly adjusted in risk terms. The idea of using an externally derived required rate in a financial project is to help investors select from options. These are standardized in a manner ensuring that different risks are recognized (e.g. by CAPM). Projects giving greatest net present values in excess of 0 are selected, with NPV = 0 as the rejection point. Stock market prices (which, by definition, refer to surviving companies), have a strong element of quasi-rents, values in excess of the minimum financing level required. Something must be added to the allowed revenue stream.

There is another important reason to do this, namely its possible effects on incentives which will, hopefully, increase the size of the pot which both shareholders and consumers can share. A regulator having the temerity to push prices sharply towards levels indicated by future financing requirements alone without reference to the shareholders' existing position, would be ignoring how incentives work in practice. Economists, because they are necessarily forward looking in their arguments, would normally say that such behaviour would indicate an increase in perceived regulatory risk, having effects on the future required cost of capital. No one has ever quantified change in 'regulatory risk' on required rates. This is a useful project for a university finance department, difficult as event analysis is. My own belief is that a far more important effect is psychological.

A workable incentive system which is entirely forward looking is an impossibility. Motivation to do well is destroyed by rewarding 'success' by snatching away the prize. Hence the principle of 'no clawback' is rightly stressed. Of course, this also implies attempting to measure the 'prize' to be preserved. In the RPI−X context, it is the gain, if any, made in the last period by unanticipated cost improvements (that is, not already defined in the previous 'X') which company managements have been responsible for. Here is another question to which regulators were not handed the solution on taking office. I add some ideas of my own about this later on. That the art is not yet very sophisticated does not mean that regulators and regulated cannot agree on what is a reasonable approach in this area, and judgements are in effect made now in the exchange between the two.

The parallel question is over what period unexpected efficiency gains should be transferred to customers. Something of a consensus among regulators seems to be emerging that this should be done so that gains in the last period are exhausted by the end of the next. This seems a sensible approach. I note that in making the two projections – attainable productivity gains able to be made by a competent management in the future, plus some rent of past efficiency which will continue – redefines the meaning of a favourite maxim that regulators do (or should) 'mimic competition'. The competition which is being 'mimicked' is not neo-classical competition, but Schumpeterian. The regulator is playing both the role of creating the possibility of earning innovatory gains and that of the 'perennial gale' of competition which tends to then wash away over time.

When the question of what to add to the cash flow to respond to the incentive needs is settled, there remains the final problem of how to settle the remaining zero-sum game. Some degree of freedom remains. Consumers can benefit if shareholders get less. Deciding on the final trade-off between consumers and shareholders is an unenviable, and unavoidable, task for regulators. To that extent, they do 'fix' market values of shares. But the process I have described cannot be said justly to be 'circular'. It is designed to set rationalized limits to the regulators' discretion. This is inevitable once real competitive forces are absent, as they are here, by definition. In practice, regulators value continuity, and increasingly stress predictable processes, openness and interaction with parties, all calculated to reduce regulatory uncertainty.[3]

In deciding this final trade-off, the history of how consumers on the one hand, and shareholders on the other, have fared is certainly relevant. Price trends and stock market experience will enter the scales. Here again, development of techniques will serve to narrow down areas of contention. Development is mainly needed on measuring shareholders' experience to cope with the fact that 'the shareholder' is such an abstraction. One thought on this: would a concept of a 'random' shareholder help; that is, measured gains and losses made by shareholders over whatever periods they could have held the shares? Then one could at least argue from some idea of total experience to date.

But a sense of proportion about the effects on consumer prices of these debates must be maintained. Regulators can affect prices through the forward assessment of proposed outlays far more than they can by varying shareholders' returns. This is why I have emphasized the organizational aspects of cash flow. Like the rest of us, however, regulators do not altogether relish playing the role of arbiter between consumer and shareholder. I sometimes think that the persistence of debate about this or that approach to 'asset valuation' is implicitly a search for the 'just regulatory price', to be given externally, to the relief of regulators.

To summarize my argument so far; establishing a forward-looking expenditure base is the lynch pin of incentive regulation. For regulators who deal with incumbents with interests in both contestable and non-contestable areas, even where clearly structured, it is essential to use cash as the process for adding up the likely financial effects on the group as a whole. Equally essential, it enables consistent views about pricing structure issues in both areas which can be founded in standard economic arguments about costs and mark-ups. Reporting in accounting terms is essentially secondary in the sense that it is required cash which should drive the results, not accounting conventions. If necessary, these decisions, based on cash, can lead to revisions in accounting methods, to avoid the charge of being inconsistent – as was levied against MMC in its refusal to make 'arcane adjustments' in the 1993 report. So, as long as the cash-flow focus is maintained, how one expresses the question of what to allow the shareholders is secondary. One can, as is suggested in the Ofgas Consultative Document, look at it as writing another cash line, along with future capex, etc. This merely makes explicit what is otherwise implicit. Moreover, it focuses the question of the trade-off between consumer and shareholder at the margin. Or one can translate the cash outcomes into accounting conventions, as the CD also suggests. The important point is the process by which the outcome is decided.

PRICE CONTROL FOR TRANSCO AND THE 1993 MMC REPORT

It will not have escaped your notice that what I have said is relevant to the current consultations set off by June's Price Control Review Consultation

Document.[4] I can assume that this audience will be generally aware of the approaches in the Consultation Document.

The issues I have been concerned with arise largely in Section 5 of the CD, Calculating TransCo's Required Revenue. The starting point is suggested as a long-term NPV calculation, perhaps covering 25 years, within which special attention is given to satisfying 'reasonable expectation' of British Gas's shareholders, and the difficulty of acquiring data on costs the further one looks in time. A further concern is added, about the implications of particular anticipated profiles of capex spent on revenue allowed during a forthcoming period, the first of which TransCo now faces. If allowed prices were closely to reflect the anticipated incidence within a given period they would show a perhaps unacceptably uneven profile through time. This is an independent choice for the regulator, because a long-range NPV calculation of expenditure is neutral as to when the revenues occur, so long as the NPV derived is the same.

Alternative ways of calculating the shareholders' interest consistent with an NPV calculation are presented. The first is to form a 'regulatory value' for the assets to be entered as a expenditure at the start of a period. The second is to assess a dividend stream to be added to cash flow on the revenue side over the years. These are discussed as to their respective methods of computation. The implication, from my remarks, is that the same underlying issues of incentives and distributive justice will have to be addressed whichever mode is adopted. There is no reason why the outcome, in cash terms, will be different, unless conformity with the regulatory precedents is recognized as a independent factor which should influence the results.

Most interest of course centres on TransCo's own response, in July 1995.[5] A notable feature of this is that, whereas, in commenting on the other sections of the Ofgas document TransCo could find much to agree with, the case is different when it comes to Section 5. TransCo does not attack directly the issue of whether forward-looking cash flows should be the lynch pin. But there is much in the discussion which suggests that they would be unhappy with such an emphasis. TransCo summarizes its approach in the area in five points. Of these, three are non-controversial, and incorporated in a forward-looking expenditure approach. Allowed revenue should:

- provide sufficient funds to finance TransCo's operating costs;
- provide a rate of return at least equal to the cost of capital;
- be based on a realistic forward projection of expected efficiency gains over the period of the next formula.

I would, of course, argue, as I have done, that the last point requires cash flow as the centre-piece. TransCo also says that allowed revenue should

- reflect the regulatory asset value established by the MMC and properly roll it forward to the start of the formula.

This is one form of calculating the shareholders' interests, and is obviously an option. The underlying assessment needs remain.

The real crunch comes with the third point in their list, namely 'to recognize CCA depreciation as a cost of consuming assets'. This cuts across the very purpose of setting up the expenditure approach, the essence of which is to provide a means of evaluating actual capex, etc., needs in the future and not to accept what is in the balance sheet. Past depreciation is certainly useful evidence about what may be needed in the future. But, to aim to 'recover the real cost of both past and future investment' (page 8) and, specifically, to reject using an estimate of future investment instead of the depreciation charge (page 8), is to substitute company for regulatory judgement.

My misgivings are reinforced by the way in which TransCo quotes the MMC 1993 Gas Report. In order to support its view that recognition of CCA depreciation as a cost of assets would 'build on the conclusions of the 1993 report', it quotes a passage (7.76) in which MMC is dealing with the question of how to express its approach in accounting terms. The important statement is made at paragraph 7.80, the summary of that section of the Gas Report:

> For the purpose of assessing the appropriate level of the price cap, we prefer to concentrate on two simple criteria: whether the future cash flows are adequate to sustain the business, and whether the marginal rate of profit is sufficient to induce the desirable level of investment, during the period for which the cap is set.

This is not a unique position for MMC to take. In MMC's South West Water Report (July 1995), much of MMC's work centred on reappraising the 10-year forward cash outlays, including rerunning itself Ofwat's analysis of efficiency (Appendix 8.3). 'Regulation of water undertakers is, as with other privatized utilities in the UK, based on the setting of a price cap (which) provides companies with the incentive to improve profitability by reducing costs' (2.59). It proceeds:

> the price cap approach cannot however be divorced from consideration of the rate of return on new investment, or, although this involves different issues, on existing capital.... The prices have to be sufficient to enable a rate of return which will attract sufficient finance for new investment. It is also necessary to consider what is a reasonable rate of return on existing assets and thus to shareholders, itself relevant in ensuring that capital for future investment can be attracted, assuming reasonable levels of efficiency.

As to depreciation, referring to the DG of Ofwat's common approach in this to water companies, 'in the context of our more detailed examinations...we based depreciation projections on investment levels and programmes we felt reasonable' (2.78). 'Depreciation' thus follows, not dictates, allowed cash outlays. This also seems to accord better with Ofgas's approach than TransCo's.

RELEASE OF INFORMATION

The question of using MMC's reports to support regulatory arguments raises what in many ways is a more important issue, about publication of material relevant to a price control decision. Despite the MMC gas reports having emphasized the importance it attached to the forward-looking cash needs, and regretted the inability of British Gas at the time to foresee its cash position more than 4 years ahead, the forward-looking emphasis did not get the prominence in discussion afterwards that it merited. I think a cogent reason for this is that critics had very little to go on to substantiate the concern.

All future impacts on cash flows – even for the 4 years admitted to be possible and, equally important, BG's own business plan forecasts – were deleted in the public version of the report on the grounds of commercial confidence. The only quantified clue as to MMC's concerns appear at Appendix 6.5, dealing with BG's accounting treatment of a replacement expenditure, which contains the estimates, 1993–7, of replacement and CCA depreciation referred to in Ofgas's Consultative Document.

Dearth of information about future choices is by no means confined to the 1993 report. It has been repeated in MMC publications in regulatory matters, as with all references. This raises acute problems of public interest. I think the cloak of 'commercial confidence' is far too freely used. The problem has worsened over the years. In a natural monopoly context it is inconsistent with the increasing ability of the public to criticize both regulators' and firms' positions which I have noted as a major gain for privatization.

Moreover regulators have rightly become increasingly concerned over the years that there should be informed debate, involving all interests, at a price review. The implication of my emphasis on the importance of forward-looking estimates of expenditures is that disclosure of information during a review consultation period should go beyond predictions about possible effects on accounting rates of return to the underlying projected expenditures. They should be given in sufficient detail to enable informed views to be taken and counter-views expressed. This is particularly important where competitors have a keen interest in how the computations affecting the future of competition over the pipes and wires are to be made, and so affect them and their integrated incumbent competitor. This is an issue which I hope will be dealt with in the current Gas discussions.

REVISING RPI – X

After the two summers of discontent about shareholders' and others' gains in utilities, it is understandable, and quite appropriate, to consider revisions to RPI – X. For Ofgas to raise the question in its TransCo's Consultative Document is a welcome initiative. I shall not pass judgement directly on whether some form of sliding scale or profit sharing is desirable, but try to draw out some implications for these from my remarks so far.

Ofgas proposes to build on the existing framework of RPI – X. It is common ground among all parties that the incentive properties of price control must be preserved. That means that the reforms, if any, must be accommodated in the forward-looking calculations. I have already said enough, perhaps, to indicate that much needs to be done to secure the basis for these. But I am also concerned about the fact that the stimulus for reforms was perceived gain by the company, not improvements in RPI – X.

A Windfall Tax?

This has given rise to demands for a one-off utility tax, to be applied some time in the future. This has merit perhaps as a money-raising device, but will certainly not improve regulation. Even as a proposal intended to mete out justice, it will fail. It cannot unscramble take-over deals, in which the sellers will retain their gains, leaving the buyers – who are always liable to give away too much to gain control – licking their wounds. If suspected of becoming a regular feature of UK utility operation, it will not necessarily dampen down efficiency seeking, but it will raise the cost of capital. Moreover, I think it possible that eventually some regulator is going to make a 'mistake' in the downwards direction. If so, there will be pressure to even things out by allowing clawback from the consumer. This would amount to engaging consumers in directly reducing companies' risks, which seems to negate the point of trying to enlist private capital into utility operation.

Sliding Scale Regulation

However, on the issue of improving RPI – X: the basic idea of the proposals is to anticipate net gains made by the regulated firm as a target, directed to an expected productivity/efficiency performance, presumably rather as now. Deviations upwards in the event will be limited, giving consumers more; deviations downwards will be limited also because prices will remain as set. This it is thought will dampen down, but not eliminate, the incentive properties of RPI – X.

To decide on what to allow for unanticipated efficiency gains is now performed by setting the regulated companies' experience in some norm of achieved efficiency gains and then, as I have explained, to make the gain into a quasi-rent to be passed on over a future period. The essential task is to sort out what has been attributable to management by eliminating the irrelevant noise thrown up in the last period. Regulators so far have done this as best they can, and would not seek to justify their answers to an econometric jury. It is understood that this is part and parcel of bargaining at review time, and companies of course look at the total 'deal' represented in the proposed 'X', not only the efficiency aspect.

To make an unanticipated efficiency gain the subject of a sharing scheme set in advance would place far more demands on the precise definition of the models to detect it. I think the main problem would be handling of the system as it will evolve over the price period. Logically, the regulator would be involved in a continuous re-running year by year of *ex-ante* scenarios to eliminate the factors irrelevant to management action – a very tall order. But to move the debate forward, I have two suggestions.

First, the 'deal' should be struck in cash-flow terms. This is a necessary requirement to link to the forward-looking estimates of expenditures. It would also do much to avoid the opportunism involved in reporting in profit terms.

Second, a practical way forward may be to make 'unanticipated' gain the subject of measurement at the time of a price review. One would seek to agree a set of indicators to reflect specific items involved in productivity changes. These would be derived first from physical measures which the industry and the particular regulated company have in common, and which can be given an anticipated cash-flow interpretation in industry-wide terms. A predicted physical interpretation of this would be set up for each regulated company. Thereafter, how each firm does can be interpreted in cash terms, against the progress of its individual physical 'norm'. This will separate the unrealized efficiency arguments from all the other unforeseen impacts on a company's experience.

But Stephen Glaister's warning, of a fortnight ago, of the influence of quality in utilities' performance is well taken. The issue is at base the question of trading company expenditures against consumer benefit, and he reminded us of the difficulties for measurement which different consumer valuations of quality imply. This has wider ramifications, not least in approaching the question of how to deal with failure on the part of regulated companies to spend the capex allowed for in the control. To pursue this would take us too far afield on this occasion. But I believe the priority of translating academic ideas into regulatory practice lies in this area, of evaluation of quality, rather than in devising ever more ingenious schemes which gloss over information problems.

SUMMARY AND CONCLUSION

My argument has run as follows: the RPI $- X$ incentive approach marks a fundamental change in the way the control of utilities is approached. The basic economic tool – the forward-looking estimates of required cash flow in separated uncontestable activities – has had to be constructed from a very imperfect start at privatization. This has required information development on both sides of the regulatory interface: companies and regulators. Substantial progress has been made, but much remains to be done to achieve a better system. Whatever position critics take, they wish to preserve the incentive properties of the controls. I have indicated important and needed developments in techniques, notably the detection of unexpected efficiency gains and rationalizing their dispersal to customers to preserve incentives, in which behavioural effects, as well as forward-looking inducements are important.

I drew out some implications of the fact that the regulators' task on this view is to evaluate a financial project when proposing an '*X*'. Accounts must be the servants, not the masters, of computation of allowed revenues. In the current exchanges between Ofgas and TransCo on the price control, I detected what I thought would be a difficulty, namely, the acceptance of forward-looking expenditures as the 'organizing principle for regulatory review', as I put it. I have also argued that useful debate will involve a much greater willingness to disclose information. On the question of modifying RPI – *X* I argued the case for learning more how to run with the present system rather than to set up more elaborate systems. However, the debate is well worth pursuing and I have suggested some ways forward.

Finally, because I have been dubbed the 'Austrian god-father' of UK regulation perhaps I should end by indicating where I think Austrian insights *are* essential to regulation, UK style. First, underpinning both sides of the regulatory tasks, price control and competition, is the Schumpeterian understanding of how profits are made and are dispersed; and, particularly for the competitive side, the Hayekian insistence that it is competition (i.e. entry, in the current case) which creates the information which both regulators and regulated have to use. Marrying these to neo-classical views of what is meant by costs is the main intellectual challenge now facing regulators.

NOTES

1 Lecture from *IEA Readings* 44: 'Regulating Utilities: A Time for Change?' (ed. M.E. Beesley).

2 The views expressed here are not those to which other Economic Advisers to Ofgas would necessarily subscribe; neither do they represent the views of Ofgas.

3 An important aspect of reducing regulatory uncertainty is the fact that, because utilities in practice have no foreseeable limit on their lives, the forward-looking cash flow approach must imply some recognition of funding needs beyond the forthcoming price control period. This requires an understanding on both sides about the future incidence of capital expenditure and its possible substitutes, within which the expenditures for the forthcoming control period can be set. In effect, this in turn requires a model to deal with such trade-offs in time, a technical matter to be argued between regulator and regulated. When the judgement is made, uncertainty about regulatory attitudes five years hence can be bounded by recognizing the amounts allowed into forthcoming control and those still to be funded afterwards. The regulator can never be bound absolutely to previous estimates, but transparency about the basis of the current

review decision will then be an established part of the argument next time round.

4 Ofgas Price Control Review: British Gas's Transportation and Storage: A Consultation Document, June 1995.
5 TransCo: Response to Ofgas Price Control Document, July 1991.

20 Mergers and economic welfare[1]

M.E. Beesley

Public policy should stem from the perceived relationship between mergers, including take-overs, and economic welfare. This should suggest whether government intervention is justified and what form it should take. The form and content of intervention is more important than is usually allowed in discussions of the subject. It should be seen as part of a total system of control; and the conditions for successful intervention should feed back into a consideration of the policy of intervention and its objectives.

THREE SOURCES OF CONCERN

What is the meaning of economic welfare in this context? It seems useful to distinguish three sources of concern, all essentially stemming from a potential increase in firm size from merger or take-over activity. First, there is the traditional association of increased monopoly power with higher prices and reduced output, compared with what might have occurred without the merger. This envisages conditions of demand and costs as actually experienced. Second, there is the possibility of what has now come to be known as X inefficiency – that an increase in monopoly power increases the likelihood that the best available techniques of production will not be chosen, and hence that higher costs than those potentially available will prevail in the market again compared with the situation without mergers, thus increasing the price the consumer must pay. For logical completeness, and indeed as a matter of industrial practically, one should also denote another category, which I shall christen Y inefficiency. This is the possibility that existing market opportunities will fail to be exploited to the full; and markets are not pursued with the vigour they might be. Thus, at least some potential consumers are not supplied. The X and Y sources of inefficiency closely interact in practice because one can hardly choose a different production possibility without affecting the product, and vice versa. The third possible source of welfare loss is the connection between increased monopoly and the emergence of new techniques and products previously infeasible, i.e. the relation between monopoly and innovation. Increasing monopoly, compared to a situation with less, may mean less innovation.

Clearly, there are potential offsets to these three possible sources of loss – increasing firm size may have favourable effects on costs, markets and innovation. (And we should add that, in practice, a government must go further than to concern itself simply with total welfare; who gains and who loses is also pertinent.) Thus, it can be argued that, in principle, policy decisions should be based on evidence about the likely effects on welfare of a merger/takeover policy, for the balance of advantages may or may not be positive.

EMPIRICAL EVIDENCE

Presumably, therefore, we would like policy to proceed from evidence relating mergers and take-overs to the aspects of welfare just defined. It is important to distinguish them partly because a different kind of evidence bears on each. Such evidence, in principle, again, should distinguish between different phenomena contained in the terms 'mergers and take-overs'. Most serious concern, we have seen, stems from changes in monopoly power; this in turn relates to market behaviour. Not all mergers or take-overs involve such changes; one could conceive of a spectrum of such phenomena ranging from the 'pure' take-overs, with no prospective effects on particular market power, to the exclusive merger of horizontal interests in a specific market, having increased market concentration as the principal feature. Seen in this way, many take-overs will be neutral in welfare terms. The evidence for welfare losses other than those arising from specific effects on market power is very thin. Thus, for example, the take-over bid aimed at asset stripping, but having no discernible prospective increases in market power, must be judged to have no potential detriment in these terms. Indeed, it is to be welcomed as increasing the general market pressures working in favour of eliminating the inefficiencies.

Turning now to the evidence: though studies of structure and performance have burgeoned remarkably in the past ten years or so, it is unfortunately very easy to demonstrate their strict irrelevance or tenuousness, for the most part, to our problems. Thus, the independent variables must include a change in firm size by amalgamation, and the dependent variable must be a good proxy for at least one of our categories of potential welfare loss (or gain). Most studies have been of the type where profit rates in a cross-section of industries have been related to concentration in the industries, together with other variables representing elements of industrial structure such as the height of entry barriers. The general result is a mild positive correlation of profit rates normally on assets with concentration. The dependent variable here imperfectly reflects our first category of welfare concern; it reflects the second hardly at all; and is ambiguous on the third. The relevant independent variable is not, strictly, represented either, because we are interested in *change* of monopoly power within a given industry. Also, most of the evidence is American, and leaves open the question of how far to attribute the results to the effects of relative firm size in industry (concentration) or to absolute scale of firm, so that there are difficulties in interpreting the results for conditions, as in the UK, where there may be higher concentration but smaller absolute firm size. (This defect is in principle remediable by suitable tests on US data.)

INNOVATION AND FIRM SIZE

The relationship between innovation and size of firm is rather better established. There is, it seems, a non-linear relationship in which research productivity tends to fall in the largest firms in an industry, and with very high concentration. But again, the dependent variable, usually some measure of research and development productivity, is not the same as a successful innovation. Where this has been tackled directly by defining the success of innovation – as notably in pharmaceuticals in which the recent work for Great Britain reported by the Monopolies Commission in the Beecham/Boots/Glaxo mergers report confirmed earlier American findings – the relevant dependent variable (scale of firm) is still a poor proxy for mergers.

So it is that considerable importance attaches to studies in which mergers and take-overs are measured directly. Two lines of attack seem to have been taken: before and after merger/take-over studies of firm profitability, and comparison of profitability of pairs of firms by industry, where one of the pairs represents low merger activity and the other high. A recent and well-popularized example of the former is given in a book by Gerald Newbould,[2] and the most important example of the latter is E.M. Kelly's *Profitability of Growth Through Mergers*.[3]

Both debunk mergers. For example, often it seems, impossibly high net gains are required from merger entities to justify the bid price. Merged firms do not perform well in terms of earnings per share even if they are good for shareholders whose directors resist bids, or where contested bids arise. But of course, again, the relationship between these studies and our welfare concerns is tenuous, to say the least. To name but some of the difficulties: mistakes in asset valuation only affect their use very indirectly; profits do not equate easily with X and Y inefficiency and innovation. At most one can say that there is no evidence that merger activity significantly increases producers' profits. Taking the mergers investigated as a whole, indeed, these studies are more interesting for the issues of who gains and loses than for the problem of potential effects on inefficiency. Clearly, the parties to the bids may gain or lose considerably, but many would judge that, if all mergers did was to provide widely differing outcomes to the immediate parties, such as shareholders, but little overall increase in producers' profits, then no strong reason for intervention in mergers exists. However, though the available studies do not help our problem much, we should note that the paired comparison method is probably the most satisfactory methodologically in principle, and could, were it pursued, yield possibly more significant indications for relevant welfare effects.

INTUITIVE ARGUMENTS

Meanwhile, with the unsatisfactory state of the evidence, we are thrown back on more intuitive arguments about the effects of mergers. A wealth of experience and common sense tells us that a prospective increase in concentration, especially horizontal, bodes ill for welfare, especially when, as in many mergers, there are existing plants, distribution systems, etc., in the merging entities. Direct competition is a better way of ensuring a spread of low-cost techniques and more vigorous marketing than is merger. Mergers, it may be argued, are principally sought not to exploit the consumer in the first sense defined above; rather the intention is to reduce an important area of risk. The increased market power, if any, will be used only in a defensive sense, especially if the looked-for benefits do not accrue. Potential market leverage, increased by merger, is thus a kind of insurance, valued for its potential. Where innovation is concerned, common sense would agree with the broad import of research findings which, to quote F.M. Scherer,[4] indicate little more than that *some* monopoly power is good, but very high concentration is bad; barriers to entry should be high enough to ensure some protection from competition, but should not be *too* high. In other words, there is a sort of Schumpeterian ideal market structure inhabited by four to eight companies backed by largish resources.

This is something of a caricature of the present state of economic advice in this area, but not much exaggerated. The general basis for policy now does not go much further. But the failure of studies to provide systematic evidence does not remove the need for a policy towards mergers. An important feature of the increasing study of mergers of recent years, including in particular the Monopoly Commission's reports, cannot fail to impress in detail, with the apparent general lack of economic planning by parties contemplating merger. With some notable exceptions, mergers are not, it seems, the result of well-thought-out corporate acquisition strategies. Little discounted cash flow or other rational aids to financial calculations are used. Few concrete plans are laid for the realization of putative economics, technological gains, etc. Still less are *alternative* partners or victims appraised. The average period from idea of merging to actuality is about eight weeks, according to Newbould. In short, the economic information flow used for prospective mergers is usually quite inadequate to support their economic rationalization. The bid situation also imposes constraints. A rule-of-thumb like 'only bid where the victim's price–earnings ratio is lower than yours' limits the choice of the victim. A defensive counter-bid must often be made with virtually no time for reflection. A fall in the price of the bidder's shares due to general stock market change, causing a postponement of merger, is not wholly correlated with the economic case; a merger good for economic welfare may be missed; and so on. One cannot resist the conclusion that there *is* a potential divergence between private merger activity and the wider economic good. Even the most telling *laissez-faire* argument, i.e. that 'good' management ousts 'bad' via the bid mechanism (thus incidentally giving some economic justification for financial rules of thumb which are based, if only indirectly, on proven managerial performance), loses some force when one considers that it is based on the notion that good management is a scarce commodity. The wider economic good indicates that the choice of *any* victim will not do; the scare talent should be applied where it will do most good. Therefore selection of the victim is important. And the area to which the managerial talent is to be applied *should* include those at present relatively invulnerable to bids, i.e. the biggest firms; so that the bid mechanism's scope is not wide enough as things stand.

CASE-BY-CASE APPROACH

Now, a natural reaction to the lack of general guidance, and the acceptance of the need for interference based on common sense, arguments, has been, as in the UK, to seek a case-by-case, cost–benefit appraisal approach to mergers. This is not however the conclusion I would draw. First, the Monopolies Commission experience has shown that an impossibly difficult task of cost–benefit analysis is required for a case-by-case approach. Certainly it is inconceivable that case studies could assemble the relevant evidence, including merger options not the direct subject of a reference, and interpret it in the time-scale required not to frustrate merger bids. Academic critics of the Monopolies Commission have been even more severe than industrial in pointing to the inadequacy of the typical analysis. But it is certain that the critics, in the Monopolies Commission's place, would have done no better. The task of economic prediction is simply too complex, the possible outcomes too many. Given the frequent lack of investigation by firms themselves, I think it unlikely that the Monopolies Commission, by having more investigation and time to investigate, can much improve on its own fairly quick collective hunch, even if that were practicable.

Second, any merger control system must have a trigger mechanism to check which mergers shall be investigated. This must be in response to rather crude *a priori* judgements, based on cumulated economic evidence of the type outlined earlier. If, as I believe, most mergers must be dealt with by the trigger mechanism in any system, there seems little to be lost by making the rules enshrined in it universal. Thus I would see no harm, and some advantages, in instituting in the UK something akin to the US Justice Department's merger rules, which are based likewise on conventional economic wisdom. The rules would be strict against horizontal merger, less so against vertical, and neutral for mergers not involving specific increases in market power. The economic reasoning underlying the rules would be at about the same level of sophistication and (necessarily) limited use of information as the usual arguments about 'industrial logic' which are used by their instigators to justify mergers. It is characteristic of such rules that they operate in established markets; they bear on the mature rather than the new market situation. Hence they are more significant for the traditional welfare concerns and for X and Y inefficiency than for innovation. Explicit rules about merging also have the advantage that they are reasonably easy to interpret from the merging parties' viewpoint, and are the same for all comers. (This is an advantage, that is, relative to the present merger policy situation, where a reference to the Monopolies Commission is only one possible outcome of a notification to merge. How, for example, can industry clearly interpret the recent conflicting decisions about reference of the Glaxo case to the Monopolies Commission and the Commission's findings?)

CONCENTRATION ON POST-MERGER ACTIVITIES

If, as I have argued, the highest potential welfare losses are likely to come from defensive action after mergers, then it would be logical to concentrate specific case-by-case action on firms' post-merger activities. Again, this does *not* imply follow-up studies by a control body, or instigating efficiency audits, or the like. These have all the difficulties of the *ex-ante* cost–benefit investigation, with the added methodological complications of controlling for alternatives in the before and after situations. *A fortiori*, the prospects of useful *post-hoc* analysis are even dimmer than for those before the event. Instead, I would emphasize the discovery and *consequential* punishment of specific anti-competitive actions, i.e. those in which a firm attempts to stifle *individual* competitive entry or expansion in its market. The distinction between action to defeat competition in general as against action to defeat one competitor in particular looks replete with difficulties. In practice, I do not think this is really so. Thus, if price cutting were the only evidence against a suspect firm, then this, being possibly interpretable as a market-wide effort to increase sales, would not be sufficient. But if there were also evidence of attempts to cut supplies to a competitor, or to foreclose market outlets to firms, etc., an attempt at specific harassment could be inferred.

This kind of inference, however, is best drawn by legal processes; the Courts are experts at assessing whether or not a group of actions is directed at a particular target and constitutes guilty conduct. If the responsibility is to be placed in the Court, there will also be room here for some improved version of the US Robinson–Patman rules against discriminatory pricing. The attempt there to ground these rules in the differences of costs of supplying to different customers has led to notorious paradoxes, where effective competition is stifled. But there is a case for the addition of price discrimination to the list of possibly objectionable acts which, taken together, might constitute illegal harassment. One might well also borrow from the US the feature of liability of incurring triple damages, payable to the injured party, arising from conviction under laws of harassment. The reason for this is essentially that an effective system of control depends on making certain lines of conduct very high-cost ones, and therefore liable to be avoided by those formulating firms' post-merger policies. Whether actions are made criminal is secondary. The best deterrent to objectionable actions is removing the 'insurance' given to merging by enhanced chances of defensive action. 'Better' private merger decisions will thus be promoted.

To sum up: one must be modest in ambitions to underpin and operate a merger policy. The market process of take-over should not be discouraged *per se*. The argument of this paper is for a two-part system of control, based on general economic argument, and run with a weather eye open for practical operations, as a system likely to lessen uncertainty for the controlled, and be feasible to manage for the controller. As presented, it will have one obvious drawback to some: it involves extending the ambit of the Courts to embrace one aspect of merger policy and removing that aspect from the present administrative area of competence. But I think that, in contrast to the fears expressed when restrictive practice reform was first mooted, the role outlined is a feasible one for the Courts. And most liberals will account the removal of action from the administrative to the judicial sphere a positive gain too.

NOTES

1 Chapter from *IEA Readings* 10: 'Mergers, Take-overs and the Structure of Industry', 1973.
2 *Management and Merger Activity*, Guthstead, 1970.
3 Pennsylvania State University, College of Business Administration Centre for Research, 1967.
4 *Industrial Market Structure and Economic Performance*, Rand McNally, 1970.

21 Abuse of monopoly power[1]

M.E. Beesley

INTRODUCTION

I deal in this lecture with one aspect of pro-competition legislation – countering abuse of monopoly power held by a single, or few, interests. This choice is in part because the other main area of the legislation – countering collective monopoly power – has been a central concern of UK legislation since the original Monopolies and Restrictive Practices Commission (now MMC) focused on it in the early 1950s. That area is rather easily aligned with European Commission procedures, a motive which has strongly influenced discussions on current reform. But it is mostly because, after all the brave words of the November 1992 Green Paper on *Abuse of Monopoly Power*, which I will call AMP, there is a good question of whether a mouse has appeared – namely the new measures announced by Mr Hamilton in April this year.

I review the options in the November paper, to compare the possibilities mooted there with what was actually selected. Then I canvass possible reasons for the omissions, stressing in particular the failure of the review process to deal adequately both with principles and the evidence on practices available to it. From this, I suggest a revised agenda for reform. I hope this will stimulate a useful debate in an area in which none of us can claim to be all-wise.

WHAT IS THE PROBLEM TO BE TACKLED?

Before embarking on the comparison, an excursion into some relevant concepts will be helpful. What *is* the problem with which we want regulation to help? By 'regulation' I mean at this point any means intended to bear on commercial decisions on specific markets, whether they be administrative or legal. Whether one means is more apt than another should emerge from analysis of the task deemed to be necessary. In practice, the potential task is to intervene in relations between an incumbent or incumbents and entrants and would-be entrants, entrants who will be wishing to expand. For convenience, I shall henceforth speak in the singular, to epitomize what is usually thought of as market power. The task is likely to arise in the following way. In general, I believe we may rely on Schumpeter's perennial gale of creative destruction to undermine monopoly.[2] Indeed, we have no choice; the vast bulk of capitalist rivalry happens in that way – and certainly before governmental processes can perceive problems which need to be addressed. The task arises where there is an established and successful incumbent, whose market position may be attacked. The possibility of anti-social behaviour by the incumbent is strongly related to the conditions of symmetry or asymmetry as between incumbent and entrant, and how these bear on each party's search for profit.

Symmetry, or lack of it, applies to each of the principal dimensions determining profit – revenues and outlays, which economists think of as demand times quantity, costs. In general, entry becomes more problematical (and of dubious worth) the greater the symmetry between incumbent and entrant on each of the profit determinants. At the limit, we have identical demand–cost conditions as seen by each. This is the set-up beloved of modern industrial economics, in which the entry problem can be reduced to a kind of timeless game between incumbent and entrant. To be sure, some deviation from symmetry can be, and is, explored, and with great elaboration. But its starting point – symmetry – makes the analyses of small actual assistance in our problem. The real world is likely to display a great variation in the conditions, and takes place in real time. The incumbent, by definition, is already *there*. The problem is not at the extremes of the spectrum of symmetry to asymmetry. Profit makers are deterred if they perceive neither a cost nor a market advantage relative to the incumbents; they will not trouble a regulator; they will not think it worth while to take the risk. At the other extreme, regulation is irrelevant; incumbents will be relatively powerless to affect the search for profit. So regulation has to inhabit the half-world of partial overlap on the profit dimensions as between incumbents and entrants. This, as we shall see, has important consequences for the possible reform of regulation.

THE GREEN PAPER'S CONCERNS

The Green Paper[3] was concerned with conduct aimed at potential or existing entrants, and the consequences of incumbent power deemed unattackable, and therefore requiring price and/or quality control. There was some unnecessary confusion between these requirements by referring to the first as 'anti-competitive' and the second as 'exploitative' conduct. The principal dimensions of an 'effective' system were described as 'adequate powers to investigate and remedy abuse' aimed at stifling competition 'in different market structures and in all areas of economic activity'. It should deter abuse as well as tackling detected abuses. The system should be clear and certain in its application and should not unduly burden business or inhibit entrepreneurial behaviour. 'There may be benefits in aligning this aspect of competition law with EEC law and the laws of other member states'. Respondents to the Green Paper were offered a choice between three options, the tests of which were proposed as:

- effective deterrence and control;
- range of conduct embraced; and
- complexity and therefore cost to companies (and to governments!).

The three options comprised:

- strengthening the existing system;
- a prohibition system; and
- a dual system.

Deterrence was deemed a function of:

- scope for private action;
- investigative power;
- power to impose fines for abuse; and the ability to order divestment remedies, or, alternative price control.

Range or scope was a function of the ability to tackle, respectively:

- exploitative behaviour;
- anti-competitive behaviour;
- joint dominance (that is, parallel action between incumbents);
- market power based on property rights; and
- the market share level at which actions could be triggered. The likely cost was judged in terms of conformity with EC or existing UK powers, and thus the weight of regulation burden on firms; and the costs of administration to be shouldered by the government.

There is some overlap between these dimensions which need not detain us; but a comment on the concern about the property rights is perhaps needed. At first sight, restraint on the use of these rights could be construed as a remarkably radical suggestion, considering the prominent role of property rights in explaining market power. It appears, however, that what was in mind was rather limited transactions based on land (the example given, which is already in the scope of UK laws, was grants of rights in land to be used in letting pitches for holiday caravans). The potential Pandora's box opened up by thus addressing a basic problem of monopoly power was not explored in the Green Paper. That is a symptom of one of the main limitations of the whole exercise, namely failure to consider how underlying barriers to entry could or should be tackled, which I shall consider, alongside other limitations, later. (I do not intend to open the box, either, in this lecture – at least not directly.)

Annex C of the Green Paper evaluated the three options, and do-nothing (the current system) on a 4-point scale from weakest to strongest. I reproduce it here.

ANNEX C

Option 1 meant:

- giving OFT stronger investigative powers;
- greater coverage of property rights;
- scope for the DGFT to accept binding undertakings in order to shorten investigation;
- provision for damages, and 'perhaps' civil penalties (but *not* private actions, as Annex C makes clear. These were to be reserved for Options 2 and 3. The proposal was to link undertakings with the point at which the Director General of Fair Trading (DGFT) refers a case of abuse to the Monopolies Commission (under the 1980 Act), that is, where the firm whose conduct is complained of has failed to concede to DGFT's proposed remedies.

Option 2 envisaged a wholesale substitution of the 1973 and 1980 Act procedures to mirror as closely as possible the Article 86 provisions of the Treaty of Rome. Prominent among them are prohibitions of specific conduct backed up by fines and appeal to the European Court. But Article 86's scope would be widened in the UK case to catch parallel action among a few incumbents ('joint dominance', now limited in European law to cases of common ownership or specific agreements). The Green Paper clearly wished at this point to side-step the present difficulties of dealing with 'complex monopolies' under the 1973 Act, by referring to a 'narrower focus than the sectoral investigations undertaken in the monopoly provisions' (page 9). Remedies would include divestment and price controls. It might be possible to have a trigger at a lower level than that (40 per cent market share) deemed 'dominant' under Article 86. Fines along 86 lines could be imposed (up to 10 per cent of turnover).

Option 3, the dual system, essentially added to Option 2, specifically to preserve, alongside the Article 86 derivatives, the present powers of MMC for 'in depth investigation', including investigation of close oligopoly. This would also bring in divestiture and price control as remedies.

AFTER THE GREEN PAPER

I will not go into the views expressed in the consultation, except to remark that collectively they are a striking testimony to the insights of the public choice theorists. Each interest – including regulators, general or specific, not only commercial and industrial interests – argued for the system most suited to its individual position. Its lines of criticism and its constructive suggestions followed. A wide range of opinion duly emerged, leaving the government more or less where it had been before the whole exercise, but giving plenty of scope to justify particular outcomes in terms of representations. In the event, Mr Hamilton announced, in effect, that the choice was Option 1 –

with some modification. He 'would build on the strengths of the existing legislation' instead of more radical action.

I wish to comment at this point on the three most important proposed changes, namely: first, stronger investigative powers, to enable the DGFT to establish more quickly whether there should be a full investigation; what these are has yet to be disclosed. Two specifically involve the Competition Act. The DG is to be enabled to accept enforceable undertakings before his formal investigation under the Competition Act, and in lieu of a monopoly reference under the Fair Trading Act. Breach would be enforceable in the Courts. This presumably is also to be a trigger for civil actions for damages. Also he is to be able to make interim orders under the Competition Act which would prohibit specified activities where a complainant 'risked suffering serious damage during the period of the MMC investigation'.

Thus the present two-stage procedure of investigation – the DGFT's and the MMC's, after a reference – was to be preserved, with the differences that the DGFT would have a stronger hand to seek compliance, both directly on seeking enforceable orders before his 'full scale investigation' and later, with respect to referring disputed findings to the MMC. Reaching the latter stage was to be made more formidable to incumbents because of the possible affect of interim orders during the MMC's investigation. The obvious implication is an intention to increase the DGFT's powers, in that, because the prospective penalties are to be higher, the probability of an incumbent accepting undertakings are also increased. One effect of this, as I am sure was part of the intention, is to lessen both the DGFT's and the MMC's burden of work. It was not made clear whether, as now, the DGFT's investigation would be published, but it seems to be likely that it would not. I understand that the DGFT's powers are to be borrowed at least in part from his merger powers, which do not provide for publication of his findings. Perhaps more significant an addition to his Competition Act armoury is the power to negotiate specific changes in behaviour by the incumbent in lieu of a reference to MMC.

What was not spelled out was the nature of the undertakings the DGFT was to be able to require. His powers in mergers stem principally from the ability to negotiate a modification of a proposed merger, in particular by persuading the parties to divest that part of their joint activities liable substantially to increase market power. This ability to negotiate divestment does not sound like a mouse. But, as applied to suspected AMP, it is surely too much of a steam-hammer to be wielded without a full MMC investigation. One of the conveniences of these proposals is that, as again I understand it, they can be incorporated in the forthcoming deregulation bill. This is convenient, especially in view of the fact that, thanks to pressure on Parliamentary slots, one could not reasonably expect new legislation to deal with the whole pro-competitive area at least for the next (1994–5) session of Parliament.

So now we have collected at least three items calculated to provoke discussion: If indeed there is to be a significant increase in the DGFT's influence, is there to be a commensurate increase in accountability to balance it? Maybe this, however, will also be dealt with under the bill. (Perhaps someone will tell us!) Second, we have what some would regard as the paradoxical position that legislation on Restrictive Trade Practices is to be delayed, while some reform of dealing with abuse is given priority. Perhaps Sir Gordon Borrie was aware of this in his recent urgent plea to get moving on the former. But I wish at this point to concentrate on a third question – has enough been proposed for dealing with AMP?

THE GREEN PAPER'S VERDICT

As we saw, the announcement sticks closely to Option 1, so the Green Paper verdict on the Government's response to its concerns has already been given, in effect, in Annex C. As we can see, on deterrence and scope of power, Option 3 dominated Option 2 in the ranking. Option 1 is deemed 'fairly weak' on deterrence, 3 is strongest. The scope of 2 and 3 is identical. Option 1 is clear in its expected operation; Option 3 is 'uncertain initially' here. So the Green Paper's *ex-ante* verdict must have been that the choice for Option 1 trades off better deterrence in favour of saving costs of operation, including that of reducing regulatory uncertainty, which would be relevant mainly in the short run. Specifically, more complicated overlaps between UK and EC powers and increase in the 'regulatory burden' on firms would be avoided.

There was to be, it seems, no new help to private actions beyond that which could follow breach of undertakings, and no fines which would follow prohibition of nominated, but there would be 'illustrative' items of conduct, such as those emerging under EEC case law, as in the Green Paper's Options 2 and 3. These are the familiar themes of objectionable conduct which, by now, include discriminatory pricing, fidelity rebates, oppressive discount policies, predatory pricing, tie-in pricing, and withholding supplies, as found in particular commercial situations. The ground for rejection of prohibition was given as the difficulty of assessing in advance what will be regarded as anti-competitive, and what is acceptable, behaviour. Also 'a prohibition would bite on fewer market situations than our present legislation'. The latter point was unfair to Green Paper Option 3, which would not, like 2, leave everything to an EEC look-alike.

Thus, the obvious question about what is intended which is raised by the Green Paper's analysis is the rejection of its emphasis on deterrence. But the prior question must be – what was conspicuously missing from the Green Paper's analysis in the first place, and what lessons, if any, should have emerged? My own problems with the Green Paper were its failure to start with the fundamentals of large firm power, and its failure to ask what were the weaknesses of the Competition Act in particular – weaknesses which are only very partially addressed by the DGFT's proposed new powers. It also failed to take on board the question of altering company behaviour in the area I have defined as critical, namely what to do (if anything) when there is considerable, but not too much, asymmetry of conditions facing the incumbent and entrant. The characteristic beliefs of incumbents in these situations will be that, on the demand side, there are no worthwhile unexpected Y inefficiencies they have neglected, that is, entry to the market must be rivalrous, and seriously damage profit prospects, and, on the cost side, a firm disbelief in the possibility of X inefficiency. Entrants will tend to believe the opposite. The competitive public interest question is – will intervention to increase the probability of entry be beneficial, net, to consumers?

COMPLEMENTING THE GREEN PAPER'S ANALYSIS

Most of us, I think, assent to the view that the essence of incumbent power is entry barriers, ranging over a vast array of possibilities, from unique property rights, and government regulation, to those immediately affecting the incumbents' costs, and in particular sunk costs which entrants may have to face, but incumbents do not. A 'barrier to entry' denotes a particular condition of asymmetry between incumbents and entrants, favourable to the former. Correspondingly, an aim of creating more competition should address the question of whether, and how, the barriers can be lowered – while, of course, at the same time taking on board the reality that the new competitors, too, will require their own means of defending, for a suitable time, the quasi-rents which induce them to enter. Obviously one way to encourage entry (depending on the entrant's own needs for defence) is to lower the barriers. The scope for general competition authorities to do this unilaterally is often quite narrow – so much depends on other legislation, other sponsoring Departments, etc., and will often require primary legislation. In practice, the need is for a regular review of legislative and other entry barriers as revealed in monopoly cases, so that suitable pressures to reform can be mounted. (The scope is rather wider for utility regulators, who can do more to negotiate to alter the rules set out in licences or authorizations; but they too in the end will hit the buffer of the needs for primary legislation if they wish to do more than use the licence that mechanism allows.)

The scope for conduct amounting itself to a barrier for newcomers depends on the underlying asymmetry of rights. The potential use of conduct by an incumbent to create a barrier is by acquiring a reputation for behaviour which will sacrifice his profit. If this is not backed by underlying barriers of other kinds, this reputation will not survive long as a barrier itself.[4] The more important possibility is making use of that part of the entry conditions which are common, in order to deter those which are not. It is clear then that, in the real world, judgements about what is, and what is not, likely to affect entry by prohibition of aspects of conduct is a very nice one, calling for a good deal of expertise and commercial knowledge in working out what will be its effects.

So far as this argument goes, then, the government was right to reject the idea of nominating forbidden items of conduct for prohibition in advance. It throws equal doubt, however, on the practicality and efficacy of any 'interim orders'. The snag is the proviso that there must be 'good reason to believe' in damage to an entrant. This is rarely, if ever, possible before a thorough investigation, which must be very exacting. If ever there are to be items of conduct 'prohibitable' *ex-ante*, these, I would argue, must emerge from a series of test cases, as they do, in effect, from EEC case law. There are, of course, also the familiar arguments for such tests more appropriately to emerge from a formal legal process rather than as part of an administrative process. Since I doubt whether conduct can be usefully codified in that way, I think the use of the courts is more important in other aspects of the overall problem, as we shall see.

The second failure of the Green Paper was to consider systematically where the Competition Act 1980 was weak. In particular, it failed to draw the lessons available from the utility regulators' origins, structure and experience. They were regarded, it seems, as interests to be negotiated with rather than to be learned from. The powers given to the specialist regulators (Oftel, Ofgas, Offer, etc.) in important measure stemmed from the perceived weaknesses in the Competition Act. In each case, the judgement was made that the Act was inadequate to deal with an incumbent starting off its privatized existence with 100 per cent market share. The objective possibilities of competition, and its speed of development, varied widely among the several regulators' industries. One might, for example, have expected the Green Paper to have given special attention to telecoms, where potential for competition was strongest, and the track record of dealing with an incumbent longest.

Telecom is a good witness to my thesis of the importance of asymmetry in entry problems. For example, though it has been possible to mimic existing voice services since simple resale was allowed in 1989, there is very little interest in doing so; there is little profit in it. On the other hand cellular, substantially innovative, grew rapidly. Cable operators can add their telecom business to an independent market, Cable TV. PCN offers are in the gap between Cellular and POTS ('plain old telephone service'). But all, of course, also depend on incumbent services, prices, etc., to operate. Here lies the main regulatory work. The big initial entrant, Mercury, which *was* meant as an intended duplicate of the incumbent, was in effect trying to substitute for what *should* have been done before privatization, namely vertical, and to some degree horizontal, divestment of the incumbent. A corollary of negotiating an entry of that degree of parallelism with the incumbent, was that a doctrine of subsidy for entry through favourable interconnect terms had to be put in place, even if covertly. The idea of 'help' for entrants in this way is very dubious. It is far better to rely on anti-trust principles to encourage competitiors. And we have to live with the difficult consequences of such a deal when further entrants come along, as Martin Cave's paper showed.

I think telecoms' and, indeed, all the other specialist regulators' experience would also have pointed to another asymmetry – that of information between the regulator and incumbent, and to a lesser extent that between incumbent and entrant about demand and cost conditions in the industry. There is no question in this respect where the advantage initially lies. It is with the incumbent. On the other hand, the regulator starts off with a clear, but virtually uninformed mind; the would-be entrant does not know, at the beginning, much in detail about whether opportunities along the demand or cost dimensions will be worth the risk of commitment. I come back to the problem of how learning could be made speedier later. Here, I wish to note that, more by happy accident than design, the regimes have turned out to be rather good – some would say too much so – in dealing effectively with the incumbent/entrant interface.

Partly this is due to the licence or authorization which the regulators police. The licence terms announce general categories of potentially abusive behaviour (undue discrimination, tie-in behaviour, undue preference for one's own ownership interest, etc.) but wisely refrain from being specific. Regulatory action is triggered by entrants' complaints. A recent telecoms example is reported in *Oftel News*, 24 September 1993, giving an insight into what is implied in running such a system. The incumbent in this case was Mercury, defending its MOTO service, which had its own licence. Complaints concerned: offering terms putting newcomers wishing to resell MOTO capacity at a disadvantage to MOTO's own direct sales division, unfair advantages in provision of handsets, and unfair cross-subsidy of handsets. Don Cruckshank decided, initially, that these were unfounded fears. But the striking thing for my argument is that all this took place *before* Mercury launched MOTO; and the manner in which, though prima facie, there was no intended excessive undue preference, more information for MOTO bearing on the entrant DSB's profitability could be and was exacted. The moral is – effective real-time intervention on behalf of entrants requires a continuously acting regulator able to decide promptly on the implications for both incumbents' and entrants' profits. But I find it inconceivable that – whatever its merits in the telecoms case, and these are undoubted – this type of action and its context (a licence attuned to the general needs of the entrants) would be replicated to deal with all possible cases of 'abuse' in the commercial world at large. The costs would be prohibitive. One should try to incorporate the specialist regulators' ability to influence company decisions as far as possible, in the general law.

A PROGRAMME FOR REFORM

So the lessons for AMP I would draw from the specialist regulators' experience are as follows:

First, that experience would have indicated the necessary conditions for exacting 'undertakings', the main innovation proposed for adding to the 1980 Act. Undertakings certainly work in the regulators' cases, but only because of the framework in which they are set – namely, of licences, with the credible threat of reference to MMC, which will escalate the possible disadvantages of not agreeing. I do not think that it will be practicable for DGFT to repeat the success he had when he was the Telecom regulator with the newly proposed powers for his present office. The necessary framework is missing.

Second, the regulators' and MMC's experience is very useful in indicating how relevant evidence in monopoly cases can be revealed. Much was made in the Green Paper and subsequent discussions of the need to strengthen powers of investigation on the EEC model. I would make a distinction here between the evidence of a kind conclusive, or nearly so, in itself (the 'smoking gun') and that which needs to be interpreted, often subtly, in a context. The first type is more likely to be found by the 'dawn raid' if collusion among firms is a condition of exercising power – that is, in Restrictive Trade Practices cases. There, as widely agreed, the additional powers will be useful. MMC (and the regulators) have wide powers to call up evidence, backed by sanctions they very rarely (if at all) have to invoke. Neither, it seems, feels that its present powers are inadequate. They consider, rightly, that the utility needs of interpreting conduct are adequately served by their ability to hear from all interested parties, and their ability to consider many hypotheses about conduct.

However, it is again true that the regulators are those who have to work day-by-day on the coal face of incumbent/entrant problems. It has turned out that in this work the burden of proof has been critical. The effect of general prohibitions in the licence conditions is, of course, to shift the burden of proof – to disprove a hypothesis about conduct – onto the incumbent. This mechanism notably increases information provision, thus substantially reducing the disadvantage from which regulators suffer when they commence operations. Again, I do not think the proposed stronger powers of investigation match up to this experience.

The important question here, of course, which always raises lively debate, is whether a shifting of the burden of proof to incumbents could or should be adopted for application in the general competition laws. I think there is no doubt that if it is to be done, it has to be in the framework of a court, or the nearest equivalent. Since I also think the chances of a substantial shift towards substituting the High Court for present administrative procedures approach zero – desirable as this might be in principle – we have to look to the MMC still to perform the function of weighing up the evidence. To what extent, however, can the MMC operate more effectively without the formal framework that is available to the specialist regulators to evoke evidence? Here I must be careful not to fulfil the expectations of the public choice theorists by special pleading! I must say, however, that what has impressed me most in my time at MMC is the breadth and depth of experience the members bring to their task. I certainly view them as capable of sorting out the very tricky question of interpreting conduct in cases of entry asymmetry; indeed, they are probably uniquely capable. MMC's strength here really depends much more on its collective business judgement than on the economic analyses it prompts, though both are necessary. This judgement would be very difficult to replicate in the High Court. Thus I envisage more monopoly references for the MMC in cases where DGFT suspects abuse, not less.

But I do think a change in MMC's procedure here would do much to reinforce its ability to evoke the kind of evidence possible with the burden of proof upon the incumbent. I have in mind promoting, and putting earlier in an inquiry, the exploration of remedies, thus making them more integral to the MMC's learning process. It would then also be possible to narrow down remedies early enough to put them to the parties more firmly, inviting more and richer arguments in rebuttal where the incumbent (or incumbents) disagree. The Commission's final proposal – and its wider observations on matters affecting entry – would be the more effective.[5]

I pointed also to the asymmetry of information as between incumbent and entrant. In a practical case, reducing this is critical to an entrant's profit calculations. I do not refer here to a knowledge of the incumbent's intentions. In a competitive economy, each actor is entitled to keep his own counsel about strategy. The need for correcting the imbalance is simply overcoming the problem that the incumbent *is* largely the industry, holding extremely valuable data in assessing its potential. There is a need to tackle this which goes to the wider problem of disclosure of commercial information. In the UK, as in EEC, far too much weight is put on so-called protection of commercially sensitive material. And it is no better than it used to be. It may well be true, for example, that the numbers of blanks in the average MMC published report has grown over time. (Utility regulators are no less bound by the current conventions.) To pursue this line would take us too far afield; no doubt a complex cost–benefit calculation would be argued for. But it should certainly not be ignored – as it was – in the context of reforming competition law.

PENALTIES AND COMPENSATION

Discussions of the Green Paper are much exercised by the perceived need to strengthen financial penalties on the wrong-doer and, to a lesser extent, on the need for the 'victim' of abuse to get financial compensation. These ideas were dropped in Mr Hamilton's statement. It may be that the drafters of the Green Papers were over-impressed by the experience in the Competition Acts' operation, which was heavily weighted by the crop of predation cases involving the bus industry. These certainly highlighted the possibility of losses to small entrants via incumbent reaction to entry. They also, however, aptly illustrated the point that alleged predation is difficult not only to demonstrate but that a long time must elapse before the consequences of the conduct complained of can be shown. In particular, in the referred cases, MMC accepted the OFT's conditions for showing predation, including the critical one that predation must be 'feasible', that is, shown to be profitable to the incumbent. Predatory behaviour in those cases was, in effect, seen as the incumbent's front-end investment for a later pay-off when, among other things, his reputation for attacking entrants would postpone possible future entry. The trouble is, of course, that in none of the cases was the evidence pushed through to demonstrate the pay-off. This would not only have been extremely difficult to show, but it would in any case have required a much longer history of incumbent action. Meanwhile, the unlucky first entrant might well be pushed towards bankruptcy.[6]

Since the decision was to drop prohibitions, the possibility of fines was dropped too. So was that of compensation for the victim of AMP. In view of my earlier arguments about the conditions for making appropriate judgement, especially ahead of argument before an appellate mechanism, that levying fines was dropped is just as well. One also has to face the objections of principle on the compensation side, namely that since the essence of capitalism is the possibility of making losses as well as gains, it is wrong to intervene to modify the process. But if one starts with the proposition – as did the Green Paper, which did follow a broad consensus – that more should be done to encourage entry (i.e. there is not enough challenge to incumbents in general), then it is appropriate to approach the problem of penalties and compensation more fundamentally; that is, through considering profit incentives.

At base, the consensus is, on the one hand, that on the incumbent's side abuse is not costly enough; and, on the other, that it would be useful to lower entrant's risks, specifically to hold out better prospects of compensation if failure occurs. I would argue that we wish not to empower regulators to levy penalties as a possibly abusive story unfolds, or to perform the impossible task of assessing what a fine should be in the absence of a direct test of damage caused. We should look to a more general means to do this. As a principle of fairness it must be applied simultaneously to both sides. So we are led to a system in which aggrieved entrants may sue incumbents for compensation. The appropriate forum is one in which the whole course of conduct can be reviewed, 'guilt' established or not, and judgement made accordingly. Such judgement is clearly a role for the courts, and in the UK context would have to be added to the administrative process in the form I have described earlier.

The snag is, of course, that as a deterrent/compensation system the costs and pay-offs to actions for damages are, at any one time, fairly remote. So we are also led to a US-style solution – the possibility of multiple damages. [It would also obviously help the possibly impecunious entrant if cases were to be taken on a no-win-no-fee basis.] I think that the UK's administrative system can very usefully be extended to add this weapon to the pro-competitive armoury. I have in mind that the question of establishing the facts about a case of abuse should, as now, rest with the administrative system, and in particular, MMC. An adverse judgement by MMC in that system, as now, would lead to the formulation of appropriate remedies within the administrative system's scope, and (I would hope) to trenchant opinion about the need for action, including primary legislation, to correct the underlying entry conditions. Also implicit in this judgement will be varying degrees of guilty intent. Quite often, damage is done unwittingly to entrants; often the fault, if any, lies more in the consequences of following constraints imposed exogenously rather than imposed by the incumbent, etc. Any of these may lead to proposed remedies, as they should, without raising the question of culpability.

But many cases do raise the question, of course. This is where MMC judgements are likely to be seen as fair, particularly if, to reach them, the procedures I have suggested are adopted. A critical part of preserving MMC's reputation for fairness is its manifest independence. It neither triggers nor influences its own involvement, and it has no part in enforcement of its proposed remedies. It was for mainly this reason that I viewed with alarm suggestions, as the Green Paper was being formulated, that MMC or its members should become involved in a fine-setting process.

The degree of guilt displayed in an adverse MMC judgement should in my view be the central concern of the High Court in which cases following the administrative process could be brought. I have considerable sympathy with the arguments, strongly expressed in the Green Paper discussion, that vexatious proceedings should be avoided. Accordingly, the rights to sue should be dependent on the outcomes of an adverse finding by the MMC. The court would always have the prerogative, when a private action is brought, of disagreeing with the precedent administrative judgement, but would be rather unlikely, I judge, to do much second guessing of a thorough report like MMC's.

Since the train of action following what turns out to be 'guilty' practice is likely to be prolonged, there is a strong case for multiple damages, say to the three-fold level of the US, if 'guilt' is indeed confirmed by the Court. I also have a suggestion on the Court's problem of assessing the losses to the plaintiff. The damage actually done to a plaintiff in the particular case should be viewed in the context of the plaintiff's net worth. What is established as a cash loss because of the conduct is a disaster to one entrant but a pin-prick to another. So in terms of its ability to pursue further commercial ventures the full triple damages would be payable to the entrant most harmed; simple damages to the least harmed. As this suggestion may well have shown, I am no legal expert. But I *would* claim that it follows the logic of bearing on the problem as a real exercise in commercial incentives. Once the system is going, the possibility of adverse outcomes and compensation will – as in the USA – become a normal part of corporate decision making. The desired shift towards competition will have been accomplished.

CONCLUSION

I hope that my own programme for replacing the mouse with a rather more formidable animal will lead to a lively discussion. I have concluded that progress in dealing with AMP depends on improving the present administrative process, while raising the prospective costs of AMP to incumbents, and lowering those to entrants. The MMC should be used more, not less, as in effect now proposed. Its own procedures should be sharpened to shift more of the burden of showing that conduct is not an abuse to the incumbent. More relevant commercial information should be made available. On the most neglected issue – of penalties and compensation – I would like to see private actions to claim up to three-fold damages, depending on the degree of culpability disclosed by an MMC investigation. The High Court, in awarding damages, should tailor them to the entrant's lack of means.

But I would like to close by recalling that there has been much discussion recently of the need for the utility regulators to aim to create conditions in their own industries where, having sorted out the problem of natural monopoly control from that of promoting competition, they can yield matters of the control of AMP to the wider competition authorities. My argument, in effect, has been that this will only become practicable when the lessons of their experience have been absorbed, and duly turned into reform of that wider framework.

As a postscript to the lecture and discussion that followed it, I have been presuaded by Sir Sydney Lipworth's comments that, in addition to my proposals, it would be necessary to change the law in order to create the ground for the High Court's decision. I think this could be simply accomplished by making abuse of monopoly power (with no further specification) as the offence, and providing for the MMC's prior participation in investigating a case as a condition for recognition of an 'abuse'.

NOTES

1 Lecture from *IEA Readings* 41: 'Regulating Utilities: The Way Forward' (ed. M.E. Beesley).
2 J.A. Schumpeter, *Capitalism Socialism and Democracy*.
3 *Abuse of Monopoly Power*, Department of Trade and Industry, November 1992, HMSO.
4 There is an analogy here with restrictive trade practices. Entry can be deterred by an agreement to deter, but this agreement will not last long without props based on underlying entry barriers.
5 Traditionally, MMC has proceeded by first making its enquiries, hearing evidence from the referred 'monopolist' and any other interested parties, deciding on the

basic question of whether the conduct that is revealed is against the public interest, and if so then proposing 'remedies' on which the 'monopolist' makes observations rather late in the inquiry.

6 One of the further difficulties in these cases was the active possibility that the conduct was supported by the incumbents' exceptionally weak bankruptcy constraint – especially where public owners were the incumbents.

22 Media concentration and diversity[1]

M.E. Beesley

INTRODUCTION

Concern for concentration of media ownership, and devising rules to deal with it to lessen perceived threats to the public interest, have been long-running themes in UK competition policy.

In contrast to the treatment of mergers in industry at large, the Fair Trading Act 1973 contains specific interpretations of the public interest in newspaper cases: such mergers have been subject to automatic referrals to the Monopolies and Mergers Commission (MMC) since 1973. In May 1995, the Government's White Paper on Media Ownership concluded that 'to preserve the diversity of the broadcast and press media in the UK', there is a 'continuing case for specific regulations governing Media Ownership beyond those which are applied by the general competition law' while proposing some liberalization of existing ownership rules 'both within and across different media sectors' in the context of extended regulation. The Government is contemplating abolishing 'the existing structure of detailed rules', substituting a set of triggers on ownership levels in the 'media market' as a whole, and sector triggers, which when actually or prospectively exceeded would mean the merger would be 'subject to approval by an independent media regulator' to determine 'the public interest'.[2] Thus, 'in the long term' the special treatment of newspaper mergers in UK law would be extended, in modified form, to other media. A separate Quango might be established alongside the other 'UK authorities', or incorporated in them.

In the light of the long history of UK competition policy cases, including the cases on newspaper mergers dealt with by the MMC, one might have expected such important proposals to have been accompanied by an analysis of why present concentration in media ownership and increases in it do represent a threat to 'the public interest'. The MMC, in newspaper mergers, has frequently made judgements about that interest. These may be summed up as the advantages of any prospective economies versus threats to the accurate reporting and presentation of views, and to the diversity of views on offer. MMC has also commented on aspects of market conduct, for example, in its reports on *Television Broadcasting Services* (Cm. 2035, 1992) and, in response to a reference under the Broadcasting Act of 1990, networking arrangements (*Channel 3 Networking Arrangements*, April 1993). However, since there have been no monopoly (as opposed to merger) references under the 1973 Fair Trading Act, MMC has not reviewed the fundamental underpinnings of power presumptively exercised, and the recent White Paper certainly does not do so either. Moreover, as the other contributors to this *IEA Readings* amply attest, there is good reason to doubt whether there really *is* an issue about media concentration; if there is, it may well be due *to* regulation, not to the lack of it.

This chapter begins by putting the issues in the framework of analysing suspected monopoly power. The practical question facing all governments, or their competitive policy agents such as OFT and MMC, is: What is the gain, if any, from a new rule or a rule change in terms of the applicable public interest criteria to be set against the cost, if any, also associated with the change. With respect to media ownership the procedure should be to assess the significance of proposed ownership changes in the light of underlying barriers to entry. Do these inhibit challenge? How may a change of rules be devised to affect the position beneficially? If action is found to be desirable, the 'change in the rules' can be directed *either* to affecting the conduct of the players, *or*, more fundamentally, to altering existing entry conditions. In the choice between means to the desired end, the power of competent existing competition authorities is highly relevant. If they are perceived to be inadequate, there is a case to legislate afresh.

Ownership concerns property rights. In the case at hand, 'media' means the transmission and receipt of written or spoken words, pictures and music, which is of central concern to the sought-after diversity in the generation of rival views and access to them. (I include music as an important vehicle of persuasion.) The 'media industry' or industries consist of a chain of production, at each level of which property rights are held. Proceeding down the chain, the principal levels are:

- *Copyright holders* of the property rights which are required to create and maintain personal incentives to invest time in developing new ideas;
- *Publishers*, including record companies, and makers of presentations or programmes, who are responsible for gathering and converting the views expressed to widely assimilable forms, or formats. There is a close link with:
- *Delivery systems*, which provide the means to reach audiences – for example, by hard copy, satellite, wires, telecommunications network or cable TV;
- *Receptors* – notably radios, TV sets, telephones and other means – needed by audiences to select among and respond to the views, including 'entertainment' as well as 'serious' productions.

Are there now significant barriers to entry at one or more levels? If there are, competition may be inhibited by vertical ownership. Otherwise, with no significant barriers at one horizontal level, observed vertical integration is due to economies in transactions. In themselves, such economies are rare enough to constitute an independent competition inhibitor.

The above formulation poses the question in terms of what competition is now possible. It outlines the *potential* for challenge. There is also a second question: How do the incumbent property-right owners *now* stand in relation to this potential? Inherited market power is counteracted only with a lag, even if entry is now free. Is there a reason for concern that powerful incumbents, if any, can delay entry for a significant period? If underlying entry conditions are likely to become less hostile to newcomers, there is less concern about present ownership and vice versa.

So the question whether a change in the rules will be beneficial is not only one of deciding whether or not entry is now, or is becoming, freer. If current entry conditions are favourable to newcomers, there is a strong presumption not only in favour of avoiding future interference, but also of dismantling regulation. But if current concentration is high, the large incumbent has incentives to use high market share to put further obstacles in the way of newcomers, so intervention may be justified. The distinction between newcomers' and the incumbent's positions thus turns on conditions of entry which are common to all market participants, and on the particular advantages of incumbency to generate barriers. But even where there is a 'dominant' incumbent now, one must be careful not to read too much into the present state of concentration. Market positions crumble much faster than is usually predicted, especially where technology is rapidly changing. However, government-based barriers to entry may not be so readily challengeable.

ENTRY CONDITIONS

Our contributors throw considerable light on the significance of entry conditions at the different ownership levels.

New ideas: the incentives

At the first level (investing time in producing and developing new ideas), diversity and challenge in intellectual products depend on the motives of the producers. In part, the inducement to such producers is to be heard, and in part economic. Rewards in the form of widespread access to the ideas and views put forward, in whatever format they are expressed, normally go hand in hand with greater remuneration. Copyright is the traditional vehicle to ensure the originator duly gets the monetary rewards. Dan Goyder points out...that, as means of communicating ideas have proliferated, so has protection for the 'effort invested in the creative act'. The range of material protected has increased, notably in computer software and data bases. The degree of protection afforded to literary work by the longest running regulation has markedly increased. UK law, in contrast to EC and US law, has also avoided making protection a function of judgements about 'intrinsic work in', or 'merit of', the 'creative act'. Clearly there is, as he shows, some danger that adoption of such rules will enhance this implicit censorship. But he also illustrates the tendency to reaffirm the rights of the original creator. And he shows the tendency to limit the manner in which a party further down the chain of production can build on the original rights to benefit from their purchase.

That there must be some exemption from competitive forces in order to generate remuneration (in the form of a 'quasi-rent', as economists term it) is widely agreed, and so is the proposition that exemption should be limited in the interests of diffusing the results of the 'creative act'. Hence, for example, patent protection which lasts only for a term of years, and the adoption of compulsory licensing procedures. There are very few 'barriers to entry' to creation itself, though there may be limits to the reservoir of creative talent because, for example, of the quality of early education and training. Since protection of the act of creation has, in general, increased, both by extension of rights and more effective means of collecting dues (as in performing rights), as Goyder shows, inducements to entry at this level have been improved, and there is little reason to fear any regression in the future.

A specific problem with media industries is that the means to realize the intellectual quasi-rents from creative acts depend extensively on the property rights held at the next level of production – the newspaper proprietors, record companies, radio and TV programme producers – all of which, to varying degrees, provide the means of dissemination and act as the effective gatekeepers of ideas. It is surely no accident, as Goyder points out, that the original 'Statute of Anne' of 1709 was propagated by publishers, not by their authors, though the latter were presumably content to see their intellectual returns increased. So the 'creative' person's practical course is either to agree to an agency relationship with the disseminator or to turn the quasi-rents into paid employment (for example, by becoming a journalist). Publishers have used the legitimacy of creativity to pursue their own search for further profit, from restrictions in book-selling. It is at the gatekeeper level that the contrasting public interest in both the protection of 'creative acts' and in competition to broaden dissemination tends to appear.

Goyder shows the ebb and flow of this conflict, in which rules about the balance to be struck are being worked out in a way reminiscent of older battles in another intellectual property rights area, that of patents. What matters more in the present context is what barriers to entry exist at the level of the producer. If the gatekeeping function is difficult to enter, there is a threat to diversity in dissemination of ideas.

Producers of formats and transmission

It is difficult to detect in any of the principal producing media types – newspapers, films, television and radio presentations – serious entry barriers stemming from the economics of production.

The most significant potential barriers are property rights giving control over the supply of factors of production and distribution and the size of economies of scale or scope, relative to the prospective market sizes. In newspapers, the succession of MMC merger cases referred to later reveals that entry to newspapers is not inhibited from the supply side. Printing is highly competitive, and whether national or regional newspapers are at issue, cheap access to localized markets is possible from any given production location. The traditional inhibitions on free entry upstream in labour supply have been undermined. In producing material to be transmitted by radio, television or films, the requisite techniques are freely available. Anyone with the ability to persuade capital suppliers can attempt to make output which will attract enough takers to pay back the funds. Economies of scale or scope are very small; they may indeed be negative, as the success of shoestring productions against the failures of attempted blockbuster productions shows. The MMC's report on Compact Discs[3] demonstrated the process by which risk capital is invested in production in advance against the hope of a large, if highly uncertain, return. It also found that a rather high concentration amongst the companies providing the downstream opportunities for marketing did not dull the competitive processes in production. Despite the persistence of artists' practice in assigning copyright to the record-making companies, returns to the artists with the better track records have tended, over time, to yield larger rents to them and to their partners in the creative act.

Traditionally, ownership links with the next level of property rights (delivery systems) has given rise to the perception that entry is difficult at the production stage. For the first 50 years or so of UK broadcasting and world-wide film making, integration ruled. The perception that integration is necessary is now, Malcolm Matson tells us, mistaken. But, at present, entry to terrestrial and non-terrestrial transmission of radio and television is limited. The reasons – and more important, the future prospects for entry – exercise Matson and Shew and Stelzer.

Matson points out that in telecoms and radio, the supply of spectrum relative to the technical means to use it, originally created strict rationing and associated licensing and incumbent property rights. But technological development has dramatically eased the problem. He also implies that with these 'wireless' processes the cost of dispersed rather than central despatch to serve the given market has fallen sharply. The prospect is for high frequency radio transmissions to become more economically feasible, even for such large users of capacity as colour TV. Presumably, rival networks built up with small-scale units for the most local distribution will become possible, perhaps borrowing from other technologies for the higher level links in the hierarchy.

Matson also stresses two-way flow use of the low frequency spectrum. Traditionally, radio and television (and newspapers) are means of communication from the few (gatekeepers) to the many (the rest of us). The costs of one-way have been far lower than those of two-way communication. Two-way capability affects the outcome in policy terms in at least two significant ways. *First*, if 'we' can return our own messages, we are enfranchised more effectively. *Second*, two-way capacity undermines the control of a given network. Erstwhile passive receivers can choose the destination and even the routeing of messages. In telecoms, where two-way communication is of the essence, this means the hierarchical, star-like system of communication, with the central owner/operator deciding on switching and routeing, becomes a more totally interconnected system with switching and routeing decided anywhere. The required logistics of operation no longer support the property rights of the network owner.

The prospect of challenge to existing network owners has also intrigued other observers of telecoms policy. In telephony, the most solid base for monopoly power has always been – and still is – ownership of the local telephone loop. Anyone proposing to enter the telecoms business against the established network must be able to offer, from the start, access to all connected to that network. The UK has, by common consent, the most freely entered telecoms market in the world. But 97 per cent of all calls still use BT's network, because of its ownership of near-universal call delivery in particular. The confrontation of a 'free' entry policy and the incumbent position centres on the interconnect problem – the terms on which the incumbent's network can be used: the conflict is even now being argued as an outcome of Oftel's December 1994 paper on the future 'Framework for Competition'.[4]

Developments in spectrum use

With respect to developments in spectrum use, were all players convinced that the alternative radio means provides an imminent threat of effective, nationwide local entry in telecoms, telecom policy could proceed on the assumption that competition will soon rule. Sub-conflicts, like the position of a national wire-based player such as Mercury, and the terms of competition between cable TV providers and BT, would then become much simpler to solve. However, uncertainty about the scope of radio-based competition, its further technical development and cost, mean it is officially judged that this simplifying assumption cannot at present safely be made.

As regards media policy, the prospects of telephone entry via radio are also important in determining whether the assumption can be made that rival radio transmission means are easily entered. Telephone experience is useful because the incentive to test its feasibility is so high, and entrants are free to do so. The way competition has developed in telecoms has meant that entrants have so far not sought to substitute for 'plain old telephone service' to fixed points, even though that still far outweighs, by an immense proportion, the more sophisticated add-on services which have proliferated in recent years. They have instead chosen to compete in mobile telecoms, requiring the capacity to hand on calls from cell to cell at high cost. Entrants' choices may change, depending on prospective profits. It is probably true, however, that the contribution short wave radio can make to building alternative media networks for two-way communication is too limited now to make a substantial difference to media supply.

Meanwhile, the impact of telephone policy on access to the media has not been helpful. The first effective rival entrants to the local loop were cable TV companies, sufficiently important now to be a focus of concern in BT's latest annual report.[5] Their entry was at least greatly helped, and perhaps entirely conditional upon, regulatory rules which bar BT from transmitting TV programmes, while cable operators could offer telephone service over their own newly-laid wires. If there were no impediments of this kind, no doubt the entry of BT would mean more competition. But the other side of the coin is that producing entry against an incumbent itself requires a likelihood of profit. This in turn requires that the entrant has his own form of at least temporary protection against competition. In the cable companies' case this took the form of banning BT from replying by entering TV programme delivery. This particular form of protection may well have been too drastic and prolonged. Nevertheless, without some form of shelter, entry does not occur. The incumbent's position *vis-à-vis* entry, and vice versa, has to be considered explicitly.

Importance of optical fibre

While impediments to entering broadcasting transmission are declining, Matson clearly thinks the most important contribution to freer markets will be the potential of optical fibre in terrestrial supply. This has always been regarded as a field in which there are great advantages to a first mover in supplying networks. As Martin Cave notes:

> ...traditional terrestrial delivery offers unlimited economies of scale (a zero marginal cost of extra viewers) within the reception area; it also offers an economy of scope (falling average cost per channel as the number of channels increases), through joint use of transmission facilities.

The same has been held to apply in cable provision. Though each household must have its own connection,

> it is highly plausible that the cost per channel of constructing a cable system would decline as the number of channels increased, especially as

the cost of laying a cable system is independent of the number of channels carried.[6]

With optical fibre as the cable, there is a vast extension of the capacity to carry messages at near zero cost; the initial cost of laying down is further spread. Even where applied to 'one-to-many' distribution (as in TV) and thus not requiring two-way capability, optical fibre, once laid and connected, offers a substantial challenge to traditional terrestrial broadcasting. Often the vision goes further, to think of a dominating, national broadband information highway, on which all will depend. But there are two reasons why what are essentially economics of system fill (adding extra customers) would not lead to natural monopoly problems – and to the allied question of which property interest gets the first mover advantages – thus foreclosing further entry.

First, how rapidly do average costs decline as customers are added? Virtually every economic activity has economies of scale and scope. The real question is how important they are in relation to potential market size at a given price, which must include all the necessary value-added items. It is significant, as Cave reports:

> the fullest study of US cable systems (in 1981) found that while the costs of operating a system did indeed increase less than proportionately to the number of homes passed, it was rather small.[7]

The advantages lay, rather, in falling costs per customer as more services are packaged and sold per customer. In other words, the conditions for increasing returns lie elsewhere than in transmission, a result which Cave found rather surprising, but which is surely better viewed as a part of Matson's vision of a very large variety of services subject to competing suppliers over the network.

The competing potential cost functions for the rival technologies – such as conventional and optical cabling, terrestrial transmission for radio and TV, two-way radio networks, satellite supply – appear never to have been systematically explored. The reason is partly the sheer complexity of modelling cost with appropriate market scale and value assumption built in as a feedback, as must be done in assessing business viability. This, no doubt, helps explain why those in a position to build the dominant first-mover position in optical fibre have not taken the plunge. BT, for example, has been notably equivocal, very largely because of its huge stake in conventional wires, which has drawn it towards the alternative strategy of digital compression (giving conventional capacity extended application).

Second, and more fundamentally, from the point of view of costs, the question is the absolute size of the transmission element in the average final price of output. If infinite capacity is cheap, then very many will supply it. Hence the proliferation of optical fibre networks in the USA for telephony, particularly in densely populated areas, but also in long-distance provision now entry is much freer in telecoms. Feasibility of entry depends, rather, on the problem of wayleaves – how to avoid having to create them. When the issue of entry of competing networks in UK telephony first arose in the 1980s, it was widely felt the incumbent's possession of all suitable telecoms wayleaves might cause problems. Would it not therefore be necessary to force BT to share? (BT itself, of course, sturdily refused to incur 'the technical risk' to its own system if such interlopers were allowed.) In the mid-1990s this problem seems to have solved itself. Even in longer distance transmission, Energis boasts of its low-cost optical fibre network, courtesy of National Grid's pylons. Wayleave rents are settled now by potential competition, not the exercise of exclusive rights. In practice, much of the attractive market (in urbanized areas, where the bulk of the population resides) has a rich set of utility wayleaves already, which can much reduce overall costs, even if not serving one's new network wholly.

Receptors

Removal of one potential bottleneck to entry serves to highlight the next bottleneck. The leading candidate seems to lie on the border between property rights in transmission and those in receptors (the fourth level identified above, . . .). It is the encryption required to be incorporated in receivers if exclusivity of reception-transmitted information is to be preserved. This, in turn, is a necessary condition for payments to be exacted from TV viewers for transmitted programmes.

Since much of the diversity which is sought in media policy hinges on providing alternatives to transmission not paid for directly by viewers, for instance, by advertising, this appears an important issue. But it is so principally because 'free' consumption of programmes at the point of viewing – either from the BBC or from backing by TV advertising – happens to have come first. Pay-as-you-view or subscription TV has still to arrive. By contrast, in newspapers, freely entered and open to competition, the paid-for instrument came first; then absorbing advertising lowered the price; then, finally, free newspapers funded entirely by advertisements entered, and are now able to give at least some additional diversity. All this happened without appearing, at any one point, to be a 'problem'. However, technical advance in newspapers is not likely to inhibit competition whereas there is some fear that encryption may do so. Shew and Stelzer raise the problem and Goyder's findings are also relevant.

A particular encryption device can become a source of restraint on rival entry, first by establishing the right to prevent copying and second by combination with a distribution system which promises first-mover advantage. The combined effect critically depends on how far rival encryption systems, which do not infringe original rights, can be substituted at similar cost. Goyder's discussion of developments in computer software copyright protection indicates that recent developments in EC law have substantially strengthened such rights; no doubt the same would be held were encryption rights to be tested. A potential policy problem is that such rights are deemed industrial property. Instead of falling into that category of intellectual property rights (such as patents) where monopoly rights are modified by explicit limitations, for example on duration and exercise, they are held without restriction as to their commercial negotiation.[8]

However, Shew and Stelzer are reassuring. Not only is present encryption supply 'highly competitive' but in the example of Videocrypt, the 'dominant' analogue standard in the UK, complaints are not about refusal to supply, but about the price of acquisition, which does not appear sufficient to inhibit rival satellite channels from using it. Furthermore, imminent use of digital encryption will not create substitute market power; the rival potential systems are many. The prices charged, even by a very limited number of successful suppliers, will not seriously affect the price of the final customer's receptor. Thus there seems no reason to intervene in the exercise of the property rights involved. Specifically, there is no case for granting monopoly and then applying rules for commercial use, as in patent law, because the required quasi-rents can be generated without such intervention, and rivals will limit their significance. Nor is there a case for using the general pro-competition regulatory mechanism which, as Goyder illustrates, is deemed necessary in analogous situations. At the level of receptors, policy can assume there is no important constraint on rivalry.

This review of the several levels of production indicates that, looking forward, there is little threat of damage to accurate presentation of rival views or their diversity, from commercial constraints on entry. Had the authors of the Media Ownership White Paper undertaken such a review, it would, of course, have been far more exhaustive than is possible here; potential means to create a future 'natural monopoly' problem might have been detected, unlikely as that may seem. More likely, present constraints on entry would have been revealed as the regulatory devices themselves, as in the restriction of the numbers of TV channels and the division of the country into franchise TV areas. These devices, our contributors imply, were means to deal with real or imagined past problems. They are no longer needed.

ARE INCUMBENTS A PROBLEM?

Even though the future appears potentially highly competitive, there may be fears that strong present players, reflected in a substantial concentration level, may threaten policy objectives, and that higher ownership concentration in the future must be avoided. The rationale is that, in particular, a powerful incumbent might be able to build upon existing market share to create new barriers to entry in the future, postponing the benefits of rival production and diversity. Incumbents, through their share of the market, will also enjoy an asymmetry of information about markets (present customers) which can be protected by appeal to commercial confidentiality. A more likely reason for concern about concentration is probably the political need to recognize incumbents as claiming special consideration, because of the costs of change. For either, or both reasons, economic or political problems in the transition to competition may be deemed to exist, requiring special regulatory attention.

The economic arguments do not seem well-founded with respect to television, radio and newspapers. In telecoms, there was, and may still be, a stronger case for pro-competitive regulation. But since the speed of arrival of competition is a matter on which different opinions can legitimately be held, there is always a difficult choice to be made. The bold course is to deregulate, and leave subsequent market relations to be dealt with by general competition law. A second course is to accept that existing regulations do deal with entry restrictions, and to attempt to ease entry nevertheless. A third course is to ignore underlying barriers to entry and to devise new rules to add to the old.

Shew and Stelzer take the second line, when they embrace the idea of auctioning existing spectrum, to organize competition for the scarce 'slots'. They describe this bidding as potentially 'the greatest fillip to competition' in broadcasting, to embrace actual as well as potential broadcasters. If it can be effectively conducted – which, given US experience in the cable TV industries, is uncertain – auctioning would certainly transfer monopoly profit to the auctioneer (the UK government in the case at hand). But such an auction would not only perpetuate the myth, if myth it really be, of scarcity; it would do nothing directly to attack the diversity problem. It would merely substitute a different set of broadcasters. There is, however, a more fundamental objection to auctions in the UK case, namely that because of the special status of the principal incumbent, the BBC, there would be no 'level playing field' among bidders with, for example, similar commercial pressures and bankruptcy constraints. As argued below, problems posed by the BBC, if any, must be attacked directly.

The Government's White Paper on Media Ownership[9] would add to regulation. It is regrettable it did not try to justify extended regulation by analysing underlying entry conditions. Because it failed to do so, it is not surprising that it did not embrace a strong deregulation line. But, in order to develop the argument, it is useful to accept its premise that new rules to trigger regulatory action are needed to safeguard diversity. Do the White Paper's proposals promise effective action?

The White Paper focuses on market shares above which a regulator must 'assess' the public interest, whether the level is reached already or by 'proposals for merger or acquisition'.[10] The market shares for triggering intervention are defined by a mixture of shares in media as a whole (defined as television, press and radio) and shares of these sectors individually. The triggers for the media sector as a whole (embracing all three) are defined as 10 per cent of the UK market, or 20 per cent of a geographical market embracing all three; 20 per cent of an individual sector – meaning it seems the UK as a whole – is also a trigger. Thus 'in the long term' the media will be incorporated into the body of UK competition law as it affects monopoly and merger. There may or may not be a specialist regulator: one option is to extend the OFT's remit.

UK competition law mechanisms

Effective action will depend partly on these triggers – how to define them specifically, and who they will catch – and partly on what happens to the 'assessment' when made. On the measurement of media markets, the White Paper does not back a particular measure. However, its candidates[11] are dealt with by Shew and Stelzer who argue convincingly for the 'hours of use or audience time of the media', as the White Paper puts it, as the correct measure. They effectively dispose of the White Paper's rival suggestions, advertising or consumer expenditure, and the British Media Group's approach.

Shew and Stelzer's results clearly set out the incumbent problem, measured relevantly over the media as a whole. Their results may be put in MMC terms as a conventional four-firm concentration ratio of about 61 per cent or, as in more relevant recent MMC practice, a Herfindahl index[12] of about 2,100. This would indeed be sufficient to 'cause concern' in the typical MMC monopoly inquiry and exceeds most analysts' trigger levels. But the significant point is the influence on the concentration measure of the largest 'firm' – the BBC, with 44 per cent of the 'market'.[13] Were it not for the BBC, there would be no concern at all over concentration (as conventionally measured). The next biggest firm, Carlton TV, has only 6.9 per cent of the market. So, the answer to the question of who the proposals are designed to catch is, in part, easily answered. The BBC, the only significant source of concentration, is excluded as outside the private sector. I come back to this important point later. But, meanwhile, it is useful to pursue the White Paper's position in its own terms.

Data underlying Shew and Stelzer's Table 2 show that only in (national) newspapers does one group have more than 20 per cent of the audience. News Corporation (embracing *The Sun, The Times, News of the World* and *The Sunday Times*) has 37 per cent, and the Mirror Group (*Daily Mirror, Daily Record, Sunday Mirror, Sunday Record, The People, The Independent* and *Independent on Sunday*) has 26 per cent. Excluding the BBC, the largest share in television is Channel 4's 10 per cent, and in radio Capital's 10 per cent.

The immediate main target of the White Paper appears to be the two large newspaper groups which, in effect, are put on notice that further mergers in the sector or integration into other media will be scrutinized. The BBC, because it is in the public sector, is not affected by the proposed triggers. TV rivals have too small a national share to be caught by that trigger, but might qualify under the geographical rule which is obviously defined (albeit tentatively) with the existing regional TV licences in mind.

The package, by raising the possibility of an 'assessment' and refusal, targets newspaper entrepreneurs, inhibiting their freedom to buy into major TV stations. Lesser cross-media moves will be able to proceed without this inhibitor. Shew and Stelzer's work demonstrates that News International has only 3.4 per cent of the media market and the Mirror Group 2 per cent. Their possible integration into TV must, therefore, be intended to be caught by the White Paper's provision that the regulator would have to 'assess' existing holdings above the thresholds, where the relevant threshold could be deemed to be the individual media 'sector'.

The concern about a maximum of (say) 7 per cent of the national media market (for example, Carlton) being added to the 3.4 per cent or less held by a big newspaper group may seem odd in normal UK monopoly control terms, especially when entry conditions are becoming freer. But how are the rules, in the context of traditional UK competition law, likely to operate? Specifically, how far will they, in practice, inhibit concentration change? The rules must be assumed to operate rather as in the past. They are an extension of the special treatment for newspaper mergers, where we have 20 years' experience and 31 cases to draw upon.

The newspaper experience

The record does little to explain how the leading newspaper groups – which are the principal targets for the new triggers – have reached their present market shares. If the control is competent to catch all significant cases, the implication is clearly that the growth of these groups must have been almost entirely due to their success in building up against competition without merger. What the control did catch was not the evolution of concentration at the national level, but many cases of shifts of ownership of regional and local newspapers.

The important point about a control is its limits – what does it not permit? Four cases of the 31 were found to be against the public interest.[14] In these four, as with all the others, the criteria considered were effects on accurate presentation of news and free expression of opinion; on employment and efficiency; on competition; and on concentration of ownership. The central grounds for rejection were, in effect, the issue of diversity, as reflected in concentration of ownership. The cases in the 1980s were strongly influenced by concerns of the 1977 Royal Commission on the Press, about local and regional concentration.[15] The nearest MMC came to a *per se* rule, expressing its priorities amongst the criteria, was in the West Somerset case:

> there are *prima facie* reasons on public interest grounds against any individual acquisition of a local newspaper which carry the process of concentration further.[16]

Two of the later cases took a less open and shut line, but still focused on the diversity rather than the competitive aspects of concentration. The very high levels of concentration found did not inhibit competition, but did threaten diversity. As the latest case put it:

> although there will be little effect, at least in the short term, on readers' choice of newspapers... there will be a significant increase in the concentration of ownership of newspapers in an important region of the country.[17]

In three other cases there was a conditional judgement requiring conditions to be met for approval.[18] Two of these again concerned local concentration; certain local titles had to be dropped from the merger. The other case should be of great interest to those who believe internal arrangements within companies can surmount the common ownership threat.[19] The majority of the group considering the case worked out a very elaborate set of rules to be attached to the consent centring on independent directors as observers.[20] Dr R.L. Marshall's note of dissent is a classic rebuttal.[21]

The newspaper cases indicate that the diversity issue will be prominent among the MMC's criteria, but that the Commission mechanism will be at best a mild deterrent, to rein in further shifts in an already extremely high level of concentration. Concentration ratios of 40 per cent to 100 per cent were frequently encountered.[22] The overwhelming impression from the 31 cases is that MMC judgements had little impact on diversity.

UK competition law practice

Moreover, even when the MMC has reported, whether there is consequent action depends on the Secretary of State of the day. The implications of this, and the degrees of freedom a Secretary of State has to avoid a reference in the first place, were well illustrated in the last newspaper merger case of 1994.[23] Though MMC made an adverse finding, and held that no conditions could be devised to mitigate the effects of the proposed transfers of ownership, the Secretary of State allowed the transfer, praying in aid sections of the 1973 Act which allow mergers or transfers of assets if he is satisfied there is a danger of a newspaper's failing because of its economic difficulties. This recourse is one of the main reasons why mergers involving major independent but financially insecure titles have seldom been referred. The White Paper on Ownership proposals will, in effect, embrace this aspect of the system.

That a regulatory system works as a minor brake on shifts of ownership is, in view of the findings about entry conditions, something of a relief, though it is unnecessarily expensive and raises questions about the accountability of politicians.[24] But a major doubt remains: the failure of present UK competition law and related administrative procedures to provide a means by which the principal assumption which should underly regulation of the media (namely, the conditions of entry) can be revisited and, if necessary, acted upon.

Because of its continued focus on acquisitions and mergers, serious consideration of what underlies market power may well continue to be bypassed. That is the province of the monopoly reference; in the case of newspapers no such reference has been made because, if it is recognized at all, the ground is deemed adequately covered by the merger provisions. True, the Director General of Fair Trading came close to having the issue opened by referring 'the supply of National Newspapers',[25] as noticed by Shew and Stelzer. But this was not an inquiry into concentration of newspapers *per se*: it considered 'supply from publishers to wholesalers' and from 'wholesalers to retailers'. It thus considered newspaper distribution, and was directed to a particular aspect of conduct ('practices in the supply of newspapers'). The MMC had to be satisfied as to concentration to required levels at newspaper publishing and wholesaler levels, and thus was led to downplay Shew and Stelzer's relevant points about what the 'market' to which newspaper ownership levels apply really is.

The White Paper on Media Ownership[26] refers to an intention to ask 'the regulator' to assess existing holdings above the thresholds as well as mergers or acquisitions. As explained earlier, this could provide the basis for assessing a large newspaper's proposal to acquire a major TV station. It could also be read as inferring that, in contrast to past practice, a fundamental monopoly inquiry would, if necessary, be mounted. But the power has always formally been available. The point of the White Paper is to bring non-newspaper media into the control. That the 1973 Act has not been used, for example, to explore TV concentration, is simply because when the BBC is easily the market leader and is exempt from such an inquiry, there is no point (and dubious legitimacy) in trying to refer much lesser concentrations, even though they might at some point technically themselves comprise a 'complex monopoly'. As things stand and are to be carried forward, we may never see a straightforward monopoly reference, even of newspapers, unencumbered by the rest of the mechanism.

But again, undue alarm about this is lessened because in newspapers, as in other media, underlying competitive prospects are found to be good. Three practices were complained of: newspaper owners setting cover prices, setting retail margins, and exclusive supply arrangements. However, the MMC felt it could not propose means to make competition more effective, except for a reform (minor in the context of a highly perishable commodity), namely, giving retailers the right to move supplies between outlets and to sell on to other retailers.[27] The central point is that the practices, which supported wholesale and retail margins to limited numbers of handlers in the past, are far less effective nowadays in stopping entry. So far as newspaper owners themselves are concerned, no-one doubted their vigorous competition.

THE BBC AND MEDIA CONCENTRATION

If there is an incumbent problem in a world of potentially free entry it must, as Shew and Stelzer demonstrate, first and foremost concern the BBC. In this respect, *Media Ownership* is a Hamlet without the Prince. The BBC appears but fleetingly in it. It says:

> Public Service Broadcasters will be included in market share calculations, but will be excluded from regulation because the government already has direct control over their ownership. (p. 6)

In other words, we (the government) will be responsible for the BBC's conduct, not the regulatory mechanism. The BBC is also mentioned (at page 20) as 'to be consulted over proposals to raise equity ceilings between an independent producer and a broadcaster'. The BBC is easily the biggest producer, so the Government's own incumbent is to be given at least rights of veto. How this is consistent, if it is, with encouraging 'joint ventures between public service broadcasters and private companies' (p. 21) is not shown. The reason for this conspicuous offstage player is, of course, that the BBC charter is being renegotiated. *Media Ownership* has to be read in concert with July 1994's White Paper on the future of the BBC.[28]

FUTURE PUBLIC POLICY TOWARDS THE BBC

Policy towards the BBC is David Sawers's principal concern. For him the central problem is how to end public broadcasting. He proposes that the BBC's licence fee should, as soon as the new Charter would permit, be run down, to a fixed timetable. The BBC must then substitute advertising, sponsorship, pay-as-you-view or subscription fees to survive. I thoroughly agree with David's insistence on consumer sovereignty and his strictures on the pretensions of paternalism; and he shares the other contributors' view about the capacity of markets to respond competitively.

However, the two White Papers suggest that the notion of continuing the fee is now firmly decided upon by this Government for the immediate future, with some effort over time to substitute alternative means of funding the continuing 'public broadcaster'. 'If the BBC services are to remain widely accessible, there is no practical alternative to the licence fee before the end of the century, and possibly for some years after' (p. 31). Though the BBC has failed so far in providing commercial encrypted subscription services, 'there may be other opportunities' for making money commercially. There is no intention to allow the BBC to be a competitor for TV advertising. Much attention is devoted to how to revamp the payment of licence fees (needless to say, a change of government would be highly unlikely to modify the basic position). Even more significantly, the Government used the 'recent developments in broadcasting internationally' in which 'new multi-media organizations are linking programme making, the provision of broadcasting services and the means of distributing them, whether by conventional terrestrial broadcasting or by cable and satellite' (p. 26) to throw doubt on its own 1989 policy of privatizing the BBC's transmission services. Here it feebly concludes 'it is not clear whether the audio-visual industry will be more closely integrated or more fragmented in the longer term' (p. 26).

A cynic might well conclude that since conditions for entry into conventional transmission's rivals are now easier, the smaller prospective quasirents have dampened the resolve to privatize! But there may, belatedly, be a recognition that direct government rules to regulate entry are superfluous in emerging technical conditions; the market will be more freely entered but the Government has decided that the BBC must be maintained as a large public sector operator. That would explain the 1995 White Paper's silence on the BBC.[29]

Retaining a large public sector operator is not consistent with allowing competition law to rule. To apply the full ambit of the 1973 Act, implies making the BBC subject to normal monopoly inquiries. Along with other public corporations, the BBC is exempt from them, though subject, as all public organizations now are, to criticism and comment on their conduct (for example, via the Competition Act 1980). Rather like the Post Office, the BBC has claims on public approval which severely limit the present Government's scope for manoeuvre in fundamental matters like privatization and phasing out of particular public bodies. It seems worthwhile, therefore, to consider what issues arise when free entry is combined with a large, publicly funded operator, bearing in mind the principal policy objectives of generation and dissemination of new ideas and enhancing diversity and access.

The prospects are for a considerable period in which the BBC will maintain its output, from a set income capped by the RPI change, substituting over time some of that revenue by commercial partnership ventures, where these can be struck. Substitution will be limited because of the inherent difficulties of allocating risk.[30] Also (regrettably in my view), BBC production of TV and radio programmes will remain integrated with transmission. My regret is because of the opportunity lost to expose the transmission to capital market disciplines via privatization, rather than the fear from effects on entry conditions which, as argued earlier, will become easier.[31]

In any case, it is doubtful whether hiving off transmission would greatly diminish the scale of the BBC's activity. Because the BBC is under no obligation to approach the standards of disclosure required nowadays of leading private sector firms, it is impossible to tell how much the BBC puts into the stages of production, the programmes, and how much into transmission. Even the biggest single source of information, the Peacock Committee on Financing the BBC,[32] contains no means to decide this. But the 1994 BBC White Paper[33] does say: 'The BBC has some 700 engineers employed on operating and maintaining its television and radio transmitters' (p. 26). This was some 20 per cent of the BBC's current full-time employment in 1994. The Peacock Committee gives, but for as long ago as December 1978, percentage breakdowns of 'total expenditure'. This gives 57.3 per cent to staff costs, 24.9 per cent to 'programme allowances' (artists' fees, and so on), 3.3 per cent to the Performing Rights Society and the 'House Orchestra', and the rest (13.5 per cent) to various overheads. If we allocate 25 per cent of staff to transmission activities, the rest to programmes and apportion overheads according to relative staff costs, we arrive at an overall split of roughly 18:82 per cent transmission to programme production. If these proportions are even approximately valid, and hold, the BBC would still be easily the largest single force in producing what is seen and heard in the UK, even if transmission *were* privatized.

Significance of BBC's continuance as large-scale subsidized operator

What is the significance of the large-scale subsidized activity for a diversity of views, and the range and quality of programmes? Views on the BBC's output have been strongly influenced by two perceptions. *First*, it is commonly held that faced with competition, the BBC is motivated to cling to market shares as a target, because of the link between that and its probability of retaining or increasing fees. *Second*, it is committed to raising the quality of output. This was, for example, the position taken by Hughes and Vines.[34] Much of the heat in discussions before and after the Peacock Committee was concerned with the BBC dilemma – how far to pursue quality at the risk of losing support for its preferred subsidized operation. What the Government has now done is to weaken the first motive and, therefore, the constraint on the BBC's behaviour. Normally, with public organizations, some *ad hoc* ministerial objectives fill the vacuum in giving the organization direction, especially if under financial pressure from the Treasury. Where there is no such pressure the organization substitutes its own objectives. So, in public UK utilities before privatization, because they were no threat to the public purse, what dominated production decisions was pursuit of technical excellence allied to views of what the balance of the public interest required.

BBC's 'Morrisonian view of public enterprise'

The BBC is the epitome of this Morrisonian view of a public enterprise – indeed, it is the last great bulwark of this 1920s idea. And its charter, when finally renewed, is most unlikely to shift this view. The current intention in the White Paper to make clearer distinctions between management and Board functions will make it more business-like. There is, for example, an intention to give the Board responsibility for appointing the Director General.[35] Otherwise, the emphasis is on retaining the governors' 'due impartiality'. The BBC's independence 'should be recognized in the new Agreement (effectively its licence), with the expectation that the Board of Governors and the BBC managers will take account of Parliamentary comments on the BBC's activities' (p. 45). As for selection of those to whom the public interest will be entrusted, the governors, there are still in effect to be '12 good men [and women] and true': 'The Government will continue to look for people with varied experience and backgrounds'. There will be no Select Committee approval of appointees – this is 'too political'. To all intents and purposes, there will still be a Morrisonian devolution of the public interest to a set of guardians. The outcome will certainly be welcomed by creators of programmes, innovative or otherwise; they will have captive transmission, not greatly subject to commercial pressures, as their show case. We can expect little threat to programme diversity, and possibly the contrary, from this prospect, for several reasons.

The usual worries about large subsidized activities are, *first*, that they represent opportunities for effective price cutting on the outputs they choose, to the detriment of competition, and, *second*, that they represent unfair competition in the attraction of inputs, notably productive talent in this case. As to price cutting, that there is, in some sense, a weak bankruptcy constraint in the BBC's case cannot be denied. However, since the total budget is to be so circumscribed, there cannot be 'a long-purse' strategy to knock out competition unless a particular line of output is targeted. Then one might indeed encounter the problem which followed deregulation of the long-distance bus industry (alone) in 1980, but which left the National Bus Company to pursue whatever tactics it liked. (It duly went for retaining market share in inter-city buses regardless of profit, because profits from most other activities, themselves heavily subsidized, were not affected by deregulation.) But one cannot see agreement in the BBC to a particular target area, to be funded at everyone else's expense. The governors would not find this consistent with their public duties. Probably more important, there would be debilitating strife among the professional programme-makers within the BBC.

As to 'unfair' buying of talent, of course, the principal effect of such large subsidy is (artificially) to increase the overall available supply of talent. This may be regrettable waste, but it is hardly likely to make it too costly to enter into competition for the talent. In sum, this particularly large incumbent is unlikely to be a serious threat to diversity; the contrary is more likely. The increasing opportunity for entry at each productive level will make it more and more a large-scale subsidized cultural centre, with an enviable ability to air its own productions. The natural question to ask is whether this should be recognized explicitly – for example, by merging the BBC licence fee with the rest of cultural funds. The Peacock Committee considered briefly the possibility of the BBC's relying on a national lottery for funds, but concluded that the latter was not likely to be successful enough. In 1996, this opinion might be revisited! But the die is probably cast.

The foregoing paragraphs pursue a different line from Sawers'. They do not deny it would be better if his solution to the BBC's problem were to be adopted – in effect, one of privatization over time. I would have added, following his line, that there should be immediate privatization of transmission and at least structural separation of television production and radio down to the requisite of financial reportage, an obligation which should be put upon the BBC immediately. But, given the Government's 'vacuous' White Paper, as he calls it, we are probably obliged to consider the BBC's status as given in the short term. The logic of freer entry implies that even as a large subsidized organization, it must adapt: it can no longer drive the market. Its significance will be more and more as an independent supplier of programmes *not* subject to the demands of the *existing* market-place. It will be a major source of innovative programming and views, some of which will strike subsequent market support, possibly large-scale support. This may well be an extravagant way of subsidizing cultural diversity and, as Sawers argues, be redundant in those terms. But it is unlikely to be a commercial menace, if governments follow the 1994 White Paper's intentions. Rather, the danger lies in failing to dismantle present regulations because of the Government's reluctance to confront *Media Ownership* with *The Future of the BBC*. On this, much hinges on what is being inserted in the new 1996 Charter, at the time of writing known only to insiders.

SUMMARY

To summarize, the argument of this chapter is that concern about media concentration is misplaced unless there are substantial barriers to entry. An examination of the four levels of production involved – using material from the other chapters in this volume – shows clear evidence of weakening constraints to entry, likely to gather momentum because of technological change and entrepreneurial response. It follows that concern about movements towards integration across the media is similarly misplaced.

It is logical to consider the existing incumbent position (the degree of concentration now) as an independent factor because of the possibility that strong incumbents could develop fresh barriers to entry on the basis of present market shares. This is equally improbable now, but there remains the need for a mechanism to review this possibility at intervals in the future. The most cogent reasons why the 1995 White Paper on Media Ownership fails to be relevant is its neglect of basic economic issues, and even more important, its failure to confront the commercial implications of the BBC's being easily the largest player in the media scene (a failure found also in the 1994 White Paper on the BBC's future).[36]

The 1995 White Paper proposes, in the long term, a substantial prolongation and elaboration of regulation, involving the present UK competition law process not, as economic logic suggests, seeking a way forward in dismantling regulations as no longer needed. Even arguing from its own premise of the need for such elaboration, its proposals are likely to be ineffective. There is a long and neglected history of newspaper merger cases, which suggests little substantial effect on concentration in either direction and, more significant, too much dependence on ministerial decisions to allow cases to go forward to, or take action following upon, MMC reports. Essentially this position is to be carried forward in the proposed regulatory régime.

Moreover, the proposals do not provide for an effective confrontation of future technical constraints on entry, should these emerge. In this the White Paper merely reflects the general failure of UK competition law to provide properly for incumbent market power. As I have argued elsewhere, this should be overhauled to drop attempts to prescribe and regulate that power only when it is manifest, as UK policy now does, in favour of measures which will greatly increase the prospective costs of exercising monopoly power, including far more reliance on private actions to recover damages for losses incurred, which could well be punitive.[37]

But a focus on regulating the private sector in the media industries misses the main point about concentration – the very large share held by the BBC, whose future as a subsidized, large-scale producer is underwritten in the 1994 White Paper. This prospect does not, as many have argued, pose an economic threat to other players. I do not disagree with Sawers's preferred treatment of the BBC, of a timed transition to private funding; indeed I would urge, in that context, immediate reforms such as the divestment of transmission and far more stringent financial reporting standards. But if the Government persists with its 1994 line (and there is no sign yet of a divergence in favour of privatization), the practical focus of further policy reform should be the present Government-inspired impediments to entry, notably in licensing networks of all disciplines including telephony, radio and TV channels.

NOTES

1 This paper was my contribution as editor to the book on 'Markets and the Media', *IEA Readings* 43, 1996, Chap. 1. The paper refers to other contributors' essays as follows: Dan Goyder, 'Copyright Competition and the Media'; Malcolm J. Matson, 'Digital Technology in Media Markets: The Consumers' Liberator?'; David Sawers, 'The Future of Public Service Broadcasting'; and William B. Shew and Irwin M. Stelzer; 'A Policy Framework for the Media Industries'.

2 *Media Ownership*, Cm.2872, London: HMSO, 1995, pp. 1, 2.

3 MMC, *Supply of Recorded Music*, Cm. 2599, London: HMSO, June 1994.

4 *A Framework for Effective Competition: A Consultative Document*, Oftel, December 1994.

5 'The main threat continues to be posed by other network operators [meaning Mercury, principally] and the growing number of cable companies, the majority of which receive financial backing from abroad.' (BT *Annual Report 1995*, p. 8.)

6 Martin Cave, 'An Introduction to Television Economics', in Gordon Hughes and David Vines (eds), *Deregulation and the Future of Commercial Television*, Hume Paper No. 12, Edinburgh: David Hume Institute, 1989, pp. 13, 14.

7 *Ibid.*, p. 14.
8 A similar position is emerging in the UK with respect to the Trade Marks Act 1994, intended to align UK policy with European, which has, in effect, strengthened Trade Marks as industrial property rights, while ignoring the question of whether there should be an analogy with the patent law's limitations on these rights.
9 *Media Ownership. The Government's Proposal*, Cm. 2872, London: HMSO, May 1995.
10 *Ibid.*, p. 22.
11 *Ibid.*, para. 6.13.
12 A concentration measure which sums squares of market shares, thus giving greater weight to the size distribution of firms as a whole.
13 See Shew and Stelzer's, Table 3.
14 The four were:

1. *West Somerset Free Press and Bristol United Press Ltd*, HC 546 (1979–80), London: HMSO, 1980.
2. *Century Newspapers Ltd. and Thomson Regional Newspapers Ltd*, Cm. 677, London: HMSO, 1989.
3. *Mr David Sullivan and Bristol Evening Post plc*, Cm.1083, London: HMSO, 1990.
4. *Daily Mail and General Trust plc and T. Bailey Forman Ltd*, Cm.2693, London: HMSO, 1994.

15 Cmnd. 6180, July 1977.
16 MMC, *op. cit.*, para. 7.18.
17 *Daily Mail & T. Bailey Forman, op. cit.*, p. 17.
18 The three cases were:

1. *The Observer and George Outram & Co. Ltd*, HC 378 (1980–81), London: HMSO, 1981.
2. *The Berrow's Organisation Ltd. and Reed International Ltd*, Cmnd. 8337, London: HMSO, 1981.
3. *T.R. Beckett Ltd. and EMAP plc*, Cm. 623, London: HMSO, 1989.

19 *The Observer and George Outram & Co. Ltd, op. cit.*
20 *Ibid.*, pp. 75–7.
21 *Ibid.*, p. 78.
22 This is not surprising if one is prepared – as some group members of MMC will always be – to take a focus as local as Eastbourne or Seaford (as in the T.R. Beckett case, *op. cit.*, para 6.23).
23 *Daily Mail and General Trust and T. Bailey Forman Ltd, op. cit.*
24 A theme explored by C.D. Foster in *Utility Regulation: Challenge and Response*, IEA Readings No. 42, London: Institute of Economic Affairs, 1995, pp. 135–39.
25 Cm. 2422, December 1993.
26 *Op. cit.*, p. 22.
27 Cm. 2422, *op. cit.*, paras. 11, 117.
28 *The Future of the BBC*, Cm. 2621, London: HMSO, 1994.
29 *Media Ownership*, Cm. 2422, *op. cit.*
30 The Treasury's idea of a collaboration is to remove all the risk onto the commercial partners that are paying for the higher risk they take, whereas commercial interests want the assurance of public sector backing to reduce their risk, without sacrificing profit.
31 The line taken here contrasts strongly with those who believe – wrongly in my view – that somehow one can eat one's cake (a publicly governed BBC) and have it (an expanding, commercially active BBC competing on level terms with the

private sector). The basic idea is that if one splits up the BBC, so that the publicly funded BBC is the sole shareholder of subsidiaries with the normal accounting requirements for reporting, that this isolates the latter satisfactorily. This is mistaken; a 100 per cent shareholder carries the basic bankruptcy risk, and all the problems of isolation remain. Proposals like this are normally coupled with a far too optimistic view of how governance mechanisms in the 'public' part of the BBC can be made more open to public influence than now, and, at the same time, maintain the public/private internal split. For a contrary view, see Richard Collins and James Purnell, 'The Future of the BBC: Commerce, Consumers and Governance', Institute for Public Policy Research Discussion Paper, 1995.

32 Cmn l. 9824, 1986.
33 Cm. 2621, *op. cit.*
34 *Op. cit.*, p. 49.
35 White Paper on the Future of the BBC, Cm. 2621, *op. cit.*, p. 53.
36 Two further official statements relevant to this paper appeared in 1995. In July, Oftel produced its response to the December 1994 Consultative Document, *Effective Competition: Framework for Action*, Oftel, July 1995; and in August, the Government's Proposals on Digital Terrestrial Broadcasting (Cm. 2946) were published. They do nothing to meet the needs for analysis argued for here. The context taken is still that of the 1994 White Papers. The tendency to look for more elaborate control mechanisms to go alongside increased competition is reinforced, particularly in the case of Oftel.
37 M.E. Beesley, 'Abuse of Monopoly Power', in *Regulating Utilities: The Way Forward*, IEA Readings No. 41, London: Institute of Economic Affairs, 1994, pp. 139–60.

23 Schumpeter and UK pharmaceuticals

M. E. Beesley

INTRODUCTION

This paper considers how Schumpeter would have tacked the problem of giving policy advice to governments about the pharmaceutical industry, singling out the UK government in particular. It would be impertinent to claim that what follows is anything more than Schumpeterian in spirit. Had he now been given the problem directly, we may be sure that he would have surprised us with new insights. He would, however, have recognised what follows as closer to his teachings than most contemporary arguments about the industry.

Fifty years on from *Capitalism Socialism and Democracy*, (CSD) Schumpeter would have been pleased to acknowledge too pessimistic a view of the longevity of capitalism. He certainly did not visualise how its international competition with socialism might go. From the viewpoint of this paper, we can assume that he now would have set the problem in a context of continued capitalist economic organisation. Specifically, he would have started from the perception that the 'perennial gale of creative destruction' was operating. That is, all firms have to conduct their affairs in the knowledge that whatever their economic strengths now appear to be, all, sooner or later, will be threatened, and many depleted, by exogenous changes in technology, organisation, shift in consumer preferences and the rest. One can safely guess that Schumpeter, taking the broad sweep of post-war industrial development, would have regarded Japan in particular as the outstanding example of the inexorable pressures on established positions of the 'new men'. As we shall see, there are difficulties in making this idea of generalised competitive pressure operational, particularly in a given industry context. But Schumpeter would have stoutly resisted any temptation to throw out the baby with the bathwater in order to make a problem more tractable.

Profits were at the centre of Schumpeter's general view of how the capitalist system works. Innovation of all kinds, organisational as well as research for new products and services, provided the opportunity to make profits. Profits, however are subject to decay from the activities of forces over which the innovator has no influence – the 'perennial gale of creative destruction' (CD) as Schumpeter called it. The latter is basically a function of that freedom to engage in economic activity which is also characteristic of capitalist societies. Entrepreneurs search for (or are given by Governments) commercial shelter to stave off the tendency for profits to dissipate. Among these will be patents, and any device against direct competition that firms can muster, including the whole gamut of devices usually thought of as anti-social, for example restrictive collusion and merger.[1] Thus, in dealing with 'cases', as he would have called them, of a particular industrial phenomenon, Schumpeter was working with two parallel ideas. The first was CD, always in the background, always strongly influencing firms' strategies. The second was the idea of prospective profit as a motive for action. Monopoly devices were to be seen essentially as alternative forms of shelter, necessary to yield a prospective profit. We can add that entry into an activity, where this was not itself innovative, had similarly to be profitable, or in other words itself anticipating some form of shelter, if only in the guise of first-mover advantages, as they would now be called, as for example in an industry which expands too fast for earlier incumbents to mop up all the demand. The famous, and for many devastating, critique of the neoclassical competitive paradigm in Chapters VI through VIII of CSD consists of *both* the assumption of CD and of 'monopolistic' practices as alternative forms of contemporary shelter. Indeed, with respect to the latter, Chapter VII stands up very well today as a first primer in investment strategy for individual firms – patents, secrecy, various forms of restraint of trade, long term contracts, and the rest, are all to be viewed as devices for keeping up the prospective cash-flow, otherwise likely to be dissipated.

Any government has to consider its policy in what is in effect a cost-benefit framework, which considers what will be the impact of change in a given policy instrument open to it on an industry's performance, and thus upon the welfare of the (usually many) parties whom the government feels obliged to consider. In pharmaceuticals, governments have characteristically thought of the pharmaceutical industry as posing a trade-off which they have to evaluate, namely that between the production of new effective ethical drugs, requiring considerable investment in research and development over an extended period, and the price of existing drugs. The connection between these is recognised as profits, from which the bulk of research and development is funded. Lower prices for the set of drugs now available, *cet par*, will reduce the profits ploughed back into research and development. Policy instruments may be brought to bear through effects on prospective profits. The most important of these in the international arena is changing the effective length of the patent life which a successful drug may have, a change that is correlated with profit prospects. In the United Kingdom a second important policy instrument bears on the prices paid for the current portfolio of drugs, namely the price negotiated with the industry under the National Health drugs purchasing scheme, the PPRS.

A common way to formulate the policy problem posed by Schumpeter's critique has been to speak of a 'Schumpeterian trade-off', namely the welfare losses to be anticipated from exploiting monopoly pricing versus the 'dynamic' gains to be anticipated from innovation.[2] In this it must be said that to anticipate any serious sacrifice from the 'exploitation' side of this is greatly to exaggerate Schumpeter's own position. His acknowledgement of such a trade-off seems at best grudging. He clearly did not weight the 'losses' at all heavily.[3] It would be truer to say that his attitude was that the burden of proof for policy intervention, e.g., in an anti-trust mode, was firmly on the proposer. 'If it ain't bust, don't fix it', better characterises his position. Of course, he never denied that policy choices do face governments, and would, I believe, have been quite content to think of their task as essentially arguing a cost-benefit analysis directed to specific proposals for policy change.

Had he reviewed the literature since CSD, the problem for him would have been that neo-classical traditions have, on the whole, triumphed. In particular, the essential CD element of his thinking, and indeed a determination to see particular industrial situations as the creation and defence of profit, has not been a central concern for economists since. On the contrary, most explanations of 'Schumpeterian' hypothesis have picked up the 'monopolistic' sides of his argument and turned them into standard neo-classical enquiries.[4] Creative destruction, and thus the fundamental explanation of what makes capitalism work has simply been dropped from the main stream. The CD process has been, rather, the concern of studies in research policy. A prominent example, bearing on the pharmaceutical industry, is Kenney's description of the rise of the bio- technology industry from 1970 as an independent challenge to the traditional organic processes (Kenny 1986). Also, the notion of a probability of success in research activity drawing from an unchanging state of nature, and hence a profitable exploitation, and, by extension, of liability to attack from other successful firms similarly placed has been used, for example, to stimulate the effects of policy changes on firms' willingness in R and D (Grabowski and Vernon 1987) and as an element in determining outcomes from trade between countries (P. Segerstrom *et al.*, 1990). But CD has not been incorporated explicitly in attempted judgements about whether intervention is needed in a particular industry. To do this some means must be found to (a) characterise it in concrete terms, and (b) to describe its past changes, so that some predictions, even if only simple extrapolations, can be made.

A 'Schumpeterian' policy analysis of the UK pharmaceutical industry would, then, have the following elements. First, one requires a description of recent changes in threats to incumbent firms' positions. The CD elements must incorporate all important factors incumbents will consider that their behaviour has to be adapted to, because basically beyond their influence in a manner which will be directly translatable to cash flow. These may be direct, as in displacement of sales; or indirect, as in increases of R and D expenditure directed to pharmaceuticals, but not under the control of incumbents; or latent, as in changes in prescribing habits of doctors (that is, change in what appropriate treatment is deemed to consist of); or substitute technology not in present R and D portfolios. Changes may be observed to go in either direction. CD can be more or less menacing at a particular time. On the other hand, we have a set of factors which relate to the incumbents' prospective and alternative shelters when proposing to invest in R and D and subsequently in marketing their products. Government's policies are relevant if they are capable of influencing these commitments.

In pharmaceuticals, the principal available shelter is patent protection. It is prominent because it is a particularly appropriate form of shelter where profits will depend on using research and development expenditure to discover, from a large number of possible products, the relatively few which will in the event succeed. Patents can be taken out on a large set at very low unit cost; but shelter will be available and potentially valuable when the 'winners' are defined. (Patent protection on the failures will then be revealed as worthless.) For the winners as for the failures patent life is limited, so the question of building substitute shelters will assume increasing importance with respect to given products, the winners, as time passes. These can in principle range from alliances of various forms up to and including merging of ownership interests to ad hoc agreements to limit price competition.

The second element in a Schumpeterian analysis will, then, be a description of how these alternatives may, at different times, be deployed and to explain why some are more likely to be adopted than others. The explanations are necessary when considering the likely effect of a government's policy changes on firms' actions. In response to a given policy change, firms will adopt the course that will most likely be profitable, involving a review of the alternative shelters which may be available.

The policy model suggested by applying Schumpeterian thought is thus for a government, at the time of decision, to predict future changes in the CD elements, which will indicate favourable or unfavourable pressure on future profits. If it wishes to compensate for these pressures, say to affect the prospective rate of drug innovation, it will consider policy changes affecting the 'shelters' prospectively available, e.g., by changing patent lives, or by action (or forbearing to act) along conventional anti-trust lines. It will, at the same time presumably consider, and weigh appropriately, the effects on the prices of the current set of available drugs. In all this, views on CD are essentially driving both firms' adaptive behaviour and the indicated direction of government action. The distinctively Schumpeterian elements in this form of policy analysis are expected shifts in the exogenous elements bearing on profits, and foreseeing what firms could do themselves to influence profit prospects.

This chapter therefore sets out to explore the possibilities of setting up such a policy model for pharmaceuticals. The information requirements are likely to be formidable, so it is hardly worth making the attempt if pharmaceuticals do not already display convincing evidence that a Schumpeterian description of the industry is a plausible one. Accordingly, the second section investigates whether the industry has indeed displayed symptoms which in particular show the outlines of creative destruction – challenge, decay of incumbent positions etc. Duly encouraged by the results, the third section considers the problem of predicting the likely direction of change in leading elements in 'creative destruction'. The fourth section describes how the search for profits is likely to work out in terms of the alternative available shelters. The final section considers the bearing of the analysis on policy issues important for the UK pharmaceutical industry, namely the change of patent lives proposed by the European Community, and the implications of the highly concentrated purchasing of drugs in the UK by the Department of Health and Social Security (DHSS).

I think there is also a highly practical reason, connected with the application of policy, for coming to terms with Schumpeter's thoroughly realistic view about the way in which profits are generated and protected, their source in innovation and their defence in shelter of many kinds, including anti- competitive devices like mergers and collusion. This involves an academic aside. The starting points for a Schumpeterian analysis – innovation and change – are of course very different from that adopted in neo-classical analysis, in which the method is to explore the consequences of deviation from an ideal, perfectly competitive industry. My own experience in the anti-trust field in particular is that while neo-classical procedures are useful, indeed possibly indispensable, in the posing of questions to put to participants in an enquiry process, the question of what to do to remedy the situation inevitably must address itself to the basic Schumpeterian question of how and why profit prospects for incumbents and potential challengers are changed by a given policy proposal. But I have to acknowledge that to adopt a wholly Schumpeterian stance involves accepting that analysis must be much more ad hoc and difficult. And using it implies forgoing the direct link with higher level principles of resource allocation which is the strength of neo-classical analysis. Thus before launching on it, one is, again, faced with a need to be convinced that a Schumpeterian policy model is really apt for the industry in question. Looking at past behaviour, does it strongly display the symptoms one would expect from an industry in which Schumpeter's view of capitalist development fits well?

THE PHARMACEUTICAL INDUSTRY AND THE SCHUMPETERIAN VIEW

This section considers the evidence for a Schumpeterian view of pharmaceuticals. Such a view might well run as follows: In ethical pharmaceuticals in particular, profits depend on generating winners from Research and Development expenditure. The means to establish rights to profits (patents) are available, but the pay-off is delayed and highly uncertain with respect to a particular tranche of R and D expenditure. Expenditures on R and D can be made by incumbents or new-comers; no substantial obstacles to entry in this sense exist. At any one time one expects to see many firms with R and D capability. Since the (remote) pay-off to a 'winner' is also difficult to impute in present value terms at that point, one expects there to be a reluctance among firms to merge to reduce R and D risks inherent in pursuing a line of research; the basis of a deal is too uncertain. For both these reasons, conventional measures of concentration will be low, whenever a cross section at one time is reviewed. At any one time there must be a high dependence on the particular product or products which happen to have achieved success. The firms should be rated by the markets as shouldering above average risks. Viewing the industry over time, one would expect to see no or little tendency for overall concentration to increase.[5] There should be marked shifts over time in the firms' ranking by size, and most important, shifts in the market pecking order for particular products, as challenges to previous market leaders succeed. To what extent are these expectations fulfilled? The evidence is far from satisfactory in many ways, as we shall see, but the cumulative picture is fairly convincing.

Concentration in R & D

First, on the overall concentration issue: Concentration among the leading owners of pharmaceutical research establishments is very low when measured in world terms. Thus, data for 1988 listing the top 22 companies in R and D expenditure terms, show these to have had 46 per cent of the world pharmaceutical sales.[6] The largest reported share is about 4 per cent.[7] The Herfindahl index is so low as to be negligible (less than 0.01). Systematically tracing ownership on the world scale is extremely time-consuming; data based on ownership for earlier years are not available, but there can hardly have been any significant shift towards concentration. Also, all sales, including over-the-counter pharmaceuticals are included. The exact proportion of ethicals is unknown in such detail, but the increasing dependence on ethicals is widely accepted, and hence the importance of R and D in company strategy.

Dependence on assets not related to ethical pharmaceuticals also complicates attempts to test the perception that the firms are distinguished by acceptance of high risk, high return projects. The obvious source of this would be appropriately adjusted estimates of beta in pharmaceutical company stock-exchange prices. There is some, but not very persuasive evidence of this in raw UK figures. But the process of disentangling effects of company gearing and varying elements in risk among the company's total assets is a formidable task which I have not attempted.[8] However, R and D has been shown in general to be riskier than other assets, e.g., by G. Wedig.[9]

There is some evidence to support the notion that the companies choose to accept fluctuations in net cash flow in order to gain a higher return in total. One of the most remarkable consistencies across leading pharmaceutical companies is the ratio of R and D expenditure to sales. In 1988 the top 28 world companies, domiciled in USA, Germany, Switzerland, UK, France, Japan and Sweden, averaged R and D expenditures of 16 per cent of their sales revenues. Sales among these ranged from £460 million to £2,200 million; R and D expenditures from £101 million to £341 million. The standard deviation of the respective percentages was 3.8 per cent; the coefficient of variation 0.238. Much of the observed variation was in fact due to the inclusion of the smallest company in revenue terms.[10] That companies have to adopt some rule of thumb, and not formal forward looking cash flow estimates, when deciding to invest from gross revenues for R and D is understandable when the principal pay-off is a hoped for success of a very few drugs some years hence. The only reference point may indeed be comparative – i.e., not to stray too far from what other companies are doing. Whatever the rationalisation, unless other costs are similarly strictly proportional to sales, acceptance of such a rule-of-thumb will increase the fluctuations in cash flow available to bond and shareholders when other costs are stickier in response to changes in sales, i.e., contain rather invariant outlays. This seems quite likely, on a year to year basis.[11]

Dependence on 'winners'

High dependence on particular successful, drugs in total ethical sales is well established. One indication of this is the systematic increase in observed concentration as the ethical market is divided in sub-groups. Drugs are grouped according to therapeutic area, of which some 17 are generally recognised. These refer principally to body systems or particular general conditions between which there is normally little possibility of drug substitution, but within which such substitution can and does occur. Within such area, more or less closely competing prescriptions occur. Thus Wells describes pharmaceutical market shares in 6 therapeutic areas in UK, for 1984 as follows:

Table 23.1 Therapeutic area, submarket 1

	Sales of leading product in therapeutic areas as per cent of		
	All ethical drugs	Sub-market level 1	Sub-market level 2
1 Alimentary tract and metabolism	2.32	15.0	49.1
2 Cardiovascular System	2.36	10.7	40.8
3 Systemic anti-invectives	2.30	27.1	70.1

4 Musculo skeletal system	1.7	14.3	16.5
5 Psycholeptics	0.7	5.5	15.4
6 Respiratory System	2.7	20.4	33.1

At level 2, the sub-markets are: 1 antiseptic ulcerants: 2 plain beta blocker agents; 3 broad spectrum penicillins; 4 non-steroidal anti-rheumatics; non-narcotic analgesics and anti-pyretics; 6 Bronchodilatory and other anti-asthmatics.

Source: Nicholas Wells 'Innovative Chemical Extensions: Office of Health Economics', December 1988.

The therapeutic area (sub-market 1) normally defines market scope at which the decision to invest in R and D is directed; the sub-market level 2 represents successful marketing of a product which may prove superior to other drugs, on average, in prescribers eyes, as remedies for a given condition. It represents the importance of the successful drug in the general portfolio of drugs being produced at any one time as a result of previous R and D expenditure. A well-publicised recent example is Glaxo's success in the first therapeutic area, where its Zantac outsells rivals at thÍ sub-market 2 level (Zantac's world shares in 1988 and 1989 of this sub-market were estimated at 52 and 44 per cent respectively.[12]

Dependence upon a successful drug at one time by particular firms is clear. Thus Wells for 1980 quotes the 10 leading UK pharmaceutical companies' dependence on their first and second rating products as follows:

Table 23.2 Dependence of companies on individual products

	(Per cent of sales)		
Company	*Product 1*	*Product 2*	*Total, 2 leaders*
A	49	22	71
B	73	8	81
C	63	23	86
D	77	15	92
E	32	19	51
F	80	8	88
G	70	20	90
H	89	7	96
I	29	16	45
J	45	33	88

Some further estimates for 1990, concerning the worlds best selling single drugs are: for Glaxo 59.4 per cent of sales; B-M Squibb 33.8 per cent: Bayer 28.6 per cent: Smith-Kline-B 30 per cent.[13]

A further implication of the reliance on one or two successful drugs from a search among a wider ranging set generated by R and D is of course a considerable tally of failures. Only those attempts which have been promising to a late stage in development, or are in fact marketed but withdrawn, are likely to be widely known and reported. A recent example of such listings of drugs is Barclays de Zoette's.[14] The ratio of discovery of new marketable ethical pharmaceuticals to new compounds found by research is very low.

Challenge over time

If companies, however large a size they may reach at any one time, are in fact challenged over the long term by the success of others, we would expect to see evidence of waxing and waning in their relative positions as time passes. Changes in companies' relative standing can be measured either at the level of the company, or with respect to their experience within a given therapeutic area. Again, the evidence is limited, particularly on the company level. It is impracticable, without considerable resources, for example, to trace the destinations of assets of those companies which have given up the area. It appears however that the pecking order of the leading companies in the top ten companies world wide, and their presence amongst the top ten, is subject to marked change. Thus, if we take the ten world leaders measured by revenue, in 1990, we can compare their position ten years earlier, in 1980, as follows:

Table 23.3 Top ten companies worldwide, in 1990 and 1980

World Leaders, 1990	Position in 1980
1 Merck	4th
2 Bristol Myers/Squibb	8th
3 Glaxo	not in 1st 10
4 Smith Kline/Beecham	10th
5 Hoescht	1st
6 Ciba-Geigy	3rd
7 Johnson & Johnson	not in 1st 10
8 American Home Products	6th
9 Sandoz	7th
10 Eli Lilly	not in 1st 10

Source: Paul West, op cit., p. 6

There seems to be a considerable churn in leadership positions. This kind of material is available with respect to the experience of companies in a particular market, UK. For non- hospital sales it is possible to compare the positions of the top 20 corporations in 1990, tracing back their positions in 1980 and 1970.

Measures of instability in rank order are admittedly difficult to encapsulate formally and to compare, say, with other industries. One could conceive of a measure which incorporated a random change in the pecking order, with deviation from this for the observed change, but that would require a full ordering of positions, not easy to acquire. Nevertheless, the impression that much change is going on is reinforced. With the experience of two decades thus represented, a natural question is whether there is evidence of the propensity to challenge changing as between 1970–80, and 1980–90. The formal answer is that between 1970–80, the sum of the rank changes displayed was 149: in 1980–90, 96. This result, however, is almost entirely dependent on the meteor-like performance of 1990's second ranking firm in the earlier decade. Dropping the most extreme observation, in each case, the two decades displayed almost exactly the same degree of 'churn'.

Table 23.4 Market position of top twenty corporations (excluding hospital sales), UK

Corporation	1990 Rank	1980 Rank	1970 Rank
A	1	2	4
B	2	7	76
C	3	1	2
D	4	4	5
E	5	6	11
F	6	20	34
G	7	3	1
H	8	8	7
I	9	5	10
J	10	21	17
K	11	30	21
L	12	32	37
M	13	14	12
N	14	17	13
O	15	15	16
P	16	18	32
Q	17	9	6
R	18	12	8
S	19	16	14
T	20	19	18
Percentage of market accounted for:-	70.5 %	67.1 %	67.5 %

Source: Office of Health Economics, London.

The same kind of approach may be applied to experience in particular therapeutic markets, this time working from the rankings of the top ten companies at 1970 and 1980 respectively, taking their experience over the subsequent decade. We have data for eleven of the seventeen therapeutic areas, covering sales in the UK, within which products may vie for acceptance. As will be seen from the details in Appendix 1, to hold one's leading market position over 2 decades was rare: it happened only in dermatologicals. A first position was held over a further five separate decades. In the rest of the 22 decades represented, first place shifted in 5 cases. In 92 cases out of a possible 220 companies appearing in the top 10 lost their position amongst the set over a decade. (Detailed figures show a much greater movement within the decade, year by year.) By adopting the convention that a firm missing in a given year's list of 10 had a rank of 12, we can sum up the 10 year changes in rank, by therapeutic area, in the following table, 5.

For comparison, a complete reversal of ordering 1–10 over the decade would produce a score of 50. The average, following the tables conventions, for all eleven areas, is 35, 1970–1980; and 34, 1980–1990. Only sensory organs in 1980–1990 and respiratory in 1970–1980 have a score of less than 25. An apt conclusion seems to be that here, again, there was considerable successful challenge in each market. There is little to suggest a trend in either direction as between the 2 decades. The small average difference is due to the exceptionally disturbed decade of 1970–1980 for the alimentary area.

Table 23.5 Changes in rank position of drugs in therapeutic markets: UK 1970–1980, 1980–1990

Therapeutic area	Rank changes 1970–1980	Rank changes 1980–1990
Alimentry	65	38
Blood and blood forming	34	40
Cardiovascular	28	39
Dermatological	33	36
Genito-urinary	44	28
Hormone preparations	27	32
Anti-infective	34	34
Muscular-skeletal	35	37
Central nervous system	36	44
Respiratory system	24	33
Sensory organs	36	22
	—	—
Total	386	373

Source: Appendix 1

CREATIVE DESTRUCTION AND PREDICTION

The previous section has demonstrated that pharmaceuticals displays many of the symptoms one would expect were a Schumpeterian interpretation appropriate. So it seems worthwhile to explore the appropriate policy model. This section considers the exogenous factors, those of creative destruction. There are three candidates for consideration: change in the aggregate demand for ethical pharmaceuticals, change in the structure of demand, and change in the quantity and distribution of research activity. They will be related in that realised demand will, at the time the current products of research and development come to market (perhaps 10 to 12 years hence, as shown later), largely determine net cash flow at that time (as also seen later, avoidable production costs at that time will usually be relatively small). The realised productiveness of present R and D effort is also an unknown quantity now. However, its present distribution and structure will indicate how rivalrous with respect to the demand its product innovations are likely to be. We consider these factors, as far as the evidence takes us, in turn.

Demand for ethical pharmaceuticals

The overall demand for ethical pharmaceuticals, as it relates to innovation in ethical drugs, is both hard to define and to capture statistically. We are essentially interested in that part of demand which relates to the prescribing habits of doctors who, in Western medicine at least, are the sole judges for consumption, and the terms of substitution between different drugs deemed to be capable of affecting illness. This is a subset of pharmaceuticals production and, for many of the world's markets, part only of the drugs commonly used, because of surviving traditional medical methods. So while world demand for ethical drugs is thought to be rising rapidly, we lack reliable figures for total world consumption for years earlier than 1989. We do have data, however, for the major western drug consumers, who also house most of the worlds expenditure on pharmaceutical R and D. Thus W Germany, France, Italy, Japan, Switzerland, UK and USA comprised 74 per cent of world ethical drug consumption in 1989.[15] Their consumption was £26.5 billion in 1980 and £70.1 billion in 1989 in nominal terms: real consumption rose by about 47 per cent.

The factors underpinning this growth are widely discussed. In these developed countries, for example, a principal driving force is a derivative of growth of income per head. The income elasticity of demand for health care for individual countries as measured by time series of expenditure, and real income, is probably greater than 1, even though countries at comparable income levels devote widely differing amounts of income to health care. Indirectly, income growth is associated with ageing in the population and ageing sharply increases the demand for drugs, as well as all other forms of health care. In this way, a growth of capacity to provide the means to prolong life as with innovations in drugs is a self-powered virtuous circle. There is no reason to suppose that widening ability to prolong the life, and to improve the quality, of the population will not continue apace. Indeed, the pressures cause never-ending embarrassment to public providers of health services, as in the UK. Success in developing particular new life-enhancing drugs has a ratchet effect, creating further drug demands later not normally related to the original innovation. However, these conventional wisdoms about what drives demand have, so far as I am aware, been tested formally, still less incorporated into a formal predictive model. There is certainly a great need for this.

Changing demand structure

Of equal interest in judging how demand will develop is the prescribing behaviour of the final consumers' principal agents, the doctors. This has been changing over the long term in a way significantly affecting prospects for the output of R and D. The history of medical prescribing is one of a long term shift from naturally based to synthetically based drugs, i.e., towards typical R and D outputs. Fundamentally also, there is a long-term shift towards adopting practices, and thus prescribing, based on Western medical techniques. To the extent that prescribing habits converge, differentiation of drug markets based on prescribing divergence will diminish. Convergence is very probably reflected in the long term trend for imports of drugs to form a greater part of total drug consumption in each country. The 7 nation data certainly shows this over the period 1980–1989, as in Table 23.6.

Table 23.6 Share of imports in drug consumption by country, 1980–1989 – percentages

	1980	1989
West Germany	17.4	26.5
France	8.3	21.8
UK	12.2	28.2
Japan	6.9	7.0
Italy	15.2	26.0
Switzerland	36.5	85.3
USA	4.1	5.1

Source: Office of Health Economics, London, based on UN commodity Trade Statistics.

Most countries show a continuous shift towards imports over the twenty year period 1970–1989, as Table 23.7 shows.

It will be noted that Japan is an exception to the continuous trend of rises in imports. The check between 1985 and 1989 was probably the result of decisions taken there in the mid- 1980s in an attempt to reverse the heavy adverse balance of payments against Japan in drugs. This adverse balance had been sharply growing over the 1970–1985 period. In 1970 it stood at £63 million, in 1985 £694 million. Indeed in yen, with 1970 as 100, the adverse balance increased fourfold to 1985. The reason for imports was again most probably a shift towards Western type prescribing, allied with a strong rise in domestic drug demand. Japan's intention to reverse what was for it a most exceptional industrial experience had long been known, together with its encouragement of local R and D spending from at least as far back as 1970. (Its expenditure on R and D, again indexed in local currency, grew faster than the other 6 countries. See table 23.9 below.) The intention, presumably, was to divert the shift into Western style medicine to more home sourcing of the products demanded.

Table 23.7 Ethical pharmaceutical imports, 1970–1989. Index based on local currencies 1970 = 100

	1970	1975	1980	1985	1989
West Germany	100	205	368	626	705
France	100	184	372	888	1440
Italy	100	247	624	3059	3044
Japan	100	169	315	398	393
Switzerland	100	131	205	361	382
UK	100	284	653	1722	3167
USA	100	272	923	1975	2433

Source: UN Commodity Trade Statistics.

This throws into relief the importance of trends in doctors' prescribing habits. We know that at one point in time, doctors do diverge considerably both in diagnoses of illness and, within a given diagnosis, tend to favour different prescriptions. We would like to know, in particular, whether these are tending to converge across the major markets, or the reverse. If the former, the international share of the total market will increase further, unless subjected to government intervention of the Japanese type. And, more important, there will be a further erosion of distinctions which create separate markets to supply idiosyncratic diagnoses. If doctors come to agree more about appropriate diagnoses, and reach greater agreement on the merits of alternative treatments, both risks and rewards to develop particular drugs will be increased. Competition will be based less on persuasion and more on consensus about therapeutic values. The importance of price as a competitive weapon will increase.

The most comprehensive evidence bearing on this issue seems to be Bernie O'Brien's 1984 study of the Patterns of European Diagnosis and Prescribing.[16] On diagnosis, widely varying rates of diagnosis of illnesses were observed. 'Essential benign hypertension' was the leading diagnosis in 3 out of the 5 countries, with a range of 433 per thousand population in Italy and 244 in Spain. 'Acute chronic and unqualified' bronchitis ranged from between 413 Spain and the UK's 214. Even the existence of particular conditions is moot; 355 per thousand population diagnosed in the UK with neuroses, but not listed as a leading diagnosis in France and Germany. Prescribing frequency varied widely, total annual prescriptions per capita at 6.5 UK, 11.3 Italy. Within agreed areas of illness, treatments also vary widely. In hypertension for example, German doctors favoured centrally acting hypertensive drugs, UK (this was 1982) thiazides and diuretics. In the treatment of bronchitis, 49 per cent of Italian scripts were for expectorants; 12 per cent in Spain and UK.

Recognising the difficulties in sampling efficiently and in interpreting across languages, we have to assume that real and significant different diagnoses exist, as indeed they do within a country to a lesser extent. We do not know how, if at all, they are changing; apparently no follow up study has been mounted. This is particularly unfortunate as the question of whether there is in fact a convergence has still to be shown. There probably is, because of the spread of common medical knowledge, but how fast it is progressing is critical.[17] Lacking direct comparisons over time we have to make do with a somewhat distant proxy involving the 7-country trade in pharmaceuticals.

The reasoning is that if there is a tendency towards uniformity in prescribing, this should be reflected not only in imports rising as a share of drug consumption in a given country, but also there should over time be a tendency towards countries' reducing their variance in the sources of their drugs. In a world in which all doctors in all countries took the same view, these sources be alike. Starting from a large discrepancy of views as now, there should be a change towards stability as attitudes across countries converge. We have already commented on the rise in the proportion of imports, with Japan as perhaps an emerging exception. We have matrices of imports between the 7 nations for 1980 and 1989. Are there signs of reduced variation of sourcing between these dates? Table 23.8 gives data measuring the coefficient of variance for imports from the 6 other countries at the 2 dates.

Table 23.8 Coefficients of variance in imports from other countries, 1980 and 1989 (standard deviations in brackets)

	1980	*1989*
Germany	1.21 (67.2)	1.25 (188.0)
France	1.26 (46.4)	1.02 (129.8)
Switzerland	1.54 (185.4)	1.91 (153.2)
UK	1.89 (44.7)	1.25 (113.6)
Japan	2.01 (108.4)	2.06 (405.6)
Italy	1.67 (61.7)	1.41 (219.5)
USA	1.09 (27.2)	1.19 (166.6)

Source: Calculated from UN Commodity Trade Statistics. The standard deviations are of imports valued in £ millions.

Signs of convergence appear in only 3 of the 7, but those that do appear are quite marked, viz in France, UK and Italy. This suggests a contrast which could be formally tested by further direct enquiry. Meanwhile we are left with uncertainty about change in a key area.

Research and Development – growth and dispersion

On the third factor, the growth and distribution of R and D, we again are unable to bring data to bear at a sufficiently disaggregated level to form a fully satisfactory view. The problem is that knowledge of R and D expenditures involves reporting at company levels, tends to be confidential and is not necessarily disclosed in formal accounts. Moreover, for this critical element of the source of property rights, we would wish to be very careful about assigning R and D to a group of companies, at least where there is a majority shareholding link. Instead, information which can be used to measure change over time derives from pharmaceutical Associations in the several countries. It may not be complete; there is no reason to suppose bad misrepresentation but it has to be treated at country level. We must again do our best with the material at that level.

First however, we may note the state of concentration in R and D at one year, 1988, on which there are comparable data for the top 28 spenders on R and D worldwide. The total R and D expenditure was £5,409 million valued across the exchange rates then ruling. The relevant measure of concentration for our purposes is again the Herfindahl. Since the largest single company expenditure (£341 million by Myers-Squibb) represented only 6.3 per cent of that total, the Herfindahl is very low, at about .028 (though confined to a R and D subset by omission of the 29th and subsequent smaller R and D company expenditure, the omission will affect the index only trivially). The assumption that firms must regard the total investment as outside their influence therefore seems safe.

Overall growth in R and D can be measured for 8 leading countries from 1970, and 12 from 1980. Measuring this over time presents obvious difficulties in dealing with inflation and exchange rates. An estimate for 8 countries over 1970–1990 and for 3 others, from 1980–1990 is in Table 23.9.

The 1990 expenditure for the 11 nations totals £10,895 million, a very high proportion, though unknown precisely, of the world's R and D effort. The growth overall is marked, far outstripping that of drug consumption. As noted above, drug consumption rose in real terms in the 7 countries by about 47 per cent between 1980 and 1989. Over those countries as a whole real expenditure on drug R and D rose by 151 per cent between 1980 and 1990. In no country was the increase less than 47 per cent. The range was from 64 per cent in Germany to 287 per cent in Switzerland. From the 5-year changes, any reasonable prediction must be for substantially greater R and D expenditure.

In deciding what this implies for the underlying threats from research in the therapeutic areas, in which research tends to be focused, it would be most useful to have an appropriate breakdown by ownership interest with respect to the therapeutic areas. This cannot be done. However, we have sub-sets of research activity by country. R and D measured at that level does indicate capacity by country to engage in relevant research. As this increases in real terms, it probably increases in potential scope. If so, one would expect an increasing internationalisation of research potential, and that such a convergence of international capacity would be reflected in

Table 23.9 Real expenditures on R and D, 1970–1990.[18] Local currencies, adjusted for respective consumer price indices 1970 = 100

	1975	1980	1985	1990	% change 1980/90
West Germany	136	173	214	283	+64
France	148	211	338	483	+123
Italy	131	159	252	440	+177
Japan	168	244	383	516	+112
Switzerland	86	85	253	329	+287
UK	147	240	371	573	+139
USA	135	155	217	360	+132
Denmark	132	160	223	467	+192
7 countries (excluding Denmark)	133	136	265	342	+152
Holland	223	467			
Sweden	111	173			
Finland	192	275			

Sources: Associations' Annual Reports and IMF.

Table 23.10 Pharmaceutical – R and D. Indices of concentration across countries 1970–1990

	1970	1975	1980	1985	1990
8 countries: West Germany, France, Italy, Japan, Switzerland, UK, USA, Denmark	.302	.226	.203	.235	.188
11 countries: West Germany, France, Italy, Japan, Switzerland, UK, USA, Denmark, Holland, Sweden, Denmark	–	–	.187	.215	.175

Source Calculated from Associations' annual reports and IMF.

more dispersion. This expected outcome can be tested. Is R and D becoming more dispersed as well as growing? Table 23.10 presents R and D based Herfindahls, measured across the R and D expenditures by country. Alternative accounts, based on 8 and latterly on 11 countries, also are shown.

Individual years are much affected by exchange rate fluctuations. In particular, the index is strongly affected by the largest constituent (in this case USA). Nineteen-eighty-five happens to be a year which weighted the US heavily. As Table 23.9 shows, for example, US real expenditure on R and D from 1980–1985 failed to keep pace with the index for 7 countries as a whole. But the general trend seems clear – for a rise in the dispension of effort, as seen by the fall in the indices. Of particular interest is the latest period of great real increase in R and D expenditures, 1985–1990. This was accompanied by a substantial increase in dispersion.

Summary

To summarise the findings of this section: Of the three elements in a prediction of the future impact of 'creative destruction', the clearest relationship is that between overall demand and total research and development expenditure. If the former continues to grow at its recent pace, when the very marked recent increase in R and D expenditure begins to yield its products, the drugs available to doctors will be substantially more in relation to that demand than they are now. But on the issue of how the structure of that demand will respond in prescribing habits, a critical matter in forecasting drug demand, no strong evidence for or against convergence emerges. On the likely impact R and D on the future supply of drugs, there seems little doubt of its strong growth and greater dispersion. On balance, therefore, it would be a reasonable position to approach policy formulation on the basis that there is no adverse trend in creative destruction. The more probable prospect is for an increase; profits will come under greater pressure.

DRUG COMPANIES AND SCHUMPETERIAN 'SHELTERS'

For pharmaceutical firms, the question of specific action to increase the chances of a good pay-off to a potential 'winner' drug or drugs will arise at the time when research and biological testing has reduced the set of candidates to relatively few, compared to the initial set of entities found and patented. Figure 23.1 is a useful stylisation of the 'discovery and development' of a new medicine, due to the Centre for Medical Research.

In terms of Figure 23.1, patent protection on a relatively large number of chemical entities will have been taken out, earlier in the process. At about years 3–4 of patent life the winnowing process will have left the few serious candidates for the increasingly expensive later stages. The management of development is recognised as requiring, as West describes it, a 'different management style and indeed a different type of scientist'. In Glaxo, for example, 'two out of three new chemical entities', submitted by research laboratory heads, 'failed to pass the Central Exploratory Development committee's scrutiny'. At about this stage the options for involving marketing and detailed possible financial pay-offs begin to be considered, anticipating the later development stages which, as Figure 23.1 shows, involve increasing number of tests on patients, until the hoped for single 'winner' is defined and sent for product licence application. In the Centre's account, regulators' deliberation on licensing is set at two years, after which selling can begin.

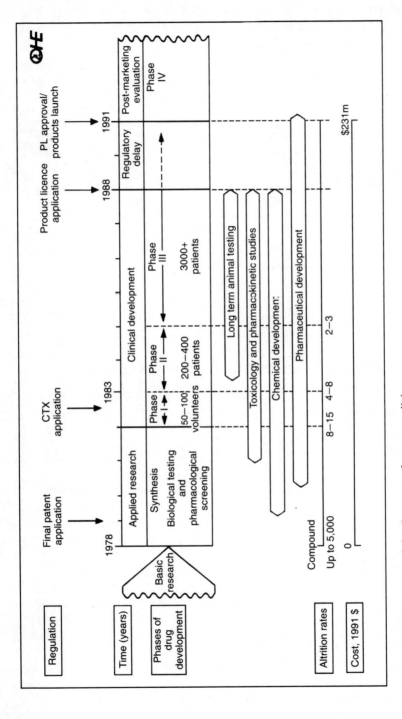

Figure 23.1 Discovery and development of a new medicine
F: Update to Figure 1.13 ' Innovation and New Drug Development' S.R. Walker and J.A. Parrish in *Trends and Changes in Drug Research and Development* eds B.C. Walker and S.R. Walker 1988.
Source: Centre for Medicines Research

Using shelters

Not noticed in Figure 23.1, which rolls back, as it were, the history of the single product which eventually gets marketed, part of the strategy to create returns includes the possibility that additional patent shelter can be erected, by parallel research effort into 'improved chemical entities' (ICE's) which might substitute for the lines developed so far. At this stage, when the latter have become very few, the fact that patents are also a means of publishing information assumes great importance. The patent information is readily mapped to the knowledge that the developing company is indeed pressing ahead with the small subset of original possibilities. This is the signal for other companies too to attempt to develop ICEs of their own. (These will not necessarily be patentable as products, as they well might infringe the patents of the older rivals, but may well be patentable as processes). These imitative efforts (or 'me-too' products as they are unkindly called) will, if they survive the testing course, have a patent life extending a few years beyond that of the 'original'. Perhaps the most important recent example of a (very) successful ICE was Glaxo's Zantac, which followed the more original Tagamet (Smith Kline) to the market after 2 years delay in 1983. This was a case in which an independent ownership interest won the race to develop a successful ICE. An example of the reverse case, of common ownership of the 'original' and the ICE, was Valium following Librium.

The 'original' compound producer can thus also deploy a hedging strategy, in the light of judgements about the cost of such developments on the one hand, and the extra effective patent protection on the other. But patent strategy is not the only important dimension of profit seeking at this stage. By the time candidates have become few, it is possible to focus on actions which might advance the marketing date in a particular market and by expansion reduce the time taken to market in other countries. If this can be done, profits accrue earlier. A possibility here is putting more resources into speeding up the clinical trial phases. Companies can similarly shorten the regulatory delay, again with respect to a single country market and, at greater cost by attacking countries simultaneously. The choices in strategy are now richer, and there may well be trade-offs between them; for example, if extending effective patent protection has a present value of costs roughly the same as that of speeding up acceptance of a drug, the latter will be preferred simply because the revenues arrive sooner. With respect to regulatory delay, and to US conditions in the early 1980s, such a trade-off has been noticed in the context of public policy to patent extensions. Grabowski's and Vernon's simulations calculated a company's break even between shortening of regulatory lag versus patent extension by a given amount of time as at 5 or 6 to 1 in the former's favour.[19]

If the decision is to increase resources applied to testing, the problem will be to deploy a large extra capacity to do the testing at the appropriate time. In the later 1980s there seems to have been a growing attention to this process. Pharmaceutical companies have realised better the advantages of a capacity to switch manpower from drug to drug as the potential of each comes clearer, so as to shorten the expected average testing period. The superior logistics have essentially stemmed from applying management skills more rigorously. Schumpeter might well have recognised this as an organisational innovation providing an extra shelter. Its effect is to improve profit prospects for the larger firms having a diversified portfolio of up-coming drugs.

The more remote event of marketing the product will arise at the time of concentration on a few front runners. Hence the question of marketing alliances arise, that is collaboration with firms willing to provide the required manpower for tackling the job of persuading doctors to prescribe a new drug. These are likely to be alliances confined to the need to speed action in particular markets. An alliance us unlikely to extend to sharing of the basic property rights in the drug or drugs, because at this point there must be lively hopes of very high pay off to the drugs while, at the same time viable options among established networks may well exist, so that there is no need to share in ownership of drugs involved. In 1991, for example. Scrip reported many such marketing oriented deals. Examples are the Sanofi–Sterling alliance giving Sanofi access to the US market. 'Both parties have insisted on retaining separate identities and headquarters' (Feb. 27, 1991). AHP set up a joint venture for the distribution of ethical and nutritional products in Japan with Eisai (20 September 1991). Astra bought Simes from Zambon to give 'access to its own marketing channel in Italy' (25 September 1991).

Generic competition

Whatever marketing alliance has been formed at this stage (of a decision to major on a very few drugs) it will assume much greater importance at a later stage in the sequence, namely the time at which sufficient approvals have been acquired to begin active marketing. In terms of Figure 23.1 this might well arise at about years 10 to 12. At this stage, the disposition of own and competing ICE's will be known, and the time of effective patent shelter available determined. The principal further question affecting future profits will then be strategy with respect to prospective generic competition which may ensue when patent life expires. How acute this is at the time of market-ing will of course depend on how successful a firm has been in shortening the previous stages. It will also strongly influence the price at which the product is brought to market and its desired future price path.

One would suppose that the most usual course would be to work back from the presumed date of generic entry and decide the pricing path for the future in the light of that. Generic production has its own of costs of entry, principally of testing for licensing. At that point all the development costs put into the patented drug have been sunk. The current production costs will normally be very small. True, marketing costs will still be among the avoidables then to be taken into consideration. But there is no reason to suppose that possible generic manufacturers production or marketing costs will be much, if at all lower, at that point than those of the patented drug. The problem is largely one of maintaining exposure to drug prescribers to whom visits will have to be made at reasonably frequent intervals. Such visits are the more effective, of course, if the drug has an individual designation, not a simply generic one, so that the impact of the visit is not lost during the intervals of calling. (This is no doubt a reason why generic manufacturers have increasingly branded their products.) With a very large number to be called upon, in different geographical locations, the cost per call for generic or patented drug will not vary very much. So, relative to prospective generic competition, the patented drug will face lower avoidable costs at that point, because of the testing costs to be faced by the prospective generic rival.

In the case where the generic competitor is expected to have exactly the same therapeutic value as the patented drug, the implication for setting the most profitable course seems clear. One aims at an entry-forestalling price at the time when generics could enter and still make profit because the generic costs of seeking approvals is avoided. If the low price then anticipated stimulates so much demand that to serve it would seriously over-weight a firms' commitment to manufacturing then the profitable course would be to licence the brand, which carries the tag of approval, to an independent manufacturer or manufacturers.

Until the point of a shift to generic production or licensing, one simply charges what the market will bear. This is basically a function of how superior the prescribers perceive the drug to be as compared to other treatments in treating illness. A doctor will, explicitly or implicitly, make the patient's trade-off between price as an efficacy of treatment. What the revenue-maximising price (or prices) are likely to be is no doubt judged by a combination of past experience and test results coming from early market experience. Because of the low avoidable costs at that point, at least in established sophisticated drug markets, the exercise is essentially one of revenue maximising. In this, one expects the principle of price differentiation to be uppermost – output and revenue are increased thereby. (Public sensitivity about drug prices in individual countries probably dictate that this differentiation is largely confined to separate countries).

However, an assumption of an exact therapeutic replication is extreme. More frequently, one would expect to encounter differences in perceived quality between the patented and generic drug. If, as one would suppose, this difference lies in favour of the previously patented drug (or the relevant ICE's) then it is possible to sustain a price differential against the generic. Backing up the differential with persuasive advertising and promotional visits will often make this sustainable over a considerable time into the generic period. The important point of difference from the exact replica case is that the differing qualities/price mix which generics often have ensures that they too have a (differentiated) market opportunity, and will enter. Eventually the pressure of entry by many differently specified generics will erode the pay-off to support the original patent brand. Viewed *ex post*, the price patterns over time displayed by patented drugs will have in common a period of high price exploitation of what the market will bear, followed however by differing patterns of relative decline, depending on the factors just described. There are several descriptions of completed cycles of this sort.[20]

Alternative sources for shelter

At any time when Government policy decisions are made, drug firms will be managing the profit seeking process at each of these periods in market development. The parallel question to that of predicting the future of exogenous influences on profit is: will there be a further application of sources of shelter? In this period of what might be called 'managing the pay-off' to a bonanza and bonanzas, a natural Schumpeterian question is whether other possible sources for profitable shelter can be erected to increase it. The candidates of conventional importance in public policy are organising merger and collusive activity. As argued earlier, proposals to merge are unlikely to be seen as useful (as distinct from buying, in one form or another, perhaps through 'alliances', extra capacity to sell one's product). They not only dilute the winner's prospective profit to new ownership interests but are also costly and time consuming to bring about, delaying changes in working practice. Mergers are more likely to be relevant for application at a much earlier stage in the process, and are most likely in order to hedge against the threat from a completely different R and D base. An outstanding example of such a merger appeared in 1991, relating to biotechnology, American Home Products acquisition of 60 per cent of the Genetics Institute for a reported $600 million (Scrip 4 October 1991).

At the point of confrontation with potential generic competition, there is little to be gained from merger with a revealed generic opponent, useful as this might have been had it happened at an earlier stage. The important potential for sustaining profits is that described earlier. With the winner in place, one is as likely to be discarding a generic as acquiring it – as is perhaps indicated by Glaxo's recent disposal of its antibiotic generic interest to Swedish interests. Similarly, probably nothing to be gained by formal or informal collusion on prices at this stage, when the large pay-offs are occurring. As seen earlier, the very success means that the vying products are few, and if there are generics, they will be occupying separate market positions dictated by price trade-offs determined exogenously. These market forces, and outcomes of the players' signalling, are sufficient to reach the most profitable outcomes. Collusion in an anti-trust sense is not required. As we shall see in the next section, in the UK, public drug

purchasing policy has necessarily created the structure for cartel-like operation among drug manufacturers, by requiring joint negotiation between the
DHSS and the industry. Despite this infrastructure, no suggestion of collusion on pricing has, to my knowledge, been raised, at least in recent years.

The further question arises of whether the responses to opportunities to
increase profits by shortening delays to market entry can themselves be
elevated to an independent source of Schumpeterian shelter. These were
earlier identified as acquiring the means to test products in several markets
simultaneously, and, applicable to the later stage, ability to speed up market
acceptance after final approval. The former was argued to be an advantage
of a diversified portfolio, and therefore an advantage to size. The latter was
not so clearly prone to a size advantage, though there may well be some
economics of scale in marketing across products, there may even so be some
economies in combining the two functions. Acquiring the means of inte-
grating to substantial operations of this kind, across the many cultures, is
clearly an exacting task, as is its coordination to respond to fluctuating
market needs. The critical question is whether the instances of those we
have cited represent a one-for-all-shift in conditions to which the industry in
general will quickly adapt, or whether some exclusive, long-lasting, and
therefore independently profitable rights can be attached to the developments. At the limit, one could conceive of these new found abilities to
organise testing and marketing as potential substitutes for a strategy
which is, as we have seen, based on R & D and patenting. A well known
proposition in dealing with vertical chains is that most monopoly profit is
likely to be exacted at the point in the chain where there are most obstacles
to free supply. Is it conceivable that this could shift to the later stages of
production and marketing in the drugs case?

Any judgement must be tentative, but there are two reasons for supposing the answer to be 'no'. First, no one has suggested that resources needed
to establish the required positions in testing and marketing are in restricted
supply. The skills involved are readily available; indeed the consumer
industry itself – the hospitals and doctors' practices constitutes a vast
reservoir of such skills. A small differential pay-off offered in switching to
drug companies' employment should find many takers. The second reason
is that even large drug companies are each individually small in relation to
the whole testing and marketing effort required. There then arises the
possibility that independent organisations might well specialise in the functions required, acquire considerable size, and yet offer many alternatives to
both large and small drug companies. The benefits would then be externa-
lised, in so far as the R and D winner seeking mechanism is concerned.
There is already at least one potential example of such specialisation.
Innovex is a product of the mid-eighties, offering a marketing service
particularly of regular visiting to doctors in which a large portfolio of
drugs can be incorporated. It gained market entry through offering to
represent manufacturers of 'non-winner' drugs – i.e., those drugs having

small but useful potential niches in the market. It is moving to overseas representation on the same principle. Clearly the skills, once established, can be upgraded to appeal to more substantial lines.

Summary

This selection has shifted the focus from the exogenous forces comprising elements of creative destruction to elements manipulable by companies in their search for profits. The problem was seen as a conversion of a set of property rights (patents) of highly uncertain, and for the most part zero, value to eventual profit. Decisions at two points of time were seen as important, the first relating to alternatives to extend prospective patent life, or shortening time to market; and the second, around the point of marketing, when the best strategy *vis-à-vis* impending generic entry is faced. The purpose was to develop a plausible account of behaviour useful for judging issues of public policy, an assessment which has to be taken with the predictions of the previous sections in mind. A particular concern of this section has been that of whether the behaviour imputed to drug companies might be the basis of raising shelters from competition, which would add significantly to the protection given by patents. In the event, the picture is of a single-minded exploitation of these rights. Profiting from them tends to preclude the seeking of alternative shelters. There has emerged a relatively recent emphasis on shortening lead times to market. Here there is a pay-off scale in vertically managed operations. This was interpreted as realising a previously unexploited opportunity. The minimum required scale for most profitably exploitation may well have risen in the 1980s; however, this does not necessarily imply a commensurate rise in the scope of single ownership interests.

The conclusion of the previous section was that, if anything, the future prospects are for a strengthening of the forces of 'creative destruction'. The individual firms' strategy reviewed in this section are probably properly viewed as prospectively the best available adaptations to that shift. In other words, it would be quite logical for a particular pharmaceutical firm to hold the view that the prospects are for more effective competition in the industry and that realised profitability from dug production will be protected so long as the down-stream market position is strengthened alongside continued generation of products from R and D. If that R and D base is itself threatened, e.g., by biotechnology, then a further defensive strategy may be to widen the R and D base, perhaps by merger, so concentrating more on ethical drugs, amongst other things by divesting irrelevant activities. This seems to characterise the recent actions, for example Glaxo and Borough Wellcome. (Both firms announced aims to concentrate on ethical drugs, widening the R and D base at the same time as strengthening the vertical relations through to markets.)

However, public policy concerns in this area are only, at best, indirectly expressed via the issues which concern anti- trust agencies, those which would be immediately concerned in any big shift in the exogenous and endogenous factors affecting an industry's competitive behaviour. Rather, the policy issue is seen as a broader cost benefit one – will drug consumers benefit from a given proposed change in rules which apply to the industry? As pointed out earlier, governments have universally accepted the basic modus operandi here – the patent system. For the most part, a government, like the firms themselves, will be operating on matters which can be modified, accepting that basic framework. In the UK, drugs are not seen as an important anti-trust issue, though to be sure before MMC there is a question (of merging wholesalers of drugs) which could effect the terms on which distribution is conducted and there is the question of whether pharmaceuticals position as the only product (alongside books) for which resale price maintenance is legally approved should be challenged. As elsewhere in Europe, a major issue is the length of patent terms, and, peculiar to UK, is the impact of the National Health Services' purchasing policy, expressing the power of an exceptionally big buyer. This are instruments whose use will principally affect the outcomes for drug users. The next, concluding section addresses these issues briefly.

CONCLUSIONS

This paper has explored the application of Schumpeter's thinking to policy issues concerning industries, by concentrating on pharmaceuticals. It has not followed the convention of most industrial economic contributions in testing various 'hypotheses' culled from Schumpeter's views on monopoly. Instead it has attempted to apply directly the two complementary and essential strands of his thought, on the one hand the continuous action of 'creative destruction' and on the other firms' actions in building various forms of shelter from it, usually monopolistic in character, and always involving innovation. The simple Schumpeterian policy model deduced from this is that judgements about a particular industry should be formed from characterising the elements of creative destruction, deciding upon their future direction, and interpreting firms actions with respect to shelters in the light of this. In all this firms are motivated to realise the (necessarily temporary) profits innovation can give them.

Policy must assume such motivation to continue. A particular policy maker, e.g., the UK government, can do far more to affect the terms on which firms can negotiate the profits from 'shelters' than it can the more fundamental forces of 'creative destruction'. In a nutshell, the indicated line for policy is to act in the light of assumptions about the latter. If the major issue for example, is the effect of intervention on the results expected of competition (e.g., lower prices, more innovation) one might well conclude that if the forces described in 'creative destruction' are predicated to rise, there will have to be compensating relaxation in the degree to which firms are permitted to profit from 'shelters'. Schumpeter never attempted, so far as I am aware, to apply his arguments specifically to a current industrial policy issue, but they would surely have run along these lines. The paper attempted to define the relevant elements of 'creative destruction' against which to interpret firms' actions to realise profits from innovation. As we have seen, the evidence which can be brought to bear is limited, so the ambition of these conclusion is likewise limited, namely, to establishing broadly whether the analysis gives reason to intervene currently and in what direction. The policies involved the European Commission's recent proposals for lengthening effective patent lives in pharmaceuticals; and the question of whether there is case for modifying the National Health Service's scheme for purchasing drugs.

It is worth pursuing such a Schumpeterian line for pharmaceuticals only if there is evidence that the scheme of thought reasonably well describes the outcomes in the industry. The second section reviewed this, coming to the conclusion that, indeed, characteristic symptoms were present – for example changing fortunes for individual firms over time and much displacement in pecking orders in therapeutic groups. The overall picture fits well with the vision of individual firms using the patent mechanism to innovate in competition with each other, continuously having to renew innovations to get shelter from the market power, which in the end, will inexorably drive the returns from particular innovations down. If ever there was a 'Schumpeterian' industry, this is surely it. The third section, however, took up the more difficult question of predicting the future course of 'creative destruction'.

This involved defining the factors involved to which firms essentially have to adapt. Four were identified – shift in overall demands; change in demand structure; and shifts in the amount and total distribution of research and development activity. Unsurprisingly, since the problem has not hitherto been posed in this form, evidence was far from satisfactory. Particular future needs for clarification were identified, particularly in the question of changing structure of demand, specifically in doctors' prescribing habits. We also had to develop measures of R and D dispersion, which, at the national level, were distant proxies for what was required, namely distributions at different points in time related unequivocally to ownership. However, a reasonable verdict seems to be that the prospects are that the 'creative destruction' elements on balance are now set to rise.

The following section traced the likely course of firms' strategy to seek the gains from innovation. It affirmed that, after the committal of R and D, used to set up many patented options for development, there were two chief periods at which decisions bearing on future profitability were made, at the point of narrowing options to a few and, later, in strategy vis a vis the ending of patent protection and (if successful) the onset of generics. Among the options to improve prospects which seemed most important for 'shelter' were extension of effective patent cover through ICE's; alliances designed to shorten effective time taken to get to market, and variations of limit pricing when facing the genetic threat. Forms of 'shelter' which have most excited anti-trust authorities – merger of ownership interests and collusive practices were argued to be of little importance because of little bearing on pay-offs, with the exception of merger to hedge against extreme threats to existing R and D expertise, as in biotechnology. It seemed unlikely that recent moves towards marketing alliances, useful for shortening market lead times, would themselves become an independent major source of shelter. They would not challenge R and D plus patents in this role.

With these indications, then, we may comment briefly on the two policy issues. The EC's decision was to issue complementary protection certificates, equal to the period between the start of the patent term and the date of the first authorisation to market the medicines, obtained anywhere in the EC, less four years, with a cap of 10 years total extension. This will imply for firms the second patent relief to apply in UK in recent years. (In 1988 the right of genetic companies compulsorily to acquire a licence after 16 years was withdrawn.) The straightforward implication of the analysis of this paper is that, since 'creative destruction' is set to increase, there will indeed be mounting pressure on realisation from innovations now in the pipe line at some future date. Governments might thus logically decide that compensation in the form of extra patent protection now will prevent some reduction in R and D investment in the future which would otherwise occur. But the analysis stresses the dissociation of realising returns from the commitment of previous investments, and the Schumpeterian-like emphasis on acting in hope for the future bonanza. Particular incumbents have no monopoly of future R and D investment. In practice, no better explanation can be offered for the willingness to commit the original funds than a faith in the productivity of scientific thought. Moreover, the firms have already moved to improve the effective patent life by measures to shorten the time taken to get to the market. It is difficult to see in these circumstances, why a refusal to extend patent lives would have very serious effects on R and D expenditure. Nevertheless, so far as it goes, there is some support here for the decision.

The second policy issue concerns the UK drug price regulation scheme, the PPRS, which covers 85 per cent of ethical drugs sold in the UK. The PPRS may, or may not, succeed in what is in any case inherently an arbitrary decision, in keeping down drug prices below what they would otherwise have been, but it does offer drug firms more confidence in pursuing an internationally differentiated price policy, and it tends to stabilise income year to year, whilst giving companies useful degrees of freedom to improve home margins. UK drug companies can use the stability in income it generates either to accept greater risks in marketing efforts abroad or in increasing their R and D commitment. One would suppose that UK manufacturers would oppose any root and branch reform which might bring more independent purchasing, for example by breaking up the central price control mechanism. Their interest more certainly lies in pursuing opportunities to lever the price up through the bargaining mechanism, whilst leaving the structure essentially intact.

But if there were to be more effective measures on prices currently paid by creating say, more competition in purchasing, this has to be seen in the light of the policy model. What happens when one form of profit shelter is removed? The price control scheme is one such shelter: the central question is, if it is replaced, what moves are then open, if any, to UK firms to restore prospective profits necessary to generate the incentives for R and D? Clearly, much more work has to be done on options then facing firms before these questions can be answered satisfactorily. But an effective reduction in current drug price levels must, *ceteris paribus*, adversely affect willingness to take on R and D risks, given the earlier findings about the exogenous pressure tending to worsen profit prospects. Another such shelter which could be removed is resale price maintenance for drugs. In saying all this, one is very conscious also of the gaps in the analysis of the forces of 'creative destruction'. One can claim, however, that by using both strands of Schumpeter's thought, 'creative destruction' and the shelters from it, one at least puts the policy questions in the right form.

APPENDIX I

Table A23.1 Market leaders by Therapeutic Group

Market position in 1970	Position in 1980	Position in 1980	Position in 1990
1	Not in top 10	1	2
2	Not in top 10	2	4
3	Not in top 10	3	5
4	Not in top 10	4	6
5	Not in top 10	5	Not in top 10
6	2	6	10
7	Not in top 10	7	Not in top 10
8	Not in top 10	8	Not in top 10
9	Not in top 10	9	Not in top 10
10	6	10	3
	Ranks missing in 1980 – 1, 2, 3, 4, 5, 7, 8, 9	Ranks missing in 1990 – 1, 7, 8, 9	

Table A23.2 Blood and blood forming Organs

Market position in 1970	Position in 1980	Position in 1980	Position in 1990
1	3	1	6
2	1	2	Not in top 10
3	2	3	Not in top 10

4	Not in top 10	4	1
5	Not in top 10	5	4
6	5	6	7
7	Not in top 10	7	Not in top 10
8	Not in top 10	8	Not in top 10
9	Not in top 10	9	9
10	8	10	Not in top 10
	Ranks missing in 1980 – 4, 6, 7, 9	Ranks missing in 1990 – 2, 3, 5, 8, 10	

Table A23.3 Cardiovascular system

Market position in 1970	Position in 1980	Position in 1980	Position in 1990
1	2	1	8
2	5	2	4
3	1	3	2
4	4	4	7
5	Not in top 10	5	Not in top 10
6	Not in top 10	6	Not in top 10
7	8	7	1
8	Not in top 10	8	Not in top 10
9	6	9	Not in top 10
10	Not in top 10	10	Not in top 10
	Ranks missing in 1980 – 3, 7, 9, 10	Ranks missing in 1990 – 3, 5, 6, 9, 10	

Table A23.4 Dermatological

Market position in 1970	Position in 1980	Position in 1980	Position in 1990
1	1	1	1
2	8	2	3
3	2	3	Not in top 10
4	4	4	10
5	Not in top 10	5	2
6	Not in top 10	6	Not in top 10
7	3	7	Not in top 10
8	Not in top 10	8	Not in top 10
9	Not in top 10	9	9
10	Not in top 10	10	Not in top 10
	Ranks missing in 1980 – 5, 6, 7, 9	Ranks missing in 1990 – 4, 5, 6, 7, 8	

Table A23.5 Genito-Urinary

Market position in 1970	Position in 1980	Position in 1980	Position in 1990
1	1	1	2
2	10	2	4
3	Not in top 10	3	1
4	Not in top 10	4	6
5	6	5	Not in top 10
6	Not in top 10	6	Not in top 10
7	Not in top 10	7	Not in top 10
8	8	8	7
9	Not in top 10	9	10
10	5	10	Not in top 10
	Ranks missing in 1980 – 2, 3, 4, 7, 9	Ranks missing in 1990 – 3, 5, 8, 9	

Table A23.6 Hormone

Market position in 1970	Position in 1980	Position in 1980	Position in 1990
1	4	1	9
2	1	2	8
3	2	3	2
4	Not in top 10	4	5
5	3	5	3
6	8	6	7
7	Not in top 10	7	4
8	6	8	Not in top 10
9	9	9	Not in top 10
10	7	10	Not in top 10
	Ranks missing in 1980 – 5, 10	Ranks missing in 1990 – 1, 6, 10	

Table A23.7 Anti-infection preparations

Market position in 1970	Position in 1980	Position in 1980	Position in 1990
1	2	1	2
2	9	2	4
3	3	3	1
4	7	4	6
5	8	5	Not in top 10
6	Not in top 10	6	8
7	6	7	Not in top 10
8	5	8	7
9	Not in top 10	9	5
10	4	10	3
	Ranks missing in 1980 – 1, 10	Ranks missing in 1990 – 9, 10	

Table A23.8 Muscular Skeletal

Market position in 1970	Position in 1980	Position in 1980	Position in 1990
1	1	1	10
2	2	2	5
3	6	3	2
4	Not in top 10	4	8
5	Not in top 10	5	7
6	Not in top 10	6	1
7	4	7	Not in top 10
8	Not in top 10	8	Not in top 10
9	Not in top 10	9	Not in top 10
10	Not in top 10	10	9
	Ranks missing in 1980 – 3, 5, 7, 8, 9, 10	Ranks missing in 1990 – 3, 4, 6	

Table A23.9 Carpal Nervous system

Market position in 1970	Position in 1980	Position in 1980	Position in 1990
1	1	1	10
2	2	2	1
3	6	3	Not in top 10
4	Not in top 10	4	2
5	10	5	3
6	3	6	Not in top 10
7	Not in top 10	7	Not in top 10
8	4	8	Not in top 10
9	Not in top 10	9	Not in top 10
10	Not in top 10	10	Not in top 10
	Ranks missing in 1980 – 2, 7, 8, 9	Ranks missing in 1990 – 4, 6, 7, 8, 9	

Table A23.10 Respiratory system

Market position in 1970	Position in 1980	Position in 1980	Position in 1990
1	2	1	1
2	3	2	3
3	6	3	Not in top 10
4	1	4	Not in top 10
5	7	5	6
6	8	6	4
7	4	7	Not in top 10
8	Not in top 10	8	Not in top 10
9	Not in top 10	9	Not in top 10
10	Not in top 10	10	10
	Ranks missing in 1980 – 5, 9, 10	Ranks missing in 1990 – 2, 5, 7, 8, 9	

Table A23.11 Sensory Organs

Market position in 1970	Position in 1980	Position in 1980	Position in 1990
1	Not in top 10	1	1
2	2	2	4
3	9	3	6
4	5	4	2
5	3	5	5
6	8	6	3
7	Not in top 10	7	10
8	Not in top 10	8	Not in top 10
9	Not in top 10	9	Not in top 10
10	Not in top 10	10	Not in top 10
	Ranks missing in 1980 – 1, 4, 6, 7, 10	Ranks missing in 1990 – 7, 8, 9	

Source: Office of Health Economics, London.

APPENDIX II

THE UK PHARMACEUTICAL PRICE REGULATION SCHEME

The British National Health Service accounts 85 per cent of ethical drug sales in the UK. Of NHS sales, hospital purchases account for 15 per cent. The rest are prescribed by primary level doctors, local practitioners. Hence the principal instrument available to the Government is the bargains struck annually by DHSS with representatives of the industry, the ABPI, on which all suppliers of more than £4 million's worth of drugs have the right to be represented. The significance of the large proportion destined to be prescribed by the 25,000 local doctors lies in the mechanisms designed to control the quantity of drugs supplied, which must bear principally on their behaviour. The DHSS/ABPI confrontation is concerned solely with the price of branded, non generic drugs. For the balance – the 15 per cent of the drugs sold for hospital use – more widely spread bargaining exists, in the sense that purchasing is done by NHS regions, or sub-sets of the regions, who are free to negotiate the prices and quantities, including proportions of generics, that they wish. There is nowadays little central pressure to buy British, so sourcing for hospital is quite free. There is little doubt that the price bargaining done through the 85 per cent under the PPRS – the Pharmaceutical Price Regulation Scheme, which is as old as the Health Service itself – sets the dominant ruling prices which concerns ethical R and D firms.

    In terms of recent history, the PPRS has become markedly more detailed in its control mechanism. Each pharmaceutical firm must submit each year its past results. These must be presented to sum to UK operations in 3 categories, Home NHS, Export NHS and other businesses (which will include over the counter sales). Export NHS are those drugs sold at home, but also exported, so if a drug is sold abroad exclusively, its 'results' will not be under scrutiny. An overall target profit varying recently between 17 per cent and 21 per cent on historical cost valuation of assets is set. If for any drug the firm's forecast is more than 50 per cent above target, an immediate reduction to apply in the current year is made. In between, the target and 50 per cent is a 'grey area' which becomes the subject of detailed bargaining. If the firm can persuade the other side that the superior profit is due to efficiency, not cover pricing, the profit is allowed. Some compromise is of course normally reached. If, for example, the firm is on the contrary forecasting an overall current loss, and this is assented to by the other side as a reasonable view (perhaps there has been a substantial exogenous rise in costs), then the firm is allowed to compensate by raising prices in the current year on whatever drugs desired, subject of course to the 50 per cent profit rule's not being breached.

Not suprisingly, arguments over the years have become very detailed and sophisticated. There is no easy route for 'creative accounting' to pull the wool over the DHSS eyes. By now, it is probably not worth the candle to try, because every year's submissions divulge more comparative information; and there is a full cross-section of drug firms to which the DHSS can refer. Previous attempts have simply produced more breakdowns by ratio of types of cost to sales. Nowadays, each part of cost has its permitted margin – R and D capped at 17 per cent, Distribution at 3 per cent. Sales (e.g. the tally man) at 9 per cent and even as far as 'Information' at 1 per cent. The DHSS, in all this, take a view on what, in the circumstances, is reasonable. In effect, rule by exception, year on year, prevails. It is unlikely that a large shift in ratios would be allowed in one year.

Quantities taken are not directly affected by the bargaining . Doctors still determine these. This is not to say that there are not DHSS inspired attempts to influence doctors. On the contrary, the aim for some time has been a target that 60 per cent of prescriptions be generic as opposed to about 40 per cent now. A very elaborate system of persuasion is deployed to try to achieve this influence. This mainly consists of arranging for increases in the information reaching doctors, so that they may compare their own prescribing with that of some local average. Reasons for diverging from averages are legion of course. But there is a system of tracking high prescribers. Since April 1st 1991, Indicative Prescribing plans have been instituted. This involves justifying to a local District Medical Adviser large deviations from plans which a doctor has put forward. Disputes about alleged over prescribing can be raised to regional level and ultimately to the centre. However, action to respond to disapproved-of-behaviour by docking doctors remuneration is still very rare. Since some famous cases in the 1950's, when bizarre anomalies in prescribing quantities were discovered, there are no recent cases of actual financial penalties. Firms may still assume quantities to be unaffected by what is done centrally year by year.

The bearing of the operation of the PPRS on the concerns of this chapter seem to be as follows. The price negotiation fixes UK prices of drugs. This is an important part, but by no means all, of the UK manufacturers market. Among the 7 nations which are referred to in the text, UK's exports of drugs amount to more than 50 per cent of home drug consumption, a figure only exceeded by Switzerland. At the point of the generation of profits on which the negotiation bears, vis, the production of drugs, the manufacturers problem is to determine mark-ups over very low avoidable cost. Differential mark-ups across main markets will increase the gross revenue, and therefore profits. The negotiation fixes one of these mark-ups in a way which in effect compensates companies for sunk R and D costs. There is no way of knowing whether this is 'generous' or not. Indeed the problem is in practice quite insoluble in terms of cost *now* relevant – i.e. forward looking cash flow. Working out a 'proper' remuneration would involve making central judgements on individual firms corporate plans and indeed double-guessing them. (It would also, I would argue, require adopting a Schumpeterian view of the industry.)

Nevertheless conventional mark-ups are adopted and back-up by scrutiny of accounting costs is now quite detailed. Quantities are left in effect as a free variable, the control system for prescribing can have little effect on the bulk of prescribing decisions. Companies are constrained in making use of this by the allowed limits on sales expenditure, but they can attempt to improve efficiency in their appeal to doctors, so are not entirely without influence on prescription. Basically the quantity supplied must be viewed as a variable neither side of the negotiation can influence much. Companies are, however, free to vary patterns of integration. The PPRS fixes retail prices from which wholesale mark-ups are given. Companies can acquire the margin for example by take over of wholesaling or, as Glaxo recently did, decide to adopt direct selling. These moves are profitable if some new source of distribution efficiency accompanies them.

Drug companies, then, have part of their total pricing problem of mark-ups solved, even if arbitrarily, by the price negotiation. The context in which these decisions are taken makes it very likely that quantities will not be susceptible to changes in individual selling. There is every prospect of year to year stability of individual prices if the companies so desire. Net income from the UK portion of drug sales can be relied upon to be reasonably stable. There are two probable effects: the drug manufacturers can (differently) price in other markets with confidence generated by relative certainty in a main one. Moreover, a significant part of net income is not subject to much perspective variation from year to year. Less risk is faced at home, or, to put it another way, greater marketing risk can be accepted abroad, or indeed more risky R and D than would otherwise be done can be undertaken. Companies are quite free to choose between these uses of the 'comfort' that the scheme brings. They are able to pursue some prospectively profitable actions within the scheme without possible adverse feedback.

In short, the PPRS may or may not succeed in pressing down on drug prices: the question is probably unanswerable. What it does do is to induce a useful element of stability in income, and simplifies the task of setting prices to all markets to which drugs may be sent. How firms use this is, no doubt, quite different across the set. Whether as a whole, UK manufacturers fare better or worse than other country's drug manufacturers faced with similar problems (e.g. the French) is another story. But one would guess that UK manufacturers would be loath to see a root and branch change in the scheme. It is far better to concentrate on small favourable changes in applying price conventions.

NOTES

1 'Collusion' might well include agreements between firms to cross-licence patents, where such collective shelter promises better profits than refusal to share. For reasons explored in W. Baumol's contribution to this book, and for reasons explained later here, pharmaceuticals is not characterised by such behaviour. However, I think such behaviour is quite consistent with Schumpeter's view of the sources and protection, of profits.
2 Examples are Tandon (1984), Grabowski and Vernon (1987), P. A. Geroski (1990).
3 See the discussion at pages 101–103, CSD.
4 For a review of this tradition, see P. A. Geroski, (1990) op cit.
5 The caveat 'little' is entered because finding a zero concentration trend depends on continued free entry to pharmaceutical R and D. If incumbents can build superiority over outsiders, and thus the initial set of firms is given, the process might better be described by exposure to random growth on that set. This could lead to greater concentration over time. There is some evidence in UK experience that the concentration over time. There is some evidence in UK experience that the pharmaceutical firm population has changed considerably over a 30-year period. There were 98 manufacturing companies in 1962 and 1990 in 1991, as judged by membership of the Association of the British Pharmaceutical Society. In between these years 64 ceased trading individually, 30 survived, and there were 56 new entrants. 'Ceasing trading' includes withdrawal and takeovers.
6 Source: Office of Health Economics, London.
7 Depending on source, this can vary.
8 The London Business School's Risk Measurement Service, July–September 1991, reports betas for the best-known UK specialist drug companies as follows: Glaxo 1:13; Wellcome 1:10; Smith Kline: 81. These are equity, not asset, betas.
9 G. J. Wedig, 'How Risky is R and D? A Financial Approach', *Review of Economics Statistics*, 1990, pp. 296–303.
10 Omitting this outlier, the standard deviation was 2.74 and coefficient of variation 0.173. Data from Office of Health Economics, London.
11 The effect would of course be dampened by tax reliefs.
12 Source: F. Dell'Osso, 'When Leaders Become Followers: The Market for Anti-Ulcer Drugs', London Business School, Case Series No. 12, Feb. 1990.
13 Source: Tables 6 and 14, Paul West: *Glaxo – a preliminary review*, Mimeo Centre for Business Strategy, London Business School, August 1991.
14 Barclays de Zoette Wedd Research: 'Glaxo: Phenomenal Financial Flexibility', Autumn 1989, p. 7.

15 The respective figures were £70.1 billion and £95 billion.
16 Office of Health Economics, London.
17 Establishing the European Common market implies standardisation of medical school training, a development difficult to accomplish, but as in other community matters, subject to an increasingly urgent timetable.
18 Real Index in Sterling.
19 H. Grabowski and J. M. Vernon, (1987).
20 The discussion in the text underlines how difficult it is for drug interests to defend their position in neo-classical terms. At the point of anticipation of generic competition, prices for the patented drug will get little support from what are *then* avoidable costs, which will be very low. The actual mark-ups are justifiable only in the fuller, Schumpeterian, context.

REFERENCES

Barlays De Zoette Wedd (1989) 'Glaxo's Phenomenal Financial Flexibility', Research Mimeo.
Baumol, W. (1992): Contribution in this volume.
Centre for Medical Research: Innovation and New Drug Development, S.R. Walker and J.A. Parrish in *Trends and Changes in Drug Research and Development*. Ed: B.C. Walker and S.R. Walker 1988.
Dell Osso. F. (1990), 'When Leaders Become Followers: The Market for Anti-Ulcer Drugs', London Business School, Case Series No. 12.
Geroski, P.A. (1990), 'Innovating Technological Opportunity and Market Structure', Oxford Economic Paper 42, 586–602.
Grabowski, H. and Vernon, J. (1982), 'Pioneer Imitators and Generics – A simulation model of Schumpeterian Co-operation', *Quarterly Journal of Economics*, Vol. CII. pp. 491–525.
Kenny, M. (1986), 'Schumpeterian innovation and entrepreneurs in Capitalism. A case study in the US Biotechnology Industry', *Research Policy* 15, 21–31 North Holland.
O'Brien, B.J. (1984), Patterns of European Diagnosis and Prescribing: Office of Health Economics: London.
Schumpeter, J.A. (1950), 'Capitalism Socialism and Democracy', 3rd Ed, New York, Harper and Bros.
Segerstrom, P.S. Anant, T.C.A. and Diropoulus, E.G. (1990), 'A Schumpeterian Model of the Product Life Cycle', *American Economic Review*, Vol. 80, No. 5, 1077–1091.
Tandon I.G. (1984), 'Innovation, Market Structure', *American Economic Review* Vol. 74, No. 3, June 1984, 394–403.
Wedig, G.O. (1990), 'How Risky is R and D? A Financial Approach', *Review of Economics and Statistics*, 276–303.
West, H. (1991), 'Glaxo: A Preliminary Review II', *Centre for Business Strategy*. London Business School, Mimeo.

Name index

Subject index